GEOGRAPHY

THE STUDY OF LOCATION, CULTURE, AND ENVIRONMENT

McGRAW-HILL SERIES IN GEOGRAPHY

EDWARD J. TAAFFE AND JOHN W. WEBB, *Consulting Editors*

GEOGRAPHY

THE STUDY OF LOCATION, CULTURE, AND ENVIRONMENT

John F. Kolars
John D. Nystuen

Professors of Geography
University of Michigan

Drawings by
Derwin Bell

Department of Geology
University of Michigan

McGRAW-HILL BOOK COMPANY

New York	St. Louis	San Francisco	Düsseldorf	Johannesburg
Kuala Lumpur	London	Mexico	Montreal	New Delhi	Panama
Paris	São Paulo	Singapore	Sydney	Tokyo	Toronto

Credits

Cover and chapter opening illustrations from
Metamorphose. *M. C. Escher, Escher Foundation
collection Haags, Gemeentemuseum, The Hague.*

Part I illustration from **Tower of Babel.** *M. C. Escher,
Escher Foundation collection Haags, Gemeentemuseum,
The Hague.*

Part II illustration from **Day and Night.** *M. C. Escher,
Escher Foundation collection Haags, Gemeentemuseum,
The Hague.*

*This book was set in Palatino by Black Dot, Inc.
The editors were Janis Yates and Helen Greenberg;
the designer was J. E. O'Connor;
the production supervisor was Joe Campanella.
The printer was Federated Lithographers-Printers, Inc.;
the binder, The Book Press, Inc.*

GEOGRAPHY
THE STUDY OF LOCATION, CULTURE, AND ENVIRONMENT

1 2 3 4 5 6 7 8 9 0 F L B P 7 9 8 7 6 5 4

LIBRARY OF CONGRESS CATALOGING IN PUBLICATION DATA

Kolars, John F
  Geography: the study of location, culture, and
environment.
  (McGraw-Hill series in geography)
  1. Cities and towns. 2. Human ecology.
I. Nystuen, John D., date joint author.
II. Title.
GF125.K64   910   73-11262
ISBN 0-07-035309-3

*To
Jeffrey,
Leslie,
and Christine*

CONTENTS

PART TWO
NATURE AND MAN IN A SPATIAL CONTEXT

Contents

xiii

PREFACE

The purpose of this book is twofold: to introduce modern geography to students with no previous knowledge of the subject and to demonstrate how a geographic point of view can enhance our understanding of the world around us. To do this, we discuss social and physical systems and the interaction between them in terms of their spatial attributes, including their dimensions, densities, scale relationships, associations, and patterns. In this way, we come to our definition of geography as *the study of man-environment systems from the viewpoint of spatial relationships and spatial processes.*

We make no claim that geography offers the only valid view of man and nature. But geography does provide an important and basic approach to such matters. We hope that this book will present insights into spatial behavior and that the ideas elaborated in the case studies can be transferred to situations relevant to you. At the same time, we try not to present any simple world view as the correct and only one. Phrasing this in the vocabulary of the geographer, we do not try to point the way; we only try to help you find out where you are. You must choose your own goals, your own destinations. Our only word of caution is that human activities invariably take place in an environmental framework and have environmental consequences. In order to appreciate this, let us consider three events which emphasize different aspects of the interaction between social and physical systems.

On a summer afternoon, August 24, A.D. 79, the people of Pompeii, a town of about 40,000 at the foot of Mount Vesuvius, went about their lives much as city folk have done for thousands of years. Messages scrawled on those ancient walls are still preserved for us to see and give us some feeling for those vanished lives: fans praise their favorite gladiators; people urge each other to vote for their candidates; children pick out nonsense rhymes and phrases. On that fateful day, food was laid out on supper tables; goods were being bought and sold; and friends made plans for the evening's entertainment. Though the mountain above them had been grumbling, no one really anticipated what happened next. Suddenly the volcano let loose a great cloud of fiery ash that quickly buried the town. At least 2,000 people died under a thirty-foot mantle of volcanic debris which preserved much of the settlement intact for the next two millennia. Now we can go as tourists and see where the life of that town so abruptly ended. Seldom are we presented with such a vivid demonstration of nature's impact on man.

Humans can also be caught up by social forces remote from nature which nonetheless pattern their lives, influencing where they live and work. Consider the following example of the interaction between people and social institutions.

It is a dark night on the outskirts of Ankara, Turkey. As a police patrol moves through the empty lots and open fields on the city's edge, its progress is followed by a dozen watchers concealed among the bushes and rocks. When the patrol has disappeared into the night, one of the watchers in the shadows signals with a flashlight. Instantly, the scene changes. Trucks pull in from the highway down below; workers emerge from the darkness; materials are unloaded, and in a few hours a small, but solid, house has appeared where none stood before. A light glows in the window and a single family goes about its business of tidying up. Though the cement is still wet and the raw odor of disturbed earth still clings, a look of permanence is nevertheless there. When the patrol returns the next night, its leader does not break stride at the sight of the new house. Why should he? Every night on his patrol the same thing happens. Another family has arrived and started life in the city.

In many parts of the developing world the migration of rural folk to city homes has swollen to a flood. Squatters have quickly learned that where public land is found in and near large settlements, once a roof is over a family's head, the task of eviction by the courts is long and complicated. Faced by thousands and thousands of such cases, city and national governments in developing nations have given up trying to break the log jam in the courts. The result is a new pattern of urban growth with new strains placed upon the physical and social structures of the city. This is only one of many ways in which people react to new developments in their social, economic, and political environments.

A third scene, familiar to many American readers, shows how our search for what we perceive to be most desirable can sometimes destroy the very thing we seek. An aircraft factory worker and his family move from St. Louis to Southern California in order to enjoy a high salary, the year-round sun, and warm beaches. So have many million more recent arrivals in the "Sunshine State." Each family insists upon its right to own a private automobile and to visit the seaside and mountains whenever its members wish. But the environment cannot easily cleanse itself of the added burden of exhaust fumes and sewage that such

Squatter Settlement in a Part of Ankara, the Capital of Turkey. None of the people in these houses have a valid title to the land on which they built their homes.

numbers bring. The air becomes murky and unpleasant to breathe; the beaches are fouled and often unsafe for swimming. The very conditions of the natural environment which have lured a generation of Americans to California are beginning to alter under the impact of too many people. In this case, the value system under which the newcomers operate leads them to unwittingly alter and degrade the environment which they originally sought. This is Pompeii in reverse, where man overwhelms nature.

A GEOGRAPHICAL POINT OF VIEW

In order to understand the chains of linked processes which bind man and nature so effectively together, we must consider both human and natural systems. Many disciplines study one aspect or another of humans and their environments, but only a few have traditionally considered both man and nature in a single context. *Geography* is the oldest of such efforts to understand the total processes by means of which man will survive or perish on earth. Geography's role as a unified discipline is one thing which we wish to make clear in this text.

We attempt this in several ways. Our primary concern in this book is with spatial and environmental models of human and natural systems. This book breaks with geographical tradition by talking first of mankind and then of the land he occupies and utilizes. We do this for a specific reason. *Man is the ecological dominant.* No other agent on earth has so modified the total environment in so brief a span of time; no other environmental agent has the potential for ending all life on earth. Only the unlikely event of a solar flare or other disaster of nearly cosmic magnitude could exceed man in his role of altering the face of the earth.

We begin our discussion with considerations of the city, for mankind's urban life-style has evolved rapidly and overwhelmingly in recent decades. At the same time, we introduce the reader to a series of increasingly complex spatial insights which represent geography's special contribution to both the social and physical sciences. Chapter by chapter throughout Part One of this book, we build a spatial picture of human activity. Our basic premise, however, is that the spatial insights provided by geography apply not only cross-culturally to human systems but also with appropriate modifications, to those in nature. Thus, Part Two presents some basic underlying facts about natural systems as they operate upon, within, and above the surface of the earth. We specifically emphasize the flow of energy, primarily solar energy in many forms, through the natural systems that shape earth environments. We then introduce the role of plants and animals in the creation of various life environments. Throughout the book we make frequent references to the impact that man has upon natural systems and to how human and natural systems in combination create the human ecosystems upon which we depend. In the final chapters we combine our views of human spatial organization with our knowledge of natural systems in order to give a more complete picture of man's impact on earth environments. Readers will find direct discussions and explanations of the physical phenomena which help shape earth systems in Chapters 14, 15, 16, and 17. We have kept this material separate for two reasons. It is necessary to understand something about nature before attempting to change it. This book does not claim to exhaust the subject matter of physical geography, but we hope that these chapters will sensitize the reader to the importance and complexity of such things. We also feel that for a one-term introduction to geography, the student specifically interested in human geography can skim or skip the above four chapters without losing the narrative thread of the discussion. Likewise, the student primarily interested in environmental systems can omit Chapters 6, 7, 8, and 9, which deal directly with problems of communication, industrial location, and economic development. We have tried in this way to present a manageable integrative approach to geography combining the concept of environmental unity with the insights offered by locational analysis.

Any attempt to present the richness and complexity of modern geography in a single text is a formidable task. Whatever success we have achieved in this book is due less to our own efforts than to the many people who have helped us along the way. We first wish to thank the students at the University of Michigan who have taken the introductory courses upon which our effort is based. The constant challenge of their critical and inquiring minds has been a spur to our ambitions. Equally important to us has been the advice and criticism of our consulting editor, Arthur Getis, who has successfully alternated as devil's advocate and staunch friend. The actual presentation of the subject matter in graphic form could not have been done without the advice and help of Waldo R. Tobler, whose new *Hyperelliptical Map Projection* was especially created to serve as the base for the world maps throughout most of the text.* Many of the other base maps have also been provided by Waldo Tobler, whose knowledge and ability in computerized mapping have allowed flexibility in our choice of map projections. In the same manner, we feel that the illustrations and maps prepared by Derwin Bell will long survive the words that accompany them. Finally, we wish to thank our many able assistants at the university, and especially Gwen Nystuen, as well as the staff at McGraw-Hill who have provided support, advice, and encouragement above and beyond the call of duty. If errors, omissions, or oversights vex our critics, only the authors are to blame.

John F. Kolars
John D. Nystuen

*W. R. Tobler, "The Hyperelliptical and Other New Pseudo Cylindrical Equal Area Map Projections," *Journal of Geophysical Research*, vol. 78, no. 11, April, 1973, pp. 1753–1759.

1 | LOCATION AND ENVIRONMENT: A GEOGRAPHIC POINT OF VIEW

It is convenient to begin this book with a discussion of human activities before introducing natural processes. We do this by making some simple assumptions about human behavior in space. This is accomplished by constructing models in which the natural world is reduced to a featureless plain. Once we have gained some insight into human behavior on this homogeneous surface, we are able to reintroduce the complexities of nature in order to see what changes result from their presence. Thus, not only do we go from human systems to natural ones, we also begin with simple models of reality and proceed to more factual descriptions of the complex whole. We hope in this manner to show how a *geographic point of view* increases and enriches our understanding of the world in which we live.

Numbers Without Dimensions

In order to understand the expression *a geographic point of view*, let us consider the following list of numbers:

49 72 34 31 31 74 69 39 60 44 56 67

This sequence might represent many things: the age of participants in a panel discussion, the number of houses in a sample of Chinese hamlets, or the distance traveled daily by commuters to Wall Street. These numbers are, in fact, average monthly temperatures in a mid-latitude or temperate location. No discernible progression appears associated with them. Yet the list as set down is a sequence, in this case ordered by alphabetizing the months of the year. How much more logical to arrange the numbers as they occur chronologically (Figure 1−1), for the temporal arrangement carries with it additional information about the seasonal values of the figures.

In the same way, many lists are ordered alphabetically which might better have some other arrangement. This is particularly true of things relating to the earth-space in which we live. Census tables showing population and other characteristics of various political units often list Alaska next to Alabama and Ethiopia after England. Geographers find this practice no more logical than alphabetizing the months of the year. Examples showing the importance of the location of things in space, just as in time, are found everywhere. The clustering of the poor in "poverty pockets" and of minority groups in "ghettos," and the congregation of major industries within a small portion of the world's nations, as well as the fact that we recognize areas by such regional phrases as "the Corn Belt"

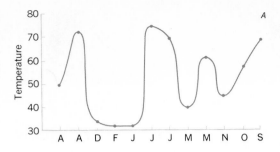

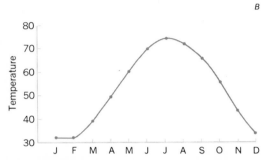

Figure 1-1 Average monthly temperature (*A*) Monthly temperature arranged alphabetically by month. (*B*) Monthly temparature arranged chronologically by month.

and "the Holy Land," immediately suggest that spatial ordering has taken place in the real world. The problems of Alabama and the problems of Alaska are very different although their juxtaposition in alphabetized lists falsely suggests some type of continuity nonexistent in reality. Alabama and Georgia, Alaska and British Columbia, England and Scotland, and Ethiopia and the Sudan are all more logically paired than any alphabetically associated countries.

Another example of the need to identify places by location, as well as by name, occurs when international data are presented. Table 1–1 shows the per capita income for selected European countries. On the left, the values are arranged by listing the countries alphabetically with names designated through common English usage. The same values are listed on the right, but the list has been alphabetized using the official names which

each country chooses to use for itself. Which alphabetical listing is correct? By whose criteria should information be compiled?

Still another example of this problem will occur if you travel to Europe next summer. At that time will you stay in Cologne or Köln, Florence or Firenze? The latter names are locally correct; the former are, at best, rather poor English transliterations.

Cross-cultural confusion like this can be overcome by locating cities, countries, and other places using spatial coordinates such as latitude and longitude. While a number of geographic techniques exist for recording, storing, and analyzing information through the use of coordinates, maps are the most familiar way in which this is done. The figures given in Table 1–1 have been plotted in Figure 1–2. Notice that in addition to overcoming the language difficulties inherent in the alphabetical lists, the distribution of per capita income on the map of Europe suggests additional information that the lists conceal. Per capita incomes are highest in northwest Europe and diminish to the east and south with surprising regularity. In the same way, per capita incomes for all the countries of the world show a distinct spatial ordering (Figure 1–3).

Now compare the world per capita income map with the one showing population growth rates throughout the world (Figure 1–4). The corresponding patterns on these two maps indicate a strong correlation in geographic space between high growth rates and low incomes. In the same manner the average consumption of proteins and calories shown on the world nutrition map (Figure 1–5) indicates greatest need in the developing nations of the world. The grouping of problems such as these in specific areas suggests that it would be useful to study the patterns formed by various geographic distributions. However, map patterns are not always simple or easy to understand. Figure 1–6 demonstrates world variations in population densities. Large numbers of people live in some areas, while other places are empty, or nearly so. But notice that both the rich nations and the

Table 1-1 Per Capita National Income for Europe (U.S.$)*

Common English Name		Official Name as Designated by Each Country	
Country	Income	Country	Income
Albania	400	Bundesrepublik Deutschland	1,970
Austria	1,320	Československá Socialřstická	1,240
Belgium	1,810	Deutsche Demokratische Republik	1,430
Bulgaria	770	Éire	980
Czechoslovakia	1,240	Estado Español	730
Denmark	2,070	Federativna Socijalistička Republika	
Finland	1,720	Jugoslavija	510
France	2,130	Kongeriget Danmark	2,070
Germany (Dem. Republic)	1,430	Kongeriket Norge	2,000
Germany (Fed. Republic)	1,970	Koninkrijk der Nederlanden	1,620
Greece	740	Konungariket Sverige	2,620
Hungary	980	Llydveldid Island	1,680
Iceland	1,680	Magyar Nepköztársaság	980
Ireland	980	Narodna Republika Bulgaria	770
Italy	1,230	Polska Rzeczpospolita Ludowa	880
Netherlands	1,620	Repubblica Italiana	1,230
Norway	2,000	Republica Popullore E Shipërisë	400
Poland	880	República Portuguesa	460
Portugal	460	Republica Socialista România	780
Romania	780	Republik Österrich	1,320
Spain	730	Republique Française	2,130
Sweden	2,620	Royaume de Belgique/Koninkrijk België	1,810
Switzerland	2,490	Schweiz/Suisse/Svizzera	2,490
Turkey	310	Soyuz Sovyetskikh Sotsialisticheskikh	
United Kingdom	1,790	Respublik	1,110
U.S.S.R.	1,110	Suomen Tasavalta	1,720
Yugoslavia	510	Türkiye Cumhuriyeti	310
		United Kingdom	1,790
		Vasileion Tis Ellados	740

*National income—value of the nation's output of goods and services, including balance
of income from abroad.
Source: *Statesman's Yearbook, 1967*; Population Reference Bureau, 1971

poor nations have areas of sparse as well as dense population. Variations such as these complicate our understanding of the distribution of the world's problems.

Spatial patterns, like those revealed to us on the accompanying maps, attract the geographer's attention. Almost all phenomena, from the level of nutrition to population densities, cultures, and political ideologies, can be better understood when considered in a spatial context. Most of the problems facing mankind have a spatial character, an analysis of which will help with their solution. The *analytical techniques* referred to later in this book are useful in understanding complicated spatial relationships, but mastery of techniques is only one part of problem solving. It is also necessary to have available the *facts* which relate to the problems. Equally important are *theories* to suggest how the facts should be arranged and which analytical techniques are most appropriate. The combination of geographic facts, techniques, and theories presented in this book establishes a *geographic*

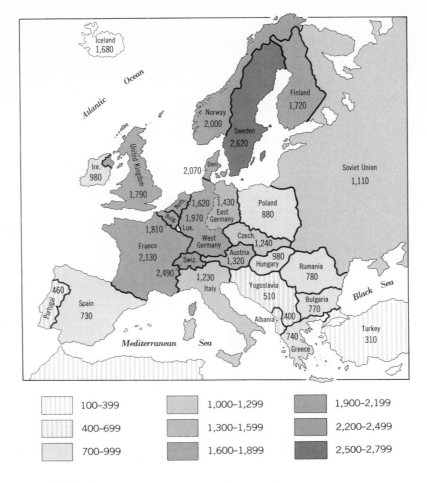

Iceland
1,680

Atlantic Ocean

Norway
2,000

Finland
1,720

Sweden
2,620

United Kingdom
1,790

Ire.
980

Den.
2,070

Soviet Union
1,110

Neth.
1,620

East Germany
1,430

Poland
880

Belg.
1,970

Lux.
1,810

West Germany

Czech.
1,240

France
2,130

Swiz.
2,490

Austria
1,320

Hungary
980

Rumania
780

Portugal
460

Spain
730

Italy
1,230

Yugoslavia
510

Bulgaria
770

Black Sea

Albania
400

Turkey
310

Greece
740

Mediterranean Sea

	100–399		1,000–1,299		1,900–2,199
	400–699		1,300–1,599		2,200–2,499
	700–999		1,600–1,899		2,500–2,799

NATIONAL INCOME (In U.S. Dollars Per Capita)

Figure 1-2 European per capita national income in U.S. dollars, 1968
(Population Reference Bureau, 1971; based on 1968 data supplied by the
International Bank for Reconstruction and Development)

Figure 1-3 World per capita national income in U.S. dollars, 1968   (Op.
cit., Figure 1-2)

Figure 1-4 Annual rate of population increase, 1971   The darker the area,
the greater the birthrate. If the annual birthrate remained at a constant
value of 2.0, it would take thirty-five years for the population to double. At a
constant rate of 3.0, the population would double in twenty-three years.

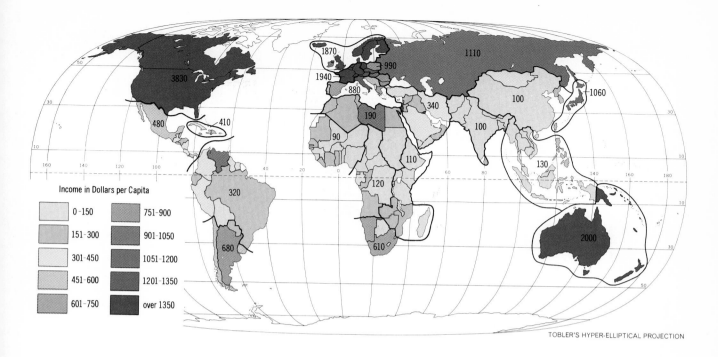

Income in Dollars per Capita

0–150	751–900
151–300	901–1050
301–450	1051–1200
451–600	1201–1350
601–750	over 1350

TOBLER'S HYPER-ELLIPTICAL PROJECTION

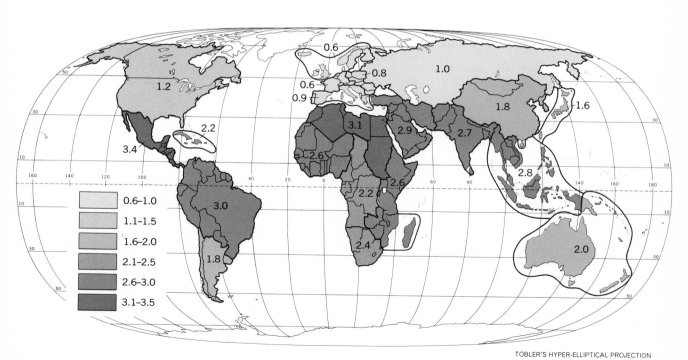

0.6–1.0
1.1–1.5
1.6–2.0
2.1–2.5
2.6–3.0
3.1–3.5

TOBLER'S HYPER-ELLIPTICAL PROJECTION

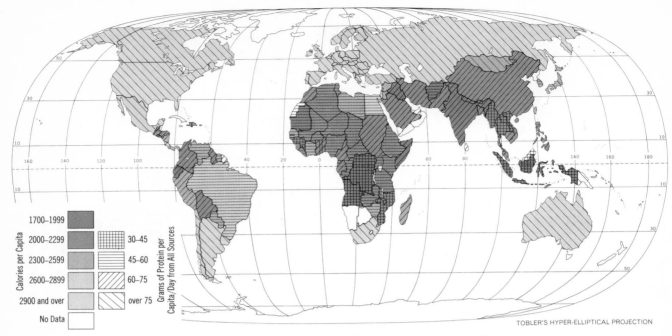

Calories per Capita
■ 1700–1999
■ 2000–2299
▨ 2300–2599
☐ 2600–2899
☐ 2900 and over
☐ No Data

Grams of Protein per Capita/Day from All Sources
▦ 30–45
▤ 45–60
▧ 60–75
▨ over 75

TOBLER'S HYPER-ELLIPTICAL PROJECTION

Figure 1-5 World food supply (net food supplies per capita at retail level) Statistics on food consumption are for the latest year available, mainly from 1960 to 1970. They are not uniformly reliable, since they generally reflect over- rather than underestimates. They are also averages by country; great variations exist in almost every country, so that even in countries which have average surplus consumption there are undernourished people. (Prepared from data in *UN Statistical Abstract 1970*, Table 161)

point of view, particularly useful for understanding the kaleidoscopic world in which we live.

Nominal versus geographic locations

The first insight associated with the geographic point of view is a simple but important one. We must distinguish between words implying places as nominal classifications and words referring to specific locations. Place terms used in nominal or nonspatial classifications cannot be located on maps. Phrases like

the rural and urban sectors of the economy
the developed and developing worlds

Western civilization
black America
suburbia

use place terms nominally. Obviously, these words indicate different sorts of environments, but beyond this distinction what do such words tell us? Where are the *rural and urban sectors* of the economy located? Are the country-dwelling commuters of Connecticut and Michigan who travel each day to offices and factories in the city better assigned to rural or urban America? How many factories must a nation have to be located in the *developed* rather than the *developing* world? Why do courses in *Western civilization* include Meso-

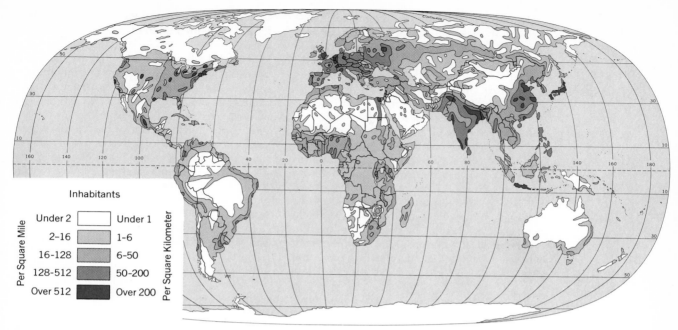

Figure 1-6 World population density.

Inhabitants

Per Square Mile		Per Square Kilometer
Under 2	Under 1
2–16	1–6
16-128	6–50
128-512	50-200
Over 512	Over 200

potamia, Egypt, and sometimes Persia, but not Sub-Saharan Africa? What happens when *black America* wants to become part of suburbia?

The use of place words in this manner presents an abstract division of data. There is nothing wrong in using words this way, but it is important to remember that abstract words often have as many connotations as there are people using them. Distinguishing place terms with real locations from place terms used nominally is one way of clarifying our thinking. Trying to define the geographic locations of place terms used nominally gives us additional insight and information—even if we find the real locations of certain nominal terms as elusive as *the end of the rainbow*. On the other hand, learning to think about real space in abstract terms is an important step in understanding spatial theories and analyti-

cal techniques, which, in turn, lead us to new insights about the real world.

Dimensional Primitives: A Way of Looking at the World

We all use words referring to location in our everyday speech. Proper nouns like *New York* and common nouns like *country* and *city*, as well as adjectives like *near* and *far*, occur in nearly every sentence. We also use a variety of spatial words with strong emotional overtones. The umpire shouts, "You're out," meaning the player must leave the field. He is literally sent out of the area of action. To be *on the in* is to be well-informed. In medieval Europe, to *sit below the salt* was to be placed in a menial position at a lord's table. *Right* and *left* have strong political connotations which we read about every day.

Location and Environment

9

The problem in dealing with terms like those above is to make them exact. In this task, we may turn to mathematicians for help. We do not intend to assign numbers to the world around us; rather, we shall consider mathematicians in their role as logicians and philosophers. In considering the nature of the world and their attempts to describe it, mathematicians long ago realized that for consistency and logic every word in every theorem must be defined. This led to the dilemma of defining every word of the definitions defining the words. Since this exercise could go on and on like the ever-diminishing images in two barber shop mirrors, a solution to the problem of ultimate definitions was needed.

The practical solution found for this problem was to agree that the meaning of certain terms should be accepted intuitively. These undefined terms, upon which the subsequent logical structures of mathematics are built, are called *primitives*. In like manner, certain basic statements which describe the fundamental conditions held to be constant throughout any sequence of mathematical reasoning are called *axioms* and are composed of *primitives*. In these axioms, each word is required for a complete description but does not duplicate the meaning of the other words; that is, each word is necessary and independent. Having been given this start, and carefully staying within the original limits of the axioms, we can evolve elaborate systems of logic from such terms.

In much the same way it is possible to describe the world in all its geographic complexity and yet to begin with only a limited number of dimensional *primitives* arranged to

Figure 1-7 Cities with over 2 million population.   Notice that although there is a concentration of very large cities in the Eastern United States and Western Europe, there is actually a greater total in the non-western world. Even so, these many large cities contain a much smaller proportion of the total population of the non-western world, which is still largely rural. (1970 data.)

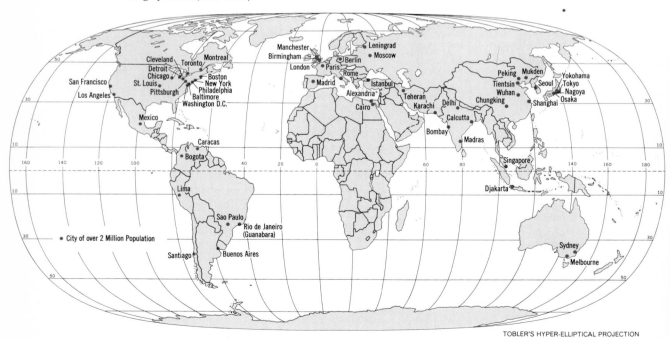

TOBLER'S HYPER-ELLIPTICAL PROJECTION

form a small set of *basic spatial concepts*. Consider Figure 1–7, "Cities with Over 2 Million Population." At the scale[1] of this map the entire world can be depicted on a single page. The cities which interest us appear as a series of dots or points when drawn at this scale. But in reality they cover many square miles and are of various shapes. On this map, city area and shape are not considered important. The number of very large cities and their location are the data the map is meant to present, so it is sufficient to designate each city as a point without size or shape. Here, then, is the first of the primitives with which our geographic viewpoint can be created: A *point* is considered to be a dimensionless location.

Beginning with the concept of a point, we may then derive two additional elements so essential to geography that they can be considered primitives in their own right. A series of points arranged one after another creates a *line*. A collection of adjacent points arranged in a nonlinear fashion, or a line which closes upon itself, defines an *area*. Imagine a plain, smooth tabletop. If one grain of salt is placed on this surface and viewed from a distance, it will, for all practical purposes, appear as a dimensionless point. A row of salt grains viewed from the same distance will appear as a line. A dense sprinkling of salt, one grain in depth, when viewed from across the room will define an area on the tabletop; when seen from only a few inches or feet away, this same area will visually decompose into individual grains or points.

Point, *line*, and *area* concepts are important to geographers for several reasons. Not only do they form the basic or primitive elements in various systems of geometry and topology, but they may be used to describe all manner of things in the real world. In Figure 1–7, the *points* marking the cities represent foci of human activity and wealth, as well as concentrations of people. *Lines* on maps represent everything from transportation routes to national boundaries. *Areas* stand for nations, re-

gions, forests, oceans and continents, and every other feature extending in two dimensions. We can think of cities as *points* linked by transportation *lines* to each other and to farming *areas*. There is another dimensional primitive with which we will be concerned as our discussion unfolds. *Volume* follows logically after area. However, we will limit our present argument to points, lines, and areas, for those are the spatial elements upon which map making relies. Later in this book we will talk about spatial variation in the distribution of many things, such as income, population, air temperature, and precipitation. Such distributions can be shown on two-dimensional maps just as we can depict plains, contoured surfaces, hills, and mountains. Two-dimensional, or flat, distributions are plotted along two axes designated x and y. The third dimension is plotted on a third, or z, axis.

The most direct linear value that can be shown on the z axis is elevation. Measures of vertical values, such as for building heights or volumetric relationships which might be needed to understand air pollution problems or the movement of air masses, are also shown on the z axis. Very often the value plotted on the z axis represents an abstraction, for example, population density. On the other hand, geographic locations in the form of points, lines, and areas always are shown by x and y coordinates. Therefore, we will begin with the first three of these primitives and return to considerations of volume in the following chapters.

An orderly view of relations between dimensional primitives

The most common of everyday things can be viewed spatially. Consider the campus where you are now studying. You and your fellow students can be thought of as concentrations of biotic energy endowed with the desire to learn. At a map scale suitable for showing the entire campus, people appear as points. On good days, two things may happen: the sun will shine, and your professors will give brilliant lectures. From a geographical point of

[1]An expression which we must accept without definition until Chapter 2.

view the difference between lecturing professors and sunshine is that the professors are *punctiform*, or pointlike, while sunlight washes in upon the earth as an areal phenomenon. That is, for our purposes sunlight cannot be separated into individual points of light but equally covers the entire area of the campus. A lecture is generated at a point, the professor's head. When students wish to enjoy the sun, the geographical relationship can be described essentially as one of point to area, since they will disperse across the lawns in a fairly even distribution in order to sun themselves. If you attend a lecture, the spatial patterning is one of many points clustered around a single point.

In summary, points may be thought of as concentrations or foci. Lines represent a double function as either paths of movement or boundaries. Areas show the extent of things and represent distributions or dispersals. Another way of looking at areas is that they are used to generalize and classify the world around us. This is the campus; that is the town; beyond is the countryside.

Now let us consider Figure 1–8, "Dimensional Relations," which shows all the possible combinations of points, lines, and areas. One-half the table is empty; it would be redundant to fill it in completely.[2] The various relationships are illustrated by selected urban examples. The number of such examples is almost endless; each reader should develop his own conceptual skills by thinking of his own examples. Note that these relationships appear in the world of nature as well as the world of man.

In the upper-left-hand corner is the cell representing point–point relationships. While we have already discussed one point–point example—the lecturer and his audience—urban examples are plentiful. The relationship between a wholesale establishment, such as a bakery, and its retail outlets can be thought of as points relating to points. An example of point–line relationships would be the prob-

lem of locating bus stops along a bus route. Should they be stationed at every block, which would make the trip very slow, or should the stops be far apart, which would allow quick trips but be inconvenient for the people walking to the bus stops? A similar problem would be to find the best locations for several ice cream vendors on a boardwalk. Point–area relationships are illustrated by the problem of the optimal location of television stations. The transmitter is located at a point but broadcasts over a more or less continuous area. (Viewers within that area may be thought of as points, which opens up the possibility of interpreting problems in several ways.) Ideally, television stations should be located at the center of the most dense concentration of population. But high population densities mean high land values and taxes, which might make the station unprofitable. These factors must be taken into account in finding the best location.

At the intersection of the second row and second column the line–line relationships that interest city dwellers include the problem of interchanges where superhighways cross each other. Other examples would include the problem of bridge building where canals and streets intermingle. Line–area examples immediately call to mind all manner of traffic problems. Anyone who has been caught in the five o'clock rush as the central business district empties out along limited-access highways into the suburbs can vouch for the frustrations of inadequate line–area relationships.

The complexity of area–area relationships stems from the inherent difficulties of defining areas in terms of logical sets of variables as well as of defining their extent and boundaries. A relatively straightforward example of area–area relationships which results in complex interactions is the city of Berlin (Figure 1–9). Although the entire prewar city originally functioned as a single urban entity, subsequent political differences have separated the two parts. Their zone of contact is the infamous Berlin Wall. Other urban examples of area–area relationships are the ways in which major cities divide the space intervening between themselves and their neigh-

[2]Any such array as this is often referred to as a *matrix*. Individual squares or boxes are called *cells*. The horizontal lines are called *rows*, and the vertical ones are called *columns*.

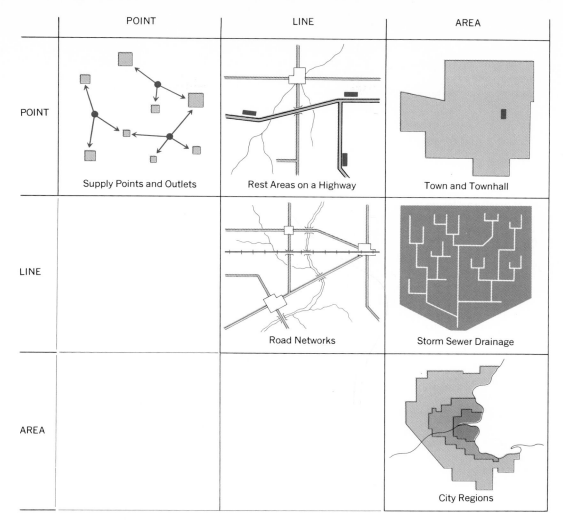

	POINT	LINE	AREA
POINT	Supply Points and Outlets	Rest Areas on a Highway	Town and Townhall
LINE		Road Networks	Storm Sewer Drainage
AREA			City Regions

Figure 1-8 Dimensional relations All spatial phenomena can be characterized by their spatial dimensions. When spatial elements interact, the dimensions involved will influence the geographical pattern that results. The table shows point–point, point–line, point–area, and other kinds of elements in some type of association. The classifications could also be extended to include volumetric relationships by the addition of a row and a column to the table. For example, air pollution problems could be considered a point-to-volume or a line-to-volume interaction depending upon the dimension of the pollution sources.

bors, thus dividing their customers, water supplies, and room for expansion. On still another level, the maintenance of gang territories, or "turfs," within major cities results in street violence and even deaths when rival groups attempt to extend the areas under their control.

Some Basic Spatial Concepts

Once we have learned to think about the world in terms of its point, line, and area characteristics, these dimensional primitives can be used to define basic spatial concepts or axiomatic statements. When geographers talk about space, they do not mean astronomical space. The exploration of interplanetary and interstellar space is the work of astronomers and engineers, not of geographers. Geographers also do not consider space as an object or condition which exists of itself. The space which concerns us is defined functionally by the relationship between things. It is the nature of this geometric and topological relationship that forms the basis for the study of geographic space.

Let us take a simple example to show some geographic concepts. Imagine a large room, either a ballroom or a gymnasium. The empty room provides no clues or directions on how a crowd might behave if gathered there. Now imagine that a dance is to be held in the room. Musicians enter and choose a position at random along one of the walls. Once they have

established themselves, the crowd which has come to listen and dance does not behave randomly, but arranges itself in a very determinate fashion. Nearest the music are those people who want to watch the musicians. In order to see as well as hear, this group will form a semicircle around the orchestra. Before the semicircle is complete, a second rank of listeners may build up near the center, rather than remain too far toward the side. In this area the people will be packed closely together.

Beyond the watchers will be couples more interested in each other and in dancing. They will tend to remain in an area beyond people who are just listening, but within easy range of the music. Here every couple will need a larger space in order to dance, but the total area—while filled with fewer people—will be completely appropriated. Finally, in the areas along the walls and farthest from the musicians will be small groups of people talking or waiting to dance. In this last area there may be empty, unused floor space, as well as clusters of people.

What, then, are the spatial concepts which relate to this scene? First, directional orientation. There is a directional quality to the orchestra. Those spectators interested in the music not only will crowd as close to the musicians as possible, but will also face them. The musicians, in turn, will orient themselves toward the crowd. The human form has a natural orientation—a front and a back—which defines a line of sight. A location or a point

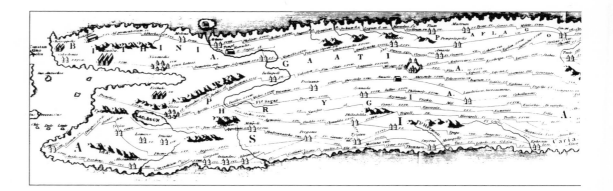

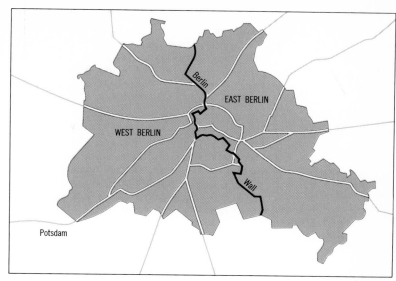

Figure 1-9 The Berlin Wall   West Berlin is a spatially separated enclave of West Germany in East German territory as a consequence of the termination of World War II. Germany was divided into two parts by Western and Communist powers; Berlin, the former capital, also was divided. In the following years, thousands of East Germans fled Communist control by crossing into West Berlin despite efforts to halt them. Eventually the East German regime erected a solid, fortified, and patrolled wall between the two halves of the city in order to prevent the escapes. The wall remains a real and symbolic barrier between the two Germanys. The unusual geographical circumstance is a major factor in the political tension generated by this situation.

Figure 1-10 Peutinger map (*E. Tabula Peutingeriana*)   The map shows routes across Asia Minor in classical times. It contains information about the route network or connections but none about true distances or directions. (*Journal of a Tour in Asia Minor*, William Martin Leake, London: John Murray, 1824)

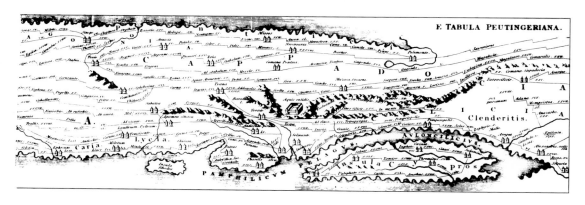

and a line of sight or ray are necessary and sufficient to define orientation. Thus, *direction* is of critical importance in understanding the spatial organization of the scene we are considering.

Distance is another important spatial quality. The sound of the music varies with distance. If the musicians are thought of as communicating to the crowd, they speak most directly to the semicircle of listeners, and somewhat less directly to the dancers beyond, who also are distracted by their own interests. Finally, on the edges of the scene, where the music is soft enough to allow conversation, the people are less directly involved with the musicians.

Intensity of communication falling off continuously with distance is a property shared by many, but not all, phenomena. An example of the opposite effect of distance is a transportation cost which normally rises with distance. Other phenomena are invariant with distance —at least within some range. Legal jurisdiction is as binding at the borders of a state as at its center.

Despite variations in behavior within the room, all the people are there because of the musicians' presence. If the orchestra leaves, the spatial patterning of the people within the room dissolves, for the functional associations which brought them there no longer exist at that place. The room will soon become empty. This relationship between the people and the musicians may be spoken of as a *functional association.*

There is a special type of functional association specifically spatial in character which is referred to as *connectivity*. By this we mean a special relation which objects in space have to each other. Look at Figures 2–3 and 1–10: one is taken from a railroad time schedule; the other is a twelfth-century copy of a third-century A.D. Roman road map. In both maps, although they were drawn seventeen centuries apart, certain spatial qualities are present, just as other spatial qualities are absent. The first shows the Green Bay and Western Railroad which connects Lake Michigan with the Minneapolis–St. Paul area, and the second shows roads in Asia Minor. In both maps, cities and routes are of major interest. In both maps, true proportional distances are lacking. In both maps, true directions or map orientation are also absent. And yet both maps contain significant amounts of information and provide keys to successful travel between the towns they show. Although true portrayals of distance and direction are absent, each shows the correct relative position or adjacency between cities. The *connectivity* of their space has been maintained. No matter how distorted their portrayal of the world, a traveler could find his way from city to city using these maps, for each city maintains its connectivity with its neighbors.

These, then, are the first three spatial concepts with which we are concerned: *distance*, *direction*, and *connectivity*. They will appear again and again in the following chapters. In combination with point, line, and area dimensional concepts, this provides a beginning for all kinds of geographic analysis.

2 | CITY SPACE — CONCEPTS OF SCALE

The Importance of Scale in Human Affairs

Suppose a spaceship operated by alien creatures visits Earth, their mission to seek intelligent life on the planet. While in orbit they remain too high to observe detail on the ground. During the landing phase of the journey, heat-shield problems prevent their monitoring the surface. Once on the ground they immediately find life, but detect only creatures of low intelligence having a simple form of social organization. The alien creatures are tiny; their ship, no bigger than an acorn, has landed in a grassy meadow, and those ant-sized explorers have indeed discovered ants. Upon leaving the earth they record that the planet lacks a developed civilization. They never see humans, and so they are unable to judge what mankind has achieved.

Their scale of observation has been inappropriate. If they had been able to look from their portholes at certain elevations during the descent, they might have noted human figures and the geometric forms of man-made structures. But even then they might not have noticed us, for their own technology might produce a landscape composed of curved forms and irregular elements. In such a case, they would not recognize the crystallike and geometric structures characteristic of our settlement patterns as the products of intelligent life or life at all. Their mission might fail because of two types of problems: one related to the scale of observation and the other to pattern recognition.

Surprisingly, all humans are like those alien creatures. Earth phenomena, both physical and cultural, often occur at scales vastly different from the range within which our unaided senses function. Thus, we frequently fail to make accurate observations of the world in which we live. Sometimes instruments allow us to change our scale of observation and to broaden the range of signals we can monitor. For example, telescopes allow us to see long distances into the hugeness of the universe, while microscopes let us probe into the world of microbes and molecules. Nevertheless, we run the risk of failing to observe the phenomena which interest us most because we may choose the wrong scales of observation. We also may not perceive a pattern when we see one if we fail to recognize that a particular form or arrangement has significance. Finally, patterns may be so obscured by unwanted information that we may need special devices to filter out all but the critical data.

Instruments for changing the scale of observation

Telescopes and microscopes are familiar scientific instruments which change the scale of observation. At the scale at which geographers

Figure 2-1 (A) Apollo VI space photograph of the Dallas–Fort Worth, Texas, area Large roadways are only partially visible. The photograph is an example of a geographical data display in which distance and direction are close to being correctly represented, whereas connectivity is uncertain and fragmented. Other notable features are the light areas, which are devoted mainly to commercial and residential land uses, and the dark areas, which are agricultural fields and groves of trees. Notice how the area between the two cities is built up with urban land uses. This is a physical reflection of the interaction which exists between the two cities.

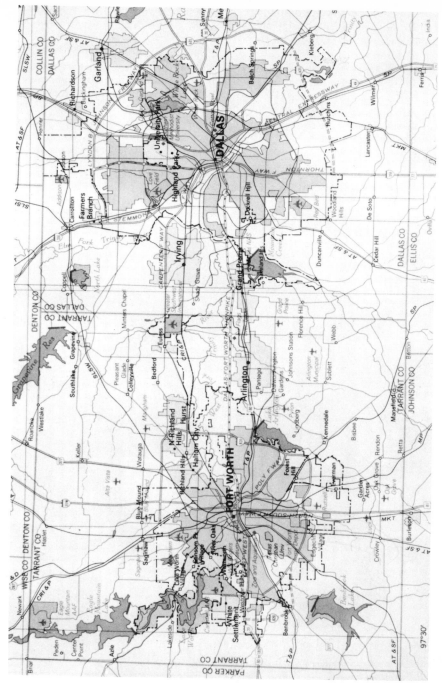

(B) Map of the Dallas–Fort Worth area The map shows the same area as the space photograph above. Notice the similarities, but also notice that additional sets of data have been added to the map; to name a few: political boundaries, railroads, airfields, and place names. Connectivity of transport lines is much more complete, compared to the space shot. The photograph, on the other hand contains information not on the map: for example, the texture, or mosaic, of land uses present and the grid pattern of the roads, which are best seen in the upper-right-hand corner. (Photo by permission of the National Aeronautics and Space Administration; map from *National Atlas of the United States of America*, U.S. Dept. of the Interior, Geological Survey, Washington, D.C., 1970)

observe things, air photographs and maps are similar instruments of observation. Both maps and photos allow us to record very large areas of the earth's surface. Maps much more than air photographs, however, are selective filters which can be used to enhance important elements and to diminish or eliminate unimportant ones. Figure 2–1*A* and *B* shows a satellite photo and a highway map of the Dallas–Fort Worth area of Texas. Notice how each presents a large, different set of information.

Space, when portrayed on maps, may also be stretched and transformed in a controlled manner. Such controlled distortions of map space are called *map transformations*. Figures 2–2 and 2–3 show familiar types of map transformations: one, a Bostonian's view of the United States; and the other, the area served by a particular railroad company. In each case, the area most important to the map maker has been enlarged at the expense of other places. While these illustrate subjective map transformations, Figure 2–4 shows a map which emphasizes southern Michigan according to a

Figure 2-2 *A* **Bostonian's view of the United States** (Daniel K. Wallingford, Columbia University Bookstore, New York)

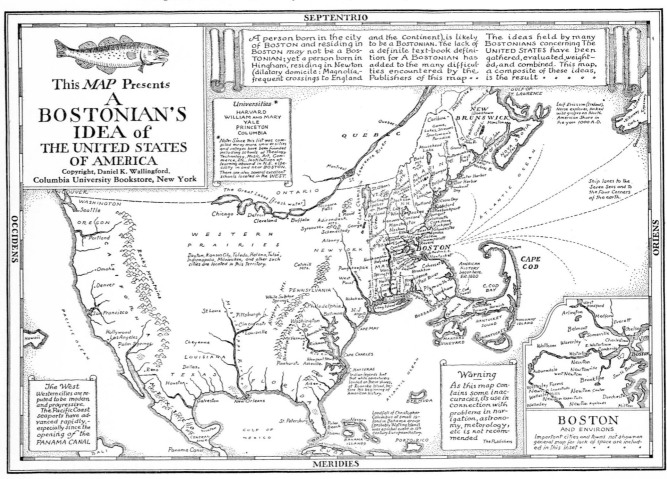

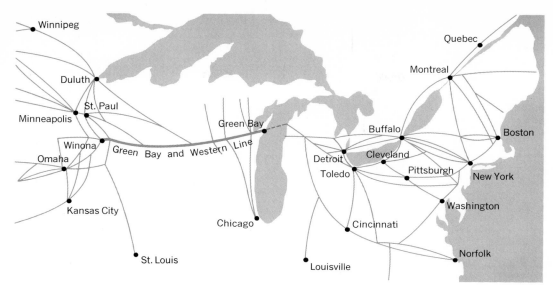

Figure 2-3 The Green Bay and Western Railroad Distances, direction, and area are distorted on this map, but connections are correct. The purpose of the map is to show the connectivity of the railroad company's rail network. (By permission of the Green Bay and Western Railroad Company, Green Bay, Wisconsin)

mathematical formula. Conversely, inappropriate choice of transformations can obscure meaningful patterns. Thus, the Bostonian's map would not serve the needs of a traveling salesman.

Any collection of information recorded by areal units may be considered an instrument of spatial observation. The United States Census Bureau reports information by census tracts, which are small areas within which the number of houses, the number of people by age distribution, and many other facts are listed. Information is also sometimes presented in city, county, state, or national units. For cities of more than 50,000, "block statistics," which describe the units defined by intersecting streets (i.e., city blocks), are also available.

There are many similarities between mechanical instruments, such as cameras, and the charts and tables produced by census enumerators and social scientists. Just as you may place a filter over the camera lens to re-move unwanted wavelengths of light, census enumerators may choose to list only certain kinds of phenomena. The photographer may use other optical devices to enhance the edges of photographic images; the choice of enumeration categories may similarly enhance or delete particular census data. For example, businesses below a certain size may be omitted from an enumeration; or census tracts which have a few nonfarm families but which are still mainly used for farming may be counted as completely agricultural for some purposes.

Limitations on scale change as an analytical device

Just as both optical and census instruments perform transformations on data, each instrument has its own peculiar limitations which distort the information transmitted. For example, data about a city are often reported only for the area within the city limits. Although city boundaries define the legal jurisdiction

Figure 2-4 Map emphasizing southeastern Michigan In this map projection centered on the state of Michigan, distance from the center is plotted as the square root of actual distance. The effect is to enlarge the center of the map at the expense of its edges.

of the municipality, the city as a unified place of settlement may extend far beyond its limited political jurisdiction. Data reported for the political unit alone—that is, the municipality —may be incomplete in terms of the city as a regional entity with far-reaching functions. The nature of the census unit is just as important as the speed of a camera lens, and one must be very aware of the characteristics and capabilities of the statistical instruments used in order to avoid errors of observation.

In the motion picture *Blow Up*, the story line centered on a photographer who took a picture of two people in a park. Later he discovered the real story in the picture—the image of what appeared to be a body lying in some bushes in the background. The size of the body was very small relative to the field of vision. Because of this, and to learn if there really was a body in the picture, the photographer enlarged the photograph in order to see more clearly the segment which had attracted his attention. The first enlargement he made was more enticing, but still the picture was too small for him to be certain that a body

was truly shown in the photograph. Eventually, however, he enlarged the part of the photo showing the body so many times that, just as the information he sought was within his grasp, the grains of the photo emulsion and the other optical and technical characteristics of the instruments he used for enlarging and processing blurred the picture into a random pattern of gray tones. In other words, just as his choice of scale was about to reveal the truth, the ratio of unwanted to needed information became too great to retain the pattern. At the movie's end the photographer still was uncertain about what he had photographed and was unable to learn whether a crime really had been committed.

This scenario reveals the necessity for establishing upper and lower bounds on what we wish to observe. If a subject is too small a part of the total picture, it will be lost in an overwhelming flow of useless information. If it is too large, only one small portion of the whole will dominate the entire picture. The end result will be like the blind men and the elephant, each of whom could describe the elephant only in terms of the one part he could touch. In the same way, maps and other instruments used to record and display facts are heavily dependent on their inherent limitations as well as on the perceptions of the researcher using them. To have confidence in facts, one must be sure of the methods employed to gather and present them.

Site and Situation as Changes in Scale

Spatial observations involve both positional control and identification of local values or intensities. Positional control means keeping track of the location of each observation relative to other observations or to some fixed delineation of earth-space. Knowing the location of each observation allows preservation of spatial order, the importance of which was discussed in Chapter 1. The major reference system for knowing where things are in the world is the latitude and longitude coordinate grid, which uses the equator and the prime meridian as its reference bases. But it is not always necessary to know the latitude and longitude of a place to maintain positional control. All that is needed is information about the relative locations of elements under study.

The situation and site of cities as a problem of scale

To speak of the relative location or situation of things is to comment on the properties of the space in which they are found. Spatial properties need not be constant. In one context we may be concerned only with linear distance; in another, travel time may be the best way to measure functional distances. Other attributes of the space, such as direction and connection, may also be involved. With good locational control one can speak of the shape or pattern of spatial systems. Without such control only intensity measures at given sites remain. Geographers distinguish relative location and intensities at specific places by referring to *situation* and *site* characteristics.

The character of a site is also obtained by observation. Site data include the quantity and type of all manner of things found at a given location. For example, such data might include the number of people living in a house, the ethnic character of those same people, their income, and many other attributes. Site observations may also include the number of houses in a city, the energy produced at a given place, the total built-up area of a city or region, or the proportion of multistory buildings to single-story structures. That is, any identifying characteristics can be used to describe a site. The choice of what is described depends upon the needs of the observer and the problems he wishes to solve. When measuring site characteristics, there is no concern for positional control. The important feature is the quality or intensity of the thing observed.

In summary, geographers speak of site and situation. Observations of site refer to the qualities or attributes of a place; observations of situation refer to the position or location of a place relative to other places. A site is best thought of as an area with particular attributes.

If the same place is thought of in relation to other places, it is best considered as a point location. This involves a change of scale. Figure 2–5 illustrates such a transition from point to area. At a scale of 1:500,000 the town of Gettysburg, Pennsylvania, appears as a point connected by lines (roads) to other settlements also shown as points. At a larger scale, 1:130,000, the town appears as an undifferentiated built-up area with roads radiating from it. At still larger scales it is seen as a heterogeneous area composed of streets, houses, public buildings, and parks.

Characteristics of site and situation

Site and situation characteristics can be both good and bad. Cities may prosper from being well situated and from having pleasing site conditions. They may also encounter difficulties from being poorly situated or from having negative site characteristics. Calcutta, India, for example, is located in a swamp, a poor site. Because of its site, clean drinking water is scarce, waste disposal is difficult, and special precautions must be taken with the foundations of buildings lest they crack or sink into the soft ground. The situation of Calcutta, on the other hand, is a good one. The city is located at tidewater and can be reached by oceangoing vessels. Upstream from the city are the Ganges–Brahmaputra river system and the Gangetic Plain, populated by millions. Thus, Calcutta's situation is a good one, allowing it to serve as the major commercial gateway between a large population and the rest of the world.

Other places which are important because of their location come easily to mind. The barren, steep-sided Rock of Gibraltar is a poor site for normal activities. At the same time, its location at the entrance to the Mediterranean Sea gives it great strategic value and makes it well suited to serve as a fortress. Similar rocky eminences in remote deserts and along open, empty shores have no situational value and are avoided because of their difficult site properties. But like Gibraltar, the port of Aden, located at an inhospitable site, is occupied

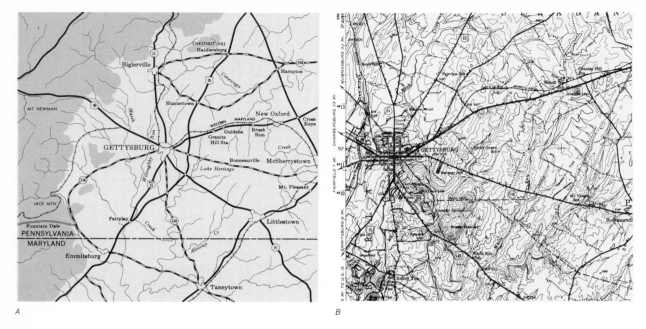

A   B

because of its position at the entrance to the Red Sea.

Some places have good sites but poor locations. A familiar example is beautiful Rio de Janeiro with Sugar Loaf Mountain rising above its curving beaches. But Rio de Janeiro is badly located with respect to the rest of Brazil. It is on the eastern coastal periphery, cut off from the interior by a difficult mountain range. To counteract these qualities and to promote the development of the interior, the capital of Brazil has been moved from Rio de Janeiro well inland to Brazilia. Situation, not site qualities, led to this move.

In any investigation, the classification of phenomena according to site or situation depends upon the scale of observation. If the internal pattern of Calcutta is to be considered, a large-scale map is necessary. This choice of scale would allow a close inspection of Calcutta and would reveal the city as a heterogeneous set of areas constituting business districts, caste neighborhoods, and transportation networks, all of which have either high or low population densities with people who can be described as rich or poor.

A further enlargement of a given district within the city would reveal the location of individual buildings or activities. A particular hotel might be the one used most by foreign visitors. This could be explained either by the quality of service available—a site attribute —or by the convenience of its location relative to points of interest within the city—a situational attribute.

Knowing the character and location of all the parts of the city has little meaning in discussing the role of the city in world affairs. At such a scale Calcutta is better considered a point, well located with respect to world trade and the pattern of population distribution in India.

The Scale at Which Things Happen

Scale considerations are important in two ways. We have seen that the scales with which we choose to observe the world influence our interpretations of it. In much the same way, the behavior of an individual can vary significantly from that of the group or population to which he belongs. What a person says as

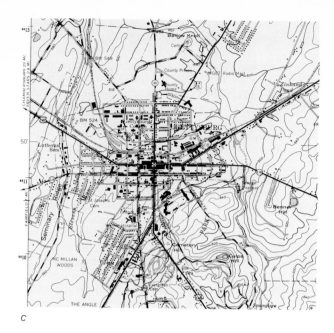

C

Figure 2-5 Scale transition from a point to an area   Gettysburg, Pennsylvania, at three different map scales: (A) 1:500,000, (B) 1:130,000, and (C) 1:48,000. Notice that the total area covered gets smaller as the scale of the map enlarges. Large-scale maps are close-up views. Small-scale maps are distant views. (U.S. Geological Survey topographic maps)

an individual may not match what he does as the elected chairman of a committee; what he does as chairman of a committee may not match how he votes as the member of a political party; how he acts as the member of a political party may be different from his response as a loyal citizen to international conditions. Such changes in behavior do not mean that this person is inconsistent or hypocritical, but rather that different types of events take place at different scales or levels of organization and his responses to those events may vary accordingly. What may be appropriate at one level can be inconsistent at the next. An appreciation of the different scales at which things happen can be useful in understanding the nature of the world.

Personal space

The analysis of the personal space in which individuals function is of interest to anthropologists and sociologists as well as geographers, and is sometimes referred to as the study of *proxemics*. Each one of us surrounds himself with a small territory which he feels

to be his own. We have all experienced the feeling of uneasiness when we suddenly find our elbow in competition with that of some stranger for the same armrest in a theater. This "bubble" of personal space is very important to us. We prefer that strangers "keep their distance," although friends may come closer. In American society, the only people whom we readily welcome within touching distance are our close relatives and loved ones. The next time you attend a ball game or movie, observe the way in which the crowd shares the limited space which it occupies. Dates and married couples may hold hands or walk with their arms touching, but strangers will attempt to preserve their own personal spaces, although the distances which separate them may be reduced to a few inches or less. In order to do this and to minimize the flood of sensation that accompanies any crowd, people will take evasive action. Their movements will become restricted; they walk with short steps and keep their arms close to their sides. If inadvertently touched by someone, they will draw back as sharply as the confined space allows. Conversely, within the limits of this most intimate

*City Space—
Concepts of
Scale*

of personal spaces nothing is more pleasant than the awareness of the touch and perhaps even the aroma and warmth of someone you love.

Living or work space

Beyond the more intimate limits of each person's space are the areas or territories within which we live our daily lives. The classroom and the dormitory, as well as the office and the rooms of your own home, represent another and larger type of space which has special meaning. Within this living or work space, distances are measured from about two to three feet for conversations between casual acquaintances, to perhaps tens of feet for lectures, group activities, and parties. Conversations are carried on in normal tones, and individuals respect each others' personal "bubbles" of territory; office workers can exchange information, meetings are carried out across conference tables, and students and counselors interact comfortably at these distances. We are able to focus our gaze upon the facial expressions of the people with whom we are communicating. Slight movements and changes in the tone of a person's voice give clues to the way in which he is reacting to the situation. Living spaces are controlled by the construction of soundproof walls and doors that can close off rooms for greater privacy. Under these conditions members of a family may choose to come together to share their feelings, such as on Christmas when presents are opened around the tree. At other times, an individual will feel a need to be alone and may lock the door of his room to ensure privacy.

These units of personal, working, and living space are the indivisible building blocks which society uses to organize the areas which it occupies. Be sure to keep them in mind as you consider how larger spaces such as urban areas are organized.

House and neighborhood space

A group of houses upon their individual lots or several apartment buildings and other structures along a street constitute still another type of space, which might also include large lecture halls, auditoriums, gardens, and small parks. Distances here may range from 100 to perhaps 1,000 feet, the outer limit often being the limits of line-of-sight recognition. Where living units are concerned, territories of this size are often thought of as neighborhoods. Larger groups of people can meet under these circumstances. Usually an individual will not know all the other persons gathered nearby but will share some common purpose with them. A speaker can be recognized from a distance, but friends may become lost in the crowd. Communication becomes more difficult; sound amplifying devices become necessary for public meetings. If you wish to talk with someone, you may have to walk within speaking range, and often we telephone our friends next door rather than visit them. Under these conditions contacts between people become more specialized and less casual. We designate certain places for meetings, others for private domiciles, still others for parks and playgrounds. In this way, spatial specialization exerts an increasing control on human communication. Symbols such as the standardized shape of traffic markers often supplant lettered signs, and messages are more often directed from one person to many listeners rather than on a person-to-person basis. The neighborhood may become an important feature of city life within these distances, and the distribution of minority groups can often be mapped at this scale.

City-hinterland space

The scale of change between neighborhood and city marks a transition where the study of face-to-face behavior, sometimes called *proxemics*, gives way to more specifically geographic spatial considerations. A city consists of many neighborhoods and specialized areas which function together in a manner different from that of a cluster of households. In addition, the city occupies a central focus within a region or hinterland which it serves and which in turn is dependent upon the urban center.

The extent of the city and its hinterland is fixed in large part by the distance which commuters will travel to and from work. Research has shown that the average American commuter will travel no farther than about 60 minutes either going to or coming from work. Depending upon road and traffic conditions, this means that the linear commuting distances traveled in and near a city vary from 4 to 40 miles. Beyond this distance communication becomes more difficult, and it is within this range that local news media, radio and television, daily newspapers, and urban institutions—such as local and metropolitan governments—are effective. Crowding, traffic congestion, and possible bottlenecks in communication must be overcome by routine channelization. Superhighways, one-way street systems, Federal Communications Commission regulations, and many other devices are used to expedite the movement of people, goods, and information under these conditions.

Regional-national space

Nations can be thought of as clusters of cities and the regions which they represent. The distances at which humans interact in terms of regional and national systems vary from a few hundred miles to several thousand. In order to tie such vast areas together, news media—such as nationwide broadcasting and television networks—must be organized. In the same way, political parties need not only "grass roots" organizations but also nationally organized superstructures to coordinate the efforts of the thousands of local groups. Nations need carefully designed chains of administrative command and clearly defined relationships between local and national governments in order to function effectively. Highways physically bind the nation together. A strong constitution and legal system, which clarify and standardize numberless individual differences in human behavior, are other means of communication within the nation. Thus, the type of human activities served at this level can be thought of as nationwide

transportation, political, legal, and economic systems, to name a few of the possibilities.

Global space

Finally, individual nations and international blocs relate to each other on a global scale. The world itself is the limit of the distances involved, with 12,000 miles the farthest that one point can be from another on the surface of the globe. World affairs of all kinds are carried on at this scale. Trade agreements and cultural exchanges are the alternatives to misunderstandings and warfare. In this case, international communications systems, including satellite relay stations and transoceanic cables, facilitate the exchange of information. Translation from one language to another is essential, and international organizations like the United Nations and the International Red Cross help coordinate the efforts of individual countries. In the same way, trade and customs barriers, as well as visa and passport requirements, can restrict travel and the flow of goods and ideas. The ever-increasing improvement in transportation and communication technology draws the world together, but the subsequent sense of crowding and the urgency of instantaneous news coverage may unnecessarily magnify the problems of organization at a global scale.

The representative fraction

Table 2–1 shows the relationship of these scales of human activity to each other. It should be recognized that the transition from one scale to another is continuous and that all of the indicated scales are ranked along a continuum rather than existing in reality as discrete pigeonholes or quanta. Special attention should be given to the column labeled "representative fraction." This term is used particularly by cartographers on the maps which they prepare. It is a way of accurately indicating the relationship between the real world and its graphic representation. The numerator, the number which appears before the colon, indicates one unit of *linear* measure (inches, centimeters, etc.) on the map; the second number, the denominator, represents the number of inches or centimeters (or whatever *linear* unit is specified) of the real world indicated by one map unit. Thus, if we were to draw a life-sized picture of a man, 1 inch on the paper would represent 1 inch of the man's actual measurements. If his nose were 2 inches long in reality, it would appear 2 inches long in the drawing. This would be indicated by a representative fraction 1:1, or 1/1. If we were to draw a very large map of a room in which everything appeared one-fourth actual size (e.g., a table 4 feet square would appear as a rectangle 12 by 12 inches on the paper), the representative fraction would be 1:4, or 1/4. Maps of manageable size must be quite small regardless of the areas they represent. Thus, most representative fractions are very small by the above standards. Maps which show 1 mile equal to 1 inch on paper have an R.F. (the common abbreviation for representative fraction) of 1:63,360. The range of representative fractions shown in the table suggests the scale of the maps which could be used to plot the corresponding activities. Maps of personal space are seldom if ever made, but in order to complete the table, an R.F. of 1:1 has been included.

How Scale Changes Operate in Human Affairs

Many of the problems which human beings must solve pertain to the scales at which various processes operate. We quickly learn not to trim our fingernails with dressmaking shears—there are smaller scissors designed to do the job. The difference between the two types of tools is a matter of scale, and the problems encountered when we use the wrong-sized tool for the job are occasioned by a lack of fit.

After recognizing that human activities proceed at different scales, we are faced with trying to understand how communication across scales works. Communication is often not very successful because the media involved do not match the job to be done.

Advertising: An economic example

Many activities demand a proper fit between the processes and equipment involved. One example of this is the problem faced by firms wishing to advertise through magazine ads. A large metropolitan bank may wish to gain the prestige of advertising in a nationally recognized magazine. Such publications may have circulations in the millions and distribute copies in all fifty states as well as throughout the world. Page rates for advertising in these magazines are predicated on very large audiences and are extremely expensive. In fact, banks seeking customers in only one city or one metropolitan area may find such costs prohibitive. When national-level magazines first began to be published, very few local firms could justify the expense of advertising in their pages. And yet this source of income was desirable for the publishers, just as the prestige of their pages was desirable to potential advertisers. The problem was a lack of fit in the scales at which the two institutions functioned. In recent years this problem has been largely overcome by publishing regional editions of national magazines. Thus, the major news stories, feature articles, and fiction appear in the copies printed and bound in every region in which they are sold, but the advertising is solicited locally as well as nationally. Special pages are inserted in editions meant to be distributed within restricted areas. In this way a metropolitan bank may place an advertisement which will reach only those customers within range of the bank's services. At the same time, larger companies selling automobiles or soap on a national basis will also place advertising in the same issue. Rates are adjusted according to the estimated customer potential for each used, and all the parties benefit from the adjustment in scale which has been made.

Metropolitan versus local city government: A political example

A second example illustrating this point relates to the problems of local and regional

Table 2–1   Relationship of Population Groups, Types of Activities, and Scales of Interaction

Type of Space	Spatial Range	Characteristics of Interaction				
	Radius from person (representative fraction)	Primary modes of interaction	Selected controls	Type of function	Number of people involved	
Personal space	Arm's length 1:1	Voice, touch, taste, smell	Evasive movement	Intimate contact	1, 2, 3, . . .	
Living or working space (private space)	10–50 feet 1:50	Audio and visual (sharp focus on facial expression and slight movement or tonal changes)	Impervious walls, doors	Effective personal conversation, 1-to-1 exchanges	. . . 50–400 . . .	
House and neighborhood space	100–1,000 feet (line of sight) 1:500	Audio-visual (sound amplification)	Spatial specialization	Impersonal interactions symbol recognition, many-to-one exchanges	. . . 100–1,000 . . .	
		Limit of Proxemic Interaction				
City–hinterland space	4 to 40 miles (60-minute one-way commute) 1:50.000 1:63.630 = 1 inch = 1 mile	Local news media, TV, urban institutions, commuter systems	Routine channelization	Mean information field, daily contact space	. . . 50,000– 10 million	
Regional–national space	200–3,000 miles 1:500,000	National network of news media, national organizations, common language desirable	Hierarchies	Legal-economic-political systems	200+ million	
Global space	12,000 miles 1:50,000,000	International communication networks, translator services, world organizations, international blocs	Travel restrictions, trade barriers and trade agreements	War, trade, cultural exchanges	3+ billion	

government. In years past, central cities such as St. Louis and Chicago were largely self-sufficient in terms of the services which they provided for their inhabitants and the local tax base which met the expenses of city government. This was particularly true in the period before mass transportation and the automobile. At that time, most people who worked in the city shopped there and took advantage of its streets, parks, schools, and playgrounds, and also lived within the legal limits of the town. The taxes they paid were directly available as payment for the services they received. Moreover, the population represented a cross section of the settlement's economy. The rich, the poor, and the middle

City Space— Concepts of Scale

class, as well as businesses, factories, and residential areas, were found within the city boundaries.

Recent developments have greatly changed the situation just described. As city populations have increased, more and more of the wealthy and middle class have moved to the suburbs and now commute to work. This has had a multiple effect upon the central city. New suburban towns are growing up on the perimeters of the cities. Such settlements frequently incorporate and became legally independent communities with the power to levy taxes on their inhabitants. The central city thus loses suburban taxpayers as a source of revenue, particularly with regard to property taxes. At the same time, because the suburbs have become legally independent, the city is no longer able to expand outward and incorporate recently settled areas. There is an absolute outward limit placed upon the city's growth as a legal entity. However, many suburbanites continue to travel to the city for employment. Ever-increasing numbers of automobiles necessitate new access highways and terminal facilities such as parking structures. The central city is strangling in crowds of cars and clouds of exhaust fumes. Funds to pay for the new roads and parking structures and for the upkeep on the overburdened pavements must be provided by the central city government—not by the commuters, who are taxed at their places of residence in the independent suburbs. Many factories and businesses which in turn wish to expand seek the congestion-free suburbs with their lower land values and tax rates, and another source of revenue is denied the central city. Finally, new migrants to the city generally come from poor rural areas. Many of these newcomers are from culturally disadvantaged groups which present the inner-city schools with an additional educational burden. Suburban schools often offer higher salaries and better working conditions which in turn lure teachers away from the city.

As the inner city and its government groan under this collection of woes, new solutions to the problem are sought. One suggestion has been the idea of metropolitan governments. Such governments would be organized much like that of the federal government of the United States. That is, while maintaining local independence in many things, the suburban city governments would unite with the central city to form an overall governing body which could levy certain taxes and redistribute resources for the good of the entire community both within and without the central city limits. This in essence constitutes a scale change in the approach to urban problems. Metropolitan governments as such, however, have until very recently met with no success in their formation. (In Canada, metropolitan Toronto seems to be a successful exception to this observation.) The people of the suburbs have been unwilling either to share their taxes with the inner city or in turn to accept responsibility for the special problems found at the core of the urban region.

As the white flight to the suburbs continues, the proportion of poor black residents increases within the central city. Where once this group represented a minority, the roles of white and black are being reversed and some cities are now electing black mayors for the first time. In other cities councilmen and high officials are being chosen from minority groups.

Parallel to this latest set of changes is the growth of a new attitude toward metropolitan government. Where once nonwhite groups constituted an unrepresented minority, they now are a major political force within the central city. The formation of metropolitan governments would allow suburban candidates the chance to win office and to control the inner city, once more placing the black minority at a disadvantage. In this way, the scale change from small local governments to larger units not only offers potential aid to the central city but also threatens the role of inner-city residents in representative government. Thus, black leaders of the core areas are now being faced with a new set of political problems which further demonstrate how the many parts of an urban area are mutually interdependent.

3 | CITY SPACE — MODELS OF CITY GROWTH

Politics, planning, and survival all relate to the size, shape, and growth patterns of urban areas. If we are to survive as urban dwellers and urban neighbors, we must understand as much as possible about the growth and function of cities. Inevitably, three questions must be answered about urban places whenever we attempt to understand how they prosper or decline. Where do urban people come from? What forces help to create the general character of cities? What tangible shapes do cities take, and are such shapes clues to the processes underlying city growth? The concern of this chapter is largely the third question, although the first two are dealt with briefly.

Sources of Urban Growth

The growth of urban population has already been discussed in Chapter 1. Let us only remind ourselves of the general origins of urban people and of the magnitude of urban population growth, particularly in America. Cities increase in two ways—through migration and through natural increase. At present, natural increase accounts for the greater part of urban population growth, but in earlier decades and in the eighteenth and nineteenth centuries migration was more important. Such migration consisted of two types: the movement of

rural people into cities and the mass movement of urban and rural populations from one region or country to another as the result of political, economic, and other pressures.

Typical of this latter type is the migration to the United States of more than 34 million immigrants between 1841 and 1930. More than 80 percent of these migrants come from Europe (Table 3–1).

Earlier migrations had peopled the thirteen colonies with smaller groups of white and black people, but no other population movement in history can compare with that great journey from the Old World to the New at the end of the nineteenth and the beginning of the twentieth centuries. Two out of three foreign-born residents of the United States chose city homes in 1900 although the nation as a whole at that time was only 40 percent urban. By 1950, 64 percent of our population was urbanized and 36 percent rural. At the same time in 1950 about 80 percent of all foreign-born Americans lived in the nation's cities.

For the present discussion of city space, we need only be aware of the numbers of people who arrived and that they came to America to live primarily in its cities. This international migration temporarily eased Europe's population crisis. Such relief was short-lived, however, and later internal migration from farms to

Table 3-1   Immigration to the United States, 1820–1968

Period	Europe	Asia	America	Oceania	Africa	Total
1820	7,691	5	387		1	8,084
1821–1830	98,817	10	11,564		16	110,407
1831–1840	495,688	48	33,424		54	529,214
1841–1850	1,597,501	82	62,469		55	1,660,107
1851–1860	2,452,660	41,455	74,720		210	2,569,045
1861–1870	2,065,270	64,630	166,607	36	312	2,296,855
1871–1880	2,272,262	123,823	404,044	10,914	358	2,811,401
1881–1890	4,737,046	68,380	426,967	12,574	857	5,245,824
1891–1900	3,558,978	71,236	38,972	3,965	350	3,673,501
1901–1910	8,136,016	243,567	361,888	13,024	7,368	8,761,863
1911–1920	4,376,564	192,559	1,143,671	13,427	8,443	5,734,664
1921–1930	2,477,853	97,400	1,516,716	8,726	6,286	4,106,981
1931–1940	348,289	15,344	160,037	3,011	1,750	528,431
1941–1950	621,704	31,780	354,804	19,242	7,367	1,034,897
1951–1960	1,328,293	147,453	996,944	16,204	14,092	2,502,986
1961–1968	904,965	255,289	1,390,603	15,900	17,395	2,584,152
Total	35,479,597	1,356,061	7,143,817	117,023	64,914	44,161,412

Does not include 269,321 "Not Specified" immigrants for the years 1820–1968.
Source: *Annual Report*, U.S. Immigration and Naturalization Service, 1968.

factories had the same result in Europe as in America. Everywhere towns and cities expanded at an astonishing rate.

Processes of Urban Growth

It is risky to describe the physical growth of a single city or single type of settlement and to say with confidence that the pattern described fits more than a few real examples. On the other hand, we need a general description of the development of American cities to serve as a background for more abstract theories of city growth. The following characterization of urban development in America is intended not so much as a complete picture, but rather as a frame for the theories which conclude the chapter.

Cities at the beginning of the Industrial Revolution

In accordance with our ideas of point, line, and area relationships, cities may be thought of as being tied together by routes along which move people, supplies, products, and messages. At the beginning of the Industrial Revolution, water transport predominated, and the carriers on such routes were oceangoing ships, riverboats, and canal barges. River and canal towns as well as seaports were of great importance, and their core areas grew up within easy reach of good docking facilities. When railroads appeared somewhat later in the nineteenth century, the first engines were underpowered, and trains had to seek out the lowest mountain passes, the flattest land, and the gentlest slopes. This meant that the tracks often followed the rivers or coastlines and entered settlements at points near existing port facilities. In other settlements lacking water transport, railroads also kept to the lowest ground and avoided hills and steep grades. Factories, warehouses, and businesses which depended upon rail and water transportation for raw materials and the shipment of finished goods were located along the waterfronts and near the railroads. Businesses also were concentrated near the docks and rail lines. As a result, business districts were often

*Spatial
Design
in World
Society*

32

pointlike clusters or linear in form, following transportation lines. These historic core areas were often noisy, dirty, and unhealthy, with fevers and poor drinking water adding to the problems of the inhabitants, the more fortunate of whom moved to higher ground and commuted to work by horse and buggy. The poorer working class, with little or no public transportation, had to live within walking distance of the factories. Thus, the idea of the "other side of the tracks" or the "poor in the hollow and the rich on the hill" became an established fact in early industrial society.

Other nineteenth century urban characteristics

Coal-burning steam engines were another factor contributing to location of the working population in nineteenth century cities. These steam engines were used to turn drive shafts, which in turn were connected by means of moving belts to individual looms, drill presses, sewing machines, and all other types of factory equipment. Such belt-driven mechanisms presented particular problems to the designers of factories. If the belt-drives were too long, they sagged and either dragged on the ground or had to be held up by auxiliary rollers. In either case much power was lost. A better design was to run the main belt-drives vertically from an engine in the factory basement to machines and equipment located directly overhead. Factories were stacked vertically floor above floor, with the source of power in the basement. Raw materials had to be lifted to the upper floors, while semifinished and finished goods were lowered to waiting transport at ground level. This constituted an inefficient system which constantly fought the pull of gravity. When new sources of power became available, this style was rapidly abandoned, but in many older American cities multistoried red-brick factory buildings dating from the nineteenth century can still be found near the railroad tracks and along the waterfronts.

All these conditions resulted in cities at the beginning of the nineteenth century which were constricted and crowded. Clusters of vertical, belt-drive factories, located in low-lying areas along transportation routes, were surrounded by the densely packed dwellings of factory workers, who could travel no farther to work than they could walk at the end of a long, hard day. Better neighborhoods, which accommodated the wealthy, were removed from the original factory and business districts and often located on higher ground. Under such crowded conditions, population growth forced the cities to expand outward from their historic cores. Such expansion depended in turn upon new developments in the technology of manufacturing and transportation.

Late nineteenth and early twentieth century cities

The distances mechanical energy could be transmitted and workers could travel to their jobs were severely limited at the beginning of the Industrial Revolution. New inventions in the century that followed rapidly changed the internal design of factories and the commuting patterns of their employees. Knowledge of how to produce, transport, and use electricity became important. Centrally located plants, dependent upon falling water or burning coal, made available electric power which could be transported along cables or overhead wires. This in turn allowed a new form of mass transportation to develop; the electric interurban train and the electric trolley soon changed the American city landscape. Commuter lines extended outward from the original city centers along lengthening radial lines. As Figure 3–1 shows, small suburbs sprang up along these electric interurban lines, and cities grew outward in response to the new means of transportation. Electricity also meant that machines no longer needed to be attached to steam engines by unwieldy belt-driven mechanisms. Instead, machines powered by electricity could be located wherever their owners wished. It became a simple matter to lead power to the machine by means of an insulated cable. This meant in turn that factories no longer had to be stacked floor on

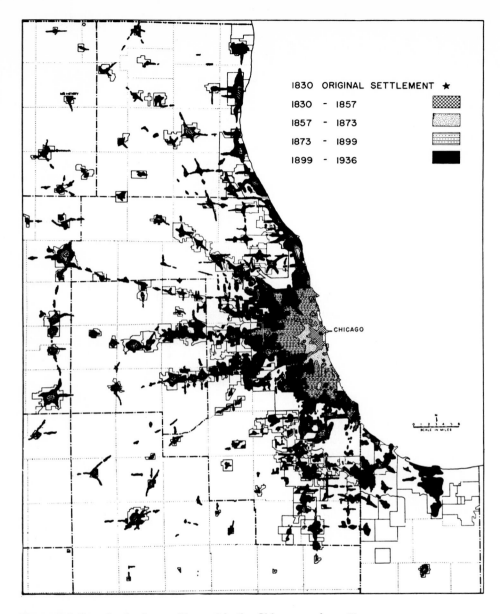

Figure 3-1 Growth of urban settlement in the Chicago region The concentric rings of growth are clearly visible. Also apparent is the heavier growth along the lake shore to the north. The linear development radiating from the center is the effect on suburban land use of the electric interurban railways and, later, of the United States highway system.
(*The Structure and Growth of Residential Neighborhoods in American Cities,* Homer Hoyt, Federal Housing Administration, U.S. Govt. Printing Office, Washington, D.C., 1939, p. 98)

floor above steam engines. Gravity became much less of an enemy as factories went horizontal, with products moving from point to point on the assembly line along moving tracks. Thus, the familiar one-story industrial plant filling many acres of land became a working reality. However, the construction of such buildings required large tracts of cheap land, unavailable in the crowded cities. In addition, taxes were increasingly levied by larger cities to pay for improvements in transportation and social services demanded by a better organized and educated labor force. The suburbs offered not only land in sufficient quantities but sometimes tax advantages as inducements for luring new business their way.

The twentieth century city

The movement of industry and business to the suburbs might not have been possible but for parallel improvements in transportation. By 1910 the internal combustion engine was developed to the point where the private automobile became practical. Parallel developments in petroleum refining and road building helped create a new urban environment characterized by increasing numbers of automobiles. After World War II, lighter, stronger steel alloys, aluminum, and other modern metals replaced heavy, brittle cast iron; synthetic rubber reduced the price of tires. The price of cars went down relative to the income-earning ability of the workers who produced them. The electric interurban train had lost popularity and streetcar tracks were torn up as private autos and public trolleybuses carried more and more of the public to work, market, and play. Eventually, the interurban lines were replaced with high-speed limited-access highways which also radiated outward from the central parts of cities.

In interurban times, once the commuter arrived at his suburban station, he had to find his way home on foot or by horse and buggy. Suburban towns, as a result, were restricted to areas very near the electric train tracks. This meant that as the radiating rail lines pushed farther and farther from the cities,

the distances between the various branches increased. More and more inaccessible farmland remained between the lengthening spokes of the wheel-shaped network of facilities. Since the advent of the auto, the commuter no longer has been restricted at the homeward end of his trip from the city. After leaving the expressway, he simply drives a few miles farther into the previously inaccessible land near the centers of the pie-shaped sectors between the major highways. The unused farmlands away from major routes have already begun to fill up, and today cities spread outward in all directions from their cores. Factories once located outside of urban areas are now far behind the advancing built-up edges of the cities. Workers commute by automobile laterally around metropolitan perimeters as well as along radial routes leading to and from city centers.

The inefficient factories of the nineteenth century are largely abandoned and often torn down, and the tenements near the center of the cities no longer house immigrants from Europe. Now a new wave of poor people, both black and white, often rural and largely from the South, or Spanish Americans from the Southwest and Puerto Rico, have arrived. The workers' tenements of yesterday have become slums and black ghettoes, while the children and grandchildren of poor first-generation Irish, Italian, and Polish immigrant workers now are substantial middle-class suburbanites. But the city as a dynamic ever-changing entity continues to expand.

A Simple Model of City Growth

This thumbnail sketch of urban events in America over the last 1½ centuries scarcely indicates the complexities of the changes that have occurred. Geographic theories help us to order and then interpret the kaleidoscopic urban world. In this way we come to the third set of questions posed at the beginning of this chapter. How does a spatial point of view enlarge our understanding of city processes?

City Space—Models of City Growth

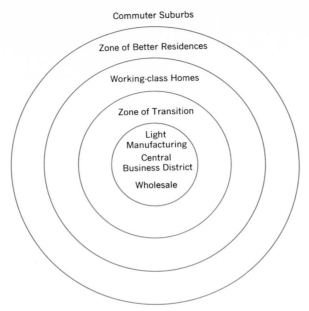

Commuter Suburbs

Zone of Better Residences

Working-class Homes

Zone of Transition

Light
Manufacturing
Central
Business District
Wholesale

**Figure 3-2 The concentric ring model of city
growth** (After Ernest Burgess, "Growth of the
City," *Proceedings of the American Sociological
Society,* vol. 18, 1923, 85–89.

The concentric ring theory

Just as we can tell the age and fortunes of a
tree by looking at its rings, cities also have
telltale patterns by which they reveal themselves to us. In fact, a "concentric ring" theory
of city growth was suggested by Ernest Burgess in the 1920s (Figure 3–2). Burgess and
his colleagues at the University of Chicago
conducted a number of studies of their city.
Their conclusions reflect the particular nature
of Chicago and its surroundings, but also
provide a useful, if undetailed, model of city
growth. Chicago is located on the southwestern shore of Lake Michigan on a level
lake plain. Expansion away from the original
settlement core near the lakeshore is limited
only to the east by the lake itself. In all other
directions the level plain offers few barriers
to urban expansion, and according to Burgess's
model of city growth, cities should grow outward evenly in all directions from a central

nucleus or core. Over a long enough period
of time, and given several successive stages
of growth, the city will develop a series of concentric rings or zones surrounding the central
business district (often referred to as the
CBD). In the CBD are found the major retail
functions and government services associated
with large cities. Department stores, good
restaurants, and specialty shops will cluster
there along with government buildings, courts
of law, hotels, museums, and theaters. According to Burgess a mixture of light manufacturing
establishments and wholesale businesses is
found immediately surrounding the CBD.
These two sets of establishments in combination are the ones most able to pay the high
rents characteristic of the city center. In turn,
all these establishments depend upon the centrality of their location and their easy accessibility to large numbers of potential customers.

At an early period in the history of the city,
the zone ringing the central core was occupied
by workers with residents of higher economic
class just beyond. Cities, however, constantly
grow and change, and additional firms seeking
the locational advantages of the city center
have only two choices. The CBD can expand
vertically to accommodate new businesses in
skyscrapers, or it can expand horizontally,
encroaching upon the residential areas surrounding it. In Burgess's concentric ring
model, emphasis is placed upon outward
horizontal growth. As a result the compound
core, or CBD, is ringed by a *zone of transition.*
Private homes become rooming houses; businesses exert more and more pressure for land;
and residential blight characterizes the area.
It is in this zone that the ills of the city are most
evident. Disease and poor health accompany
tenements and slums, while illiteracy, unem-
ployment, and crime go hand in hand. In this
home for recent immigrants is one of America's critical problem areas, for which various
"treatments" such as *urban renewal* and the
model cities programs have been suggested.

If we were to travel directly away from the
center of Burgess's hypothetical city, the next
ring beyond the zone of transition would

contain working-class homes of increasingly good quality. Signs of urban blight would give way to lower-middle-class respectability. The quality and cost of homes would continue to increase with distance from the center and would be matched by a decrease in residential density. Next, a zone of better residences would ring that of the established working class. Finally, on the edges of the city the commuter suburbs would present an incompletely built up area with small satellite towns and intervening empty fields.

Density and density surfaces

One way in which to think of what the Burgess model tells us about cities is to consider the distribution of people within a growing settlement in a succession of time periods. Figure 3–3 shows population densities at increasing distances from the CBD. In this case, the definition of density is the number of people counted at their place of residence and living on a given unit of land. This can be represented as a number of points located within a given area. This could be measured, for example, in terms of hundreds of people per city block, but since city blocks vary in size, we most often refer to the number of people per square mile. (In any case, this represents a *point–area* relationship like those discussed in Chapter 1.)

Line t_1 in Figure 3–3 shows the distribution of people within the original settlement. When the town was first founded, everyone lived within walking distance of its center. Even then central locations had added value, although in general there was plenty of room for all. Latecomers, the poor, and full- or part-time farmers were most likely to live farthest away. In any event most of the population lived close to the center; their numbers diminished regularly with increasing distance.

A somewhat later period is shown by line t_2.[1] The city has continued to grow both in

population and in area. The center is filling with nonresidential uses. Increasing rents and competition for land have forced residents to seek homes farther from the CBD, and population densities are increasing rapidly at the edges. Line t_3 shows population density and distance relationships still later. The town is becoming a city, and the characteristic rings described by Burgess are beginning to appear in a more complete form. The outer edge of the city continues to grow, and population densities there continue to increase in a regular manner. Nearer the center, the *zone of transition* with its packed tenements and slums accounts for the crest of population densities somewhat away from the actual center. The CBD is shown by lower density values. This is because the office buildings and shops at the very center of the city allow fewer apartment buildings and other residences. Line t_4 represents the contemporary city with a relatively empty CBD, a ring of slum housing just beyond, and steadily diminishing residential densities stretching out to the remoter suburbs. Urban expansion can thus be imagined as a wave of population density moving outward from some central point.

In this two-dimensional graph the area beneath the line represents the total number of people found along one radius leading directly outward from the center of the city. Although a line has no width but only length, we assume that the area on the graph is one unit wide, since measures of density are in points per square unit. This diagram can be thought of in three dimensions if the area defined by the abscissa and one of the lines t_1, t_2, t_3, etc., is revolved around the vertical axis, or ordinate.[2] A cone-shaped volume, or

[1]*Technical note*: The use of a small t with a numerical subscript (read: "t sub one, t sub two . . .") is a standard way of indicating successive periods of time or stages.

[2]*A useful suggestion*: In all graphs the two lines at right angles to each other are referred to as the y, or vertical, coordinate, and the x, or horizontal, coordinate. These lines are also called the *ordinate* and the *abscissa*. Nearly everyone has trouble remembering which is which. If you remember that your lips form a vertical "O" shape when you say ordinate, and a thin, flat line when you say abscissa, the distinction can be easily remembered.

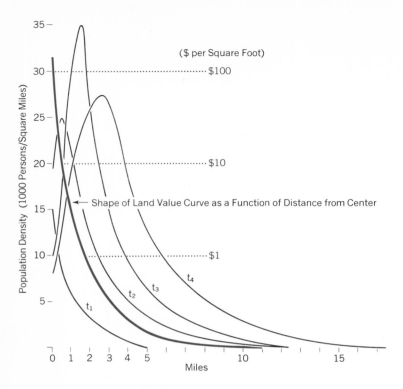

Population Density (1000 Persons/Square Miles)

($ per Square Foot)

$100

$10

← Shape of Land Value Curve as a Function of Distance from Center

$1

t_1 t_2 t_3 t_4

Miles

Figure 3-3 Urban population density radially from city center at different time periods in growth process The family of curves represents a hypothetical change in residential density as the city grows through time periods t, t_1, etc. The decline in population density at the center is caused by displacement of residences by business and industrial uses. These curves may be described by varying parameters of a mathematical expression relating population density to distance from the center of the city. This expression is the gamma distribution $d_r = ar^b e^{-er} + d_o$, where d_r is population density at radius r; d_o is central population density; and a, b, and c are parameters. A central crater is formed when $b > o$. See S. Angel and G. M. Hyman, ''Urban Spatial Interaction,'' *Environment and Planning,* vol. 4, 1972, p. 107.

witch's hat, results from this revolution (Figure 3–4). The volume of the space beneath the surface of the cone will be equal to the total population of the city.

Note how the less densely populated CBD at period t_3 forms a hole in the center (Figure 3–4). This does not mean that land has grown less valuable at that point. Non-residential activities are able to pay more for use of centrally located land than can households. If we were to measure land value, the line showing this in dollars per unit area would have its highest point at the very center. This is represented in Figure 3–3 by the red line measured on its own vertical axis in dollars per square foot.

Obviously, the real world varies enormously from the orderly picture presented by Burgess, and the concentric ring model has been criticized for its failure to describe the true complexity of modern cities. It should be remembered, though, that simple models have advantages as well as drawbacks. In this case, the model recognizes the desirability of a central location and the historical realities of city growth. Establishments which can afford to pay the highest rent command the most central positions. Residents and smaller businesses must seek locations on the edges. As the city grows, land use changes occur with some lapse of time between one major use and another. For example, abandoned higher-class residences may eventually be torn down to provide space for office buildings, but meanwhile poorer immigrants find shelter in the former mansions of the rich just as hermit crabs live in the castoff shells of other sea creatures.

The Burgess model assumes city growth unhindered by variations in the physical environment in which the city exists. Thus Burgess's model is symmetrical in all directions. This symmetry is the result of two qualities. The first is the assumption that all building sites are exactly alike. This results in a *homogeneous surface* having everywhere the same *site characteristics* such as soils and drainage. The second quality refers to uniform ease of transportation in all directions at every point. A surface with this quality is called an *isotropic surface* or *isotropic plain.* This condition would cease to exist if transportation were improved in one direction but not in others—for example, by building a north-south road but not an east-west one.

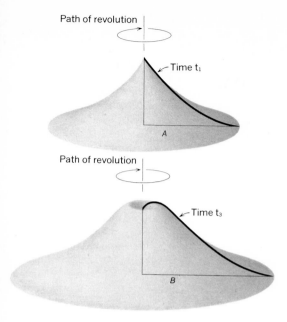

Figure 3-4 Urban population density surfaces
(*A*) Density surface at time t_1. (*B*) Density surface
at time t_3. These surfaces are three-dimensional
representations of two of the curves shows in
Figure 3-3. They are formed by rotating the curves
in a complete circle around the center of the city.

Models of City Growth More Closely Approximating Reality

By ignoring the complexities of the real world,
isotropic surfaces allow us to concentrate
on simple processes of city growth. Other
models more complex than that of Burgess
consider the environments in which cities
exist. Let us now examine some of these additional ideas of city growth which more closely
approximate the real world.

As cities grow, their several functions become separated by greater and greater distances and the role of high-speed transportation becomes more important. Today access
highways link suburban homes with downtown offices. Access provided by these routes
is not everywhere equally available, and
some parts of the city will be better served
than others. The first modification of the
isotropic plain upon which our model city

stands is therefore a simple one. Transportation will be cheaper and better along some
routes leading from the center than along
others. Further complications might also include the presence of steep slopes, bodies
of water, and other physical barriers to expansion. However, if only differences in
transport are considered, the concentric ring
pattern will be drawn out along major routes
until the city pattern becomes more star-
shaped. This is shown in Figure 3–5, which
continues to resemble Burgess's model because of its symmetry around a central point.

Figure 3-5 (*A*) Concentric zone model   Under
the assumption of equal transport costs in all
directions, the ideal concentric ring pattern is
deduced.
(*B*) Concentric zone model modified by radial
transport routes   Transport costs along the six
evenly spaced radial routes is assumed to be
less than in other radial directions. The resulting
land use pattern is extended along these routes.

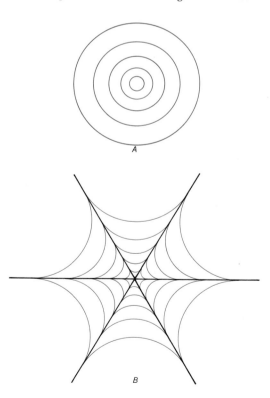

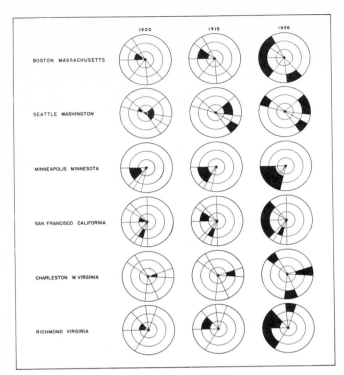

**Figure 3-6 The radial sector theory
of Homer Hoyt** Shifts in location of
fashionable residential areas in six
American cities, 1900 to 1936.
Fashionable residential areas are
indicated by solid black. (Op. cit.,
Figure 3-1, p. 115)

The radial sector theory

In 1939 Homer Hoyt suggested a variation
of the earlier symmetrical models of city
growth. Hoyt was employed by the Federal
Housing Administration to learn more about
the areal distribution of home mortgage risks
within expanding cities. Using large quantities of *block census data* he determined that
high-value residential neighborhoods tended
to grow outward from the city center within
limited wedge-shaped sectors along radial
transport lines. In other words, while a concentric ring pattern does occur, there is at a
given distance from the CBD considerable

lateral variation within any zone. Figure 3–6
shows the variation found by Hoyt in the
distribution of high-rent neighborhoods for
a number of cities. It should be noted that
the value of land, or rent, grades downward
in all directions from the most valuable sectors.

It is important to remember that the theories
and models of city growth which we create
may best represent conditions for a particular
time or place. Both the zone and sector theories
thus far discussed seem to fit earlier periods
of city growth better than the present one.
Some cities have now reached such giant
sizes and are so complex that simple models
are no longer adequate. The next three theories
of city growth more nearly match the conditions and problems inherent in Megalopolis
(see Figure 3–7) and other major conurbations.

The multiple nuclei theory

Modern cities have grown so large that they
have absorbed or captured many of their
smaller neighbors. At the same time, distances from the CBD to outlying areas are
often too great for casual shopping trips.
Factories and businesses located at suburban
sites generate new need for local services.
These and other factors help to create a new
type of city with not one but several core areas.
These multiple centers of activity are tied
together by superhighways and serve a far-
flung urban population. Many residents of
modern cities may visit the main or central
business district only on special occasions.
This results in a city with not one but many
nuclei around which growth occurs.

Chauncy Harris and Edward Ullman first
described this type of city in 1945. They
recognized an urban land use pattern with
several discrete nuclei which develop for
different reasons (Figure 3–8). Some parts
of their model city grow because of specialized
facilities. These might include the water-
front district, specializing in shipping, or
the main CBD, which possesses the advantage
of greatest accessibility. Other places through
historical accident accumulate many businesses of the same kind and offer customers

*Spatial
Design
in World
Society*

a wide selection of similar goods and services. These focal points within the city attract customers by having many similar or related offerings and can provide a wider range of goods and services at lower prices than more isolated facilities. Still other types of urban activities are detrimental to each other and seek to locate maximum distances apart. For example, factories and better-class retail shops are seldom if ever found close together. Finally, certain activities can afford to pay high rents while others must seek the cheapest land possible. High-rise office buildings occupy valuable land near the center of urban areas, while used car lots, which require large amounts of relatively cheap land, must seek peripheral locations.

This idea of the *multiple nuclei city* describes large modern settlements more accurately than do the models of Hoyt and Burgess. However, none of these models completely meets the needs of city planners or informed citizens who must make decisions about the urban environments in which they live. The Burgess and Hoyt models have the advantage of simplicity, but they fail to describe reality sufficiently. The model of Ullman and Harris describes the land use pattern in modern cities but does not suggest any spatial order to the process which might allow us to predict future conditions beyond a simple extension of the existing pattern. We have yet to consider urban models which can help us to anticipate future needs in terms of not only quantity but also location. For example, we may be quite certain that the city in which we live is growing outward from its center in a complex way, but in ten years or twenty how many more schools and shopping centers will be needed and just where should we put them?

Population densities and processes of city growth

In order to answer the above questions it becomes necessary to carefully reexamine the *processes* of city growth. One way to do this is to consider the basic spatial concepts

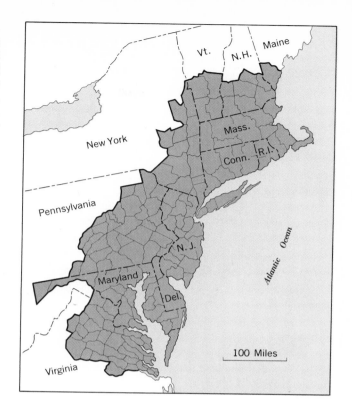

Figure 3-7 The original Megalopolis Professor Jean Gottmann defines a nearly continuous built-up area on the Eastern seaboard of the United States as *Megalopolis*, a new urban form of coalesced metropolitan areas. The areal units used to identify Megalopolis are counties which meet certain criteria of urbanism, such as a low percent of the work force in agriculture, high population densities, etc. This does not mean that the region is a solid mass of people and urban facilities. There are considerable areas of farms, forests, and empty land in Megalopolis. Gottmann has defined an urban region of great complexity and interaction. He argues that it is useful to consider it a single entity for many purposes. (After Jean Gottmann, *Megalopolis*, The Twentieth Century Fund, New York, 1961)

which are involved. Among such concepts the idea of population density plays an especially important part. Density has been defined as the number of points per given area. Population density is the number of people

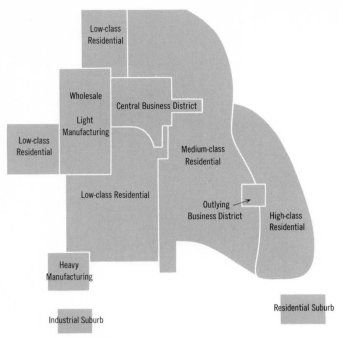

Low-class
Residential

Wholesale
Light
Manufacturing

Central Business District

Low-class
Residential

Medium-class
Residential

Low-class Residential

Outlying
Business District

High-class
Residential

Heavy
Manufacturing

Residential Suburb

Industrial Suburb

3-8 Urban land use pattern showing several discrete nuclei (After C. D. Harris and E. L. Ullman, "The Nature of Cities," *Annals of the American Academy of Political and Social Science* CCXLII, Nov. 1945, part of figure 5.)

per given area. Figure 3–9*A* and *B* shows two areas within urban Detroit. Part *B* depicts the distribution of households in an older, built-up portion of the city. It is easy to see that densities are everywhere great and relatively uniform. Part *A* shows an area 10 miles farther from the center of Detroit, where the city is penetrating rural areas. Such great

variation in density is typical of large cities. All cities show unequal distributions of people. If we understand such variations, we will have made a step toward understanding the processes of city growth.

Figure 3–10*A* and *B* shows population densities within the entire Detroit metropolitan area. The two lines of Figure 3–10*B* represent density profiles plotted from the CBD to the suburbs. Both lines have a shape similar to the curve illustrated by line t_2 in Figure 3–3. In terms of actual types of housing and numbers of people, we find that near the center of the city multistory apartment buildings create population densities of 25,000 people per square mile. Beyond the ring of apartment buildings come individual houses on small lots with nearly 10,000 inhabitants on each square mile of urban land. This would be similar to the densities shown in Figure 3–9*A*. Finally, suburban population density drops to less than 500 people per square mile in some places but rises again to minor peaks in the vicinity of satellite cities. These profiles confirm the observations of Harris and Ullman about multicored metropolitan areas.

The exponential decay function

The above relationship of residential densities to distance from the city center can also be conveniently expressed by a mathematical formula suggested by Colin Clark:

$$y = ae^{-bx}$$

which can also be written

Figure 3.9 (*A*) Distribution of households in the expanding suburban edge of the Detroit metropolitan region At the suburban edge of the metropolitan region, housing developments often can be distinguished by their curving street patterns. Areas of low housing densities and curving streets contain high-income housing. A scattering of housing is found along the square section line roads in the open land to the west.

(*B*) Distribution of households in an older, built-up portion of Detroit, Michigan Household density is uniformly high in solidly built-up areas of Detroit. The density declines with distance from the central business district, which is off the map to the southeast. The empty spaces are given to nonresidential land uses, such as industrial and commercial sites and parks.

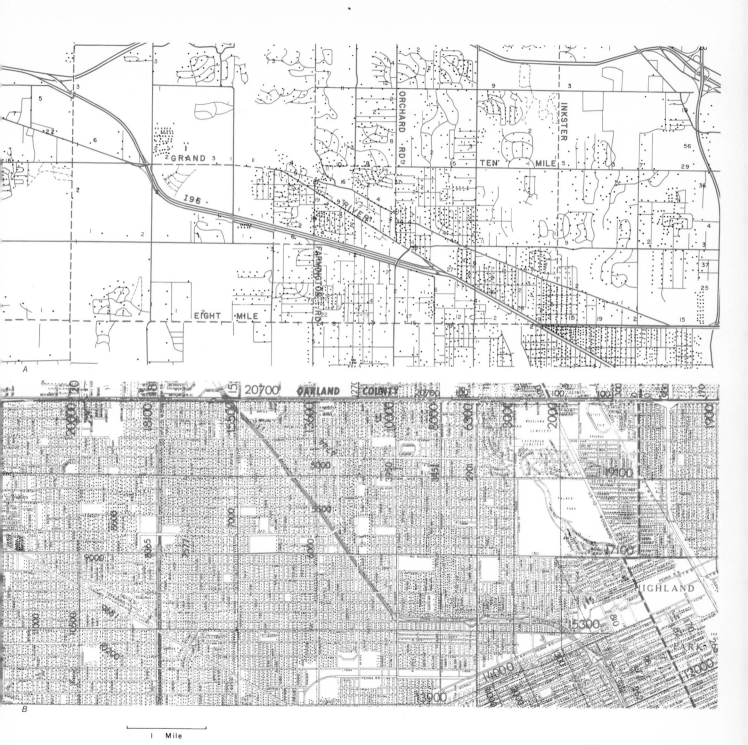

A

B

1 Mile

43

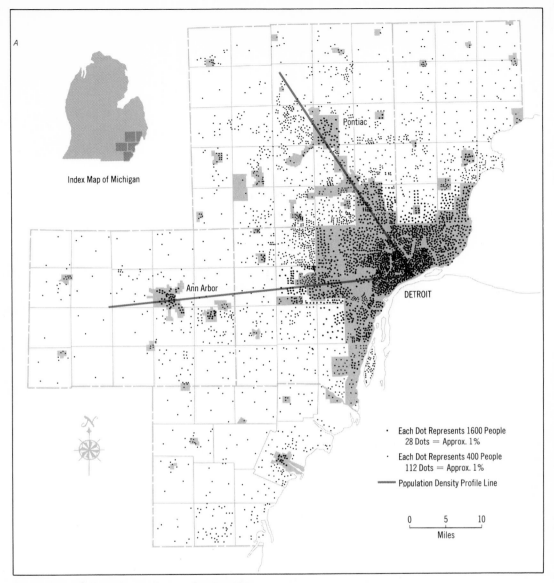

A

Index Map of Michigan

Pontiac

Ann Arbor

DETROIT

- Each Dot Represents 1600 People
  28 Dots = Approx. 1%

- Each Dot Represents 400 People
  112 Dots = Approx. 1%

— Population Density Profile Line

0   5   10
Miles

Figure 3-10 (A) Detroit population density, 1960 The Detroit metropolitan region extends into a five-county area in southeastern Michigan. The population density is greatly variable, with a high peak in the center of Detroit and lower peaks centered on satellite cities in the suburbs. The pattern is typical of American cities.

(B) Profile of Detroit population density Population density levels along two lines shown on the map in part A. The lines extend through two satellite cities (p. 45). (Donald R. Deskins, "Settlement Patterns for the Detroit Metropolitan Area 1930–1970," paper for the Metropolitan Community Research Project and Department of Geography, University of Michigan, Ann Arbor, June 1963, graph pages 80–81 and map series, map 5.)

$$\log y = \log a - bx$$

In this formula y equals the density of residential population, x equals the distance from the city center, and a and b are constants which must be defined in terms of the particular urban system for which the formula is being used. A line representing this formula resembles the slope of the cone in Figure 3–4A but differs from the schematic representation in Figure 3–4B in that it does not include the "backslope" or hole in the donut indicating the lower population density in the central business district. Slightly more complicated functions could be used to describe this condition as well as to add the effects of satellite cities. While some readers may wish to further explore the mathematical implications of these expressions, it is only necessary for us to emphasize two things with regard to Clark's idea. First, the distribution of residential densities can be described mathematically. Land values, rents, the amounts invested in buildings, and other variables are similarly distributed. Second, these generalized distributional patterns are symmetrical with respect to the city center.

An important thing to remember about the application of the exponential decay function to urban models is that curves described by the function always represent *average* conditions. At any given distance from the center, the height and slope of a line in Figure 3–3 will be the average of all the lateral sectors in a given ring such as is shown in Hoyt's diagrams. Although such averages cannot tell us what to expect to find at a specific location, they offer insights into the nature of American cities. We can expect curves similar to the one shown for almost every large settlement whether its population is 500,000 or 5,000,000.

The law of allometric growth

We note that regardless of size, all large cities in a particular economic and cultural system have the same general characteristics. All their parts or functional areas share relatively

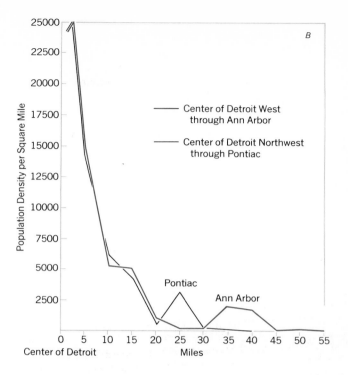

fixed proportions of the total area of each city. For example, in the United States, regardless of city size, the total area devoted to commercial activities occupies about 3 to 4 percent of the entire built-up area. Single-family dwellings use up about 40 percent of the entire city space, while streets and highways account for approximately another 28 percent. The total allotment of various land uses by area is shown in Table 3–2. These figures may seem strange and may not match our views of reality. For example, the CBD in a large metropolis may not be large enough to account for 3 percent of the area of the city. However, if the areas of all the outlying shopping centers and small neighborhood business districts are added to that of the CBD, the estimate will be approximately correct. This means that even the multiple nuclei model of city growth can be described in a regular or mathematical manner if it is viewed as a set of aggregate conditions.

City Space—Models of City Growth

Table 3-2 Land Use in American Cities as a Proportion of Total City Space

Residential	39.6
Streets	28.2
Public-Semipublic	11.0
Parks, playgrounds	6.7
Commercial	3.3
Heavy and light industry	6.4
Railroads	4.8
Total	100.0

Source: Harland Bartholomew, *Land Use in American Cities*, Harvard, Cambridge, Mass., 1965, from table 3, app. C.

This principle can be better understood by drawing an analogy with biologic growth. For example, when a child is about two years old, parents can tell what its mature height will be by doubling its height at that time. Moreover, if the child is normal and healthy, all its parts will continue to share approximately the same proportion of its total stature and weight no matter how large an adult it becomes. This rule is generally true for animals of the same species and is called the *law of allometric growth*. Swedish farmers measure the chest circumference of cows in order to estimate the amount of edible meat which the animal will produce. It does not matter whether the cow is large or small: the proportion between chest girth and the final weight of butchered meat will remain constant. By the same token, paleontologists can reconstruct the general appearance of prehistoric men from a few bones or teeth. All that is necessary is that the organic proportions and the size limits of a particular species be known.

To summarize we can say that, within a given species, if the size of one part is known, it is possible to predict the size of the entire individual or of its other parts. If the total size is known, it is possible to predict the size or proportion of one or more of its parts.

Stig Nordbeck has applied this law of allometric growth to many inanimate things, including volcanoes and large cities. His reasoning is that while a city grows and maintains its same general shape and function,

the various parts within it will retain the same proportion to each other regardless of city size. It follows that if the size or rate of growth of one type of land use is known, it is possible to predict the total size of the city or the size of the various areas devoted to other land-using activities. Conversely, if a city planner has an estimate of the future population of the city, he can also estimate the total increment of streets, shopping centers, sewers, and residential areas which must be added to accommodate that future population.

Applications of the law of allometric growth

There are many interesting applications of the idea of allometric growth. Geographers have shown that for every settlement there is a regular relationship between the size of the built-up area and its population. Although most cities are irregular in shape, this relationship can be thought of more clearly if we assume that settlements are all shaped like perfect circles and let the size of the circle be proportional to the total area of the city we wish to consider. In this case, the circle representing the city would be proportional to both the size of the built-up area and the population living in the built-up area. The radius of such a circle can be expressed by the formula

$$r = aP^b$$

P is the population, and r is the radius, while a, the maximum density, and b, the rate that density declines with distance, are coefficients based on empirical observations of the particular cities being considered. If the area of the city is known and we wish to estimate the population, the same formula can be written

$$P = \left(\frac{r}{a}\right)^{1/b}$$

Waldo Tobler has demonstrated this application of the law of allometric growth for the cities of Fort Worth and Dallas, Texas. Using an Apollo VI photograph of the two cities (Figure 2–1) he estimated their built-up areas, which appear as lighter shades of gray on the photograph. Coefficients *a* and *b* were supplied by previous studies of American cities. It took only 15 minutes to estimate a total population of 668,000. This number is within 2 percent of the 1960 census figure! Since people constantly come and go from large cities, and since the census itself has some margin for error, this figure estimated by Tobler is as reasonable or accurate as that compiled over many weeks by hundreds of census workers. The implications of this are important because it means that in the near future it will be possible to take gross census measures of city populations simply by repeating Tobler's method of analysis using low-cost satellite photographs of every part of the world.

The disadvantage of predictions based on Nordbeck's model of city growth is that his is in no way a positional theory. By this we mean that it does not allow us to specify locations for the component parts of the city but deals only in total values. A projection of future needs in terms of shopping centers can show that 10 million additional square feet will be needed by 1980 in a particular city, but not where to locate the new shopping facilities, or whether there should be one large center or several smaller ones. This is particularly true when we consider Ullman and Harris's observations about modern cities. The more multinucleated a city becomes, the more scattered and divided will be its functioning parts. Another note of caution is that if a city undergoes an important cultural or technological change, its patterns of growth may suddenly begin moving along a new and unexpected path. The invention of the internal combustion engine and the automobile caused such a dislocation in earlier patterns of city growth. Though we know much less about the significance of cultural changes, it is likely that as one subculture replaces another within a city, changes in the basic system may make prediction by

use of the allometric model difficult. However, deviations from a predicted growth pattern may be used to identify significant cultural shifts.

Urbanization Defined

To further understand the environment in which we live, we must consider the themes of urbanization and population growth as cultural processes. By urbanization we mean the manner in which populations change from rural life patterns to those of city dwellers. From our geographical point of view, urbanization may be described as the process by which humanity gathers into point locations or urban clusters rather than remaining thinly distributed across agricultural areas. As Kingsley Davis points out, a careful distinction should be made between the absolute growth of cities and the process of urbanization. In an urbanizing society, the proportion of city dwellers within the total population increases steadily, sometimes dramatically. Countries which have already gone through this process can no longer be said to be urbanizing. Such populations are urbanized. In this case, the proportion of city to rural population remains constant, and the nation is predominantly urban. For example, 80 percent of the population of England and Wales lives in urban agglomerations of 100,000 or more, a proportion which has remained almost constant for the last 25 years. England is thus urban, no longer urbanizing.

In countries which have already been urbanized, cities can continue to grow in absolute size along with overall population growth. This does not mean that the population is becoming proportionately more urban. Figure 3–11 shows the rates of urbanization for four countries: Japan, the Union of Soviet Socialist Republics, the United States, and England and Wales. Note that the percentage of urban population in England and Wales in recent years has remained nearly constant. Japan's urban population is increasing most rapidly relative to its total size. The United

City Space— Models of City Growth

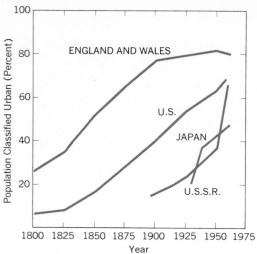

Figure 3-11 Rate of urbanization of four countries Most nations are undergoing a process by which an increasing proportion of their population is living in urbanized areas. This change in the percent of urban people to total population is called *urbanization*. It occurs primarily because of rural-to-urban migration, although it is also influenced by regional differences in natural increase of the population and by changes in the size of urbanized places. The rate of urbanization varies greatly from nation to nation. It is slow in some highly urbanized nations, such as England and Wales, and most rapid in nations with rapidly growing economies, such as Japan. (Kingsley Davis, "The Urbanization of the Human Population," *Scientific American*, vol. 213, September, 1965, pp. 40–53, copyright © 1965 by Scientific American, Inc.

States and the Soviet Union are increasing their urban populations at about the same rate, although in absolute terms the United States is more urbanized.

England is typical of the distinction between urbanization and absolute city growth. For example, the constancy of urban population within the British population is in sharp contrast with the growth of the London region. Within this region, defined as an area within 40 miles of Piccadilly Circus, population grew by 800,000 in the period 1951–1961. It is estimated that in the next 20 years the population of the same area will increase by 1,900,000. At the same time, England's urban-rural population ratio may actually decrease.

The adjustment of people to the geographical space in which they live reflects their economic activities, life-styles, and total numbers. The transition from rural to urban ways of life has already brought about significant changes for much of the world's population. As cities increase in number and size, they coalesce to form urban areas which may become as large as some agricultural regions. Thus, as shown in Figure 3–12, the spatial form of the dominant life-style on earth has changed from *farm areas* with scattered punctiform settlements to contemporary cities serving as major foci for human activities. In the foreseeable future, the dominant life-style will be found in vast *urban areas*.

The two processes, urbanization and the growth of very large cities, create overlapping sets of problems. Urbanization is associated with questions of migration and changes in life-style. Very large cities create problems of access, high densities, and overburdening of the environment. These two sets of problems will be examined in many ways in the following chapters. Let us first review the nature of world population growth, which is closely associated with them.

The explosion that isn't

Perhaps the most common term used by social scientists with grim predictions for the future is the expression *the population explosion*. The cataclysmic overtones of that phrase nevertheless hold out nuances of hope. Surely after the catastrophe, some lucky survivors will pull themselves from the ruins, dust themselves off, and start over again. To a human observer far enough away to be safe, a conventional explosion displays maximum violence simultaneously with the triggering action, and thereafter the force of the blast rapidly depletes itself. In other words, if you and the structure you're in survive the initial destruction, you are among the survivors—you are alive.

This is simply not an accurate analogy for the growth of world population. The sequence of events taking place around us, and to which

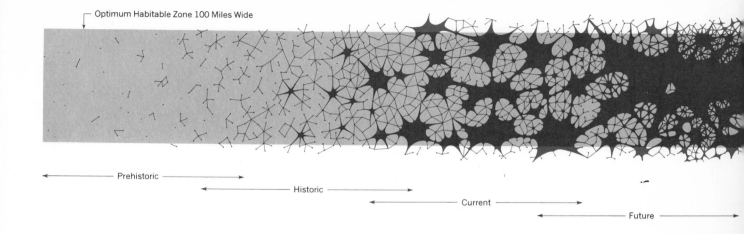

Optimum Habitable Zone 100 Miles Wide

←———— Prehistoric ————→

←———— Historic ————→

←———— Current ————→

←———— Future ————→

Figure 3-12 Evolution of urban form This is an abstract representation of the change in human organization of space through time. The organization proceeds from scattered punctiform settlements in prehistoric times to a predominantly rural agricultural landscape organized by a network of transport lines and urban points. Currently, the urban landscape is expanding in large areas. In the future, the dominant life-style and spatial organization may be urban. The figure is meant to show settlement in a 100-mile zone best suited for habitation. In the future, even with a greatly increased population expected, the world will have vast areas with inhospitable conditions nearly empty of people. The implication is that future populations will have to extend the urban order into the poor resource areas to some extent.

we contribute by our own presence, is actually the reverse of any known explosion. An explosion rapidly dissipates its energy and loses its potential for further damage or further growth; world population increases daily, and every increase magnifies its potential for disaster.

The upward sweep of the world population curve, shown in Figure 3-13, is familiar to most readers. While world population growth estimates vary according to the viewpoint and techniques employed by various demographers, the story is always much the same. Ten thousand years ago, at the time the domestication of plants and animals was first taking place, the world was inhabited by perhaps 5 million people. By the beginning of the first millennium A.D., more certain supplies of food, improved technologies, and

more efficient forms of political and urban organization had helped increase world population to perhaps as much as 275 million, although other estimates for this period are as low as 133 million. For the next ten centuries, until A.D. 1000, the total population of the world scarcely varied. Deficits in some places were countered by local surges of population in others, but the overall pattern was one of relative stagnation. Thereafter, from A.D. 1000 to about 1650, world population doubled in size, but it was only in the nineteenth century that the 1 billion mark was passed. Sometime between 1930 and 1940, population had again doubled. By 1970, more than 3.5 billion people were alive, and all of you who read this book may expect to share planet Earth with more than 6 billion neighbors if you survive until the year 2000.

City Space— Models of City Growth

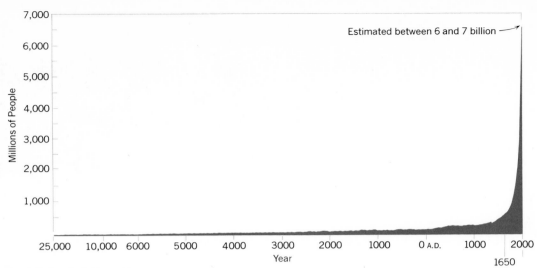

Figure 3-13 World population growth The long-time view of world population growth emphasises how unusual current conditions are. The current rate of growth has no precedence, and it cannot continue very long. On a different scale, the smaller graph shows changes in the past three centuries with a forecast to the year 2000. (References: William Petersen, *Population*, 2d ed., Macmillan, New York, 1969; Glenn T. Trewartha, *A Geography of Population: World Patterns*, Wiley, New York, 1969; Edward S. Deevey, Jr., "The Human Population," *Scientific American*, vol. 203, September, 1960; John D. Durrand, "A Long-Range View of World Population Growth," *Annals of the American Academy of Political and Social Science*, vol. 367, 1967; *U.N. Demographic Yearbook 1970*)

This spectacular and ominous increase in population can be better appreciated in terms of the survival rates of various groups of people throughout history. Figure 3–14 shows the longevity, or average life expectancy, of eleven human groups in ancient and modern times. Illness, warfare, malnutrition, and famine were everyday occurrences for all our ancestors. The selection process was brutal and only the strongest survived.

Contrast the longevity of preindustrial societies with that of Americans in recent times. The results of the Industrial and Scientific Revolutions of the nineteenth century are demonstrated here. Improvements not only in the means of production but also in the fields of agriculture, transportation, banking, trade, communications, and medicine all serve to extend the life-span.

One important element of these examples must not be overlooked. Just as the growth of world population has been sporadic through time until the last few centuries, so has the average length of life and the increase in numbers of people varied from place to place at any given period in history. This is illustrated in part by the variations in life expectancy at birth, as shown in Figure 3–15. We must also remember that local variations are hidden within data compiled for large political or census units. The survival rate in Appalachia is not the same as in New England.

In the same way that we may subdivide the world into geographical regions for which we show survival rates and other demographic characteristics, we may also want to talk about populations in terms of their urban and rural qualities. People, in changing their life-styles, also change their geographical locations. American cities have, in the last 70 years, sheltered a larger and larger proportion of the American population. In 1890 approximately 18 percent of the total inhabitants of the United States lived in its cities; by 1900, 40 percent; by 1930, the urban segment had increased to 56.2 percent; while in 1970, 69.9 percent were classified by the census as urban dwellers. The same trend is found everywhere in the world. Table 3–3 gives some indication of the magnitude of this change from rural to urban modes of life.

An example from the non-Western world illustrates these startling trends in the redistribution of population. During the 10 years from 1941 to 1951, more than 9 million people in India moved to the cities. Their destinations were the larger urban places; their origins, the poor and isolated hamlets and villages scattered across the countryside. This was approximately 3 percent of the 1941 rural population which generated the move and 20 percent of the original urban population in the same year.

Urbanization has become one of the most important issues of the last 150 years. World population in that time increased about 3.5 times, from 960 million in 1800 to 3.6 billion in 1970. During the same period, the total population of cities and urbanized areas with more than 100,000 inhabitants grew nearly 43 times, from 15.6 to 669.0 million. The distribution of urbanization by world regions is shown in Table 3–4 and Figure 3–16. The pattern of this distribution is similar to that of the distribution of per capita income. This suggests that it is more than coincidence that the developed countries of the world are the urbanized ones.

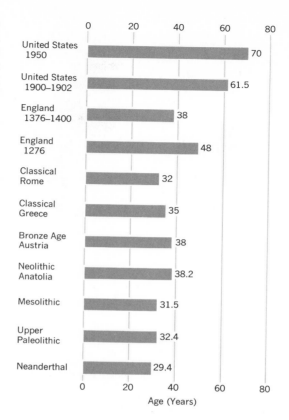

Figure 3-14 Longevity in ancient and modern times Longevity, or average life expectancy, is a useful population statistic established by means of life tables. Life tables include records of the number of people alive in each age bracket, the age-specific death rate, and other data. The average number of years of expected life at birth may be derived from these data. Life insurance companies use them to determine life insurance risk rates. Longevity is usually calculated at birth. One of the main reasons for the longer life expectancy in modern times, compared with earlier periods, is the reduction in infant deaths. Considerable data are needed to calculate accurate life expectancy rates. Since these data clearly are not available for ancient times, the rates quoted in the graph must be taken as gross approximations. (Edward S. Deevey, Jr., "The Human Population," *Scientific American,* September 1960, copyright © 1960 by Scientific American, Inc.

City Space— Models of City Growth

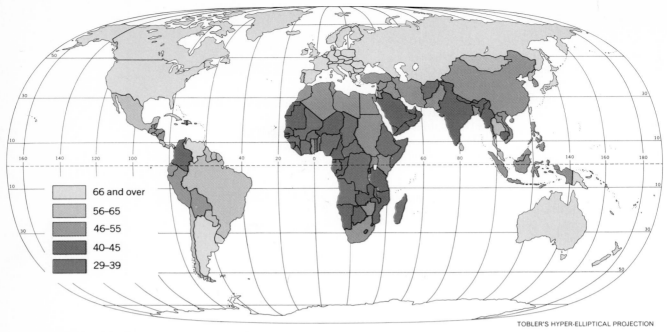

WORLD LIFE EXPECTANCY AT BIRTH 1970

66 and over
56–65
46–55
40–45
29–39

TOBLER'S HYPER-ELLIPTICAL PROJECTION

Figure 3-15 Life expectancy at birth, by nation, 1970 The values shown on this map are subject to the measurement errors described in the text and in the caption of Figure 3-14. Nevertheless, a clear spatial pattern is observable. Life expectancy is generally less in the underdeveloped countries of the world. The darkest areas indicate places where infant and child mortality rates are high. In these societies, the commonplace loss of children through death is in great contrast to the experience of people in more advanced economies.

Table 3–3   Development of Urbanism

Region	% of Total Regional Population in Cities over 100,000			
	1850	1900	1950	1970
Africa	0.2	1.1	5.2	10.2
America	3.0	12.8	22.6	24.7
Asia	1.7	2.1	7.5	10.1
Europe and U.S.S.R.	4.9	11.9	19.9	27.1
Oceania		21.7	39.2	44.6

Source: 1850 to 1950: Gerald Breese, *Urbanization in Newly Developing Countries,* Prentice-Hall, Englewood Cliffs, N.J., 1966, p. 22. 1970 data: *U.N. Demographic Yearbook 1970, U.S. Bureau of the Census 1970, Statistical Abstract of Latin America 1969* (U.N. data are for latest available year, mainly 1965–1970).

Figure 3-16 Percent of urban population, by nation, 1970
Definitions of urban areas vary from country to country and over time. The map shows the latest available U.N. statistics for countries and employs slightly different definitions of urban area as reported by each country. The countries are grouped into world regions, with their average percent of urban population shown. Variation of tones within regions shows something of the range in values which exists. Especially in the large countries, subregions would also show great variation in percent of urban population. (Data: *U.N. Demographic Yearbook 1970*)

Table 3-4   World Urban Population, 1970

Region	Total Population (millions)	Urban Population (millions)	% Urban
Northern Africa	82.2	27.6	39
Western Africa	90.8	12.5	15
Eastern Africa	92.0	8.7	9
Middle Africa	28.2	5.1	18
Southern Africa	26.4	7.7	42
Northern America	199.3	140.0	70
Middle America	65.5	35.7	54
Caribbean	20.7	8.2	40
Tropical South America	121.4	60.1	49
Temperate South America	34.6	24.8	72
Southwest Asia	51.9	21.8	42
Middle South Asia	713.8	138.1	19
Southeast Asia	186.5	31.4	17
Mainland East Asia	658.0	99.4	15
Island East Asia	116.4	78.3	67
Northern Europe	80.1	56.6	71
Western Europe	145.5	80.8	56
Eastern Europe	102.4	53.1	52
Southern Europe	119.2	49.1	41
U.S.S.R.	241.7	136.0	56
Oceania	14.9	11.5	77

Source: *U.N. Demographic Yearbook 1970.*

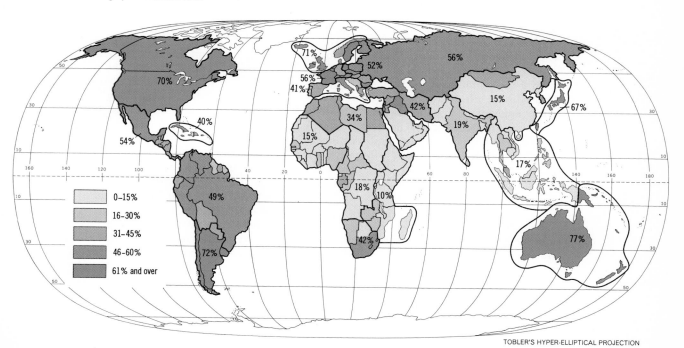

TOBLER'S HYPER-ELLIPTICAL PROJECTION

PERCENT POPULATION CLASSED AS URBAN

4 | THE CITY AND ITS HINTERLAND—
THE EFFECTS OF DISTANCE

Cities are places to live. Whether it is Park Avenue in New York, a crowded street in Naples, or your own neighborhood, more and more of the world's people call the city and its suburbs home. In fact, it is safe to say that a majority of the students who read these lines already live in a metropolitan area or will move to one sometime during their lives.

Cities are places to sell and buy goods and to provide and utilize services. Employees in the Paris Bourse and the New York City Stock Exchange, seamstresses in the garment district and salesmen on Saville Row, bowling alley operators, insurance salesmen, grocery store cashiers, and air traffic controllers perform a few of the many activities that characterize urban life. Cities also provide people with enjoyment and education. Museums and zoos, theaters and restaurants are among the goals of tourists and weekend vacationers. No metropolis is without its colleges and at least one university.

Dominant Trade Areas

While the residents of cities fill some of the jobs and utilize part of the services offered by the urban places in which they live, the use of cities is not limited to urbanites. Neither are the manufactured goods produced in cities reserved only for local citizens. Every city reaches out to serve and influence the area surrounding it. In return, what goes on in the city reflects the resources and character of the surrounding region. Midwesterners are familiar with the popular term "Chicagoland," which refers to the vast area dependent upon Chicago for supplies and services. New York City has a similar dependent area stretching far beyond its legal borders. In fact, every settlement has some geographical area larger than itself with which it interacts.

The ability of cities to reach beyond their legal limits can be illustrated by considering the distribution patterns of their daily newspapers. If a person traveling by car from New York to Chicago were to check the newsstands in all the towns along his route, he would find New York papers predominating on the "out-of-town" rack in New Jersey and Pennsylvania. As he moved westward, Chicago papers would begin to appear until finally their presence would predominate in Ohio and northern Indiana. The same relationship exists between Chicago and St. Louis or between San Francisco and Los Angeles, or between any two major cities. The dynamic activity and excitement of major metropolitan centers are of concern to the people living in the areas around and between them as well as to their own inhabitants.

Just as rural people depend upon cities,

cities must reach out for the supplies which support them. While a small town will usually use dairy products from some nearby source, large cities must depend upon distant farms. Figure 4–1 shows the sources of milk for the New York City area.

Figure 4–2 shows the area served and influenced by Mobile, Alabama. The complex nature of such urban influence is partially revealed by the seven boundary lines drawn about the city itself. Nearest to the city is a line showing the extent of the area in which

Figure 4-1 Sources of fluid milk for the New York area The fluid milk marketing area is a receiving zone for fluid milk in which wholesale milk prices are agreed upon under federal marketing orders. New York City is by far the largest market in this receiving area. Most of the milk destined for this area (89 percent) comes from the source areas shown under the federal marketing orders. Eleven (11) percent of the milk received comes from producers *not* under federal milk-marketing orders. Their sources are unknown, although very likely they are located in the same general territory. (Data from "Sources of Milk for Federal Order Markets by State and County," U.S. Dept. of Agriculture Consumer and Marketing Service, Dairy Division, C & MS-50, 1969)

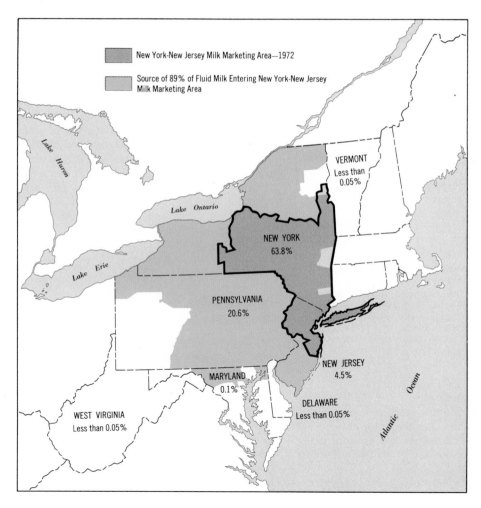

New York-New Jersey Milk Marketing Area—1972

Source of 89% of Fluid Milk Entering New York-New Jersey Milk Marketing Area

Lake Huron

Lake Ontario

VERMONT
Less than 0.05%

NEW YORK
63.8%

Lake Erie

PENNSYLVANIA
20.6%

NEW JERSEY
4.5%

MARYLAND
0.1%

DELAWARE
Less than 0.05%

WEST VIRGINIA
Less than 0.05%

Atlantic Ocean

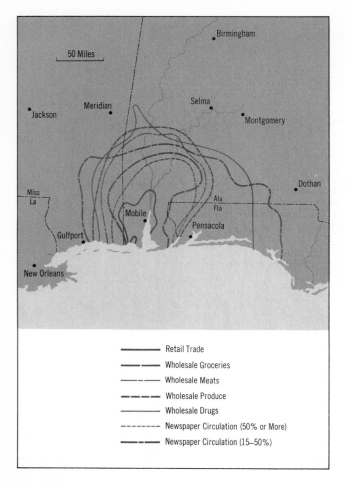

- —————— Retail Trade
- — — — Wholesale Groceries
- —— - —— Wholesale Meats
- — — — — Wholesale Produce
- —————— Wholesale Drugs
- - - - - - - Newspaper Circulation (50% or More)
- —— - —— Newspaper Circulation (15–50%)

Figure 4-2 The areas served and influenced by Mobile, Alabama The first six lines are boundaries of territories around Mobile, Alabama, within which Mobile has 50 percent or more of the business in the particular trade or activity listed in the legend. (Edward L. Ullman, *Mobile: Industrial Seaport and Trade Center*, bound dissertation, University of Chicago, 1943, p. 58)

Spatial Design in World Society

56

the people spent 50 percent or more of their retail dollar in Mobile. Although the area it encloses is smaller than those for other types of urban-based activities, it is still many times larger than the city itself. The outermost

lines mark the boundary of Mobile's immediate influence. In some places the area served by the city's wholesale drug firms reaches farthest; in other places the farthest reach is shown by those places where more than 20 percent of all out-of-town newspapers originate in Mobile. At varying intermediate distances a variety of other indicators show the extent of the city's hinterland.

Each settlement, however large or small, influences and relates to the area surrounding it. Where wholesale and retail services are concerned, the area which a city serves is called its *dominant trade area*. Small settlements reach out only a few miles, while a city the size of Mobile, 70,000 at the time of the study, has an area of influence that extends more than 100 miles to the north and east. City size alone, however, cannot explain in every case the extent of the trade area or hinterland of a particular settlement. Distance measured in terms of the ease or difficulty of travel is also important. So too the influence or competition of neighboring settlements is significant in determining how far a city will reach beyond its borders. The effect of size, ease of travel, and location relative to dominant centers is shown by the newspaper distribution areas in the vicinity of Frankfort, Germany (Figure 4–3). Every aspect of cities and city-oriented life is influenced by population, travel conditions, and intercity competition. The sections which follow clarify the interrelationship of these and other variables and show how in combination they define the areas cities serve.

City-Hinterland Connections: The Journey to Work

Let us consider a trip with which nearly everyone is familiar. *The journey to work* may be nothing more than a housewife's walking from the bedroom to the kitchen in the morning. It may be as unusual as the travel pattern of one professor who teaches both in New York and at the Sorbonne in Paris and makes two round trips by air each week across the Atlantic. Between these extremes are found millions of American commuters who move daily by car from their homes in the suburbs to their jobs in the cities. This is, in fact, such a common occurrence that one way of functionally defining a *metropolitan area* is in terms of the commuting range of its inhabitants. This range is measured not so much by straight linear distance—since traffic conditions vary from place to place—as by the actual time required to drive to work. The average commuter will willingly drive about one-half hour both to and from work. Very few will consider extending the time for a one-way trip to an hour or more. This is also true for commuters who travel by train.

Figure 4–4 shows the frequency of commuter travel by train to New York City. The number of commuters declines rapidly with distance. Notice, too, how individual commuter stations appear like loosely spaced beads along some parts of the rail network. Figure 4–5 shows the commuting areas around various cities in the southern Great Plains and Rocky Mountains. In this figure cities with large commuter areas are most likely located in level areas and have good highways leading into them. Those cities with asymmetric commuting zones are often located adjacent to mountainous areas where driving is slower, or they may be connected to their hinterlands by poorer road systems in certain directions. Just as the unequal distribution of population within a city can be aggregated and shown by a smooth curve, the density of commuter travel as a function of distance (i.e., the number of commuters traveling between a city center and a particular distance ring) can be expressed by a similar curve (Figure 4–6).

Distance, travel effort, and distance decay functions

When we speak of the frequency of commuter travel and the spatial extent of city hinterlands, we are actually referring to varying degrees of participation in the processes which define urban life. A number of curves similar to that in Figure 4–6 describe the degree of partici-

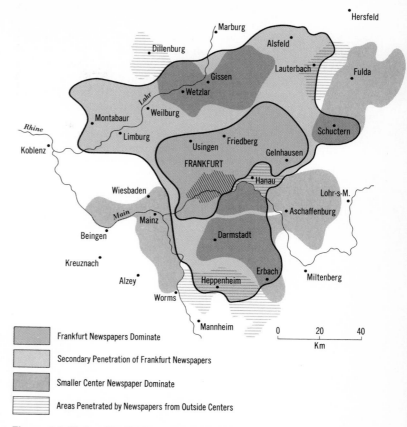

Frankfurt Newspapers Dominate

Secondary Penetration of Frankfurt Newspapers

Smaller Center Newspaper Dominate

Areas Penetrated by Newspapers from Outside Centers

Figure 4-3 Major distribution area for Frankfort newspapers (After J. Beaujeu-Garnier and G. Chabot, *Urban Geography*, Wiley, New York, 1967, fig. 38, p. 403; and W. Hartke, *Die Zeitung als Funktion sozial geographischer Verhaltnisse im Rhein-Main Gebiet*, Rhein-Mainsche Forschungen, 32, 1952, p. 21)

pation of people in an activity at a given site in terms of the distances they must travel to reach that point. A simple exercise will illustrate this on a regional and national scale. Plot the home addresses of a random selection of students attending your school. The largest proportion of students will come from nearby counties in the state in which your college is located, fewer will call states at intermediate distances "home," and people from the opposite side of the country and foreign students will appear least frequently. If you perform this exercise, however, you will notice exceptions to the regular diminishing of student numbers with distance. This can be accounted for in several ways. Obviously a nearby state with a very large population will be over-represented in absolute numbers because of its size. If the number of students from a given political unit is expressed as a proportion of the total population of that state or country, the participation curve which you plot will be much smoother. Other factors which might further influence the regularity of such a curve will be the per capita income of each state and perhaps the number and quality of its schools.

Figure 4-4 Frequency of commuter travel by train to New York City
Frequency zones have a maximum radius of 2½ miles from each station. Only trains entering within 5 miles of the city center (the area marked by the inner circle) are considered. (Adapted from David Neft, "Some Aspects of Rail Commuting: New York, London and Paris," *The Geographical Review*, vol. 49, no. 2, April, 1959, part A of plate II, figs. 3 and 4, copyrighted by American Geographical Society of New York)

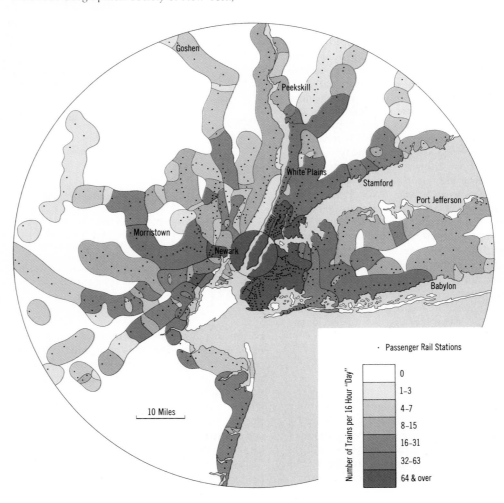

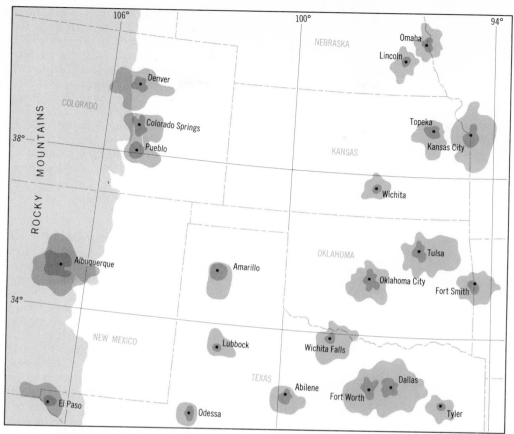

Figure 4-5 **Commuting areas of some metropolitan centers in the Southern Great Plains and the Rocky Mountains** (After Brian J. L. Berry, U.S. map in "Commuting Fields of Central Cities," University of Chicago, Social Science Research Council Committee on Areas for Social and Economic Statistics, in cooperation with the Bureau of the Census, Dept. of Commerce, Wash., D.C., April, 1967)

The same comments hold true for commuters to a city. The closer and/or larger the commuter suburb, the greater will be the absolute number of people traveling from it to the city each day. The number of job opportunities at home compared with those in the city will also be important. So too will be the nature of avail-

Figure 4-6 **Frequency of commuter travel as a function of distance** (Adapted from *Chicago Area Transportation Study,* vol. 1, parts of fig. 32, p. 61, published by the State of Illinois, 1959)

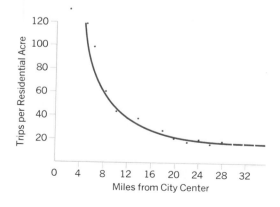

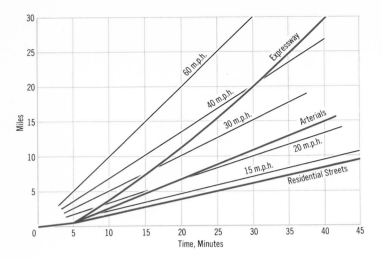

Figure 4-7 Time required to travel the same distance under varying road conditions On gravel and/or winding mountain roads, one can average between 15 and 30 miles per hour, depending upon conditions and number of stops. (Source: *The Dynamics of Urban Transportation*, Symposium of Automobile Manufacturers Association, Inc., October, 1962)

able transportation facilities and route conditions.

Variations in travel effort

We live in a non-Euclidean world where a straight line is seldom the shortest distance between two points. In order to understand this statement it is necessary to consider the *travel effort* instead of the linear distance involved in moving from place to place. If you have ever driven to the city during the morning rush hour, you will know how long it took you to fight the traffic and to find a parking place. On the other hand, if you have been fortunate enough to be leaving a city at that time and have moved swiftly along the nearly empty outbound lanes, it will be clear that the distance from city A to suburb B measured in time or effort may be much less at eight o'clock in the morning than it is from suburb B to city A. Just the opposite may be

true during the five o'clock rush to get home. Thus, crowding and traffic help to skew the even geometry of the world in which we live.

Road conditions as well as traffic density also alter the symmetry of the commuter's world. Poor surfaces and narrow lanes will make certain routes slower than others. Steep road gradients, numerous sharp curves, and busy intersections can also delay the traveler and add extra costs of time and fuel to his trip. Figure 4–7 shows the total time required to go the same distance under varying road conditions.

Directional Differences: Geographic Circles

Variations in travel effort find expression in a variety of ways. City hinterlands as determined by commuter trips would be symmetrical about the center of a city on a theoretical isotropic plane. That is, if linear distance were the only consideration, all city hinterlands would be round.

Directional differences in travel effort act to create asymmetrical areas of influence. Thus, a geographic circle measured in terms of equal travel effort about some central point will rarely, if ever, resemble the perfect circles of Euclidean geometry. Figure 4–8 shows a set of geographic circles centered upon a business in a metropolitan area. Each line represents one minute of driving time away from the business under normal conditions. Such lines showing equal *time-distance* are referred to as *isochrones*. Travel along main boulevards and highways is easier and faster than on side streets. Generally speaking, this map shows that it is easier and faster to drive in an east-west direction than in a north-south direction. A major exception to this is travel along the northwest-southwest trending streets which cut across the area. The distribution of customers patronizing the business upon which this map is centered would conform closely to the asymmetric travel pattern shown by the isochrones. Such isochronic analysis can be a useful tool in understanding

Labels on map: Eight Mile Road, Telegraph Road, I-94, BANK

Figure 4-8 A set of geographic circles centered on a business The lines represent one-minute driving time intervals away from the business location at the origin, under nonpeak-hour traffic conditions. The values were determined empirically by actually driving over the roads and measuring the number of seconds between checkpoints. The time lines were then determined by totaling the number of seconds from the business location along the shortest time route. Connecting the set of equal time points into a continuous line is obviously an abstraction because the vehicle cannot travel off the road network. This technique adds to the readability of the map, although adding an unreal character to it. Some interesting time-distance inversions occur as a consequence of a network of roads in which travel along some segments is much faster than along others. This is, however, the nature of the urban space in which we live.

patterns of retail trade. By simple analogy, if we equate all the services offered by a city with those provided by a single store, it becomes easier to see why cities develop irregularly shaped hinterlands.

The geometry of city hinterlands

Not all variations in the shape of city hinterlands need be explained by variations in travel effort. A few simple geometric relationships also help to explain asymmetries such as the

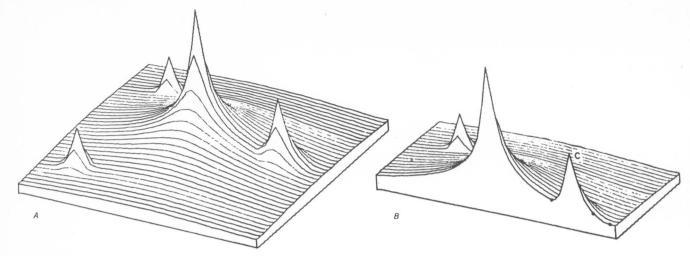

A

B

Figure 4-9 (A) Generalized population density surface of a metropolitan area. (B) Cross section of metropolitan density surface This model is a computer-calculated and computer-drawn density surface of a hypothetical metropolitan area. The model does not take into account nonresidential land use at the center of the cities and therefore does not contain the depressed central density pattern described in Figure 3-4B. The shape shown could be thought of as the rent surface or density of interaction in a metropolitan area with a central city and three satellite towns. (Robert S. Yuill, *A General Model for Urban Growth: A Spatial Simulation*, Michigan Geography Publication No. 2, Depart. of Geography, University of Michigan, Ann Arbor, Mich., 1970)

lopsided north-eastward extention of Mobile's influence (Figure 4-2). In order to examine this idea, let us return to our theoretical world with its cities situated upon an isotropic plane.

Figure 4-9 shows a generalized population density surface for a metropolitan area. A major city can be seen dominating the area along with three smaller suburban towns. This surface could also depict the total influence of each settlement and its inhabitants. If there were a single isolated settlement, a symmetric and circular cone of influence would extend outward from the CBD. In the example shown in Figure 4-9 cones of influence intersect one another much as the cones of adjacent volcanoes might build up around each other. This is further illustrated in Figure 4-10. Notice how the larger city at

point A generates an area of influence which nearly engulfs that of the smaller settlement at B. Only the crest of city B's cone of influence rises above the slopes of A. The allocation of influence between two cities, or in this case between a major city and its satellite, can be visualized by drawing the line of intersection between the two cones. Thus points x and y in Figure 4-10 correspond to x' and y' in Figure 4-11, which is a map representation of the preceding three-dimensional view. Since the influence of the central city is greater on the side of the satellite settlement nearer to the larger city, the extent of the area of influence of the smaller place is less on that side. Conversely, the area of influence of the smaller, suburban town extends farther on the side away from the larger city. The resulting map pattern shows an asymmetrical hinterland belonging to the smaller town.

Figure 4–12A to D shows the relationships between a large isolated city and its hinterland, the hinterlands of two cities of equal size, the hinterlands or areas of influence of a large- and medium-sized city, and a large city and a smaller satellite suburb. Compare these figures with the map of Mobile. The presence of New Orleans to the west of Mobile suggests that the asymmetry of its area of influence results from the proximity of the larger metropolitan center.

Breaking points between city hinterlands

If two urban places have essentially the same number of shops and the same type and range of goods and offer the same services, how will customers located between them decide which center to patronize? In the real world, personal preferences as well as a host of other conditions play an important part in these decisions. Employment opportunities as well as consumer shopping habits vary considerably, and workers may commute from long-established homes in one town to new jobs in another city rather than change their residences. This process of city selection for work and shopping is extremely complicated and can be described in probabilistic terms as well as deterministic. If we think deterministically, it is possible to draw a sharp dividing line between two such cities; a probabilistic model, on the other hand, would show zones of overlapping influence. In both cases the extent of influence will be a function of their characteristics. Population alone may give an indication of their relative attractiveness, or variations in job opportunities or the number of commercial establishments may also be used. Let us also assume that the number of opportunities for work and trade is directly proportional to city size. In this case, if transportation facilities are everywhere the same, the boundary between the market areas of the two cities will be a line marking equal travel effort in either direc-

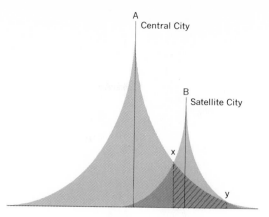

Figure 4-10 Allocation of influence between a central city and a satellite town Profile view of the zones of influence of a central city and its satellite town. The satellite's area of dominance is asymmetrical, being offset in the direction away from the central city.

Figure 4-11 Areas dominated by central city and satellite town Plan view of the zones of influence of a central city and its satellite town. At a distance beyond the satellite town, the central city reestablishes its dominance.

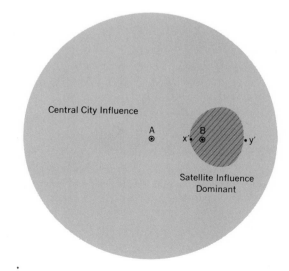

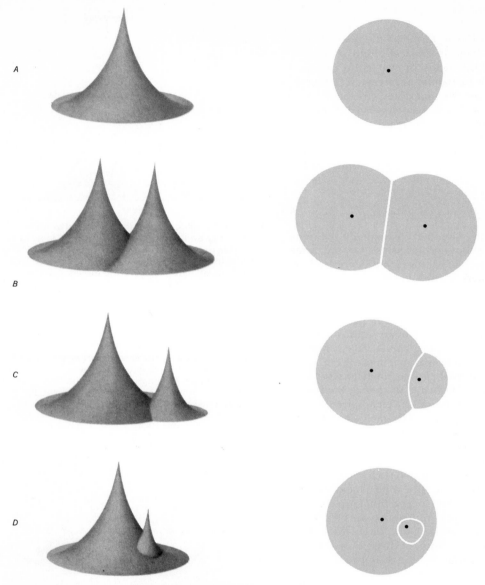

Figure 4-12 Cones of Influence around cities of varying size (A) single city, (B) cities of equal size, (C) city and independent small town, (D) city and satellite town.

tion. If the distance between two such places is 50 miles, then each will dominate an area 25 miles in depth. On the other hand, if one settlement is larger than the other and offers a larger number of more varied employment and customer opportunities, the market area or hinterland of the larger place will reach out farther from its CBD than that of the smaller. These relationships can be recognized in Figure 4–12.

Retail Gravity Models

The areal extent of city hinterlands can be estimated with the help of what are called *retail* and *social gravity models*. This approach for measuring the interaction between cities was first suggested by Henry C. Carey in 1858. Carey reasoned that an analogy might be drawn between the attractive force between two physical masses as stated in the physics equation

$$F = G \, \frac{M_1 M_2}{d^2}$$

and the interaction of two urban places. In this equation—which is familiar to all students who have had introductory physics—F is equal to the attractive force, M_1 is equal to the mass of the first body, M_2 is equal to the mass of the second body, and d^2 is the square of the distance between them. The constant G is an additional factor, the force of gravity, which must be included to make the computation correct.

William J. Reilly rewrote this equation in 1929 using populations instead of mass in order to describe the retail interaction between two cities. In his equation

$$I = \frac{P_i P_j}{d^2_{ij}}$$

P_i is the population of the first, or ith, city and P_j is the population of the second, or jth, city. The square of the distance between the two cities is shown by the notation d^2_{ij}. This

says: The retail interaction between two cities i and j is equal to the product of their populations divided by the square of the distance between them. The interaction I may be a measure of the number of customers, sales, or some other exchange between the two places. Thus two towns of moderate size which are located a short distance apart may have the same amount of goods passing between them as two larger places separated by a greater distance.

Problems associated with the gravity model

If only trips for one type of item are considered, and that item is readily available at all places with little or no variation in price and quality, then distance alone will usually determine the consumer's choice of market or market town. On the other hand, people will try to combine several errands on a single shopping trip, and larger towns with more choices and a greater variety of goods and services will attract customers from greater distances. As a result, the gravity model can only work where many trips and many travelers are concerned. A farmer may one day go to the nearest town to buy only groceries. Another time he may travel to a larger and more distant place not only to buy groceries but also to purchase a replacement part for his tractor and a pair of shoes for his child. More complicated models devised to take this type of human behavior into account are described in advanced texts.

A few moments' thought about the basic gravity model described above will reveal other complications. For example, is straight linear distance a good measure of true geographic distance? Ease of transportation may be very important. A superhighway leading to a farther city may offset the proximity of nearer places reached only on narrow, crowded county roads. If we consider city merchants who make deliveries to stay-at-home consumers, directional variations in freight rates or shipping charges may also make a significant difference in the customers' choice of stores. Several researchers have suggested that distance should be given greater or less importance depending upon the true effort required to overcome space. In order to do this the value d^2 might better be replaced by d^b where b would be some other value than the square of the distance. This might be the distance cubed in some cases where road conditions were poor, or the value might be something less than the distance squared where travel conditions were especially good.

Another thought to make us pause before using the simple gravity model would be the character of the populations involved. If three cities of equal size are equal distances apart but the average income in one city is considerably lower than those in the other two, the interaction between the two wealthier places might be much greater than between the poorer place and its richer neighbors. If we consider interaction on a world scale, cities of the same cultural background or ethnic composition might well interact with each other much more than with other urban populations speaking different languages or having different political beliefs. For greater accuracy an attempt must be made to weight each population according to some estimate of its potential for interaction. In one study of this kind cities in the South in the United States were considered to be less in the mainstream of national activity and were discounted by giving them a value only eight-tenths their true population size, thus reducing their interaction potential. In this manner some effort was made to adjust the gravity equation to assumed variations within the United States.

The subtle role of perception also must be taken into account. Many people say, "New York is a great place to visit but I wouldn't want to live there." This indicates a value judgment about the character of New York by nonresidents. In much the same way, our grandfathers longed to visit "Gay Paree" and made Paris the goal of European travel. Similarly, the public's image of certain national parks as desirable places to visit accounts for inequalities of recreational land use. On

days when Yosemite National Park is so crowded that hikers and campers are being turned away, other beautiful campgrounds in the same area remain unfilled. The role of perception and attitude in spatial decision making is, thus, very important in accounting for real world patterns which otherwise might seem to contradict what we have said about the effect of distance on human affairs.

Social gravity models

Variations from culture to culture and between cities with different levels of income further complicate the basic equations of retail gravitation. John Q. Stewart and other social scientists more than 30 years ago recognized the need to take such factors into consideration. They suggested that the analogy with the equation for gravitation force can be used to measure many kinds of influence and interaction between population groups in addition to the retail function of cities. Several variations on Reilly's original equation have been put forward. One of the simplest, but more comprehensive, of these social gravity models takes the form:

$$I_{ij} = K \frac{P_i P_j}{d^b_{ij}}$$

In this equation the interaction I may be a measure of the number of telephone calls, intercity migration, commercial exchanges, or any of the multitude of ways in which society interacts. The constant K describes the intensity of interaction in a particular society. Its value must be carefully derived from field observation, for people interact with their neighbors in ways which vary significantly from culture to culture and from activity to activity. P_i and P_j are measures of size, and d^b_{ij} is the distance between the two places weighted by some exponential value b which again depends upon variations in travel effort.

Market Areas and Transportation Costs

The retail and social gravity models discussed above work only when aggregate conditions are considered. That is, the preferences and choices of individuals are so varied that for the purpose of understanding the spatial character of cities we must view society only in large groups. In this way personal and random variation in behavior is averaged, and we may look at the total behavior of a city's population as matching some type of normal distribution. While a few people may act in extreme and seemingly illogical ways, the average citizen's actions can be anticipated, although we cannot identify him as an individual.

Gravity models do not help us understand the *processes* underlying retail and social behavior as much as they provide *descriptions of the behavior* of large populations. Another way in which it is possible to view the delimitation of city hinterlands or market areas is to understand the role played in their formation by transportation costs. If we consider each urban place as a collection of stores or sales outlets for services and manufactured goods, we can simplify our discussion by considering the case of a single factory producing one particular manufactured item. Once we understand the processes by which one establishment defines the area in which its output is distributed, it becomes possible to view each city as the sum of all the stores and factories it contains. The total commercial activity within the city and the area served by such commerce in essence defines the hinterland or trade area of the city.

The threshold of a good

Every factory and every store must begin with certain basic necessities. Land on which to locate, a building or buildings to house the firm, equipment of all kinds, and a labor force and sales personnel must all be provided before the success of the establishment can be assured. All these things cost money, and all the money originally invested must eventually be returned to the investors through sales. If production costs are not met and exceeded by the returns from sales, failure results.

The minimum number of sales or the smallest total volume of sales which will allow a commercial establishment to prosper and give an adequate return to its owners is called the *threshold of the establishment*. This idea may also be expressed in terms of a single sale or a single item if the total costs of production are divided by the number of units produced. This establishes the lowest price which may be charged for an item at the threshold volume of production which will meet production costs and also provide a reasonable return on the initial investment. This may be thought of as the threshold price of the good. From the customer's point of view every good and service has some maximum price more than which he is unable or unwilling to pay. When the price is unreasonable, the customer will go without or substitute something more reasonably priced. Obviously, to allow the firm to stay in business the threshold price must be less than the maximum a customer is willing to pay.

The range of a good

The above discussion omits one important cost in every transaction. Transportation must be paid by either the customer or the producer of every good and service. Shoppers must travel to the store, or the merchant must ship the purchase to the customer. Less tangible services are affected in the same way. You must visit your insurance salesman, or he must come to you. Medical doctors charge more for house calls than for office visits. The difference in price is their evaluation of the cost of their travel effort.

The cost of transportation varies considerably from item to item. If we consider only material goods for the moment, we can understand such variations in terms of the relationship between the volume or weight of an item and its total sales price. Generally speaking, small, lightweight goods with high value may travel long distances, while bulky or heavy items having a low value per pound or per cubic foot will travel less far. This simple relationship is shown in Figure 4–13. A fine

Value of Good		
	High	**Low**
High	Good Shipped Intermediate Distance Ornamental Building Stone Appliances	Good Shipped Short Distance Bricks Bottles
Low	Good Shipped Long Distance Cameras Watches Radios	Good Shipped Intermediate Distance Table Salt ˙ Fertilizer

(left vertical axis label: Volume or Weight of Good)

Figure 4-13 The relationship between volume of weight and value on the distance a good is shipped

camera with an expensive lens weighs at most 2 or 3 pounds. Even with adequate packing, equipment like this can be mailed long distances for only a few dollars. If we imagine a camera shipped from Japan to the United

Figure 4-14 Transport cost increment in relation to shipping distance The transport rate is the dollar charge per unit distance or the slope of the line. For linear transport rates of the type shown here, the total transport cost for shipping a given distance is found by multiplying the rate by the distance shipped.

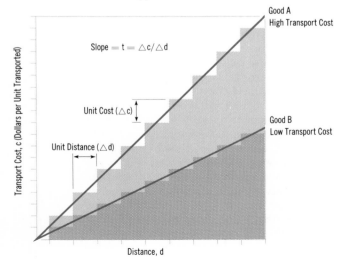

Slope = t = △c/△d

Good A
High Transport Cost

Unit Cost (△c)

Good B
Low Transport Cost

Unit Distance (△d)

(vertical axis: Transport Cost, c (Dollars per Unit Transported))
(horizontal axis: Distance, d)

States by air, its total cost might be 300 dollars, of which 5 dollars might cover the necessary postage. Heavy bulk items such as bricks sell for only a few cents apiece. If a brick were shipped more than a few miles from the kiln in which it was baked, the price of transportation would soon exceed the cost of production and the combined production and transportation costs would be more than anyone would be willing to pay. Many items fall within this category. Soft drinks are essentially water with flavoring added. The bottle in which the beverage is shipped to the consumer also constitutes a significant part of the total weight. Glass and water are low-priced items and cannot be shipped long distances without unnecessary expense. Thus bottling works and brick kilns must be located close to their customers, while camera factories, in terms of transportation costs, can afford to locate in a few select places.

The unit cost for shipping various items 1 mile can be shown on a graph by vertical lines of different lengths. For each unit of distance involved an additional vertical transportation cost increment is added. Figure 4–14 shows this for two unlike types of goods. Notice how the resulting lines resemble two steps of stairs, one very steep and the other much more gentle. Since it is awkward to use stepped lines such as these on graphs, sloping lines representing the average increase in transportation cost with increasing distance are substituted in their place. In Figure 4–14 t equals the ratio of the cost of transportation Δc per unit distance Δd and is shown by the slope of the line.

When the transportation costs are added to production costs, it becomes apparent that goods can be shipped only finite distances before the costs of shipment make the products so expensive that customers will no longer buy them. This absolute limit on the demand for an item is called the *maximum range of a good*. Figure 4–15 shows the relationship between production costs, profits, and transportation costs for two hypothetical products, both of which cost the same amount to produce, both of which sell for the same price, but one of which is easily transportable and the other expensive to ship.

Let us now translate these ideas into an areal context. Imagine a factory located on an isotropic plain across which potential customers are evenly distributed. Let us assume that 100 sales per year are necessary to offset the initial investment in the factory and all subsequent production costs: that is, the *threshold of the establishment* is 100. In order to meet these initial costs the factory must be able to ship its products a distance r which represents the radius of a circular area surrounding the factory which will include 100 customers. This distance is called the *minimum range of the establishment*. Another distance r' is called the *maximum range of an establishment* (Figure 4–16). All else being equal, in a densely settled area the minimum range of a good will be considerably less than in a region with sparse population. By the same reasoning, establishments with identical maximum ranges which operate in sparsely and densely settled areas would serve small and large numbers of customers, respectively.

A Regular Shape for City Hinterlands

Some commercial establishments in a city will have limited ranges, while others may serve

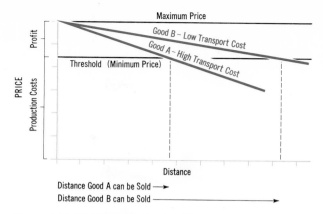

Figure 4-15 Relationship between production costs, profits, and transportation costs for two hypothetical products If two goods are sold at an equal price and profit but with a different transport cost for delivery, the good with the lower transport cost can travel farther.

the entire globe. This is shown in part by the varying ranges of the activities plotted on the map of Mobile (Figure 4–2). If we return now to our idea of the city as a collection of stores and factories, it is possible to think of the market area of an urban place as a combination of the maximum ranges of many different goods and services. A settlement of a particular size might be characterized as having a typical

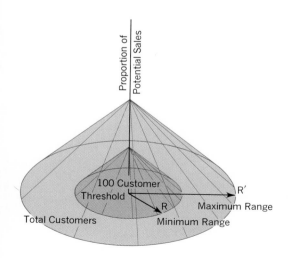

Figure 4-16 The relationship between the threshold number of customers and the minimum and maximum range of a good The proportion of potential sales realized will fall with rising prices. This decline will occur as the base price is raised or as the delivery price is increased by the addition of the transport cost. The diagram shows both conditions. The base price cannot be so high that the firm is unable to achieve a market penetration of at least 100 customers—that is, its threshold of business. The customers are assumed to be spread evenly over the surface. Taking into account transportation costs, this threshold is met at the minimum range r. If the base price is lowered, greater market penetration is achieved locally and more distant customers will find it worthwhile to buy the good. At some distance r', the transport cost precludes effective market penetration regardless of the base price (presuming it stays positive). This is the maximum range of the good.

The City and Its Hinterland— the Effects of Distance

69

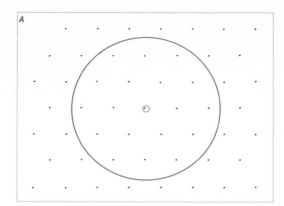

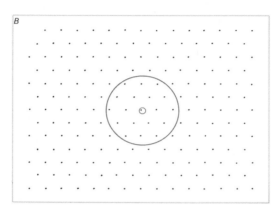

Figure 4-17 Minimum range of a good as a function of density Assume that an activity requires contact with eighteen locations other than its own to reach its threshold of business. The diagram illustrates that the range of the good, the radius of a circle centered at the firm, is inversely related to the density of customers. (*A*) Low density, large minimum range. (*B*) High density, small minimum range.

with the regularity shown in Figure 4–17. People cluster together in settlements or along transportation routes, and near natural resources such as ore deposits or recreation sites. If every irregular distribution required a city hinterland with a new, perhaps unique shape,

Figure 4-18 Minimum market areas remain circular in a region of uneven population density An even population distribution is not a necessary condition for the existence of a circular market area. Parts *A* and *B* of the diagram show minimum market areas for firms with a threshold need for eighteen neighbors. Region *A* has an even distribution of population, and region *B* has an uneven distribution of population. It is always possible to draw a circle around the *n* nearest neighbors (ignoring ties for last place). The larger circles encompass eighteen additional neighbors for firms with double the threshold of the first case. Different radii are necessary, but the shape remains circular.

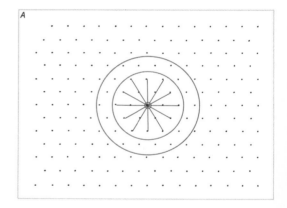

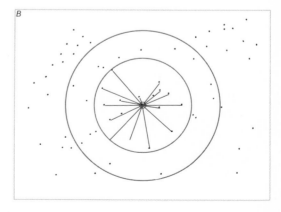

average range for all its activities. Small settlements with few establishments would reach out a much shorter distance than larger ones with many specialized activities. This brings us to the question of how urban places share with their neighbors the territories which surround them.

The first consideration is the most efficient shape for the hinterland of a single settlement. Real world populations are seldom distributed

it would be extremely difficult for us to seek regularities in the spatial character of cities. What we need to find is a universal shape which will fit all hinterlands and yet contain the necessary number of customers to reach a given threshold requirement. On a plain having an evenly distributed population (Figure 4–18A) a circle meets these requirements. The only exception to this would be where two or more points might be exactly the same maximum distance from the center. If the threshold requirements were to change, the circle might grow larger or smaller, but we would not have to find a new shape.

It may come as a surprise to learn that regardless of the irregularity of population distribution, a circle is still the simplest universal shape that can be drawn to contain any specified number of points or customers. Naturally, odd shapes with all sorts of indentations and bumps might be drawn that could still contain a set number of points, but this could be done only by introducing confusing variety into our analysis. Figure 4–18B shows a highly irregular distribution of points within two circles, the smaller containing exactly eighteen and the larger exactly thirty-six. The circle drawn through the eighteenth most distant point from the center includes the other necessary seventeen but excludes the nineteenth, twentieth, and so on. The same is true of the larger circle for the thirty-sixth point. Experimentation with an irregular point pattern of your own will quickly show that this holds true in every case. This means that in our search for universal conditions or constants we may take the circle as a possible regular shape that the hinterlands of settlements might take.

The next problem we must consider is how a collection of settlements with circular hinterlands might occupy a large area and share its resources, including space itself, or provide services and goods for the population distributed across it. We have dealt with single firms and single settlements in this chapter; therefore, a consideration of multiple settlements comes next.

5 | HOW CITIES SHARE SPACE: CLASSICAL CENTRAL PLACE THEORY

Cities and their uses of space are so complex that it is wise to begin our discussion of how urban places divide up the territories they occupy by looking at the simplest type of settlement. In most parts of the world subsistence-level farm villages provide shelter and basic needs but no real retail services for the peasants who inhabit them. Nevertheless, a hinterland, however small, is just as important for a village as a city. After all, the villagers depend upon the fields surrounding them for their very lives. At the same time, villagers "commute" to their fields rather than living near or in the center of their property. The village hinterland of fields and the farmers' daily trips to them are thus in many ways analogous to our preceding discussion of cities and commuters. Once we have established some basic rules about the spacing of villages, we can more easily move on to a consideration of larger settlements.

The Basic Pattern

What would be the optimum arrangement of farm villages across an isotropic plain of uniform fertility? Let us make the four following assumptions. (1) The land supports a uniform number of people per square mile. Let us assume in this case that the number is 25. Such an exact figure is solely a matter of con-

venience for the argument that follows. Poorer land would have lower population densities and greater distances between villages. (2) The typical farmer can afford to walk no more than 2 miles to work in the morning, nor can he trudge more than 2 weary miles homeward at the end of a long day behind plow or harrow. This distance represents the *maximum range* of the village as a self-sustaining farm community.

It follows from these two conditions that the total land available to a village must fall within a circle having the village at its center and a radius of 2 miles. The total area of such a circle is 12.56 square miles, which at 25 persons per square mile would provide for a population of about 314 people.

Our next assumption (3) is a simple one, that life is reasonably good and that there is slow but steady population growth. Eventually our 300-plus people will become 450 and even more—30 new families of 5; 150 new mouths to feed; an additional 6 square miles of land needed! Since the original population of 314 utilized all the land within 2 miles of the village center, young husbands and wives and their children who are old enough to work must walk more than 2 miles each way every day to find available land. When this trip to work becomes too great, the excess population will be forced to move. Let us assume that a *hiving-off* process will take place and a new village will be formed. But where?

The answer to this question in part depends upon our next and last assumption. (4) Villagers who hive off will try to stay as close as possible to older settlements in order to maintain important social bonds and linkages. The minimum distance between any two villages must be 4 miles, that is, at least twice the village radius. This distance allows adequate land for food production. At the same time, villagers will not move farther apart since they wish to minimize the travel distance required to maintain social contacts. Now let us see how the "offspring" of one parent village might fill up an empty and inviting area.

If we start with an empty plain and randomly place one "seed" village upon its surface, in succeeding generations that settlement will grow, hive off, and grow again. In turn, it will be joined by younger neighbors who grow and hive off in ever-increasing numbers. As each settlement grows beyond an optimum size defined by the trip to work and the carrying capacity of the land, it will become a mother for new colonies. This is shown in Figures 5-1A to D. In illustration 5-1A the primary settlement—designated A— reaches the hiving-off point and sends forth a nucleus which establishes itself two radii away at B. This distance will allow B when fullgrown to extend toward A without competing for land needed by the mother community. In the next generation A again surpasses optimum size and hives off settlement C, while at the same time its first colony reaches optimum size, although it does not yet need to hive off excess population. In the third generation, A again sends out a colony which locates at D. In this and all subsequent cases new colonies are located so as to maximize contact with the most senior of the already existing settlements. B, having reached the point where hiving is necessary, sends out its own colony D', while C reaches but does not exceed the population which can be supported on land within 2 miles of its center. Subsequently, colonies are estab-

lished at all the points E, F, E', and F'. The pattern formed after eleven generations by villages following the above rules of growth is shown in Figure 5-1B. Notice too that by the time settlements E, E', F, and F' have been formed (Figure 5-1A), villages B and C are completely surrounded and will have to leapfrog their neighbors in order to send out colonies. Such a predicament would represent a resource shortage—in this case farmland. When this happens, the parent settlement has a limited number of possible actions. Its people may move beyond their neighbors to more remote resources, or new population increments may stay at home. In the latter case population densities will increase, and if no new sources of income are found, the general level of living will inevitably drop. Sometimes this crisis is met by an intensification of farming. Sometimes services and activities may develop with increasing settlement size, and a basic shift may take place in the pattern of living within these larger places. Figure 5-1C shows the accumulation of population in the original model assuming that everyone stays at home once empty neighboring land is used up.

Space packing: Circles into hexagons

Before leaving this example, let us consider the villages both as focal *points* and farm *areas*. Viewed as points, the pattern generated is a latticework consisting of equilateral triangles, each apex of which represents a settlement. When each point is thought of as the focus of a system of farming which utilizes the space around it, then the entire plain must be divided up among the settlements. This is shown by the neatly packed circular farm village areas in Figure 5-1A. One problem remains. Since circles do not fit tightly together, small open spaces, or interstices, exist everywhere. If these open spaces are divided equally among their neighbors (Figure 5-1D), the field of packed circles is transformed into a neat arrangement of hexagonal areas with no unaccounted space (Figure 5-1C). Locations within the small subdivided areas will be more than

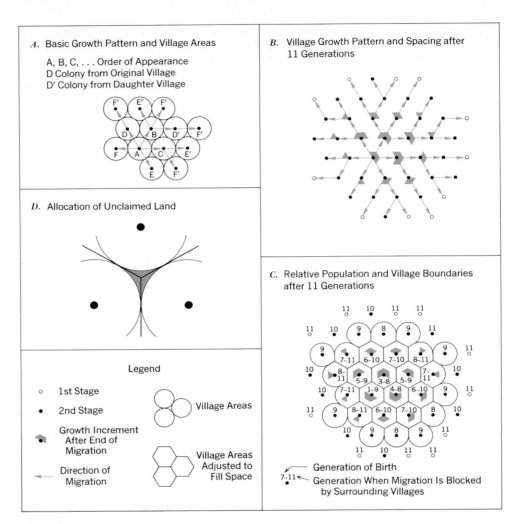

Figure 5-1 A growth model of village spacing Classical central place theory assumes as an initial condition that the underlying settlement pattern is an array of farm villages distributed at the nodes of a hexagonal lattice. A simple model of a settlement growth process that would result in such a pattern can be postulated. The key spatial assumptions necessary are that (*A*) each settlement requires a compact, finite, and local unit area for its functioning; (*B*) daughter colonies locate as near as possible to the parent colony when splitting off; and (*C*) an optimum size exists for the basic settlements. The process is described more fully in the text.

2 miles from any village center in our original model, but such excess distance will be very slight indeed; and in a more complex model we might start with slightly smaller circles which when changed to hexagons would not exceed a maximum distance of 2 miles. In any event, a triangular network of points and a field filled by hexagonal areas provide the best geometric solution to our original problem of farmers, farms, and farm villages.

Only three regular geometric shapes can be used to fill space without overlaps or leftovers: equilateral triangles, squares, and regular hexagons. Hexagons, being most nearly circular in form, are the best of the three shapes for minimizing the distance between a central point and the surrounding area which it controls. Thus, our model, generated with a simple set of geographic, social, and demographic rules, results in a pattern fulfilling the requirements of pure Euclidean geometry.

A Classical Theory of Central Place Hierarchies

The village pattern with which we have filled our isotropic plain relates man spatially to the land he occupies. But such settlements would be simple places where a traveler could find no cafe or teashop, no cobbler to mend his boots, nor any store to sell him provisions. The most humble peasant is linked to some sort of market economy which provides him with necessities, be they only flint and steel to light his fire, or, in more prosperous and modern times, a transistor radio with which to learn the latest news. In like manner, money for goods and services, and to pay the tax collector, marriage broker, and doctor, comes from his sale of crops. Such produce goes to middlemen who buy from many farmers and pass what they have collected to larger-scale wholesalers in their turn.

If we are to pull this simple model of spatial organization nearer to reality, we must provide our villagers with what they need; and we must also furnish goods and services necessary and suitable for a more urban life-style to the townsmen who supply the farmers. To do this let us introduce into our model a complete set of firms which will supply the entire population with whatever they need and can afford. In other words, the problem is *to find the best locations for a variety of establishments which have different thresholds and ranges for the goods and services which they provide.* While this complicates our model, we can continue to impose a certain simplicity

upon it by assuming that the population served by the necessary firms is evenly distributed in geographic space. Our network of villages will serve this purpose.

An interesting answer to the problem of regularly arranging points (firms) across an area (in this case represented by an evenly distributed population) was offered by Walter Christaller in 1933. Christaller, a German geographer, had noticed regularities in the settlement pattern of Barvaria in southern Germany. He attempted to explain these regularities deductively by creating a settlement model with certain fixed qualities and assumptions. At the same time, Christaller was interested in the distribution of different-sized settlements, villages, cities, and towns, which sometimes cluster together and sometimes are found far apart.

Another German, an economist named August Lösch, in 1945 independently derived an answer similar to Christaller's. Both concluded that *the best way to spatially provide a population with all types of services is to place such activities in a nested hierarchy of increasingly larger central settlements located at the nodes of a hexagonal network.* Both Christaller's and Lösch's schemes are essentially static. That is, their models are presented full-blown in all their complexity with no reference to how they might change through time. Christaller himself observed, "The state of rest is only fiction, whereas motion is reality." But both scholars stopped short of more dynamic models, and it may be said that their contributions have been as much to stimulate further geographic thought as to give us any absolute explanations of the real world.

Their answer, as given above, is phrased in a kind of geographical shorthand which needs clarification. To do this we will first give Christaller's rules and assumptions. We will also use this opportunity to follow through a sequence of theoretical reasoning in considerable detail. By doing this we hope to make the thought processes behind such exercises more explicit and understandable in order to demonstrate the value of this type of thinking. Next we will describe the system of central places which he proposed, and finally we will leave the static models of Christaller and Lösch and attempt to create a more dynamic description of a similar system as it might have developed in an imaginary kingdom, a useful place where everything goes according to plan. The remainder of this chapter will present examples of central place systems as they have been perceived and described in the real world.

The conditions underlying Christaller's model

Christaller began his deductions by limiting his model to the following conditions:

1. There exists an unevenly spread market on an isotropic plain.

The character of an *isotropic surface* should already be clear to us, and *an evenly spread market* simply means that everyone within the population has the same purchasing power and the same set of needs and desires.

2. There exists an equally spaced, discontinuous population.

All the conditions implied by this are met by the model of village distribution which has already been presented.

3. There exists a set of central place activities with different thresholds; these activities are point occupying and are ordered according to the size of their thresholds.

A central place activity or good is something needed by members of a population which they* cannot provide for themselves. Such things can be material goods such as groceries, clothing, or equipment. They can be less tangible services like dentistry, haircuts, or insurance. They can also be socially defined, as are church services, Saturday night dances, or social clubs like the Elks, De Molay, and the Knights of Columbus. Such activities are considered to be *point occupying*. That is,

the spaces needed for their realization are so small when considered at the scale necessary for viewing the area in which their customers or participants live that they are reduced to dimensionless locations or points. In reality, such points are settlements of different sizes whose strategic central locations allow a maximum number of people to participate in the activities which take place there as well as to consume the goods and services they produce. Such settlements are referred to as *central places*. Thus, theory relating to them is known as *central place theory*. The notion of *different thresholds* relates on one hand to the number of participants necessary to make a social function succeed. For example, too small a crowd can turn a dance floor into an empty and echoing barn, while a congregation consisting of only a few people cannot support the regular services of a priest or minister. On the other hand, where goods and services are concerned, the number of people necessary to provide a living for a dentist will be different from the number needed to keep a barber in business. A small grocery store can survive on sales made within the local neighborhood of which it is a part, but a furniture store or farm tractor salesroom must draw its customers from a far larger population in order to survive. If we take a set of activities which we assume includes all those necessary for leading a complete social and physical life, some will be able to get by with a low sales volume or with a few participants; others will need a great many. If in considering this set we rank its members in order of sales volume or number of participants from largest to smallest, we will have fulfilled Christaller's final condition.

We should also note in passing that with an unchanging and evenly distributed population *the threshold of a good determines the minimum range of a good*. For example, if a small grocery store needs 1,000 customers to survive (i.e., its threshold is 1,000) and every member of the population is a customer, then the minimum range of the grocery will be the radius of a circle the area of which includes exactly 1,000 people. Assuming a fixed and evenly distributed population, this area and therefore its radius will always be the same. Another establishment, needing a larger sales volume, would for the same reasons need to include more people within its sales area and therefore would need to be at the center of a circle with a larger radius.

Assumed relationships within Christaller's model

When Christaller specified the characteristics of his model as we have just described them, he created the environment in which his settlements, their activities, and their populations might interact. Such interaction depended in turn upon a set of *assumed relationships* which describe the manner in which all action would take place. These relationships can be summarized by the following four points.

1. The population of each central place is a function of the number of goods and services it offers.

By this is meant that a settlement offering few goods will be smaller than one offering many goods. The difference is in the number of storekeepers, service workers, and their families needed to offer a larger number of goods and services. In order to live continuously at a given place people need jobs. The population size thus depends upon the number of goods and services offered.

2. The central place hierarchy operates as a closed system.

Christaller, in simplifying the world in which his model operates, chose not to take into account the full activity of towns and cities. In this scheme his settlements serve only their own immediate hinterlands. They neither produce goods or services for national or international distribution nor import anything from beyond the limits of their own interlocking network of settlements. A second

major simplification made by Christaller is that his cities exist as dimensionless points serving the areas surrounding them but not serving themselves. This notion creates a contradictory situation within Christaller's logic which needs further discussion. The existence of cities with large populations within the model would contradict a basic characteristic of its environment, that is, an evenly distributed population. In order to avoid this paradox, settlements must be treated as points with populations which have no needs of their own. This shows something important about deductive and theoretical reasoning. The abstract world of the theoretician also can have its pitfalls as well as its advantages. In the final analysis the real world is the absolute standard against which all our ideas must be judged.

3. A minimum number of central places operates within the system. (That is, each central place offers all goods offered by lower-order places plus an additional set with a larger threshold.)

This condition recognizes what economists sometimes call *economies of scale*. Every new firm will have overhead costs. These will be both in the construction and maintenance of the establishment itself and also in the provision of roads, new energy and water supplies, and other urban services for which the general population must pay. Therefore, the social and economic objectives of the population will be to cut down overhead wherever possible by clustering and sharing facilities. In terms of the settlement hierarchy, this means that each central place will offer as many goods and services as it can within the limits of the system. It also means that larger settlements offering very special services which have higher thresholds will also offer all the goods and services available in smaller settlements. To illustrate this in the briefest possible way: A small town might have a grocery store but little else; a larger town might have a barber but would also have a grocer; a

How Cities Share Space: Classical Central Place Theory

city would have a dentist, and a barber, and a grocer. It also follows that dentists would not set up practice in isolated locations since that would necessitate new roads and other facilities already available in existing settlements.

4. The system operates under perfect competition and complete information.

Every firm and every customer will have complete and accurate information about all other customers and firms. This rather unrealistic but useful assumption means there will be no "shopping around" by customers. They will know beforehand that the goods and services they want will be exactly the same everywhere. Moreover, they will know which establishment is the nearest source for what they desire and go directly there. In other words all movement will be to the nearest place where the good or service is offered. No one will ever unnecessarily cross boundaries into another firm's hinterland. In the same way, *perfect competition* means that each establishment is so small when compared with the entire system that prices cannot be influenced by a single firm's dumping goods on the market to lower the price or hoarding goods in order to drive prices up. Likewise, firms cannot form monopolies for the same purpose. They all will be completely independent of each other, and all will have profit as their only motive. Finally, no establishment can have a price advantage because of differences in the quality of its product or through arbitrary price changes. In this model the only advantage which firms can experience is that of better or worse relative locations. Another way to say this is that all firms operate exactly at their thresholds, making just enough profit to survive. Since the *threshold of a good* determines the *minimum range of a good* where population is evenly distributed, the market areas determined by the minimum range will remain as small as possible and the maximum number of firms will be packed into the area served by the system.

Christaller's spatial model

Once Christaller had so carefully set the scene, there remained the task of constructing a spatial model matching the assumptions he had set forth. Given a set of activities ranked according to the size of their market areas, Christaller chose to begin with the largest settlements, while August Lösch began his considerations with the smallest. In this account, we will briefly describe the formal or geometric construction of a central place hierarchy from Christaller's point of view, while Lösch's choice—from small to large— forms the basis for the spatial history of our imaginary kingdom.

According to Christaller, each central place provides a complete set of activities associated with settlements smaller than itself. In addition, it has certain activities which can only flourish in places its size or larger. High-order central places (that is, very large towns and cities) are located across an isotropic plain, as were the villages in our earlier example. This results in a series of widely spaced settlements, each surrounded by a hexagonal market area representing the service with the highest threshold and the largest minimum range. In addition to their specializations, these large central places offer a *complete* selection of services to the population immediately adjacent to themselves. But because the market areas of these secondary services are smaller than those of the highest order, much of the population is not provided with these lesser activities. This is because the high-order centers are too far apart (Figure 5–2A).

In order to fill the needs of this unserved portion of the population, firms offering goods and services with smaller market areas are located in the unserved spaces between the largest market centers. The problem is to identify the most spatially rational locations for these smaller centers. Points farthest from the highest-order centers are logical places for the next tier or level of establishments. Such points of least accessibility are found at the exact center of each equilateral triangle

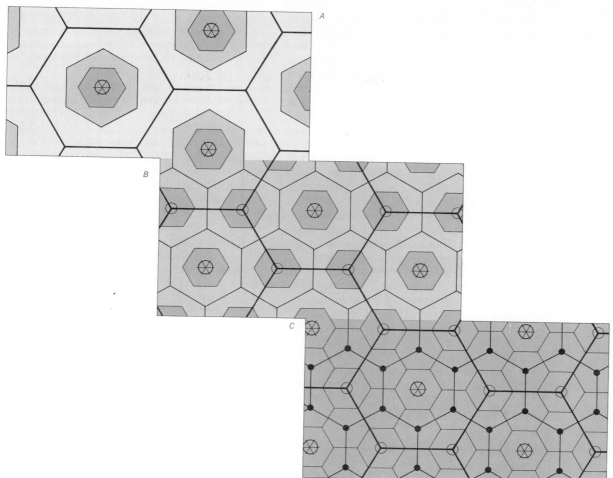

Figure 5-2 Nested hierarchy of central places and their market areas
(*A*) Partial hierarchy showing the network of largest market places and their
market areas. This includes high-order goods (lightest shading), which
require wide spacing of centers in order to reach their market threshold,
intermediate-order goods (intermediate shading), and lower-order goods
(darkest shading), with their shorter ranges. (*B*) Partial hierarchy showing
the network of large and intermediate centers forming a nested hierarchy,
which provides high-order and intermediate-order goods for the entire
market area and low-order goods in their immediate locale. (*C*) Complete
nested hierarchy in which the entire region is serviced with high-,
intermediate- and low-order goods from a three-level hierarchy of central
places. Close spacing of low-order centers allows goods with short ranges
to reach the entire area.

formed by three adjacent higher-order places in the network. Figure 5−2B shows the total market area covered by high- and intermediate-order places. Finally, small towns and perhaps large villages (that is, low-order central places) are located in the unserved areas between large- and medium-sized settlements. Again, the best locations are the center points of the equilateral triangles formed by every three adjacent settlements in the existing network. This results in a landscape (Figure 5−2C) in which every place receives all the goods offered by the system. In this hierarchy a few large settlements furnish all customers with specialized services and also provide populations immediately adjacent to themselves with middle-range services and basic necessities. Medium-sized settlements in turn supply similar middle-range services to all customers not served by the largest centers; they also provide basic goods and services to their own neighboring populations. Finally, a network of small central places fills in the remaining gaps, thus bringing basic services to the rest of the population. The sum of all these settlements, the market areas of the small nested inside those belonging to higher-order central places, creates a *nested hierarchy of central places.*

Imaginary History of A Central Place System

There once was a Prince who lived in a kingdom which in the beginning had nothing but farm villages. He was industrious and imaginative, and liked a good time as well as the next fellow. Thus, it came about that the Prince began making mead in order to celebrate the good harvests, the coming of spring, summer, fall, and winter, and sometimes just to celebrate, so cheerful was his mood. Now mead is a drink made from honey; and honey, with an assist from the bees, comes from flowers. But flowers, belonging to that happy class of plants known as heliophytes, or sun lovers, cannot cluster at points but must grow widespread in order to soak up the sun which floods down everywhere. At the

same time, bees, being busy but exceedingly small, do not fly long distances from flower to hive; and so it happened that honey was found everywhere in small quantities but never in large amounts at any one spot.

Thus many people in the kingdom could have made mead; but, strangely enough, few did. Our Prince's was the best. In fact his mead was so good he was soon not only providing drink for himself but also selling it to other people in his village. Now, this suited him very well, and he was soon referred to as the Merchant Prince by all the villagers, a title which was quickly shortened to Merp. Unfortunately, there were not enough customers in Merp's village alone to justify his becoming a full-time and profitable mead maker. In other words the threshold of his mead establishment was higher than the population of mead drinkers in his immediate village. Now it so happened that Merp's mead was very good and justifiably famous. Soon people from the neighboring villages closest to his own were walking across the fields to patronize his shop. In fact, some people from each of the six villages surrounding his own became regular customers. The fame of Merp's mead spread, and people from villages even farther away would send word that they wished that they too could buy some of his mead. But distances were too great, and so Merp's customers were limited to those in the nearest villages.

Now Merp fell to thinking about the meadless, thirsty people beyond the range of the good he had to sell. "Why not," he said, "set up branch mead shops in other villages in order to help the people celebrate their weddings and festivals and at the same time turn a pretty penny for myself?" (For the kingdom's coinage was particularly beautiful and the pennies were loveliest of all.) Merp quickly visited other villages beyond his nearest neighbors and found in them potential mead makers eager to give up farming for another way of life. Merp gave these people, one in each of the villages he chose, a franchise to become a mead maker using his famous recipe. In no time at all the landscape was filled with a network of mead shops serving the mead needs of the populace.

Now, in placing his branch mead shops Merp had had to take into account the short distance that customers were willing to walk. This meant that his network of mead shops was a closely spaced one and that shops in villages just one tier beyond his nearest neighbors became his competitors for the trade of the villages which lay between them. It fell out that people in a neighboring village who wished to purchase mead could choose one of three equally near mead-selling villages from which to make their purchases (Figure 5–3A).

The result of this was that one-third of the customers in each such village journeyed to a different neighboring mead center. And so it came about that there developed a spatial hierarchy with mead-drinking villages representing first-order places and mead-selling villages becoming second-order centers.

This meant that Merp soon shared his customers with the six mead shops nearest his own. In other words, his shop could depend upon all the customers from his own village and one-third of the customers from each of the six surrounding villages. All in all, he could look forward to having the equivalent of cus-

Figure 5-3 The three basic central place hierarchies The diagrams show the meaning of the K = 3, K = 4, and K = 7 central place hierarchies. These are the three smallest regular hierarchies that can be defined on a hexagonal lattice. A regular hierarchy is one in which the number of immediate subordinates is the same for each level.

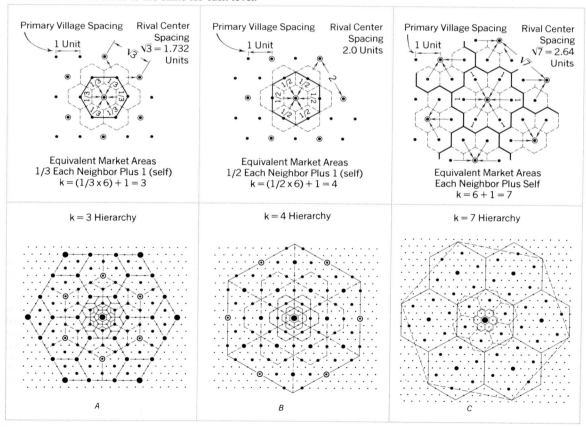

Primary Village Spacing — 1 Unit
Rival Center Spacing — $\frac{1}{3}\sqrt{3} = 1.732$ Units

Equivalent Market Areas
1/3 Each Neighbor Plus 1 (self)
k = (1/3 × 6) + 1 = 3

k = 3 Hierarchy

A

Primary Village Spacing — 1 Unit
Rival Center Spacing — 2.0 Units

Equivalent Market Areas
1/2 Each Neighbor Plus 1 (self)
k = (1/2 × 6) + 1 = 4

k = 4 Hierarchy

B

Primary Village Spacing — 1 Unit
Rival Center Spacing — $\sqrt{7} = 2.64$ Units

Equivalent Market Areas
Each Neighbor Plus Self
k = 6 + 1 = 7

k = 7 Hierarchy

C

tomers from three villages patronizing his own establishment. This was also true for mead shop operators in all the other mead-selling villages throughout the land.

Time passed, and with the increase in mead sales in every corner of the province there soon developed a shortage of copper kettles suitable for brewing mead. Merp had for a long time dabbled in copper kettle making for his own needs, and being farsighted, he anticipated that soon mead shops all over the land would feel the need for mead pots just as their customers had long before experienced an unsatisfied mead need. This was fortunate, for in order to justify the expensive equipment necessary for copper kettle making Merp had to provide copperware not only for his own village market area but also to the market areas equivalent to at least eight additional copper kettle-using villages. At the same time, his copper pots were heavy and hard to carry, and the farthest he could profitably transport them was just two times as far as people were willing to travel to obtain mead. In other words, he could sell his pots in his own village, in the six mead-selling villages closest to him, and in the six mead-selling villages beyond them. But this left the rest of the country without copper kettles. Thus Merp found himself once more doing for copperware what he had done for mead shops. He traveled throughout the land and set up a network of subsidiary copper pot emporiums in mead-selling villages beyond the maximum range of his own goods. Soon copper shops were flourishing in another, larger, more widely spaced network similar to the one he had set up for selling mead.

Again Merp felt the competition of the businesses established just beyond the maximum range of his own copper kettles, and again he found himself sharing customers from the outermost ring of villages with the subsidiary copper kettle makers nearest him. When things had sorted themselves out, he found that he was selling copper to his own village and the six mead-selling villages nearest him and winning one-third of the customers from the second tier of six mead-selling villages beyond them. Thus, his copper shop depended upon

a number of customers equivalent to those found in nine village market areas.

Merp's Amalgamated Mead Makers were becoming famous, and their slogan, *Never a Greater Mead,* was on everyone's lips, just like their product. As Merp's enterprises became more and more prosperous, he realized that much of his success was due to the hard work of his helpers. Wishing to recognize their efforts, he designed a golden mead mug which he awarded for long and meritorious service. Since these mead mugs were solid gold, they were very valuable and could be shipped long distances for a small proportion of their total worth. Not every employee received a mug, however, and this last of Merp's products had the highest threshold of all. At the same time, its maximum range reached as far as the farthest person to whom one might be awarded. At last Merp had found something which he could supply without his having to set up subsidiary firms in other parts of the country. In fact, he supplied all the the twenty-seven village market areas which had developed within his province.

The $K = 3$ hierarchy

Let us end our story of Merp, the Merchant Prince and President of Amalgamated Mead Makers, with the above episode. Our point has been made. Starting with the smallest mead-drinking settlements (that is, villages or first-order central places), we have seen the progressive buildup of larger places offering mead to drink. These could be considered second-order central places. Thereafter, the addition of copper kettle manufacturing to another, less numerous set of settlements established a third order of central places, each containing mead drinkers, mead makers, and pot manufacturers. This process was repeated again for Merp's own settlement, a fourth-order central place, which produced in order from smallest to largest market areas mead, kettles, and golden mead mugs. This progression of central places offering more and more specialized services and goods depended upon a regularly increasing progression of customers. If these populations are thought of in terms of the number of village-sized market areas served in each case, the sequence is 1, 3, 9, 27, 81, . . . This progression by the square of 3 indicates the total effective market area which each order of central place serves (Figure 5-3A). Lösch recognized this and gave systems incorporating this type of expansion a kind of shorthant designation. They are called K=3 *networks* and follow a *marketing principle* which had been recognized earlier by Christaller.

K=4 and K=7 hierarchies

Two similar progressions are described in Lösch's shorthand as K=4 and K=7 systems. The progression of market areas in the K=4 system is 1, 4, 16, 64, . . . , while that of the K=7 is 1, 7, 49, . . . Christaller also recognized these and suggested that the K=4 would also be useful for transportation networks and the K=7 for administrative purposes, although his comments predated Lösch's labeling.

In the K=4 network all settlements are located on roads leading directly away from the highest-order centers. This means that straight-line routes can reach all places, a situation unlike that in the K=3 network, where a zigzag route must be followed to reach all sizes of settlements. Central places in the K=4 network also provide a ranked order of goods and services. Starting at the bottom and moving upward, the minimum range of the lowest-order good is one-half the range of the next highest, which is in turn one-half the range of the third-order good, and so on for as many orders as are found within the system. Lower-order settlements are located exactly halfway between places of the next highest order and lie on the boundaries separating the market areas of those higher-order places (Figure 5-3B). It follows that a central place of a particular size has within its own market area the equivalent of four market areas of the next smallest size. It is this progression by fours which leads us to call this a K=4 system.

The K=7 network changes by a rule of seven. That is, each central place of a given size contains within its boundaries the equivalent of the areas associated with seven central places of the next smallest order (Figure 5-3C). This system is unlike the K=3 and K=4 networks, for each central place is located at the center of the area with which it is associated and is never divided by boundary lines of higher-order places. The advantage of this for administrative purposes can be seen at once. If a village or town lies equidistant from two or three larger places, its inhabitants, when shopping, can utilize some freedom of choice and go to whichever place they choose as long as their travel costs remain the same. Where administration is concerned and questions of legal jurisdiction are important, higher-order centers cannot share the allegiance of some smaller place's population, nor should questions of which code of laws, which police force, which tax collector be allowed to arise if the society is to function at all well. This is because law and administration in theory do not experience exponential decay with distance but remain fully enforced up to the boundaries of the administrative units in which they are applied. Thus, it is most efficient if each higher-order place clearly controls the territories of those places beneath it in the system. An examination of Figure 5-3C will indicate that the K=7 network satisfies this condition.

Other geometric progressions using still larger numbers are possible but not practical to present here. On the other hand, while our tale of the Merchant Prince may have seemed fanciful at times, there are many examples where knowledge of the geometry of central place systems can help clarify seemingly unsolvable complexities. The next section of this chapter discusses possible applications of central place theory to different societies.

Examples of Central Place Hierarchies

Relaxing the basic assumptions

The world is a chaotic place, and models of it which are useful because of their rigorous assumptions are remote from reality because of that rigor. We have seen the crystalline harmony of K=3, K=4, and K=7 networks.

What happens when the assumptions which protect them are stripped away and we seek their counterparts on the face of the earth? Christaller viewed his cities as dimensionless points serving the areas which surround them but not serving themselves. This is clearly unrealistic, but was allowed in order to maintain everywhere an even distribution of population. This also permitted the basic hexagonal market area of the smallest size to be everywhere the same. But we know that population clusters in cities. If we maintain a fixed unit of population, the hexagonal areas necessary to contain that basic population unit will be smaller where populations are large. That is, the minimum range of any good will become less as population density increases even though the threshold of the

Figure 5-4 Modular hexagonal pattern An example of a hexagonal network constricted around certain cells and enlarged around others to adjust for differences in underlying density of central place customers.

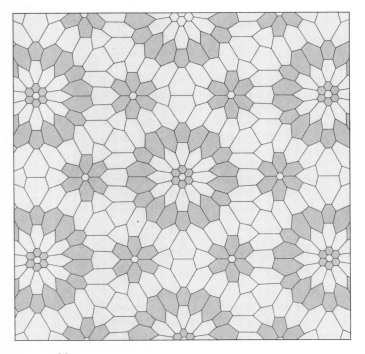

establishment remains the same. For example, if our basic threshold unit were 1,000 people, those thousand customers might live on one square mile in eastern Pennsylvania or the bottomlands of the Po Valley in northern Italy, or they might live on one city block in Chicago or Paris. It is more realistic to recognize that the basic unit of the hexagonal pattern will contract around cities and expand when far from urban places. Figure 5−4 shows a modular hexagonal pattern of this type which can be repeated over and over in all directions. Variations in this snakeskin allow adjustments to be made to the hexagonal network wherever sparse or dense populations appear.

Population density varies from place to place throughout the world as the result of many things besides urbanization. Some causes of this are cultural, some economic, some natural. Most often it is a combination of these and other conditions. An examination of the distribution of world ecotypes and world population on maps will show many different examples of population's becoming more sparse in very cold, very dry, or very mountainous areas. This thinning out can be shown graphically by the gradual change in size of a hexagonal network, with smaller hexagons representing wetter or warmer or more productive areas with dense populations and larger hexagons indicating colder, drier, or rougher areas with sparse populations (Figure 5−5).

Changes in the size of the basic network help us to relax some of the assumptions in the central place model, but as long as central place hinterlands are defined by simple patterns, we must continue to assume that customers remain neatly at home in their own market areas. This is not the case in the real world. A distant store will offer credit while one nearby will not. The children like *that* dentist and can't stand *this* one. Vegetables are always fresher in the supermarket on the other side of town. At the same time, people will combine trips for the sake of convenience. Few customers would travel miles and miles just to buy a toothbrush. But if someone has made a long trip to a regional shopping cen-

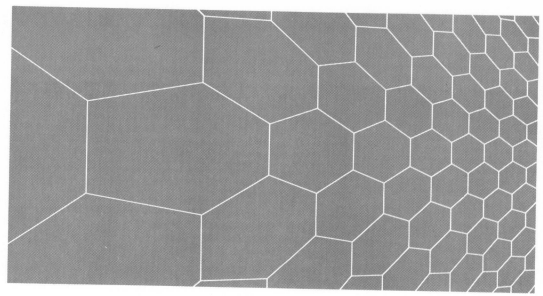

Figure 5-5 Logarithmic expansion of a hexagonal lattice A hexagonal network expanded by a logarithmic function in one direction. This network would be suitable for an underlying population that varied from dense to sparse along the east-west dimension.

ter in order to buy a color television set, it is quite reasonable for him to step into the pharmacy adjoining the furniture store to make such a smaller purchase. When several similar errands are combined in one trip which thus has several purposes, boundary crossings can occur at any and all levels of the hierarchy.

Still other adjustments in the basic hexagonal network of settlements might deal with frontier situations. As settlement extends into less and less hospitable places, fewer and fewer amenities become available to the population. One might expect to find trading posts selling matches and ammunition, but sterling silver and vintage wines are only found for sale in large cities. In other words, lower orders of the central place hierarchy exist almost everywhere, but the complete system is limited to the most commercialized areas. The frontier development of a central place hierarchy is illustrated in Figure 5-6.

Random events or "shocks" may well skew or otherwise distort regular central place hierarchies into unrecognizable forms. In fact, it seems quite remarkable that there are locations where theory seems to be reflected in reality. This is due in part to the relative regularity of the underlying environment in those places. Szechwan Province in China, Iowa and the northern Great Plains, and Ontario, Canada, provide us with a few such examples.

Permanent settlement hierarchies: China

A heap of flesh and a pile of bones, no matter how cleverly arranged, are not a living body. If the intended creature so described is to have life, blood must pump through veins and arteries and muscles flex in response to messages from the brain. So too with urban systems. In order for our ideas of settlement hierarchies to have validity and use we must be able to plot the paths taken through the

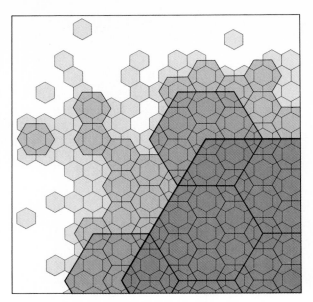

Figure 5-6 Frontier development of a central place hierarchy The assumption underlying this pattern of settlement is that usually only basic, low-order goods are offered on the frontier or edge of a settlement system, whereas larger thresholds are met in the central commercial areas and the full range of high-order goods is offered.

system by people, goods, and messages. We turn now to mainland China, where over the centuries a hierarchy of central places has had an opportunity to develop an easily discernible pattern involving all sizes of urban places and levels of society. These elaborate systems of markets were described in locally prepared gazetteers, while additional information is available through newspaper accounts, some rural surveys, and personal information obtainable from Chinese emigrants now living outside the mainland. Among the scholars who have studied this subject is G. William Skinner, whose analysis includes much information on the spatial organization of traditional Chinese peasant society. The Chinese example is valuable for another reason besides its completeness. The age and stability of Imperial China allowed

its system of settlements to attain a kind of spatial equilibrium of great interest.

Periodic markets Imagine a morning, dew-wet and bright, with the sun risen across the Chinese plain. We are standing at the edge of a small market town. It is one of the regularly scheduled market days, and since the harvest is nearly complete, the roads are busy with peasants bringing produce to sell and returning to their villages with their meager but necessary purchases. This is considered a "hot" day—not because temperatures are high but because business is flourishing within the market. On so-called "cold" days the market is nearly empty and local wholesalers may be on their way to nearby villages to bid for and buy the farmers' peanuts and grain. Barbers and blacksmiths also leave town on "cold" days to visit customers who ordered their services on a previous visit, usually during some "hot" market day.

The market undergoes regular or periodic changes. On certain days itinerant peddlers line the streets, making them noisy with their offers of manufactured items and goods not produced within the local region. The comings and goings of these footloose sellers follow complex and regular schedules. The low level of living and the frugal life of the village farmers generate only a small demand for imported wares at any given place at any particular time. The *threshold* or lower limit of sales needed to sustain such a peddler could not be met if he were to remain in one town waiting for his customers to come from villages within one day's walking distance. In theoretical terms the maximum range of the activity has fallen below the minimum range required to meet the threshold of the business. As a result, markets in the small towns of China as well as many other places in the world meet periodically rather than continuously. Towns with many nearby customers may have markets which meet every other day. Fewer potential customers result in markets' being scheduled less frequently, perhaps three times or six times each lunar month. On days when a market is not in progress in one town, the itinerant shops will travel to another "standard" market which is in session. In this way, by visiting a number of *periodic markets*, salesmen who might otherwise fail for want of sufficient trade manage to survive (Figure 5–7).

Standard markets If we were to walk through the market itself, we would see not only the temporary stalls of the peddlers but behind them a few permanent shops where tobacco and matches, candles and lamp oil, needles and thread, and brooms and soap can be purchased any day, "hot" or "cold." Teahouses and wineshops are often crowded with townsmen and villagers, while odors of cooking in food stalls and small restaurants season the morning air. Home workshops and small establishments also offer an irreducible minimum of needed goods and services. The carpenter's saw and the coffin maker's hammer sound in the street. In another shop, paper religious objects are made and sold. Other services, needed less frequently, are provided by the occasional visits of folk healers, tinkers, scribes, fortune-tellers, and musicians.

The business of the town is by no means limited to commercial activities. Eating and drinking establishments serve as headquarters for rotating credit societies where peasants can borrow money. Rich landlords may maintain an office for collecting rents, and merchants and landowners may lend money or extend credit to their regular customers. Marriage brokers frequent the teahouses in market towns in order to learn of marriageable girls. Chinese secret societies which once controlled all aspects of life in the countryside also had headquarters or lodges in market towns. The control of commission agents who weighed the grain and dealt in livestock fell to these groups on market days. Religious festivals were often combined with annual fairs held in the standard market town. The local temple was the concern not only of townsmen but also of pious leaders from nearby farm communities. Thus a variety of social needs and obligations were met within

the town, and the peasants in the surrounding countryside were dependent as much on their local market town as on their own small farm communities. At the same time, local officers of the imperial government collected taxes and administered the law, thus linking the peasantry and townsmen to the remote capital.

Higher-order markets Market towns like the one described above did not provide all the needs of every Chinese. Members of the educated and wealthier elite would have to seek still larger *intermediate* market towns if they wished to buy books and writing materials. Better-quality cloth, unusual foodstuffs, and luxury items also seldom found their way to local markets and were supplied only in the larger towns and cities. The local elite and leisured class were accustomed to drinking their tea and wine in the establishments of larger towns where there was an opportunity to meet others of their class. Beyond such *intermediate markets* were those in larger cities which offered still rarer goods and more specialized services. A many-tiered system of markets, often paralleled by matching social and religious organizations as well as by progressively higher levels of government offices, spread its network across the Chinese landscape. *Minor markets* in villages where a peasant might trade a few eggs or vegetables with his neighbor were at the bottom. Next came *standard markets* and market towns which have occupied most of this discussion. Above them, *intermediate* and *central markets* were found in progressively larger towns. Beyond them, local and regional cities supported a complex variety of markets which supplied local, regional, and perhaps even national needs. Goods, money, and information moved both up and down through this system of settlements along paths, roads, and rivers.

China: K=3 and K=4 systems The mapped distribution of *standard* and *intermediate* market towns and their market areas located southeast of Chengtu in Szechwan Province in central China is shown in Figure 5–7A.

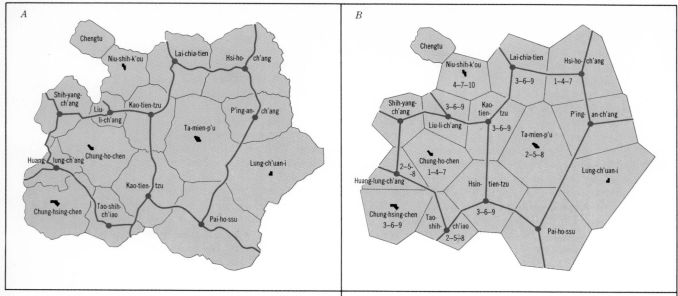

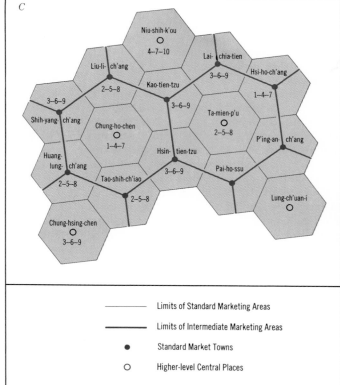

Figure 5-7 K=3 marketing structure in rural China (after Skinner) (*A*) Map of a portion of rural Chinese market towns and their hinterlands. (*B*) Periodic market fair days for a two-order hierarchy of central places. (*C*) The abstract K = 3 nested hierarchy corresponding to a portion of a rural Chinese marketing system. (G. William Skinner, "Marketing and Social Structure in Rural China," *Journal of Asian Studies*, vol. 24, 1964, pp. 22–26)

——— Limits of Standard Marketing Areas

——— Limits of Intermediate Marketing Areas

● Standard Market Towns

○ Higher-level Central Places

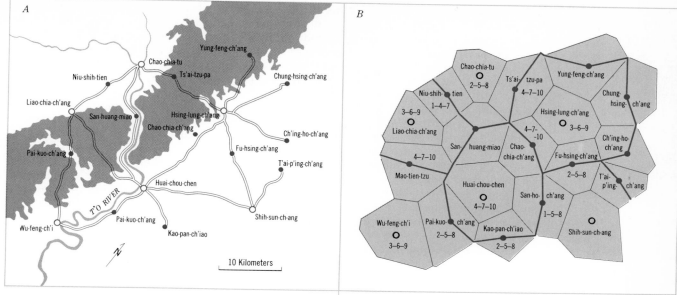

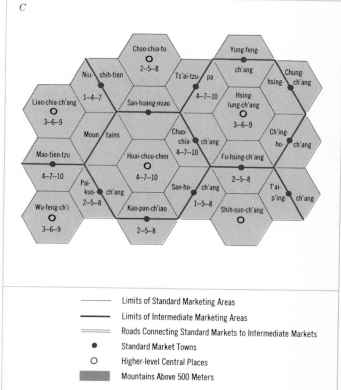

Figure 5-8 K=4 marketing structure in rural China (after Skinner) (*A*) Map of farm markets and their hinterlands, including a mountain zone. (*B*) Periodic market fair days for a two-order hierarchy of central places. (*C*) The abstract K = 4 nested hierarchy corresponding to a portion of a rural Chinese marketing system. Note the empty cell due to the presence of a sparsely settled mountain zone. (Op. cit. Figure 5-7)

Two simple analytical steps allow us to see the emergence of a K=3 network from the original map. In Figure 5-7B the boundary lines of the approximate standard and intermediate market areas have been straightened. (Numbers at settlements indicate the days within a 10-day cycle on which markets are held.) In Figure 5-7C the same boundaries have been standardized and reduced to diagrammatic form. These simple maneuvers quickly show the underlying order of the system. It should be noted that adjacent standard market towns may hold markets on the same days—for example, Kao-tien-tzu and Hsin-tien-tzu—but that the scheduling of such markets rarely coincides with market days in the intermediate market towns (i.e., those in the next highest order) with which they are associated. Conflicts are thus minimized vertically throughout the system, while horizontal conflicts are of little importance owing to the lack of lateral connections between settlements of the same order.

The same analytical steps have been repeated in Figure 5-8 for an area located northeast of Chengtu. In this case a two-step abstracting of the original map reveals a K=4 network with one market area unoccupied because of mountains. Notice that the only roads mapped connect higher-order and standard market towns, but that these direct routes join all the settlements with no detours except those imposed by topography. Again, market day scheduling conflicts for settlements within the same vertical systems are kept to a minimum.

Iowa: Crossing market boundaries

In matching our theoretical notions of settlement hierarchies to real world consumer patterns we need information about the actual shopping habits of the population. Recent investigations by Brian Berry and his associates near Council Bluffs, Iowa, tell us a great deal about Midwestern Americans and the hierarchy of settlements which they utilize. Figure 5-9A shows the area, while Figure 5-9B to F uses a series of star diagrams to indicate the origin of the rural customers and the settlements which they visited to obtain particular goods or services. This information was obtained by personally interviewing individual householders or by checking the addresses of customers or subscriber lists and charge account files at stores and offices. Once the origins and destinations of shoppers were learned, a straight line was drawn from each customer's residence to the urban place visited by him. The subsequent arrays of points and lines tell us many things about central place hierarchies.

The sequence of such goods and services in order from smallest to largest market areas is grocery shopping, office calls to physicians, women's coats and dresses, hospital services, and newspapers. This list, while incomplete, represents an entire hierarchy of central place functions from those with very short minimum ranges and low thresholds to others with high thresholds and large minimum ranges. Notice, for example, that many people subscribe to newspapers originating in Des Moines, Iowa, far off the map to the east. This is interesting in itself, for Des Moines is smaller than Omaha, Nebraska, which is much nearer. However, in-state news originating at the state capital and presented by an excellent newspaper outdraws publications from the larger, closer city. Here is another place where simple theory and reality can differ. Affiliation with a political unit may influence consumer behavior to a degree which overcomes the friction of distance.

Figure 5-9 Consumer travel in southwestern Iowa The lines represent a shopping trip from home to the central place offering the good or service listed. A variation in the range of the goods is clearly observable. Also, the market areas overlap to a considerable degree. (Brian J. L. Berry, *Geography of Market Centers and Retail Distribution* © 1967, pp. 11–12. Reprinted by permission of Prentice-Hall, Inc., Englewood Cliffs, N.J.)

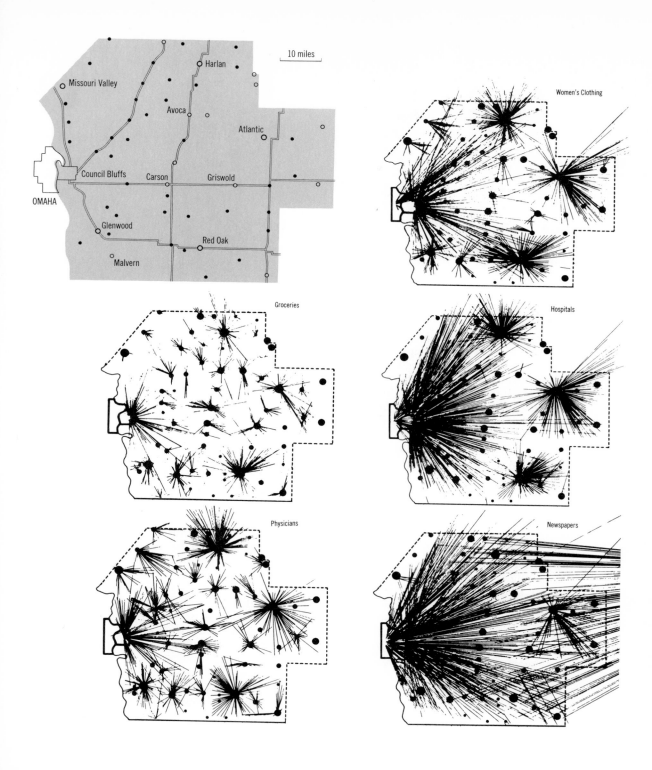

10 miles

Missouri Valley

Harlan

Avoca

Atlantic

Council Bluffs

OMAHA

Carson

Griswold

Glenwood

Red Oak

Malvern

Women's Clothing

Groceries

Hospitals

Physicians

Newspapers

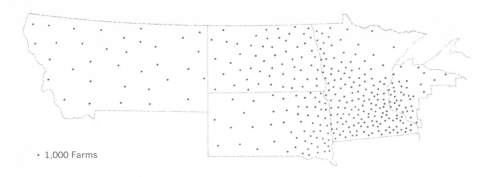

• 1,000 Farms

Figure 5-10 Distribution of farms in the upper Midwest region The resources become more sparse to the north and west in the upper Midwest region, and the number and spacing of farms reflect the underlying resource base.

One of Christaller's original assumptions was that perfect competition existed and that consumers would not cross the boundary lines of their market areas. An examination of the Iowa maps shows that this is generally true but that there are enough exceptions to the rule that our theory needs some modification to match reality. Notice how in every diagram many of the rays emanating from urban places cross each other, clearly indicating that decisions were made on the basis of other criteria besides that of physical distance between customer and producer.

Given some knowledge of the expense of the item to be purchased and the number of times per year that such shopping might be done, we can understand differences in travel behavior. Grocery stores which are patronized on a regular daily or weekly basis have short minimum ranges, and settlements containing them are more or less evenly spaced throughout the study area. Clothing stores (Figure 5–9D) on the other hand are limited to far fewer places, attract more customers, have higher thresholds, and can expect customers to come greater distances but much less frequently. It is also important to note that while few customer triplines cross each other on the grocery map (Figure 5–9B), many more do so on the map showing trips for women's clothing. This is generally true, for as specialization increases and considera-

tions of travel time and short-run convenience decrease, the overlapping of market areas becomes greater and greater. This is also true where the investment required in the establishment providing the services becomes larger. Physicians' offices attract patients from medium-sized market areas, while larger, more expensive hospitals are fewer in number and reach out long distances for those who use their services.

The upper Midwest: Network distortion

The apparently endless, level miles of the northern Great Plains would seem a natural place to find an expression of Christaller's and Lösch's orderly landscapes. But subtle changes in the grassland's environment can create distortions in its settlement network just as certainly as do the high mountains which rise west of those buffalo-haunted plains. While the eastern half of this area is relatively flat, topographically speaking, rainfall along a line drawn between Minneapolis, Minnesota, and Great Falls, Montana, decreases steadily from 28 inches per year in the east to 12 inches in the west. At the same time, average annual temperatures decrease slightly from south to north. There are about 160 frost-free days at the southern limit of this area and approximately 110 such days along the United States–Canadian border.

While most of the land is relatively fertile, northern Minnesota and Wisconsin are marked by the rocky outcrops of the Laurentian Upland or Canadian Shield. Aridity, cold, and poor soils all mean lower yields per unit of farmland. Lower yields mean reduced carrying capacities for the land, and if a high level of living is maintained by the population, farms must be correspondingly larger. As a result of this, it is reasonable to anticipate that farm populations will decrease from east to west and from south to north within this area. Figure 5–10, showing the distribution of farm units in thousands, confirms our expectations. At the same time, if the population is organized according to the spatial principles outlined so far, we would expect to find the basic Christaller network concentrated most densely in the southeast and most open or sparse in the northwest. This can be seen in Figure 5–11, where a regularly enlarging hexagonal network has been adjusted to match variations in the distribution of farm population. The resulting pattern is reminiscent of the expanding hexagonal lattice shown in Figure 5–5.

The upper Midwest: Hierarchies of functions
The distorted pattern in Figure 5–11 is admittedly a cartographic device meant to illustrate our argument. There is, however, a relatively simple way of testing the notion that a

spatially organized hierarchy of central places exists in this area and that its network varies in size from southeast to northwest. This test necessitates understanding another aspect of central place hierarchies. When we spoke earlier of *nested hierarchies*, we indicated that in a particular culture and economy the smallest settlements offer a few basic goods and services to the population adjacent to them. Larger central places offer the same things and, in addition, provide more and more specialized goods and services for bigger and bigger populations in increasingly larger areas. Since each good or service has a particular threshold which characterizes its place within the hierarchy, it is possible to compile a list of central place functions which allows us to predict what we should find in a settlement if we know its population.

In their investigation of Snohomish County, Washington, William Garrison and Brian Berry determined the threshold urban populations for fifty-two different urban-based activities. These are shown in Table 5–1, along with the average minimum populations associated with their first appearance in a central place hierarchy. For example, hamlets with populations of at least 275 people will contain some sort of restaurant or snack bar. Veterinarians' offices do not appear in settlements smaller than 575 people, and public accountants open offices in central places larger than

Figure 5-11 A hexagonal net conforming to the underlying rural population pattern in the upper Midwest region

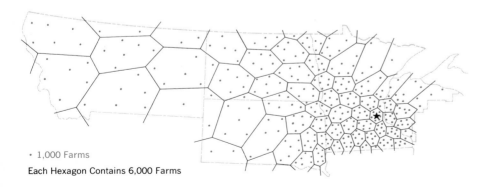

• 1,000 Farms

Each Hexagon Contains 6,000 Farms

Table 5-1 Threshold Populations for Fifty-two Urban-based Activities

Class I₁		Furniture stores, etc.	546
Filling stations	196	Variety stores, "5 & 10"	549
Food stores	254	Freight lines and storage	567
Churches	265	Veterinaries	579
Restaurants and snack bars	276	Apparel stores	590
Taverns	282	Lumberyards	598
Elementary schools	322	Banks	610
Class I₂		Farm implement dealers	650
Physicians	380	Electric repair shops	693
Real estate agencies	384	Florists	729
Appliance stores	385	High schools	732
Barber shops	386	Dry cleaners	754
Auto dealers	398	Local taxi services	762
Insurance agencies	409	Billiard halls and bowling alleys	789
Fuel oil dealers	419	Jewelry stores	827
Dentists	426	Hotels	846
Motels	430	Shoe repair shops	896
Hardware stores	431	Sporting goods stores	928
Auto repair shops	435	Frozen food lockers	938
Fuel dealers (coal, etc.)	453	Class I₃	
Drug stores	458	Sheet metal works	1,076
Beauticians	480	Department stores	1,083
Auto parts dealers	488	Optometrists	1,140
Meeting halls	525	Hospitals and clinics	1,159
Feed stores	526	Undertakers	1,214
Lawyers	528	Photographers	1,243
		Public accountants	1,300
		Laundries and laundromats	1,307
		Health practitioners	1,424

Source: William Garrison and Brian J. L. Berry, "A Note on Central Place Theory and the Range of a Good," *Economic Geography*, vol. 34, no. 4, October 1958, pp. 304-311.

1,300 people. On the other hand, a town with a public accountant will very likely have both a veterinary and a restaurant. This list is based upon a somewhat complicated technique for determining average populations which need not concern us here. It should be noted, though, that these threshold numbers are not intended to be absolute or unchangeable. The important thing to realize is that the role of a settlement within a central place hierarchy can be roughly determined by learning the number of people living within its boundaries. If the type and number of functions available are known, the settlement's position within the hierarchy can be determined.

Figure 5-12 shows forty-six central place functions found in settlements across the northern Great Plains. They are grouped in the order of their appearance along with their approximate thresholds. Each general category of functions: convenience, specialty, and wholesale, indicates a higher level in the hierarchy. This list is not meant to be complete. It also varies somewhat from that of Garrison and Berry, but this might be expected as the result of regional differences in economic and social activities. The diagram also identifies four classes and six subclasses of settlements, from hamlets with nothing more than service stations and lunchrooms

Figure 5-12 Trade center types (central place functions in the upper Midwest region) This graph is a summary of the central place goods and services offered by the towns and cities of the upper Midwest region. There is considerable variation from town to town, but in general, the expected low-order goods and services are available in nearly all small hamlets and villages, with increasingly more specialized, higher-order goods entering in towns and cities with greater populations. A population scale is shown on the left of the graph and the order of appearance of central place goods and services on the right. (John R. Borchert, "The Urbanization of the Upper Midwest, 1930–1960," *Upper Midwest Economic Study*, Urban Report No. 2, University of Minnesota, Minneapolis, Minn., 1963)

to wholesale-retail cities offering all forty-six types of functions as well as many more not listed. Again, our notion of a nested hierarchy of functions is confirmed.

The upper Midwest: Central place sequences The spatial distribution of settlements in the upper Midwest classified according to their place in a functional hierarchy is shown in Figure 5–13. The twin city metropolis of Minneapolis–St. Paul dominates the area and constitutes a special case not shown in the preceding diagram. Far to the west, Spokane, Washington, is a similar regional metropolis, although its population is considerably smaller than that of the Twin Cities. Beneath the Twin Cities are ranked four levels of commercial centers. Wholesale-retail centers, shopping centers, and convenience centers are subdivided for greater clarity, while hamlets constitute a single subdivision. The map shows that wholesale-retail centers are few in number and widely spaced. Shopping centers are more frequent; convenience centers more numerous still; and hamlets occur in the greatest numbers (Table 5–2).

Cross-cultural Variations: Ontario

One important departure from theory may result from cross-cultural variations in the use of space. Much of our discussion of central place theory has emphasized cross-cultural

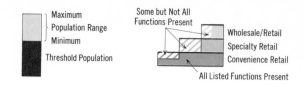

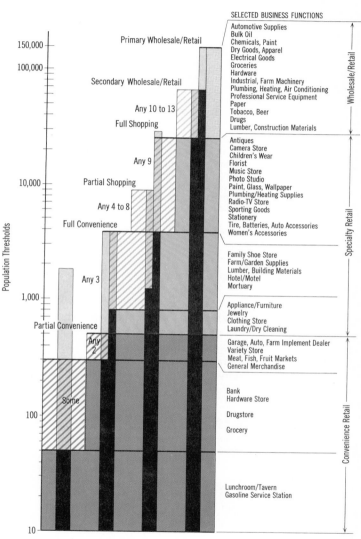

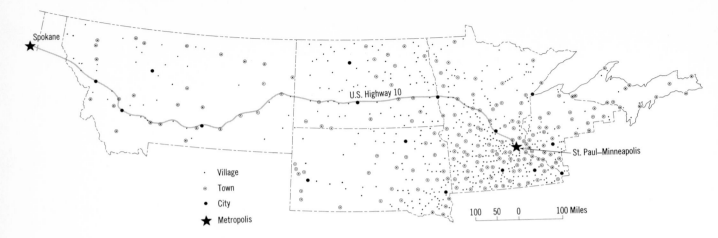

- · Village
- ⊙ Town
- ● City
- ★ Metropolis

Figure 5-13 Upper Midwest settlement patterns   The pattern of towns and villages in the upper Midwest conforms roughly to central place theory expectations. The wider spacing of towns to the west reflects the lesser resource base. The number and placement of villages, towns, cities, and metropolises also resemble a central place pattern. Obvious exceptions are the clusters of mining towns in southwestern South Dakota and western Montana. Mining is not a central place function. The sequence of villages, towns, and cities along U.S. Highway 10 may be taken as a sample central place sequence. (Op. cit., Figure 5-12)

similarities rather than differences in spatial behavior. This is particularly true for certain types of periodic markets and the development of higher-level market centers. An interesting and relatively unexplored subject is the point along a continuum of spatial behavior where cultural regularities give way to cross-cultural differences.

A comparison of Old Order Mennonite and "modern" Canadian consumer travel in Ontario Province will serve to illustrate the importance of cross-cultural spatial studies. Old Order Mennonites are known for their conservative religious beliefs, which are reflected in their homemade and somber clothing, their use of horse-drawn vehicles rather than automobiles, their very restricted use of electricity, and their rejection of much of the modern

Table 5-2   The Frequency of Trade Center Types in the Upper Midwest

	Type of Center				
	Regional Metropolis	Wholesale-Retail	Shopping Centers	Convenience Centers	Hamlets
Number of Centers	2	17	169	482	1,647

Source: Opt. cit. Figure 5-12, Report No. 3.

world with its temptations such as moving pictures and television. Many Mennonite communities still provide their own teachers and education for their children. They are less conservative than other groups like the Old Order Amish in that they utilize modern farm machinery. All such groups are in sharp contrast with the other Canadians who surround them. These latter "modern" people have no religiously inspired restrictions of dress, nor do they shun contact with the outside world. In fact, differences between the two groups are great enough for us to talk of a *dominant culture* and a *subculture* where they are concerned.

The accompanying star diagrams (Figure 5–14A to G) of an area near Waterloo and Kitchener in Ontario are similar to those for Iowa and illustrate the shopping habits of the two diverse groups. A comparison of the origins and destinations of shopping trips made by the Mennonites and modern Canadians reveals cross-cultural differences. Distinctions in the two travel patterns are not in every case tied directly to settlement size or level in the hierarchy. Both modern and Mennonite Canadians travel intermediate distances for banking services and very little difference can be seen in their habits. In this case the service sought is relatively high in the spatial hierarchy and is impossible for individuals to do for themselves. In the case of travel for food, visible differences can be seen between the longer trips made by the modern Canadians as opposed to Mennonite journeys. This is a reflection of the Mennonites' simpler food preferences, greater self-sufficiency, and reliance on horse-and-buggy transportation. The use of horse-drawn conveyances for frequent shopping trips places time restrictions on Mennonite travel. It also means that whenever possible they will avoid going through busy Waterloo to reach Kitchener although it has a greater selection of goods and services. It is no fun trying to drive an easily frightened horse through downtown traffic. In much the same way a study of the Old Order Amish in Indiana shows their preference for a supermarket on the same side of a busy highway

as most of the Amish colony's houses. A similar supermarket on the far side of the road had few Amish customers because of their reluctance to take horses into a dangerous situation. Finally, Mennonite trips for yard goods are in sharp contrast with modern Canadians' trips for clothing bought off the rack. Most Mennonites dress conservatively and make their own clothes. They create little demand for store-bought attire, and there is little or no commercial response to their slight needs.

This part of Ontario has a well-developed spatial hierarchy of urban places just as our other examples have had. But differences can be found between Ontario and Iowa. Most important for our purposes are variations in consumer travel patterns between the two culture groups in Ontario. In many ways the spatial behavior of modern Canadians resembles that of people from Iowa more than it does the use of space by their Mennonite neighbors. Where modern goods and services are required, such as banking, both groups behave very much the same. But where traditional functions are carried out—and what could be more traditional than a culture group's habits of eating and dress?—modern Canadians travel much farther than do traditional Mennonites, who still live almost as their grandfathers did. We learn from this that even in a relatively small area with a single set of urban places, interesting and perhaps significant differences can exist on a cross-cultural basis. On the other hand, many spatial similarities seem to be shared by unlike cultures.

The way in which people communicate, the messages they send, and the way in which they organize space to do this are of great interest to geographers. Spatial hierarchies can be thought of as elaborate communication systems. Their design may help or hinder a group in its efforts to define and reach its goals. The next chapter examines the idea of human communications and the spatial systems which serve societies in their attempts to survive.

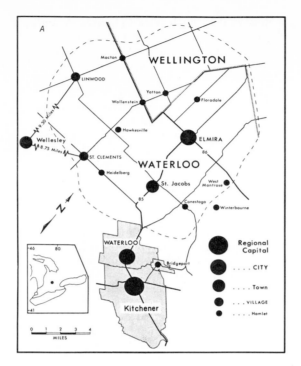

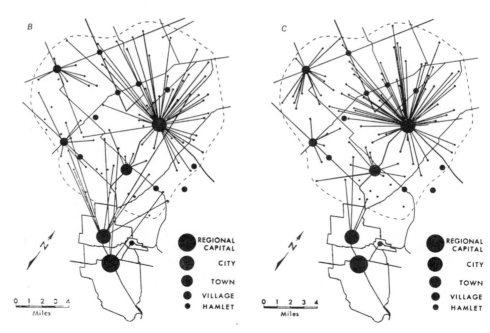

Figure 5-14 Shopping habits of Mennonites and "modern" Canadians near Waterloo, Ontario, Canada (*A*) The study area, (*B*) "modern" Canadian travel for banking service, (*C*) Old Order Mennonite travel for banking service, (*D*) "modern" Canadian travel for clothing and yard goods, (*E*) Old Order Mennonite travel for clothing and yard goods, (*F*) "modern" Canadian travel for food, and (*G*) Old Order Mennonite travel for food. (Robert A. Murdie, "Cultural Differences in Consumer Travel," *Economic Geography*, vol. 41, no. 3, July, 1965)

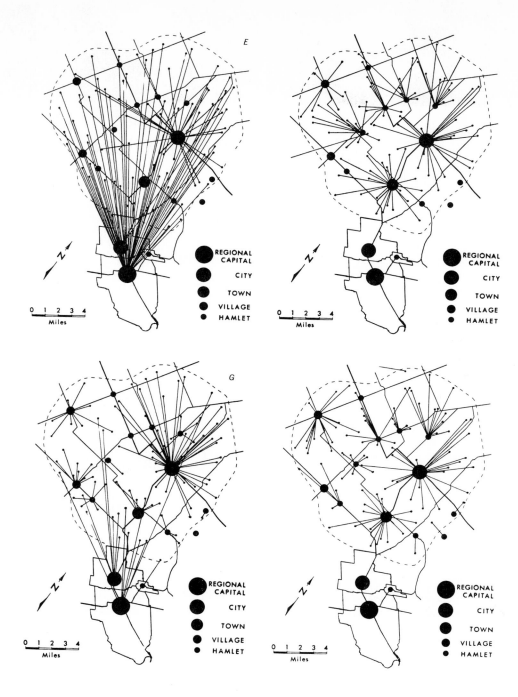

D

E

REGIONAL
CAPITAL

CITY

TOWN

VILLAGE

HAMLET

N

0 1 2 3 4
Miles

REGIONAL
CAPITAL

CITY

TOWN

VILLAGE

HAMLET

N

0 1 2 3 4
Miles

F

G

REGIONAL
CAPITAL

CITY

TOWN

VILLAGE

HAMLET

N

0 1 2 3 4
Miles

REGIONAL
CAPITAL

CITY

TOWN

VILLAGE

HAMLET

N

0 1 2 3 4
Miles

*How Cities
Share Space:
Classical
Central Place
Theory*

99

6 | COMMUNICATION AND ORGANIZATION: CHARACTERISTICS OF INFORMATION SYSTEMS

The Importance of Connectivity

As I was going to St. Ives,
I met a man with seven wives.
Every wife had seven sacks,
Every sack had seven cats,
Every cat had seven rats.
Rats, cats, sacks, and wives,
How many were going to St. Ives?

St. Ives is everywhere. The man of St. Ives, trailing his retinue of wives, cats, and rats like a comet's tail, might be taken as symbolic of communication hierarchies. In pages past we have talked about the organization of space with strong emphasis upon *distance* and *direction*. Only when we maintain those two basic elements are we able to discern portions of the hexagonal networks by means of which space is most efficiently organized. But those qualities are no more important than a third: *connectivity*. In some static system, a picture in *Mother Goose*, with all the characters frozen at one moment in time, the man of St. Ives might have his wives and their minions ranged around him in some neat geometric pattern. But once we start the cadence of the verse and begin chanting it like a marching song, sending all those people and creatures jogging and skittering along imagination's winding roads, all spatial order will be lost. The wives will gather and gossip, or hurry to harrass their man. The cats and rats will do all the things cats and rats have always done, and the scene will appear to be near chaos. And yet the connectivity is there that links them all into an old and familiar rhyme. The whole thing is much like an army on the parade ground and an army caught up in battle. On parade the relationship between staff and officers and men, divisional headquarters, regiments, companies, platoons, and squads is given some spatial expression. That regularity is soon lost when army meets army in battle, but the connectivity of the system, in this case expressed as a chain of command, keeps the whole organization operating through charge and countercharge, defeat and sometimes even victory.

Administrative hierarchies are what we are discussing here. They might be expressed in terms of locational analysis as $K=7$ systems. At the top is a central figure or a central place which administers its immediate surroundings as well as having authority or dominance over six adjacent places or positions of the next lowest order. Each of those six would in turn administer its own area and six still lower-order places. A message starting at the top and moving through the chain of command outward and downward would split and split again until every level, place, or person was reached. This pattern is shown in Figure 6–1. We have returned momentarily with this figure to a geometric ordering of space to make a by now familiar point. If this diagram is redrawn in a more abstract form, emphasizing the system's connectivity, the subsequent pattern resembles the orderly branching of a tree. Figure 6–2 shows such a diagram that matches a K=7 network, but many systems can be diagrammed in tree form.

It should not be thought that hierarchies shown as trees are necessarily one-way systems. The election of the President of the United States every four years is a good example of the reversal of such a system. Ideally, every person casts one vote, which is recorded at some local polling place. Counts from neighborhood polls are aggregated at city and county and state levels, until finally the nation as a whole learns what party and which man the populace has chosen. In this case many small messages start at widely dispersed points. By virtue of their aggregation at higher and higher levels they become a single directive by means of which the President receives his power. The people's decision is then given expression by means of Presidential decisions

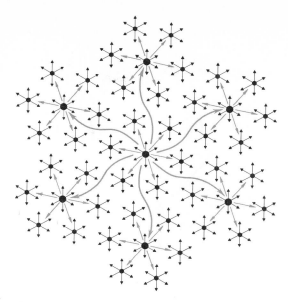

Figure 6-1 Flow pattern for a K=7 spatial hierarchy

or commands sent back down through the hierarchy until individual voters are again involved, this time by the need to comply with new laws or to pay new taxes.

Figure 6-2 K=7 tree hierarchy   This hierarchy may be thought of as representing an organization chart of a regular K=7 hierarchy. The circles could be foremen or supervisors. Topologically it is identical to the spatial hierarchy shown in Figure 6-1.

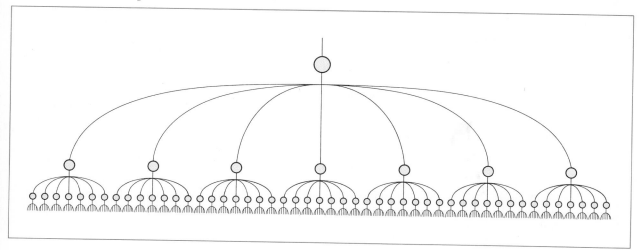

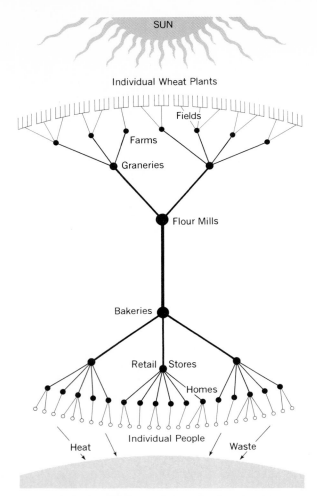

SUN

Individual Wheat Plants

Fields

Farms

Graneries

Flour Mills

Bakeries

Retail Stores

Homes

Individual People

Heat

Waste

Figure 6-3 Energy pathways in the wheat-to-bread food chain Many systems display a dumbell, or "complete tree," spatial network. Energy and material are assembled, change of state occurs, long transport hauls are completed, and products are distributed for use and, finally, returned to the environment after use.

plants — fields — farms — graineries — mills — bakeries — stores — homes — individuals — heat and waste—can be shown as a complete tree (Figure 6-3). Tiny increments of solar energy and soil nutrients are concentrated by each wheat plant into kernels of grain. Grain is harvested and concentrated in grain elevators for shipment to flour mills. Flour in turn moves to bakeries from which bread is shipped to numerous retail outlets and finally to individual homes. Once eaten, the energy is released; everything else that remains is waste. The energy is used to perform work which creates heat as its final by-product. The waste, either garbage or sewage, eventually breaks down into its component parts, releasing a final increment of heat energy back into the earth environment. Thus the whole system represents a coming together and a dissipating of energy through space and time.

This forms a basic dumbbell-shaped system of concentration and dispersion similar in form to a real tree with both roots and branches. Consider how leaves concentrate the sun's energy for long trips to the tips of root tendrils, and roots in turn absorb moisture from the soil to help maintain the tree's metabolism. On the next warm day lie down on the grass near some tree, and in your prone and sideways view see both ends of the tree, one in air and the other in soil. Imagine the system in its entirety and enjoy seeing birds and worms as similar, each species living in and around the energy system that is the tree, and each an energy system organized in its own way along hierarchial lines (Figure 6-4).

In brief, hierarchies are an efficient way to fill space with different-sized settlements. Settlements are typified by different types of activities or by different stages in the same system of activities. Thus our wheat — bread — energy system in Figure 6-3 could be shown in part as a farm — village — town — city — neighborhood — house settlement system. Neat and formal arrangements of space are often lost or undecipherable, but in any system, either natural or social, the connectivity which binds its many parts together can be shown

Another way in which hierarchies as systems become important to us is the gathering, processing, distribution, and use of resources of all kinds. This is such an important point that we will return to it again and again, but a single example will suffice for now. The following simplified food system—sun and

as treelike series of paths or links connecting together hierarchically arranged focal points. At such foci, energy, materials, or ideas are concentrated, perhaps changed into another form, and sent along to higher or lower centers for further concentration or distribution. *Trees* of this kind are found everywhere and ultimately can be thought of as communication and transportation systems which organize and hold together all human and natural phenomena.

Types and Techniques of Communication

If someone you love reaches out and touches your hand as you pass by, you have received one of the best kinds of messages. When a relative telephones and says, "Come home, we need your help," you have received another communication. The world is full of communications and messages, many of which we scarcely recognize and some of which we fail to realize at all. Each one of us at least once in our lives has given a message, perhaps not in words, to someone we hoped to know much better. And too often from the sender's point of view the message is never read, the invitation to friendship passed over. On the other hand, stop and consider the next time you get a parking ticket that you have received a message. Not just to "pay the two dollars," but a more complex communication, a comment by society about the values it places on transportation and terminal facilities, and another one in which a whole system of courts and agencies combines to enforce a tiny part of our culture's code of conduct.

Table 6–1 gives examples of the means of communication employed and the numbers of people between whom messages are sent. The columns are divided between *personal means*, in which nothing gets between the sender and the receiver, and *mechanical means*, in which mechanical and electronic devices are used to move messages. The *Mechanical* column is further subdivided into *Instant* and *Stored* categories to accommodate obvious differences in types of communications.

Going from left to right in every row of the

Figure 6-4 A complete tree system The tree is a system which transfers energy and material between two volumetric domains via a hierarchical network.

table leads us from immediate face-to-face experiences with strong emotional overtones to more and more remote events. Since electronic communication is for all practical purposes as quick as or quicker than direct human speech, the difference between the first two columns in any row is one of increasing distance. The third column, *Mechanical-Stored*, indicates that senders and receivers can be far apart in time as well as space. It is very hard for us to predict where we, the authors of this book, will be when you, the reader, see these pages. Many miles and many years may separate us. It is the same with old letters and diaries. Some of the most evocative reading materials available are your own old messages to others and to yourself.

Similarly, the quality and nature of messages change from the top to the bottom of the table. The ideas and emotions exchanged between two and only two people have elements lacking in mass communication. The reverse is also true; mass media can do things personal chats never could. President Franklin D. Roosevelt, in the early days of radio, recognized these differences and bridged the gap between face-to-face and mass communication by holding "fireside chats" on national networks.

To summarize the characteristics of communication as arranged in the table, in the upper left we find face-to-face spontaneous, repetitious, fluctuating, give-and-take between couples. The lower right is reserved for the massed voices of society speaking across the years. Information flow between sender and receiver changes from the upper left to the lower right of the table. Going from conversations to constitutions, such flow becomes increasingly more routinized, more inflexible, and more one-directional in char-

acter. This accounts for the frustration felt by individuals when they attempt to deal with communication elements further and further along this continuum. Student protestors are less successful than they wish since they almost always use face-to-face–personal–instant communication techniques in their attempts to change many-to-many–mechanical-stored messages embodied in laws and constitutional articles. The best political strategists will choose a variety of types and techniques of communication in order to achieve their goals. Successful politicians are also realists about the social inertia of the things they want to influence and change. Each one of us operates across this spectrum of communication, and our happiness and sense of personal effectiveness are tied largely to our ability to send appropriate messages along the right channels.

Overload in Information Systems

All systems must have a constant flow of messages, materials, or energy moving through them in order to function. Flows move from focal point to focal point along routes or paths. The carrying capacity of these routes is finite, and there are limits above which they cannot operate. Some examples where breakdown results when these upper limits on the carry-

Table 6–1   Means of Communication by Numbers and Types

Number Involved in the Exchange	Type of Contact		
	Personal	Mechanical	
	Instant	Instant	Stored
One to one	Talk, touch	Telephone	Letters
One to many	Lectures	Television	Textbook
Many to one	Town hall meeting	Group lobbying by telephone and telegram	Contracts
Many to many	Symphony and applause	Conventions	The law

ing capacities of systems are exceeded include blowing a fuse just as you plug in the iron after turning on the air conditioner, a traffic jam, and a flooding river. People as part of communication systems are also affected. A worker pushed beyond endurance by the increasing tempo of his task refuses to continue working or behaves irrationally and botches the job. The latter situation is one of the high points of Charlie Chaplin's film *Modern Times*, in which he is overwhelmed by his work on the assembly line and goes temporarily insane. In every case, when the upper limit is exceeded, the system suffers from *overload* and breaks down.

While every system which includes paths with finite carrying capacities is subject to overload, whether it is a highway network or the human body, for the moment we will consider *information overload* rather than the physical overwhelming of some system. Information overload can be defined as *receiving too many bits of information per unit of time for adequate appraisal, processing, and response.*

To understand this, let us consider automobile driver reaction time. A good driver must be constantly aware of the events surrounding him and be able to respond to them quickly and rationally. The more events or objects per mile, the slower a person must drive in order to see and safely respond to his environment. There is a definite upper limit on the number of things a driver can take into account. If he speeds up, the flow of information bits past his eyes becomes too great, and then he may well have an accident.

The main difference between an expressway with limited access and a city street is reduced information per unit distance. On a freeway, the number of information bits and subsequently the number of necessary choices per mile which face the driver are reduced and the speed with which the system operates can be increased. But this also means that the choices open to a driver on an expressway are decreased. Efficiency, measured in terms of the time necessary to cover a fixed distance, is improved, but at the expense of decreased

flexibility and an accompanying hazard, boredom. Seemingly endless miles of uninterrupted superhighways can induce drowsiness which spells disaster or at the very least the utterly frustrating experience of missing your exit and having to drive on another 12 miles to the next turnoff.

There is a trade-off between freedom of choice with less efficiency and greater efficiency but increased inflexibility. Ultimately, however, nearly every system can be subjected to intolerable loads. Cities as communication systems are no exception, nor are their inhabitants safe from similar stress.

Increasing System Capacity

The efficiency of any communication system is proportional to the number of messages exchanged between its participants. Of course, this means messages which are understood and acted upon. Too many messages, too much information, as we have already said, will simply break down the system. As organizations grow larger and more complex, new ways to increase capacity must be found. This becomes evident, for example, if we contrast ancient and modern forms of government.

A Greek city-state (*polis*) could operate democratically by calling an *assembly* of all its citizens in the marketplace or amphitheater in order to carry out the business of legislation. To be sure, not every inhabitant of a *polis* was a citizen. Citizenship belonged only to adult males whose fathers were citizens before them. Given this Greek definition of the electorate, the number of decision makers remained manageable. In all of what is now Greece only Athens had 30,000 or more citizens so defined. And in all the Greek world just two other city-states, Syracuse and Agrigento (Acragas) in Sicily, were as large. At the time of the Peloponnesian War, Athens's total population numbered perhaps 175,000 men, women, and children, who were slaves, alien residents, and free Athenians. This meant that one in every five or six inhabitants had the right to vote. Since not every citizen could regularly find time to help run the government, daily business was conducted by an appointed *Council of 500*, 50 from each of 10 tribes. Turnover in the council was rapid, and every citizen had to serve his turn. The arrangement, therefore, was relatively fluid, and each participant knew and could actually see and hear all other persons who debated and cast ballots.

The city of Socrates and Plato was a far cry from modern nation-states such as our own. In the election of 1972 more than 73 million voters cast their ballots for President, and even then, less than 70 percent of those eligible to vote did so. Such populations are far too large to gather at one place, let alone give every citizen a chance to be heard. Instead, we must use telephones, radios, and teletype machines to gather and tabulate votes beyond the precinct level, while voting machines are used almost everywhere. Sheer size forces us to use new methods of decision making and vote taking. If governments are to represent the will of the electorate, the channel capacities of their political systems must be increased to accommodate more and more people.

How then can we alter the systems we use to meet new demands? An obvious answer is to enlarge the channels through which information flows. This could mean larger auditoriums for public meetings. Another way would be to add additional, parallel channels the same as those that already exist. In this case we might try to hold duplicate city council meetings to handle overflow crowds of citizens. However, simply increasing the size of a system will not necessarily increase its efficiency. There are other ways in which the capacities of systems can be increased without making them larger.

Standardization and *routinization* are two such means. The degree to which these qualities exist within systems imparts particular characteristics to them. Therefore, it is important to recognize such features, their attributes, and the advantages and disadvantages which accompany them.

Standardization

A standardized system is so designed that it has only a limited number of types of inputs and outputs, whether this refers to information or material objects. By doing this, fewer choices need to be made within the system and a smaller number of steps can be taken in order to process information and materials flowing through it.

We constantly encounter standardization in our daily lives. We may complain of the dreary sameness of major motel chains offering bland anonymity in every corner of the land. This is not a conspiracy of mediocrity. This is a prime example of standardization and its advantages and disadvantages. If travelers want and demand a certain level of comfort within a fixed price range, and if they want reliable food every meal and not a gourmet's delight one night and a ptomaine parlor the next, they seek out standardized hotels and restaurants.

Companies that deal in nationwide accommodations must be able to provide reliable food and lodging in every location. They tend to avoid local or regional variations, no matter how picturesque or appetizing they may be. Thus a chain restaurant may be nothing to write home about—since there is probably one back home anyway—but it is almost always dependable and reasonably priced, and offers those same French fries that always keep Junior quiet at meal times. Travelers who want variety and higher quality must pay for it with time, by seeking out good restaurants in unfamiliar places; with money, since unusual and good-quality items almost always come in smaller quantities at higher prices; and with patience, for if we experiment we inevitably make some mistakes.

Other systems using standardization include buses which require exact change when you board them and colleges with rigid entrance requirements. In each case—and you can add dozens of examples with a few minutes' thought—the system more efficiently processes customers, passengers, or students by limiting the type of inputs it will accept. In every case freedom of choice is sacrificed for increased carrying capacity.

Routinization

Routinization limits the number of paths through a system. We have already noted than an expressway will take you quickly from one side of a city to the other but offers only one path with few entries and exits. Freedom and flexibility are sacrificed for efficiency. The same is true at another scale for assembly lines. Factories produce enormous quantities of standardized products by limiting the number of paths materials can take through their systems, and workers must perform the same task over and over at an appointed spot along the line. Engineering and medical schools which train students to meet certain specific and rigid standards of performance set by the state offer fewer electives than do departments in the humanities which follow different standards of excellence and attempt to graduate no two students exactly alike. By reducing the number of paths through a system, the number of decisions open to the participant are limited and the efficiency of the whole operation increases. Improvements are gained by adopting *standard operating procedures*, whether these are routines operating within the system or actual physical pathways along which things move.

One further way in which efficiency is gained is by making the boundaries of the routes or paths more and more impenetrable. This can best be explained with the help of a simple example. Consider three kinds of garden hose: The usual kind is an impervious tube, another has holes regularly spaced along its length, and a third is made out of heavy canvas through which water can seep at any and every point. The force of the water reaching the end of the hose farthest from the faucet is greatest in the first kind and least in the third. Conversely, water reaches the ground along the entire hose when it is made of permeable canvas; only the ground at the far

end of the impervious hose receives liquid. There is a trade-off here between efficiency, measured as the force of the water at the far end, and linear coverage, which is greatest where the walls of the hose are easily penetrated. End points, remote from each other, are best served by paths with impenetrable boundaries or walls. An example comparable to the garden hoses is the role of different types of boundaries in transportation networks. City streets have low curbs, few protective devices, and many open driveways. On the other hand, the borders and median dividers on superhighways are very often reinforced concrete posts with corrugated steel panels in between. The latter boundaries are literally impenetrable in most cases. City streets provide access to local areas; expressways connect widely separated points. Their boundaries match their functions.

Changing capacities of carriers and terminal facilities

We must be careful not to assume that specialization applies only to routes and not to carriers and terminal facilities. In fact, whole systems can become so adapted to a single use that their specialization makes them unsuitable for any other purpose. Iron ore shipment on the Great Lakes is a good example of this. This system, by means of huge ore boats, supplies iron ore from the Mesabi Range near the western end of Lake Superior to steel mills along the shores of Lake Michigan and Lake Erie. Similar cargoes of coal are carried from railroad terminals on Lake Erie in Ohio and Pennsylvania to other points farther removed from the coal fields of the central and eastern United States. At first, ore and coal boats were more or less motorized barges of relatively small size. With the passing of time, the ships became larger and larger. At first they became wider, deeper, and longer, but the physical geography of the Great Lakes imposed certain design limits on these lake craft. The ship locks at Sault Sainte Marie and the channel in the Detroit River between

Communication and Organization: Characteristics of Information Systems

107

Lake Huron and Lake Erie are relatively narrow and shallow. Furthermore, it would be exceedingly expensive to enlarge these bottlenecks in the natural system. After the ore boats had reached the maximum width and depth permitted by the narrows described above, their capacity was further increased by making them longer and longer without changing their draft or beam. By mid-century these ships had become so long that they were unseaworthy in the open waters of the Atlantic, where the crests of large ocean swells can be far apart and the ships could literally be broken in two. Along with this set of interacting constraints special docking and loading and unloading facilities were developed at both ends of their voyages. The mass movement of bulk ore and coal has been highly perfected, but the ports specializing in these cargoes cannot be used for any other type of vessel or activity. Thus, the bulk movement of raw materials on the Great Lakes has become highly specialized, but the system is inflexible to the point of being unable to accommodate other cargoes or to use its carriers elsewhere. If the sources of coal or iron were to drastically change, or if new technology ruled out ore or coal in their present form or quantities, the system would automatically become obsolete. Here again the choice has had to be made: specialization with greater capacity and accompanying inflexibility; or more general, less efficient, but more flexible and lasting carriers.

Institutions as Communication Systems

Institutions of all kinds, public and private, may be thought of as communication systems. Routes, terminals, and carriers can be identified within them, and in every case information flow is an important part of their functioning. Institutions are organized for special purposes and are always standardized to some degree. Prisons, factories, armies, and universities are all institutions. Different as are the purposes they serve, they still resemble one another, for all of them are hierarchically organized and structure the space they occupy according to their functions.

Prisons

Prisons represent one extreme along a continuum of institutional systems. When society decides that one of its members is dangerous or should be punished, he is put in prison—that is, he is denied the unlimited use of space. At the same time, if too many prisoners are kept together in one area, they may become unmanageable. Prisons are spatially organized into separate buildings or wings, cell blocks, and cells. The warden is aided by assistant wardens, who in turn direct guards and trustees in the prison routine. Thus the spatial organization and administrative hierarchy parallel one another. Traditionally, prisons have had almost no methods for their inmates to communicate upward through the hierarchy. Since prison conditions often give much for prisoners to complain about, prison riots should not come as surprises. Such disturbances serve as mechanisms for penetrating the nearly impervious boundaries imposed on information flow by stone walls and an inflexible chain of command.

Factories and armies

Factories and armies are very similar. In each case their members are given greater freedom of movement than prisoners. But specialization and routine are built into each system. Participants must be in proper places at appointed times in order for both these systems to work.

In either case, highly organized hierarchies must send information from the top to the bottom of the system. There must also be some feedback. Quality control tells factory management when production processes are going astray. Shop stewards and union representatives keep the owners aware of the workers' feelings. One of the reasons for strikes is the breakdown of normal information flow between management and labor.

Army terminology—front, flank, rear, advance, retreat, strong point—is particularly spatial in character. Generals must know the progress of battles, which are in turn made up of thousands of individual encounters. Movement through space is a key factor. Reinforcements must be sent to bolster weak points or to take advantage of the enemy's mistakes. Supplies and ammunition must go forward, and intelligence and the wounded need to be sent to the rear. Here again, information flow directs the movement of men and materials just as management needs information to run a factory. *Regimentation* is important in both examples. In fact, the words *regime* and *regiment* share a common root with *regimentation* and provide clues to the way in which these and similar institutions are organized.

Universities

Universities are also hierarchically ordered institutions which occupy space. They, however, are found near the opposite end of the continuum along which we have ranked communication systems. Their goals are to maximize independent and imaginative thought. To do this, freedom of choice and independence of decision are most important. Here, as in our other examples, we are talking about an ideal situation. Freshmen, particularly, may find it hard to believe the above statement, but even an underclassman will appreciate the freedom of university life if he has just come from the army or an assembly-line job.

The main purpose of a university is to generate new ideas and change in the minds of students and faculty. This is done in order to create new knowledge which may eventually find practical application, or to bring forth works of art with which to satisfy our innermost needs. The university, then, is ideally a place where the minds of men are allowed complete freedom to generate new ways of looking at the world. Once imagination has produced ideas, they must stand the test of debate and challenge in the academic

cockpit. Professors and students should challenge each other. Out of such interchange will come new and better ideas. The best and most efficient way to do this is by prolonged face-to-face communication with as many different people as possible.

The spatial and functional organization of the university matches these needs. A large number of classes meet every hour. At regular intervals participants change classes and rooms, and new combinations of students and professors are formed. A single student may hear three or more teachers in a single day and may come in contact with completely different students in each class. The frequency of contact with bearers of new ideas is enhanced by this continuous shifting about. Certain other focal points exist on campus for the exchange of information. The library, a storehouse for knowledge, is one of these. Students and professors come and go during their lifetimes, but the materials in libraries generally remain in one place longer and are more available than humans. Thus, books and documents have a kind of inertia which places them on the lower right side of the table of communication types (Table 6–1). Access to information of this sort gives stability and continuity of academic life, although even printed knowledge ages, becomes less pertinent, and, as it were, dies.

On the other hand, cafeterias and coffee shops are also important parts of universities. At these points intense, fleeting, face-to-face encounters take place between students and faculty. The university in this way has a full range of information exchange mechanisms from very large, highly structured introductory courses through smaller classes, seminars, and libraries all the way to personal conversations and arguments. All such exchanges take place in an ever-changing variety of locations. The effect is kaleidoscopic and may seem confusing to new students until they realize that the strength of the university as an information and communications system is in its flexibility and freedom.

Communication and Organization: Characteristics of Information Systems

109

The Balance between Routine and Change

Even universities need some routine and specialization. In this way the capacity of the system is increased in order to provide more and more people with the educations they want. This imposes problems of increasing systems capacity while maintaining an opportunity for innovation. Sometimes whole schools are organized to meet the needs and purposes of students and faculties. Dentistry, engineering, and medicine are examples of more highly structured, tightly organized parts of the university. In such cases, the students must prepare for examinations imposed by external licensing agencies like state governments. We would scarcely want to drive across an imaginative but untested bridge, or have our tonsils removed by someone long on imagination and short on skill.

This brings a basic problem in universities to our attention. Universities, like any other institutions, need to be organized. Their students need to learn basic skills, be they surgery or sonnets. But all such organization stifles the opportunity for radical new departures, that is, the imaginative breakthroughs by which mankind always advances. To the extent that students are not allowed to make their own choices, the university becomes a think factory turning out identical products who may serve society but not advance it. On the other hand, to the extent that students have absolute freedom, there is less and less chance of any finished product. In other words, institutions of all kinds in order to survive and improve must find a balance between routine and change.

Every one of us constantly works within or alongside not one but many institutions. If we think of them as spatial systems with routes and walls, terminals, and carriers, as well as feedback and storage mechanisms, our ability to understand and cope with them will improve. In every case, institutions, like any systems, can suffer from overload and breakdown. Since cities are in large part collections of institutions, all that we have said so far about information flow and communication systems applies to urban places. The concept of settlements' being organized into spatial hierarchies is particularly useful at this point. In the pages that follow we will consider cities as communication systems which are in turn nodes in the overall system which makes up the modern world.

7 | URBAN COMMUNICATION: INFORMATION FLOW AND THE MEAN INFORMATION FIELD

Switching Points

Cities are like the refreshment table at a party. When you want to meet that fascinating person across the crowded room or escape a boring conversation in which you're mired, you excuse yourself and go get something to eat or drink. Somehow you don't return to your original partner but begin talking to someone else. If that new conversation doesn't work out, there's always the need for another sandwich, another trip to the switching station. Even at room scale, space is not homogeneous. Certain places offer more opportunities for contact and exchange than do others.

Cities are the same. Their huge daytime populations, the pedestrians crowded together on the streets, thousands of stores, hundreds of institutions, and scores of theaters and museums all provide the opportunity for face-to-face contact between people. Karl Deutsch likens the metropolis to a telephone switchboard with hundreds of lines leading into it and an efficient means of making connections between any two wires. The potential for communication in such a system is enormous.

Transactions and Commitments

In every society communication fills a variety of needs. At the simplest verbal level a baby gets pleasure from hearing his parents exclaim and coo over him and from goo-goo-gooing in return. Adults participate in what are sometimes called *idiot greetings* when they say "Hi" and "Hello" to the same classmate or co-worker whenever they see him, even if it's twenty times a day. All these constitute verbal assurances that we are part of a social group and that we are approved of and loved.

Almost every communication is intended as a *transaction*; it is part of the way in which the business of living is conducted. We communicate our needs and desires; we ask, plead threaten, fuss, and persuade. We listen, in turn, to countless messages directed at us. Such exchanges of messages are transactions and often result in one or both parties committing themselves to do something or provide something for the other person. Transactions and commitments can be between individuals or between people acting for firms, corporations, institutions, and all manner of social groupings. The marriage vow formalizes a commitment between two people arrived at after lengthy transactions. Contracts and mortgages are similar formal statements of agreements between people and institutions. Business deals, life insurance sales, and theater tickets and the performances that follow all can be thought of as transactions and commitments. The opportunity for these interactions is greatest in large cities, and is one of the major reasons for their existence.

Quaternary Urban Activities

The words *quarternary activities* are a convenient way to say *information handling and management*. Our use of *quaternary* implies that *primary, secondary,* and *tertiary* activities also exist. Let us place these terms and the activities for which they stand in a proper context. If we consider all the pursuits in which man engages, all the different jobs he does, we can order such activities along a continuum of resource manipulation. For example, a man can be a miner, a metal worker, a steel salesman, or an economist for a firm which buys and uses structural steel. Each type of activity relates to the same resource, but as we move along the above list, we find that each subsequent person's contact with the actual physical resource has grown less. At the same time, influence and decision-making ability increase steadily from miner to salesman to management economist.

Activities involving the actual procurement of raw materials—for example, mining, farming, and lumbering—are designated *primary activities*. Those during which raw materials are physically manipulated and changed into more refined and manufactured products— iron and steel, furniture, bread, gasoline—are called *secondary activities*. All the jobs which relate to the buying, selling, transporting, and stockpiling of manufactured items can be called *tertiary activities*. We also include under this designation all services such as repair and maintenence, clerking, and entertainment. Many of these jobs are not directly concerned with the manipulation of physical resources. The term *quaternary activities* refers to the handling and management of information and knowledge. Thus, most managerial positions would be included under this phrase. Accounting, banking, stockbroking, publishing, librarianship, basic research, and teaching are also included. The term *quaternary* was suggested by the geographer Jean Gottman in his attempt to describe the characteristics of Megalopolis.

Generally speaking, the larger the settlement, the greater the importance of information handling to its survival. Nevertheless, it is difficult to show the role of quaternary activities, for to do so we would have to follow various important messages and orders for goods and services step by step from desk to desk, from office to office, from town to city. If we plotted enough of these routes on maps, we would see lines converging on major metropolitan areas. Unfortunately, information suitable for making such maps is often confidential and, usually, almost impossible to track through the administrative labyrinths of big business and government. We must try instead to find *surrogate measures* of the central role played by cities in quaternary activities. Such *surrogates* would stand in place of more direct measures; that is, they would be *reliable substitutes for the real thing.*

Certain things suggest themselves as reliable substitute measures for information flow and handling. The quantity of mail sent and received, the number of library books available to the public, the number of books, magazines, and newspapers published or the number of publishers, the number of computers in use at a given location, the number of telephones and/or telephone calls, and the points of origin of television programs and radio broadcasts all serve to show where the action is in today's world.

It would belabor the obvious to display elaborate statistics proving that New York City is the source for an overwhelming majority of direct news broadcasts and "live" radio and television shows. Prerecorded programs such as "specials" and weekly series may be made in Hollywood or elsewhere but almost always are sent to New York City for rebroadcasting down through the hierarchy of television and radio stations. Figure 7–1 shows two major broadcasting networks, both originating in New York City, the home of all major broadcasting companies in the United States. Just as New York City dominates

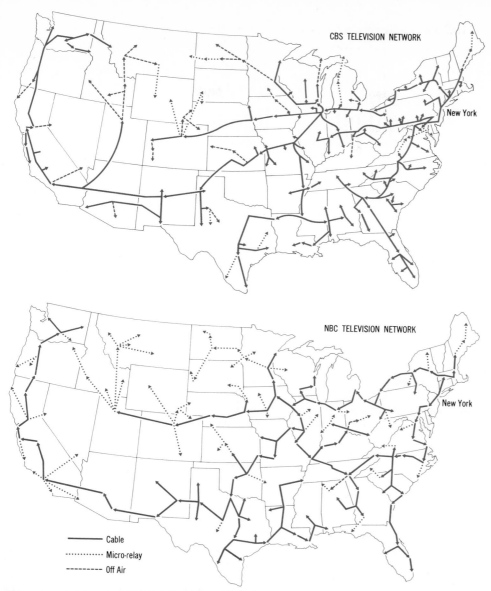

CBS TELEVISION NETWORK

New York

NBC TELEVISION NETWORK

New York

——— Cable
············· Micro-relay
--------- Off Air

Figure 7-1 NBC and CBS national television networks These networks
consist of line-of-sight microwave connections or physically connected
cables. Both networks originate in New York City. They employ quite
different route patterns to reach the same areally spread TV market.
Neither network is very redundant; that is, there is usually only one route
from New York City to a given station. This implies either that their
equipment is very expensive and alternative routes are not financially
feasible, or that the equipment is very reliable, or both. (*International
Television Almanac 1967*)

113

Table 7-1 Dominance of New York in Communication Industries and Services

City	Population of Surrounding SMSA (nearest 1/10 million)	No. of Textbook Publishers	No. of Daily Newspapers	No. Employed in Printing and Publishing	No. of Companies in Data Processing Products and Services, 1968	No. of Airlines
New York	12.0	131	11	125,100	236	63
Los Angeles	7.6	1	3	42,400	49	31
Chicago	7.0	18	7	96,900	115	26
Philadelphia	5.0	12	3	38,600	36	26
Detroit	4.3	1	2	19,800	17	17
Boston	2.8	11	4	24,100	18	16
Washington, D.C.	2.9	7	3		29	17

Source Data: *Editors and Publishers Market Guide 1970*; textbook publishers: list of members of the American Textbook Publishers Institute; data processing–computer companies: *Computer Yearbook & Directory 1968.*

communication media in America, every nation has a major city which is its communication hub. London, Paris, Rome, Tokyo, Moscow, and Buenos Aires, for example, dominate the electronic flow of information in their own countries.

Table 7-1 shows the dominance of New York in book publishing and data processing companies. The major urban areas of the country account for a very high proportion of all communication industries and services.

Another measure of the information-handling potential of a population is its accessibility to private means of communication. The telephone is most important. Figure 7-2 plots the number of telephones of all kinds (private, commercial, government) for a selection of cities in the United States and Turkey as a function of their size. The first thing that we see is that the data form two discrete groups. Turkey, an emerging nation, has fewer telephones per capita in every case. Generally speaking, in both the United States and Turkey there is a direct relationship between city size and the number of telephones. However,

New York City, Washington, D.C., Istanbul, and Ankara all have proportionately more telephones per capita than the other settlements. This is a clear indication of their central role in the communication complexes of their respective countries.

The emphasis placed upon large cities can be shown by another, more comprehensive measure. Large companies maintain their headquarters offices in major cities. This is confirmed by the data shown in Table 7-2 and Figures 7-3 to 7-5. The data given in Table 7-2 clearly indicate the predominant role played by New York City and Chicago in business management. Other American cities also serve as headquarters for far-flung business empires, but to a lesser degree. The maps that follow illustrate the connectivity which exists between New York City, Chicago, Pittsburgh, Los Angeles, Detroit, and the rest of the coterminus United States and Canada.

This clustering of management results in a geographic focusing of information flow upon a few large cities. When the absolute numbers of people and messages in the world

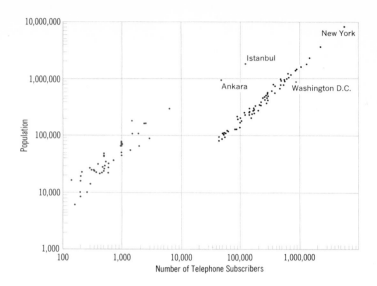

Figure 7-2 The number of telephones by size of city in Turkey and the United States, 1970 The number of telephones as a function of the size of a city in Turkey and the United States yields linear but separate trend lines when plotted on double logarithmic graph paper. The difference in the location of the trend lines reflects the much greater use of communication in the advanced nation compared with the emerging one. The closeness of the points to each regional trend line indicates a unity or system of communication in each region, with the two largest cities far and away the most important communication centers. In Turkey, Istanbul is the largest city and Ankara is the capital. The same relationship exists in the United States between New York City and Washington, D.C. As one would expect, Washington, D.C. has more telephones per capita than normal. This can be seen by its location off the trend line to the right, even though there are other cities which both are larger and have more telephones than the capital city. (Compiled from data in *Statistics of Communications Common Carriers*, Dec. 31, 1968; Turkish telephone directories; *Census of Population by Administrative Division*, Republic of Turkey Prime Ministry, State Institute of Statistics, 1965)

were small, the urban experience within such central places was comprehensible and manageable. Now that we are undergoing runaway growth of both population and information, cities are becoming more difficult places in which to live.

The communication revolution

The communication revolution which has taken place in the last few decades has changed all our lives. The invention of new ways to record, store, and transmit information, as well as the development of additional approaches to logic and thought, has accelerated the world's flow of information. Every century has seen an increase greater than the one before. Every decade, particularly in the last hundred years, has experienced a geometric growth of information handling. For example, in the nineteenth century type was set by hand at a top speed of about 1 character per second. Mechanical typesetting machines built during the last 75 years have raised this to about 5 characters per second. At the present time photographic typesetting machines with mechanical character selection achieve rates of 500 per second, and electronic composing

machines have reached speeds of 10,000 characters per second. This increase in the ease and speed of typesetting is paralleled by improvements in high-speed presses, publishers' accounting procedures, and the shipment of books and newspapers to readers throughout the world. The resulting flood of reading materials of all kinds is illustrated by two sets of data shown in Tables 7–3 and

Table 7–2   Location of Headquarters of the 500 Largest U.S. Industrial Corporations, 1971

City	No. of Corporations
New York	115
Chicago	38
Pittsburgh	15
Cleveland	14
Los Angeles	11
Philadelphia	11
St. Louis	9
Detroit	8
Minneapolis	8
Milwaukee	8
Other cities	263

Source: *Fortune*, May 1971.

Urban Communication: Information Flow and the Mean Information Field

Figure 7-3 Location of plants, by state, for the 500 largest U.S. corporations with headquarters in New York City (After William Goodwin, ''The Management Center in the United States,'' *The Geographical Review,* vol. 40, no. 1, January, 1965, pp. 8–10; data from *Moody's Industrials,* 1962; and *Thomas' Register of American Manufacturers,* 1961, copyrighted by American Geographical Society of New York)

Figure 7-4 Location of plants, by state, for the 500 largest U.S. corporations with headquarters in Chicago (Op. cit., Figure 7-3)

Figure 7-5 Location of plants, by state, for the 500 largest U.S.
corporations with headquarters in San Francisco and Pittsburgh
(Op. cit., Figure 7-3)

Table 7-3   Pounds Shipped by Mail at the Libraries Materials Rate in the United States

1948	5,746,751
1953	7,133,881
1958	45,586,019
1963	69,327,734
1968	101,240,000

Source: *The Bowker Annual of Library and Booktrade Information* Bowker, New York and London, 1970, pp. 59.

Table 7-4   General Books Sales of All Types in the United States

1963	1,673,000,000
1968	2,568,000,000

Source: Table 7-3, op. cit., p. 28.

7-4. The United States' mails are a major means by which publications reach the American reading public. In the 20 years between 1948 and 1968 the volume of materials shipped at the library postal rate increased 20 times by weight! In the 6 years from 1963 to 1968 the value of all types of books sold in the United States rose by more than 50 percent.

This incredible increase in communication by the printed word has been matched by similar increases in radio and television. Here, as in any communication system, terminal facilities are important. Commercial broadcast stations in the United States and its territories increased by nearly 1,000 from 1965 to 1968. Receiving sets of all kinds increased by more than 250 million in the period from 1950

Table 7-5   Increase in Communication Media for Selected Countries

Country	1972 Population (millions)	Per Capita Gross Natl. Income (U.S. $)	Radio Receivers				Television Receivers			
			Thousands		% Increase	Per 1,000 Inhabitants	Thousands		% Increase	Per 1,000 Inhabitants
			1960	1970			1960	1970		
United States	209.2	4,240	170,000	290,000	71	1,412	55,600	84,600	52	412
Sweden	8.2	2,920	2,744	333*		41	1167	2513	115	312
France	51.9	2,460	10,981	15,796	47	314†	1902	10,121†	432	201†
Japan	106.0.	1,430	12,410	25,742	107	255†	6860	22,658	230	215
U.S.S.R.	248.0	1,200	58,600	94,600	61	390	4788	34,800	627	143
Argentina	25.0	1,060	3,500	9,000	157	370	450	3,500	678	144
Mexico	54.3	580	3,300	14,005	324	276	650	2,978	358	59
Turkey	37.6	350	1,352	3,072	127	87	1	25†		0.7†
Colombia	22.9	290	1.971	2,217	12	105	150	800	433	38
Algeria	15.0	260	596	700†	17	52	60	100†	67	7†
Egypt	35.9	160	1,500	4,400	193	132	50	475	850	14
Kenya	11.6	130	57	500†	777	48†		16		1.5
India	584.8	110	2,148	13,387	451	22	0.4	25		0.05
China	786.1	Est. under 100	7,000†	115,000		16	10	300†		0.4†
Nigeria	58.0	Est. under 100	143	1,275	791	23	1	75		1.4
Afghanistan	17.9	Est. under 100	24	248†	933	16†				

*Decrease due to combined radio-TV licenses.
†1969 data.
‡Estimate.
§1965 estimate.
Source: *U.N. Statistical Yearbook 1971* and Population Reference Bureau, Inc., 1972.

to 1967. Tables 7–5, 7–6, and 7–7 show similar increases for other countries throughout the world. The number of phonographs in use in the United States in the same 18 years rocketed from 16.8 to 51.0 million. In banking, another area of communication and information handling, similar expansion has taken place. Examine the next check that comes your way. You will notice a set of numbers printed in the lower-left-hand corner. Those numbers are printed with a special shape so that optical scanners can read and sort them. All such checks are routed to their home banks by automatic devices which sort and channel thousands per hour. An indication of the explosion in information handling that has taken place is that if all such checks were sorted by hand, this job alone would require the labor of every man in the United States between the ages of eighteen and forty!

And so we arrive at another paradox in our lives. We cannot handle, unaided, the immense communication burdens within a mass society. But as we solve problems of volume by greater and greater standardization and by substituting more and more machines to do our work for us, we inevitably change our life-styles. There is no way to go back to the simple agricultural world of our grandfathers and still keep the conveniences which serve us. Who among us is ready and willing to sacrifice automobiles and airplanes, radio and television, credit cards and checking accounts for the quiet life? And yet part of

Table 7–5 (cont.)

Country	Newsprint Consumption Kilograms per capita		Telephones			
			Thousands		Per 100 inhabitants	
	1955–1959	1970	1966	1970	1966	1970
United States	35.7	43.5	98,789	120,218	50.3	58.7
Sweden	23.8	42.7	3,573	4,307	46.0	53.7
France	10.4	11.9	6,554	8,774	13.3	17.2
Japan	6.0	19.1	16,012	26,233	16.1	25.1
U.S.S.R.	1.6	4.0	7,872	11,000	3.4	5.0
Argentina	6.7	10.8	1,527	1,748	6.7	7.5
Mexico	2.4	3.1	928	1,506	2.1	3.1
Turkey	0.7	2.0	386	577	1.2	1.6
Colombia	1.7	2.4	500	809	2.8	3.8
Algeria	0.7	0.3	143	184	1.2	1.3
Egypt	1.0	1.0	335		1.1	
Kenya	0.3	0.4	57	77	0.6	0.7
India	0.2	0.4	927	1,175	0.2	0.2
China		0.7				
Nigeria	0.1	0.1	73	80	0.1	0.1
Afghanistan		0.04	9‡		0.1	

Table 7-6 World Distribution of Telephones

Region	Thousands 1966	Thousands 1970	% Increase 1966 to 1970	Telephones per 100 inhabitants 1966	Telephones per 100 inhabitants 1970
Africa	2,618	3342	28	0.8	1.0
North and Cen. America	108,151	132,294	22	36.1	41.2
South America	4,469	6,137	37	2.6	3.2
Asia	20,603	33,229	61	1.2	1.6
Europe	59.720	80,776	35	13.3	17.4
Oceania	4,540	5,879	29	25.4	29.1
U.S.S.R.	7,872	11,000	40	3.4	5.0
World	208,500	272,700	31	6.2	7.4

Source: *U.N. Statistical Yearbook 1971.*

our modern world is a nearly unmanageable flood of data and information which all these things pour in upon us. What happens to human beings in the path of such an onslaught and what alternatives do they have?

Information Overload in City Systems

If the average person lives 75 years and sleeps one-third of each 24 hours, his waking life will be 50 years long. Within this period of consciousness it has been estimated that 10^{16} (ten thousand trillion) bits of information will be processed by him. The rate at which this huge store of information can be handled depends upon the means by which the information is transferred, the individual's health, and his skills. Experiments indicate that reading is perhaps the fastest and most effective way for humans to process

Table 7-7 Estimated world book production, 1955-1969

Region	Book Production by Number of Titles 1955	Book Production by Number of Titles 1969	Number of Titles per Million Inhabitants 1955	Number of Titles per Million Inhabitants 1969	Percentage Distribution of Book Production 1955	Percentage Distribution of Book Production 1969	Percentage Distribution of Population 1955	Percentage Distribution of Population 1969
Africa	3,000	8,000	13	23	1.0	1.6	8.3	9.7
America, North	16,000	71,000	66	226	5.6	14.3	9.0	8.8
America, South	9,000	12,000	72	64	3.2	2.4	4.6	5.2
Asia	70,000	100,000	47	50	24.6	20.2	55.0	56.0
Europe	131,000	225,000	320	489	46.0	45.4	15.2	13.0
Oceania	1,000	5,000	68	265	0.3	1.0	0.5	0.5
U.S.S.R.	55,000	75,000	279	313	19.3	15.1	7.4	6.8
World total	285,000	496,000	106	140	100.0	100.0	100.0	100.0

Source: *Unesco Statistical Yearbook 1970.*

Table 7-8   Information Transmission in a Metropolitan Area of 5 Million Population

Mode of Reception of Social Communications	Time Allocated (in millions of person-hours per year)	Estimated Receiving Rate (in bits per minute)	Estimated Flow (in millions of millions of bits per year)
Reading	4,000	1,500	360
Television	6,000	400	144
Lecture and discussion	4,000	200	50
Observation of environment	3,000	100	20
Radio	1,500	300	30
Films	160	800	8
Miscellaneous	5,000	100	30
Total			642
Per capita average—100,000,000 bits per year.			

Source: Richard L. Meier, *A Communications Theory of Urban Growth,* published for The Joint Center for Urban Studies of the Massachusetts Institute of Technology and Harvard University by the M.I.T. Press, Cambridge, Mass., 1962, p. 130.

information. If we take this as the optimum case, then a well-trained speed reader might average 3,000 bits of information per minute. Not everyone can read so rapidly, and the prospects of bringing every reader up to his fastest reading rate through special training are slight. It is reasonable, therefore, to take the average reading rate for the general population as closer to 1,500 bits per minute. Richard L. Meier suggests that at this rate a person who reads 350 days per year for 12 hours each day could accommodate an information flow of 400 million bits of information per year. Even at double the assumed rate the total figure still would be less than 1 billion per year. We must also keep in mind the rather unrealistic assumptions that our subject would read without stopping, that he would not have to react to what he read beyond passively assimilating the information, and that all forms of communication could be made as efficient as reading.

Meier further estimates that the current growth rate of per capita information transmission is between 3 and 6 percent per year. Furthermore, there is no indication that this rate will diminish. Table 7-8 shows his estimate that the per capita flow of information in a modern city is about 100 million bits

of information per year. At a conservative growth rate of 3 percent the information available per person would reach 200 million bits in 36 years and the practical limit of human processing in 72 years. If the faster rate is selected for our calculations, the 400 million limit would be reached in 24 years— just about the year 2000. Obviously, something will happen before urban man is faced with such an overwhelming and unrealistic flow of information! Automation and computers may relieve us of some of the burden but cannot spare us completely. Other psychological defense mechanisms exist within us to protect us from too much stress. The unconscious use of such defense mechanisms accounts in large part for what we take for granted as typical urban behavior.

Responses to urban overload

The moose challenges Captain Kangaroo to a game of catch and tosses him a table tennis ball. The captain catches it and returns it quickly. Moose then tosses two at once; again returned. Four, five, a dozen, the captain frantically grabs at the cascade of balls and flings back a few. Finally a flood of table tennis balls pours down on a silent, unresisting fig-

Urban Communication: Information Flow and the Mean Information Field

ure. The captain, overwhelmed, has *turned off.* His response to too many table tennis balls may be a standard joke on children's television, but the effectiveness of the scene comes from how well it matches realities we all have experienced. When too much of anything comes our way, something has to give.

Stanley Milgram has suggested a number of ways in which city dwellers adjust to conditions of urban overload. A person walking near Times Square in New York City will have the opportunity of face-to-face contact with 220,000 people within 10 minutes of his hotel room or office. Across the Hudson River in Newark, New Jersey, he would be able to meet only 20,000 people in the same 10-minute walking radius. Still farther out in the suburbs this figure would decrease to 11,000 or less. The hordes of pedestrians encountered near Times Square are overwhelming. In order to accommodate themselves to such numbers New Yorkers have adopted patterns of behavior for which they are famous. First of all, they always seem to be in a hurry. Another way of stating this is that city dwellers apparently *allocate less time for each transaction or casual contact.* Money is thrown down on the counter and a newspaper snatched up; subway tokens are purchased hurriedly and without comment. When the number of contacts or information inputs increases drastically, less time can be allocated to each encounter.

City dwellers are often accused of being callous and unconcerned with the plight of their fellow man. At face value, this may well be true. But in terms of the community or social group of which they feel themselves a part, they will be no better or worse than rural folk. When a New Yorker steps over a drunk collapsed in the entryway of his apartment building, he is again responding to urban overload by *disregarding low-priority inputs.* Energy and time, money and emotion must be carefully parcelled out when there are so many drains upon each person's limited supplies.

City living forces people to constantly *redraw the boundaries that define their lives in order to spare themselves and shift the burden to the other party.* Stores selling faulty merchandise will disclaim responsibility and send the frustrated buyer to the factory representative. The City Department of Streets will tell an apartment dweller that the broken sidewalk in front of his building is the responsibility of the landlord. The landlord will reply that it is the job of the city to repair such things.

Urbanites reduce or block off reception of all kinds before it's allowed to happen. Everyone seems to wear sunglasses in the city. All the pretty girls have blank eyes like plexiglass curtains drawn between themselves and the passing crowd. No businessman, lawyer, or doctor will see anyone without an appointment; and the usual comment of the famous to the press is "No comment."

Associations within the city are often fleeting and superficial. *The intensity of inputs is diminished by filtering devices.* Many people seek the anonymity of city life. Both fugitives from justice and celebrities weary of recognition welcome city crowds into which they can merge unnoticed. Friendships are formed among a person's co-workers and not geographically. People can live for years in the same apartment building, pass each other in the halls, stand together in the elevators, and never become acquainted.

Finally, *special institutions are formed to absorb inputs that might otherwise overwhelm the city dweller.* Peddlers and parades must be licensed, and police enforce noise abatement laws. Welfare departments care for the poor, who might otherwise ring every doorbell and stop every pedestrian in search of alms. Everyone "lets his fingers do the walking" in the classified pages rather than personally traveling from store to store in search of what he needs.

On another level of interaction, ethnic neighborhoods can be considered informal institutions which have grown up over long periods of time. These neighborhoods become habitats which are familiar and therefore less stressful for specific social groups. Greenwich Village with its counterculture and the Bowery with its bars and bums tend to segregate and institutionalize life-styles in New York City just as do the Left Bank in Paris and Soho in London. In this way, ghettoes may represent in part the self-imposed, protective clustering of minority groups. This is not to deny that powerful forces beyond the control of minorities constantly work to keep them contained in undesirable areas. But just as the dependents of American military personnel form "little Americas" in foreign cities, so may people speaking the same language or practicing the same religion voluntarily seek each other out for protection and relaxation. Zoning laws provide a more formal way of institutionalizing certain kinds of land use. This creates special city environments by excluding industry, determining street widths and property setbacks, and providing open space in the form of parks. All these measures tend to lessen the density or rate of information flow, thus protecting the individual.

The relationship between cities, information flow, and people can be outlined quite simply. One of the chief reasons for the existence of cities is the opportunity for face-to-face contacts which are important for service (tertiary) and information-handling (quaternary) activities. So many people and so many communication outlets may accumulate within the city that its inhabitants become overloaded with information. The alternatives resulting from conditions of information overload are the breakdown of the system or the creation of mechanisms and attitudes which protect or buffer individuals. Flight to the suburbs and special institutions are two of many such mechanisms. An entire set of attitudes which distinguish city dwellers from their country cousins may also develop. These distinctions are described below.

Urban and rural attitudes

It is possible to characterize the sharp contrast between urban and rural society by the phrases *city slicker* and *country bumpkin*. Other contrasting pairs of words like *cosmopolitan* and *bucolic* also suggest themselves. The city is thought of as a place of innovation and change, while the small town stands for tradition and stagnation. The city dweller is sophisticated; his behavior is *cool*. That is, little or nothing surprises him or makes him flustered. The tourist from the small town, on the other hand, is overwhelmed by the tall buildings, the crowds, the thousands of sights. He is what comedian Fred Allen called a *yuck*, the provincial who gapes at skyscrapers. These contrasting behavior patterns are easily explained in terms of adjustments to information overload. The city dweller, accustomed to the flood of contacts at the urban core, has developed attitudes which protect him, His noncommittal sophistication is simply one way of making a virtue out of omitting what he can't handle. The unsophisticated visitor has not yet had time to overload and responds to the same situations in a naïve manner.

Personal appearance becomes very important in the city. Since most contacts are fleeting in urban situations, the clothes one wears become symbols of status and attitude. Hair styles, particularly men's hair length, also assume the function of costumes telling the role a person plays. In the small town, conformity to some accepted norm is more important. Everyone knows who everyone else is, so why hide it? Along with all of this is the utilitarianism of city life. It's not a man's background that counts, but rather his skills, accomplishments, and bank balance. In small towns, conversely, family ties and length of residence are more important. There are still some places in New England where people, residents for 50 years or more but born elsewhere, are considered newcomers or strangers.

The city dweller views the world as changeable, and he values material progress. This comes in part from his emphasis on the material appearance of the people with whom he has brief contacts. Anything goes as long as it leads to success. Geographically speaking, high land values near the city center increase competition for land use. Buildings are continually being torn down and new ones built in their places. The actual environment in which the city person lives is more likely to change than are the ageless country hills.

On the other hand, truly rural people, subjected to the unpredictable whims of weather which make or break farmers' fortunes each year, may be more fatalistic. That is, they accept whatever fate has in store for them, for their chances of changing the course of events is slight. This notion is again reinforced from a geographical point of view if we consider the high population density of cities combined with the immense concentration of wealth in these central places. A natural disaster which might wipe out a few rural families and go unnoticed except by the unfortunates will evoke massive efforts of aid and reconstruction if it strikes a city. Not only is the city able to marshall people and wealth, it is also located at a focal point of communication lines and news media which report its condition to the world. Some cities dominate the world news. For example, while New York City's problems are of spectacular proportions, New York City is not alone in its troubles. And yet for every newspaper article or news item telling about the woes of Pittsburgh, Calcutta, or Buenos Airies, there are several relating Manhattan's problems. This is in large part a reflection of the concentration of news media, writers, and broadcasters in the area.

Contrasts between rural and urban life-styles and attitudes result many times from differences in the geographical scales at which people view their environments. Inhabitants of both very large and very small settlements identify with events occurring in their home areas more than they do with those in other places. A man may think of himself as a New Yorker, or he may identify himself, for example, as a Shadypointer if he happens to live in Shadypoint, Oklahoma. New York City has a population of nearly 8 million; Shadypoint has only 300. And yet if a New Yorker reads of crime or violence anywhere within the far-flung limits of his city, he will feel his security threatened just as much as would the citizen of Shadypoint if trouble happened there. It matters very little that New York is 25,000 times larger than Shadypoint, for the *vulnerable space* of each person

matches the approximate dimensions of the settlement in which he lives.

The boundaries of the world perceived by people in large and small settlements vary in much the same way. The big-city dweller will be accustomed to seeing strange behavior and dress; his perceptual horizon will extend to include other city modes in the world system of which he is a part. Rural people, at the other extreme, draw the perceived boundaries of their world along nearby landmarks. Even if the daily mobility of two people from large and small settlements is much the same— let us say each travels 5 miles to work and 5 miles home—the richness of the urban scene will expand the worldly experience of the city dweller more than any village environment will.

The Mean Information Field

Frequency of contact between people, their mobility or use of space, and the richness of information within their environment all play a part in shaping a population's life-style. The geographical concept of the *mean information field* (MIF) of the individual can be used to operationally define the relationship between human contacts, mobility, and information availability.

Nonspatial variables

Every environment contains information of many kinds in very large quantities. Only a portion of the total amount of information which surrounds a person will be available to him. Just as we receive information from all sides, so do we communicate messages to the people and environment which surround us. Not everything we transmit outward is received or understood. Sometimes we refuse messages; sometimes our own messages are rejected by others. The ability and willingness of people to receive and send information depend upon their education, training, and culture. This ability to communicate is also a function of a person's chronological age. Very small children find little to enjoy at motion pictures. An illiterate wandering in a library will be as isolated from information as he would be on a desert island. An observant, well-trained farmer reads much more from the landscape than does a city dweller.

Daily contact space

Our ability to communicate with other people also depends upon our ability to overcome the *friction of distance*. Distance as a geographic variable has been discussed at length in Chapters 3 and 4. We can translate those ideas into the individual's ability to communicate with others by observing that the people we contact most frequently are those closest to us in space. The farther from us a person is located, the less likely are our chances of communicating with him. Our ability to communicate across space depends upon our access to means of transportation and communication. If you do not own or drive a car, if you cannot write letters or read, or if you do not have the price of postage or of a telephone call and can't afford a bus ticket, the range of your communication is very limited. The *mobility* or *space-using capability* of each person is important in determining his ability to send and receive information. Shut-ins and stay-at-homes lead impoverished lives. Housewives detained by small children in suburban kitchens sometimes show signs of having been kept in solitary confinement. On the other hand, people commuting to the city share two worlds, suburban and urban.

The average or usual area across which a person moves each day enhances to a greater or lesser degree his ability to communicate, for the size and character of this area will help to determine the number and type of people with whom he comes in contact. This *daily contact space* of the individual deals with regularly occurring events rather than those which are out of the ordinary. In other words, the daily contact space of a person would be defined by his trip to work, shopping trips, and normal journeys for social purposes. Once-in-a-lifetime migrations and

unusual trips such as journeys while in the armed services are excluded. To create or draw the daily contact space of an individual, his usual trips are plotted on a map. This may be shown as an actual pattern of moves or generalized as a simple form such as an ellipse (Figure 7–6).

The daily contact space of people varies with age, occupation, and culture. A baby's contact space is limited at first to his crib and his mother's arms, then to one or two rooms, next to a house and yard, and finally to a neighborhood as the child grows older. Young adults are probably the most mobile in American culture, while increasing old age restricts the geographical area which people utilize in their daily lives. Businessmen commuting to the city cover more space than do their wives, while traveling salesmen see more of the world than do typists and desk-bound administrators. Women in some cultures are confined for most of their lives to harems visited only by husbands, sons, and brothers. Nomads may wander over miles of pasture, while peasant farmers tend only a few restricted acres of land. The *daily contact space* of people is shown in Figure 7–7 as part of their *personal communication fields*.

The mean information field

We may think of each person as standing at the center of a cone-shaped tent, the inner volume of which represents all the contacts he makes with others. This tent (Figure 7–6) can be referred to as his *personal communication field*. Its shape describes the *allocation* of his contacts over space. The height of the center pole is proportional to the general probability of his communicating with someone nearby in contrast with his communicating with someone farther away. The slope at which the walls of the tent fall away is the rate at which his contacts diminish with distance. The diameter of the tent is a measure of his ability to overcome distance through his own mobility and his use of communication devices. However, the actual number of people contacted by an individual varies as a function

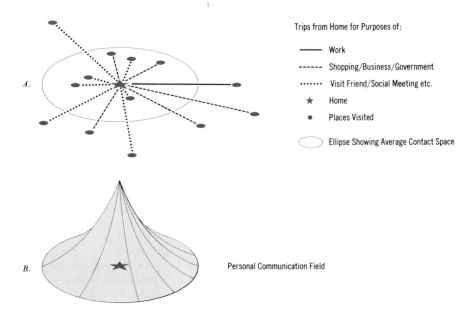

Trips from Home for Purposes of:

——— Work

- - - - - Shopping/Business/Government

·········· Visit Friend/Social Meeting etc.

★ Home

● Places Visited

⬭ Ellipse Showing Average Contact Space

Personal Communication Field

Figure 7-6 Daily contact space and personal communication fields A person is usually counted for census purposes at his place of residence. But people are not always at home. Part *A* of the diagram represents a typical collection of other places visited at varying frequencies and distances from home. The ellipse shows the average distance to these other locations appropriately weighted by frequency of contact. It is only with in this space that a person has contact with other people and with communication devices. Part *B* shows an idealized personal communication field which indicates the range and intensity of potential contact. This idealized cone would vary by culture and by individual.

of his age, occupation, and culture. Therefore, we must multiply this personal communication field by the total number of contacts made by the individual in a given time.

Obviously, a baby will interact intensely with an extremely limited number of people nearby. His *actual contact field* will be very peaked, steeply sloping, and small in volume. An urban middle-class adult will occupy a communications tent with more gently sloping walls, a larger diameter, and a significantly larger volume of contacts. Conversely, as the elderly communicate with fewer and fewer people, their fields become smaller. The size of actual communication fields also varies from one socioeconomic group to another and from culture to culture. Figure 7–7 also shows the actual communication fields of people

from different cultures at different ages. Because personal and actual communication fields vary greatly from individual to individual within any culture, it is useful to aggregate or summarize such fields in order to show the behavior of particular populations. Each of these aggregates is referred to as a *mean information field* (or by its abbreviation, MIF).

Communication and spatial diffusion

When gold was discovered at Sutter's Mill in California, relatively few people knew of it for the first week or two. This was because, regardless of the discoverer's desire for fame or secrecy, there were not many persons nearby to receive and pass on the message. As

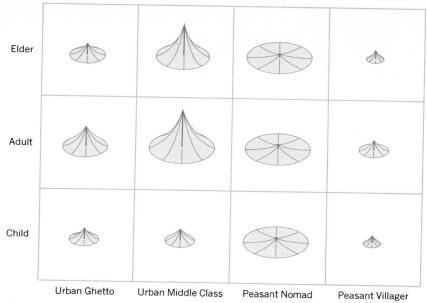

	Urban Ghetto	Urban Middle Class	Peasant Nomad	Peasant Villager
Elder				
Adult				
Child				

Figure 7-7 Hypothetical communication field, by age and culture
Personal communication fields can be expected to vary by age, occupation,
and culture. In most societies, working adults have the greatest spatial
range and are engaged in more transactions than the young and old. Nomads
travel widely but with fewer transactions per day.

word reached San Francisco and finally found its way to the Eastern states, more and more carriers and recipients became available. The news *diffused* to every corner of the land, and the gold rush was on. The rate at which that information spread was a function of the MIF and the population distribution of the people involved. Once the idea reached densely populated areas, it spread rapidly. We can imagine how this process works if we consider that each person who receives the message immediately becomes a new sender. As more and more senders are created, the news descends from all sides upon those still ignorant of it. At the same time, the advance of the news into untouched territory proceeds in a stepwise fashion from one communication field to the next. The greater the overlap of communication fields, the faster it will spread.

Geographers are concerned primarily with the spatial aspects of diffusion processes. They share this interest in particular with anthropologists who have studied the idea of *culture hearths* and *culture areas*. A culture hearth can be thought of as some location on the earth's surface inhabited by a group of people whose inventiveness creates ideas, traits, customs, and inventions which move or diffuse outward until people in possibly remote areas also utilize them. Similarly, a culture area is a geographically defined portion of the earth's surface the population of which shares a set of ideas, traits, customs, and inventions which distinguish that group from all others. The distinction between the two is the *originality* of things moving outward from the hearth; the inhabitants of a culture area in most cases share a collection of things which have come from all over, though a few may have originated at home.

In this respect, culture hearths are thought of as generating *diffusion waves* which, moving outward from their source, carry "messages" like ripples expanding outward from

*Urban
Communication:
Information
Flow and
the Mean
Information
Field*

127

SPATIAL PROCESS

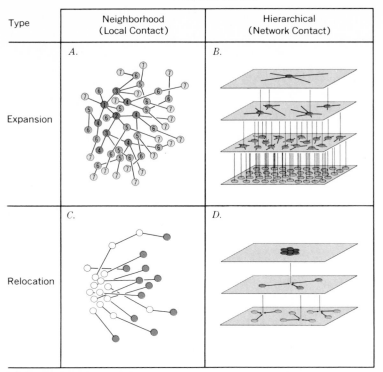

Type	Neighborhood (Local Contact)	Hierarchical (Network Contact)
Expansion	*A.*	*B.*
Relocation	*C.*	*D.*

Figure 7-8 Types of diffusion Examples of each type of diffusion include: (*A*) neighborhood spread of a rumor or disease, (*B*) spread of a national fad, (*C*) shift of frontier homesteads, (*D*) migration to a metropolis.

a rock thrown into a lake. While these ideas were originally discussed in qualitative terms by anthropologists Clark Wissler and A. L. Kroeber, it was the Swedish geographer Torsten Hägerstrand who presented quantitative measures of diffusion. Hägerstrand's treatment of diffusion looks at the process over a number of time intervals. At every succeeding time the "wave" moves farther through space from its source. Models such as this are *distance-dependent* and *spatial* in character.

Another type of diffusion study derives more from the work of sociologists who view diffusion as an interaction process between individuals which can take place between peers without reference to their geographic

locations or by moving up and down social or administrative hierarchies. Such models are *hierarchial and nonspatial* except in the sense that movement from one level of a hierarchy to another represents changes in scale. Another aspect of diffusion studies concerns whether the number of people sharing the thing diffused increases with each move or time period or whether the number of such "knowers" remains constant.

Various combinations of these traits are possible. For example, the movement of styles from one metropolitan center to another and then outward from those points to surrounding cities and thereafter to towns is both hierarchical and spatial. Figure 7–8 presents four basic combinations: in two the "knowers"

Spatial Design in World Society

128

remain constant in number but move either spatially or hierarchically; in the other two the numbers increase with each time period although the process can be either distance-dependent or hierarchically structured. The diffusion processes where numbers increase have particular significance in terms of human and other ecosystems. The two examples given below illustrate how environments can be affected both positively and negatively by the growth and diffusion across space and time of ecological elements.

Our first example of spatial hierarchical diffusion is the growth of the Sierra Club, an organization dedicated to helping people explore and protect wilderness areas (Figure 7-9). The club was founded by John Muir and a group of friends in San Francisco in the year 1892. For many years it remained only in that vicinity. However, individual membership became increasingly widespread. In 1906 the members living in the Los Angeles area wished to form their own local chapter. Thereafter, there was a short-range diffusion of chapters in California. By 1930 a chapter was opened in New York City. Several years later the Great Lakes chapter located in Chicago was organized. In 1960 the club members decided that they could become an effective national organization, and further hierarchical growth took place from New York, Chicago, and other early centers. At the present time the Sierra Club is among the major environmental lobby groups in the United States.

Figure 7-10 shows the distance-dependent diffusion of the Brazilian honeybee *Apis mellifera adansonii*. Technically speaking, these bees are not "knowers" but, rather, an expanding life-form. However, the diffusion they follow in hiving off and swarming to

Figure 7-9 Growth of the Sierra Club—an example of hierarchical diffusion The hierarchical diffusion linkages are defined wherever a descendent chapter is formed from territory previously assigned to antecedent chapter. An example is the Mackinac Chapter territory in the state of Michigan, which was formerly a portion of the Great Lakes Chapter, including eleven states with chapter headquarters in Chicago.

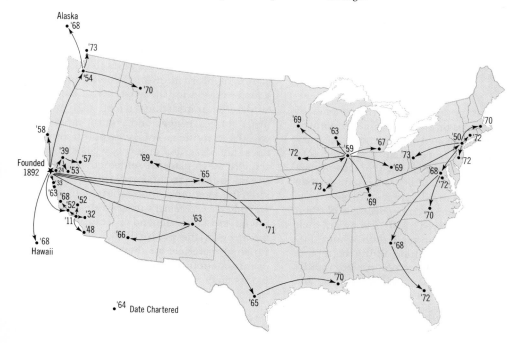

Figure 7-10 Spatial diffusion of the Brazilian honeybee This honeybee, which is unusually vicious, poses a threat to the people in the areas it invades. There is a proposal to try to halt its advance at the Isthmus of Panama, thus preventing its spread to Central and North America. (Gerald S. Schatz, "Countering the Brazilian Honey Bee: Aftermath of a Biological Mishap," *News Report, National Academy of Sciences*, vol. 22, no. 8, October, 1972)

new locations is analogous to the spread of disease or rumors or even the spread of knowledge of domesticated plants among early man. This bee was originally imported into Brazil from Africa in 1956. In 1957, twenty-six swarms were accidentally released in São Paulo, Brazil. The rapid spread of these insects is of particular importance because of their aggressive and unpredictable behavior, their danger to man and animals with whom they come in contact, and their ability to replace other bees. These bees have spread rapidly through the mechanism of hiving off and swarming to new homes over relatively short

distances. This process is a distance-dependent one typical of contagious expansion diffusion. If this bee were to reach North America, it might well mean the end of the beekeeping industry in the United States, since their visciousness would necessitate their destruction. The resulting loss to American agriculture through inadequate plant pollination has been estimated at as much as 5 billion dollars annually. A committee of the National Research Council has monitored the advance of these bees across South America. The committee points out that control of the bees in the vastness of the Amazon basin is beyond anyone's means. They recommend that every effort be made to stop them at the Isthmus of Panama by placing new types of breeding bees with more desirable genetic characteristics in their path. Some colonies will also have to be killed or given new, less dangerous queens in order to control the menace in the heavily populated areas of South America. In any event, knowledge of diffusion processes provides scientists with better means of becoming ecological watchdogs.

Communication as a Catalyst for all Urban Activities

Geographic theory suggests that the manipulation of information and knowledge has been a major reason for the existence of cities. Certainly, the transactions which take place in urban places trigger and control most of the world's activities. This viewpoint, however, does not describe or explain most of what actually takes place in settlements of all sizes. In fact, quaternary and tertiary activities provide the economic foundation only for what we call *service centers* or *central places*. Many towns and cities depend instead upon manufacturing or the production of raw and semi-finished materials for their survival. The flow of information through the hierarchy of urban places may direct all such activities but in most cases furnishes them with very little direct economic support. Information, rather, serves as a catalyst producing much greater reactions. While centrality and connectivity are significant in hierarchies of central places, other factors are important in the location of primary and secondary industries. The next chapter looks at additional elements which help to create patterns of production. But no matter what other geographic elements fall within the limelight, no matter how slight the role played by information flow seems, we must remember that without a steady flow of messages nothing would take place.

Come to the highest peak in the land and view the sweep of the continent. Let imagination extend our vision in order to see not only the plains, mountains, and coastlands with their routes and cities, but also the origin and movement of messages, goods, and materials everywhere across the land. If we exercise our wits a bit more, we can liken the scene in its entirety to some complex form of life with nervous and circulatory systems, in fact, to one endowed with all the parts necessary for maintaining its dynamic, moving form.

If quaternary activities and the cities which support them can be compared to the brain and nervous system of this gigantic organism, then the tertiary services are analogous to the functions performed by veins and arteries distributing oxygen, nutrients, and fluids throughout its body. In this fanciful comparison, the raw materials produced by fields and mines become similar to the food and water consumed by every living thing. There remains the role played by the digestive tract and glands, for which we need seek a comparison. And such a comparison comes immediately to mind: The manufacturing complexes of the world and their activities can be easily equated with those organs which change raw food into substances the body can use. Finally, of course, both the body and the land must be able to dispose of waste products quickly, easily, and safely.

It is not our intention to carry this comparison any further. We use it only to point out the interrelatedness of urban activities with those in rural areas and of the important systems, both man-made and natural, which bind them together. If the world is to remain healthy and suitable as the home of man, its many parts must function well together. If each of us is to contribute to this state of global health as well as help to maintain and restore it, we must understand earth's physiology and metabolism. Nor is it worthwhile or practical to separate man and his works from those of "nature." Ultimately, we live in and with nature and are part of it. If it falters or perishes, so too, inevitably, will we all.

The centers of secondary production where manufacturing takes place are just as important as quaternary and tertiary activities within the man-land global system. The ideal function of manufacturing complexes is to provide for all material human needs in a manner and at a rate which will bring no cumulative harm to the total life-support system on earth. This aim may be further divided into two interdependent ones, the first being to maximize production while minimizing economic cost, the second to assure continuing production at a minimum of costs or damages to society and nature. This second aim has received scant attention until recently.

Part One of this book, with its emphasis on

location theory and spatial organization, is primarily concerned with economic maximization. This emphasis is made in large part because the beginnings of modern location theory were in the subject area still often called *economic geography*. Part Two enlarges on this theme, and among other things discusses the problems associated with attaining a balance between manufacturing, society, and nature. Since only a few short centuries ago North America and the other parts of what is now the modern industrial world contained only the simplest of Neolithic or preindustrial manufacturing activities, it is worthwhile to consider the patterns of industrial growth in space and time that have led to the present world condition.

The Economic and Technical Growth of Regions: The United States

The United States is among the great manufacturing countries of the world. However, within its boundaries there is great variation in production from region to region. What characteristics describe those parts of the United States that grew into powerful commercial and industrial centers? Why did some places never grow industrially and why have some declined?

Some historical conditions

The United States is rather a special case, for it is one of the few countries which was "born free." That is, the growth of the nation and the nation's industries coincided with the general rapid increase in technological and productive skills which we have come to know as the Industrial Revolution. The American population from the very beginning had no significant traditional society of peasants and nobility within it. At the same time, like it or not, the native American Indian population had been in large part removed from its original lands and partially destroyed. The formative years of industrial development needed an enormous labor force which was supplied by the importation, family by family, of the uprooted masses of Europe. We often refer to the America of the nineteenth and early twentieth centuries as *the melting pot*, wherein people of many backgrounds and persuasions were merged. But it might be more accurate to call it the *grinding mill* between the stones of which immigrants, largely stripped of their native cultures, had of necessity to conform to new modes of life. The changes in society necessary for industrial development were harder to bring about in complex traditional societies such as those which existed in Europe and Asia.

The economic growth of America can be viewed in terms of three factors or inputs designated by classic economics: capital, labor, and raw materials or resources. A fourth element worthy of consideration is the role of the entrepreneur, who provides managerial and organizational skills. As geographers we will consider the importance of relative situation or locational advantage in the growth of industry. It is also important to consider the way in which political processes influence development. These factors are intertwined in every system, whether "Western" or communist or feudal.

In the early United States private profit was the major motive underlying the growth of industry. The rapid influx of unskilled workers provided a labor surplus available at low wages. Before union organization forced a more equitable distribution of profits (an issue still considered unresolved by many), wealth went to the organizers of industry and commerce. This was the era of *robber barons* and *captains of industry*. The former raped the land of its natural resources; the latter ground the faces of the workers in the quest for profits.

Stage one: Initial exploitation

At first, direct exploitation of natural resources was the means of gaining wealth. The gold fortunes of California are a prime example, but there are many others, including those made from:

Fish and lumber in New England

Coal in West Virginia

Lumber, iron, and copper in Michigan

Silver and gold in Colorado

Lumber in the Pacific Northwest

Grasslands and petroleum in the Great Plains

The soil itself throughout the South and Midwest

Development of these resources took capital which came from (1) foreign investment, (2) Eastern financiers in well-developed areas far behind the advancing frontier, and (3) local money, especially from *nouveau riche* entrepreneurs first on the scene. It was not the miners, or lumbermen, or fishermen who got rich. It was the saloon keepers, merchants, and early manufacturers.

Stage two: The takeoff point

In every case the accumulation of capital led to a *takeoff stage* marked by a period of rapid expansion and enormously wasteful exploitation of resources. Only the cream of the land was skimmed off. The buffalo were slaughtered; Michigan white pine and California redwoods devastated; the seas emptied of herring and the whale herds reduced to isolated individuals. It was a time of *once-and-for-all, git-and-git-out* exploitation of nonrenewable resources. High-grade gold, silver, and copper were taken, shallow petroleum fields emptied, hardwood forests cut; and even now the fossil water from beneath the high plains of eastern Colorado is irrigating fields from subterranean reservoirs never to be refilled.

But we must not be completely harsh in judging the pioneers and early businessmen. Hindsight is easy, and current standards may not have always applied. The rapid exploitation of a resource to exhaustion sometimes yields another cycle of growth *providing the profits earned are reinvested in productive local industries.* For example, the hardwood forests of Michigan and Indiana provided

profits which helped to create the furniture industry for which Grand Rapids is famous. In much the same way, white pine and copper fortunes were subsequently invested in the Detroit automobile industry. Early investments in machine industries, buggy manufacturing, and marine engines were an intermediate step between the mines and lumber camps and the assembly lines at Willow Run and River Rouge (Figure 8–1).

Stage three: The drive to maturity

A drive to maturity characterizes manufacturing's third stage of growth. Industry begins to import raw materials and to export finished products beyond the limits of the region. With standardization and routinization, low labor skills are required of a large labor force. This pool of workers is usually encouraged to immigrate by increased job opportunities. European migrants working in the late nineteenth century textile mills and garment factories of New York and Boston are a good example of this. Black people and Southern whites flocking to the mills and factories of Detroit and Chicago also fit this roll. At this stage organizational capacity becomes the key to development.

At the international level, raw materials often move between countries. In this case, most of the profits will accumulate at the point of manufacturing rather than at the source. This might be described as *economic imperialism,* and in the past was accompanied by the military occupation of the resource-producing regions and the development of classic political imperialism. Nearly every large manufacturing country which has passed into the third level of industrial growth has trod the boards of this stage. The role is not always a comfortable one, as the British learned with their Empire, the French with their colonies, the Russians with East Europe and parts of inner Asia, and the United States with its many international woes and responsibilities.

At the regional level, to again cite the example of Michigan's industrial development,

Figure 8-1 Aerial view of the Ford Motor Company complex, steel mill, and auto assembly plants at River Rouge, Michigan The Ford Motor Company's River Rouge industrial complex near Detroit, Michigan, is a vertically integrated system in which basic raw materials, including iron ore, limestone, and coal, are used to produce steel which, within a few days, is incorporated into the engines, frames, bodies, and parts of completed automobiles. (Photo courtesy of the Ford Motor Company)

automobile manufacturing arose as the second great source of wealth in the state's history. Thousands of migrants were drawn there. As long as the expectations of the newcomers remained low, or as long as the environments from which they came offered an even less attractive mode of living, Michigan's urban areas and industries seemed to prosper. However, the auto industry soon became too large for the region, and remote investment opportunities had to be found for the new profits. Funds were dispersed to far-flung stockholders, were invested in national and international enterprises, and also went to create nonprofit organizations such as the Ford Foundation. From a global or national point of view these activities were quite rational,

but seen regionally perhaps too little was reinvested in creating the social infrastructure necessary for further growth potential in the immediate area. As the third stage of regional development reached its peak, education became more and more important at all levels. It may be argued that not enough was invested in local schools and training programs to ensure the ultimate health of the region. More of this in a moment.

Stage four: Specialized industrial development

As the fourth phase, *specialized industrial development*, is approached, less and less depends upon the presence of unskilled labor. Automation begins to take over, and machines become more and more complex in their operation. The resulting vision of the future is a technological one. A skilled and affluent labor force becomes more and more a necessity. It must be skilled to increase productivity per worker as well as the valued added through manufacturing, and it must be affluent in order to purchase the products which result. Automobiles are again a prime example of this. Approximately 20 percent of the United States' gross national product is derived from automobiles, roads, and associated activities. (An interesting comparison can be made with the federal budget, which also represents about 20 percent of the gross national product. Since about half of the federal budget is allocated to the Department of Defense and aerospace industries, this means that the automobile industry and all its accompanying activities are twice the size of our defense effort.) The working middle class buys most of the cars produced in America and must, in turn, earn wages which allow it to support the industries which employ it.

Thus, the ideal preparation for the fourth stage of industrial development should include investment in the education and aspirations of the general population. Let us phrase this for a final time in terms of Michigan and its industry. This single industrial state is only one of several such in the United States, and yet it is more powerful, more populous, and more affluent than most nations of the world. In fact, it consumes more electrical power than all but twelve nations. In other words, more than 90 percent of all the nations use less. Detroit, its largest city, is the largest automobile manufacturing region in the world. The rest of Michigan is the world's second largest automobile manufacturing region. We say this not out of some chauvanistic or hucksterish pride but rather to emphasize that this industry and its region are sustained by an innovative, skilled, organized, and wealthly population. *Yet each generation is born without skills.* Training a stream of young people in the intricate ways of a complex industrial society is one of the most important tasks within this sort of region. Without a continuous flow of new talent as well as materials and investment funds, such a region may eventually decline.

Meanwhile, another element in the equation of success is the social and natural environment which results from industrial activities. The migrant poor, filling the lowest ranks of employment, are least likely to receive the education so necessary for future success. The pattern of movement of the wealthy owners and managers to the suburbs is followed in succeeding generations by the flight of affluent workers from the inner city. We need not recount the resulting urban woes discussed in earlier pages. We simply want to point out again the interconnectedness among the elements introduced in this book as it progresses.

Spiral and Cumulative Patterns of Growth

The preceding account of growth in an industrial region is largely literary in content. It will help to order some of our thoughts about the subject before moving on in the next chapter to specific and more technical details concerning the location and growth of manufacturing firms and complexes.

Following the model suggested by W. W. Rostow, we have described the four stages of growth as *initial exploitation, the takeoff stage, the stage of maturity or sustained growth,* and *the stage of specialized development.* It is tempting to add a final stage, decline and death, but such a fanciful addition would carry our analogy with the history of some living organism much too far. Since the time of the Industrial Revolution, and perhaps since the foundation of modern West European society in the Middle Ages, there has been no major geographical shift from the centers of industry which were first established. New ones have been added in America, South Africa, Australia, and Japan, but there seems no immediate or predictable demise in store for any of the world's major industrial regions.

We can picture the region of our choice and its stages of growth as a stack of horizontal slices in time. This is shown in Figure 8–2.

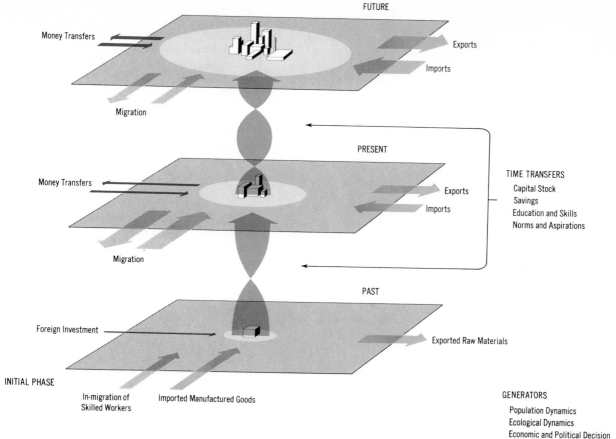

FUTURE

Money Transfers

Exports

Imports

Migration

PRESENT

Money Transfers

Exports

Imports

Migration

TIME TRANSFERS

Capital Stock
Savings
Education and Skills
Norms and Aspirations

PAST

Foreign Investment

Exported Raw Materials

INITIAL PHASE

In-migration of
Skilled Workers

Imported Manufactured Goods

GENERATORS

Population Dynamics
Ecological Dynamics
Economic and Political Decision

Figure 8-2 Regional development—circular and accelerative growth
Population dynamics include demographic change, levels of education and
skill, social norms, and aspirations. Economic and political dynamics include inertia of venture capital and labor, piecemeal innovation, uneven
writeoff, social overhead investment, neighborhood copying effect, changes
in business thresholds, and supportive and social legislation. Ecological
dynamics include depletion, overload, pollution and concentration, and
secondary effects.

In the lowest of our time slices the region is
a small one, based largely on the exportation
of raw materials. This outward flow is indicated by the broad arrow leaving the designated surface. At the same time, other elements
are moving into the picture. Foreign investment, imported manufactured goods and
machines, and migrants are represented by
the three flow arrows focused upon the re-

gional center. All these inward flows serve
to build up the region. Local entrepreneurs
accumulate savings and seek outlets for venture capital. It is not unusual for these frontier
types to like to keep close track of their money
and to seek nearby investment opportunities.
At the same time, capital in the form of machines, buildings, and stocks of goods may
gradually accumulate. Population may grow

*Patterns of
Development:
Process of
Regional
Growth*

through continued in-migration and natural increase, and with luck, the people's skills and education, aspirations and ability to consume more products will also grow. Increases in the size of the market will allow businesses with higher thresholds to appear. That is, the first firms to appear will supply the basic needs of the original population. Grocery stores, hardware shops (or historically, blacksmiths' forges), and food and drink establishments, all with very limited ranges and all needing relatively few customers to survive, will come first. Thereafter, firms needing larger and perhaps wealthier populations from which to draw their support will be established. Now dressmakers will appear as more women enter the population. Select foods instead of pork and beans will be stocked for the more affluent, and doctors, dentists, and printers will get their start. As the service population and the population served increase, the need for other kinds of goods will grow, and at some point local raw materials will be used for the internal production of goods once shipped in from outside the region.

While the above description has been given a slightly "boomtown" flavor for effect, the story is a true one. In pre-Revolutionary America raw materials were sent to England for manufacture into clothes and equipment which were then returned to the colonies. In a short time Yankee merchants and manufacturers had taken over the production of most imported goods, and even fine glass and silver, such as the metal work of Paul Revere, were being produced in New England. In more recent times, California exported fruit and gold and lumber in exchange for almost all manufactured goods from the East. Then, as population increased, automobile and other *assembly plants* were established. Machine and automobile parts were shipped to the West and put together there, a practice which resulted in considerable savings on freight. Finally, independent branch plants of large Eastern firms were established to fabricate the parts themselves from local raw

materials or those shipped in bulk from great distances. Last of all, special industries such as electronic equipment and aircraft were located particularly in the Los Angeles area. The same story could be told of countless developing countries which before their independence provided raw materials for Europe but which following the establishment of their autonomy developed industries of their own, often out of national pride and an urge for self-sufficiency.

In this sense the pattern of growth which develops is both spiral and cumulative. It is spiral in the sense that each stage leads to the next and provides the seeds for further growth; it is cumulative in that growth allows new activities and attracts additional businesses and factories which could not exist under previous conditions.

The middle time slice shown in Figure 8–2 illustrates this stage of sustained growth. Now imports and exports of materials and goods more nearly balance each other. The region may continue to provide raw materials for other places, but it also exports finished products in large quantities. Two additional transfers keep these flows in balance. On the one hand, money transfers move capital in and out of the region as it accumulates or is needed. At the same time, migration now moves in both directions as demands for more labor develop locally or as surpluses of particular types of workers develop. All in all, the region continues to grow in wealth, complexity, and area extent.

Next the possibility for specialized development becomes apparent. Local capital still will be available for investment, but even more money from outside the region will become available if things look good to national and international investors. A labor pool with specialized skills may also form and provide incentive for other firms to open nearby. Less-skilled workers will move away to regions where earlier stages of growth still exist. Typical of this would be the continuing emphasis in Connecticut and Massachusetts on skilled artisans. At first gunsmiths, brass workers, and clocksmiths developed a tradition of precision work in that area. Subsequently the emphasis on precision, control, and feedback mechanisms required in the work led to present-day electronic firms and the production of modern precision instruments. At a still later date, the growth of research firms and universities further increased the emphasis on data handling and decision making and provided new paths for development. Knowledge becomes a commodity, and a shift to quaternary activities may result.

Inertia and change

Various forms of inertia work for the smooth flow of events described and illustrated above. Labor and venture capital have strong tendencies to stay at home. People become committed to a region for reasons other than their jobs, and few want to move, once having invested in homes and schools. We have already mentioned the conservatism of local investors. Similarly, the amortization of industrial investments, that is, the time necessary to "write off" the initial costs of equipment and structures, is slow and uneven. Nothing ever wears out all at once, and it is usually cheaper to keep making replacements and repairs rather than to abandon a site and begin over again somewhere else. Meanwhile, people nearby learn by watching the earlier firms, and a *neighborhood copying effect* further increases the size of the region as observers become participants. Finally, the investment in social overhead may be immense. As we have already mentioned, schools and homes all cost money. So do highways, shopping centers, museums, and cinemas. The inertia exerted by all these things serves to keep industrial regions intact.

Perhaps the major negative forces which may cause the modern industrial world to rethink its priorities and to seek new spatial locations are the ecological dynamics which inevitably accompany partially planned industrial growth. By "partially planned" we mean development without due regard for the total balance of man and nature. Sometimes the depletion of a raw material will cause the decline of an industrial center, but this is rarely the case. American and European steel mills as well as those in Japan depend now upon ore and scrap from sources halfway around the globe. It is more likely that the overloading of the environment with pollutants from factory smokestacks and workers' automobiles as well as with wastes of other kinds will eventually create environments which neither management nor the workers can tolerate. Moreover, if the concentration of firms demanding commonplace yet essential resources such as pure water and fresh air becomes too great, the firms themselves through overcrowding will ruin the environment that originally made the site so desirable. This sequence of urban growth and decay in its entirety can force or induce firms to shift their sites to more favorable areas. In the final analysis, it is these factors which may well tell the story of success or failure for the developed world in the decades ahead—or perhaps for the entire world.

The reader may ask at this point, "Yes, but what about development in socialistic and other economies different from our own?" We recognize that such cases have unique problems, but the important thing in every economy is to get the profits from resource use into the hands of people who are able and willing to reinvest the money in further development. In nineteenth century America those were the captains of industry whom we have already mentioned. In other places and at other times the entrepreneurs may have the guise of bureaucrats or national planners. We are not saying that all the profits in socialist economies are spent wisely or for the good of the people; we simply imply that the flow of resources, both natural and financial, needs to generate new cycles of growth rather than being hoarded, squandered in the pursuit of pleasure, or transferred out of the region. At the same time, we are not defending this spiraling cycle of growth; we are simply describing it. The ecologic implications of unlimited growth will be discussed later in the book.

Transportation and Regional Development

One might think that the character of a region depends solely upon its own resources, but its external relations are just as important. A significant element in the diagram "Regional Development, Circular and Accelerative Growth" (Figure 8–2) is the movement into and out of the developing area at any given time. Such movements are often taken for granted, but the role of transportation is too vital to leave unnoticed.

We have already shown how interaction and connectivity are essential elements of city growth. In much the same way, in order for a nation or the regions within a nation to grow there must be a progressive extension of the transportation network binding their respective parts together. This can be thought of as the spatial consolidation of the areas involved. With time, more and more point locations will be served by more and more carriers. Similarly, carrying efficiency and capacity will increase as the travel time and cost between places diminish.

"The Role of Transportation and the Bases for Interaction"

We have already seen that increased transportation allows people at greater and greater distances to share goods and ideas. The result is that the world is becoming more homogeneous. On the other hand, regions no longer need to be self-sufficient; their populations can specialize in doing the things they know best and import whatever else is needed. This tends to make the world more heterogeneous. Thus, we can think of two opposing processes at work, one resulting in regional similarities, the other in regional differences. Both are important in regional development, and both depend upon the intensity of spatial interaction. Edward L. Ullman, whose definitive essay provides the title for this sec-

tion, describes three factors which relate to the growth of interaction between people and between industries.

Complementarity is the first factor which stimulates interaction and subsequent regional development. This means that if one place has a surplus of a material or product and a second place has a matching need, an exchange will take place. However, just being different is not enough. The surplus of milk in New Zealand does little to encourage the shipment of dairy products to China. Even if politics and economics permitted, the avoidance of milk and milk products in the Chinese culture would prevent such an exchange. There must be a *supply* in one place and a *demand* in the other for interaction to occur. Where modern transportation allows the shipment of low-value bulk materials for long distances, strange alliances occur. West African iron ore finds its way to American steel mills, as does ore from Venezuela and Labrador. On the other hand, where two places produce similar things, the likelihood of exchange becomes considerably less. While some wheat is shipped in both directions across the Canadian-American border, the amount is slight compared with the amounts that are sent to other destinations.

The second factor which may promote or inhibit interregional exchanges is a presence or absence of *intervening opportunity*. This is a question of relative location—if a demand exists at some place and two or more sources of supply are available, all else being equal, the source nearest the consumer will be used. We have already seen how the Mennonites of Ontario trade in Waterloo rather than go farther to Kitchener with its more numerous stores (Chapter 5, Figure 5–14). The world is full of other examples. The forests of the Pacific Northwest became a source of lumber for Eastern states only after the forests of the upper Midwest were depleted. The iron ores of Africa and South America were sought out only after the great deposits of high-grade ore in Minnesota were essentially exhausted. At a personal scale, analyze your own use of space. How often do you go across town to a more distant park to walk your dog or play ball if some nearby place will serve just as well? Recreation places can be considered as resources, and in order for their users to travel from afar the sites must have some unique quality, like the slopes of Aspen or the geysers of Yellowstone. Otherwise, remote areas will go unused while nearer spots will attract all the customers.

What about winter ski trips to the Alps instead of Aspen, or exotic cheeses available in the supermarket next to those produced in Wisconsin or New York? Reasonable transportation cost, or *transferability*, accounts for such movements. The Alps have become available to some people for Christmas skiing as the result of large, fast aircraft, charter flights, and comparatively low prices for food and lodging in foreign areas. In other words, modern air technology has made people more transferable than before. Cheeses from France and Germany compete with American products because of low sea transportation costs. Coal and iron ore are available from remote sources because the technology of transportation has made their bulk shipment possible at low cost. In these examples low-cost transport makes it possible to supply materials in sufficient quantities. Conversely, if a product is too bulky or heavy and its market price too low to sustain proportionately large transportation payments, it cannot be used and a less expensive substitute must be found to take its place. For example, poor populations in developing countries find it difficult or impossible to pay the proportionately high costs of shipping lumber and coal and oil from distant sources. Because of this, throughout much of the arid parts of the world where trees are scarce dung is burned for fuel and mud or adobe used for building walls and even roofs. It may seem incongruous that the beaches of the Pacific Northwest are piled with driftwood free for the taking while elsewhere poor families use animal droppings for fuel. But driftwood's low value and great bulk create a lack of transferability which makes all the difference. Similarly, the plastic bottles thrown out in such profusion from American homes would be considered valuable containers anywhere in the developing world, but the cost of moving cheap plastics farther than the nearest refuse heap places them impossibly out of reach for those unable to pay the costs of transportation. Free for the taking at one point does not mean free delivery at another.

Thus for development to take place with the aid of transportation: (1) *complementarity* must exist between the developing region and other areas; (2) there should be no *intervening opportunity*; in other words, there must be a need to develop the resources within the region rather than seeking similar materials at some place nearer the market; and (3) the cost of transporting materials, people, and information must be such that they have a high degree of *transferability*. Only after these conditions have been met can development become reality. In the next chapter we will return to our isotropic or homogeneous plain in order to see how such conditions, stated in theoretical terms, influence the location of industry and industrial complexes.

Parallel to the growth of cities is the increasing complexity of the regions which contain them. This is particularly true of the industrial concentrations around which so much of the modern world revolves. We have already mentioned that in wealthy economies labor becomes its own best market. When many industries cluster together, they not only share a common labor pool and market but also reinforce each other by supplying component parts for each other's products. Since the suppliers are close to the consumers, transportation costs of such parts are low and another advantage is gained. Industries in modern times have moved closer to centers of population. It is true that there has been a recent shift of some factories from the city to the suburbs, but on a regional scale such moves are relatively insignificant. The map of the industrial regions of the United States (Chapter 10, Figure 10–16) could almost be used to show the concentrations of population in the nation.

Nevertheless, the location and procurement of raw materials and energy supplies cannot be overlooked. Every factory must in some way solve the problem of where to locate in terms of materials, labor, and customers. Some succeed; others do not. While a variety of reasons account for the location of industry, transportation plays a particularly important role. In order to fully appreciate this, we now examine several theoretical examples of industrial location.

The Spatial Equilibrium of Individual Firms

Let us start on a flat plain with a single factory utilizing an evenly distributed raw material such as some agricultural product. In this general case, the consumers and the labor force are also spread evenly over the plain. Factory operations involve three types of costs: the cost of procuring the raw material, production costs, and the cost of delivering the finished product to the consumer. For the firm to stay in business the market price must cover these costs plus a reasonable profit. Let us assume such a balance is achieved. This would result in a finite supply area around the plant from which the raw material would be provided at some average price. If this supply area were enlarged, the average price for the raw material would go up by the additional transportation cost involved. The factory would also be a definite size, that is, capable of a certain volume of output at a given cost. Everything else being equal, an equilibrium would be established which would result in a fixed wholesale price. If in order to expand the size of the market area production were suddenly increased many times without a parallel price increase, the firm would find itself in trouble. Difficulties would occur from an inevitable rise in the cost of raw materials as well as from problems in procuring additional labor and capital equipment. Management, as it sets about establishing a firm's scale of production, must therefore keep in mind the spatial constraints on procuring raw materials and labor.

The market area served by a factory is also finite. Management must take into account the number of customers who will purchase their product at the price offered. At a given factory price, additional customers are available only by enlarging the market area. This, however, would mean a price rise for all the customers in order to absorb added delivery costs. Thus, for the factory to operate successfully, all these factors must be in balance spatially as well as economically. Under such conditions it is not very practical for management to tell their salesmen to "go find new customers," for they could only find customers by going greater distances. The resulting rise in travel costs would require a price increase, which, in turn, would very likely reduce the number of customers per unit area in the original market zone. Another way to describe this is to say that most products are *price elastic*. This is an economist's term indicating the change in volume of sales that accompanies a change in price. As the price rises, more and more customers will switch to other products or do without the commodity. In our example, if the price becomes too high because of increased transportation costs, the market area will yield fewer and fewer customers and the firm's sales will drop below the break-even point.

The economics of business are embedded in a matrix of spatial constraints. The equilibrium of a firm can be upset by spatial changes such as innovations in transportation, changes in population density, and raw material yields per unit area, just as dislocations can result from changes in nonspatial attributes such as shifts in the elasticity of demand or improvements in internal economies. Similarly, nonspatial innovations may often improve a firm's productivity, but sometimes such changes have accompanying spatial consequences that can make the firm's location no longer tenable. Both parts of the picture must be clear for management to prosper.

Methods of Solving Locational Problems

The linear case

Imagine an electronic parts manufacturer serving a number of assembly plants located along a single-track rail line. The industry is a *footloose* one: that is, it can locate anywhere it chooses without changing its production costs. Parts must be delivered from the factory to each of the firms it serves, but deliveries are limited to only one firm on each trip. Where along the line should the factory be located in order to minimize the distance traveled in delivering parts to all its customers?

If it is not possible to concentrate the factory and all its customers in the same place, thereby doing away with transportation costs, travel efforts may be reduced by locating the factory at the point of *minimum aggregate travel, the point at which the sum of the travel efforts to all points in the system is at a minimum.*

Figure 9–1 shows the situation graphically. Firms F_a to F_g have fixed locations along the route. Our factory can be placed at any point along the line, including the same point as one of the assembly firms. There are at least two points which may suggest themselves to the reader. Most of us might think that the *mean*, or *average*, location along the line would be most efficient. Others might think the *median point*, with the same number of firms on each side, would represent the solution. Who is right?

We compute the *mean value*, that is, *center of gravity*, by starting at either end, summing up the distances to each firm, and dividing by the number of firms. The mean location is at the sixth unit of distance from the left. The median location with three firms on either side would be at F_d. If we compute the aggregate distance to each milepost along the line from all of the

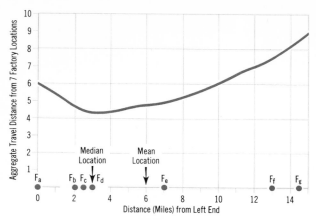

Figure 9-1 Locating the point of minimum aggregate travel for an odd number of factories along a line In a linear pattern with an odd number of elements, the point of minimum aggregate travel is the median point, that is, the point at which half the distribution is on one side and half on the other. For an asymmetrical distribution, the mean location will be some distance from the optimum aggregate travel location.

Figure 9-2 Locating the point of minimum aggregate travel for an even number of factories along a line The optimum location for the aggregate travel distance in a linear pattern of an even number of elements is indeterminate. It is located at any point along the line between the two most central elements in the distribution. The zone of optimum location could be quite large if these two points happen to be far apart.

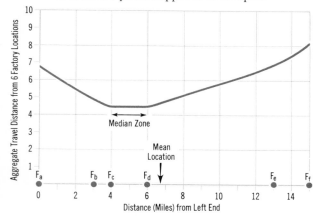

firms, we can plot the values as a curve shown on the upper part of the figure. Notice that the minimum total distance coincides with point F_d.

The situation is not so simple when an even number of points must be served. Let us consider the same case, but with six firms instead of seven (Figure 9–2). Now the median point of the distribution lies somewhere at or between the two most centrally located firms. In fact, there is no median point; rather, there exists a line segment with half the firms to the right of it and half to the left. The factory supplying parts may be located at either of the two centrally located firms or anywhere along the space between them. As long as the factory is located between the two central firms, the increased distance incurred in moving from one central firm's location is compensated by a decrease in distance from the other central firm. In other words, there is a stretch of spatially neutral territory along which any location will do. While this may seem somewhat contradictory, we will see a similar situation in the two-dimensional example that follows. The real world implications of this are important. Within industrial regions there are sometimes large areas which have such nearly equal transportation advantages that other factors, such as environmental conditions, become more significant in the final process of location.

The two-dimensional case

Let's face it, geographic reality is almost always areal rather than linear. How do we find the point of minimum aggregate travel when the points are in an area instead of along a line? Where in a park would we put a hotdog stand? Where is the best spot in a city to locate a bakery? Where in the nation should we build our assembly plant? Let us mention in passing that *the mean value, or center of gravity, of a two-dimensional distribution does not necessarily coincide with the point of minimum aggregate travel.* This is simply an extension of our same observation for the linear case.

It would be useful if there were some quick and simple way to extend the analysis of the median point from one dimension to two, but none is known. The problem is that as the observer moves around the periphery of an array or cluster of locations, the point which appears to be the median shifts according to his location. A simple example will explain this. Imagine that you are standing at the edge of a field upon which are growing a random scattering of trees. Looking straight at the field and viewing it from right to left or left to right you see a fixed sequence of trees. But since some of the trees will be nearby and others far away, as you stroll around the edge of the area the trees will appear to change their relative positions.

Because there is no simple method for finding the point of minimum aggregate travel for a set of locations on a two-dimensional plane, it is necessary to use some sort of *iterative solution*. By an iterative solution we mean a method which first approximates an answer, and thereafter, using the first results, attempts to find a better answer the second time, and so on, and so on. Each time an approximation is attempted, the results come closer to the correct answer, although it may never be reached exactly. The process of iteration is stopped when the approximate answer falls within some limits of acceptability determined by the needs of the person solving the problem.

One firm with several customers

Imagine that the electronic parts manufacturer in the linear example now wants to locate within a region across which are randomly scattered the same seven assembly firms mentioned in the linear case. This situation is shown in Figure 9–3A. Where should the manufacturer locate in order to minimize transportation costs, all else being equal? The answer to this question is the point of minimum aggregate travel. To find such a point we must use an iterative solution. One simple rule to start with is that the point of minimum aggregate travel must lie within the polygon formed by lines connecting the outermost of the scatter-

ing of customers (Figure 9–3A). Consider the sum of the distances from all of the firms to each of a set of regularly spaced points covering the entire polygon. One such set of distances is shown on the diagram. Each point has associated with it a total travel distance to all the customers. Some of these values will be relatively large and others small. The one with the smallest value is our first approximation of the point of minimum travel. If we think of the values at each of the points as tent poles of varying height sticking up above a flat plain, then we can imagine the cloth of the tent touching the tops of the vertical lines. This forms a continuous surface like the one in Figure 9–3B, which is really more like a sagging awning than a peaked tent. This surface shows the continuous change in aggregate transportation distance from any point on its surface to all the firms. If we made a physical model of the surface and released a steel ball upon it, the place where the ball would come to rest would be the point of minimum aggregate travel. This would not necessarily correspond with our shortest tent pole, but it would be nearby. This is because in the first step of the iteration the regularly spaced points are relatively far apart. To improve on this we may repeat the process by centering upon the first solution a smaller lattice with points closer together. Once more we measure and sum up the travel distances to the points in the finer lattice. A finer-grained estimate thus becomes available in the vicinity of the first minimum. We repeat this process until the change from one iteration to the next is so small that further improvement would not be worth the effort. The surface which we have constructed showing aggregate travel effort is a smooth one shaped like a shallow bowl. All the down gradients lead to the minimum point. There are no rolling hills; nor are there pits or wells on the surface. This is because there are no significant differences in the character of the transportation surface from one place to another.

A special difficulty can occur in finding the point of minimum aggregate travel if the bowl-

A. Locating Mean and Median Centers

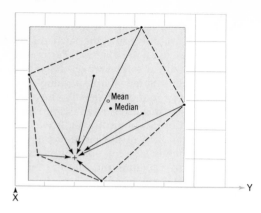

B. Aggregate Travel Surface

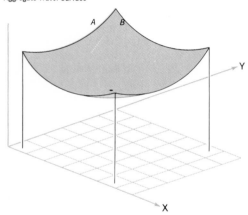

Figure 9-3 Finding the minimum aggregate travel location and the mean location of a two-dimensional point pattern (*A*) An iterative search solution is suggested for finding the point of minimum aggregate travel in a two-dimensional pattern. A lattice of points is constructed over the region in which the elements are located. Distance and travel effort are measured from each element to a lattice point, and the sum of these values is determined. The procedure is repeated for each lattice point. This set of values lies on the surface shown in part *B*, and the surface can be approximated from them. The procedure may be repeated in the vicinity of the lowest value for increased accuracy. The minimum point found in this manner is always only an approximation of the true optimum.

An analytical solution for finding the mean location is available. Project the location of the elements on two perpendicular axes. Find the ordinary arithmetic mean of the projected values on each axis. The two mean values will be the coordinates of the mean location in the two-dimensional array. This will not ordinarily be the point of minimum aggregate travel.

(*B*) An aggregate travel value may be calculated for any arbitrary point in the region in which a collection of elements is located. The collection of all such values would trace out the surface shown in the diagram. The problem then is to find the lowest point on the surface. The surface contains an infinite number of points, and therefore, the approximating method suggested above is used to approach the optimum as closely as desired. Other search methods could also be employed.

like surface is extremely shallow or perhaps even flat over part of its area. Think again of the steel ball analogy. If a ball were released at the lip of a nearly flat bowl, it would travel in a complex pattern rolling back and forth many times. Its path would depend upon where and in what direction it was started, and it would take a long time for it to settle down. If the surface were in part actually flat, there would be an area where the ball could settle just as well at one place as another. Contrast this situation with that of a funnel-shaped surface with steep sides. On such a surface

the ball would reach a single resting place almost immediately (Figure 9−4*A* and *B*).

The lesson we learn here is that if there is very little difference in the values near the absolute minimum, a zone of indeterminate location will exist which depends upon the cutoff value chosen for the iteration. In a situation where there is no marked difference among several near-optimum locations, it may be a waste of time to search for the absolute value or optimum. A typical problem in the real world would be evaluating the location of a new regional hospital. It would make sense

to locate such a facility at the point of minimum aggregate travel since the time used in an
emergency trip to the hospital might be very
critical. However, if the gradient of the aggregate travel surface were nearly flat in the vicinity of the optimum site, alternate locations
nearby might be just as good for all practical
purposes. If the exact optimum point were
already occupied by another building or function which could not be easily displaced, then
another one nearby would do nearly as well,
and would be much less expensive.

A further step in this type of analysis might
be to deal with several variables simultaneously. That is, we might first want to solve
the problem in terms of the point of minimum
aggregate travel and then consider land values
as shown by a rent surface similar to those discussed in Chapters 3 and 4. The two surfaces
could then be added together, or to look at it
another way, they could be stacked on top of
each other and their depressions and elevations combined. This is shown in a simple case
in Figure 9–4C. A major problem in such a
maneuver is to find some unit of measure com-

Figure 9-4 Monotonic statistical surfaces A
surface is monotonic if there is always a downward path from any point to the minimum point
on the surface. Clearly, search procedures are
much simplified if the surface is monotonic. It may
be monotonic but very flat in the vicinity of the
optimum, as in part A of the diagram. A rather
broad zone of indifference regarding the separation
of the true and approximated optimum may be tol-
erated with such a surface. This would not be the
case when a steep gradient to the surface exists
near the optimum, as shown in part B. In some instances, but not all, the sum of monotonic surfaces is also monotonic. Simple search procedures
may then be employed to find the minimum. The
usual problem in adding statistical surfaces is
finding a proper weighting of one relative to the
others. If one rides higher or lower on the others,
the minimum point will be shifted. If the choice
of relative value involves some ethical or moral
judgment, a scaling factor may be impossible to
determine. The researcher must then seek a consensus of opinion. Objective procedures will not
suffice.

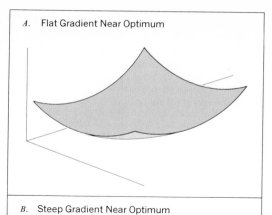

A. Flat Gradient Near Optimum

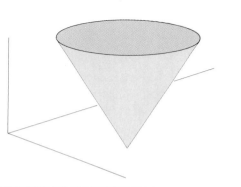

B. Steep Gradient Near Optimum

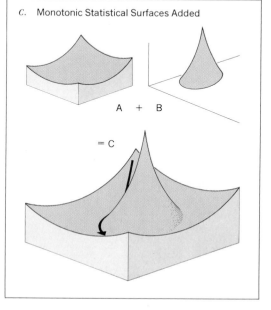

C. Monotonic Statistical Surfaces Added

A + B

= C

*Transportation
and Location:
The Search
for Optimum
Sites*

mon to both surfaces. In the case of the hospital, one measure is in value or rent per acre; the other is in minutes or seconds of accessibility. How much is a minute less in an ambu-

Figure 9-5 Production and transportation costs associated with a single firm (A) Profile of production, terminal, and carrier costs. (B) The profile rotated through a full circle. Contour lines on the surface projected to the plane show costs rising with the distance from the production location.

A. Production, Terminal and Carrier Costs

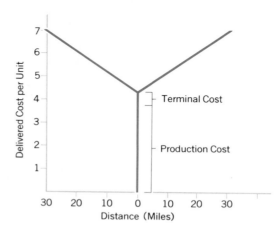

B. Total Delivery Cost in Two Dimensions

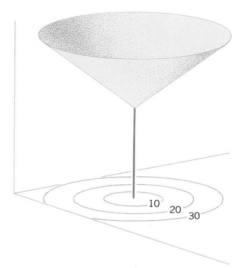

lance worth to an accident victim relative to the cost of buying more expensive land for the hospital? In cases like this, no analytic method will by itself give an answer. This is the kind of decision making that requires inputs other than those provided by science.

A panel of citizens would probably be needed to render such a decision. Medical personnel might give the panel some idea of the cost in lives attributed to the length of time between accident and hospital treatment. A cost analysis would indicate the land cost contribution to anticipated daily patient costs. Some relative weight would have to be assigned to the two types of surfaces in order to add them together. Once this was agreed upon, the analysis could be completed. The problem would not be avoided by simply adding the two surfaces without considerable soul searching. Lack of such an effort would imply that money and lives were exactly equal and the same. One value of the initial analysis is that it at least pinpoints the alternatives and forces the decision makers to consider ethical and human values. As in most things, there is no final, easy path to wisdom.

If the surfaces we add together are complex or numerous, the end result will be a rough terrain with many possible choices. At the same time, it would be nearly impossible to consider surfaces with fifty or a hundred points without the assistance of electronic computers, for thousands of calculations would be required for each iteration. In this case, we have been considering the location of a factory or business serving a number of scattered customers. Another, similar problem arises when we wish to locate a single firm having several sources of raw materials.

Best locations given multiple transport costs

Consider a mine or other source of raw materials. In order to extract the substance and prepare it by concentration, refining, or other means for shipment, certain terminal costs are inevitable. These might be shown by a vertical line such as that in Figure 9–5A. Once the material has been loaded on a carrier, transportation costs will make it increasingly expensive with each mile it travels away from its source. This is also shown in Figure 9−5A. Terminal and carrier costs combined make up the total cost of transportation. If we picture such costs three-dimensionally, they will take a shape much like an umbrella blown inside out (Figure 9−5B). Such costs can be mapped on a two-dimensional surface as a set of concentric rings (sometimes called *isotims*) increasing in value with increasing distance from the center. Now let us consider a factory which uses three such raw materials, each of which has different production and terminal costs and different shipping costs and originates at a separate point location. In all three cases, the shipment costs could be shown as a set of concentric rings increasing outward from the center (Figure 9−6). It is possible to determine the combined costs of bringing all three materials together at any point. In Figure 9−6 the combined cost of transporting materials to point A would be 10 dollars a ton for the first material, 10 dollars a ton for the second material, and 15 dollars for a ton of the third material. If we assume that all three materials are needed in equal quantities, the best location for a factory would be where the sum of these three transportation costs is least. The way to determine this point or area is to add up the three values at a large number of points on the map (Figure 9−7A). These summed costs can then be used to draw another map of the combined transportation cost surface (Figure 9−7B). Points having the same values may be joined by lines (sometimes called *isodapanes*) similar to those on a contour map. The lowest point on such a map is the ideal spot for a factory if transportation costs are the most important factor. This would be point X in Figure 9−7B.

We know that in reality such regular conditions as those just described rarely if ever occur. Special transportation rates may be assigned one material or another. Terminal costs may depend upon whether a port or mine has automated loading facilities or whether the work is all done by hand. Moreover, some shipments may travel by rail, while others come by barge or truck. In every case the sur-

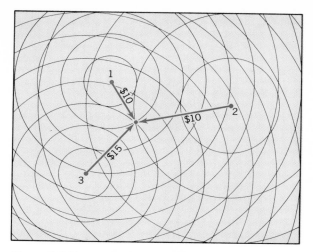

Figure 9-6 Transportation costs from three separate raw materials sources The total cost of moving raw materials from each point source to an arbitrary location, such as point A, can be estimated by use of the cost contour lines (isotims).

face representing the combined transportation costs shows high costs in some places and low costs in others.

The same thing is true for the distribution of finished goods. In this case we might consider three major cities, each representing a consumer market. Where should we locate our factory in order to minimize the costs of reaching the entire market? Isotims can be constructed around each city, and summing their values at any point, as described above, allows us to construct isodapanes similar to those describing least-cost locations for assembling raw materials (Figure 9−7B).

The principle of the *median location* can be important in the two-dimensional as well as the one-dimensional or linear case. If a particular city has more customers than the other market cities combined, it may be considered as the median location and the best spot for the factory. This can be easily illustrated. Suppose three cities, A, B, and C, have 200, 300 and 600 customers, respectively. If the factory is located in city C, there will be zero transport costs for 600 customers and some other com-

Transportation and Location: The Search for Optimum Sites

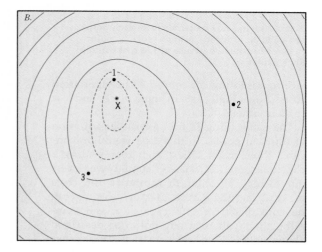

A.

```
 +71.0    +58.0    +55.3    +63.1    +76.9    +95.4

 +57.5    +40.2    +37.7    +48.9    +63.6    +85.3

 +52.3    +36.4    +35.6    +46.0    +61.0    +83.2

 +56.4    +37.4    +43.1    +54.0    +69.5    +89.3

 +71.3    +59.9    +60.6    +69.4    +83.5    +100.8
```

B.

Figure 9-7 Least cost location for assembling raw materials from three separate sources (*A*) Estimating cost surface by calculating assembly costs for a lattice of points in the space. (*B*) Contouring the statistical surface estimated in part *A*. The contours are called *isodapanes*. The minimum point may be found by the methods described in Figure 9-3.

bined cost based on a total of 500 customers located in cities A and B. If we were to move out of city C and approach cities A and B, no matter how much we saved reaching the customers in A and B we would have an additional loss of 100 units in departing from C. In the real

world this is one of the most persuasive arguments for large population concentrations attracting more and more industry, particularly if consumer goods are the item of production.

A final case might be where some of our centers represent markets and others are sources of raw materials. A contour surface showing increasing transportation costs could be constructed for each type of center. All such surfaces could be added together, and the resulting map of aggregated costs for both getting to the factory and getting from the factory to the market would indicate the places with lowest total transportation costs. All else being equal, the low spot on this map would be the best location for a factory.

Differential Transportation and Production Costs

Suppose we have two factories in direct competition with each other. How will they divide up their market areas? The simplest case would be where both have the same terminal costs of assembly and production and the same transportation costs for the finished product. Figure 9−8*A* illustrates this example. Factory F and factory F′ have equal production and terminal costs shown by the two stems; their transportation costs increase regularly with distance from their locations. The point *X* at which the transport lines intersect represents the limit of each factory's market in the area between them. The lower part of the figure

Figure 9−8 Competition for market area by two firms under varying conditions of production and transportation costs (*A*) Transportation and production costs are equal for the two firms. The market boundary is a straight line dividing the space between the two firms. (*B*) Transportation costs are equal; production costs are unequal. The market boundary is a hyperbola bending in the direction away from the firm with lower production costs. (*C*) Transportation costs are unequal; production costs are equal. The market boundary is a circle surrounding the firm with higher transportation costs. (*D*) Transportation and production costs are unequal. The market boundary encloses an egg-shaped region surrounding the firm with higher costs.

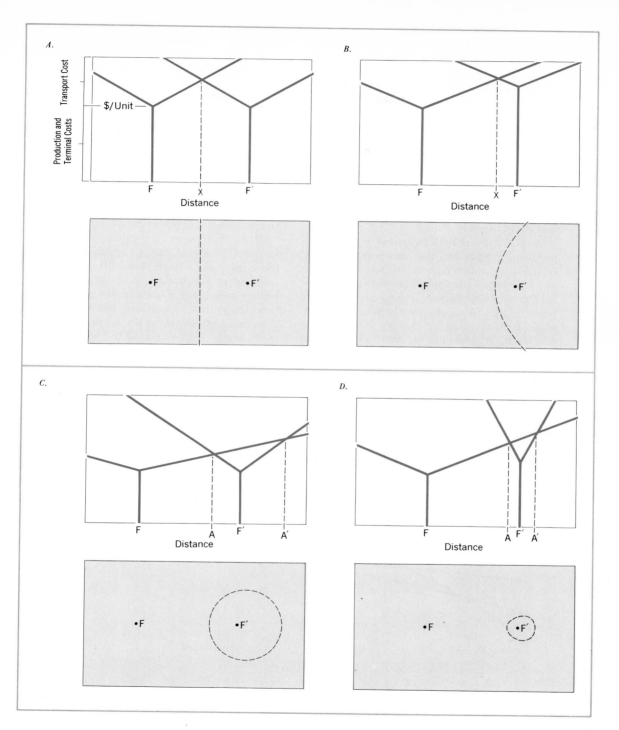

shows a map view the same situation. Note that the intersection of the two sets of equal cost lines is a straight line. This is a reflection of the complete symmetry of the costs involved.

Now suppose that one factory has substantially greater production costs although transportation remains the same for both. In this case (Figure 9–8B), the factory with lower costs has a distinct advantage in the area between the two. The point X has now shifted at the expense of factory F'. Again the lower portion of the figure shows a two-dimensional view. But now factory F has an advantage which allows its market area to partially enfold that of factory F'.

In the third case both factories have the same production costs but the transportation rates which they must pay are different. This is shown by the variation in the slope of the lines in Figure 9–8C Factory F has an advantage both in the area between them and also at some distance beyond factory F'. The two points of intersection of the transportation lines (A — A') show the limit of the second fac-

tory's market area in the linear view. The map illustrates how an advantage in the transportation costs allows factory F to completely encircle the market area of factory F'.

The progression we have followed leads inevitably to the fourth, most complicated case. In this, the factories have unlike terminal costs and unlike transportation rates for their products. Obviously, given these conditions many variations are possible. A typical case might resemble that in Figure 9–8D, which is similar to the pattern formed in Figure 9–8C. In the third example the smaller hinterland is circular in form; in the fourth the hinterland assumes a more complex egg shape.

Other variations complicate things still further. The above analysis applies only when the customers directly bear the costs of increasing transportation. In many instances a factory will have a fixed or list price for its products within a given area. If that is the case, then management must decide just how far it is willing to ship goods, all the while absorbing increasing transportation costs. If two or

Figure 9-9 Comparisons of transport costs by different types of carriers
Truck transport generally has lower terminal costs but higher carrier, or over-the-road, costs than the other types of carriers. Railroad carriers are intermediate in terminal and overhead costs between truck and ship. Water transport has very low distance costs but high terminal and overhead costs. The result is that trucks compete most efficiently at short distances, rail carriers at intermediate distances, and water carriers at longest distances.

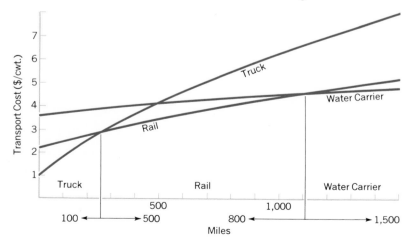

more firms are engaged in a price war, customers at considerable distances may benefit from not having to pay increased transportation. Such benefits are usually short-lived, however, and once a firm has driven its competitors out of a territory, prices may suddenly go up. In fact, subsequent prices charged by a victorious firm may actually include the costs incurred during the previous battle and pass them along to the customer! One indication of differentials in pricing based on transportation is the legend seen in certain advertisements: "Prices higher west of the Mississippi."

Variations in the Cost of Transportation

No interaction can take place without movement, and no movement has zero transportation costs. In the preceding sections we have been primarily concerned with the location of raw materials, industries, and markets. Let us now consider some basic differences in the transportability of materials and goods. Different types of carriers offer different advantages; at the same time certain commodities or materials are either more expensive or less expensive to ship than others. Finally, institutional arrangements such as special rates or other preferred treatment impose variations on the cost of transportation. Figure 9–9 illustrates differences in the cost of several types of carriers. Some commodities may serve the same end purpose but may have different forms, different content, and different degrees of transportability. Table 9–1 illustrates this for one of the most general of all commodities, energy, in some of the many forms in which it is moved. In this instance, terminal and over-the-road costs have been included in a single figure. We have omitted human porters from both figures, for their use results in astronomical costs. If a coolee or a porter on safari were to eat 1 pound of rice per day and could carry a 100-pound load, and if his trip out and back from his starting point were to last 50 days with no "refueling" stops along the way, half his load on the trip out would be "fuel" for the journey!

Table 9–1 Costs of Moving Energy*

Type	Cost, $
Coal by oxcart (labor only)†	190,056
Lignite by rail	4,456
Fuel wood by rail	3,866
Manufactured gas by pipeline	3,866
Electricity (at 60% load factor)	2,345
Oil by tank truck	2,005
Coal by rail	1,725
Natural gas by pipeline	1,720
Oil by rail	1,372
Oil by pipeline (high estimate)	600
Coal by freighter (normal)	483
Oil by tanker (high estimate)	170
Oil by pipeline (low estimate)	105
Oil by tanker (low estimate)	85

*Various fuels converted to electrical equivalents. Dollars per million killowatthour moved a distance of 500 kilometers. Assumed rate of energy return: 20 percent of the contained energy. Loading and carrying costs combined.
†Estimate by Kolars based on criteria similar to those cited in the source note below. Oxcart, labor only: per ton per kilometer, $0.62; with 1,220 pounds coal (yielding 1,000 killowatthours) gives $0.378 per kilometer for 1,000 killowatthours. Loading cost assumed to be the same as fuelwood: $1.056 per 1,000 killowatthours.

Source: *Energy Sources of the World*, U.S. Department of State Publication 3428, June 1949.

Weight-gaining and weight-losing industries

Certain products weigh more and more as they move from one stage to another of their production. These are called *weight-gaining* commodities. Other finished products weigh less than the original materials from which they are made. These are called *weight-losing* commodities.

Bottled soft drinks are a good example of a weight-gaining commodity. The initial ingredient is usually a concentrated syrup produced at a few regional locations. The syrup is shipped to local bottling plants where locally available water—by far the largest and heaviest ingredient—is added. Bottles, another heavy part of the end product, are also most often procured locally, even from the market

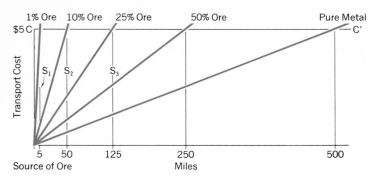

Figure 9-10 Adjusted transport rate, by grade of ore and distance range, for a constant transport charge The diagram shows the effect of ore grade on the distance an ore can be shipped. An ore is valued by the amount of pure metal it contains. It takes twice as much ore to get the same amount of metal from an ore with half the metal content of a higher-grade ore. Consequently, for a fixed transport cost on the usuable part of the ore, a low-grade ore cannot travel as far as a high-grade ore or the pure metal. Very low-grade ore—e.g., 1 percent or less—can hardly be moved from the ore deposit. Therefore, smelters for low-grade ores are found at the ore deposit. Higher-grade ores may be moved toward the market.

itself in the case of returnable bottles. Most of the total transportation costs are incurred in the last few miles between the local plant and neighborhood retail outlets. Such industries will be consumer-oriented.

The iron and steel industry is a good example of a weight-losing activity. Ore, coal, limestone, scrap, water, and other materials are used in very large quantities to produce smaller amounts of the end product. In cases such as this, producers will try to minimize the distances that raw materials are hauled, while finished goods will travel farther. In other words, the factory will be located nearer the raw materials than the market.

This relationship is clearly shown in Figure 9–10. This diagram assumes the location of a mine or metal source at the intersection point of the two axes. The rays or lines extending outward from that point indicate the accumulation of transportation costs with increasing distance for five kinds of mate-

rials ranging from a completely pure one ready for further processing to an ore containing only 1 percent of the desired substance. This figure assumes that the cost of moving a ton of pure substance will be the same in all cases and that the cost of moving less than pure materials has been *adjusted* in direct proportion to the amount contained. That is, it will cost twice as much to move a ton of iron in the form of 50 percent ore as it will to move a ton of iron in the form of 100 percent pig iron. Typical metals in the form of ore would include high-grade hematite ore, which is 50 percent iron; bauxite, which is approximately 25 percent aluminum; and copper ore, which often contains 1 percent or less of the sought-after metal. The cost of moving a ton of pure material is shown by the horizontal line c—c'. If that cost represents the maximum amount allowable for transporting any raw or semi-finished material, then the intersection of each of the transportation cost lines with c—c' will mark the farthest that that particular substance could be shipped from its source. Thus, hematite could travel from the mine to a smelter at S_1; bauxite from the mine to S_2; and copper ore from its source to S_3. In all these cases, the more waste material accompanying each pound of metal, the more quickly the allowable transportation costs of the metal will accumulate and the closer to the mine will the smelter or refinery, of necessity, be located. Though in reality such shipments become much more complicated, the above conditions are still the essential reasons that the processing of weight-losing raw materials is located far from the market and nearer to the sources.

A special case of particular historical interest is manufacturing prior to the Industrial and Transportation Revolutions. In the Middle Ages and before, the materials used and the goods produced by a single craftsman weighed considerably less than the food consumed by him during the year. Thus, the total transportation costs involved could be minimized by locating the workshops of artisans in agricultural areas. The term *cottage industry* takes on a new meaning when viewed this way. It was cheaper and more efficient to bring the materials to the workers than to transport food long distances to workers living near sources of raw materials. It was also less costly to move the finished products to the cities than it was to support large numbers of workers in urban areas. Only with the improved transportation and manufacturing techniques developed during the nineteenth century could settlements grow through large cityward migrations of workers. Before then the cost of moving food and raw materials was greater than the cost of transporting the finished goods.

Rate structures

Another important variation in transportation costs results from different rate structures, that is, different methods of assessing aggregate transportation costs. In general three types of rate structures are used for determining the cost of transportation. The first is a *postage stamp* rate in which a single charge for transportation is made regardless of the distance the item is shipped. The second is a *blanket rate* in which the area served is divided into zones or regions, each with a uniform freight rate throughout but with farther zones having higher rates charged. Figure 9–11 shows a typical blanket freight rate structure for lumber originating in the Pacific Northwest. The third type of charge is a *mileage rate*. In this type there is some direct or proportional charge made for each unit of distance a commodity is shipped.

Rates often vary from straight linear relationships, for economies of scale are gained by shipping the same quantity of something longer and longer distances. Most carriers charge high per mile costs for local shipments, intermediate costs for shipments to somewhat farther places, and relatively low

Figure 9-11 Blanket freight rate structure The map shows freight rates for lumber, in cents per 100 pounds, originating in the Pacific Northwest. Large sections of the country can be reached for the same cost. Values for the nearer Western states are not shown. Flat rate zones are much smaller for shorter hauls, if they exist at all. (R. J. Sampson, *Railroad Shipments and Rates from the Pacific Northwest,* Bureau of Business Research, University of Oregon, Eugene, Ore., 1961, p. 45, map 1)

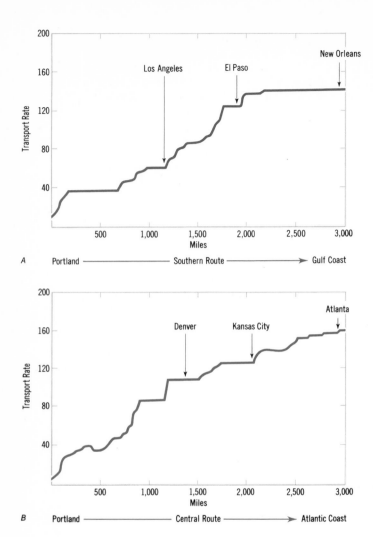

Figure 9-12 Freight rate profiles for the transport of lumber and plywood from Portland, Oregon, across the United States via the central route to the South Atlantic Coast and via the southern route to the Gulf Coast. (Op. cit., Figure 9-11, pp. 40-41, charts 2 and 3)

utilized. This results in an irregular, gradually flattening profile for the transportation cost line leading away from the source of the materials shipped. Figure 9-12 shows this for lumber and plywood from Portland, Oregon, destined for the southern United States. Imagine the complications encountered if transportation lines as irregular as the one shown here were to be used in the figures illustrating the models in the preceding section. In the real world not only do the complications increase, but strange situations are often found. Notice in Figure 9-12B how it is actually cheaper to ship things 500 miles from Portland than to ship them 400 to 450 miles. A similar example exists for an area beyond Kansas City at a distance of about 2,300 miles. In these and many other cases the rates charged by shippers reflect the competition of local products or other means of transportation. Thus, railroads often lower their rates on routes parallel to navigable waterways so that they can compete with the water transportation.

The role of competition between carriers in industrial locations

Most industries have stages of production in which logistics enter as an important variable. All such firms are concerned with seeking the best location for their facilities and with obtaining the best transportation rates bargaining can provide.

The American aluminum industry offers an example of this point. Aluminum is made from bauxite, a 25 percent ore, the bulk of which is now imported from Caribbean and South American deposits (Jamaica, Surinam). Bauxite is processed mechanically and by heat to yield aluminum oxide (alumina) which is 50 percent aluminum by weight. Facilities for this stage are found in the Gulf port cities such as Mobile, New Orleans, and Baton Rouge. The final stage of reduction to pure aluminum is accomplished by electrolysis and requires a large energy input. It takes 13,000 kilowatthours of electricity to make 1 ton of aluminum. The industry has great

costs per unit distance to remote places. This has the advantage to the shipper of extending his market area beyond its normal limits. Nearby customers may actually underwrite the transportation costs of customers at greater distances when this type of shipping rate is

incentive to locate this stage of production in a region where energy is plentiful and cheap. For a time the Pacific Northwest was the best location for aluminum reduction mills because of the low-cost electricity made available by the well-developed hydroelectric power plants of that region. In the 1960s, however, advances in the generation of electricity by coal-fired steam plants made the Ohio Valley, with its cheap coal resources, attractive to aluminum companies. The Pacific Northwest plants require a very long rail haul from the Gulf ports, and then much of the finished aluminum must travel back across the country to the industrial East with its aluminum fabricating plants which make up a large part of the wholesale market. A considerable transportation savings was achieved when most of the new aluminum plants ended up on the banks of the Ohio. Not only could the river water be used for cooling, but also it made possible barge delivery of the aluminum oxide processed on the Gulf. The railroads offered rail rates competitive with the barge rates, and as a result, none of the aluminum plants use the Mississippi-Ohio river system for barge traffic. One could still say, however, that they have benefited from the presence of the river, for if the threat of barge transportation did not exist, the refining mills' bargaining power with the railroads would be diminished.

One of the results of optimizing locations is that certain areas of the world become identified with particular activities. These areas can be thought of as land use *regions*. The next chapter describes methods of identifying types of regions whether they are formed by spatial optimizing activities or other unrelated processes.

10 | DIVIDING SPACE AROUND AND WITHIN CITIES: REGIONAL ANALYSIS

Regions as Mental Constructs

We succeed as living creatures largely through our ability to impose some sort of mental order on the infinite combinations of reality which surround us. We do this by continuously learning to classify and categorize all our impressions and perceptions of the world. A baby soon learns that the world it inhabits does not consist of an immense number of unique items and actions but rather is made up of sets of similar things. Thus, the first door a toddler sees may seem entirely different from the second one, but in a very short time he learns to lump all such contraptions into a single set called *doors* with certain attributes.

Space is one of the most important things about which babies and children learn, and as they grow up, they acquire more and more knowledge about the locational geography of their environments. All of us go through similar stages of development. These processes are usually intuitive and take two forms. We construct maplike images based on the geography we have encountered. Such *mental maps* help us to navigate from place to place. In all cases, we identify specific portions of the earth's surface, place limits of some sort around each one, and form emotion-filled value judgments about every area thus identified.

Areas to children may have the rich nuances of the playpen, living room floor, grassy yard, city street, or playground. For adults, areas may evoke all manner of responses from fear and anger to pleasure and longing. This is particularly true as we begin to think about and become concerned with areal locations such as *the Deep South, the industrial Northeast, Harlem and Westchester, North and South Vietnam*, and *the Near East*. Whenever we identify some geographical area, we are *regionalizing* earth-space. That is, we are categorizing and assigning qualities and values on a locational basis. We are delimiting *regions*, however intuitively, and as a result have become practicing geographers.

We regionalize our environments in order to simplify, understand, and manipulate them. That is, once we have identified a specific area and assigned certain attributes to it, we can act in terms of the good or bad qualities it represents to us. This is such a natural way to behave that we seldom stop to analyze the process by which we perceive and identify these regional constructs which bring order to our lives. If we do think closely about what we are doing, we soon realize that regions are strange things. We could not survive without our ability to categorize space, and yet as we attempt to be more and more precise in defining the places important to us, the less successful we become. Ask yourself a few questions about the regions which concern you most, such as the area in which your house is located, the political unit in which you pay local taxes, or any of the potential war zones throughout the world. Where are the exact boundaries of your neighborhood? If you are now part of a college community, is your town geographically split between "town and gown"? If so, can you draw the geographic border between the two sectors? If you want to move to the suburbs or you already live there, where is the line separating them from the city?

If we are going to organize our lives geographically by means of regions, we should know more about them. Let us look at some examples of how the regions important in our lives can be most evasive mental constructs and why we need to be more specific in their use. This entails several problems, among them problems of regional definitions, problems of scale, and problems of distributions and their intensities.

Problems of Defining Regions
The Near East

For years the newspapers have been filled with stories about the latest crisis in the Near East. Just to confuse matters, the same crises are occurring in the Middle East, which apparently is the same place; or is it? Let us simplify matters for the moment and call the region by either term. The United States and Russia have come close to war as the result of power struggles in that part of the world. If the area known as the Near East is so important, it should be easy to define.

What do you think constitutes the Near East? There is desert there, so we might be able to define it by drawing a line on a map marking the areas with 10 inches or less of rainfall per year. But such a line does not do the job. The areas of the world falling within the 10-inch rainfall line include deserts on every continent except Europe. That will not do!

The Near East is where the Arabs live. But Arabs also form a significant minority in part of East Africa. At the same time other places which we might have strong intuitive feelings for including in the region are populated almost entirely by Jews (Israel), Turks (Turkey, Northwest Iran, Soviet Central Asia), Persians (Iran), and Copts (Ethiopia). Try again.

Well, the geographical distribution of Islam, one of the great monotheistic religions of the world, should identify the Near East. But Islam is the major religion of both Bangladesh and West Pakistan, Indonesia, and much of East Africa. Besides, what about the beliefs of the Black Muslims in America?

It is clear that aridity, ethnic origin, language, and religion do not define the Near East. What about purely political definitions which give simple lists of countries within the region? Table 10–1 lists some of the various country-by-country definitions of the Near (Middle) East during the last 75 years.

We cannot exhaust all the possible definitions of the Near East at this point. For the moment we wish only to emphasize that the confusion outlined here is not unusual when it comes to defining particular regions. Let us just remember that when the fate of nations hangs in the balance, we need to keep our terms straight—and that includes regional definitions.

Nodal regions and uniform regions

Regions are one way of simplifying and describing phenomena which are distributed through space and which, therefore, have the potential for being locationally defined. If we turn to the earlier chapters of this book, we quickly see that two classes of map patterns have been used to illustrate the many different comments regarding man's use of space. The first shows the extent and linkages of hierarchially organized systems. Typical of these would be the maps in Figure 5–14 illustrating the shopping preferences of two culture groups in Ontario, Canada. The second type of map includes all those showing the spatial distribution of sets of like objects, activities, and conditions. These distributions appear on the maps as intensities such as those in Figure 1–3,

Table 10–1   Political Definitions of the Near (Middle) East

Source	Countries
D. G. Hogarth, *The Near East,* 1902	Albania, Montenegro, Southern Serbia, Bulgaria, Greece, the Ottoman lands of Asia, the entire Arabian peninsula, the southern two-thirds of Persia
Middle East Air Command (Great Britain, on the eve of World War II)	Egypt, Sudan, Kenya
Commander in Chief, Middle East Operations, World War II	Egypt, Sudan, Cyprus, Iraq, Aden, British Somaliland, the Persian Gulf area (a region within a region!), Eritrea, Lybia, Greece, Crete, Iran
Middle East Institute, Washington, D.C. (post-World War II)	Morocco to East Pakistan and Russian Turkestan
American Friends of the Middle East—Executive Vice President, 1953–1954	"The Middle East can be defined as comprising those countries between the Pillars of Hercules and the Straits of Macassar in which, if an injustice is perpetrated in one, a protest will be raised in the others— plus Israel"

Source: After Roderic H. Davison, "Where is the Middle East?" in *The Modern Middle East*, Richard N. Nolte (ed.) Atherton, New York, 1963, pp. 13–29.

where per capita income is divided into subclasses ranging from poor to rich. Another kind of intensity shown by maps is a binary or dichotomous one. That is, every observation has simply a *yes/no* or *exists/does not exist* value. Political units are good examples of this. Point Barrow, Alaska, is just as much in the United States as is Topeka, Kansas. But cross 1 inch beyond the border into Canada and you are absolutely in another country with different rules based on a different government.

In the first type of map, movement, linkages, and organization are important. The regions depicted by these maps are organized around foci or nodes and are called *nodal regions*, or sometimes *functional regions*. The second type of map shows regions which are uniform or homogeneous throughout and which are not thought of in terms of their organization. Regions of this latter type are called *uniform regions*; they are also sometimes referred to as *formal* or *homogeneous regions*.

In a few minutes you will probably lay down this book and casually glance at the tabletop upon which it rests. Your immediate impression of the table's surface will be one of a uniform or homogeneous surface. But look closer; stains and scratches, differences in the finish, perhaps variation in the material from which it is made, create a kind of heterogeneity. Now stand back from the table. Its surface will again assume a uniform appearance. In turn, the table will become part of a mixture of furniture and furnishings which make up your room. Similarly, every part of the building in which you live will seem unique and designed for a particular purpose. But if you leave your residence and travel some distance from it, you may very well think of it and the property upon which it stands as a single unit called *home*. Thus at each successive change in scale we alternate between heterogeneous and homogeneous interpretations of the world.

When we view the human organization of space, we see areas composed of many similar units, such as farms, having little horizontal connectivity but with major linkages leading to distant focal points. The repetition of like objects in general creates an impression of areal uniformity. If we look at a larger, more encompassing area, the focal point of the system becomes apparent and appears as a nodally organized portion of a hierarchy. The alternation of our view is between uniform regions and nodal regions.

Multiple property regions

The hinterland of Mobile, Alabama, discussed in Chapter 4 is an example of a nodal region. In this case, a complex city forms the central hub from which all manner of things, including newspapers and services, flow outward and into which supplies and customers find their way. One set of preference lines or linkages cannot show all the activities which define the city and its hinterland. Neither does a single boundary serve to delimit the farthest

reach of Mobile. Here is a case where multiple criteria define the urban region which interests us. The problem is to choose an average boundary for the city's hinterland representing several factors instead of a single boundary for a single activity.

There can be as many boundaries drawn around a city as there are types of retail, wholesale, service, administrative, and all other functions available within it. Because of this, Ullman's study of Mobile shows a kind of transition zone marking the outer limits of the city's influence. This zone is actually defined by several boundaries, not just one. Regional boundaries are often delimited in this manner. An analysis of the boundary between the hinterland regions of New York City and Boston further illustrates this point. Figure 10–1 shows the division of southern New England between the two metropolises based on seven indicators. Three areas are clearly defined: a region belonging exclusively to Boston, another to New York City, and a wide transition zone between the two. There is considerable areal overlap between many types of nodally organized hierarchies centered in Boston and New York. The solution to the problem of assigning areas to either of these two central nodes is found by determining the direction of dominant movement for whatever indicator is used. For example, the suburbs of Boston are classed within the hinterland of that city because an overwhelming number of telephone calls are directed from them to Boston's downtown area. A very large number of calls are also made from Boston's suburbs to New York City, but the dominant direction of movement is to Boston. This same idea of dominance determining association can apply to many kinds of indicators and to many problems of regional delimitation.

Continuous and discrete observations

Consider two uniform regions: a field of wheat and the climatic zone within which it is found. If we walk through the field, we will see that it is composed of individual plants largely independent of their neighbors. Now let us

Dividing Space Around and Within Cities: Regional Analysis

161

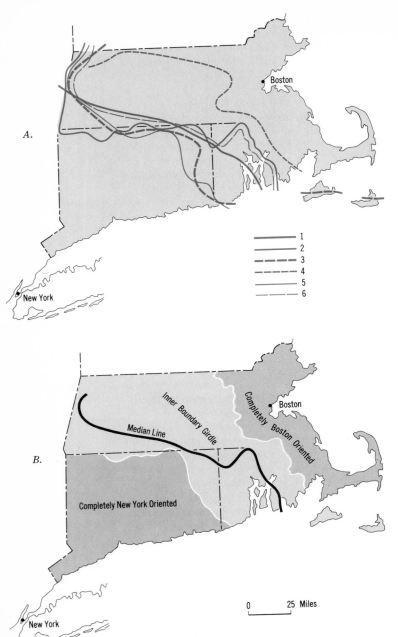

consider temperature, one aspect of the climate of area. Since the sun shines everywhere upon the air above the field, there is no part of it which is not affected by radiant energy. In fact, by definition, even the absence of radiant energy constitutes a measure of temperature. No matter how small an area we choose to observe, no matter how finely we subdivide our climatic area, we can always assign a temperature to the area under observation. This is not to say that the temperature will be everywhere the same. Differences in the slope of the ground, the reflectivity of the surface, and numerous other conditions introduce variations from place to place. But temperature will exist everywhere; only our observations of it are discontinuous. In other words, phenomena such as temperature are continuous variables over space. This is true of human as well as of natural phenomena. We have previously referred to the dichotomous and therefore continuous character of political jurisdictions. You cannot for purposes of observation subdivide a nation into areas so small that they will fall through the sieve of political jurisdiction and land in some apolitical space. On the other hand, almost all economic observations, whether per capita income, productivity, or capitalization, are based on discrete units of observation. We may describe Appalachia as a poverty region, but in the last analysis our figures are based on the incomes of individual human beings. Furthermore, the uniformities we plot on per capita income maps are aver-

coach passenger flows, (2) newspaper circulation, (3) telephone calls, (4) business addresses of directors of manufacturing firms, and (5) correspondent banks. Two other indicators not shown on the map were metropolitan origin of vacationers and an estimate of truck freight movement. (B) The median, or middle line, of the seven functional indicators was then used to define the boundary between hinterlands of the two metropolises. The boundary zone on either side of the median line shows the zone of partial dominance. (Maurice H. Yeates and Barry J. Garner, *The North American City*, Harper & Row, New York, 1971, p. 102; after H. L. Green, "Hinterland Boundaries of New York City and Boston in Southern New England," *Economic Geography*, vol. 31, no. 4, October, 1955)

Figure 10-1 Delimitation of hinterland boundaries between Boston and New York City (A) The median boundaries for a selection of activities were established in New England between Boston and New York City. The activities were (1) railroad and

ages or means and incorporate paupers below the level shown as well as rich people hidden in the crowd. In every case where we deal with uniform regions it is wise to keep in mind whether the phenomena dealt with are discrete or continuous.

The space-time framework for regionalization

The frequency and timing of our observations will also affect our interpretation of whatever we analyze. Both of these conditions can be thought of as scale differences, but one operates in time while the other operates in space. The two together constitute a space-time frame of reference of immense importance.

If we study the expansion of the United States across North America and choose to view the process only at 100-year intervals beginning in 1776, we will learn few details about the order in which statehood occurred (Figure 10–2). The time interval chosen is inappropriate for our purposes. We would do better to look at the country every decade, as in Figure 10–3. On the other hand, if we wish to study commuter patterns in metropolitan areas, we must sample the area at least every six hours. Measures made by the decade are of scant use for planning better traffic patterns and controls.

Returning to our spatial point of view, we must study the territorial expansion of the United States using all North America as our spatial frame and using states, whatever their size, as the statistical subdivisions. To make sense out of commuter patterns we need to look at entire metropolitan areas with reasonably small subdivisions, since most commuters leave the central cities when their work is done but at the same time do not travel far from them. As in all research the upper and lower limits of the scale of investigation should be carefully considered. We must always avoid using too many units or too few. This applies to time as well as space. Too many units— that is, too fine a filter—will hide significant relationships by isolating each observation in its own location and moment in history. Too few units—a sieve with too large a mesh —will allow clots and clusters of data to pass unobserved by hiding significant rela-

Figure 10-2 Statehood at 100-year intervals.

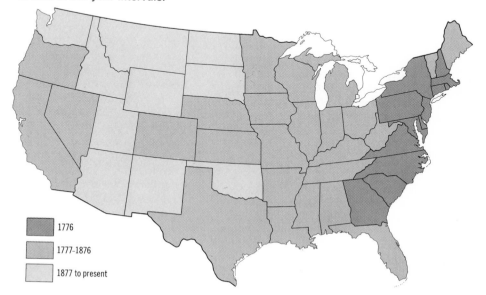

1776

1777-1876

1877 to present

Dividing Space Around and Within Cities: Regional Analysis

163

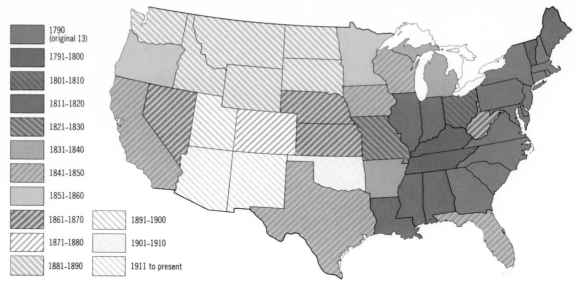

Legend:

- 1790 (original 13)
- 1791–1800
- 1801–1810
- 1811–1820
- 1821–1830
- 1831–1840
- 1841–1850
- 1851–1860
- 1861–1870
- 1871–1880
- 1881–1890
- 1891–1900
- 1901–1910
- 1911 to present

Figure 10-3 Statehood at 10-year intervals.

tionships within statistical averages compiled for meaningless aggregations.

Methods of Identifying Regions

When we attempt to identify a region, we are most often concerned with several characteristics rather than a single feature of the area. Single-feature regions like the retail outlets and customer distributions to which we have already referred are less of a challenge to define than more complicated regional types. In order to illustrate methods of regional identification we now present some problems necessitating more complicated regional analysis.

Areal overlays

One of the simplest and best ways of locating multiple uniform regions consisting of overlapping criteria is to plot each of several characteristics either on the same map or on transparent overlays which may then be superposed upon each other. The area having the greatest number of overlapping portions may be defined as the region or at least as the core of the region in question. This technique has paral-

lels in the mathematical use of Venn diagrams and in set theory, which will be commented on after the following example.

The overlay technique can be illustrated by a very practical problem recently solved by one of the authors. A large bank wished to establish a branch office in the suburbs of its home city. According to the law of its state, branch banks may be located in unincorporated suburban territories but only in *established community centers*. In other words, outside the city limits of any settlement, new banks can only be opened in recognizable settlements although such places have not yet incorporated or formed legal identities for themselves. In the case in question, the parent bank hoped to prove that a certain small unincorporated collection of homes, businesses, and service establishments constituted a viable community despite its lack of legal identity. If this could be proved, the bank could then build its branch office there and conduct business. The problem of establishing the functional validity of the settlement in question was a very geographic one.

As in any regional problem there were three steps necessary in its solution: (1) The term *established community center* had to be defined in a way which would allow the area in question to be systematically compared with the theoretical definition; (2) a suitable scale of research had to be determined; (3) actual research techniques and analysis had to be decided upon and carried out.

The problem of definition was met by use of the same kind of geographic reasoning which we have already presented in earlier chapters. The following is an excerpt from the formal argument presented to the Federal Comptroller of Currency, who decided the case.

Economic, political and social organization of metropolitan areas takes the form of nested hierarchies. Some functions are regional in scope, others metropolitan and still others local. An economic example of such a hierarchy is retail shopping centers. Some are regional in character, serving large regions in the metropolitan area. Others are community retail centers and still others serve as local convenience shopping centers. Political organization follows the same pattern. Some urban services have regional jurisdiction and taxing base, others county-wide and others local. Similar social organizations exist. Club memberships, church groups, school districts, and local businesses organize the community at the local scale for social purposes. Unincorporated villages are a type of community organization at the lower level of this hierarchy. We may claim that a concentration of such local activities, when not an incorporated place, is still the organizing focus of the surrounding territory out to at least half the distance to the next concentration of services of comparable size. Natural and man-made barriers may modify the extent of this influence. A branch bank, which is a local economic activity operating at the convenience level, may be expected to seek out such a cluster of community activities as the most effective location in which to reach the people of the local community.

By this definition, proof of the viability of the settlement in question depended upon being able to demonstrate its centrality or focality from an economic, administrative, and social point of view.

The scale of investigation was more or less pragmatically determined. An area including and larger than the settlement had to be shown. At the same time, a very large area including numerous such settlements was unnecessary since similar settlements would subdivide the area into roughly equal-sized low-order hinterlands. Therefore, an area roughly 6 by 6 miles with the settlement near its center was selected (Figures 10-4 to 10-6).

Three research techniques were used in the analysis. To begin, five overlapping service areas were plotted on the map: (1) fire districts, (2) police districts, (3) voting precincts, (4) elementary school districts, and (5) postal districts. The subsequent overlap of these services is shown in Figure 10-4. Next, the addresses of a random sample of local library patrons were plotted on the map along with similar samples of a cleaning establishment's customers, members of the local Veterans of Foreign Wars post, and members of the Rotary and Kiwanis Clubs (Figure 10-5). These distributions represent a more nodally organized set of activities but again helped to confirm the evidence of centrality presented by the first analysis. Finally, the number of urban land parcels per quarter square mile were counted for the entire 64-square-mile area. It was reasoned that urban-sized land parcels rather than farm-sized properties are a de facto proof of urbanization. The density of small-sized land parcels shown in Figure 10-6 coincides rather neatly with the overlap of service areas on the first map and the cluster of customers and members on the second. To make a long story short, the central area in question was judged to be an *established community center*, and the case was decided in favor of the bank. From the point of view of this discussion, the analysis had established the functional validity of a small, low-order urban region.

A note on Venn diagrams and set theory

Readers with some background in logic or mathematics will recognize certain similarities between the technique of overlaying one regional characteristic on another and the use of

Van Buren Township

I-94

Romulus Township

Huron Township

1" = 4000'

Areas Receiving Multiple Service from Romulus Village
Number of Overlapping Services

1   2   3   4   5

Service Areas Include:

Police District
Fire District
Postal District
Voting Precinct
Elementary School

Figure 10-4 Public service jurisdictions of the unincorporated village of Romulus, Michigan   An unincorporated village, by definition, has no boundaries. The central office or facility of each of the services listed was in the built-up section of the unincorporated village of Romulus. Each public service jurisdiction was plotted separately on the map. A functional definition of the village territory was defined as the zone with maximum overlap of the service jurisdictions.

Venn diagrams to sort out overlapping phenomena. Any collection of related or like things or activities can be thought of as a *set*. For example, all types of land use found in cities might be a single set. An individual and particular land use, such as a park or rail yard, is considered an *element* of the set. Closely related land uses—parks, playgrounds, bicycle paths, ball fields—can be thought as *subsets*

within the set of urban land uses. Sets of one kind of element may overlap other sets and become subsets of more than one set. For example, the set of land uses known as *recreational* can be found as subsets of *urban land use* and *rural land use*. The largest grouping which includes all elements under consideration is called the *universal set*.

As Peter Haggett points out, maps may be

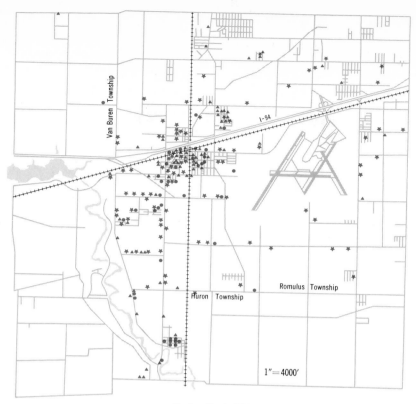

* Members Kiwanis, VFW Post, Rotary Club
• Cleaning Establishment Customers
▲ Library Users

Figure 10-5 Home place sample of members and customers of Romulus-centered activities The range of certain central place functions of the unincorporated village was established by plotting the home address of a sample of members and customers of Romulus-based activities.

considered a special type of Venn diagram. Thus you may think of all the countries in the Western Hemisphere as a universal set, the countries of South America as a subset, and a single South American country as an element within both the set and subset. In this case, spatial contiguity plays an important role. In the more general case, nonspatial characteristics define at least some of the characteristics of the elements. For example, the universal set might again be all the countries of North and South America, but the subset could be major producers of wheat and beef. Elements within the latter subset would then include Argentina and the United States, which, obviously, are

noncontiguous. This emphasizes the necessity of keeping the operational definitions of the problem clearly defined. It is also necessary to keep in mind that most Venn diagrams are maps not of geographical space but of abstract spaces often specified by nonmetric definitions.

Venn diagrams deal often with a finite and rather neat geographic world containing well-defined units with clear characteristics. Reality is messier than that.

The most widely used method by means of which complex associations of variables can be simplified is factor analysis or principle component analysis. The next section shows

Density Values Represent Number of Urban Parcels per Quarter Square Mile

■ 100 or More	▨ 50 to 100	▨ 10 to 50	□ less than 10

Large Urban Establishments

▨ Commercial and Industrial

Figure 10-6 Urban land parcel density in the vicinity of Romulus, Michigan   A land parcel map was employed to determine the density of land parcels in the vicinity of the unincorporated village of Romulus. A lattice of points was laid over the map, and the number of parcels of land within a square centered on the point and half a mile on each side were counted. A density surface was so defined, and contours on that surface revealed the contiguously built territory of the village. This method of establishing boundaries is morphological rather than functional. The two methods described in Figures 10-5 and 10-6 were functional. Counting housing density or street intersections would be two other morphological techniques for defining urban areas.

how this technique has been used to look at the distribution of economic development throughout the world.

Factor and principle component analysis

Regions, like people, are complicated and unique but at the same time share similarities. Just as everyone has a head and two arms and two legs, so may regions share commonalities such as similar population densities, climates, and vegetation. If we look closely at people, however, we observe different skin pigmentation, as well as straight hair and curly hair; blonde, brunette, and black hair; big noses and small ears; big ears and small noses. But the important thing is that despite a confusion of physical detail, we can perceive apparent if sometimes elusive patterns by means of which we can tell one group from another. For example, if we encounter a collection of people with high cheek bones, a fold of skin at the inner corner of the eye, and straight black hair, we might classify them as Mongoloid rather than Caucasoid or Negroid peoples. With additional effort and analysis we might be able to identify or categorize them as Japanese or Chinese. If we went further and took their cultural attributes into consideration, our identification would become almost positive. There would be exceptions to our general description of all people claiming Japanese ancestry, but the probability of such variations would be low, since the Japanese share a common cultural heritage as well as genetic background. To put it another way, we can describe a range of physical and/or cultural attributes belonging to a particular people by using a single comprehensive term, in this case *Mongoloid* or, more specifically, *Japanese.* The problem is to sort out the details into sets of related characteristics and to arrive at systems of classification which can account for all the details in terms of a few basic types.

One analytical technique by means of which numerous characteristics associated with any phenomenon can be compared, sorted, and accepted or rejected on the basis of the similarities they share with each other is called *factor analysis.* We might start out by observing ten different characteristics in a human population and find that of the total six features are always closely associated. We might also find that three of the remaining four features are also found in mutual association but independent of the first six. A third set of one feature also exists. That is, changes or variation in the group of 6 will not be accompanied by changes in the group of 3 or the group of one. However, all three groups are needed to describe the population. We might further be able to use a single measure to describe how much of the variation in the total population could be explained by the six characteristics in combination. Such a grouping and measure is called a *factor.* Once several such factors have been identified which characterize differences within a particular population, it is possible to determine the percent of overall variation that can be attributed to each factor.

Thus, if we take our example of ten traits and reduce them to three basic factors or patterns, we would "collapse" the ten to three and still be able to adequately describe the population. We might also be able to separate each individual from the population and describe him in terms of the three factors (let us call these *A, B,* and *C*) that we have already identified. We could thus assign him an *A* value, a *B* value, and a *C* value which taken in combination would describe him in terms of the three factors, which in turn would represent ten different physical traits.

Two similar techniques exist by means of which this can be accomplished. If *all* the variation within a population is assigned in part to each of the identified sets of characteristics, the technique is called *principle component analysis.* If some small percentage of the variation within a population is left unassigned and attributed to error, the technique is called *factor analysis.* The difference between these two techniques is a technical one, and for our purposes we will speak of the two interchangeably. Moreover, we will

Table 10-2 Indices of World Economic Development

1. Kms. railroads p.u.a.*	13. Imports p.c.	28. Crude birth rates
2. Kms. railroads p.c.†	14. % Exports to N.	29. Crude death rates
3. R.r. freight ton-km.	Atlantic	30. Pop. growth rates
p.y.p.c.‡	15. % Exports raw mate-	31. Infant mort. rates
4. Ton-km. freight p. km.	rials	32. % Pop. in cities
r.r.	16. Kw-h. electricity p.c.	>20,000
5. Km. roads p.u.a.	17. Energy cons. in kw-h.	33. Physicians p.c.
6. Km. roads p.c.	18. Energy, cons. p.c.	34. % Land area cultiv.
7. Motor vehicles p.c.	19. Comml. energy p.c.	35. Wheat yields
8. Motor vehicles p.u.	20. % Energy cons. comml.	36. Rice yields
road	21. Energy res. in kw-h.	37. Pop. p.u. cultiv. land
9. Motor vehicles p.u.a.	22. Energy res. in kw-h.p.c.	38. Newspaper circ. p.c.
10. Value for. Trade	23. % Hydro pot. dev.	39. Telephones p.c.
11. For. trade p.c.	24. Hydro pot. dev. p.c.	40. Mail flows p.c. domestic
12. Exports p.c.	25. Fiber cons. p.c.	41. Mail flows p.c. internat.
	26. Petrol. ref. capc. p.c.	42. National product
*p.u.a. = per unit area.	27. Pop. density	43. National product p.c.
†p.c. = per capita.		
‡p.y. = per year.		

avoid a detailed, "cookbook" discussion of how analysis based on these mathematical techniques is carried out and concentrate instead on the results and their regional implications.

Some nations are rich and some are poor, but are these national units clustered together geographically into regions or are they randomly distributed? In other words, are there regions of the world which might accurately be described as developing as well as those which are developed? Also, do groups of nations share nearly similar characteristics of development and closely resemble one another, or do they "string out along various continua which measure relative development"? Brian J. L. Berry in a global study of the regionalization of economic development has used factor analysis to examine these and similar questions.

The first step in this exercise in regionalization was to decide upon a broad definition of "economic development." This condition is generally thought of as a high level of production and consumption of energy and material goods matched by a high level of literacy, good health, and similar demographic con-

ditions. Next, data were collected for forty-three various measures of development for each of ninety-five world political units. A selection of these indices is shown in Table 10-2. The countries are listed in Table 10-3 and shown on the maps in Figures 10-7 and 10-8. Other indices of development and additional countries might have been added to these lists, but nearly impossible difficulties arose in getting comparable data for more political units or measures of development. It was also felt that the large number of countries would sufficiently describe the entire world, while the forty-three indices were more than adequate to indicate the relative position of a given nation.

The countries were ranked according to their position for each indicator, and a 43×43 correlation matrix comparing each of the indices with all the others was computed. Factor analysis was then used to find which combinations of the many indices best described the countries. The forty-three indices fell into four basic patterns by means of which the ninety-five countries could be described. The first factor or pattern accounted for 84.2 percent of the observed variation, while the second factor

Table 10-3 Political Units Considered in Developmental Study

1. Canada	33. Ireland	65. Rhodesia & Nyasaland
2. United States	34. Italy	66. Fr. Equatorial Africa
3. Colombia	35. Netherlands	67. Fr. W. Africa
4. Costa Rica	36. Norway	68. Madagascar
5. Cuba	37. Portugal	69. Angola
6. Dominican Republic	38. Spain	70. Mozambique
7. El Salvador	39. Sweden	71. Afghanistan
8. Guatemala	40. Switzerland	72. Ceylon
9. Haiti	41. United Kingdom	73. India
10. Honduras	42. Algeria	74. Pakistan
11. Mexico	43. Egypt	75. China
12. Nicaragua	44. Libya	76. Taiwan
13. Panama	45. Morocco	77. Hong Kong
14. Venezuela	46. Tunisia	78. Japan
15. Argentina	47. Cyprus	79. S. Korea
16. Bolivia	48. Iran	80. Br. Borneo
17. Brazil	49. Iraq	81. Burma
18. Chile	50. Israel	82. Indonesia
19. Ecuador	51. Jordan	83. Malaya (& Singapore)
20. Br. Guiana	52. Lebanon	84. Philippines
21. Surinam	53. Syria	85. Thailand
22. Peru	54. Turkey	86. S. Vietnam
23. Paraguay	55. Ethiopia	87. Australia
24. Uruguay	56. Ghana	88. New Zealand
25. Austria	57. Liberia	89. U.S.S.R.
26. Belgium	58. Sudan	90. Czechoslovakia
27. Denmark	59. Union of S. Africa	91. E. Germany
28. Finland	60. Belgian Congo	92. Hungary
29. France	61. Br. E. Africa	93. Poland
30. W. Germany	62. Gambia	94. Rumania
31. Greece	63. Sierra Leone	95. Yugoslavia
32. Iceland	64. Nigeria	

Source: Brian J. L. Berry, "A Statistical Analysis," part VIII, in Norton Ginsburg (ed.), *Atlas of Economic Development*, University of Chicago Press, Chicago, 1961, p. 110.

accounted for another 4.2 percent. Such a high percentage of explanation allows us to skip factors 3 and 4. Factor 1 indicates that among the forty-three original indicators, accessibility, transportation, trade, external relations, technology, industrialization, urbanization, national product, and the organization of the population are all closely associated along a single new measure or dimension which is referred to by Berry as the *technological scale.* Factor 2 emphasizes those indices least repre-

sented by factor 1: birth and death rates, infant mortality rates, population growth rates, population densities, and population per unit of cultivated land. This second factor is referred to as the *demographic scale.*

Once the major patterns had been identified, the countries were reranked according to their positions on these two new scales. At this point the new list of ninety-five countries were divided into five equal groups of nineteen countries each. This arbitrary

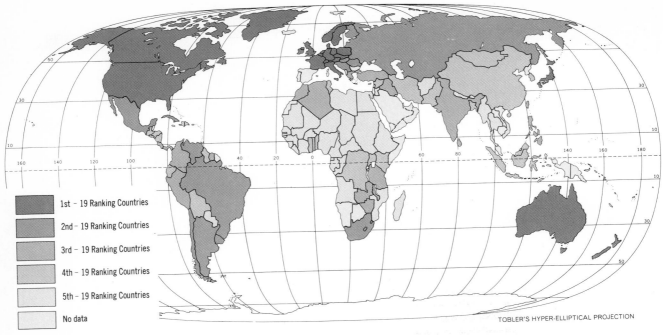

THE TECHNOLOGICAL PATTERN

TOBLER'S HYPER-ELLIPTICAL PROJECTION

Figure 10-7 The technological pattern Countries ranked according to a composite score on a "technological scale" as determined by a factor analysis of ninety-five world political units and forty-three measures of development. (Brian J. L. Berry, "A Statistical Analysis," Part VIII, in Norton Ginsburg (ed.) *Atlas of Economic Development,* © 1961 by the University of Chicago. Published 1961. Composed and printed by the University of Chicago Press, Chicago, Ill., p. 111)

division allowed a middle group and two other groups on the higher and lower sides. Maps were made using the two sets of five groups of nineteen countries each. The result is shown in Figures 10–7 and 10–8. These two maps show us that high productivity, energy use, consumption of goods, and access to transportation are accompanied by good health, literacy, and low infant mortality rates, to name a few of the indicators represented by the two factorial scales. Conversely, measures typical of low energy consumption and minimal production and consumption of goods and services are paralleled by poor health, high death rates, and high population densities per unit of cultivated land. The resulting map patterns indicate that a considerable degree of spatial contiguity or

regionalization does occur in terms of nations sharing similar characteristics. While Berry went on to test and analyze the relationship between the demographic and technological scales, our purpose is served at this point. Given refined analytical techniques it is possible to "boil down" vast quantities of data into manageable map patterns representing regions. However, in the study just described human judgment was still important, as it is in all regional analysis. The forty-three basic indices on which the analysis was made were first identified through familiarity with the phenomenon of economic development. Later in the study the division of ninety-five countries into five groups of nineteen each was again a matter of cartographic convenience. Nevertheless, the resulting maps

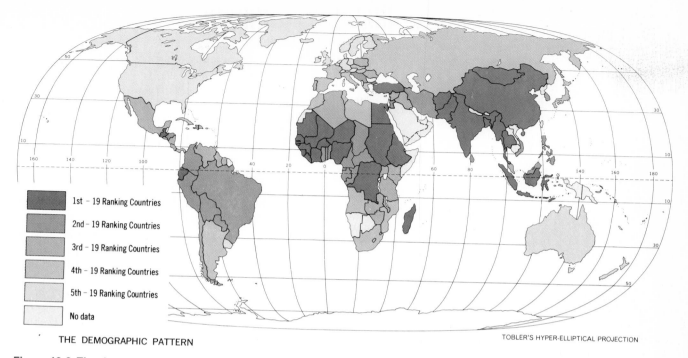

1st – 19 Ranking Countries
2nd – 19 Ranking Countries
3rd – 19 Ranking Countries
4th – 19 Ranking Countries
5th – 19 Ranking Countries
No data

THE DEMOGRAPHIC PATTERN

TOBLER'S HYPER-ELLIPTICAL PROJECTION

Figure 10-8 The demographic pattern Countries ranked according to a
composite score on a "demographic scale" as determined by a factor analysis
of ninety-five world political units and forty-three measures of development.
(Op. cit., Figure 10–7, p. 112)

confirm our notions of the distribution of
development throughout the world. In Chapter 12 we will examine a theory which accounts for the particular distribution we have
just described. In the meantime, let us continue our discussion of regionalization.

The Topology of Geography

Regionalization is a basic technique by means
of which we organize our impressions of
the world in which we live. Our interest in
regions could be justified by this aspect alone,
but a second reason exists. We might call this
reason the topology of geography: a consideration of the shapes areas take and of the real
world conditions resulting from those forms.

Gerrymandering

The most famous or infamous manipulation
of geographic shapes has been given the name

gerrymandering. This practice is essentially
the drawing of political boundaries in such a
way as to give unfair numerical advantage
to a particular party when voting takes place.
The name itself is derived from that of Elbridge Gerry, Governor of Massachusetts,
who in 1812 led his party in a redistricting
of state counties in order to gain unfair political advantage in forthcoming elections. The
strange shape given Essex County in the
northeastern part of the state (Figure 10–9)
led critics to call it a *gerrymander:* Gerry +
(sala)mander. The practice of gerrymandering
remains common today in local politics.

Spatial efficiency

Not all boundaries are redrawn for the purpose of gerrymandering. The "one man, one
vote" ruling of recent years has led many

*Dividing Space
Around and
Within Cities:
Regional
Analysis*

173

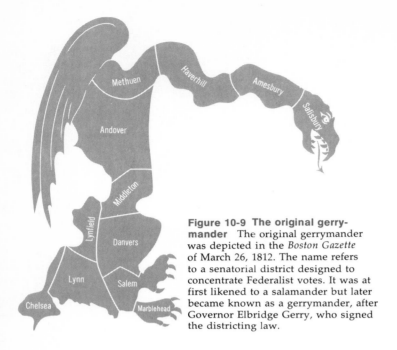

Figure 10-9 The original gerrymander The original gerrymander was depicted in the *Boston Gazette* of March 26, 1812. The name refers to a senatorial district designed to concentrate Federalist votes. It was at first likened to a salamander but later became known as a gerrymander, after Governor Elbridge Gerry, who signed the districting law.

states, counties, and cities into spatially redefining their political subunits to ensure the voting rights of citizens. In other words, the voting districts have been made more *spatially efficient*. Another subject demanding greater spatial efficiency is the matter of drawing the boundaries of school districts to minimize racial inequities and also to minimize the distances that students must travel to reach their schools. If we consider a school as a central place to which students travel, then its district will constitute a hinterland from which it draws its student population. If the hinterland is shaped in a strange or inefficient way, some students will have to travel excessive distances. In this case a measure of spatial efficiency would be the sum of the distances all students attending a school would have to travel in order to reach the school. The smaller this figure, the more efficient will be the region served by each school.

A knowledge of geography and of regionalizing techniques need not be an abstract exercise. Good regions can mean savings to

taxpayers, the more equitable distribution of voters within voting districts, and the rational matching of consumers and resources. In this way geography can create its own social topology. But regions in themselves tell only part of the story. The world is most interesting where one region or realm contacts another. In fact, the edges of regions are where the real problems of regional delimitation are found. Therefore, we next consider boundaries, their problems, and their role in the world around us.

Boundary Problems and the Edges of Regions

One example of this deals with the edges of homogeneous regions or the contact zone between them. Take, for example, the problem of defining the edge of a typical urban area as shown in Figure 10–10. Long fingers of built-up area extend into the countryside with urban outliers beyond the contiguous edge. Empty spaces form deep embayments with pockets of unoccupied land here and there within the city. Where does the city begin and end? One approach to this question might be to define the urban CBD and to work outward from the center to the edge. The techniques we have already covered in this chapter, in large part, have adopted this strategy. Another way of considering regions is to worry about their edges. That is, if we can define their edges, the centers will take care of themselves. But to define the edges of one or more regions we must consider the processes at work within them. Let us consider a configuration found in nature and how generalization can be drawn from complexity.

Epsilon measures and local operators

Suppose we wish to locate the boundary between the North American continent and the Atlantic Ocean southward from New York City. Nothing could be simpler, you might at first think. However, questions of scale would immediately raise their heads like monsters from the ocean depths. Does our map need to show all the embayments and peninsulas

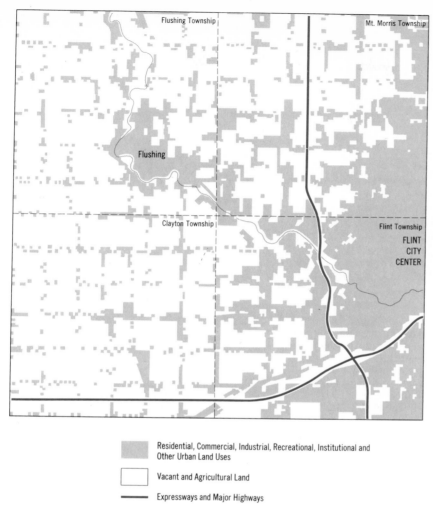

Flushing Township | Mt. Morris Township

Flushing

Clayton Township | Flint Township

FLINT CITY CENTER

Residential, Commercial, Industrial, Recreational, Institutional and Other Urban Land Uses

Vacant and Agricultural Land

Expressways and Major Highways

Figure 10-10 Urban areas of the western half of Flint, Michigan, and adjoining townships Where is the boundary of the urban area of Flint? (Based on Genessee County Metropolitan Planning Commission map, "Existing Land Use, Genessee County, 1968")

illustrated in Figure 10–11A? Or would a much smoother outline as in Figure 10–11B do? You may reply that the closer we come to reality, the better off we are, and that the first map is the best. But if we were to look at a large-scale Coast and Geodetic Survey navigational chart of a portion of the same area, we would see how lacking in detail even the first map is. And yet, armed with the best maps available

at the largest scales, if we were to walk along those same shores, we would become aware of many additional things the map makers had missed. If we were planning to sail southward along the coast from New York City in a small boat, and if that boat could turn easily in twice its own length but could never safely venture more than a few hundred yards from shore, we would be interested in all the crinkles and

Dividing Space Around and Within Cities: Regional Analysis

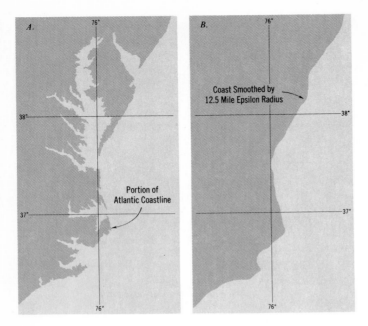

Figure 10−11 **Portion of Atlantic coastline of the United States at different levels of boundary generalization** (*A*) A detail map of the Atlantic coastline showing Delaware and Chesapeake Bays. (*B*) The same coastline as in part *A* generalized to a curve, with curvature not greater than that of a circle with a twenty-five-mile diameter.

crenulations of the coast. On the other hand, if we were skippering a giant oil tanker whose keel rode many feet beneath the surface and which needed several miles in which to turn if it were using its own engines, we would avoid the coastal shallows at all cost. Our route would take us well out to sea, and the inlets and shoals nearer in would not interest us at all.

In order to depict the coast at the level of smoothness or detail suitable to our purposes we can use a simple, mechanical technique. Let us say that the diameter of an area in which a supertanker can effectively navigate is 25 miles. Next, let us cut out a circle of cardboard the radius of which is proportionate to 12½ miles on the map shown in Figure 10−11*A*. Now let us roll that disk along the coast, marking all the while the line of contact it makes with the intricate land-water boundary shown on the

map. Notice that the edge of our disk cannot penetrate many bays and inlets. Note too that almost all the detailed features of coast fall on the landward side of the line of tangency between the effective operating radius of our ship and the heavily indented shoreline. The resulting line which we have drawn along the coast shows a much smoother contact between the continent and the sea than the one with which we started (Figure 10−11*B*). What we have ended with is a new map showing the edge of the domain of very large ships on the Atlantic. In using this method of defining a boundary we assume that the ship's captain will keep his vessel as near to the center of his circle of maneuvering ability as possible. The actual boundary falls at the perimeter of the circle, but if the ship were to be found there, it would be in dangerous waters and in trouble.

The radius of the circle used to delimit the effective boundary between two types of regions or domains is called an *epsilon radius*, sometimes simply shown as the *E* radius. This radius may differ from one circumstance to another, and the size of its circle, which effectively delimits the intricacy or smoothness of a border, depends upon the processes at work within the region or regions defined. In the case of the oil tanker it was large; in the case of a sailing dinghy it would be small. In every case, the process or agent of action by which the epsilon size is determined is referred to as a *local operator*.

Boundary dwellers and boundary dwelling processes

The zones of contact between two or more regions are places of particular interest. Let us consider perhaps the single most important boundary zone on earth. The seashore or littoral marks the contact between land, water, and air. As the tide rises and falls, sometimes more, sometimes less land is exposed to the atmosphere. The shallow waters lapping the shore of the continents conserve or store the sun's energy and often become hospitably warm. At the same time rivers and runoff of all kinds bring nutrients from the land into the neighboring seas. Such foods are particularly available at the mouths of large rivers. There estuaries and deltas often present interfingerings of land and water. If we were to choose an epsilon measure of large radius, representing the daily life space of the larger fish and sea mammals, we could define the outer limits of the coastal zone by moving such a disk along the map edge of such a shore. In the same way, if we chose another epsilon representing a continental- or land-based process, such as the outer coastal boundary for a railroad which would not require too many tight turns, causeways, or bridges, and moved this second epsilon disk along the landward side of the coastal zone, we would define two boundaries for the land and sea. These boundaries would approximately parallel each other, but in many places a kind of no-man's-land of tidal marsh and windswept headland, consisting of both land and sea and yet belonging completely to neither, would be defined (Figure 10–12).

Boundary zones such as these offer opportunities for processes which could not endure in the homogeneous environments on either side. In like manner, they are often noted for a unique set of inhabitants adjusted to peculiarities resulting from the interfingering and interaction of adjoining domains. Consider the map of Chesapeake Bay in Figure 10–13. Oysters are sea creatures which need rich sources of food as well as energy in the form of sun-warmed water. They are bottom dwellers and therefore live most often in shallow water. If the coastline is straight and steeply sloping, the zone available to them where the necessary conditions of shallow, nutrient-rich water are met is too narrow to sustain more than a modest population. At the same time, a straight coastline is more readily exposed to the pounding of surf which might easily destroy shellfish and crustaceans. The deep inlets of the estuary give protection from the sea's excess energy. This relationship of the boundary zone to its inhabitants is evident on the accompanying map. In much the same way, a major theory regarding the origins of life on the earth suggests that it may have first appeared in the shallow coastal waters of primordial continents.

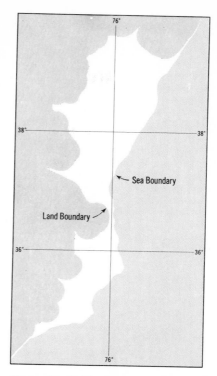

Figure 10–12 The coastline of the Chesapeake and Delaware Bay region smoothed on both land and sea sides by an epsilon radius of 12.5 miles

For our immediate purpose of understanding urbanization we should transfer these ideas into the realm of human activities and consider the boundary effect in settled areas. Certainly the zone of deterioration surrounding the CBD in Burgess's concentric ring theory of city growth represents the contact between the business district and viable residential districts surrounding it. One interesting example suggested by these ideas is in the North Beach area of San Francisco (Figure 10–14). This area, which is directly west of the Barbary Coast of nineteenth century fame, before World War II included an Italian community in North Beach, particularly along Columbus and Grant Avenues, and the well-known Chinatown to the south. In the years following the war the Chinese community held firm in its traditional location, but little by little build-

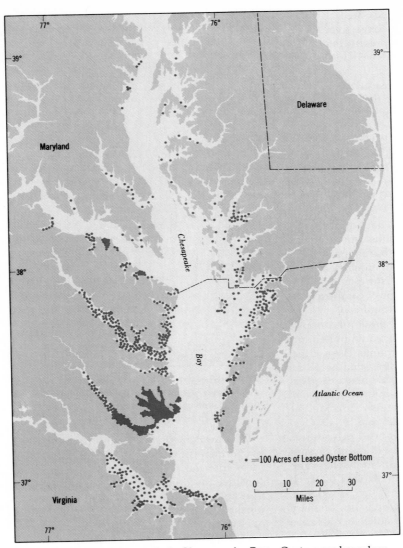

Figure 10-13 Oyster grounds in Chesapeake Bay Oysters are boundary dwellers. They live in salt water but need the protection and nutrients of a shoreline. A zone of estuaries and deltas with deep interfingering of land and water offers the best environment for them. (John J. Alford, "The Role of Management in Chesapeake Oyster Production," *The Geographical Review,* vol. 63, no. 1, January, 1973, fig. 2, p. 48, copyrighted by the American Geographical Society of New York.)

ings on the Italian edge of Chinatown were given up by their original tenants. By the early 1950s this boundary zone between the two ethnic communities had become the seedbed for the earliest beginnings of what was later to be known as the counterculture. Bohemians,

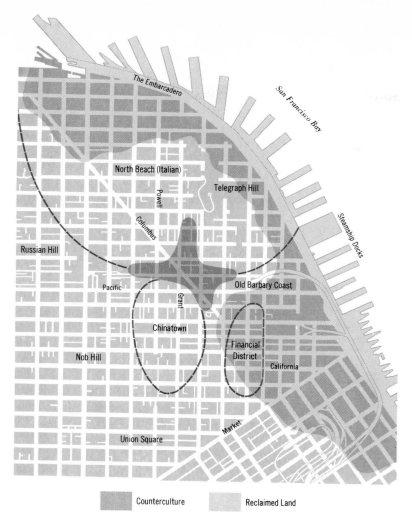

North Beach (Italian)
Telegraph Hill
The Embarcadero
San Francisco Bay
Powell
Columbus
Russian Hill
Steamship Docks
Pacific
Old Barbary Coast
Grant
Chinatown
Financial District
Nob Hill
California
Union Square
Market

Counterculture   Reclaimed Land

Figure 10-14 The North Beach and Chinatown areas of San Francisco
Boundaries of ethnic districts in urban areas may provide an environment
for boundary dwellers in society. The zone between the tightly knit ethnic
communities of Chinatown (Chinese) and North Beach (Italian) was the
location of a series of counterculture developments in the 1950s and 1960s.

who were later to be followed by beatniks, hippies, and flower children, began frequenting bars and eating places such as the famous *hungry i*. Small shops offering handicrafts and organic foods first appeared there, and until commercialization made the area a tourist mecca, people dropping out of the system and seeking a place to live often went there. Later, the developing elements of the counterculture moved westward to the Haight-Ashbury district, which flourished for a short time. Again the area sought out was in a sense a boundary zone. This time, low-cost rooms and stores were located between an expanding black

Dividing Space Around and Within Cities: Regional Analysis

179

district to the north and east and a contracting middle-class Jewish neighborhood to the south. The immediate presence of Golden Gate Park was an added inducement for street people and others to frequent the district.

Oysters, craft shops, and urban blight all can be described in terms of the special boundary environments or domains which help sustain them. In this way boundaries become a special class of regions in themselves. Where indentations and promontories are few in number—that is, where the contact zones are smooth and perhaps straight—transitions are usually abrupt, gradients steep, and zones almost linear in nature. Deep embayments very often create broad zones with shallow gradients.

Industrial Regions of the United States

Let us use some of our techniques for regionalization to find the industrial core of the United States. As we might expect, the distri-

Figure 10-15 Venn diagram of criteria defining manufacturing regions A Venn diagram represents sets of elements which share one or more attributes. In this instance, the elements are counties and the number of manufacturing employees and the value added by manufacturing are the attributes of interest. That subset of counties which exceed given levels in both attributes are chosen as the basic units of the manufacturing regions being sought.

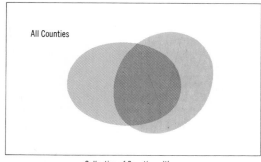

All Counties

Collection of Counties with:

Over 10,000 Manufacturing Employees

Over $100,000,000 Value
Added by Manufacture per Year

bution of manufacturing activities in America has a definite spatial expression. Knowledge that production is located in a few geographically limited regions provides useful insight into the spatial organization of not only America but the entire world.

How can we define a useful set of criteria with which to delimit such regions? Certainly the number of workers employed in industry should give some notion of where manufacturing takes place. We already know that few commuters travel more than an hour each way to and from work. Fifty miles, about the distance traveled in one hour on a busy highway, easily constitutes the outer limit that most people are willing to travel every day. The majority of workers travel somewhat less. If we locate the major centers of industry in terms of the numbers of employees and give each center a hinterland with a radius of 50 miles, we can define a region or regions based on industrial employment. But workers are only part of the total picture of industry. Certainly, the difference between the value of raw materials delivered to a factory and the price of the finished products coming out the other end will be a good measure of the importance of the industrial center under consideration. Such a measure is called the *value added*. We would expect a close correlation between sites where many workers are employed and those places where the greatest value is added during the process of changing raw materials to finished goods. The automobile industry is an example of this. In other places, particularly in those industries which are highly automated, such as petroleum refining, and others where the end product is extremely valuable yet produced by a relatively small number of highly skilled craftsmen, such as tool and die making, we might expect value added to outstrip the absolute number of workers. Conversely, some industries pay relatively low wages, employ large numbers of workers, and produce relatively bulky goods of moderate value. The textile and garment industries fall within this category.

Which measure should we use, number of workers or value added? We can resolve this choice with a simple Venn diagram. Figure

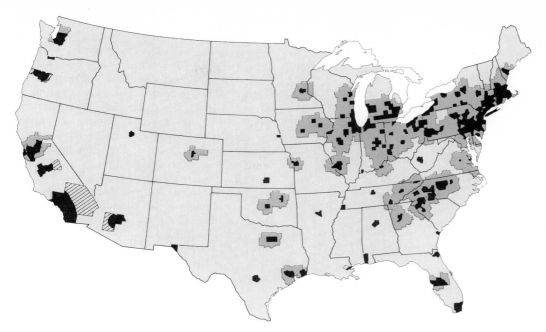

Figure 10-16 United States manufacturing regions The manufacturing regions shown are defined to include counties with over 10,000 annual average production workers and over $100 million value added by manufacturing (darker tone) and in addition, those counties whose centers of population are within fifty miles of a county of the type defined in part *A* and whose areas also adjoin one or more similarly defined areas (lighter tone). Portions of large Western counties which are beyond fifty miles of the county's population center are excluded from the region. (Compiled from data in *County and City Data Book 1967*, U.S. Bureau of the Census, Wash., D.C.)

10–15 shows value added and the number of employees in manufacturing as two overlapping sets. On the one side can be found all those instances where workers are a determining factor; on the other, all the cases where value added is most significant. The area common to both is less likely to occur and therefore is somewhat more narrowly defined than any other part of the universal set. Certainly any area sharing both characteristics can be thought worthy of inclusion in a core industrial region, so let us use both criteria in combination.

The next problem is a choice of scale. Data for the two measures we have chosen have been compiled by the census on a national, state, county, and city basis. States provide too coarse a filter to show much useful detail,

although using them we might see indications of the general location of industry. Also, anomolies like the poverty-stricken Appalachian region penetrating the well-developed Northeastern states cannot be shown at a state-sized scale. Cities, on the other hand, appear as points on the maps of the United States small enough to be used in this book. This leaves counties as the most useful unit recording the data we wish to use. County units shown in the 1967 *United States Census of Manufacturing* as having more than 10,000 employed industrial workers *and* in which more than 100 million dollars in value is added by manufacturing are shown in Figure 10–16. While clusters of counties thus defined appear with some regularity in the Northeast, many units are isolated from their neighbors. This

Dividing Space Around and Within Cities: Regional Analysis

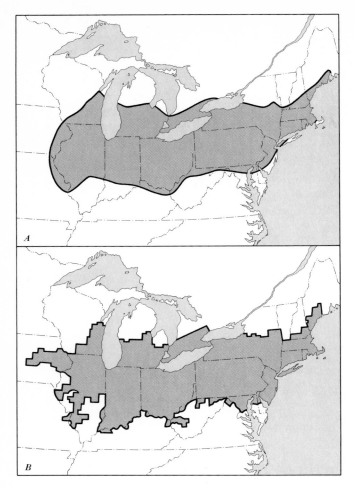

Figure 10-17 The manufacturing belt (*A*) 1919 (After de Geer), (*B*) 1958. Compare the Northeastern manufacturing belt as defined in two earlier figures with the one shown in Figure 10-16. They show nearly the same pattern. Noteworthy variations occur in southern Indiana and Ohio and in northern Pennsylvania, which are excluded from the areas defined in Figure 10-16. (Allen Pred, "The Concentration of High-Value-Added Manufacturing," *Economic Geography*, vol. 41, no. 2, April, 1965, p. 111)

leaves us with too many regions which are too small for a good understanding of the national distribution of industry.

This is where the epsilon measure of a 50-mile commuting radius serves us well. We simply roll an epsilon circle with a suitable radius around all the clusters of counties. Any county so close to its neighbors that the circle cannot pass between it and others nearby is included inside an industrial region. On the other hand, so too are nonmanufacturing counties found within the line. Empty spaces inside a region thus defined are also fitted with the same epsilon measure. Areas untouched by the inside epsilon fall within the region but are too far from industrial counties to be included in the classification. In other words, our regions can have holes in them. Finally, we add two additional rules to neaten up our presentation. First, since regionalization is putting things together, we will not include as a region any single industrial county so far from a neighboring industrial county that it stands completely alone. Second, we will carefully observe a rule that keeps our epsilon circle within 50 miles of the center of population in each unit. With small counties this will make little or no difference as to the final appearance of our regions. Very large counties, such as Riverside and San Bernardino in southern California, which have large empty tracts as well as densely settled areas will be subdivided by this procedure, and part excluded, part included.

The resulting map showing the location of industry in the United States (Figure 10-16) resembles previous maps of value added and manufacturing workers (Figure 10-17). However, it also provides some surprises and new insights. The industrial Northeast shows up very clearly. This region still dominates American industry with 58.2 percent of the workers and 61.6 percent of the value added for the entire United States. But unlike earlier presentations, the epsilon technique has clearly defined a large hole within the region in northern Pennsylvania. Also significant is the southward extension of another manufacturing region along the Carolina Piedmont into Georgia. This second region accounts for 7.1 percent of the workers and 4.7 percent of the value added in the United States and cannot be overlooked. Finally, significant islands of industry are scattered in the Midwest, in the South and along the Gulf Coast, and in the Pacific states. These account for 12.6 and 15.5 percent of the American totals and indicate the expansion of population and capital out of the Northeast into the West and South. All in all, however, the historic pattern of development in the United States remains the same.

We hope that two messages in particular are made clear in this chapter. First, the infinitely complicated world can be ordered by intuition or analytical techniques into intellectual constructs called *regions*. Second, our regionalization of industrial production indicates a significant core area in eastern North America. The two chapters that follow discuss a theory of agricultural location which in its broadest application relates urban land uses to those of rural areas besides showing how the industrial core areas of the world act, in part, as focal points of spatial organization on a global scale.

Dividing Space
Around and
Within Cities:
Regional
Analysis

11 | THE MARKET AND THE FARM: AGRICULTURAL LOCATION THEORY

A pilot flying over the cities of the North China Plain would see each settlement surrounded by a ring of green fields. The circles shade from bright green nearest the cities to more yellow hues and finally merge with browns and russets of the open farmlands far away from any urban place. This is called *green ring effect* and results from the use of human fertilizer on lands adjacent to the settlements. Soil nutrients concentrated in agricultural products are shipped to the cities, passed through human consumers, and returned in part to the fields as human waste, called *night soil*, which is collected and spread back on the land. Transportation costs are high for night soil, and it cannot be shipped long distances. Thus, the rapidly diminishing ring of green vegetation reflects the friction of distance on the return flow of nutrients to China's land.

You're on your way west. Interstate 80 stretches 2,000 miles ahead of you to San Francisco. You and your friend are driving shifts, and the road peels away at a steady 80 miles per hour. The suburbs of Chicago with their plumes and fumes drift back behind you. Tall corn rises to the right and left as Illinois swings past. You started late, and as night comes down you are still moving through the green fields of Iowa. Morning comes up behind you and you stop to walk around a rest stop, stretching and looking. Western Ne-braska now. Wheat fields. Dry and getting drier. Grasslands ahead with *Danger: Livestock on Road* signs whipping by. The farms turn to ranches and windmills set back against the hills, and then you reach the Continental Divide with little towns hot under the high sun and sheep like pillows far off where pines begin. . . .

Chinese cities or American landscapes, the great earth stretches on; band upon band of different crops, different uses for the land; each region shading into the next. Is it chance the way farm activities are distributed? Does nature alone dictate that corn grows in one place and wheat in another? Why corn, then wheat, then cattle, then sheep? What structures the country as it is? In this chapter we discuss how geographic theory helps to explain the distribution and location of different types of agriculture. In the following chapter we suggest ways in which world land use as a whole is organized. More specifically, in both chapters we will be talking about a well-known body of thought referred to as *agricultural location theory*. Such theory was formalized by Johann von Thünen in the nineteenth century. Using his ideas as a starting point, we hope to illustrate the interaction of natural and cultural systems. Man operating in the context of nature accounts for the world as we know it; this chapter begins to relate man to nature from a geographic point of view. Thünen's ideas also present an opportunity to show the relationship between nodal or hierarchically organized regions and homogeneous, multifactor regions. Finally, in the next chapter we try to place the city in the context of its total environment on a worldwide scale.

The Areal Basis of Farming

Mankind ultimately depends on farming the land. Over many thousands of years a complex relationship has developed between humans on the one hand and their domesticated plants and animals on the other. This relationship is symbiotic; that is, it is a two-way street. Good farmers and a wise society give back to nature what they take. Soil is fertilized and mulched to replace nutrients and minerals removed by harvesting. Plants and animals, in turn, depend upon the people who eat them for their survival in competition with undomesticated nature. Corn, more correctly referred to as Indian corn or maize, was originally a tiny wild plant far different in form from today's tall, tasseled giants. In the wild state it could reproduce itself annually with no help. Thousands of years of selective breeding at the hands of man have changed all that. Maize must now be harvested, and the kernels must be removed from the cob and stored and then carefully planted the following spring in well-prepared ground. If man were to disappear and maize left to reseed itself, the domesticated species would be unable to do so and would disappear within a season or two following our own demise. We eat the plant, but in turn, we nurture it and help it to survive. In fact, though some domesticated plants and animals might survive in some form without man's help, their relationship to us is symbiotic. Without man their numbers and areal extent would be vastly reduced.

Almost all domesticated plants are heliophytes, or sun lovers. Sunlight is an areal phenomenon, and as we have said before, plants must spread over an area in order to obtain enough solar energy to prosper. At very large scales, within tiny areas, we can view

plants as transportation systems. Leaves spread out to catch sunlight in order to form chlorophyll; roots bring water from below. The entire system maintains the plant in equilibrium with its environment through evaporation and transpiration. If we step back a bit and view plants at local scales incorporating slightly larger areas, we are dealing with point –area relationships: plants spread as points across fields of sun-warmed soil. This same distribution when viewed at neighborhood scales creates small homogeneous areas easily identified as corn fields, wheat fields, pastures, and so on. At a regional scale farms can be viewed as nodally organized collections of fields. The farmhouse and buildings serve as a focal point for the activities of the farmer, who makes frequent trips outward from his own shelter to tend his crops. At harvest time, the sun's energy and soil's nutrients are brought from the fields in the form of produce, which is temporarily stored near the farm's focal point before being sent cityward. If we consider the point, line, and area relationships involved at several of these levels in the scale of operations, we can see collections of plants defining fields, which in turn are nodally organized around the farmhouse and farm buildings. Collections or sets of farms make up farm regions and are joined to farm communities and local markets by roads and telephones along which messages and produce move back and forth. Agricultural regions in turn serve urban concentrations of population which in most cases are still small enough to be shown as points on world maps. Thus, at some scales the system linking the land to the city can be seen as nodally organized into functional regions; at other scales homogeneous regions of particular crops or farm types can be identified.

The geographic significance of food processing

Communication and transportation links join points and areas in all possible combinations. Messages and energy move through the system as much as produce does. At the same time, the system concentrates and alters the resources which it transports. Food processing increases the value of produce in proportion to its weight or volume. This is done by removing excess water and waste material. The result, in each case, is a more transportable commodity. Every grocery store and household cupboard is full of examples. Jam is concentrated fruit. A steak is simply a cow with its hide, horns, and viscera removed. The pound of sugar in the jar on your breakfast table is refined from 11 pounds of sugar cane taken from the field.

Perishability is also important. Fresh grapes can be shipped only with great difficulty and expense. Raisins are less perishable and more easily transported than grapes. Wines are more valuable, and properly handled, nearly as transportable as raisins. But here we must distinguish between *concentration* and *preservation*, although one usually implies the other. Preservation of foodstuffs makes them available at other times than the harvest. Large populations are thus able to sustain themselves through the lean and hungry months of winter and spring. Preservation also is crucial to the development of civilization and urban lifestyles because it allows food to be transferred to places where consumption far surpasses the ability of the local land to provide produce.

Storage and preservation of food represent a transfer through time from one season to another. *Concentration and transportation of food represent a spatial transfer* from areas of surplus to areas of need. Incidental to these processes are changes in flavor and texture, sometimes producing new foods even more desirable than the original fresh produce. In either case, concentration and preservation play important roles in the transportation and transfer systems which help to create agricultural regions.

The regionalization of farm types

When we speak of agricultural regions, we necessarily deal with abstractions born of our own imaginations. Nevertheless, we divide the world around us into homogeneous areas for convenience in classifying and understanding it. We speak casually of the *Corn Belt* or the *Cotton Belt*. We write learned papers about the types of agriculture, their numbers and spatial distribution. Even a simplified map of world agriculture identifies nine types of farming scattered across the globe (Figure 11–1).

The most interesting thing, however, is not the number or complexity of the regions we perceive, but rather the homogeneity within them and the singleness of choice which their farmers exercise. Farm numbers are limited by the availability of land, and within broad limits by the character of the physical world. A conservative estimate gives us more than 280 million individual farms throughout the world, with at least 2 million in the United States. If we were to examine these farms in more detail than shown in Figure 11–1, in order to acknowledge the variety we observe around us we might increase the number of farm types to 100 or more. The possibility of 280 million farmers choosing from over 100 types of farming leads to astronomical combinations, but similar farms are found clustered together. There is a distinct regional effect which creates the Corn Belt in the United States, the Rice Bowl of China, the dairy districts of Scandinavia, and the cattle region of Argentina, to name but a few.

Why do people making independent choices end up making the same one? Why does one farmer in Iowa decide to raise maize and soybeans and to fatten hogs, and his neighbor decide in favor of the same combination, and his neighbor, and his? These are important questions, for if the nature of farm decision making is understood, then changes in systems of agriculture can be brought about more easily.

Variables Determining Farm Production

The reasons for the choices farmers make can be subdivided into four categories. These are (1) site characteristics, (2) cultural preferences and perception, (3) available technology and organization, and (4) geographic situation or

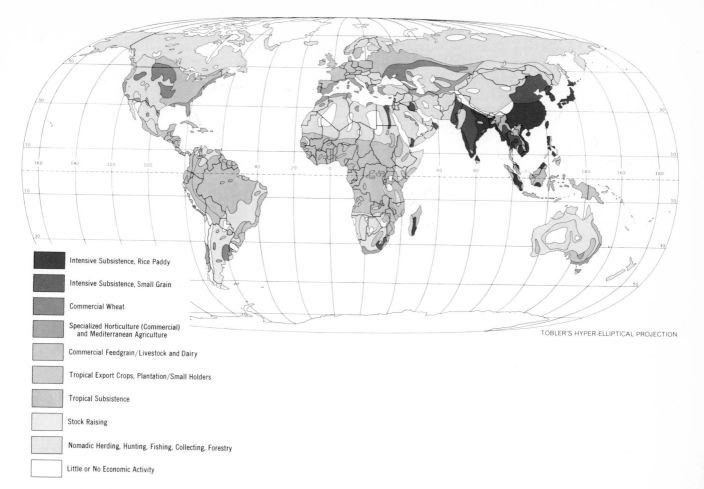

Intensive Subsistence, Rice Paddy

Intensive Subsistence, Small Grain

Commercial Wheat

Specialized Horticulture (Commercial)
and Mediterranean Agriculture

Commercial Feedgrain/Livestock and Dairy

Tropical Export Crops, Plantation/Small Holders

Tropical Subsistence

Stock Raising

Nomadic Herding, Hunting, Fishing, Collecting, Forestry

Little or No Economic Activity

TOBLER'S HYPER-ELLIPTICAL PROJECTION

Figure 11-1 World agriculture

relative position. Let us briefly survey the first three of these before considering the fourth in greater detail.

Site characteristics

Site characteristics are the *in place* attributes of a particular area viewed at large, local, or neighborhood scales. Thus, the amount of rainfall and average annual temperature of an area are considered important site characteristics. Soil type and fertility, slope, drainage, and exposure to sun and wind are also used to characterize the physical geography of each and every site. These things all relate to the amount of energy available in the physical system within which the location is incorporated. Other site characteristics could include the number of insect species, their populations, and their potential for destroying crops. The same is true for plant, animal, and human diseases. At still another level of abstraction, the human population density of an area can be considered one of the characteristics helping to determine the qualities of site. The type and intensity of pollution, the

The Market and the Farm: Agricultural Location Theory

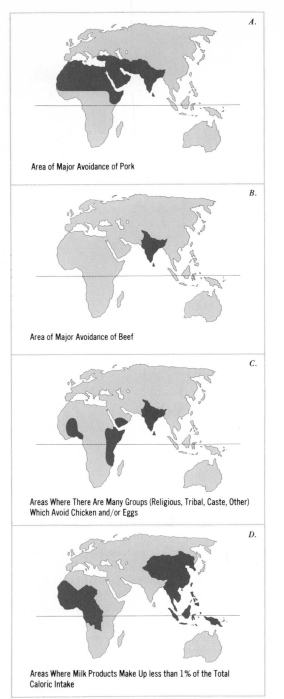

A.

Area of Major Avoidance of Pork

B.

Area of Major Avoidance of Beef

C.

Areas Where There Are Many Groups (Religious, Tribal, Caste, Other)
Which Avoid Chicken and/or Eggs

D.

Areas Where Milk Products Make Up less than 1% of the Total
Caloric Intake

amount of built-up area, and the nature of land ownership and property fragmentation could also be included in this category.

While it would be possible to devote the rest of this chapter to site characteristics, we must reserve further discussion of them until Part Two. Let us push on and review other elements which affect the nature of agricultural systems, keeping in mind that our purpose is to place *agricultural location theory* in a broad and useful context.

Cultural preference and perception

Perhaps the least known and possibly the most important of all the conditions which help to determine the type of agricultural activity which takes place at a given site are the cultural, psychological, and emotional characteristics of the people involved. For example, we do not eat everything which is available; sometimes people starve rather than consume perfectly edible but taboo food. Muslims abhor pork; certain Hindus abstain from eating all meat, but particularly beef; many Africans will not eat chickens or their eggs. The Chinese and some other peoples of East and Southeast Asia refuse to drink milk or eat milk products. Figure 11−2 shows the areal extent of some of these food prejudices.

Figure 11-2 Four food avoidance areas These represent very general regions of food avoidance; within them are subgroups with entirely different preferences and avoidances. We could also show the United States with major avoidances of nutritious meats which could be or are readily available: horsemeat, dogmeat, guinea pig meat, etc. These, as well as iguana, monkey, camel, and others, are relished by some peoples and totally rejected by others. Prejudices and sanctions for and against eating of animal foods are generally much stronger than those concerned with use of grain, fruit, and vegetable foods. Nevertheless, custom and preference play a major role in the use of all foods. (Maps adapted from several figures and references in Frederick J. Simoons, *Eat Not This Flesh,* University of Wisconsin Press, Madison, Wisc., 1961; average milk product consumption 1959−1961 from *The World Food Budget 1970,* Foreign Agricultural Report No. 19, U.S. Dept of Agriculture, Economic Research Service, Foreign Regional Analysis Division, Table 1, p. 4)

The refusal to eat certain foods places real constraints upon the agricultural systems possible within an area. Maize is scarcely considered human food in much of Europe, and therefore its production is restricted to animal fodder in all but a few places. Americans consume large quantities of meat despite its expense. A diet with greater emphasis upon vegetables and cereal grains would be just as healthful and cost much less. Most nationalities can be characterized by their food preferences and prejudices. Think of the variety of ethnic restaurants which add to the allure of any large city.

The way we perceive the resources around us is also important. For example, the European settlement of North America was largely from the northeast to the west. The firstcomers were Anglo-Saxons and other Europeans accustomed to a moist, mild climate and a tree-covered landscape. Those yeoman farmers equated trees with fertility. To them, land to be suitable for farming should, in its wild state, have a cover of trees. New England and the East Coast met their expectations when they settled there. But as subsequent waves of migrants pushed west to the edge of the central prairies and Great Plains, they encountered treeless, grass-covered areas. This lack of trees failed to meet their perception of truly fertile land. They referred to this area as the Great American Desert—which according to some people began at the Mississippi River—and pushed across it to the valleys along the Pacific Coast. There again they had to clear the land of timber before farming it, but they were satisfied. Those early farmers failed to see in the grasslands the latent fertility of what was to become the Great American Breadbasket. It took a later generation of migrants, this time people from the steppelands of Eastern Europe, to take advantage of the rich, grass-covered soils of Nebraska and Kansas. Thus, the way in which those immigrant groups perceived the environments which they encountered colored their subsequent use of the resources available to them. Many other factors influenced the pattern of settlement on the Great Plains. Certainly

technological developments such as the mold-board plow and barbed wire fencing also were important. However, it is not our purpose in this section to explore these topics in great detail. We want, rather, only to identify some of the important elements which complicate reality and make simple explanations so difficult. As part of this we should not overlook intangible but significant human interpretations of the environment.

Available technology and organization

Since the end of World War II and the subsequent creation of international development programs, whole libraries have been written about technology and organization in agriculture. It is convenient to summarize this general category by describing two types of farms and farmers located at opposite ends of the developmental spectrum. Modern commercial agriculture as it is practiced in the United States might be one case; subsistence-level farming in an emerging economy would be the other.

Modern commercial farming The modern commercial farm is characterized by the large amount of capital necessary for its operation. We describe this as *capital-intensive*. Farms substituting human labor in place of all the conveniences and mechanical aids that money can buy are called *labor-intensive*. The investment necessary to operate a viable, capital-intensive farm unit in the United States is impressive. The average value of the property and buildings on "first class" American farms in 1959 was 135,000 dollars. Table 11-1 shows the average size of and the amount of capital invested in a variety of American farms in 1963. When we compare the capital invested with gross farm income for the same properties, it is easy to see why farmers prefer to leave the countryside and take jobs in urban areas. Remember, the gross farm income must compensate the farmer for his annual investment of labor as well as capital.

The Market and the Farm: Agricultural Location Theory

Table 11-1 Size, Investment, and Returns by Type of Farm, United States, 1963

Type of Farm* and Location	Size of Farm in No. of Units	Total Farm Capital, 1/1/63	Gross Farm Income†
Dairy, Central Northeast	32.2 cows	$ 43,400	$ 14,475
Dairy, western Wisconsin	23.8 cows	37,410	10,267
Hog and beef fattening, Corn Belt	153 acres	98,920	31,024
Cash grain, Corn Belt	246 acres	137,020	24,581
Cotton, southern Piedmont	101 acres	30,750	7,153
Cotton (nonirrigated), Texas, High Plains	445 acres	84,950	19,584
Cotton-specialty crops (irrigated), San Joaquin Valley, Calif.	329 acres	305,450	112,987
Tobacco, North Carolina Coastal Plain	47 acres	27,640	12,581
Spring wheat, small grain, livestock, northern Plains	588 acres	57,540	12,384
Winter wheat, sorghum, southern Plains	684 acres	125,910	16,632
Cattle ranches, intermountain region	149.5 cows	95,550	17,460

*All except cotton farms in California are family-operated.
†Includes both income from farming and government payments.
Source: *Farm Cost and Returns Commercial Farms by Type, Size and Location,* Agricultural Information Bulletin 230, Economic Research Service, U.S. Department of Agriculture, June 1964, p. 4.

Modern farming is quick to change under the necessity to return profits on such sizable investments. Fluctuations in the market are watched closely by farmers, and for example, the number of animals they raise varies dramatically from season to season. Figure 11-3 illustrates the rapid fluctuation in the number of hogs butchered over a 19-year period. The enormous variation from year to year reflects the uncertainty of farmers' efforts to anticipate market demands and shifting wholesale prices. Animal types also change rapidly. American hogs were once fat porkers heavy with lard. Consumer tastes changed rapidly in favor of lean bacon and ham at the same time that vegetable oils provided a cheap substitute for cooking fats. Innovation plays its role here, as well. Now pigs being fattened for market are sometimes fed from raised troughs which they must reach by standing on their hind legs, thus producing lean, well-developed hams.

Not only does the market fluctuate widely, but new markets for new crops bring about abrupt changes in farming. Hybrid corn and soybeans have both made dramatic entries into American farming in recent years. Figure 11-4 illustrates the nearly geometric increase of the area devoted to soybean production. In the period between 1960 and 1965 alone, more than 10 million additional acres were sown in this crop. Changes result not only from market fluctuations but also from competition with new sources and substitute products. Rubber was originally produced from trees growing wild in South American jungles. By 1920, 90 percent of all rubber came from trees grown in orderly plantations half-

Spatial Design in World Society

190

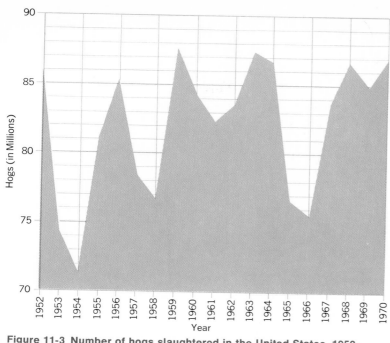

Figure 11-3 Number of hogs slaughtered in the United States, 1952–1970 The number of hogs slaughtered in the United States varies greatly from year to year. From this record, it appears to take a few years to recover from a decline, which can be as much as 20 percent lower than the previous peak year. The fluctuations are due, in large part, to uncertainty regarding future price and the fact that a farmer must start his production cycles months ahead of when he plans to market the products. (Data from *Historical Statistics of the U.S. Colonial Times to 1957: Continued to 1962 and Revisions; Statistical Abstract of the U.S. 1963–1971,* U.S. Dept. of Commerce, Bureau of the Census, Wash., D.C.)

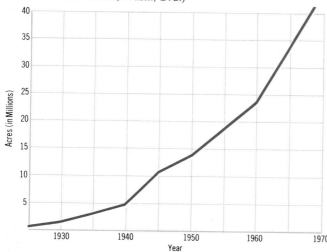

Figure 11-4 Introduction of soybeans in the United States Soybeans, a source of vegetabls oils and proteins, have become a major crop in the United States in recent decades. The consumer has shifted to vegetable oils for cooking and in margarine and has preferred leaner meats. These changes in market demand have encouraged farmers to switch from corn to soybeans, which are processed directly into foodstuff as well as providing protein supplements for animal feed. (Op. cit., Figure 11.3, and *Bulletin #951,* Dept. of Commerce, Bureau of the Census, Wash., D.C.)

Farming and Farm Regions: Agricultural Location Theory

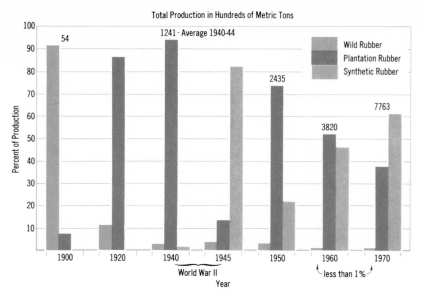

Figure 11-5 Percent of world rubber production in wild, plantation and synthetic rubber, 1900–1970 (Data from: Rubber Study Group, *Commodity Year Book 1956 and 1971*; wild rubber percentages, Jones and Darkenwald, *Economic Geography*, Macmillan, New York, 1954, and Jean le Bras, trans., *Introduction to Rubber*, Hart, New York, 1969)

way around the world in Southeast Asia. World War II reduced all production of rubber trees, both wild and plantation-grown, to only 16 percent of the total. In the decades that followed, synthetic rubber was less important, but in every case, wild rubber production remained an insignificant proportion of the total (Figure 11–5).

The modern farmer's qualities match the demands of the system within which he operates. He must be an agronomist able to assess the physical requirements of crops both new and old. He must be receptive and able to understand and accept the advice given by the Department of Agriculture's county agents as well as that from state university experimental farms and from seed, chemical, and machinery salesmen. He also must be able to think like a market economist. If his evaluation of the market is wrong, he will be left with an unsalable surplus of crops or animals. To avoid this he must utilize every source of information available. City people would be

surprised if they listened to the farm programs broadcast in the early morning over many stations. Market futures are given regularly, as are the number of animals delivered, bought, and butchered at major stockyards. The farmer listens to all this and more and must decide for himself how to operate his enterprise. At the same time, the commodities produced on modern farms travel long distances, sometimes to the other side of the world, to reach the consumer. This means that the farmer must follow not only the fortunes and activities of his neighbors but also those of farmers producing similar crops in distant states or other countries.

All these activities require financing, and the farmer must know something of the money market. Acquiring loans and mortgages is an everyday part of the farmer's life. Again, he must know where money is available and at what rates of interest. He must decide whether he should get by on what he has, or take out a short-term loan, or perhaps operate with long-term mortgages. He must be able to anticipate whether interest rates will diminish or climb, and time his requests for money accordingly, that is, if the needs imposed on him by nature and his creditors allow him the luxury of choice.

In the same way, he must be a lawyer and politician of some ability. If his farm is near an expanding city or in the path of an advancing highway, he must be able to defend himself against unfair invasions without adequate payment for land appropriated by the government or damages caused by industry and housing developments. In other cases he must struggle to defend his rights to the use of water for his crops and animals. Legal conflicts over water are particularly characteristic of drier regions. In the same way, increasing government manipulation of farming makes it vital that the farmer be able to advise his congressman and senator at both the state and national levels. Simultaneously, he must help elect representatives who will best serve his interests.

All in all the modern commercial farmer must be a superb manager if he is to survive. He must assess and juggle all the things described above and many more while balancing his decisions against a capricious and often uncooperative Mother Nature. To do this he has a variety of information sources available: radio and television, farm journals and magazines, special newspapers and stock market reports, government farm agents, and advisors sent by private industry. At the same time, his aspirations are almost the same as those of urban dwellers. He wants the same conveniences, the same family transportation, the same schools for his children, and the same high level of living. In the final analysis, the modern farmer in all ways resembles his city cousins much more closely than he does subsistence-level farmers in emerging economies.

Subsistence-level farming By subsistence-level farming we mean agriculture which provides food, shelter, and the basic necessities for its participants but which allows little or no surplus with which to enter the commercial market system. It would be difficult to find a completely self-sufficient farm anywhere in the world today. Here, however, we present a description of such a system in order to clarify the traditional characteristics which in various combinations with those of modern farming go to make up the middle and lower range of the agricultural spectrum. For our present purposes we will use the terms *subsistence level* and *traditional* agriculture interchangeably.

The traditional farmer fortunate enough to own the property he tills nevertheless works the land with his own labor and without the use of modern machines. *Labor-intensive* agriculture requires that he and his family toil long hours in order to farm fewer acres of ground than his modern counterpart. It is difficult to make direct comparisons between these two types of farming, for virtually no data exist which show the capitalization of subsistence-level farms. We can, however, make some qualitative comparisons. The Near Eastern farmer, for example, may own one or two oxen which he uses to pull a wooden plow or solid-wheeled cart. In some cases fodder is so scarce, because of the extreme scarcity of irrigation water, that only the very richest farmers can afford to feed draft animals. Lacking animal power, the farmers must spade their fields by hand. Similar conditions exist in South and Southeast Asia, where more fortunate farmers rely on oxen or water buffalo while the poor depend on the sweat of their own brows. The picture is repeated again in Latin America, while in much of Africa sleeping sickness and rinderpest disease have kept the horse and cattle population at a minimum, unavailable even to those farmers who might afford them. Particularly in Africa, *hoe culture* is common, with humans using those tools in place of plows pulled by animals.

In some parts of the emerging world absentee landlords living in the cities may own hundreds of villages. In these cases, the landlord may provide seed, equipment, land, and

The Market and the Farm: Agricultural Theory

water, while the tenant farmer invests only his own labor. The harvest, however poor, is divided into five portions; each part is allocated to one of the five subdivisions just mentioned, with the landlord receiving four-fifths and the tenant one-fifth of the produce.

All these conditions are reflected in the low per capita incomes found in the predominantly agricultural nations of the world. Figure 1−3 shows the world distribution of income. It is no coincidence that the distribution of predominantly rural populations shown in Figure 3−16 matches that of the low per capita income countries.

Subsistence-level farming with its lack of cash or surplus crops presents few opportunities for experiment and change. We should not consider this as completely bad, though, for subsistence-level agriculture throughout the world is remarkably resilient and able to survive all manner of disasters. We should not ask the question, "Why are traditional farmers so inefficient?" but rather, "How have such impoverished methods of farming survived thousands of years of drought and flood, heat, cold and storms, unfair taxation, war, pillage, and looting? Indeed, why does traditional agriculture continue to resist the well-intentioned, well-financed, and highly trained technicians who have tried to change it in recent years?"

The answer can be summed up in a short sentence: *Tradition is wise.* Subsistence-level or traditional agricultural systems lack the flow of information so necessary for rapid change. Poor education and ignorance of modern farm methods are everywhere apparent in the emerging nations. But we should not think that the participants in these systems are either stupid or lazy. Lacking capital, outside information, and scientific methodology, the farmers have learned farming strategies by trial-and-error methods over hundreds and hundreds of years. Their inherited culture, which provides them with techniques and attitudes necessary for survival, is their most valuable asset. For example, wooden needle-nosed plows without moldboards are used

everywhere in arid regions by subsistence-level farmers. While they are seemingly far less efficient than our own moldboard metal plows, which turn a deep furrow, thereby exposing the soil to sun and air, needle plows stir the earth without severely disturbing the surface. By not exposing the underlayers, valuable soil moisture is preserved for subsequent plant use. The simple needle plow is also less expensive, and can be made and repaired from local materials. When modern farm technicians first attempted to introduce the iron moldboard plow into the Near East, it was not readily accepted by local farmers, who knew more of their own environment and pocketbooks than did their would-be helpers. Similarly, when tractors were used to replace oxen in some areas, a major conflict arose. Plowing was easier and the timing of crop planting was improved, but the departure of the oxen deprived the villagers of their major source of fuel. In those treeless areas, dried dung mixed with straw was in many settlements the only material available for the cooking fires. The tractors were an improvement but necessitated an additional investment in kerosene cookstoves. In the words of one enlightened developmental technician, "There's no fuel like an old fuel." Thus farmers in the emerging world are slow to change their ways for fear of overtaxing themselves, their pocketbooks, and their resources. Given enough slack and the opportunity to change, ·they are as willing to accept new developments as are our own farmers. It is simply because they already have a system that works reasonably well that they are cautious about experimenting with irreplaceable materials and money. Tradition tells them what will succeed and how to survive, albeit at a low economic level. In other words, don't rock the boat.

In summary, the traditional and the modern farmer *viewed as stereotypes* have contrasting characteristics and skills. The modern farmer is a specialist in technology, money matters, and management. The traditional farmer is able to provide himself and his dependents with food, shelter, clothing, and equipment made with his own hands. He is at a disadvantage in the modern market system but could probably survive a major catastrophe like war as well as or better than his modern counterpart. This is particularly true when we consider the elaborate supply system which provides the modern farmer with necessities. If his communication lines were cut, he would soon run out of fuel, spare parts, store-bought foods, and clothing purchased off the rack. Traditional communities, on the other hand, depending on the outside world for fewer things, would miss it far less if cut off from central places ranked above them in the settlement hierarchy.

Geographic situation or relative position

The emphasis placed upon communication and organization in the above section brings us to the central point of this chapter. Wherever the movement of energy, goods, and information is important, so too will be the friction of distance and the relative location of the farms in question. We have already described three sets of variables which help to determine the form that agricultural land use will take. Let us now consider our fourth set, relative location expressed particularly in terms of distance. To do this, we must resort to our method of holding all other variables constant in a greatly simplified model of the world. By controlling variation in site characteristics we return to the homogeneous plain used in earlier chapters. If we assume no variation from place to place in the cultural preferences and perception of the actors involved in our drama, we eliminate, for the moment, the vexing questions which those things raise. The same is true for available technology and organization. If everyone behaves exactly the same, we have created a homogeneous cultural as well as physical space. This makes a perfect medium within which to let our farm systems grow uncluttered by any but spatial considerations. This model world can be our petri dish; let us start simply and see what develops.

Johann Heinrich von Thünen

Relative position is important in agriculture at all scales from world patterns to patterns of production surrounding a single settlement. The analytical principles underlying this statement were first demonstrated in 1826 by Johann Heinrich von Thünen, a north German landowner and farmer who wrote on the economics of production. Thünen had observed that various types of farming occurred with surprising regularity in circular bands or rings around his own settlement. The pattern was not always clear, but in his book, *The Isolated State*, he presented a logical scheme which explained what he had observed. The importance of Thünen's work, however, lies not in his explanation of the world in which he lived but rather in the fact that *his methods may be applied to other situations with other sets of data, with results differing from what he observed but consistent with the geographic theory which he outlined.*

Thünen's ideas are of particular interest to geographers because they deal with geographic rather than nominal locations. In the words of Michael Chisholm:

His argument started from the premise that the areal distribution of crops and livestock and of types of farming depends upon competition between products and farming systems for the use of any particular plot of land. On any specified piece of land, the enterprise which yields the highest net return will be conducted and competing enterprises will be relegated to other plots where it is they which yield the highest return. Thünen was, then concerned with two points in particular: 1. The monetary return over and above the monetary expenses incurred by different types of agriculture; 2. Such net returns pertaining to a unit area of land and not to a unit of product. For example, if a comparison is being made between potatoes and wheat, we will not be concerned with the financial return obtained per ton of produce but with the return which may be expected from a hectare of land in either crop. Thus, at certain locations wheat may be less profitable than potatoes because, although the return per ton on wheat is higher than on potatoes, the latter yield perhaps three times the weight of crop to a hectare of land. In this case, potatoes will occupy the land.[1]

Rentals and economic rent

In our discussion of agricultural land use we are assuming that each type of activity, each crop raised, will give a certain monetary return to the farmer. If we take the total value of production for a given farm and subtract from it the total costs involved in bringing forth the product, we will have the net return on the farm. This divided by the number of units of land the farm incorporates (acres, hectares, etc.) will give the net return per unit area, for example, dollars per acre. Economists call this the *economic rent* of the activity; we prefer the term *location rent*. If we imagine two pieces of land both being used for the production of wheat, one piece so poor and/or far removed from market that it is at the absolute margin of production and another which has the highest, best, and most lucrative wheat yields possible, the difference in profits between the two will again constitute the economic rent of the more fertile, nearby piece.

We frequently hear the term *rent* used in a different way, meaning the amount paid by a tenant for the right to occupy and use a certain property. The use of the same term for two such different concepts is confusing. In the first case the word refers to the value of production at a given site; the second term really refers to one of the costs of production which must be subtracted before net profit or economic rent accrues. For this reason we will follow the lead of Paul Samuelson and use the term *rental* for the second, reserving the term *rent* for use in place of the longer term *location rent*. One further point should be made. Rentals rarely match the absolute productive value or rent for a given piece of land. Sometimes they are far lower. Rental controls in the Neth-

erlands and England allow some farmers the use of property at a fraction of its true worth. We have all heard stories about a village rented for the price of one red rose delivered yearly from a maiden's hand. Conversely, rentals may sometimes exceed the true worth of the property and their collection can thus force bankruptcy and rapid turnover in businesses. This is particularly true for commercial properties near campuses which are valued at unreasonably high rates by their owners, thus leading to a succession of restaurants and shops being established and failing one after another. This discussion will refer only to the economic *rent* of land, not to its rental.

Characteristics of the isolated state

In order to explain the world in which he lived, Thünen had to simplify and restrict the conditions describing his model of farm production. To do this he assumed six characteristics for his agricultural region. (1) At the center of the area was a single, isolated market town. No links connected it to other settlements or to the outside world in general. Movement was only to and from this one place, with its population being the only urban one and all other people being rural farmers. (2) The area in question was a homogeneous plain having equal fertility in all its parts and neither hill nor valley to vary its surface. (3) All labor costs were everywhere equal on this plain. Nowhere were there fewer laborers or more skilled workers. No cost differential could occur as a result of competition for employees. (4) Transportation costs were the same everywhere and in every direction. This required an initial roadless condition, since roads of any kind would focus transportation into a radial pattern centered on the town. The result in that case would resemble the star-shaped diagrams discussed in Chapter 3. Thus, he assumed that all carts could go to the central market by the most direct route. (5) Within this region there existed a static economy. The entire system was in equilibrium, with no long-range trends leading inevitably to lower or higher prices, nor were there sudden shocks

---

[1]Michael Chisholm, *Rural Settlement and Land Use*, Hutchinson, London, 1962, pp. 21–22.

within the system such as depressions or inflations. (6) Finally, he assumed that the market price of any commodity was fixed for any single farmer and that farmers could not form combines or cooperatives in order to manipulate the market by holding back crops to raise prices or by dumping them to ruin their competitors.

The isolated state as an energy system

Thünen showed a city and its hinterland in an isolated and very stable condition. His model, however, cannot be considered an isolated system.[2] Although he did not consider his isolated state in modern systems terminology, it may be convenient for us to view it in that way. Energy in the form of sunlight constantly entered the area with which he dealt. Foodstuffs were shipped to the central settlement and were reduced there to waste materials and heat. The waste in turn might further decompose, releasing more heat; some of the waste would be returned to the fields. (In this latter case Thünen concerned himself only with the return of horse manure as fertilizer to the land. In the early nineteenth century the major form of power for urban transportation was horses, which required large amounts of fodder and produced equally important quantities of manure as a by-product.) Eventually, the energy which had entered the system as sunlight would escape from it as some form of reradiation back to the heavens. This kind of system, which exchanges energy but no mass with its surroundings, is called a *closed system*.

It was this flow of energy through the system which helped organize its many parts into a recognizable structure. Much as logs floating on a stream become aligned with each other as a result of the flowing water, so too do all man-environment systems reflect the particular characteristics of the energy flows which they utilize and in turn help to create. We have

[2]Systems and systems terminology are treated more fully in Chapter 13.

introduced this idea of energy movement within various system in order to familiarize and prepare the reader for more detailed discussion in the second half of the book. Meanwhile, it will help us to remember that just as a steady stream of water maintains the logs in a given orientation, so too does a steady flow of energy in the form of farm products through Thünen's model maintain it in a *steady state* or single form without change. If new conditions are introduced into the model, adjustments to new steady states will result. In the following sections we will discuss and demonstrate the Thünen model as it was originally proposed. In the next chapter we will introduce basic changes in transportation and fertility and see what happens.

Unit commodity concepts

Before we examine Thünen's model for its areal characteristics, we should define some of its basic terms. These deal with unit measures of commodities such as bushels of corn or hundredweights (cwt) of milk, liters of wine, and kilograms of butter. We also need to introduce the notation which will be used to indicate other elements such as distance. As soon as our definitions are clear, we will transform our thinking into its areal form.

Let us begin, for example, with milk. It has a market price we can call p. That would be the per unit price for any commodity, in this case, a hundred pounds (cwt) of milk. Land and labor and the cost of cows, barns, and fodder are all investments of capital that must be repaid. The total expenses necessary to produce our cwt of milk must be subtracted from the market price. Market price p minus production costs c leaves a net return r, that is, the profit for each unit of produce, in this case milk (Figure 11–6).

The above relationship assumes that the market is located at the production site. This might be true if we lived next door to a dairy and could buy our milk by leaning out the window, but in most cases the produce has to be shipped some distance d to market. This can be measured in miles or kilometers. Milk

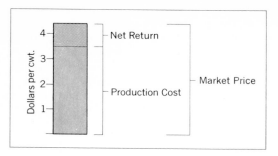

Figure 11-6 Price and cost condition at market
The market price p of a commodity at the market less the production cost c equals the net return r; that is: $p - c = r$.

is perishable, and the glass-lined, chilled tank trucks, sanitary milksheds, and everything else that it takes to get the milk from the cow to you contribute to transportation costs.

Now let us consider another commodity with different shipping characteristics. Bulk corn is much easier and cheaper to move from farm to mill or market. It can be shoveled or sucked up with vacuum hoses. It will not spoil if it is kept dry. High temperatures within the normal range will not damage it. Thus, the cost of transporting corn will be much less than the cost of moving fresh milk to market. Large or small, the cost of transporting a unit commod-

Figure 11-7 Transport rate per mile and transport cost related to distance from market The transport cost for delivering a commodity to the market is the product of the distance to the market and the transport rate per mile.

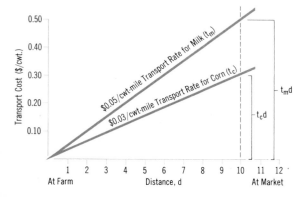

ity a given distance (one bushel or cwt per mile) is called the *transport rate* and is given the symbol t.

Let us assume that we ship a hundredweight of milk and a hundredweight of corn 10 miles. For each mile that the commodities are shipped we must add one increment of transport cost t, but each commodity will have a different value for t depending upon its perishability and general transportability. This rate times the distance shipped gives the total transportation cost td. The lines in Figure 11-7 representing the costs of shipping milk and corn have different slopes, a steep one for milk and a more gentle one for corn.

We can put the terms p, c, and td together in order to see their interrelationship when the point of production is not located at the marketplace. This relationship is stated: The net return on a unit of a commodity is equal to the price at the market less the cost of production less the transport cost. It is written thus:

$$r = p - c - dt$$

We can graph this relationship for the crop being considered. Figure 11-8 shows the unit commodity price p at the marketplace. This price is extended across the graph (line $P—P'$) to suggest the *market price* which any farmer would receive once he got his goods to the market. Line $C—C'$ represents the production costs for a commodity unit; the difference between p and c illustrates the net return r. However, this presentation shows the value of r as being everywhere the same and does not take the cost of transportation td into account. We know that transportation costs increase in direct proportion to the distance from market and must be subtracted from the net return. To show this in Figure 11-8 we have taken the transportation costs off the top of the net return. If production occurred directly at the market, the distance between market and farm would be 0 and therefore the value td would equal 0. At point A the distance would be 10 and td would be 10t. When this is subtracted off the top of the net return r, a new value r_A results.

If the sloping transport cost line is projected outward from the market, it will eventually intersect the production cost line C—C' at point X. At that intersection, the cost of transportation will equal the original net return r. In other words, all the profit earned if the market and the farm were in the same place will have been eaten up by transportation costs. Beyond that distance from market there would be no more profit, and production would stop.

Areal concepts

As geographers we are interested in giving spatial dimensions to our ideas whenever possible. Unit commodity concepts deal with *items* of production but do not relate them to the *areas* from which they come. Three basic concepts relating agriculture to area are *the intensity of inputs per unit area*; the *yield*, or production per unit area; and the *rent*, or net return per unit area. In order to understand the competition for land which exists between different types of activities we must have some notion of their rent-paying abilities.

To change our comments on unit commodities into ideas incorporating space we must multiply all the elements in the basic equation $r = p - c - dt$ by the *yield Y* or output per unit area. For example, instead of talking about bushels of wheat we must now discuss bushels of wheat per acre. We must convert measures like gallons of milk into gallons per acre. Since milk will be produced every day on a dairy farm and, on the other hand, wheat is harvested but once a year, we also need to consider production over some reasonable period of time, usually 12 months. Multiplying our original expression by yield Y we obtain:

$$Yr = Y(p - c) - Ydt$$

We can simplify this by substituting single capital letters in place of subgroups in the above equation. Let $P = Y(p - c)$; that is, *P* equals the *market margin* or profit on the amount of a crop produced per acre. For example, if farmland can produce 20 bushels of wheat per acre, then the profit per acre f.o.b.

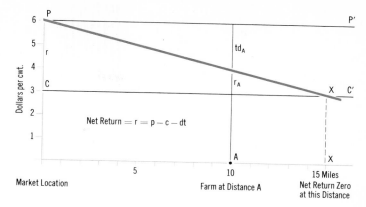

Figure 11-8 Net return relative to distance from market Net return is market price *p* minus production costs *c* minus transport costs *td*. Beyond distance *x* from the market, transport costs exceed the market margin (price minus production costs), and net return is negative. Farmers located this far away have no incentive to enter the market. In this diagram, transport rates and cost are exaggerated relative to production costs in order to show the relationship clearly. Today milk is often shipped over 100 miles to market.

the farm is 20 times the market price of 1 bushel less 20 times the cost of producing 1 bushel.

Let $T = Yt$, in other words, the transportation rate on the amount of crop produced on 1 acre of land. If it costs 1 dollar to ship 1 bushel of wheat 1 mile, then in our example *T* will equal 20 dollars.

After we have made these substitutions, it remains for us to use *R* in place of *Yr*. In this case, *R* represents the net return per unit area, or the rent. This is all expressed by a new equation very similar to our first one:

$$R = P - Td$$

Note carefully that distance *d* does not change.

We may now redraw the graph in Figure 11-8 in a simpler form showing the relationship between the market margin *P*, transportation costs *T*, distance *d*, and rent *R*. This is shown in Figure 11-9A. Again, if the farm is located at the market, distance and transportation costs are reduced to 0. This means that the market margin *P* and the rent *R* on a unit of

A. Rent and Transport Cost per Acre of Crop

$$\text{Rent} = R = P - Td$$

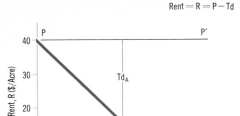

B. Rent Surface and Limit of Marketable Crop

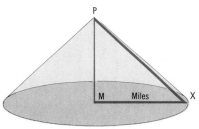

Limit of Commercial Agriculture

Figure 11-9 Bid rent as a function of distance from the market (*A*) Rent and transport cost per acre of crop. Rent is the net return of a commodity per unit area, e.g., $/acre. In order that the rent equation be in the proper units, one must think of the transport rate as the cost of moving an acre's worth of crop a unit distance. (*B*) Rent surface and limit of marketable crop.

land are the same. (Be sure to note that we have now included production costs in a single expression with the market price, and have eliminated the cost line $c-c'$ from our second diagram.) The point x where the sloping transportation rate line intersects the line of 0 profit marks the distance from market beyond which production of the crop will not be found. If we take this sloping line and rotate it around its vertical axis, the distance between m and a becomes the radius of a circle with the market

at its center (Figure 11-9*B*). This is the areal extent of crop production.

We can now draw our first two conclusions from Thünen's work. First, we see that *rent R and transport costs Td are inversely related.* As transportation costs increase, land rent decreases. Second, *given a single market taken as a point on a homogeneous plain, there will be a limit to commercial farming.* No one beyond the radius where transport costs completely eat up profit will want to try to enter the market. Thus, an agricultural region with definite limits will be formed around the city.

Agricultural interdependencies

What happens when farmers have more than one activity from which to choose? Let us return for a moment to the two commodities shown in Figure 11-7, milk and corn. We are already familiar with the steeply sloping line representing shipping costs for milk. We also have seen how that line's intersection with the 0 rent value defines a distance beyond which milk will not be produced. When we consider this in terms of yield, that distance becomes the radius of the milk-producing region around the city. Now let us superpose the sloping line indicating the costs of shipping corn onto the same diagram (Figure 11-10.) Corn commands a lower price in the market, but its transportation costs accumulate at a slower rate than do those for milk. The corn line as a result extends beyond that of the milk line. Imagine these two lines as cross sections of intersecting cones; next, imagine the two cones seen from above. Near and at the market the higher cone belonging to milk will hide that of corn. But farther from the market the situation will be reversed and the lower cone representing corn will not only extend farther from the market than that of milk but also cover or obscure the one representing milk for some distance outward from the intersection M_2. In terms of rent this means that where the milk line is highest, the greatest profit can be made in the market from dairy products. Where the corn line predominates, maize will be more profitable.

What *adjustments* occur when a second commodity, like corn, is added to a one-product system? In the original diagram milk production extended from the central market to point M_1. When corn is added, the superior profits for milk end at point M_2. Under the competition from corn the milk-producing area will be forced to shrink inward from its original boundaries (Figure 11–10). If we add a third crop, let us say wheat, the boundaries of the agricultural regions again adjust under the impetus of competition among unequal rent paying abilities of the different crops (Figure 11–11A). The amount of wheat grown on an acre has the lowest price in the market but is least expensive to ship. It will be found growing farthest from the marketplace because of the slow rate at which its transportation costs use up available profits. Now it is corn's turn to draw in its boundaries from c_1 to c_2 which mark the intersection of the corn and wheat transportation slopes. When things have settled down, wheat will be found growing from line c_2 as far out as line w_1 beyond which no profits can be made by milk, corn, or wheat. We come, with this observation, to the third conclusion provided us by Thünen's analysis. *At any given distance from market the crop with the highest rent paying ability is chosen and agricultural land use forms rings of homogeneous activity around the market.* This is illustrated in Figure 11–11B for a three-crop system.

Figure 11–12 shows the land use surrounding Thünen's original central place. Once we have seen the pattern, it is a simple exercise to reconstruct the relative value of crop types in the market and their varying degrees of transportability. Notice that the distribution of land use types in Thünen's day was somewhat different from our own. We again turn to Michael Chisholm for his commentary on this circumstance:

A point which many writers have seized upon is the fact that Thünen put forestry as the land use occupying the zone second from the central city, whereas certain types of agriculture were put at greater distances. This arrangement accords so ill with the reality of location patterns in

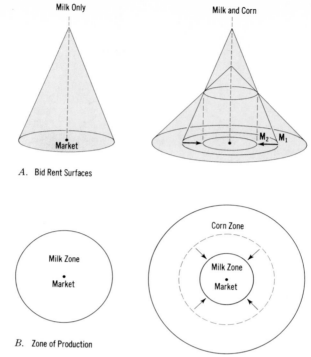

A. Bid Rent Surfaces

B. Zone of Production

Figure 11-10 Two-crop system (*A*) Bid rent surfaces. (*B*) Zones of production. The effect of adding an additional crop to the commercial agricultural system can be seen in the diagram. Corn has a lower bid rent near the market, but because this bid rent falls off more slowly with distance than the bid rent of milk, beyond a certain distance farmers receive more for corn than for milk. They will switch to corn production, and additional farmers beyond the limit of milk production will enter the market. There will then be a reduction in the size of the milk zone, with the result that less milk will reach the market. Milk prices will rise, and the market boundary will adjust outward somewhat. See Figure 11-14 for more details.

the developed parts of the world in the mid-twentieth century that people are often tempted to reject the whole analysis. A few explanatory words are therefore in place. At the time Thünen wrote, forest products were in great demand for building and, more particularly, for fuel. Large quantities of timber were required for these pur-

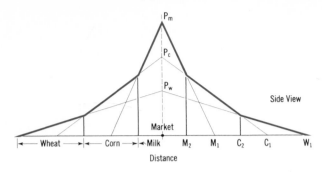

A. Bid Rent Surfaces for a Three Crop System

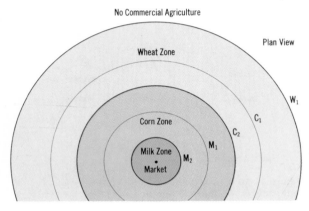

B. Agricultural Land Use Rings

Figure 11-11 Three-crop system (A) Bid rent surface for a three-crop system. (B) Agricultural land use rings. Adding additional crops to the system will cause market boundaries to adjust according to which crop has the highest rent-paying ability. Individual and independent farmers with profit motives for farming will come to the same crop decisions, depending upon their relative distance from the market, and land use rings centered on the market will form.

poses, and consumers were not willing to pay high prices. A hectare of land produced a very large quantity of lumber, even though few inputs were applied; the bulky material incurred high transport costs. Thus, the advantages of proximity to the market were such that all other types of agricultural use, except the innermost zone of intensive production, were displaced by forestry;

it produced a higher Economic Rent than any other product in the second zone. For the time at which he wrote, this arrangement was entirely logical. Since then, technical conditions have changed and forestry has been ousted from much of the land near the urban centres. This does not undermine the method by which von Thünen arrived at his circles.[3]

Thünen proposed a static model in which changes would occur instantaneously. If a system were filled with short-range uncertainties, such as the rapid variation in the price of hogs we mentioned earlier, farmers in the transition zones such as the one between milk and corn would have imperfect knowledge and always be trying to outguess the market. Thus, some would be raising cows while others would be trying grain. The two kinds of farms would be found side by side, and an interfingered boundary zone like those mentioned in Chapter 10 would result. In this case we might say that *tradition would no longer be wise*, for changes in the market, miles beyond the ken and knowledge of the farmers, would affect their lives. A farmer could make all the right decisions just as his grandfather had, but because he is a member of a market economy, forces beyond his control could change the price of his crop so much that he might find himself facing bankruptcy. In the case of market economies, we come to our fourth conclusion based on Thünen: *Agricultural industries (crop types) are interdependent*. If you change one part of the system, you will affect all its parts.

Intensity of land use

In much the same vein we may add a fifth and final conclusion: *Intensity of agriculture increases toward the market*. We have seen that a crop to be competitive must pay a high rent or profit per acre. This means that centrally located land with a subsequent transportation advantage will be high-priced. People will

[3]Michael Chisholm, op. cit., p. 30.

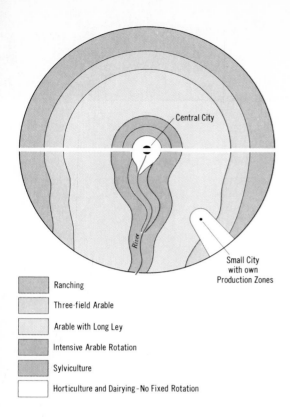

Ranching

Three-field Arable

Arable with Long Ley

Intensive Arable Rotation

Sylviculture

Horticulture and Dairying - No Fixed Rotation

Figure 11-12 Thünen's original diagram showing land use rings Half of the diagram shows the effects of lower transport costs along a navigable river and Thünen's ideas concerning the effects of a satellite city in the region. (Michael Chisholm, *Rural Settlement and Land Use,* Hutchinson, London, 1962, p. 29)

compete for property near the center to avoid high transportation costs. The actual price of land (in this case a *rental,* not a *rent*) may be bid up and up until any advantage given to it by its centrality may all but disappear. If land becomes high-priced, it will then pay the farmer to shift more and more of this total investment from actual land to other factors of production. (By *factors of production* economists mean the three basic elements which in various combinations make farming possible: land, labor, and capital.) He must increase his yields, and to do so he must invest in more and more fertilizer, greater care by men and machines,

better seeds or livestock, and dozens of other improvements. This will result in higher intensities of land use in areas nearest the market. Conversely, farms on the periphery of things will utilize more and more land with less and less investment per acre. At the same time, perishable goods will be limited in space to locations near the market unless some way can be found to make them more durable and cheaper to ship. We have already commented on the roles played by *concentration* and *preservation,* and in the examples in the next chapter these factors will again become important.

The Market and the Farm: Agricultural Location Theory

12 | THE URBAN WORLD AND
ITS HINTERLAND: LAND USE THEORY

The preceding chapter has presented a neat theoretical scheme with which to find order in the seemingly unordered world. But does it all work? The six basic assumptions underlying Thünen's initial theory restrict his model's correspondence with reality. Is there any evidence that agricultural activities really do increase in intensity toward the central point and that rent on land is greatest near the market?

Real agricultural locations at village scales

Chisholm describes various studies carried out in Finland and Sicily on the relation between distance and agricultural inputs and outputs. He discusses the land use pattern around the Sicilian settlement of Canicatti, an agricultural town of 30,000 in the central part of the island. A variety of agricultural pursuits are practiced by the townspeople. Vegetable gardens, citrus orchards, vineyards, and olive trees, as well as almonds, hazelnuts, and pistachios, dry farming (grains), and pasture and woodlots, are all ranged around the town. The pattern is at first confusing (Figure 12–1), but order can be brought from seeming chaos by drawing a series of concentric rings 1 kilometer (0.6 mile) in width around the settlement and counting the amount of land given

over to a particular activity in each zone. Table 12–1 summarizes Chisholm's findings. Looking only at the percentage of land area by distance and crop type gives us some notion of the ordering of activities. What we really need, though, is a further measure of intensity.

If you have ever gardened or worked on a farm, you know that some tasks take much more time than others. This is particularly true if we consider the inputs of labor on a per acre basis (or in this case a per hectare basis). Weeding a vegetable garden which is only $\frac{1}{10}$ of an acre may take longer than plowing the "south forty" with a powerful tractor. The National Institute of Agricultural Economics in Rome provided Chisholm with figures indicating the number of man-hours per hectare required for each of the several agricultural activities on his list. He then weighted the number of hectares allocated to each activity in each ring by the number of hours of work they require. Thereafter, he summed up all the hours for all the jobs on all the land in each zone. The resulting average number of man-days per hectare in each distance zone is shown at the left in Table 12–1. If we consider the investment of labor in agriculture a good measure of its intensity, the case is well made for the increase of intensity as we approach Canicatti, the center of the market-farm system in question.

Now let us consider whether such increasing investments are repaid by corresponding increases in rent. In this case, we will examine another example cited by Chisholm and derived from a number of Finnish farms. Here the measure of production is in net output. This would be the end value of the yield per hectare minus the costs of production and transportation to some central point like a town or village. In this case, three separate studies were made of the rent in money terms for farms located ¹⁄₁₀, ¹⁄₂, 1, 1¹⁄₂, 2, 3, 4, and 5 kilometers from some central point (Table 12–2). The net profit per acre at the very center of each of the three study areas was considered to represent 100 percent of the possible rent to be earned from any plot. Table 12–2 shows that in the first case a hectare of land in the second ring from the center (0.5 kilometer) earned only 78 percent of the amount obtained in rent from a central hectare. In the second case, rent in the second ring was only 67 percent of that at the center for equal-sized units of land. A slightly higher value (83 percent) was true for similar properties in the third example. In every case, rent as a percentage of the profit earned on a central hectare grows progressively smaller with each step outward from the center. In this Finnish study it is safe to assume that more intense agriculture was practiced near the center of each study area and that higher returns made such an investment worthwhile.

Relaxing the Basic Assumptions

Two assumptions underlying Thünen's thinking were the equal fertility of his area and equal ease of transportation in all directions in all its parts. What would happen if we introduced areas of high and low fertility into his model and also some special route, such as a navigable river, which would lower the cost of transportation in one spatial sector? Thünen anticipated these questions and commented on the most likely results.

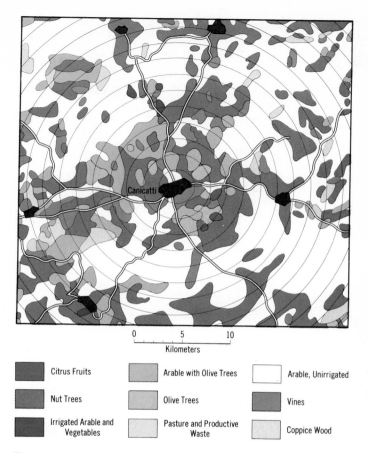

Figure 12-1 Land use pattern around Canicatti, Sicily.

Legend:
- Citrus Fruits
- Nut Trees
- Irrigated Arable and Vegetables
- Arable with Olive Trees
- Olive Trees
- Pasture and Productive Waste
- Arable, Unirrigated
- Vines
- Coppice Wood

0   5   10
Kilometers

Differences in fertility

Imagine an area with a two-crop system much as we have been considering. But in this case there is a large, infertile swamp located astride the boundary between the two crops (Figure 12–2). If the swamp remains unreclaimed, there is a hole in the productive area and the rings of production will have expanded to make up the difference by adding land at the outer edge of each crop ring. Now suppose that the swamp is reclaimed and that the costs of reclamation are charged directly against the rent which will be derived from the newly productive land. In this case, recla-

The Urban World and Its Hinderland: Land Use Theory

Table 12-1 Canicatti, Sicily: Percentage of Land Area in Various Uses and Labor Requirements per Hectare in Man-Days

Distance from Canicatti, km	Percentage of Land Area										Average Number of Man-Days per Hectare in Each Distance Zone
	Urban	Irrigated Arable and Vegetables	Citrus Fruits	Vines	Arable with Trees	Olive	Trees*	Arable, Unirrigated	Pasture and Productive Waste†	Coppice Wood	
0–1	44.7			15.8			19.7	19.7			52
1–2				18.0	16.7	8.4	41.0	15.9			50
2–3			2.6	2.3	21.8	14.4	35.4	23.6			46
3–4			2.1	13.3	18.7	0.6	47.2	18.1			50
4–5				5.1	19.2	2.4	28.4	43.4	1.4		42
5–6		1.0		6.3	4.7	1.6	17.6	64.1	4.7		41
6–7	1.3	0.7		3.3	6.7		18.3	68.7	0.9		40
7–8				4.0	7.7		23.6	62.4	0.8	1.6	39
Total‡	1.0	0.3	0.4	6.1	11.1	2.2	26.3	50.8	1.4	0.4	
Average number of man-days per hectare	300	150	90	50	45	40	35	5	5		42

*Mainly almond, hazel, carob, and pistachio.
†Sometimes sown.
‡Percent of total area in each activity.
Source: Michael Chisholm, *Rural Settlement and Land Use*, Hutchinson, London, 1962, p. 63.

Table 12-2 Finland: Relation of Production per Hectare and Distance to Farm Plots

Distance km*	Wiiala		Virri		Suomela
	Gross Output	Net Output	Gross Output	Net Output	Net Output
0–0.1	100	100	100	100	100
0.5	92	78	89	67	83
1.0	84	56	80	50	68
1.5	77	34	73	40	56
2.0	69	13	67	33	46
3.0			57	25	32
4.0			50	20	
5.0			44	17	

*0–0.1 km equals 100
Source: Michael Chisholm, *Rural Settlement and Land Use*, Hutchinson, London, 1962, p. 55.

mation will constitute an additional cost to be added to all the other ones already taken into consideration in the basic equation: $R = P - Td - C_r$, where C_r is the cost of reclamation. This is the same as raising the cost floor shown as line c—c' in Figure 11–8. If we follow the slope of decreasing rent for each crop, we find that they bump into the newly elevated cost floor, and beyond that point production cannot take place (Figure 12–3). It can be seen that the land nearer the market can be reclaimed at a profit but that swampland on the outer edge cannot meet the added costs.

Now let us suppose that the costs of reclamation will be borne by all the farmers in the entire region in the form of a fixed property tax. Since rents, intensity, and land value all increase toward the center even though the tax rate is fixed, farmers near the center will pay more money in absolute terms than those on the edge because their land will be worth more. This taxation represents an added production cost that must be charged against profits, and is shown in Figure 12–4 as an added layer on the cost floor. This will mean lower rent or profits for farmers everywhere, and since costs such as these are often passed on to the consumer, prices may go up, with temporary inflation resulting. At the same time, if the entire swamp has been reclaimed (which is possible since costs are being charged against everybody and not just against the reclaimed farmland), more land nearer the market has become available and the outer boundaries of both types of production will shrink inward. In this way consumers may experience long-range benefits as better transportation patterns form with shorter supply lines.

This simple example can be endlessly complicated in reality. The results can be good or bad, depending upon a multitude of other factors important in each individual case. One example where society as a whole has accepted the costs of reclamation and undoubtedly has benefited is the Zuider Zee reclamation project in the Netherlands (Figure 12–5). In this case valuable land adjacent

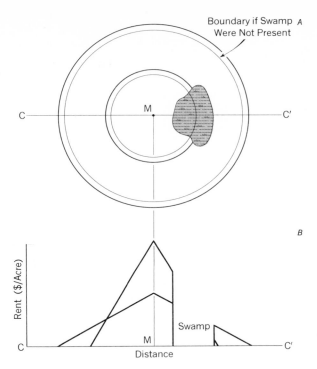

Figure 12-2 Neighboring swampland variation in the Thünen model (*A*) Two-crop system with a swamp existing near the market *m*. (*B*) Rent surface along cross section C–C'. Swampland has no value.

to the Randstadt, the Dutch equivalent of Megalopolis, has been brought into production. At the same time, internal transportation routes have been shortened in Holland. It makes good sense to reclaim lands which because of their relative location can repay the costs of putting them into production. Even if the tax burden is distributed among all the taxpayers, there will be a variety of indirect savings compensating everybody.

The opposite may be true in the United States, where Western irrigation projects sometimes reclaim arid land at tremendous investment costs. In this case, the government may provide low-cost loans to farmers within newly opened irrigation districts, or unrealistically low rates will be charged for irrigation water. Since the low rates charged some of

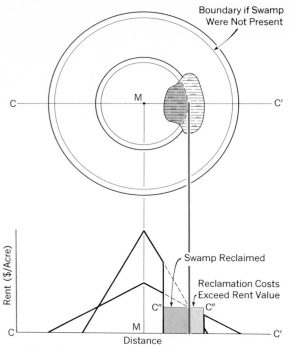

Figure 12-3 Reclamation of swampland
Reclamation costs C″–C″ added to basic production cost line C–C′. Rent-paying ability of crops justified reclaiming only swampland nearest to the market. The assumption is that the people reclaiming the swamp bear the entire cost of the reclamation.

the farmers can never hope to repay the costs of development, the difference above and beyond water sales and total costs must be subsidized by taxpayers everywhere in the country. But consider the relative location of such projects (Figure 12–6). They are often far beyond the periphery of the industrial and densely settled regions of the United States. Because of this, land rents are low and cannot compensate for the initial investments in irrigation facilities. At the same time, the remote location of the new production areas means transportation costs will be great and represent another cost that will be passed on to the consumer. Add to this the fact that

our government pays farmers *not to produce* crops on much of their land (through the soil bank and crop quotas), and many of our reclamation projects seem even more fantastic. In this way it is possible to gain some practical insights into land use and the money allocated for it. A good knowledge of Thünen's principles can enhance your decision making at the polls. Now let us see what differences improved transportation can make in our basic model.

Figure 12-4 General land tax pays for reclamation of a swampland   Tax is proportionate to land value. (Entire swamp is reclaimed.) After the project is paid for, rings contract to an ideal circular pattern. The assumption is that the entire society accepts the expense of the reclamation. For an agricultural society, this would probably mean a land tax, for that is where most of the wealth exists. The public benefit justifying such a policy would derive from the more ideally arranged land use at the end of the payment period.

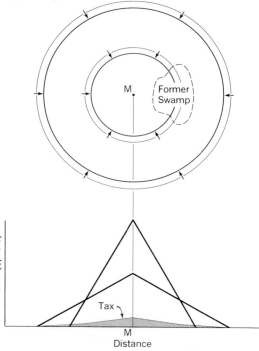

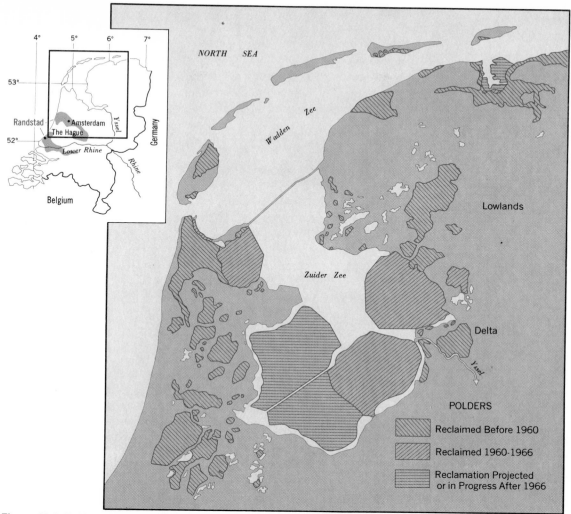

Figure 12-5 Polders of the Netherlands   Polders are Dutch lands reclaimed from the sea. They now represent a significant portion of the total land area of the Netherlands.

Differences in transportation

If we consider the nature of reality and compare it with Thünen's isotropic plain, one of the first contradictions between them will be differences in the ease of travel. We have already discussed the relationship between distance and direction and have seen how geographic circles transform space into new map patterns. Where travel costs are high in terms of time, effort, or money, the distances people travel will shrink; where a good road or navigable river makes transportation easier, trips and connectivity of all kinds will increase.

Thünen recognized this and added a river

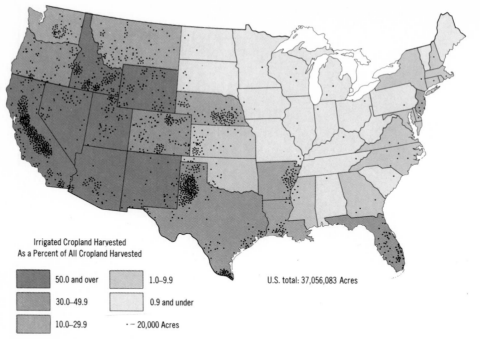

Irrigated Cropland Harvested
As a Percent of All Cropland Harvested

▉ 50.0 and over	▨ 1.0–9.9
▨ 30.0–49.9	▫ 0.9 and under
▨ 10.0–29.9	· – 20,000 Acres

U.S. total: 37,056,083 Acres

Figure 12-6 Irrigated land in farms in the United States, 1964 Most of the irrigated land in the United States is in the Western half of the nation, far away from the major Eastern market. The Bureau of Reclamation, the federal agency responsible for most federally financed irrigation projects, has authority to propose and support only projects which are located west of the Mississippi River. A government program to promote intensive agriculture far from the densest population areas would tend to increase long-haul shipment of food and add to the total transport burden. (*The National Atlas of the United States of America,* Dept. of the Interior Geological Survey 1970, plate 168; compiled from Census of Agriculture 1964, vol. 1)

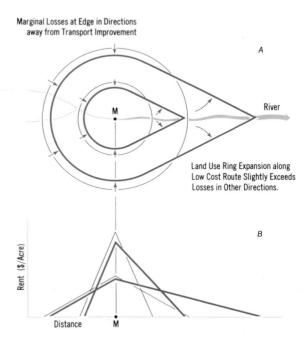

Marginal Losses at Edge in Directions away from Transport Improvement

A

Land Use Ring Expansion along Low Cost Route Slightly Exceeds Losses in Other Directions.

B

Figure 12-7 Directional improvement in transport (*A*) Effects on land use pattern of a decrease in transport cost in one direction (a navigable river route). (*B*) Adjustment in rent surface along a low-cost route. Land use margins expand in the direction of transport improvement and contract in directions away from transport improvement; prices fall; and the total volume of a product reaching the market increases.

to his landscape (Figure 11–12). The stream passes directly through his market town and has the head of navigation just at the town. This is a common condition in the real world. The tidewater settlements of colonial America were located at or near navigation headwaters on rivers flowing from the Appalachian Mountains to the sea. This led to some interesting geographic conditions, which we will soon discuss. In Thünen's case, the use of the river downstream from the market allows farmers to move goods more quickly and cheaply from points along its banks into the central settlement. The relative differences in transportation costs for a two-crop system are shown in Figure 12–7. Note how the downstream side of the cost cone is elongated. This means that additional land along the river can be used for producing the more valuable crop of the innermost ring. The same thing is true for the other zone of production. At the same time that new land comes into production downstream, farmers within a particular zone who are using land on the very periphery find they cannot compete with the newer areas of production. The boundary of the inner-ring crop will draw inward toward the center. Farmers on the edges will have to switch crops in order to stay in business. Less lucky farmers located away from the river on the outer edge of the second ring will experience the same loss from competition with new lands, but they will have no alternative crop and will have to give up commercial farming.

Spatial discontinuities

Another important variation results from different costs in unlike transportation domains. Figure 12–8 shows a hypothetical situation in which a central market is supplied in part by land continuous with it and in part by an overseas area. The crop supplied by the innermost ring is unaffected by the presence of low-cost marine transportation. Its transportation costs are so great that any possible profit would be eaten up long before its zone of production had reached the coast. On the

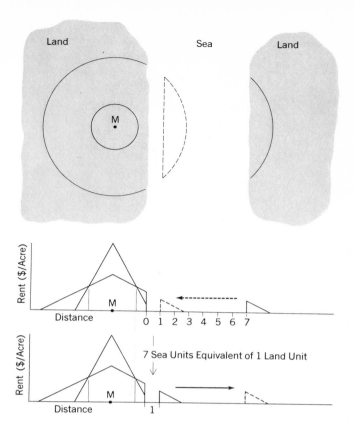

Figure 12-8 Effects of difference in transport rates in different travel domains In a region where land areas are separated by navigable seas, two transport domains exist. Sea travel is much cheaper than land travel, and distant shore areas may be able to enter the market before marginally distant land areas. It can be seen that the distant shore land is within marketing range if the sea distance is reduced by the ratio of sea-to-land transport costs. Some empty territory would exist in the ideal market ring, which implies that costs would be slightly higher for a market located in the position shown, compared with a market in the flat, homogeneous plane of the original Thünen formulation. This abstract argument helps to explain why distant places with access to ocean transport have been able to enter world commerce since the development of modern ocean travel.

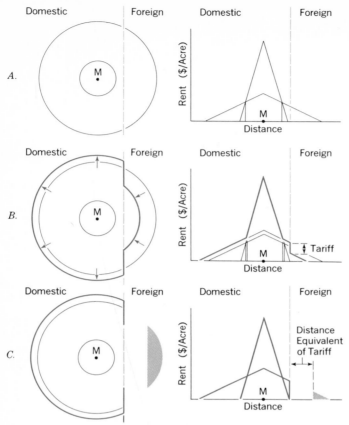

Figure 12−9 Influence of tariff on land use rings
Two-crop system. (A) No tariff, ideal ring pattern,
(B) Tariff on second crop. Rent falls and rings are
reduced in foreign supply area; prices rise and
marginal domestic producers enter the market.
(C) Distance equivalent of force of tariff. A tariff
has an effect much like that of an additional transport charge at a national border. In part A an ideal
two-crop system exists, with a national boundary
running through the region. With no tariff there is
no effect on land use pattern. In part B a tariff is
imposed and can be seen on the profile of the rent
cone as an additional depression of the rent-paying
ability of crops at the border and beyond into the
foreign land. The foreign marginal farmer goes
out of business, and, because of less product in
the market, prices rise and marginal domestic
producers are able to enter the commercial system.
The distance equivalent of the tariff can be estimated as shown in part C in a manner similar to
the difference in transport domain shown in Figure
12−8. The effect of the tariff then is to raise prices
and allow marginal domestic producers to exist in
the marketing system.

other hand, the second crop has not only a
lower transportation rate on land but an even
less costly one at sea. This would be true of
many bulk goods such as wheat. The combined costs of transportation by sea and land
are still low enough to allow some production
on the other side of the water. (In this example we have averaged special terminal
costs into the average transportation rate.)
If we project the transportation cost slope
outward and downward from the market, we
can estimate where production would end
if land rather than sea existed to the east of
the market. If we slide the fractional part of
the transportation cost cone back toward the
central market until it just fits inside the cost
cone projected on the basis of land transportation alone, we can get some notion of
the relative effects of land and sea transportation. In this case, seven sea units are seen
to be the equivalent of one unit of distance
by land transportation.

Various conditions bring about *spatial dis-
continuities* in production similar to the one
just described. Tariff barriers have the opposite effect on production areas, as does low-cost
sea transportation. Two countries with a common land boundary may raise the same crops
for a single market (Figure 12−9). With no
customs barrier at the border the area of production for each of two crops would remain
symmetrically arrayed around the central
settlement. But suppose that a protectionist
policy places heavy duties on crop imports.
This will mean that imported produce will
cost more than domestic produce, and in order
to remain competitive foreign farmers must
take less of a profit. At the same time, marginal
farms in foreign areas will become impractical
since their low profits will be consumed by a
combination of transportation costs and tariffs.
As they fail and go out of production, the
supply in the market will diminish; prices
will rise; and marginal domestic farm areas
will be able to enter the market at the expense of foreign farmers. These *before* and
after conditions are shown in Figure 12−9A
and B. It is also possible to assign a distance
which would be the equivalent of the tariff

involved. We use the same technique as in the previous case for ocean transportation. This is illustrated in Figure 12-9C.

Real Agricultural Locations at Regional, National, and Global Scales

Here, then, are several variations on the original theme proposed by Thünen. We have already seen examples of a correspondence with reality at the village and small town level; let us see what these ideas can tell us about the world at regional, national, and global scales.

Demon rum, distance, and the Whiskey Rebellion

If an insight is a good one, it should apply in many places, to different cultures, and at different times in history. It should also work at different scales of analysis or observation. This is true of Thünen's analysis of the localization of production. We have already seen how farms and farm villages in Sicily and Finland follow orderly spatial production patterns. Now let us go back in time to the eighteenth century and a newly emerged United States to find still another example of the role played by distance and transportation costs in determining farm activities. Our example concerns the drinking habits of colonial America and is told on a regional scale.

Drink, for better or worse, has always been a part of exploration and settlement. Few frontier societies have lived without it in some form. The settling of North America by Europeans was no exception, and the drinking habits of Americans have long figured in the country's history. George Stewart, in his superb book *American Ways of Life*, gives the background to the colonists' drinking habits. With a bow in the direction of the master storyteller let us summarize a few of his ideas and add one or two geographic observations of our own.

Americans in those early days imbibed four basic types of spirits: brandy, gin, rum,

and whiskey. We must skip the details about the first two kinds, which were of considerably less importance to Americans than rum and whiskey. Brandy was a gentlemen's drink, introduced by the French and difficult to make out of local materials. Gin never seemed to catch on with the American taste. Although it could be made from fermented grains grown locally rather than grapes, which were, at that time, unavailable along the Atlantic coast, the ravages it wreaked among the English poor were not repeated in the colonies. This story belongs rather to rum and whiskey, both of which are rich with geographic lore.

Rum came first. The need for locally manufactured products in the New England colonies, combined with a dearth of good farmlands and an ambitious, hard-working group of colonists, created an active if small center of industry and manufacturing in the northern colonies. Other English, French, and Dutch settlers had colonized the warmer, more fertile Atlantic shores from Maryland south to Georgia as well as the islands of the Caribbean. These latter colonists specialized in agricultural products grown on plantations which very soon were worked almost exclusively by slaves brought from Africa. While New England was becoming self-sufficient in manufacturing, the South and the islands depended upon the export of produce and the import of everything from shoes and glassware to tools from either England or the Northern colonies. In the West Indies the production of sugar from cane became so dominant that even foodstuffs such as grains and fish also had to be brought from overseas.

New England merchants soon found out that high profits were theirs for the taking through various kinds of *triangular trade*. A skipper, sailing a fine ship built in Massachusetts or Rhode Island from local timber, might take a load of dried New England cod, lumber, and some cereals to the West Indies in exchange for a shipful of sugar. This sugar would bring a high price in England and could be converted into English goods which commanded high prices in the colonies. Another, and vile, form of triangular trade also developed. Large amounts of molasses were produced during the refining of sugar in the West Indies. This syrup was taken by New England skippers back to their home ports, where it was turned into rum. Rum was cheaper than brandy and soon became the popular drink of the people all up and down the colonies from Maine to Georgia. But more rum was produced than could be locally used, and the remainder found its way in Yankee bottoms to the Ivory, Gold, and Slave Coasts of West Africa, where it was traded for black slaves. Those unfortunates were taken under hellish conditions back to the Indies and the Southern colonies, where they were exchanged for more molasses and also for silver and gold. Many different kinds of trade patterns developed as a result of the *complementarity* and *transportability* of these trade items (Figure 12-10). There were other developments as well. Viewed over a long time scale, the importation of black slaves and their subsequent victory in their struggle for freedom enriched the culture of the United States in numberless ways unforeseen at that time. In the short run, as we have said, low-priced rum became available to the colonists all along the Atlantic seaboard. In fact, rum became so much a part of American life that even today we use its name to signify all kinds of alcoholic drinks when we speak of *rum runners* and *demon rum*.

Overland transportation in those early days was difficult. The sea provided the easiest means of movement north and south along the Atlantic coast, while sailing ships, because of the relatively shallow streams, unloaded their goods only a few miles inland from the coast. Rum, like many other goods, was plentiful near tidewater, but as the frontier moved farther and farther west, transportation costs soon made it a rare and expensive drink. Scotch-Irish frontier farmers from Ulster were soon making their own brand of whiskey. Back in the old country they had made their Scotch and Irish whiskey from barley, but in America they chose rye grains, thus creating the rye whiskey so famous in folk songs. Beyond the Alle-

gheny Mountains still another grain came into use. Indian corn grew well in the hills of Kentucky, and Bourbon County in that state soon gave its name to another kind of whiskey, one which was uniquely American.

Not only had the inland farmers found a new drink; they also had solved an important economic problem which faced them. The major centers of population and major markets in colonial America were located close along the Atlantic shore. New farmlands were increasingly distant from those markets, and the costs of transporting farm products long distances overland hampered the frontiersmen. Nearest to the seaboard were located dairy farms which supplied milk and milk products to the growing cities. Beyond them woodlots supplied fuel and lumber needs just as they did in Thünen's original north German settlements. Beyond the woodlots grain fields ripened. Each of these commodities with a progressively lower rent paying ability was matched by increasing ease of transportation. Milk was perishable; firewood was necessary but heavy; grains cost less in the market but could be bagged and barged or brought on horseback down muddy mountain roads. These relationships are shown in terms of the Thünen model in Figure 12-11. Beyond the point where grain no longer could turn a profit for its farmers, cattle and hogs provided some livelihood and cash. Their advantage was that they were their own transportation. Droves of animals were walked to market from remote farms and butchered at the marketplace. Thus, meat-producing areas were found beyond the grains. But even then the advancing wave of farmers soon found themselves beyond the range of the market.

At this point whiskey became important to them. They could take the grain from an entire field and after distillation have a highly transportable product in a few kegs that could be lashed to the back of a pack animal for shipment to Eastern markets. American whiskey had established itself as rum's competitor. In George Stewart's words:

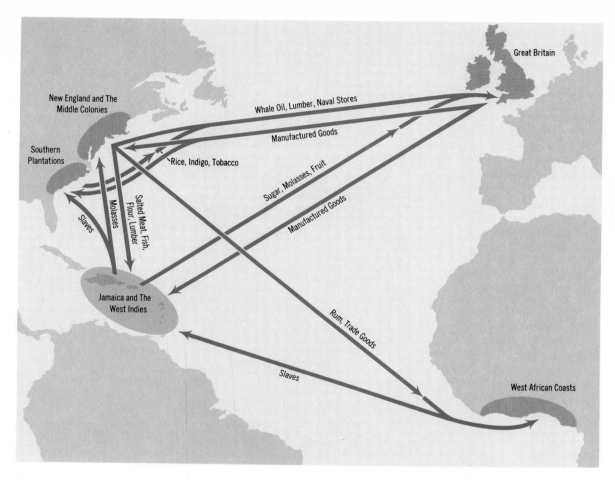

Figure 12-10 Triangular trade on the Atlantic during the colonial period.

In the middle seventeen hundreds there was a country of rum along the seacoast and a country of whiskey farther inland, but the whiskey gradually encroached upon the rum. The frontiersmen had to come down to the tidewater towns once a year anyway to get their supplies of salt, ammunition, and ironware, and they found that for those supplies they could barter whiskey as well as beaverskins. Then, the seven years' war of the Revolution must have had a great effect. The British held the sea and many of the seaports, and rum was hard to come by. War, also, is a great spreader of new ideas and new cus- *toms. Many an Ephraim Pottor or Eben Stubbs of the Marblehead Regiment must have had his first taste of whiskey when he took the proffered flask from some Patrick Wilson or Archy Loughry of the Pennsylvania Line. Moreover, the country of rum could not grow except by colonizing the oyster beds, and the country of whiskey was on the frontier and had all the West open to it.*[1]

The frontiersmen of western Pennsylvania were satisfied with their market arrangements

[1]George R. Stewart, *American Ways of Life*, Doubleday, Garden City, N.Y., 1954, p. 120.

The Urban World and Its Hinderland: Land Use Theory

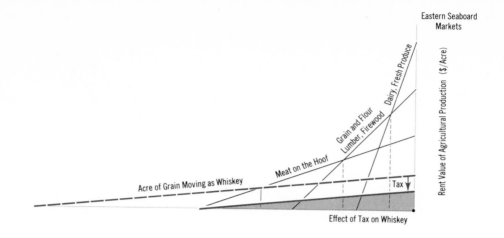

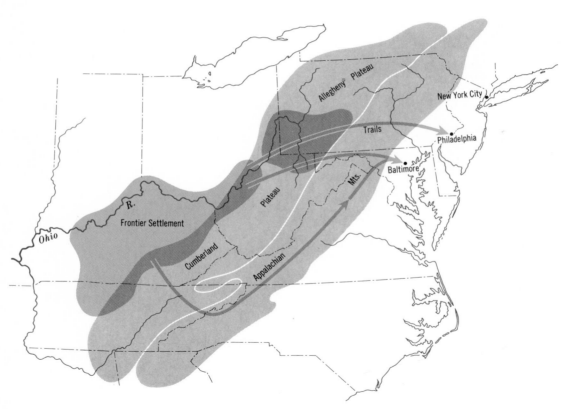

until President Washington with the help of the New Congress placed a heavy excise tax on whiskey in order to help pay the expenses of the new government. This had a similar effect on the marketing of whiskey as would a tariff. A new cost floor was added, and the margin of profit was reduced. Transportation costs could claim less than before, and the frontier Pennsylvania farmers lost their source of income as the ring of profitable farm production shrank eastward toward the coastal markets. Rioting began in western Pennsylvania in 1794, and courtrooms were disrupted and tax collectors and local law enforcement officers intimidated. Washington called out the militia and sent 12,000 men to put down the rebels. His force was so overwhelming—it was larger than any he had commanded during the Revolutionary War—that peace was quickly restored along the frontier. Happily, the tax was repealed during Jefferson's administration and the issue was short-lived.

This Whiskey Rebellion is often described as a test of power between the newly constituted government of the United States and local groups. While that interpretation may well be true, it tells us little about the causes of the trouble or of the real solutions to the problem.

The nation and its agriculture

The above discussion of the Whiskey Rebellion illustrates the application of geographic theory at a regional scale. We return now to modern times and the United States as a whole in order to see how the same basic principles apply to modern agriculture and land use. The sequence of American land use with which Chapter 11 began took us from urban landscapes, through fields of corn, to wheat ranches, and finally to open range where sheep and cattle grazed. A moment's reflection on this sequence of land uses will suggest Thünen's rings to us again. The central city with its market; high-priced but perishable corn; cheaper, more transportable wheat; and finally cattle grazing on acres and acres of unimproved range are similar to other sequences of land use already described. (We should be careful to note that the cattle referred to here are not the sleek, corn-fattened beasts kept in feedlots and destined for immediate butchering. These are, instead, yearling steers getting their first growth on cheap grass before being shipped cityward for final conditioning on special diets. Range cattle are called *stockers* and provide new stock for city-oriented feedlots, where they became *feeders* before becoming steaks and hamburgers.)

Given the concentration of industry and urban markets in the northeastern United States, we would expect that area to be the focal point for a Thünen model conceived on a national scale. Adjacent to this core area we should find perishable, high-value commodities raised for city use such as dairy products and fresh fruits and vegetables. Next we might expect high-yielding field crops, followed by less and less intensive uses of the land. Corn, wheat, and rangeland for grazing match our expectations there. Thus a completely theoretical United States would look like the map pattern in Figure 12–12. Another way of putting all this would

Figure 12-11 **The geography of the Whiskey Rebellion, 1794** The key to entering the Eastern commercial markets in the early days of trans-Appalachian settlement was to lower the transport cost on products crossing the mountains. Hogs and cattle could walk to market, but grain had to be carried. Moving grain as whiskey concentrated the value of an acre of crop into smaller loads. A tax on the trans-Appalachian whiskey reduced the rent-paying ability of grain crops to zero and the Western farmers rebelled. The face that Eastern seaboard interests could import rum by sea in competition with the inland whiskey was important in creating the political problem, a division of interests which still exists in many contexts between the seaboard and inland regions of the country.

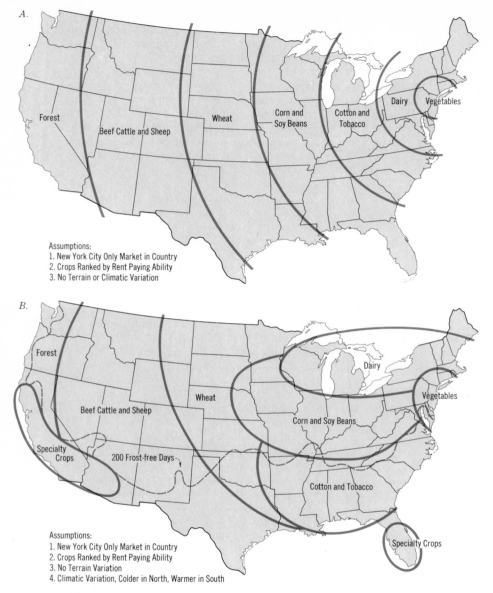

A.

Forest

Beef Cattle and Sheep

Wheat

Corn and Soy Beans

Cotton and Tobacco

Dairy

Vegetables

Assumptions:
1. New York City Only Market in Country
2. Crops Ranked by Rent Paying Ability
3. No Terrain or Climatic Variation

B.

Forest

Beef Cattle and Sheep

Wheat

Dairy

Corn and Soy Beans

Vegetables

Specialty Crops

200 Frost-free Days

Cotton and Tobacco

Specialty Crops

Assumptions:
1. New York City Only Market in Country
2. Crops Ranked by Rent Paying Ability
3. No Terrain Variation
4. Climatic Variation, Colder in North, Warmer in South

Figure 12-12 Theoretical land use rings in the United States Theoretical land use rings in part *A* become more realistic by recognizing North/South temperature variation as shown in part *B*. Rings shift around because different crops respond differently to temperature variation. Pasture for dairying can grow in short, cool seasons; corn and soybeans require 150 frost-free days and a hot summer. Cotton cannot grow north of the 200-frost-free-day line. Specialty crops exist in regions with mild winters. Adopting other assumptions, such as accounting for soil and terrain differences, would result in a more complex and realistic pattern.

be in terms of the rent paid by various land uses. Urban and industrial rents are unquestionably highest; beyond them we would expect land uses, whatever they might be, to provide less and less profit the farther we traveled from urban centers. Now let us look at the actual distribution of crops and rent earned by agricultural activities in the United States.

We should not expect reality to match the smooth rings, neat homogeneous areas, and abrupt transitions allowed us by the models we build. This becomes evident when we look at the maps in Figures 12–13 and 12–14. The first of these maps shows the average value per acre in dollars derived from all types of agricultural activity excluding livestock and poultry production. The two letters inside each state indicate the two leading money-earning crops in order of their importance. The pattern shown here is interesting both for the way in which it meets our theoretical expectations and also for the several exceptions for which Thünen's theory of land rent does not prepare us. As we expected, the highest returns per acre of agricultural land come from that part of Megalopolis between Boston and New York City. New York State itself has lower values, since the shape of the state means that most of its area is farther removed from its major city than areas of New Jersey, Connecticut, Rhode Island, and Massachusetts. Farm values fall off regularly to the west away from the urbanized Atlantic seaboard. In West Virginia and Pennsylvania the effect of the Appalachian Mountains and Appalachia can be seen in lower values that pick up again as Illinois with the major urban focus of Chicago is approached. Going south along the Atlantic coast from New York City we encounter a ridge of high rents which runs inland from the Carolinas to Kentucky. This matches the southern Piedmont and is easily explained by the presence of tobacco. Another high point over Louisiana comes as more of a surprise, although rice and sugar cane account for this rise in the topography of rents. Viewed as a whole, the United States shows a steady,

if slightly irregular, decline in rents westward across the Great Plains to the Rocky Mountains.

Idaho, Washington, Arizona, and California all seem much too high compared with expected values. Irrigation plays a significant part in raising land rents. As we have already noted, major inputs of capital have reclaimed large tracts of dry land in our Western states. In the Southwest mild winters combined with irrigation water help to produce bumper crops of cotton, fruit, nuts, and vegetables. These conditions are enhanced by modern transportation developments with refrigerated freight trains and diesel trucks which carry fresh produce to the Northeastern states. The high value in Florida also represents areas of special crops such as citrus which are possible in the subtropical climate of the area. Wheat from the rich hills of the Palouse country in eastern Washington and Idaho potatoes raise returns in the Northwest. At the same time, the mild winters and green, rain-drenched pastures of western Oregon and Washington create conditions favorable for dairy farming although the immediate market for fresh milk is very small by national standards. This problem is solved by turning fresh milk into condensed milk, cheese, and butter for shipment to the East and Southern California.

If we regionalize production by crop type for the country as a whole (Figure 12–14) and compare this map with the idealized one in Figure 12–12, we see that the general pattern is the same. However, dairy products dominate across parts of New England, northern New York State, and the upper Midwest. This is because these areas have poor soils and are north of the 90-day frost-free growing season. As a result, they are better suited for the production of hay for fodder. But even if we consider only the price structure for milk, we find our general expectations for the United States are fulfilled. Wholesale buying prices for fresh milk diminish steadily from New York State west to Minnesota in the Northeastern dairy region. Since these prices do not include transportation costs,

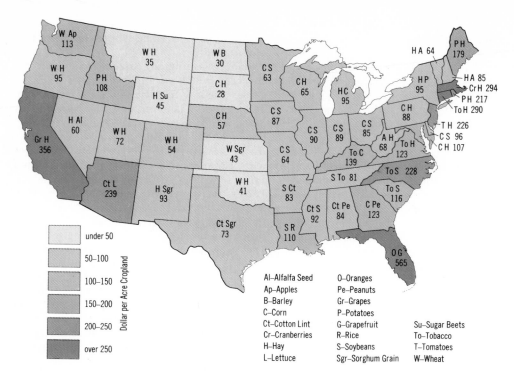

Figure 12-13 Average value ($) per acre of cropland derived from all types of agriculture, excluding livestock and poultry, 1970 (Compiled from *Statistical Abstract of the United States, 1972*, U.S. Dept. of Commerce Table 1011., "Principal Crops")

dealers must pay less for milk the farther they are from the central market area. In the South, where high temperatures make caring for dairy herds and producing fresh milk difficult, demand exceeds supply and prices are again higher.

Returning to our idealized map, we find exceptions where high-yielding cotton, tobacco, and peanuts tend to force out corn. The same is true for the specialty crops (Figure 12-12) which provide alternate choices for farmers distant from the major markets of the Northeast.

Perhaps the best way to summarize these several descriptions is to turn to the maps in Figure 12-15 which show the actual distribution of production for different categories of dairy products, corn, wheat, livestock, and specialty crops. The myriad dots scattered

like confetti across these maps could be confusing, but we hope that by now the basic processes underlying their distribution have become clear. Naturally, one theory and one approach cannot fully explain anything as complex as agricultural production in a country as large as the United States, but a geographic point of view can help. We also hope that the next time you drive across the country, your trip will be enriched when you see and understand the sequence of crop production and other activities.

Europe and the world

If our purpose were solely to describe the theory and technique proposed by Thünen, it would be repetitive to seek additional examples, but any good geography text has two

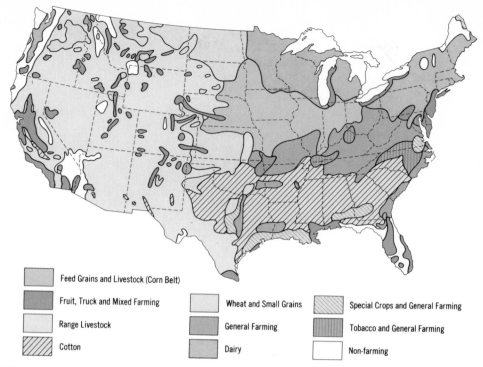

Figure 12-14 Major agricultural regions of the United States

Legend:
- Feed Grains and Livestock (Corn Belt)
- Fruit, Truck and Mixed Farming
- Range Livestock
- Cotton
- Wheat and Small Grains
- General Farming
- Dairy
- Special Crops and General Farming
- Tobacco and General Farming
- Non-farming

major purposes. One is to describe world patterns in detail; the other is to help explain the processes underlying the observed distributions. Thus we present a map of selected agricultural yields in Europe partly as description and partly as confirmation of the ideas we have already outlined.

Figure 12-16 shows the variation in yields of two major European crops. Potatoes are important across the colder, moister reaches of the British Isles, Scandinavia, and the north German plain. Wheat—particularly winter wheat, which is planted in the fall and grows all winter long, taking advantage of winter moisture until it is harvested early the following summer—is the mainstay among the cereal grains of the Mediterranean region. Because of this we might expect wheat yields to be highest in the south and potatoes in the north and northwest. Such an expecta-

tion would be based on some knowledge of the environment alone. In what way could we improve our prediction of yields of both wheat and potatoes in all of Europe? A glance at our maps of urbanization (Figure 3-16) and per capita income (Figure 1-3) reveals that even at a world scale northwestern Europe is a focal point for world organization. This is enough to let us theorize that agriculture will be most intensive near the North Sea and will diminish outward with some regularity. The map pattern once again confirms what agricultural location theory predicts. With a few exceptions such as Switzerland and northern Italy (no real surprise in either place) the bulls-eye pattern of high agricultural rents is focused on the nations adjoining the North Sea.

If we choose a smaller-scale map covering the entire world (Figure 12-17), we can put

The Urban World and Its Hinterland: Land Use Theory

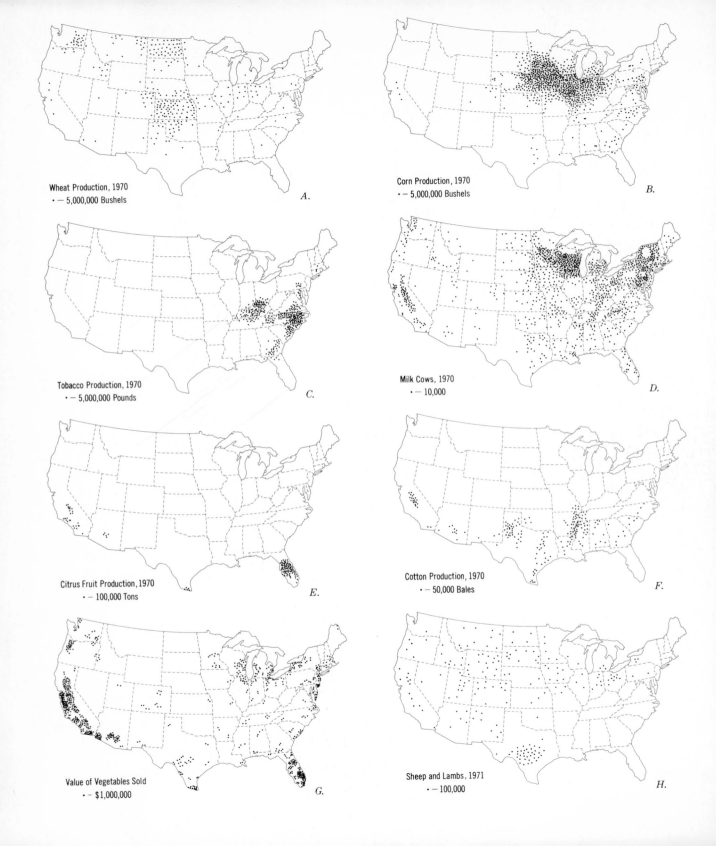

Wheat Production, 1970
• — 5,000,000 Bushels

A.

Corn Production, 1970
• — 5,000,000 Bushels

B.

Tobacco Production, 1970
• — 5,000,000 Pounds

C.

Milk Cows, 1970
• — 10,000

D.

Citrus Fruit Production, 1970
• — 100,000 Tons

E.

Cotton Production, 1970
• — 50,000 Bales

F.

Value of Vegetables Sold
• — $1,000,000

G.

Sheep and Lambs, 1971
• — 100,000

H.

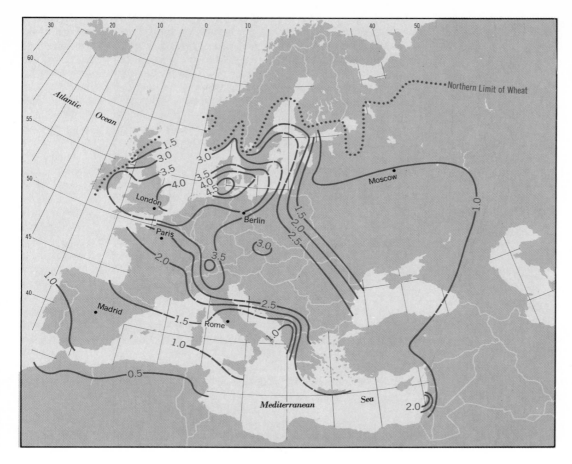

Figure 12-16 *(A)* **Yields of wheat in metric tons/hectare.** The abstract
Thünen agricultural model predicts a fall in intensity of cropping with
distance from the market. In reality, many factors influence crop choice, not
the least of which is climate. Notice, however, that the maximum yield for
wheat in northwestern Europe is not far from the northern limit of where
the crop can be grown at all. On the other hand, the high population density
and relatively affluent commercial society of northwestern Europe exert
considerable pressure on land users to be efficient in the returns they obtain
from the land. This fits well with the Thünen model. The pattern of yields in
potatoes, another staple crop in Europe, also supports this view. (*Agricultural
Regions on the European Economic Community,* 1960 Series Documentation in
Agriculture and Food No. 27, Paris, Organization for European Economic
Cooperation and the European Productivity Agency; *Annual Abstract of
Statistics,* United Kingdom, 1970, London, Her Majesty's Stationary Office,
Central Statistical Office; Tarımsal Yapı ve Üretim *(Agricultural Structure and
Production),* Ankara, Turkish State Institute of Statistics Publication No. 564,
1968)

Figure 12-15 Distribution of selected farm products in the United States
(Compiled from *Statistical Abstract of the United States, 1971,* Dept. of Com-
merce, Wash., D.C., Tables 968, 970, 977, and 989; *Annual Crop Summary,*
Crop Reporting Board, SRS, Dept. of Agriculture, Wash., D.C., January, 1972)

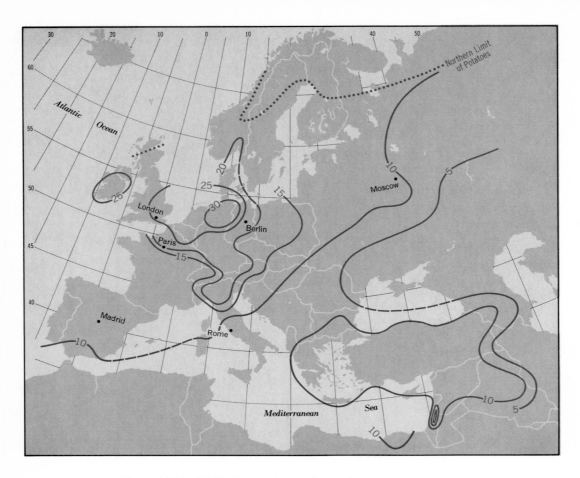

Figure 12-16 *(B)* Yields of potatoes in metric tons/hectare.

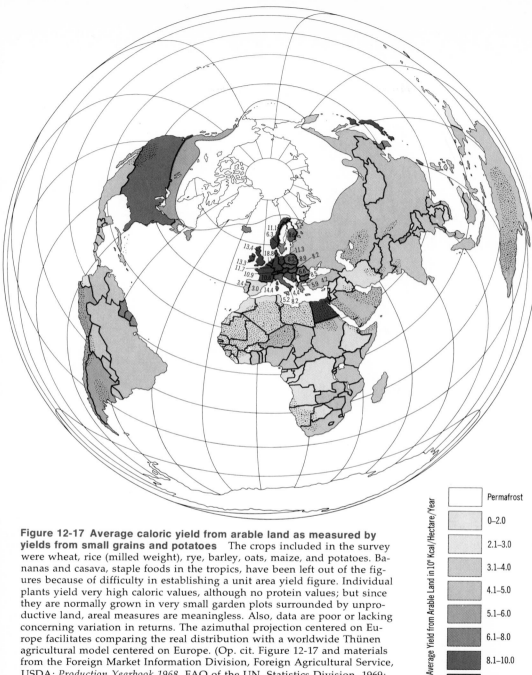

Figure 12-17 Average caloric yield from arable land as measured by yields from small grains and potatoes The crops included in the survey were wheat, rice (milled weight), rye, barley, oats, maize, and potatoes. Bananas and casava, staple foods in the tropics, have been left out of the figures because of difficulty in establishing a unit area yield figure. Individual plants yield very high caloric values, although no protein values; but since they are normally grown in very small garden plots surrounded by unproductive land, areal measures are meaningless. Also, data are poor or lacking concerning variation in returns. The azimuthal projection centered on Europe facilitates comparing the real distribution with a worldwide Thünen agricultural model centered on Europe. (Op. cit. Figure 12-17 and materials from the Foreign Market Information Division, Foreign Agricultural Service, USDA; *Production Yearbook 1968,* FAO of the UN, Statistics Division, 1969; *Statistisk Arbog 1970* vol. 74, Copenhagen; *Statistisk Arsbok 1970,* vol. 57, Stockholm)

Average Yield from Arable Land in 10⁶ Kcal/Hectare/Year

Permafrost
0–2.0
2.1–3.0
3.1–4.0
4.1–5.0
5.1–6.0
6.1–8.0
8.1–10.0
10.1 & over

Desert Climate

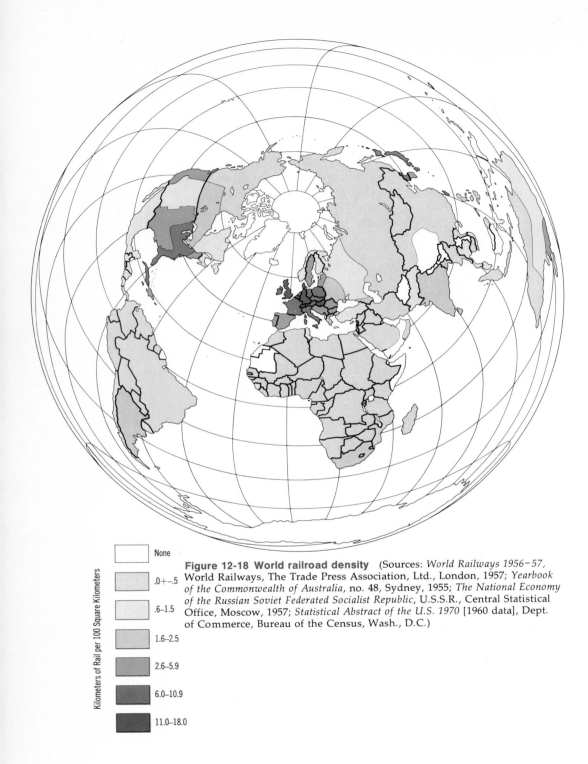

Figure 12-18 World railroad density (Sources: *World Railways 1956–57*, World Railways, The Trade Press Association, Ltd., London, 1957; *Yearbook of the Commonwealth of Australia*, no. 48, Sydney, 1955; *The National Economy of the Russian Soviet Federated Socialist Republic*, U.S.S.R., Central Statistical Office, Moscow, 1957; *Statistical Abstract of the U.S. 1970* [1960 data], Dept. of Commerce, Bureau of the Census, Wash., D.C.)

Kilometers of Rail per 100 Square Kilometers

None

.0+–.5

.6–1.5

1.6–2.5

2.6–5.9

6.0–10.9

11.0–18.0

both Europe and the United States in global perspective. Here we see the average caloric yield from both small grains (wheat, corn, barley, rye, etc.) and potatoes. Pounds and bushels per acre are converted to a more universal caloric value in order to overcome the problem of comparing unlike crops. The results of our analysis confirm what we have already anticipated. The bulls-eye pattern of intensive agricultural production centers now on the North Atlantic. Some details have been lost—for example, in the Soviet Union and America—but the general pattern of distribution focuses upon the *have* nations of the world. Outliers do exist in Argentina, South Africa, Australia, and Japan, but those places are all industrial and commercial centers which have grown up at the opposite end of the major sea routes which supply Europe.

In addition to the rings of production focused upon northwestern Europe, it is useful to note the natural limits of agriculture imposed by a short growing season in high latitudes, particularly in the Northern Hemisphere, and by extreme aridity. We will consider the effect of such conditions in Part Two of this book; but before we pass on to more complex man–environment systems, let us mention one more element spatially relating transportation costs and productivity.

Thünen and the geography of transportation

The pattern of world development emerges in terms of the rent-paying ability of various activities and of the competition among them for the lands they occupy. The pattern is skewed by culture and nature, and yet the amazing thing is the spatial orderliness which certain kinds of human activity display. It is possible now to see in simple geographic terms the connection between urbanization and agriculture as well as the association between the rich nations and the poor.

If industry forms the core of the contemporary world, and if certain kinds of urbanization go hand in hand with such activities, we have defined the focal points for centers of several bulls-eyes around which agricultural activities are ordered. Such foci can be thought of as great magnets pulling the people, produce, and ideas of the world toward their centers. This fanciful notion has an important truth in it. Huge quantities of raw and semifinished materials from the farthest reaches of the earth move by land and sea to the urban cores. All kinds of resources find their way through systems of concentration into a few select spots where they are manipulated and consumed and from which their waste products are dispersed. Thus transportation becomes a critical element in the organization of world society.

Figure 12–18 shows the number of kilometers of railroad lines per 100 square kilometers of land for each of the world's nations. Notice how the northeastern United States is surrounded by three distinct rings of diminishing railroad intensity. The same thing is approximately true for Europe and Australia. The world may be more orderly than it at first appears.

Thus, it is useful to have theories with which to organize our thoughts about our home, the earth. The patterns and principles which we have discussed thus far can be used to understand both human and natural aspects of our environment, and the problems which our use of it creates. Geographers regionalize the world in order to comprehend it, and in turn use spatial theory for insights into the way world society is organized. In Part Two we will incorporate in our thinking new patterns and complexities stemming from the natural systems which underlie all man does.

REFERENCES TO PART ONE

CHAPTER 1

Cited References

Nystuen, John D., "Identification of Some Fundamental Spatial Concepts," *Papers of the Michigan Academy of Science, Arts and Letters,* vol. 48, 1963, pp. 373–384.

Selected Readings

Abler, Ronald, John S. Adams, and Peter Gould, *Spatial Organization,* Prentice-Hall, Inc., Englewood Cliffs, N.J., 1971. A comprehensive and readable presentation of current ideas in geographic analysis for advanced students. Many interesting examples.

Bunge, William, *Theoretical Geography,* Lund Studies in Geography, ser. C, no. 1, The Royal University of Lund, Sweden, Dept. of Geography, 1966. An imaginative and influential book defining the scope and purpose of theoretical geography during a period of rapid change in geographic methodology.

Berry, Brian J. L., "The Geography of the United States in the Year 2000," *Ekistics,* vol. 29, no. 174, May 1970, pp. 339–351. A geographic view of the future of the United States, taking into account society's vastly increasing capacity for communication.

Gould, Peter, "The New Geography," *Harpers Magazine,* March 1969, pp. 91–100. Popularized explanation of current trends and subjects in geography.

James, Preston E., *All Possible Worlds, A History of Geographical Ideas,* The Odyssey Press, Indianapolis and New York, 1972. A comprehensive history of the development of geographic thought from ancient to modern times.

Myrdal, Gunnar, *Asian Drama—An Inquiry into the Poverty of Nations,* The Colonial Press, Clinton, Mass., 1968. Monumental historical analysis of social and economic processes and problems in emerging nations.

Wagner, Philip L., *Environments and Peoples,* Foundations of Cultural Geography Series, Prentice-Hall, Englewood Cliffs, N.J., 1972. A thoughtful and penetrating essay on the ideas underlying the concepts of cultural geography.

Watson, J. W., "Geography—A Discipline in Distance," *The Scottish Geographical Magazine,* vol. 71, no. 1, April 1955, pp. 1–3. A call for explicit theory in geography.

CHAPTER 2

Selected Readings

Hall, Edward T., *The Hidden Dimension,* Doubleday and Co., Garden City, New York, 1966. A discussion of proxemics and of attitudes toward the use of personal space.

Hawley, A. H., *Human Ecology,* Ronald Press, New York, 1950. A sociological view of urban communities with explicit recognition of the impact of spatial variables.

Morrill, R. L., and E. H. Wohlenberg, *The Geography of Poverty*, McGraw-Hill, New York, 1971. A recent effort to apply geographic analysis objectively to social problems, followed by policy suggestions based on their value judgments.

Sommer, Robert, *Personal Space—The Behavioral Basis of Design*, Prentice-Hall, Englewood Cliffs, N.J., 1969. Report of psychological studies of behavior and perception of immediate personal space.

CHAPTER 3
Cited References

Burgess, Ernest W., and Donald J. Bogue, *Urban Sociology*, University of Chicago Press, Chicago, Ill., 1964.

Clask, Colin, *Population Growth and Land Use*, Macmillan and Co., Ltd., London, 1967.

Gottmann, J., *Megalopolis*, MIT Press, Cambridge, Mass., 1964.

Harris, Chauncy D., and Edward L. Ullman, "The Nature of Cities," *Annals of the American Academy of Political and Social Science*, 1945, pp. 7–17.

Hoyt, Homer, *According to Hoyt*, Homer Hoyt Associates, Washington, D.C., 1966. Articles on law, real estate cycle, economic base sector theory, shopping centers, and urban growth, 1916–1966.

Nordbeck, Stig, "The Law of Allometric Growth," *Michigan Interuniversity Community of Mathematical Geographers*, Discussion Paper No. 7, 1965, available from University Microfilms, Ann Arbor, Mich.

Park, Robert E., and Ernest W. Burgess, *The City*, University of Chicago Press, Chicago, Ill., 1925.

Tobler, Waldo, "Satellite Confirmation of Settlement Size Coefficients," *Area I*, vol. 3, 1969, pp. 31–34.

Turner, Roy (ed.), *India's Urban Future*, University of California Press, Berkeley, Calif., 1962.

Selected Readings

Clark, Colin, *Population Growth and Land Use*, Macmillan and Co., Ltd., London, 1967. A reference book on world population patterns and urban density values.

Dickinson, R. E., *City and Region*, Humanities Press, New York, 1964. General reference on city form and function, worldwide and historical.

Doxiadis, Constantinos A., *Ekistics*, Oxford University Press, New York, 1968. Imaginative development of spatial concepts with good diagrams and maps of modern city structure.

Ehrlich, P. R., and A. H. Ehrlich, *Population, Resources, Environment: Issues in Human Ecology*, Freeman Co., San Francisco, 1970. Analysis of population dynamics and human pressures on world resources.

Gottmann, J., *Megalopolis*, MIT Press, Cambridge, Mass., 1964. Original study of merging metropolises on the Atlantic seaboard of the United States, evaluating their function and future.

Lynch, K., *The Image of the City*, MIT Press, Cambridge, Mass., 1960. An influential book on how people view the cities in which they live.

Murphey, R., "The City as a Center of Change: Western Europe and China," *Annals of the Association of American Geographers*, vol. 44, 1954, pp. 349–362. A comparative study of the role of cities in two dissimilar cultures.

Mumford, L., *The City in History: Its Origin, Its Transformation, and Its Prospects*, Harcourt Brace Jovanovich, New York, 1961. Very interesting and comprehensive study of the growth of cities in Western civilization.

Pred, Allan, *The Spatial Dynamics of United States Urban-Industrial Growth, 1800–1914*, MIT Press, Cambridge, Mass., 1966. An analysis of factors affecting the growth of manufacturing regions in the United States and associated urban growth.

CHAPTER 4

Cited References

Carrothers, G. A. P., "An Historical Review of the Gravity and Potential Concepts of Human Interaction," *Journal of the American Institute of Planners*, vol. 22, no. 2, Spring 1956, pp. 94–102.

Ullman, E. L., "The Role of Transportation and the Bases for Interaction," in W. L. Thomas (ed.), *Man's Role in Changing the Face of the Earth*, University of Chicago Press, Chicago, Ill., 1956, pp. 862–877.

Selected Readings

Berry, Brian J. L., *Geography of Retail Centers and Retail Distribution*, Foundations of Economic Geography Series, Prentice-Hall, Englewood Cliffs, N.J., 1967. Review of empirical and theoretical studies of the location of retail centers. A good beginning reference on the subject.

Harris, Chauncy D., "The Market as a Factor in the Localization of Industry in the United States," *Annals of the Association of American Geographers*, vol. 44, 1954, pp. 315–348. Also Bobbs-Merrill Reprint Series G-84. An excellent application of population potential ideas to market location processes.

Olsson, Gunnar, *Distance and Human Interaction*, Regional Science Research Institute, Philadelphia, Pa., 1965. A discussion and bibiolgraphy on models in geography and economics employing distance as a major variable.

Stewart, John Q., and William Warntz, "Macrogeography and Social Science," *The Geographical Review*, vol. 48, 1958, pp. 167–184. A discussion of the gravity model and population potential ideas by two leading proponents of this type of analysis.

Ullman, E. L., "The Role of Transportation and the Bases for Interaction," in W. L. Thomas (ed.), *Man's Role in Changing the Face of the Earth*, University of Chicago Press, Chicago, Ill., 1956, pp. 862–877. Well-written and seminal discussion of the role of transportation in regional interactions.

CHAPTER 5

Selected Readings

Christaller, Walter, *Central Places in Southern Germany*, trans. Carlisle W. Baskin, Prentice-Hall, Englewood Cliffs, N.J., 1966. English translation of the major portion of Christaller's original work on central place theory. Christaller presents empirical material and useful insight as well as a forceful argument.

Lösch, August, *The Economics of Location*, Yale University Press, New Haven, Conn., 1954. Another German scholar interested in many aspects of location theory. He extends Christaller's analysis in this work. It is complex and difficult to read but very rich in insight, observations, and interpretation of general location theory.

Stine, James H., "Temporal Aspects of Tertiary Production Elements in Korea," in Forest R. Pitts (ed.), *Urban Systems and Economic Development*, School of Business Administration, University of Oregon, Eugene, Ore., 1962, pp. 68–88; also Bobbs-Merrill Reprint Series G-217. An interesting analysis of periodic markets using notions from central place theory. This article and Skinner (1964, see reference to Figure 5-8) opened a new line of inquiry. See, for example, the special issue of *Economic Geography* devoted to spatial structure and process in tropical West Africa, vol. 48, no. 3, July 1972.

Wolpert, J., "The Decision Process in Spatial Context," *Annals of the Association of American Geographers*, vol. 54, 1964, pp. 537–558. An influential article about spatial behavior in an economic system, in which motivations other than pure economic determinism are explicitly considered.

CHAPTER 6

Cited References

Baumgold, Julie, "A Guide to the Hidden Meanings of New York Parties," *New York*, Apr. 28, 1969, pp. 24–32.

Meier, Richard L., *A Communications Theory of Urban Growth*, Joint Center for Urban Studies, Massachusetts Institute of Technology and Harvard University, MIT Press, Cambridge, Mass., 1962.

Miller, James G., "The Individual as an Information Processing System," in W. S. Fields and W. Abbott, *Information Storage and Neural Control*, Charles C Thomas, Springfield, Ill., 1963, pp. 1–28.

———, "Information Input Overload and Psychopathology," *The American Journal of Psychiatry*, vol. 116, no. 8, February 1960, pp. 695–704.

Selected Readings

Abler, R. F., "Distance, Intercommunications and Geography," *Proceedings of the Association of American Geographers*, vol. 3, 1971, pp. 1–4. One of the few articles in the geographic literature which considers the effect of changes in communication on spatial aspects of social systems.

Newman, Oscar, *Defensible Space—Crime Prevention through Urban Design*, Macmillan, New York, 1972. Very interesting book associating high crime rate in apartment complexes with the spatial design of public walkways, lobbies, stairwells, and hallways, and how more defensible space could be made available through improved design.

Scientific American, Special issue on "Information," September 1966. A summary of technological improvements in communications and what the consequences for world society may be.

Wolfe, Roy I., *Transportation and Politics*, Van Nostrand, Princeton, N.J., 1963.

Excellent study of the role of transportation in the economy and politics of nations. Most of the examples are Canadian.

CHAPTER 7

Cited References

Deutsch, Karl W., "On Social Communication and the Metropolis," *Daedalus,* vol. 90, no. 1, Winter 1961, pp. 99–110.

Goodwin, William, "The Management Center in the United States," *The Geographical Review,* vol. 60, no. 1, January 1965, pp. 1–16.

Gottman, Jean, "Urban Centrality and the Interweaving of Quaternary Activities," Reprinted in *Ekistics,* vol. 29, no. 174, May 1970, pp. 322–331.

Gould, Peter, *Spatial Diffusion,* Association of American Geographers Commission on College Geography, Resource Paper No. 4, Washington, D.C., 1969.

Hägerstrand, T., "Aspects of the Spatial Structure of Social Communication and the Diffusion of Information," *Papers and Proceedings of the Regional Science Association,* vol. 16, 1965, pp. 27–42.

Halpern, Jeanne W., "How Does the Law Change?" *Research News,* vol. 21, no. 8, Office of Research Administration, The University of Michigan, Ann Arbor, Mich., February 1971.

Marble, Duane F., and John D. Nystuen, "An Approach to the Direct Measurement of Community Mean Information Fields," *Papers and Proceedings of the Regional Science Association,* vol. 11, 1963, pp. 99–109.

Wagner, Philip L., and Marvin W. Mikesell, *Readings in Cultural Geography,* University of Chicago Press, Chicago, Ill., 1962.

Selected Readings

Deutsch, Karl W., "On Social Communication and the Metropolis, *Daedalus,* vol. 90, no. 1, Winter 1961. A thought-provoking theory of the city as an institution of communication.

Gould, Peter, *Spatial Diffusion,* Association of American Geographers Commission on College Geography, Resource Paper No. 4, Washington, D.C., 1969. This is a good review of diffusion studies. Most of the resource papers in this series provide a useful view of some aspect of geography. They are a good source for a student of geography.

Hägerstrand, Torsten, "Migration and Area," survey of a sample of Swedish migration fields and hypothetical consideration of their genesis. *Migration in Sweden, A Symposium,* Lund Studies in Geography No. 13, The Royal University of Lund, Sweden, 1957. An original and excellent study of migration. It is also a very good example of a scientific study of social phenomena.

———, *Innovation Diffusion as a Spatial Process,* trans. and postscript by Allan Pred, University of Chicago Press, Chicago, Ill., 1967. Another seminal work by this famous Swedish geographer. All subsequent geographical studies of diffusion have drawn heavily upon it.

Kroeber, A. C., and Clyde Kluckholm, *Culture—A Critical Review of Concepts and Definitions,* Random House, Vintage Books, New York, 1952. A critical review and detailed compilation from the works of numerous authors of concepts and definitions relating to culture.

Wagner, Philip L., and Marvin W. Mikesell, *Readings in Cultural Geography*, University of Chicago Press, Chicago, Ill., 1962. A useful set of readings on culture areas, on origins and dispersals, and on cultural elements relating to ecology and the landscape.

CHAPTER 8

Cited References

Pred, Allan, "Industrialization, Initial Advantage, and American Metropolitan Growth," *Geographical Review,* vol. 55, 1965, pp. 158–189.

Rostow, W. W., *The Stages of Economic Growth,* Harvard University Press, Cambridge, Mass., 1960.

Selected Readings

Rostow, W. W., *The Stages of Economic Growth,* Harvard University Press, Cambridge, Mass., 1960. Rostow's theory of economic development of nations, upon which our discussion of regional development is based.

Ullman, E. L., "Amenities as a Factor in Regional Growth," *Geographical Review,* vol. 44, 1954, pp. 119–132. An excellent paper discussing reasons for regional development, including noneconomic factors.

CHAPTER 9

Selected Readings

Alonso, William, and J. Friedmann, *Regional Development and Planning,* MIT Press, Cambridge, Mass., 1964. General review of regional economic processes. Chapter 4, by Alonso, is an excellent summary of location theory.

Cooper, L., "An Extension of the Generalized Weber Problem," *Journal of Regional Science,* vol. 8, 1969, pp. 181–197. Recent mathematical extensions of Weberian analysis.

Dean, R. D., W. H. Leahy, and D. L. Mckee, *Spatial Economic Theory,* Free Press, New York, 1970. A collection of classic articles on location theory from the literature of economics. This is one of three readers on spatial, regional, and urban economics. A good source for students of economic geography.

Hoover, Edgar M., *The Location of Economic Activity,* McGraw-Hill, New York, 1948. An older book frequently used as a text in location theory courses because it is well written and clear; it is still to be recommended.

Smith, David M., *Industrial Location—An Economic Geographical Analysis,* Wiley, New York, 1971. Recent book on location theory emphasizing industrial analysis. An extensive bibliography is included.

CHAPTER 10

Selected Readings

Berry, B. J. L., and F. E. Horton (eds.), *Geographic Perspectives on Urban Systems,* Prentice-Hall, Englewood Cliffs, N.J., 1970. An integrated reader on urban analysis for advanced students. Chapter 10, for example, is devoted to methods of factor analysis of urban phenomena.

Borchert, J. R., "The Twin Cities Urbanized Area: Past, Present, and Future," *Geographical Review*, vol. 51, 1961, pp. 47–70. A good empirical study of the growth of this metropolitan area. Interesting techniques are demonstrated.

English, Paul Ward, and Robert C. Mayfield (eds.), *Man, Space and Environment*, Oxford University Press, New York, 1971. A good collection of readings employing location theory ideas, more broadly applied than the typically narrow economic interpretation.

Yeates, Maurice H., *An Introduction to Quantitative Analysis in Economic Geography*, McGraw-Hill, New York, 1968. An explanation, with examples, of commonly employed quantitative techniques in geography.

CHAPTER 11

Selected Readings

Dunn, E. S., *The Location of Agricultural Production*, University of Florida, Gainesville, Fla., 1954. A modern interpretation of agricultural location theory based on Thünen's theory.

Hall, Peter (ed.), *Von Thünen's Isolated State*, Pergamon Press, London, 1966. Translation of the major analytical portions of Thünen's original work.

Higbee, Edward, *Farms and Farmers in an Urban Age*, The Twentieth Century Fund, New York, 1963. Lively discussion of modern American farming and consequences of government agricultural policy.

CHAPTER 12

Selected Readings

Chisholm, Michael, *Rural Settlement and Land Use*, Aldine, Chicago, Ill., 1970. (First published in 1962 by Hutchinson University Library, London.) A modern interpretation of Thünen's agricultural theory by a well-known geographer. Many empirical examples at different scales are presented.

Jefferson, M., "The Civilizing Rails," *Economic Geography*, vol. 4, 1928, pp. 217–231. An old, imaginative article on the role of transportation in the development of the modern worldwide society.

Kolars, J., and H. J. Malin, "Population and Accessibility: An Analysis of Turkish Railroads," *Geographical Review*, vol. 60, no. 2, April, 1970, pp. 229–246. An identification of variables which influenced the spatial development of a railroad network. The study presents a general model of the growth of transportation networks.

Stewart, George R., *American Ways of Life*, Doubleday, Garden City, N.Y., 1954. Delightful book describing origins of typical American traits as consequences of cultural diffusion and adaptation to the North American natural environment.

Webb, Walter Prescott, *The Great Plains*, Ginn, New York, 1959. A very well-written history of the settlement of the Great Plains. Webb describes the role of inherited culture, technological innovation, public policy, and attitudes toward the environment in the development of the region.

PART TWO
NATURE AND MAN
IN A SPATIAL
CONTEXT

13 | WAYS TO WEIGHT THE WORLD: A PREFACE TO MAN-ENVIRONMENT SYSTEMS

Part One introduced us to ways of interpreting the spatial organization of the world. However, the patterns it revealed were often blurred or distorted in reality. Differences between the orderly world suggested by spatial theory and the seeming disorder of reality result from three sets of conditions. (1) Events occur in a probabilistic fashion. That is, we usually know what to expect, but we should also anticipate rare happenings at less frequent intervals. Then, too, the world is in some ways random, and nothing can ever be completely certain. (2) Culture and history play their parts as well. The human mind is wildly inventive, and a portion of that inventiveness sticks from one generation to the next as learned behavior. Isolation and diffusion in time and space generate separate sets of learned behavior which we call *group culture*. The development of culture groups through time creates many histories, some of which are unique and some of which are shared. We must recognize that different people value different things and act in very different ways. (3) The world of nature with its winds and waters, mountains, minerals, and multitude of life-forms has patterns of its own which also must be considered. Man in his effort to survive and prosper rearranges nature's patterns, but in turn, the patterns of his activities are influenced and shaped by the total environment of which he is a part. This portion of our book will discuss natural processes and the part they play in the man-land system which constitutes our total environment.

Another Dimensional Primitive

Chapter 1 introduced the concept of a two-dimensional world which could be simplified and described by three primitive notions: point, line, and area. With these building blocks the basic spatial concepts of distance, direction, and connectivity rapidly took shape. Later chapters quietly added another dimensional primitive to the discussion with talk of densities and density surfaces, rent surfaces, and cones of influence.

Volume is the next step beyond area, and the volume enclosed beneath various statistical surfaces is an important geographic consideration. It is now time to formally enter this fourth primitive into our point of view. When we think of man existing in the atmosphere and upon and under the oceans, or when we consider the enormous quantities of ore and building materials which he uses, two dimensions are inadequate to describe and analyze his activities. Nature, too, involves volumes of warm and cold air, fresh and salt water, and mantles of soil and rock. It is also important to remember that just as points mark the intersection of lines, and lines mark the intersection of areas, areas are the interface between volumes. Man's home, the surface of the earth, is the interface between the spherical volume of the turning globe and the envelope of air which encases it.

Some Considerations of Scale

Chapter 2 was concerned with the importance of scale in understanding and analyzing human activities. The same considerations must be made if we are to understand and rationally approach the world of nature inhabited by man. Figure 13−1 shows the range of scales immediately important to all life-forms. As geographers we note with interest but little or no involvement the end of the continuum smaller than the individual.

Starting with the *individual*, we are concerned with how *populations* are formed by members of individual species. The social, economic, and political relationships of human populations all have spatial expression. But the world is composed of many species, and it is the relationship between population subgroups which creates *communities* of interacting organisms. For example, we might think of a group of humans relating to the plants which provide them with food, shelter, and oxygen, and which in turn are cultivated or laid waste by man. Viewing these relationships over a range of mutually dependent environments reveals important spatial distributions. If we consider the movement of food and energy into a city and the return flow of waste products to the land, we are confronted with a relationship involving both man and nature. Taken in their totality, city elements and rural elements and the relationships that exist between them create an *ecosystem*. When many local ecosystems are aggregated and viewed at regional and continental scales, we become aware of macroenvironments, which can be thought of as *bioclimates* that help define major areas of human activity. Finally, if we view the world in its entirety, we can see areas of like conditions which may span oceans or reoccur with regularity on various continents. These are referred to as *biomes*, places where life-forms face like problems.

We have complicated our trip up the ladder of scale changes by including man at every level. Most botanists, zoologists, and ecologists simplify their task by omitting man from their considerations of the world at different scales. Geographers have long recognized the interdependence of man and nature as well as the totality of the interaction between climate, vegetation and soils, and all animal life. This notion, so important that it legitimately can be described as a philosophical point of view, is called the *concept of environmental unity* and is a major theme underlying the remainder of this book.

We will discuss the world at many different scales, but communities, ecosystems, bioclimates, and biomes will be our principle concerns. At each of these scales the processes which support life can be better understood through an appreciation of the spatial relationships which exist among the actors and between actors and the lifeless, but seldom immobile, elements such as wind, water, and the earthquake-prone earth itself.

The Continents of Man

Man utilizes the resources of the earth in order to survive and prosper. The number of people living in a given area, that is, population density, is one measure of his ability to convert the raw stuff of nature into food, shelter, and all the other material things upon which he depends. His ability to organize space and to move materials, goods, and people from one place to another complicates the picture. For example, Megalopolis, Hong Kong, and many other crowded but relatively resource-poor areas could not maintain their populations without importing food and exporting services and manufactured goods to pay their grocery bills. The uneven scattering of human populations across the surface of the earth is shown in Figure 13−2A. We have omitted the outlines of the continents

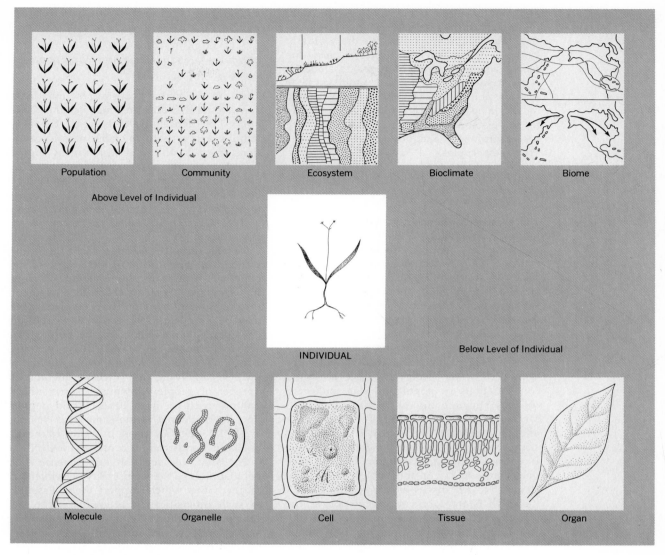

Figure 13-1 Scales at which life forms operate The individual serves as the central measure of this system. Below the level of the individual, microscopic observation becomes increasingly necessary. Above that level, geographic techniques are of great importance. Locational analysis can be used to study the life processes at every scale from that of populations to that of biomes.

and other familiar reference points in order to emphasize the fascinating, lumpy distribution that results. These are, in the words of William Bunge, the *continents of man*, the places where in terms of numbers alone he is most successful. If we can understand the reasons for the settlement pattern shown on this map, we will have come much closer to understanding how man interacts with his environment and how he organizes the space he occupies.

Environmental constraints

The presence of densely settled human populations immediately attracts our attention, but the empty areas on this map are as interesting as the crowded ones. Viewed at a global scale the effects of three environmental constraints which limit the extent of human settlement can be seen. Man overcomes these constraints only with great difficulty; otherwise, the result is either empty areas or sparse populations. Limitations are placed on human settlement by cold, aridity, and large bodies of water. Note first that no major concentrations of population exist poleward of lines showing the 90-day frost-free limit for agriculture (Figure 13–2B). Where solar energy is sparse, domesticated food crops cannot mature and ripen, and there is little incentive for human habitation. We will have much more to say on this subject in the next chapter, which discusses the relationship of the earth to its dominant energy source, the sun. In much the same way, man has difficulty supporting himself in large numbers where less than 10 inches of rain fall each year (Figure 13–2C). Finally, the constraint imposed by oceanic waters is obvious (Figure 13–2D). Similar constraints have already been mentioned in Chapter 5, where the effect of cold

and aridity on the settlement pattern of the northern Great Plains was discussed.

Resources, Technology and Population Density

The environmental constraints mentioned above establish outside limits on the distribution of densely settled areas. However, within regions with tolerable natural conditions there is still great variation in population density. To understand these variations other qualities of the global ecosystem must be taken into consideration, including man's technology and his ability to organize space and to migrate in search of perceived opportunities.

Natural resources become available to man through his application of technology to raw materials within his environment. Changes in technology result in changing increments of wealth and/or population. In fact, there may be a trade-off between new wealth and new population. That is, if the output of a system increases, such an increase may sustain more people at a fixed level of living, or the level of living may increase for a fixed number of people. Obviously, some middle ground exists in most cases. World population has increased at the same time that the level of living has risen in many countries. But both trends cannot continue indefinitely.

The only way societies can increase their populations *and* their prosperity is to intensify the activities which support them. Essential to such intensification is greater social and spatial organization with an accompanying emphasis upon transportation. Dense concentrations of people, in order to prosper, must have a rich resource base, effective technology, and efficient spatial organization. Otherwise, the price they pay for their numbers is poverty and squalor.

Figure 13-2 The continents of man—the effect of environmental constraints on world population distribution The seemingly haphazard distribution of people (*A*) can be explained in large part through a combination of low temperature (*B*), aridity (*C*), and oceanic waters (*D*).

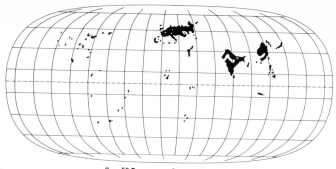

A   Over 50 Persons per Square Kilometer

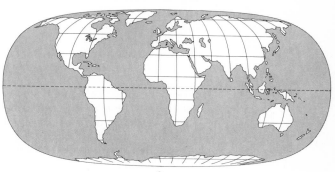

C   Less than 10 Inches Annual Rainfall

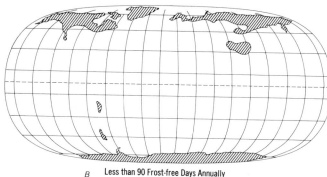

B   Less than 90 Frost-free Days Annually

D   Ocean

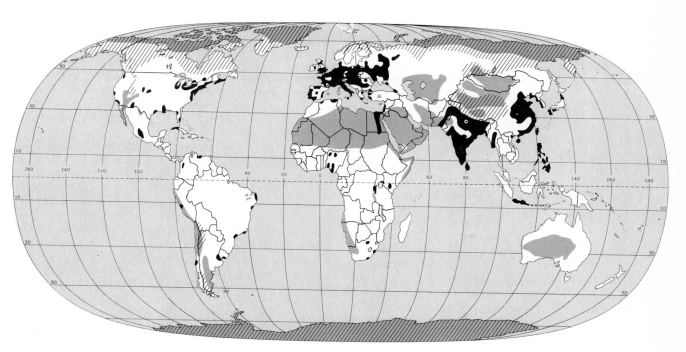

E

If we reconsider the world distribution of technical skills and natural resources, we can distinguish four major combinations of these elements. There will be those fortunates commanding a sophisticated technology who also control many natural resources. Americans are a good example of this group. Other people, such as the Swiss, may have well-developed technical skills which support them in environments having a limited or poor resource endowment. Next there are groups with few technical skills living in well-endowed areas. Among these would be inhabitants of the oil-rich nations of the Middle East. Finally, poorest of all are those who have few technical skills and who control a national territory such as Somalia or Chad with very few natural resources.

Per capita income If numbers of people alone were the measure of human success, it would be difficult to understand world population distributions. Extreme concentrations of people exist both in northwest Europe and on the Gangetic Plain of India. England, with its coal fields and iron ore deposits, has only slightly fewer people per square mile than does Japan on its mineral-poor island. The material success of mankind must, therefore, be measured not only in terms of population density but also by the level of living that groups have attained. We, therefore, add to our considerations at this point *per capita income* as a measure of a group's level of living.

Figure 13–3 brings together the four variables discussed above: level of living shown by per capita income, population density, available technology, and resource endowments. The diagram shows that countries with good resources and high levels of technology can support dense populations at high per capita incomes. It does not follow, however, that all such national groups automatically will have high population densities. Nations with many technical skills but few resources have relatively small populations (Norway), or if they are densely settled, per

capita incomes are considerable lower (Japan). On the low end of the technological and resource scale, incomes are universally small and are often matched by sparse populations.

We realize that this discussion for the time being overlooks the philosophical questions of *personal satisfaction* and *quality of life*, but the definition of these terms is so complex that we must begin with more mundane considerations like per capita income.

We also recognize the importance of other human factors that are difficult to measure. Certainly, the *aspirations* of a people are basic to their activities. Americans aspire to the lavish consumption of goods; some groups spend their time engaged in complex ritual and prayer; still others treasure leisure. But where once it was popular to point to more and more material production as a measure of progress, now only the dullest of technocrats defines satisfaction and happiness solely in terms of goods and gadgets.

Population density and the organization of space Egypt, India, and the United States, among other nations, remain somewhat anomolous when discussed in the above terms. When census data are aggregated for entire nations, the results often conceal smaller areas within their boundaries having much higher or much lower population densities. To appreciate the problem of accurately determining population densities, let us review the role of spatial organization in the utilization of resources.

The relationship between technology, spatial organization, and population densities is illustrated in part by Figure 13–4. Population densities measured in number of people per 100 square miles of territory are shown along the ordinate. Seven stages of human technological development with their attendant spatial characteristics are ranked along the abscissa. These range from the simplest ancient forms of hunting, gathering, and collecting on the left to modern and highly developed life-styles like those in the United States and northwest Europe listed on the far right. The first column corresponds roughly

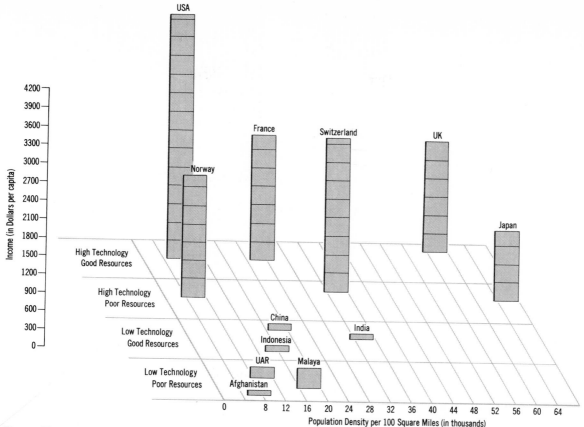

Figure 13-3 Level of technology, resource availability, and per capita income Given a high level of technology, a nation can provide its population with high average per capita incomes. This is true even when natural resources are in short supply. This is also true whether population density is high or low. The location of the nations along the population density scale would vary greatly if only arable land were considered. The United Arab Republic (Egypt) is an example of this latter point. (Data: Population Reference Bureau, 1971)

to prehistoric Indian communities such as those that once inhabited the Tehuacan Valley in highland Mexico. Those wandering microbands, operating at simple technical levels, needed extremely large territories to support their migratory existence, dependent as it was upon nature's scattered distribution of nutrients in the form of wild plants and animals. Later groups employing more efficient predomesticate systems of plant collecting are shown in the same column. All these

values represent estimates of populations using similar shifting patterns of spatial organization like those discussed in Chapter 19. The point labeled "Microbands" represents a population estimate for an early postglacial temporary campsite in what is now east-central England. The point marked "Food Gathering" is the best general estimate computed by Robert Braidwood and Charles Reed for that way of life.

The column designated "Emerging Farm

Ways to Weight the World: A Preface to Man-Environment Systems

243

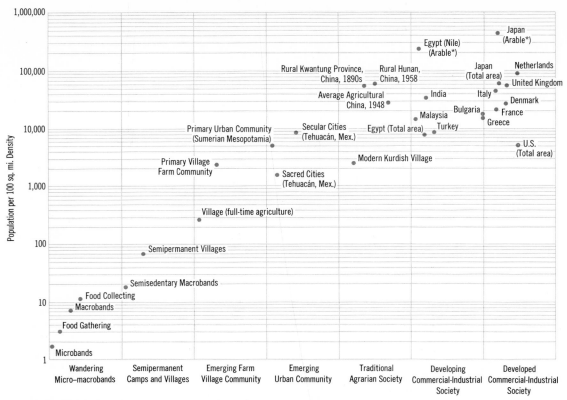

Figure 13-4 Population density and level of technology and organization
There has been an upward progression from prehistoric to modern times in
the population densities which mankind has been able to support. This is
closely linked to man's level of technology and organization of space. This
diagram should be considered with caution. No attempt has been made to
assign dates to the levels of technology ranked along the abscissa. Early
population estimates are "guesstimates" at best. Note, too, the shift in the
positions of Egypt and Japan depending on whether total areas or arable
areas are considered. (References: Edward S. Deevey, Jr., "The Human Population," *Scientific American,* September 1960; N. Ginsburg, *Atlas of Economic
Development,* University of Chicago Press, Chicago, Ill., 1961; G. W. Skinner,
"Marketing and Social Structure in Rural China," *Journal of Asian Studies,*
vol. 24, no. 1, November 1964; R. Braidwood, and C. Reed, "The Achievement and Early Consequences of Food Production: A Consideration of the
Archaeological and Natural-Historical Evidence," *Cold Springs Harbor Symposium on Quantitative Biology,* 1957, also Bobbs-Merrill Reprint A-23;
R. MacNeish, "Ancient Mesoamerican Civilization," *Science,* vol. 143,
no. 3606, Feb. 7, 1964, also Bobbs-Merrill Reprint A-364)

Community" represents a level of technology
higher than that of wandering hunters and
collectors. Food supplies are more readily
available because of man's having acquired
simple agricultural skills. Settlements with
permanent buildings begin to dot the landscape. Ancient towns and cities develop next,
and urban culture becomes a way of life for

a small proportion of the population. Now the city and the countryside surrounding it must be considered together as parts of a single ecosystem. This is followed by fully developed traditional societies like those in China described in Chapter 5. As groups gain more technical skills, nation-states emerge with most of their populations living in cities rather than on the land. Population densities associated with modern nations are shown in the last column.

We are careful not to give specific dates to any of the columns. The reason for this is that domestications and urban development took place at different times at different places throughout the world. For example, the use of domesticated plants begins about 5000 B.C. in the Tehuacan area, whereas in the Near East, Braidwood has identified domesticates occurring by 6500 B.C. at the village site of Jarmo. On the other hand, the simplest permanent settlements did not begin to appear in the Tehuacan area until about 3000 B.C. It follows that it is safer to keep our measuring units general and sequential rather than tying them to exact dates. The important thing to keep in mind is that every new state of technological development increases the complexity of the spatial organization of the society involved.

This does not mean that the quality of life necessarily improves. It is entirely possible for a nation have many technical skills and rich resources and yet to create a nightmare state similar to that in George Orwell's *1984*. Political control and economic power can be vested with the multitude or serve only an elite few. The latter is unfortunately the case in many developing countries as well as in some economically advanced nations. The result in the developing countries is a great and growing gap between the crowded poor and the wealthy few. In developed economies controlled by dictators, political organization, wealth, and technology are the means by which control is exerted. In such a society the quality of life for the common man can be unenviable as the result of his inability to control his own affairs.

Problems of measuring population density

Having observed the chart we should pause for a moment to consider the nature of the data upon which it is based. Remember, *population density* means the number of people living within a fixed unit area; often, such figures are estimated. No one has yet invented a glass-bottomed time machine with which to return to the Tehuacan Valley or any other place and moment in history in order to take an actual population census. Such figures are "educated guesses" based upon archaeological evidence and current observations of similar situations. Nevertheless, when we collect estimates and "guesstimates" from several different sources and find them all falling within a relatively narrow range, as in this case, we can have some confidence that the picture we present is reasonable.

Estimating population density figures presents problems which are particularly spatial in character. For example, Braidwood and Reed's population density figure for the emerging urban community is based on estimates of the whole of ancient Sumer including densely built-up cities and arid wasteland. The inclusion of wasteland is not some capricious whim of those prehistorians. Rather, there is little evidence with which to decide which areas were irrigated, which were pasture, and which lay waste so very long ago, and so there is little choice except to include the entire territory. The same thing is true for the Tehuacan figures which we have calculated from the author's reports.[1] For want of a better figure, we took the statement that the Tehuacan area totals 1,400 square miles and used it as the denominator in our calculations. But who knows the exact territories used and coveted by those ancient hunters, warriors, and farmers? A different number would have yielded larger or smaller densities, but again, lacking first-hand knowledge, we must go by *best estimates* if we are to go at all.

These observations remain true for today's

[1]Richard S. MacNeish, "Ancient Mesoamerican Civilization," *Science*, vol. 143, 1964, pp. 531–537.

The two Egypts. Agriculture is possible in Egypt only where irrigation water is available. Topography restricts irrigation to the valley and delta of the Nile River. Beyond those areas, "boundless and bare, the lone and level sands stretch far away." The contrast between the two environments can be clearly seen in this satellite photograph. (NASA Gemini 5 photo)

ity, we arrive at a relatively low figure of 7,600 people per 100 square miles. On the other hand, if we consider only the arable and inhabitable portions of Egypt, that is, the valley of the Nile and its delta, the population density of Egypt climbs to an astounding 236,000 people per 100 square miles of farmland. (See the photograph at the left for a view of the two Egypts.) A comparable contrast exists between total area and cultivated area for Japan (63,000 versus 433,000 per 100 square miles).

There is no pat answer to the question of which areal units to use. The terminology of answers is determined by the terminology of the questions asked. And the questions asked are in large part dependent upon the nature of the systems under investigation. Up to this point in our discussion we have used ideas and terminology relating to systems in a largely intuitive manner. In the remainder of this book we will discuss larger and more complex processes and will rely even more on systems concepts. We, therefore, need to define some basic terms relating to these ideas. In following this line of reasoning, the first concept we must understand and define is *system* itself.

General Systems Theory

Numbers of people, resources, technology, and level of living must be considered simultaneously if we are to understand the distribution of human population. To really make sense of man and his activities the above four items form much too short a list. Moreover, simply listing things tells us nothing about relationships between the various elements, and nothing about the processes which link them together. To appreciate such processes we must be able to identify cause and effect relationships: If *A*, then *B*; given *B*, then *M* or *N*, . . . As geographers, we also want to see causal relationships in terms of their spatial and environmental characteristics.

Consider the above association of wealth, productivity, and population. At a given level of technology and resource availability a society within a fixed territory may have an

censuses. Is the viable United States all the area within its legal boundaries? Or should we exclude the wastelands of Alaska and Nevada and only consider the rich fields of Kansas and Iowa? And what about calculating urban densities? Should we use standard metropolitan statistical areas or the areas within the legal boundaries of cities for computing urban population densities? Or should we compute densities using a neighborhood scale and include only residential lots in our calculations? Consider the figures shown in the right-hand columns of the chart. If the desert is included in our calculation of Egypt's population dens-

unchanging per capita income and a stable population wherein births and deaths balance each other. A subsequent technological breakthrough might make more wealth (food, money to buy food, medicine, etc.) available to the group. At first, everyone would be better off, with more food to eat and money to spend. Given better conditions, the number of deaths per thousand people might diminish and the population increase correspondingly. But if the technological breakthrough was such that the resulting productivity could not keep pace with population growth, the per capita share of total wealth would again drop. Deaths might again increase because of renewed poverty, and a new condition of equilibrium would result. The only difference between the old and the new states would be that a larger number of people would be supported; but they would be no better off than before. A pessimistic view such as this was held by many early economists and led to a laissez faire philosophy which saw the poor getting poorer while the rich grew richer. Whether or not this situation is inevitable depends in large part on the interpretation given it by the people making the decisions and the kinds of analytical thinking they employ.

This can all be summarized: Resources plus technology yield a product which in turn gives a population at a certain level of living. New technology increases productivity; increased production leads first to wealth and then to more people; more people's sharing a fixed product means lower per capita incomes. Lower incomes yield poverty; poverty yields a higher death rate. The circle is closed although the numbers involved are greater. We have here a set of things and their attributes which are linked together by a process that establishes their interdependence. However, a description such as the one just given can be awkward. It can also be difficult to repeat for another set of conditions or another time by a different person. It is important, therefore, that we establish a uniform technique of simultaneously viewing many variables and the processes which link them. To do this geographers are turning more and more to the idea of *general systems theory* and *systems analysis*.

System and environment

The processes which characterize the world of man and nature can be thought of as chains or networks of related events and material things. *Any set of objects and the relations between them can be called a system.* Humans and human artifacts make up man-made systems. Natural phenomena and the processes which link them can be thought of as natural systems. The separation of man-made systems from natural systems is ultimately impossible. The presence of man has affected almost all natural systems with which he has come in contact. In turn, man is a biotic creature dependent upon the environment for all things: light, heat, food, shelter, the very air he breathes. Part One of this book has discussed some human systems from a geographic point of view; Part Two introduces some basic natural systems and attempts to show how human and natural processes are interwined.

Let us reconsider the case of Egypt's population density. The question was whether to use the valley of the Nile or the entire territory within the nation's borders as the areal unit defining population density. To simplify things, let us assume that the population is entirely dependent on agricultural production. The critical area is defined then as those places where agriculture is possible, that is, the valley of the Nile and the delta. The total system includes the population supported by agriculture; the natural valley environment, including vegetation, soil, climate, and water; and various culturally defined pieces of equipment and artifacts, including everything from fertilizer to farm houses. The surrounding desert plays very little part in the operation of this farm system but cannot be ignored. At this point, we must make a careful distinction between the farm *system*, which is the *basic object of investigation*, and the surrounding desert, which constitutes the larger *environment*, that is, *those parts of the external world within which the system exists and which interact with it.* To be complete, we would also want to include as part of the environment the national and international economies within which the Egyptian agricultural system operates. But as is our custom, we will simplify the discussion by omitting those things. In agricultural terms, the proper areal unit for computing population density is the valley and delta where the system exists rather than the total country, which includes part of the desert environment surrounding the system.

Closed, isolated, and open systems

Now let us consider the relationship between any system and the environment which surrounds it. Imagine a theoretical city and its suburbs and the workers who commute back and forth between the two places by electric trains. In this model, no people leave for places external to the system and none enter it from outside. The thing that is imported is energy in the form of electricity which provides the means by which travel takes place. Heat, another form of energy, escapes from the system back into the surrounding environment. This is a *closed system* very much like the sealed cooling system in an automobile, in which the same fluid circulates over and over and only energy to drive a pump and excess engine heat cross the system's boundary. The mass of the cooling fluid never varies. In other words, *a closed system is one which exchanges energy but never mass with its environment.*

"But," someone will ask, "isn't the cooling system an integral part of an automobile?" And, "Isn't it impossible to find a city and its suburbs completely isolated from the world market?" The answer is *yes* in both cases. But in our theoretical example both the automobile and the world market are not the objects of study, and by definition become the environments of the smaller systems. In other words, *the environment of a system is all the systems larger than itself in which it is embedded.*

In fact, our use of a theoretical city and suburbs which exchange energy but no mass with their environment raises an important point. Reality contains some systems which for at least a limited period of time are physically discrete although energy flows across their boundaries. But it would be impossible to find a completely insulated real system which exchanged *neither mass nor energy* with its environment. Such systems can exist only in theory, as in the perfect thermodynamic models used in physics or in a total cosmology where the entire universe is treated as a single system. This type is called an *isolated* system.

On the other hand, if we consider the city and its suburbs or Egypt and the valley of the Nile as they exist in reality, we must picture them as kinetic and undergoing constant change. They grow and prosper, or decline; they exchange people, materials, goods, and ideas with the rest of the world that is their environment. Put another way, mass and energy constantly move in both directions across their boundaries. Systems of this type, which most closely describe reality, are referred to as *open systems.* Remember, Egypt's most important resource is the water of the Nile River, which originates outside the system as we have defined it here.

Dynamic equilibrium

A steady supply of water is as essential to any city as it is to any farm system. Some cities take their water directly from rivers and during periods of drought must ration its use. A more dependable way to supply water to a city is to collect it in a reservoir for release when needed. (The city and the river can be thought of here as a partial system since we do not consider where the river water comes from or where it goes after being used in the urban area.) In order to regulate the flow of water to the city as it is needed, the reservoir is used as a *storage device* to smooth out variations in the annual availability of water. Many systems include similar *stores* or *regulators* in order that the *input* to the system will balance the *output* that follows. (A budget and a bank account serve this purpose in the management of money. To paraphrase Mr. McCawber, "Happiness is spending one cent less than you earn.") A healthy city depends in part on its having enough water to meet its needs and keeping its needs within the amount of water available to it.

A city reservoir releases a varying flow of water to the city. In turn, it receives varying amounts of water from the rivers that feed it. When the rivers run low, the reservoir contributes more water than it receives. The flow to the city does not alter, but the level of the reservoir drops. When the rivers are in flood, the reservoir is refilled and excess water is allowed to bypass the reservoir. At that time, just enough water is taken in to balance the outflow at the city end without lowering or raising the level of the reservoir. If we measured the water level in the reservoir repeatedly and found no variation in its depth, we could not tell from that single set of measurements what the reservoir's inputs and outputs were. Such a condition, where a system temporarily is neither growing nor shrinking but is nevertheless in complete operation, is called a state of *dynamic equilibrium*. If the outlets and inlets to the reservoir were simultaneously closed, the system would exist in a condition of *static equilibrium*. But almost immediately evaporation and perhaps leakage would begin to lower the water level. Thus, static equilibrium is difficult to maintain, and what we most often observe is dynamic equilibrium. This is true of a person with very regular weight who must eat and drink every day in order to replace the energy he burns and the water he loses through perspiration and as a disposer of waste products.

Control and feedback

The use of water in the city varies from hour to hour, from night to day, and from season to season. An interesting example of this is the manner in which a series of small water-demand peaks occur during early evening hours in areas where television is a major form of entertainment. Every hour and every half-hour a brief, intense period of water use indicates trips to kitchen and toilet by thousands of viewers taking simultaneous

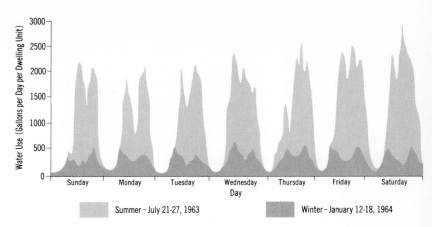

Figure 13-5 Winter and summer pattern of daily water use—Creekside Acres, California High summer water demand based largely on air conditioning, lawn watering, and swimming pool use is in sharp contrast to lower winter needs. The twin peaks for each day mark breakfast-time and dinner-time activities. Use in the early morning hours is least of all. (T. R. Detwyler, M. G. Marcus, and others, *Urbanization and Environment*, fig. 5-11, p. 121, after Linaweaver, 1965, © 1972 by Wadsworth Publishing Company, Inc., Belmont, California 94002. Reprinted by permission of the publisher, Duxbury Press.

breaks during commercials and station announcements. On a longer time scale, summer obviously places peak annual demands on a city's water supply. It follows that any active system such as a city and its reservoirs must respond to several simultaneous and continuously changing sets of demands such as those shown diagrammatically in Figure 13–5. Long-range increases in the city's water needs, perhaps dependent upon long-term upward trends in urbanization or consumer lifestyle, further disturb or alter the system.

Such fluctuations in demand require a return flow of information to the men or machines that open and close the reservoir's intakes and outlets. As water lowers in the reservoir, a signal may be given by some floating switch mechanism, or visual observation may be employed. In either case, news of the deficit finds its way back to the intake, and the gates

Ways to Weight the World: A Preface to Man-Environment Systems

249

are opened. Thus, a return track or *loop* has been activated in the system. In our human example we could say that as a person lives and does work, he uses up energy in the form of food. His stomach grows empty, and his immediate supplies of energy run low. His appetite increases, and he begins eating, largely because of the hunger message which has reached his brain, thereby triggering an activity which replenishes ebbing energy supplies in his body.

In both these examples *the presence of a loop means that the objects and events involved are mutually dependent upon each other.* An empty stomach generates appetite, which causes the person to eat, which satisfies his hunger, which reduces his appetite. The reservoir begins to empty, which causes the intake gates to be opened, which raises the level of the reservoir, which thereupon closes the intake. Since in each case information in one or another of many possible forms is fed back to a previous position in the system, this type of process is referred to as *feedback*.

In the examples just given the messages act to keep the system in equilibrium; that is, they dampen or reverse the developing condition. This form of control is called *negative feedback*. For example, action takes place to bring the water level in the reservoir back to normal. In other words, *negative feedback is deviation-correcting.*

In another case, the message which loops back can be a positive one. For example, when prospectors send the magic word GOLD! back to their friends from some remote place, those receiving the message may in turn tell their friends and relations, and they in turn will tell theirs until thousands of people get the message and a gold rush is on. In this case, a small event may mushroom into a big one. Simple models of city growth describe a similar situation. Two or three service establishments in a small settlement may lure additional customers, who in turn, by their presence, persuade a few more stores to open, which lure still more customers and workers, et cetera, et cetera, et cetera. In this way the equilibrium of the system is disturbed and a

new condition continues to grow. Just as the garbled account of one gossip may develop into a panic when passed on by other mouths, sometimes an act of little seeming consequence can bring about great changes, so that with time's passage it may become impossible to recognize the humble origins of major events. We recognize this when we say, "As the twig is bent so grows the tree," or "For want of a nail the shoe was lost. . . ." *Positive feedback is deviation-amplifying.* Only when a still newer set of messages reestablishes negative feedback—for example, "The city is a dangerous place to live," or "There's no more gold in them thar hills!"—can a new steady state or dynamic equilibrium be temporarily reached.

A structural classification of systems

Simple systems: Great Sand Dunes National Monument The feedback just described implies information flow through the system. Information carries with it a strong implication of intelligence at work. But many sets of interacting things obviously lack conscious intelligence. In fact, systems often include human participants who are so unaware of the roles they play that they become almost mindless robots in some larger scheme. The description which follows of the system at work within Great Sand Dunes National Monument, Colorado, illustrates how energy and material (mass) can move through a system independent of conscious information.

On the southwest flank of the Sangre de Cristo Mountains in semiarid south-central Colarodo, giant sand dunes 500 to 600 feet high form part of a dynamic natural system more and more influenced by the works of man. In this area, just north of the New Mexico border, the flat, 40-mile-wide San Luis Valley lies between the San Juan Mountains to the southwest and the Sangre de Cristo Mountains to the northeast. In the valley center near the town of Alamosa (Figure 13–6 *A*) is an area of prehistoric lake bottoms and natural levees, now dry, but formed in wetter times at the end of the Pleistocene glaciation. Prevailing

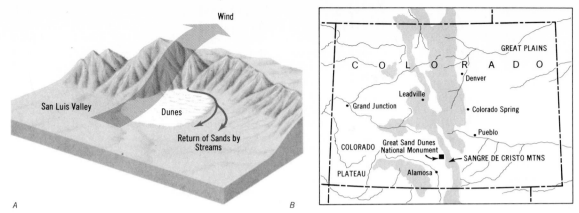

Figure 13-6 *A.* **Location of Great Sand Dunes National Monument.**
B. **Great Sand Dunes National Monument as a closed system** Wind-borne sand is carried from the valley floor to the mountain slopes where it is temporarily deposited until water returns it to lower elevations. Very little sand escapes over the mountains. This is considered a *closed system* because the sand in it is recycled again and again.

winds blowing out of the southwest carry silt and sand from this ancient alluvial accumulation in a northeasterly direction toward the barrier of the Sangre de Cristo Mountains. As the sand-bearing winds rise over these mountains (Figure 13–6*B*), their energy is insufficient to lift the burden they carry above the peaks and crests. Their load drops, as it has for thousands of years, at the foot and on the flanks of the mountains. This has resulted in an accumulation of giant transverse dunes now set aside and recognized as Great Sand Dunes National Monument. Sand from these dunes is carried eastward into the mountains up Medano Pass, which acts as a funnel for the strongest gusts. The occasional rain that falls on the mountains forms intermittent streams which return the sand to alluvial fans on the valley floor. Little or no sand escapes beyond the mountains to the east. Only the wind and its energy continue on. The sand recycles again and again.

Wind, sand, dunes, slopes, rain, and streams are the objects which taken together make up this particular natural system. The San Luis Valley and the two mountain ranges form the environment in which the system is em-

bedded. These physical objects taken by themselves form a set with little or no indication of the processes which bind them together. Such sets constitute the simplest view of systems, and as Kenneth Boulding says, make up "the geography and anatomy of the universe."[2] They represent the *frameworks* for all the other more complex views of systems we may take.

In the last few thousand years the Great Sand Dunes system has been for all practical purposes a *closed* one. Wind-borne energy passes through it, but its mass in the form of sand remains almost constant. The path through the system taken by the energy as well as the path taken by the sand itself presents a comewhat more complex view of the same system. The dry lake bottoms contribute sand to accumulation dunes just on the windward side of the great transverse dunes for which the monument is famous (Figure 13–6*B*). These accumulation dunes pass sand on to the great transverse dunes which in their

[2]Kenneth E. Boulding, "General Systems Theory—The Skeleton of Science," *Modern Systems Research for the Behavioral Scientist*, Walter Buckley (ed.), Aldine, Chicago, 1968, pp 3–10.

turn are the source of the sand found in a set of climbing dunes which endlessly advance up the slopes of the Sangre de Cristo range only to be dropped by the wind and returned by the streams to the valley below. Once again in the valley, the returned sand is subject to further wind erosion and the cycle repeats. The mapped path of energy and mass through this system describes a series of *cascades* with the output of one part or subsystem becoming the input of the next. In combination, the framework of objects and the cascades of energy and mass form a kind of *clockwork system* which operates without requiring information feedback. Systems organized at this clockwork level exist everywhere about us. In the next chapter we will discuss movements of the earth and sun in space as though they make up a gigantic clockwork system.

The above terms sufficiently describe the system operating at Great Sand Dunes National Monument. A temporary equilibrium exists, though perhaps slightly more sand accumulates each year with progressive wind erosion of the valley floor. No conscious control mechanism is necessary for the existence of the dunes. We will round out our typology of systems with more complex ones in a moment, but before saying goodbye to the Great Sand Dunes let us consider what may happen to those fragile features in the near future.

The equilibrium of the system depends upon a steady supply of sand passing through the great dunes from the valley floor to the mountains and back. One way in which blowing sand dunes are stabilized is to moisten them and to encourage vegetation to grow and fix their surfaces. The dry valley bottom near Alamosa and the alluvial outwash fans along the foot of the mountains provide sand because of their aridity. But man everywhere works to readjust nature and, to his way of thinking, improve it. This could very well happen in the San Luis Valley if extensive irrigation projects are constructed outside the national monument but well within the critical sand source area. If this happens, the sands there will be stabilized, as will the materials returned by the streams to the valley floor. With their source of supply cut off, the Great Sands would gradually dwindle away as more and more of their materials became stabilized. Conversely, overgrazing of the valley floor might possibly lead to more erosion, more sand, and bigger dunes. In either case, man would serve an almost mindless role in the destruction or enlargement of the natural feature.

Complex systems We have already mentioned many systems more complex than simple clockwork ones. They include some control mechanism or *thermostat* that operates to keep them in equilibrium, much as that name implies. The floating switch at the city reservoir which opened the intake valve when water levels dropped and closed it when they approached normal is typical of this type of *thermostat system.*

Self-maintaining systems that are able to repair themselves come next. Living and nonliving structures are usually separated from each other at this point. However, simplicity is still a determining characteristic and living cells are perhaps the best example.

Plants as self-maintaining and self-reproducing systems lacking mobility, consciousness, and intelligence, as we ordinarily recognize those properties, are more complex forms of self-maintaining systems. *Animals* with mobility, intelligence, consciousness, and a variety of sense mechanisms constitute living systems beyond the plant level. *Animals, plants,* and the *environment* which supports them form *ecosystems.* Man must be given an even higher status as a system because of his superior intelligence, his ability to abstract and symbolize, his accumulated culture, and his tools. Groups of men form *social systems,* for obvious reasons more complex than single human beings, and these in turn interact with all other systems which make up the environment of man to form the most complicated structure of all, *human ecosystems.*

Levels of generalization: Black, gray, and white boxes

The above list suggests that the more complex forms such as ecosystems and human ecosystems are in fact hierarchically arranged and include all the other simpler systems at lower levels. The problem when using a systems approach is to choose the proper scale. In fact, we might now want to take exception to the saying, "The proper study of mankind is man." It might be better to say, "The proper study of mankind is the human ecosystem." But in any event, no one can hope to look at everything there is to study. Having distinguished a system from the larger ones which form its environment, we must still decide the lower limits of the study. How deeply do we wish to penetrate into the subsystems which make up the object of our study? One way to simplify the problem is to look only at the inputs and outputs of those subsystems rather than to examine their internal workings. We may take the internal operations of such things for granted, or if we are unable to understand all there is to know about some smaller part of a system, we may simply accept the results of it. Such unanalyzed subsystems may be thought of as *black boxes* through which things pass and in whigh the conditions of things are changed, although we don't know how.

Black boxes may hold surprises. We simply observe their input-output over some range and do not know if they will work beyond those ranges. We usually have no explanatory theory of their inner workings. Nevertheless, the use of black boxes is reasonable when trying to understand the larger systems in which they are embedded. Naturally, black boxes should be treated with caution if the system to which they belong begins to change and drift into new levels. This is what is happening in the current ecologic crisis, where some unpleasant surprises are beginning to show up. The side effects of some insecticides on higher animal life illustrate the unforeseen consequences of our acts.

If the processes inside subsystems are partially understood, we can view them as transluscent if not transparent containers and call them *gray boxes*. Finally, when a subsystem is understood and mapped to our complete satisfaction, we may refer to it as a *white box*. No secrets there!

The terms defined in the previous pages describe the multitude of systems that make up the total world of man and nature. We have also roughly sketched the relationship of man and the resources which support him. The chapters that follow continue this theme by first introducing the clockwork system of the earth and sun. We then describe more and more complex systems including those of plants and animals. By the end of this section we will return to the discussion of various human life-styles and economies. We hope that by then the underlying environmental unity and spatial organization of the human ecosystem will be apparent.

14 | SOLAR ENERGY AND MAN: EARTH AS A HEAT ENGINE

Two examples of human adjustments to the basic clockwork flux of solar energy are school graduation and June brides. As the school year draws to an end, graduation and a new life loom. To some students this means freedom; to some marriage. But no matter how the year's seniors may feel about their situation, June graduation and June brides are part of a long and honored tradition tied to the passage of the seasons and to man's adjustment to the annual cycle of solar energy availability.

When most of the population lived on farms or in small towns serving the agricultural community, the need for field labor was greatest during the summer months. Schools were dismissed so that students could help on the farms. At the same time, winter was past and the quagmire roads had dried out. Families and friends could get together, and since early harvests or the promise of a good growing season were as good as money in the farmer's pockets, it was a natural time for weddings.

With the shift into an urban age the need for large, seasonally available numbers of farm workers diminished. But as we have seen, institutions are slow to change, and schools still let out in late May or June. Freedom from school reinforces the old tradition of June farm weddings, and a spate of campus marriages still marks that time of year. Of course, we are talking about the Northern Hemisphere, and of course, some schools are experimenting with new time schedules which pay little attention to the agricultural cycle.

Energy and Man

The human use of energy and the amount of energy provided by the sun offer curious contrasts in magnitude. The energy produced in engines and furnaces has made profound changes in man's life-style. Yet, in caloric equivalents, fuels and other sources of energy used by man in 1965, for example, produced energy equal to only about one one-hundredth of the solar energy arriving at the earth's atmosphere each day! For this reason alone it is important to distinguish among world energy systems and view each at its proper scale.

Man differs from all other life-forms in that he employs engines and furnaces to gain access to nonliving sources of energy. Engines convert fuels to electrical and mechanical energy; furnaces produce heat. Nathaniel Guyol summarizes the magnitude of such energy conversion:

World consumption of energy from all sources,

including non-commercial fuels, was equivalent, in 1965, to approximately 6 billion tons of coal (or 4 billion tons of oil).

To supply this energy, the world consumed 2.7 billion tons of coal and lignite; 1.5 billion tons of crude petroleum; 25 trillion cubic feet of natural gas; 900 billion kilowatt hours of hydro-, nuclear, and geothermal electricity; about 1 billion tons of non-commercial fuels; and something under 100 million tons of peat, oil shale, and natural gasoline.[1]

One of the most significant things about the above quotation is that only two words in it pertain to types of energy derived from sources other than the sun: *nuclear* and *geothermal*. These two energy sources derive directly or indirectly from radioactive materials and are assuming greater significance with every decade. Their contribution to man, however, is as yet insignificant when compared with other sources. All fossil fuels are simply stores of ancient sunlight; hydroenergy, whether in rivers or waves, derives directly or indirectly from the sun. In the former case, ancient plants and animals stored solar energy in their bodies as part of normal growth processes; in turn, their remains form deposits of coal, petroleum, and natural gas. In the latter case, solar energy through evaporation and precipitation lifts water high onto the land, thus providing the kinetic energy of running water.

The Energy Balance of the Earth

In discussing the energy relationship of the earth to the sun we will talk about *heat*, which is one form of energy. Other forms of energy include kinetic energy, the energy of an object in motion; potential energy, the energy inherent in an object due to its relative position; work, or force moved through distance (grams centimeters/second^2 × centimeter = erg); chemical energy; nuclear and electromagnetic energy; and the energy of mass, described by the familiar $E = mc^2$. Heat is measured or per-

ceived in terms of *temperature*, which is a measure of the kinetic energy of the molecules that make up the heated substance. Temperature can refer to the degree of molecular motion in gases, liquids, and solids. This temperature, particularly air temperature, is sometimes referred to as *sensible heat*.

The relationship between the temperature of the earth and the radiant energy of the sun represents a system in dynamic equilibrium. We can imagine a simple model of this system that consists of an intensely radiating sun and a solid ball representing the earth suspended in the vacuum of space some distance away. The sun radiates energy in all directions, but only a small portion of that energy will be absorbed by the earth. The amount of energy intercepted by the earth will be proportional to the intensity of the sun's radiation and the area of the earth's crosssection, and inversely proportional to the square of the distance between the sun and the planet.

As the radiant energy of the sun strikes the surface of the sphere, some will be reflected back into space; the rest will be absorbed. It is convenient to use the term *insolation* when referring to the interception of solar energy by any surface. The ability of a surface to reflect radiation is called its *albedo*. A snow field has high albedo; plowed ground a very low albedo. On the average, the earth reflects about 36 percent of the insolation it receives from the sun.

If the sun were to increase its radiation, the earth would heat up until increased reradiation once more balanced the inflow of energy; a new state of equilibrium would be attained at a higher temperature. However, as long as the elements of the system remain constant, reradiation and reflection from the sphere balance the inflowing energy and the sphere maintains itself at a steady temperature. Fortunately for us, the fusion process which converts hydrogen to helium within the sun is remarkably regular in its production of energy. The unvarying rate of flow of radiant energy that results is called the *solar constant*. It is measured as the amount of energy received on a square centimeter of surface held outside

[1]Nathaniel Guyol, *Energy in the Perspective of Geography*, Prentice-Hall, Inc., Englewood Cliffs, N. J., 1971, p. 5.

Solar Energy and Man: Earth as a Heat Engine

the atmosphere at the average distance of the earth's orbit from the sun (93 million miles) and at right angles to the sun's rays. Under such conditions 2 gram calories per square centimeter per minute are received. Since 1 gram calorie per square centimeter is a measure of heat energy called a *langley*, the solar constant is the equivalent of 2 langleys per minute.

In this example, insolation (short-wave radiant energy) is absorbed and transformed into heat (kinetic energy) and then again transformed into long-wave radiation which returns to space. These changes illustrate our need to understand the *first law of thermodynamics* when examining energy flows through earth systems. The first law states: Energy can be neither created nor destroyed. Thus, if a system has its temperature in equilibrium, neither increasing nor decreasing, the outflow of energy from the system must equal that which enters it. However, the total energy input to a system may be transformed into more than one form, and we must use careful accounting procedures to find where all of it has

gone. Also, in some cases, energy may be temporarily stored within a system as potential energy, for example, in waters ponded high above sea level or as chemical energy in the form of plant and animal materials.

The spatial and temporal distribution of solar energy

The model of the sun and earth-sphere described above has slight similarity to the complexities of the real system. The seasonal march of temperatures distributes heat unequally across the surface of our planet. The spinning globe warms each place by day and cools it at night. Low-lying areas are warmer on the average than the tops of mountains; cloudy regions receive less energy than those with open skies. Many mechanisms exist at a global scale which distribute and redistribute energy across the surface of the earth. In its grandest and most simple form, this process can be described by the *second law of thermodynamics,* which states: Of itself, the flow of heat is always from warmer to cooler areas. As with the first law of thermodynamics, the second is sometimes difficult to see clearly and immediately in action. The words *of itself* are a key to understanding this. Energy may sometimes move from cooler to warmer areas—the continued chilling of a refrigerator is an example of this—but this reverse flow is possible only with inputs of additional energy from outside the system in question.

The daily amount of insolation at a point on the earth's surface depends upon the number of hours of daylight and the angle at which the sun's rays strike the earth. The great distance of the sun from the earth results for all practical purposes in all the sun's rays' approaching the planet parallel to one another. Consider three shafts of sunlight parallel to each other and of equal diameter in space (Figure 14–1). Let one ray strike the earth at the equator, another at 30° latitude, and the third at 60°. Note in Figure 14–1 that all three cross sections in space are equal and that the energy per unit area is the same for each. Now note that where the vertical ray strikes the equator the energy arriving

Figure 14-1 Intensity of sunlight as a function of latitude   Three shafts of sunlight strike the earth centered upon 0°, 30°, and 60° latitude, respectively. Their cross sections have the same area in space, but the area each illuminates on the global surface differs from the others. Assuming a steady and equal flow of radiant energy along each shaft, insolation per unit area will be most intense at the equator and least nearest the poles. This is because of the increase in size of the illuminated areas from low to high latitudes.

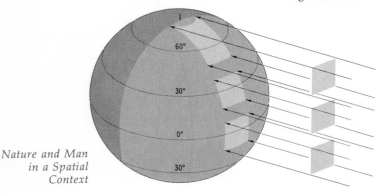

at the earth is distributed over an area the same as that of the shaft's cross section in space. At 30° the same amount of energy is distributed over a larger area, thus reducing its intensity. The third shaft hitting nearest the pole is thinly spread over a still larger surface. This effect is increased still further by the length of the path that solar energy must take to reach the surface once it has entered the earth's atmosphere. At the equator, the vertical ray penetrates the least amount of atmosphere; near the poles the path is much greater. Such distances are called the *optical air path* of sunlight.

Spatial differences in the seasonal distribution of energy will be accounted for in the next section, but for the moment let us consider the shorter days and lower angle of the sun during winter months followed by the long days and high sun of summer. This reaches its extreme with six months of darkness and six months of daylight at both the North and South Poles. Figure 14–2 shows the intensity of insolation for the entire year along a meridian of longitude from pole to pole. The elevation of the surface indicates the amount of energy received. The flat-floored basins at the extreme north and south show those months when no sunlight reaches the poles. The values shown are measured outside the atmosphere in order to avoid variations resulting from differences in optical air paths, as well as differences in atmospheric turbidity, density, etc. Global subsystems within the atmosphere and oceans constantly act according to the second law of thermodynamics to even out the differences in energy availability by moving energy from the equator toward the poles. Before considering such systems let us for a moment look more closely at the celestial mechanism through which such differences in the distribution of insolation occur.

The earth, the sun, and the seasonal cycle

The earth-sun system produces cyclical and seasonal changes which serve as the pulse as well as the inspiration of mankind. For our purposes we can think of this system as consisting of only two elements.

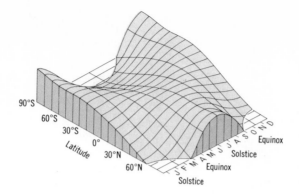

Figure 14-2 The effect of both latitude and season of year on the intensity of insolation At any given latitude and date, the relative amount of energy received is proportional to the height of the surface point above the flat base of the block. It should be noted that insolation along only one meridian is shown as a continuous surface for every day of the year. The flat areas in the northern corners and south-central part of the diagram represent the periods of Arctic and Antarctic night. This diagram is drawn looking from north to south. (Diagram by W. M. Davis. Reproduced by permission from A. N. Strahler, *Physical Geography*. Copyright 1951, © 1960, 1969 by John Wiley & Sons, Inc.)

We begin with a radiant body, the sun, which may be considered stationary in space, although in reference to other star systems it is not. A spherical earth, *rotating on its axis, revolves* around the sun. The earth's path of revolution is called its *orbit*. The plane determined by the sun and the orbit of the earth is called the *plane of the ecliptic*. The earth's axis of rotation is not vertical to the plane of the ecliptic but rather is inclined to it at an angle of 66½°. All these terms are illustrated in Figure 14–3. Though the axis of the earth has a slight wobble, the effects of which are unimportant here, its north end always points in the same direction with reference to the heavens outside the solar system: approximately toward Polaris, the North Star.

During a 12-month period the earth travels once around the sun, following an unvarying path which defines and is traced upon the plane of the ecliptic. The earth is closest to

Solar Energy and Man: Earth as a Heat Engine

257

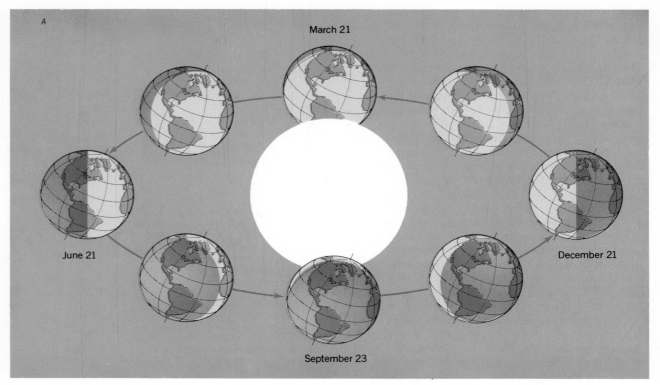

A

March 21

June 21

December 21

September 23

B

Earth Viewed from the Sun at the Time of

The Summer Solstice

The Vernal and Autumnal Equinoxes

The Winter Solstice

*Nature and Man
in a Spatial
Context*

258

the sun (91½ million miles) during winter in the Northern Hemisphere. Six months later it is farthest from the sun (94 million miles). The elliptical shape of this orbit is insignificant in terms of the effect it has on the amount of insolation received when compared with differences caused by the tilt of the earth's axis and the position of the vertical ray of the sun north or south of the equator.

The *summer solstice* (June 21 or June 22, depending upon the particular year) is a good time and place to begin tracing the annual

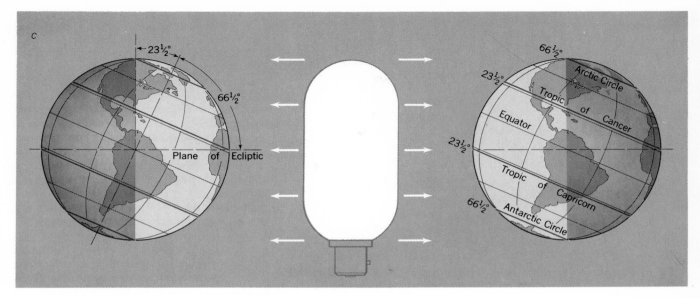

Figure 14-3 The inclination of the earth's axis and the changing seasons The north pole of the earth always points the same direction toward the star Polaris (A). The inclination of the axis from the plane of the ecliptic accounts for the north-south march of the vertical rays of the sun and therefore, of the seasons (B and C).

trip of the earth around the sun (Figure 14-3A). At that time, the north end of the axis points most nearly toward the sun. It is the longest day north of the equator, and the vertical ray of the sun has moved as far north as the Tropic of Cancer, $23\frac{1}{2}°$ north latitude. Three months later (September 22 or 23) the axis of the earth points neither toward nor away from the sun but is at right angles to it. At this time, day and night are of equal length everywhere in the world, and a ray of sunlight is just tangent to both the North and South Poles. This is the *autumnal equinox.* Three months later, December 22 or December 23 marks the *winter solstice* with the north end of the earth's axis pointing away from the sun and the vertical ray striking at the Tropic of Capricorn, $23\frac{1}{2}°$ south latitude. In ancient times this was a period of feasting and sacrifice to the sun god in order that he might be lured back from his wintry home. Three months later, the *vernal equinox,* on March 20

or March 21, again sees the earth's axis at right angles to the sun, and again the conditions that held during the autumnal equinox prevail. Finally, with the passage of another three months the earth has returned to a position at the summer solstice and its cycle is completed, only to begin once more.

To understand the effect that this annual cycle has upon the receipt of energy at the surface of the earth, consider the earth as a sphere lighted from a single source, the sun. Given these conditions one-half the sphere will be lighted, the other dark. The lighted half is called the *circle of illumination.* Now at the winter solstice the circle of illumination on the earth extends only to $66\frac{1}{2}°$ north latitude and the North Pole area is in darkness (Figure 14-3C). This is the shortest day of the year in the Northern Hemisphere. Six months later, during the summer solstice, the circle of illumination has shifted northward and the South Pole area at latitudes higher than $66\frac{1}{2}°$ is in

Solar Energy and Man: Earth as a Heat Engine

259

darkness (Figure 14–3C). The line marking the extreme extent of darkness in the north is called the *Arctic Circle*, in the south, the *Antarctic Circle*. The absence of sunlight in polar regions for long periods of time obviously accounts in large part for their extreme cold.

Meanwhile, the vertical ray of the sun, that is, the ray following the shortest optical air path, has moved from 23½° south latitude on December 22 to 23½° north latitude on June 21. As we have already seen, insolation is greatest where the vertical ray strikes. Since the vertical ray moves with the seasons, the greatest amount of incoming radiant energy per unit area per minute shifts north and south during the year and crosses the equator twice, once at each of the equinoxes (Figure 14–3B). This cyclical progress accounts for the northward movement of higher temperatures in our summertime and the reverse effect during our winter.

Figure 14-4 The latitudinal energy balance of the earth between incoming shortwave solar radiation and outgoing longwave radiation from the earth Note the predominance of incoming radiation at low latitudes and the excess of outgoing radiation near the poles. The deficit and surplus areas shown on the graph have the same areas but different shapes. If they did not equal each other, the planet earth would either overheat or become colder. The movement of energy from surplus to deficit areas drives the giant atmospheric and hydrologic heat engine described in the text. (R. E. Newell, "The Circulation of the Upper Atmosphere," *Scientific American*, vol. 210, no. 3, March 1964, p. 69, copyright © 1964 by Scientific American Inc.)

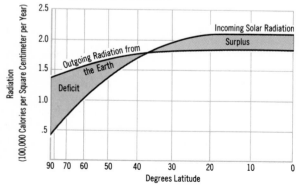

The terrestrial heat engine

During the summer the polar regions receive 24 hours of sunlight and accumulate more insolation in one day's time than does the equatorial zone, where day and night are approximately 12 hours long every day of the year. However, during the rest of the year the long polar night lowers the average annual amount of insolation received in the Arctic and Antarctic. When all factors are taken into consideration—differences in the angles of the sun's rays, differences in the length of day and night, and so forth—we find that the area near the equator has an annual heat surplus while that near the poles has an overall heat deficit. Figure 14–4 shows incoming shortwave solar energy and outgoing long-wave radiation plotted according to latitude. Near the equator the area between the two lines represents heat surplus; near the poles the area shows heat loss. Although they have different shapes, the two areas are the same size, thus illustrating the overall spatial balance and equilibrium of the heat budget of the earth. One important aspect of this equilibrium condition is the latitudinal separation of the surplus and deficit areas. Energy in very large amounts must move from place to place in order to balance deficits and surpluses. The mechanism through which this occurs is a global subsystem of winds and ocean currents which can be thought of as a gigantic heat engine constantly in motion and constantly fueled by the sun.

Budgeting the earth's energy cycle

In order to examine the components of this engine, we must understand how energy is transferred from the sun to the earth's surface, and from the earth's surface to the atmosphere and back to space. This flow is shown by the vertical cross section through the atmosphere in Figure 14–5. The horizontal patterns made by its moving parts can be seen in the maps of the winds and currents that follow.

Scale is an important consideration in the energy cycle of the earth. An ant may walk sedately beneath grass whipped by a mighty wind, and minnows may flash along the ocean bed as giant waves break above them. Only the occasional gust or eddy disturbs such creatures at home in flux of the elements. Man's relationship to the flow of energy in which he lives is much the same. Although tornadoes and hurricanes may endanger us, the energy in the fiercest winds is still only a fraction of that in which the earth is bathed each day. For example, the kinetic energy in a tornado with winds in excess of 300 miles per hour is something in the neighborhood of 7×10^{10} calories, or only about ½ of 1 percent of a summer day's insolation on a square mile of the earth.

Though the amount of radiation varies from place to place and from season to season, the solar energy intercepted by the earth equals approximately 3.67×10^{21} calories per day. The general paths of the vast amount of energy arriving at the earth are shown in Figure 14–5. Of the insolation reaching the outer edge of the atmosphere (100 percent), 41 percent penetrates the protective mantle of air, clouds, and dust and is absorbed by the surface of the earth itself. Another 25 percent is reflected directly back to space from the earth and clouds. The remaining 34 percent is either absorbed or diffused by the atmosphere. Of that, 15 percent is diffused, from which 9 percent is reflected back to space, while 6 percent reaches earth. The atmosphere temporarily retains the other 19 percent.

The subsequent path of the 47 percent which is absorbed by the earth is complex and various before it returns to outer space. For the moment we will simplify things by treating the earth as a black box in the energy system. Since 47 percent of the total insolation is absorbed by black box earth, an equivalent amount must return to the atmosphere and eventually to space in order to maintain equilibrium. Conduction accounts for 10 percent of this returning energy. This is simply the direct heating of cooler air as it comes in contact with the warmer surfaces of the earth. The warm earth also emits long-wave radiation which

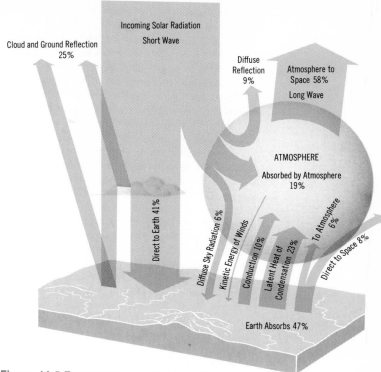

Figure 14-5 Energy balance of the earth
Incoming shortwave solar radiation is equal to 100 percent. Outgoing radiation also equals 100 percent. The paths taken by component parts of the total are simple (e.g., direct reflection back into space from clouds) or complex (e.g., diffuse sky radiation can be absorbed by the earth, is thereafter released into the atmosphere as latent heat of condensation, and finally is reradiated into space). Careful examination will show that the subtotals as well as totals on this diagram are in balance. Such symmetry is, in part, the result of the simplification by the authors of much more complex and incompletely understood processes.

accounts for another 14 percent, of which 8 percent goes directly to space while 6 percent is temporarily absorbed by the atmosphere. The remaining 23 percent returns to the atmosphere in the form of *latent heat*. This requires further explanation.

When an object either absorbs radiation or is otherwise heated, energy is imparted to the molecules making up that object. The speed of the molecules is increased, and this may be thought of as a form of kinetic energy. A molecule of water in the form of ice will have the least kinetic energy; water in fluid form will have more energy. The extra increment of energy needed to change ice to liquid is called the *latent heat of fusion*; the amount needed to change liquid water to water vapor is called the *latent heat of vaporization*. Conversely, when water vapor condenses to a liquid, its molecules move more slowly. The increment of energy originally used to change the liquid to vapor must go somewhere when vapor is condensed. When water vapor in the atmosphere condenses and becomes rain, the energy released heats the atmosphere. In the same manner, there is an increment of energy released by each molecule when liquid water freezes into ice. This accounts in large part for warmer temperatures observed during snow storms. Citrus growers, when threatened by frosts of brief duration, sometimes take advantage of the release of latent heat and may actually spray their orchards with water. As the water freezes on contact with the cold air, its latent heat is released, thus warming the surroundings. If the frost is not too severe, a little ice coating the buds and twigs may actually serve as an insulating overcoat.

The atmosphere also can be conveniently thought of as a black box in this system. Conduction, latent heat, and long-wave radiation return 39 percent of the energy from the earth to the atmosphere where it is added to 19 percent directly absorbed from the sun's rays. The heated atmosphere and the heated earth exchange energy back and forth many times in many ways. The net result of this exchange has already been mentioned as the 14 percent which is emitted from earth as long-wave radiation. Another small amount—less than 1 percent—also returns temporarily to the earth's surface as the wind energy which helps propel the currents of the world's large water bodies. Finally, the atmosphere reradiates all the energy it receives from all sources. This amounts to 58 percent of the original insolation. All these paths can be identified and cross-checked by carefully adding up the per-

centages shown at various points in Figure 14–5.

One word of caution is necessary. No one, as yet, really knows the exact percentages of energy at any given point in the system. Also, these amounts vary from season to season and from day to day depending upon cloud cover, the angle of the sun's rays, the amount of dust in the atmosphere, the reflectivity of the particular portion of the earth's surface under consideration, and many other things. Thus, these comments should be taken as indications of the amounts involved rather than as absolute values.

Composition, Temperature, and Pressure of the Atmosphere

Fifty-eight percent of all solar energy intercepted by the earth finds its way into the heat reservoir of our atmosphere for varying lengths of stay. When radiant energy is transformed into heat within the atmosphere, it is unevenly distributed because of differences in latitude, land and water distribution, cloud cover, and a variety of other causes. Air masses of different temperatures are the result, and the presence and movement of such air masses in both vertical and horizontal directions as well as the interaction between unlike portions of the atmosphere are responsible in large part for the short-term effects we call *weather* and the long-term conditions we know as *climate*. We have already mentioned how the movement of air helps to balance the heat surpluses near the equator against the deficit areas near the poles. The composition and characteristics of the atmosphere are integral components of the earth heat engine.

The atmosphere contains pure dry air, water vapor, and atmospheric solids including dust particles. By *pure dry air* we meant a mixture of gases which has changed significantly since the beginnings of geologic time, but which has remained more or less constant in composition within man's span on earth. This mixture consists by volume of 78 percent nitrogen, 21 percent oxygen, 0.9 percent argon, 0.03 percent carbon dioxide, and traces of a variety of other gases. Dust from windy deserts or plowed fields may color a sunset or blot out the sun, just as smoke particles from forest fires or factories may also serve to filter the sunlight from above. All kinds of matter are classified as atmospheric solids, including airborne salt crystals from ocean spray and radioactive materials from hydrogen bomb tests. Water vapor is most conspicuous in its associated form of liquid cloud droplets, but high humidities on any warm day also indicate the presence of water molecules in the atmosphere.

The vertical distribution of the atmosphere is of critical importance. Here at the bottom of our airy envelope the atmosphere may seem to extend above us forever, but in reality we exist within a thin gauze of gas clinging to the much larger globe. This becomes evident in the many photographs from satellites which show the thin layer of atmosphere in cross section along the limb of the earth's horizon. In fact, almost 97 percent of the entire atmosphere is within 18 miles of the earth's surface. If you have ever climbed a mountain above 18,000 feet (3.4 miles) or flown that high in an airplane, you have had one-half of the atmosphere below you. The other half extends out-

ward approximately 21,000 miles to the *exosphere*, the absolute limit of earth's atmosphere and the point where a gas molecule can, with its own velocity, escape earth's gravitational field never to return.

The atmosphere presses upon the earth beneath. The weight of a column of air from sea level extending to the exosphere is on the average 14.7 pounds per square inch. This will support a 29.92-inch (76-centimeter) column of mercury in a barometer. At an elevation of 11 miles above sea level the weight of the remaining column of air is one-tenth as much; at 20 miles, one-hundredth as much; at 70 miles, one one-hundred-thousandth as much. We are speaking here of average conditions.

Sensible heat recorded as air temperature changes regularly with elevation. In the lower atmosphere there is a steady decrease in temperature equal to 3.6°F with every 1,000 feet of increased elevation. Changes of this kind are called the *lapse rate*, and the above rate of change is called the *normal lapse rate*. Atmospheric temperatures under normal lapse rate conditions decrease regularly to an elevation of 6 or 7 miles (10 kilometers), where a low of −60 to −70°F is reached. However, beyond this elevation temperatures may stabilize, in-

Cloud formation of a low-pressure system near the Straits of Gibraltar as seen from the National Aeronautics and Space Administration's Gemini X spacecraft. The curving limb of the earth that marks the horizon is veiled by a thin layer of white, the thickness of which represents more than 90 percent of the atmosphere upon which we depend. (NASA photo)

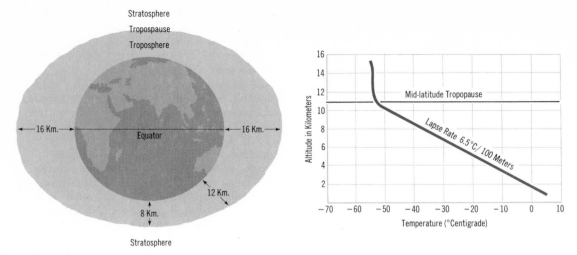

Figure 14-6 The tropopause and the lapse rate The tropopause is the elevation at which atmospheric temperature ceases to fall in a regular fashion with increasing altitude. It is highest over the equator and lowest over the poles. The normal lapse rate is the rate of decrease in free-air temperature when passing from a lower to a higher elevation.

crease, or decrease depending upon the zone within the atmosphere. The lower portion of the atmosphere within which the regular lapse rate occurs is called the *troposphere*. The portion above the troposphere to a height of about 30 miles is known as the *stratosphere*. Beyond that the *mesosphere* and *thermosphere* extend outward into space. The division between the troposphere and the stratosphere is called the *tropopause* (Figure 14–6). Almost but not quite all of the earth's weather occurs within the troposphere, and those of you who have flown in a commercial flight above 30,000 feet may have noticed how smooth your trip was, with all the clouds and air turbulence in a layer below you. You were undoubtedly winging along just above the tropopause, taking ad-

vantage of the relative uneventful conditions of the stratosphere.

The gaseous envelope, in which earth is contained like a space age parcel en route to some unknown destination, is unevenly heated horizontally as well as vertically. Air temperature varies from place to place, particularly with changes in latitude and elevation but also because of cloud cover and whether land or sea lies below. Water is a much better insulator than land, and water bodies heat more slowly under direct solar radiation than does land. Water also cools more slowly and gives up less energy than does an equal area of land surface. Water's slower rate of temperature change results from (1) the continual mixing of warm and cool waters by waves and currents, (2)

Figure 14-7 Global variation in temperature, (A) January and (B) July Variations in temperature can be mapped at global scales. The isotherms on these maps indicate the distribution of energy at the earth's surface in the coldest and hottest months in each hemisphere. Note how the isotherms bend poleward over the continents in the summer hemisphere, while low temperatures reach farther toward the equator on the earth's winter half. Sharp bends in the isotherms along certain coasts show the presence of cold and warm offshore currents.

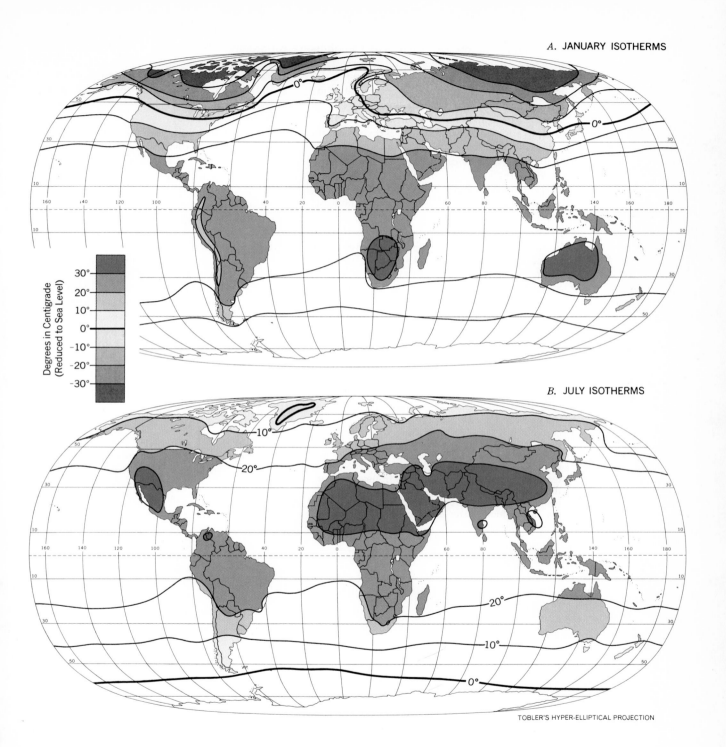

A. JANUARY ISOTHERMS

B. JULY ISOTHERMS

Degrees in Centigrade
(Reduced to Sea Level)

30°
20°
10°
0°
-10°
-20°
-30°

TOBLER'S HYPER-ELLIPTICAL PROJECTION

evaporation and the removal of large amounts of energy as the latent heat of vaporization, (3) the fact that sunlight can penetrate water to considerable depths while earth and stone are opaque and absorb most incoming energy within 1 or 2 inches of the surface, and (4) the greater specific heat of water, which requires about three times as much energy as does an equivalent volume of land to increase its temperature the same amount.

The result of all this is that land is hotter by day and colder by night as well as considerably warmer in the summer and colder in winter than water. Variations in air temperature can be mapped at global as well as neighborhood scales. Figure 14–7 shows the global variation in temperature for July and January. The lines on this map connect points having equal temperatures and are called *isotherms*. They give an indication of the distribution of energy at the earth's surface for those times. Note how the isotherms tend to bend poleward over the

continents in the summer hemisphere while low temperatures reach farther toward the equator on the earth's winter half. This differential shifting of temperatures over land and water with the seasons is shown diagrammatically in Figure 14–8.

Differential heating of the atmosphere on an earth scale results in large, distinct masses of cold and warm air. Cold air is dense and heavy compared with warm air and tends to sink earthward, while thinner, warm air rises. These differences are reflected as variations in air pressure measured by a barometer. Barometric pressure varies both above and below the 29.92 inches (67 centimeters) of mercury, which you will recall equals the weight of a column of air under standard conditions. Air pressure, like heat, tends to adjust inequalities within the system by movements from high-pressure to low-pressure areas. This endless effort to stabilize barometric variations results in winds which, in general, move down the *barometric slope* or *pressure gradient*.

The world of wind

Let us now look at both a vertical and horizontal view of the atmosphere and see how, by knowing a very few facts about the distribution of energy and the movement of air masses, it is possible to sketch a model of the global wind system. This knowledge is useful, for it is this wind system which in large part drives the ocean's currents, accounts for some important long-range climatic characteristics, and helps bring daily changes in the weather.

The direct rays of the sun fall upon the equator only twice each year. At the time of the equinoxes (March 15 and September 15) the heating of the earth is essentially symmetrically distributed between the Northern and Southern Hemispheres. The rest of the time more insolation strikes the earth on one side of the equator or the other. This makes the conditions at the equinox a good starting point for discussing the world wind system.

Despite annual variations in the symmetry of insolation, we may think of the total amount of energy earth receives as being greatest at

Figure 14-8 Latitudinal shifts in an isotherm from July to January as the result of oceanic and continental influences (hypothetical Northern Hemisphere continent) Cool offshore currents move lower temperatures southward along the west coast of the continent. Low January temperatures reach farther equatorward in the center of the continent. Conversely, warm July temperatures extend farther north in the center of the continent than on its edges. These variations result from the relatively poor insulating quality of the land, which warms and cools more quickly than does water.

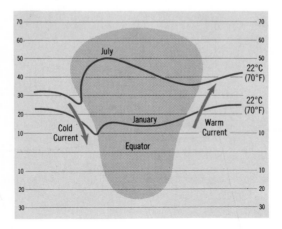

the equator and least at the poles. In this simplified model we would expect to find the atmosphere at the equator heated the most and that at the poles least of all. This results in warm, ascending air girdling the earth with an equatorial belt of low pressure (Figure 14–9). But the air cannot rise indefinitely, and as it cools at greater elevations, it spreads horizontally to the north and south. Meanwhile, the air above the poles, being coldest, is most dense and settles earthward. The pressure gradient thus created should extend from a high at the poles to a low at the equator, and the atmosphere, acting to readjust these inequalities, should move accordingly. Dense, cold air should slip equatorward near the earth's surface, while rising, warmer air should move north and south as it gradually cools. The result should be twin cells of circulating air, one north and the other south of the equator. This system was first suggested in 1735 by the English meteorologist George Hadley. However, the existence of such a gigantic cell

in each hemisphere did not fit the observed global distribution of climatic features.

An American meteorologist, William Ferrel, modified Hadley's scheme in the nineteenth century to include three such cells on each side of the equator. As we shall see in the pages ahead, his suggestion of an equatorial band of warm, rising air, a second belt of cool, dense, descending air at 30° latitude north and south, and another band of relatively warm air ascending at 60° latitude more closely matches the distribution of world climates (Figure 17–1) and the pattern of world winds (Figure 14–10). In memory of these men the two equatorial cells are called *Hadley cells* and the two mid-latitude cells are called *Ferrel cells*. The spatial asymmetry of insolation north and south of the equator during most of the year results in a rather lopsided system of pressure belts. Only one Hadley cell develops fully for most of the earth's 12-month trip around the sun, that in the winter hemisphere; the one in the summer hemisphere

Figure 14-9 Hypothetical airflow in the troposphere at the time of the equinox   The equinox has been chosen in order to give hypothetical symmetry on both sides of the equator. Vertical components of the system are high and low-pressure belts. Horizontal air movement across the earth's surface results in the world wind system discussed and named in the text. The actual system is less well defined and less symmetrical than this diagram shows. (*Vertically exaggerated and not shown to scale.*)

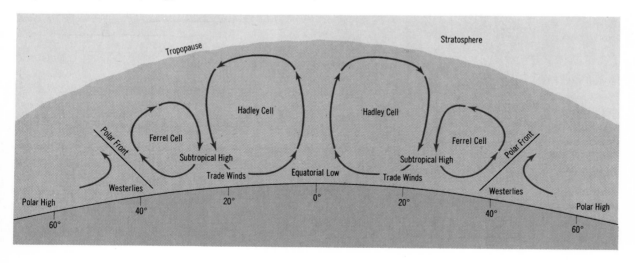

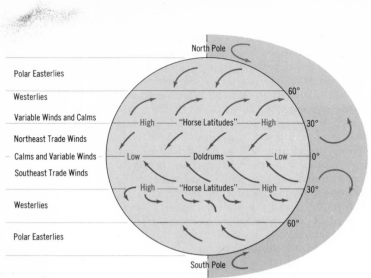

Polar Easterlies

Westerlies

Variable Winds and Calms

Northeast Trade Winds

Calms and Variable Winds

Southeast Trade Winds

Westerlies

Polar Easterlies

North Pole

60°

High — "Horse Latitudes" — High — 30°

Low — Doldrums — Low — 0°

High — "Horse Latitudes" — High — 30°

60°

South Pole

Figure 14-10 General world wind and pressure pattern This diagram shows a highly abstract and hypothetical pattern of world pressure belts and the winds which equalize their different barometric conditions. The polar easterlies are less well developed than other parts of the system, but the basic pattern prevails in a much more complicated form. Compare this with the satellite photo of the southern hemisphere for striking similarities.

dwindles until it almost disappears. Nevertheless, the energy within a fully developed Hadley cell is enormous. The mass of air circulated annually by such a cell would equal about 378×10^{15} metric tons, approximately one-seventeenth the mass of the earth! And yet the energy required to do this represents, in turn, only a fraction of the total insolation in which the earth is continually bathed.

Given the alternating belts of high and low pressure we have just described, we could also predict that winds would blow along the surface of the earth, adjusting differences between them. On a stationary globe such winds would move directly north and south. But the earth rotates, and its rotation produces an effect upon these winds, as it does on all moving objects. This effect, more specifically known as the *coriolis effect,* is stated in *Ferrel's law: A gas, fluid, or object moving in the Northern Hemisphere tends to be deflected to the right of*

its path of motion, no matter what compass direction that path may have. Moving objects are similarly deflected to the left in the Southern Hemisphere. This effect is greater near the poles than near the equator. Various results occur from the coriolis effect. For example, in the Northern Hemisphere, at high latitudes, driftwood accumulates on the right bank of rivers more than on the left, and the right-hand rails on double-tracked railways are reported to wear out more quickly than those on the left side. This same deflection affects the winds blowing between belts of high and low pressure. The resulting pattern looks something like that in Figure 14-10.

At this point we must take note of man's desire to order the world in which he lives by giving names to everything. Figure 14-10 summarizes and labels the seven pressure belts and six major winds making up the global components of heat engine earth. Note the general symmetry of the pattern on either side of the equator; also note that winds are often named after the direction *from which they blow.*

At the equator the major vector of air movement is vertically ascending. Air near the surface is often calm or disturbed by random breezes blowing every which way. Here are the *doldrums,* one of the two areas of calms at sea dreaded by all sailors before the age of steam. Many a sailing ship has been becalmed for days, weeks, perhaps even months, near the equator, and the term *doldrums,* now in general use, means any period in our lives when we just can't get started or go anywhere. The convergence of twin wind systems to the north and south add to the general condition within the doldrums. These are the *northeast* and *southeast* trade winds, which represent the lower horizontal components of the tropical Hadley cells. Within the area of the trade winds the motion of the atmosphere is relatively predictable, with a steady flow of air converging at the equator. This is called the *zone of intertropical convergence,* which is the technical name given to the doldrums. The trade winds themselves are so named because of the role they played in the early exploration and settlement of the New World. Shipmasters soon learned to sail southeasterly from Europe to America in order to take advantage of these steady winds. However, poleward of the trade winds is another belt of intermittent calms and breezes. In this case, descending cool air at 30° north and south latitude makes the ocean beneath a trap for sailing ships. Here is the *subtropical high-pressure belt*, sometimes called the *horse-latitudes*, about which strange stories are told. It is said that when the Spanish first ventured to cross the Atlantic, their galleons often were becalmed in those latitudes. Days passed, and the ships' supplies of fresh water soon became more precious than gold, too precious indeed to give to the horses on board. And so the poor beasts were jettisoned; left to drown; their bloated bodies terrible signposts of thirst warning other ships to beware a similar fate.

Still farther poleward the flow of air from northwest to southeast in the middle latitudes provides a regular wind system known as the "brave westerlies" in the Northern Hemisphere and the "roaring forties" in the Southern. These gales continually move masses of wet marine and dry continental air from west to east around the world. In the days of sail they provided a quick, rough journey back to Europe from the New World, particularly in the summer. But in the winter months, and almost all year around in the Southern Hemisphere, where fewer continental land masses block their passage, the continuous rush of air pushes giant ocean waves before it. Thus the ships involved in the triangular trade described in Chapter 12 would move from Europe to the Caribbean and Africa on the northeast trades and then northwest to the Carolina coast on a starboard tack. Once there, they would lay over in the port of Charleston until spring, when the westerlies would blow them back to Europe. The winter trip was not worth the risk and rough weather. Charleston thus became an important port in colonial America, but with the age of steam, ships no longer wintered over on the Carolina coast and the town became the quiet place it is today.

Poleward of the westerlies, the cold of higher latitudes acts to offset the regularity of winds

Two large, low-pressure cells over the North Atlantic. The counterclockwise movement of the cells is apparent from the cloud pattern. Storms and weather fronts are associated with the passage of this type of cell. (Tiros IX, 100th orbit, Jan. 30, 1965; NASA photo 65-H-136)

and pressure belts described in our simplified model. Nevertheless, a pressure belt of *relatively* warmer air ascends at 60° north and south as the *subpolar low-pressure belt*, while at the poles frigid, descending air creates two powerful *polar high-pressure areas*. The winds that circle the poles equatorward of the polar high-pressure systems are called the *polar easterlies* but are less well understood, in part because of the lack of comprehensive and continuous weather observations in those latitudes.

High- and low-pressure cells

While the above summarizes the world wind and pressure systems, there remains another basic, if secondary, characteristic of the world pressure system that we should note. The Northern Hemisphere with its continental masses alternating with the Atlantic and Pacific Oceans has a well-defined set of high- and low-pressure cells associated with temperature differences on the land and water. Particularly in its winter, the Northern Hemi-

Solar Energy and Man: Earth as a Heat Engine

Apollo 17 (72H-157B), December, 1972. The Southern Hemisphere appears
with Antarctica a prominent white patch at the bottom. Africa and the
Arabian peninsula are clearly seen. This photograph illustrates the pressure
belts and wind systems discussed in the text. The sequence, beginning in
Antarctica is (*a*) the polar high with relatively clear, dry air, (*b*) the polar
easterlies along the circumpolar low, shown as a band of broken irregular
clouds, (*c*) a series of well-developed cells marking the path of westerly
winds, (*d*) the open skies of southwest Africa, indicating the southern subtropical low-pressure zone, (*e*) linear cloud elements over the Indian Ocean
indicating the southeast trade winds, (*f*) the equatorial low-pressure belt
marked by scattered clouds formed by convectional air currents, (*g*) a less
clearly seen area of northeast trade winds, and (*h*) the subtropical high-
pressure belt in the northern hemisphere. (NASA)

sphere develops two giant high-pressure cells, or *anticyclones,* one over central Asia which is called the *Siberian High,* the other over North America called the *Canadian High.* The pressure of the descending, cold air at the center of these anticyclones forces winds outward toward their edges. The coriolis effect deflects these winds to the right, so that the entire cell rotates in a clockwise direction. At the same time, since the oceans bordering the continents are relatively much warmer in winter than the land, warm, moist, and ascending air creates an *Aleutian Low* over the North Pacific and an *Icelandic Low* over the North Atlantic. These are termed *cyclones* and have a general counter-clockwise movement of winds toward their centers (photo, page 269).

In the Northern Hemisphere in the summer months the location of high- and low-pressure cells is reversed, with low pressure developing over the hotter lands. However, cells of either kind are better defined in the winter months than in the summer. This is in part because the entire system tends to shift poleward during the high-sun period. The westerlies referred to above give impetus to the high- and low-pressure cells and help to drive them continually eastward around the world. Thus, in winter, the middle latitudes experience a continual parade of alternating high- and low-pressure systems which in large part account for the changeable weather with which most of us are familiar.

In the Southern Hemisphere the lack of large land masses leads to the development of more beltlike pressure systems, although depending on the season, smaller highs and lows do form over the continents. However, the northern winds and pressure cells are better known to mankind because most of the world's population lives north of the equator in the middle latitudes.

Eddies in the World Ocean

Anyone who has experienced the battering drive of wave and wind as a hurricane comes ashore or who has read Joseph Conrad's or Jack London's descriptions of storms at sea

knows something of the energy exchange between the atmosphere and the waters of the globe. The winds described in the previous section impart a fraction of their energy to the water surfaces over which they pass. Little is known about the actual frictional mechanism by means of which the energy transfer takes place, but the overall effect is important in directing the currents of the world ocean.

The direct effect of the wind on the water is simple to understand although difficult to test outside the laboratory. The surface layer of the ocean can be thought of as a stack of nearly frictionless sheets, one below the other. The

Figure 14-11 Ekman spiral in the Northern Hemisphere Wind moving across the surface of water imparts energy to the water and causes it to move. The coriolis effect deflects the movement of the water (to the right in this example). Since water is essentially frictionless, the water molecules at each successive depth are deflected away from the path of movement of those directly above. This results in a spiral movement imparted to the water to a shallow depth. The average direction of this moving surface layer is at an angle to the original wind direction.

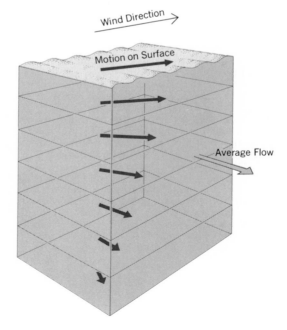

Solar Energy and Man: Earth as a Heat Engine

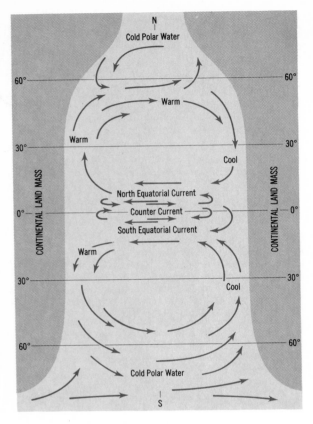

Figure 14-12 Schematic ocean currents
Two gyres are shown moving warm and cool
water into latitudes where otherwise it would not
be found. The equatorial currents are pushed
along largely by the trade winds; their east-west
direction results from the coriolis effect. The
currents, in turn, are deflected by the shores of the
continents and moved farther to the right in the
Northern Hemisphere and to the left in the
Southern Hemisphere by the continuing coriolis
effect. The westerlies drive the currents eastward
until they are again deflected and the gyre closes
upon itself. Cool water thus moves equatorward
along the western shores of the continents, while
warm water moves poleward on the eastern shores.
The west-to-east movement of the water and winds
is enhanced in the Southern Hemisphere by the
absence of land barriers at high latitudes.

top sheet slides over the others in almost the
same direction that the wind pushes. However, the water is deflected slightly by the
coriolis effect, just as it deflects the winds
themselves. In the Northern Hemisphere, each
succeeding downward sheet of water is deflected a little more to the right of its original
path of motion. However, the wind's energy
cannot directly reach the deeper waters beneath the surface layer, and the spiral of motion is relatively shallow (Figure 14–11). This
directional spiral in the surface waters is
known as an *Ekman spiral*, named after V. W.
Ekman, a Swedish oceanographer, who suggested its presence. The entire surface layer,
with its main movement at an angle to the
force of the wind, is called the *Ekman layer*.
Movements within this layer in combination
with other factors such as continental barriers
to the west and east tend to direct the surface
currents of the oceans toward the centers of
the major basins in the mid-latitudes (Figure
14–12). This results in a piling up of water,
which while slight—less than 1 meter higher
than at the edges of the basin—further results
in a downward pressure on the waters beneath.
These deeper waters must slide out in response
to the pressure from above. The entire system
operates much like an atmospheric high-
pressure cell or anticyclone. The outward
moving waters are deflected to the right in the
Northern Hemisphere and to the left in the
Southern.

The confining shape of the ocean basin
further deflects the moving waters. In the
North Atlantic, for example, the westward
flow encounters the American continent and
is turned first northward and then to the east.
The east-flowing current comes up against the
shores of Europe and is forced largely southward and subsequently back to the west, thus
completing the circuit (Figure 14–13). These
giant eddies in the world ocean are called
gyres, the most famous of which is the one
just mentioned with the Sargasso Sea at its
center.

The energy carried in these gyres—or more
accurately, variations in the energy contained
in them from one part to another—warms or

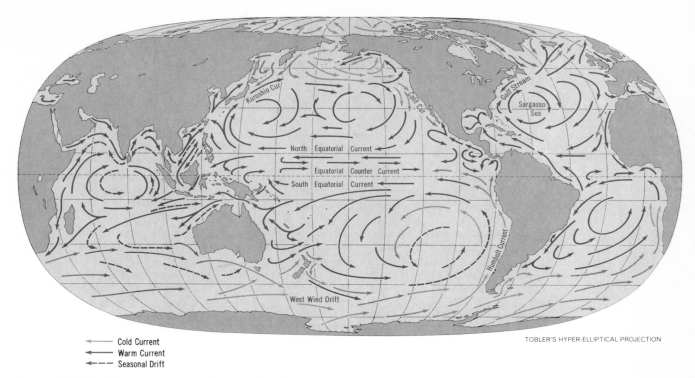

—————→ Cold Current
—————→ Warm Current
—————→ Seasonal Drift

Figure 14-13 World ocean currents The complicated pattern shown here is an extension of the simplified version shown in the preceeding figure (14-12). Warm and cool waters moving latitudinally north and south are important elements in the formation of climates utilized by man. The pattern is essentially symmetrical north and south of the equator and in both the Atlantic and Pacific Oceans.

chills the shores of the world ocean. This will become apparent as we follow the complete path of a subtropical gyre. However, the circulation of oceanic waters throughout the entire volume of the seas is little understood, and the patterns shown in Figures 14–12 and 14–13 relate only to the surface layer.

Beginning with the limb or portion of the gyre nearest the equator, the steady movement of the trade winds imparts energy to the waters beneath and sets them in motion. The coriolis effect deflects the moving water at approximately 45° to the right or left of the wind's direction, depending upon the hemisphere. The result is an east-west flow of water called the *North* and *South Equatorial Currents*. Between these, and directly at the equator, is a lesser, reverse flow, the *Equatorial Countercurrent*, which helps to equalize the return flow of water to the east. The Equatorial Currents are warmed by the high-sun insolation of the tropics. As they are deflected by the continents on the western edges of the ocean basins, they carry relatively warm water poleward along the east side of the continents. This water is a mixed blessing, for being warm, it is a major source of energy for those continental shores, while the moisture-laden air above it provides precipitation for the eastern coastlands. At the same time, however, the warm water contains smaller amounts of absorbed gases such as oxygen and carbon dioxide which are necessary for maintaining marine life. The warm, blue waters of the Gulf Stream and the Medi-

Solar Energy and Man: Earth as a Heat Engine

273

terranean may evoke the praise of poets, but they are relatively sterile, and it is the colder oceans, rich and green with microscopic plant and animal life, which sustain the fish which, in turn, help to feed the world.

The northern and southern extensions of the equatorial flow are perhaps the best known of all the world's currents. The *Gulf Stream* along the eastern United States was described as long ago as two centuries by Benjamin Franklin. A similar current in the Pacific, the *Japan*, or *Kuroshio*, *Current*, is nearly as famous. Lesser known, but important in the Southern Hemisphere, are their counterparts, the *Brazil Current* and the *East Australia Current*. Poleward of 40° latitude, the warm waters begin to contact cold currents flowing from the Arctic, the *Labrador* and *Greenland Currents* of the North Atlantic, the *Oyashio* of the North Pacific, and a general upwelling of antarctic waters in the Southern Hemisphere. The colder, gas- and nutrient-filled waters of the polar seas mix with the warmer waters and are forced to the surface where they support rich harvests of sea life.

In these latitudes the surface currents are pushed smartly along by the westerlies and take the name the *West Wind Drift*, called the *North Atlantic Drift* in the Atlantic Ocean. The West Wind Drift contains more energy than would be normally expected at such latitudes. By the time the eastern shores of the ocean basins are reached, the difference is significant. England and Scandinavia, British Columbia and Alaska, and southern Chile all benefit from the warmth thus provided. For example, January temperatures at 60° north latitude average minus 10°F on the shores of Labrador, while at the same time southern Norway and the Shetland Islands experience average temperatures of 40°F. Of course, the shores of Labrador are further plunged in cold by southward-flowing arctic waters. In general, the temperature of the ocean affects temperatures on the adjacent coasts. This is shown by the poleward shift of isotherms where warm currents flow off-shore and by the equatorward shift where cool or cold currents are found (Figure 14–8).

With their deflection equatorward along the eastern basin shores, the waters of the subtropical gyres once more enter relatively warmer latitudes. By comparison they are now cooler than their new environment, having lost much of their energy along the way. In turn, they have acquired more absorbed gases and more nutrients and are mixed in part with polar waters. The effect is shown by the cool, life-laden *California* and *Humboldt* (or *Peru*) *Currents* of the Pacific and their Atlantic counterparts, the *Canary* and *Benguela Currents*. At this point, the gyre closes upon itself like the dragon of immortality biting its own tail.

Though we close this chapter with a notion of immortality and endless process, we must avoid the notion that these liquid components of heat engine earth operate entirely outside the range of man's impact. Navies may float like tiny chips upon their surface, but oil spills from ships far at sea can be carried with disastrous effects to our shores. Battles have been fought over the control of fishing at certain critical spots such as the shallow waters off Iceland. And just as the green glass fishnet floats lost by Japanese fishermen wash ashore in the Pacific Northwest after transpacific voyages, so too can radioactive materials from island bomb tests find their way to populated shores. Nor does man's tampering end with acts such as these. Megalomaniacal schemes and dreams of some planners have included the damming of the Bering Straits, which would warm the eastern shores of Siberia by cutting off the frigid Oyashio Current. Others have talked of blocking the Red Sea near Aden in order to generate hydroelectric power by pouring the waters of the Indian Ocean into the empty basin left by the evaporation of the waters trapped behind the dam. These ideas may be the pipe dreams of bureaucrats, but with environmental control becoming more and more a reality and a political issue, we cannot entirely overlook them. We will return to considerations such as these, and more, in later chapters. For now, we have described in the briefest detail the major atmospheric and oceanic transfers of energy that help to maintain the surface of the earth in a habitable equilibrium. Our next task is to enlarge the scale at which we view the world and to consider the interaction between the atmosphere; the hydrosphere, or waters of the world; and the lithosphere, or rocky portions of the earth's surface. These interactions can be thought of as subsystems of energy and moisture flow, which sculpture and reshape the earth's ever-changing face as well as create world patterns of weather and climate.

15 | ENERGY AND THE EARTH: THE HYDROLOGIC CYCLE

In the year 1927, Gutzon Borglum, an American sculptor with a vast dream and endless ambition, started carving massive figures of American Presidents from the granite of South Dakota's Mount Rushmore. Fifty-three months later when lack of funds ended his project four great faces fit for giants 465 feet tall stood out upon the mountainside. To reveal those craggy features 400,000 tons of granite were removed from the peak in just over four years. Natural erosion processes before man appeared on earth removed an equivalent amount from the continents into the sea every 24 minutes. The activities of man have so increased the rate of erosion on earth that today the same amount is moved by the world's rivers into the world's oceans in just 10 minutes!

Two important subsystems of planet earth are highlighted by the above comments. Enormous quantities of water must move endlessly across the earth in order to transport such vast tonnages of eroded materials. Also, the continents must be constantly renewed; for at the present rate of erosion, all the land surfaces with their hills and mountains would be reduced to sea level in just 34 million years. Yet, there is no geologic evidence, that is, no proof exists, that the continents have ever worn completely away.

The endless cycling of water from the seas to the land and back again, *the hydrologic cycle*, will receive special attention in this chapter. We also have something to say about the *lithologic*, or *rock*, *cycle* in the chapter that follows. The two cycles are intertwined to various degrees, but the time span of the hydrologic cycle is measured in years, while that of the lithologic cycle is measured in eons.

The Physical Properties of Water

Before discussing the geographic movement of water, it is worthwhile commenting on this most interesting of the chemical compounds found on earth. In the outermost 3 miles (5 kilometers) of the earth (not counting the atmosphere) water is three times more plentiful than all other substances combined and six times more abundant than feldspar, the next most common compound. Water is almost alone in inorganic nature as a liquid, and is the only substance found on earth in all three states: solid, liquid, and vapor. Its heat of vaporization is the greatest of all substances, and its surface tension is the highest of all fluids. It is one of the best solvents and can dissolve a wider range of materials than any other. Water has many other special characteristics, but we will mention only one more. As do most substances, water contracts while cooling. Unlike all other materials, shrinkage ceases at 4°C (39.5°F) for fresh water. At lower temperatures expansion again occurs, and ice, which forms at 0°C (32°F), has a density 0.92 that of water. Because of dissolved salts, sea water freezes at a lower temperature than does fresh water, about −2°C (28.4°F). Sea water unlike fresh water, contracts until the freezing point is reached. As freezing occurs, however, the dissolved materials are essentially excluded and sea ice has the same composition as ice formed from fresh water. Two important conditions follow from these properties. Marine waters near the poles become denser when chilled and sink to the bottom of the ocean. This allows warmer waters to take their place, thus helping to induce oceanic circulation. The vertical component of this circulation ventilates the deeper basins, while the horizontal component helps equalize the global distribution of energy. The second condition is perhaps even more important. If ice were denser and heavier than water—a condition true for almost all other substances—it would sink to the bottom of the lakes and seas. Once there it would accumulate under the insulating layers of water above it. Gradually the basins of the world would fill with ice, and life on earth would be extremely difficult if not impossible under such circumstances. Kurt Vonnegut in his novel *Cat's Cradle* describes an imaginary ice that freezes at a temperature higher than that of the human body. The result is a dying and soon dead planet. If ice were heavier than water, the effect would be the same even if the process were somewhat slower. While we need not worry about such a predicament, it is useful to keep in mind the unique properties of water as we discuss its role in the earth's environmental systems.

Geographic and temporal changes in the location of water are characterized by many different processes, all of which become the means for channeling energy from place to place. Twenty-three percent of the sun's energy intercepted by the earth finds its way from the heated surface of the globe back into the atmosphere by means of the latent heat of vaporization. This and other increments of energy which pass through the atmospheric reservoir act as a source for power for the winds of which

Mount Rushmore Memorial, Black Hills, South Dakota   The man-made talus slope beneath the monument, while huge, is only a tiny part of the materials eroded by human activity. (U.S. Dept. of Agriculture photo)

we have already written. Wind, precipitation, changes in temperature, and many other similar phenomena combine into a set of short-term atmospheric conditions we all know as *weather*. Weather, in turn, acts upon the surface of the earth in various ways. The resulting breakdown of rocky materials, *weathering,* helps to create conditions suitable for the formation of soils and the growth of vegetation. The cumulative, long-term effects of weather are characterized as different types of *climate* most easily identified by the vegetation associated with them. Meanwhile, weathered materials and soils are constantly being removed and transported by moving water. The removal of materials by water, *erosion,* continuously planes down the earth's surface. The redeposition of these materials, *sedimentation,* continuously fills in the low-lying portions of the earth. At still another scale, water moves endlessly through the bodies of plants and animals, sustaining them and keeping them alive and healthy. In com-

Energy and the Earth: The Hydrologic Cycle

277

bination, all the processes and paths which water follows become so complex that in order to understand them we need simple models with which to order our thinking. The idea of the hydrologic cycle offers us such a place to begin.

The Hydrologic Cycle

Earth is the wet planet. More than 295 million cubic miles of water in the form of ice, liquid, and vapor lie awash the globe. Why are we constantly cautioned that humankind is rapidly "running out of water?" If we draw up a

Figure 15-1 Distribution of water on earth   So great is the proportion of the world's water that is stored within the sea that two scales have been used in this diagram. Of the 3.3 percent of the total that is fresh water, less than 1.0 percent remains unfrozen. Though earth has been described as a "wet" planet, very little fresh water is available for use. (Data from J. E. Van Riper, *Man's Physical World,* McGraw-Hill, New York, 1971, p. 174)

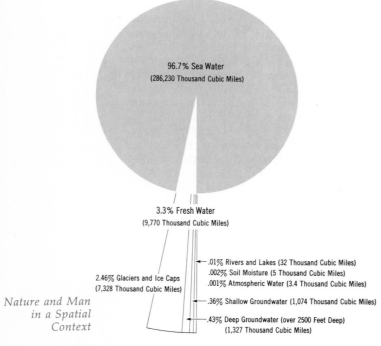

96.7% Sea Water
(286,230 Thousand Cubic Miles)

3.3% Fresh Water
(9,770 Thousand Cubic Miles)

2.46% Glaciers and Ice Caps
(7,328 Thousand Cubic Miles)

.01% Rivers and Lakes (32 Thousand Cubic Miles)
.002% Soil Moisture (5 Thousand Cubic Miles)
.001% Atmospheric Water (3.4 Thousand Cubic Miles)

.36% Shallow Groundwater (1,074 Thousand Cubic Miles)

.43% Deep Groundwater (over 2500 Feet Deep)
(1,327 Thousand Cubic Miles)

Nature and Man in a Spatial Context

budget of the world's waters, part of the problem becomes immediately apparent. Almost 97 percent of all water is the salty stuff that fills the oceans. Only 3.3 percent, or just under 10 million cubic miles, is fresh or salt-free enough to drink. But not all the fresh water on earth is available for immediate use. Three-fourths of it (2.46+ percent) is locked up in glaciers and ice caps. Another 0.43 percent is stored within the surface layer of the earth as groundwater more than 2,500 feet deep. Groundwater stored nearer the surface accounts for another 0.36 percent. Most amazing is the relatively small amount found in rivers and lakes (0.01 percent), that within the soil and available to plants (0.002 percent), and that in the atmosphere itself (0.001 percent). These proportions are shown in Figure 15–1.

If the moisture in the atmosphere, rivers and lakes, and the soil were not in constant flux, there indeed would not be enough water to meet all the demands placed upon such a small store. Fortunately, the solar energy which drives the earth system constantly recycles water and allows its reuse. Thus, while the atmosphere contains only an estimated 3,400 cubic miles of water in the form of vapor, an estimated 95,000 cubic miles of water is evaporated from the oceans, lakes, rivers and from moist lands each year. Obviously, what goes up must come down, and 95,000 cubic miles of precipitation balance the equation. It is the paths taken by this constantly recycling water that concern us here.

The oceans are the source of almost all the water moving through the hydrologic cycle. A small quantity of *juvenile* water finds its way into system from the gases generated during volcanic eruptions. Nevertheless, there is strong evidence that the accumulation of oceanic waters is very old and that the seas have lapped at the continents from at least early Paleozoic times more than 400 million years ago.

There are varying opinions on the amount of water evaporated from the ocean surface each year, but one good estimate places this at about 80,000 cubic miles. Once in the atmosphere, this water follows one of a number of

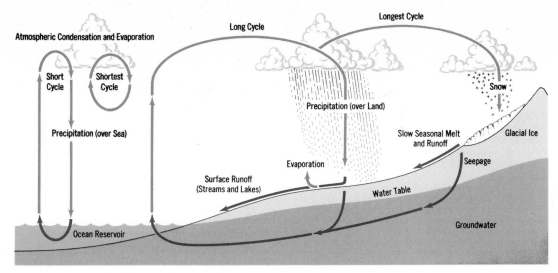

Figure 15-2 The hydrologic cycle and some of its variations   A molecule of water moving through the atmosphere and the oceans and across the surface of the land can be caught up in hydrologic cycles of various duration. The short cycles may be simply from the ocean to the atmosphere and back again or from the atmosphere to a falling drop of rain which evaporates before reaching the ground. Cycles of intermediate length would move the same molecule from the sea to the atmosphere, over the land in rain clouds, and eventually back to the sea in streams of groundwater. If the water were locked up in glacial ice, years might pass before melting released it for a return trip to the sea.

possible routes or cycles until it returns to the sea (Figure 15–2). The shortest cycle of all does not involve the ocean directly and consists of the condensation of rain and its immediate evaporation in the atmosphere without reaching the earth's surface. Nevertheless, this *shortest cycle* still depends upon the ocean's having provided the atmosphere with water at some earlier time. A more significant *short cycle* takes place when condensation occurs and rain falls upon the surface of the sea. Some of the water vapor provided by the oceans is blown inland and enters a *long cycle*. In this case, rain falls upon the land, where part of it immediately evaporates, some soaks into the earth to fill the twin reservoirs of soil moisture and groundwater, and some runs back into the sea in the form of streams and rivers. Along the way water is temporarily stored in lakes and also, in tiny but critical quantities, in plants and animals. A still *longer cycle* involves

precipitation in the form of snow and ice. In this cycle, years may pass before a particular molecule of water finds its way slowly from the head of a glacier to the point where melting occurs. After that, the return to the sea is quickly accomplished. The longest cycle incorporates all the shorter cycles within it, as does each succeedingly shorter cycle include those still smaller. Thus, in addition to the water evaporated from the oceans, another 15,000 cubic miles is evaporated from rivers, lakes, and moist lands. Since precipitation must balance this evaporation, we find 24,000 cubic miles of water precipitated each year on the land and another 71,000 onto the oceans. Moreover, since more water precipitates upon the land than evaporates from it, a final 9,000 cubic miles eventually reaches the sea as liquid runoff. The final picture is one of endless cycles within cycles, some of which we will now try to describe.

The latitudinal balance sheet

Energy is unequally distributed across the globe from the equator to the poles. Land and water are also unequally distributed latitudinally upon the earth (Figure 15–3). Moreover, the surface area of the earth itself varies with latitudinal position. While the inequalities of land and water area are self-evident from the accompanying figure, the statement about surface area and latitude needs a little more explanation. For example, a band of latitude measured from the equator (0°) to 5° north latitude is approximately 24,000 miles in circumference on its southern edge. A similar 5° latitudinal band measured between 60° and 65° latitude is only 6,000 miles in circumference along its equatorward side.

All else being equal, insolation upon the earth's surface results in water evaporation proportional to the temperature of the atmospheric cover. We would, therefore, expect to find evaporation from the seas and wetlands to be greatest near the equator and least near the poles. For the moment, let us consider only the total amount of evaporation and its inevitable parallel, precipitation, as these two processes are distributed latitudinally across the earth. Figure 15–4 shows the distribution of excess evaporation and excess precipitation north and south of the equator by 10° bands. By excess we mean whichever amount is greater when all that has gone up (evaporation) is subtracted from all that has come down (precipitation). At some latitudes much more moisture is lost to the atmosphere than is returned; at others just the opposite is true. Only between 30° and 40° south latitude is the ledger in balance. A distinction must also be made between the continents and the oceans, for the seas generally contribute and receive more water than do the continents.

Now consider the general pattern of moisture debits and credits. Between 10° and 40° north latitude and 0° and 30° south latitude the oceans give up enormous quantities of water which enters the atmosphere in vapor form. (Remember that the quantities given in this figure refer only to the absolute differences between evaporation and precipitation. Thus, the total shown for the entire world is about 22,000 cubic miles, compared with 95,000 cubic miles mentioned earlier.

Figure 15-3 Distribution of land on earth by latitude The total land mass in each five-degree band of latitude north and south of the equator is shown as a percentage of the total. The data have been grouped symmetrically on either side of the central axis in order to suggest the shield shape which we have assigned the hypothetical continent discussed throughout the book. The diminishing of the total surface area of the globe near the poles is clearly evident in the south polar region, which has only a small portion of the total land area, although that area is considered to be completely above sea level. (Based on data: Waldo R. Tobler, *Geographical Coordinate Computations Part II,* Finite Map Projection Distortions, Technical Report No. 3, University of Michigan, Dept. of Geography, December 1964, under contract with the Office of Naval Research, Geog. Branch Contract Nonr. 1224(48), Task No. 389-37)

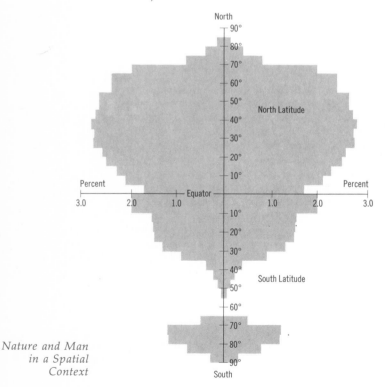

The difference between the two figures represents those waters which are recycled several times in the same immediate area within a single year.) Poleward of 40° in both hemispheres precipitation exceeds evaporation. This is clearly a function of less solar energy's being available at those latitudes. The absolute amount of either excess evaporation or excess precipitation is also less, because of the smaller surface areas involved, as discussed above. The greatest evaporation occurs near 30° north and south latitude in the belts of subtropical high pressure.

It is obvious, though, that the subtropical seas do not dry up and that the higher latitudes are not necessarily drowned in ice or water. A constant readjustment or geographic redistributing of water vapor and liquid keeps the ledger of the earth in balance. Water vapor from areas of excess evaporation is carried by the wind into areas of excess precipitation. Much of the precipitation simply falls upon the surface of more northerly and southerly seas, but another portion descends upon the land. The excess precipitation, in turn, runs off as rivers or sometimes as glaciers which reach the sea. At higher latitudes excess precipitation which falls upon the surface of the sea eventually finds its way equatorward in the form of deep sea currents. Where excess precipitation also occurs just north of the equator, runoff from the land and rain upon the ocean's surface is carried by currents toward the subtropical high-pressure belt. Once there, it again evaporates. We should not imagine, though, that these trips are direct or without interruption. The same molecule of water may travel between earth and high heaven a number of times along the way. In fact, it is estimated that the average length of time that water in vapor form remains in the atmosphere is only about nine or ten days. What we are talking about is the total picture, and as with all views of totality much detail is lost in the telling. Nevertheless, even these simple statements about evaporation and precipitation can be combined with our knowledge of the world's wind and ocean current systems to give us a

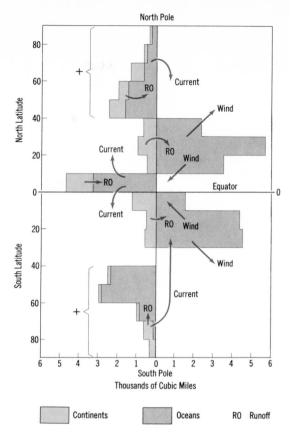

Figure 15-4 The water balance of the earth by latitudinal zones The left side of the diagram shows the areas of the world where precipitation exceeds evaporation; the right side shows the areas where evaporation exceeds precipitation. An excess of liquid water is found poleward of 40° latitude in both hemispheres. At lower latitudes, evaporation (water vapor) exceeds precipitation (liquid water). Only in the Southern Hemisphere between 30° and 40° latitude do the two balance each other. In order to redress these inequalities, water in both its liquid and vapor forms must move long distances latitudinally. The arrows indicate the direction and type of transporting agent important in maintaining a worldwide water balance. (After J. E. Van Riper, *Man's Physical World*, McGraw-Hill, New York, 1971, p. 177; taken from Wuest)

Energy and the Earth: The Hydrologic Cycle

better view of the total earth ecosystem. Having done this let us move closer and look at certain hydrologic processes at an even larger scale.

Humidity and condensation

The words *evaporation* and *precipitation* go hand in hand. We have already considered evaporation in some detail but have not yet looked closely at the causes and conditions of precipitation. Precipitation is water in either solid or liquid form which falls from the atmosphere, occurring mainly as rain, snow, hail, or sleet. Its presence depends upon the *condensation* of water vapor when the temperature of the atmosphere reaches the *dew point*. We mean by this that warm air has greater capacity to hold water vapor than does air which is cold. For every temperature there is a fixed and definite weight of water vapor which can be held in a given volume of air. When this amount is present, the air is said to be *saturated*. The proportion of water vapor present to the total carrying capacity of the air is called the *relative humidity* and is measured as a percentage. Thus, for example, at 30°C (86°F) a cubic meter of air can hold up to 30 grams of water vapor. If at that temperature only 15 grams are contained in a cubic meter, we describe the relative humidity as 50 percent. When the air is saturated and contains 30 grams, the relative humidity is 100 percent. If the temperature of this same cubic meter of air were to drop to approximately 17°C (62°F), its capacity to contain water vapor would be halved and it would become saturated by only 15 grams of water vapor. The temperature at which the carrying capacity of the air matches the actual amount of water vapor contained within it is called the *dew point*. At this temperature, saturation is reached, any excess moisture condenses, and precipitation results. The term *absolute humidity* refers to the amount of water actually present in a volume of air and is measured by *weight* rather than as a percentage.

All of this discussion assumes that the volume of air involved remains constant. But a cubic meter of air when moved to higher elevations becomes considerably larger, while one moved nearer sea level is compressed and becomes smaller in volume. As a result, the measurement of absolute humidity presents some problem. To overcome this difficulty, the *specific humidity* of the air is often used by meteorologists and geographers. This is the *weight* of water vapor contained within a given *weight* of air including the water vapor itself. Very similar to this measure is the *mixing ratio*, which is the weight of water vapor compared with the dry weight of the air which contains it. The advantage of both these measures is that they remain constant regardless of changes in volume as long as the unit of air involved neither gives up nor receives additional moisture.

What all this means in terms of world geography is that at a global scale the cold air of the poles contains far less moisture than does the warm air of lower latitudes. At the same time, the relative humidity of the atmosphere is lowest near the subtropical high-pressure belts and greater both at the equator and in polar latitudes. Not only is air more nearly saturated near the equator (relative humidity), it also contains more available moisture in absolute terms (specific humidity or mixing ratio). As we will see, this has important consequences for human occupance in those general areas.

Types of Precipitation

The processes by means of which precipitation occurs in all its forms are more complicated than might at first be supposed. In this discussion it will suffice to say that large masses of moist air must be cooled below the dew point in order for precipitation to take place. Nighttime cooling by long-wave energy reradiation into space cannot accomplish this. Instead, it is necessary for warm, moist air at lower elevations to be lifted to greater heights where suitable cooling can occur. The discussion that follows deals essentially with the lifting processes which accomplish this.

The adiabatic rate

The general decrease in temperature as one travels away from the earth's surface has already been mentioned. This is known as the *lapse rate*, normally 6.4°C. per thousand meters change in elevation, and is associated with the fact that air at lower elevations is more dense than air at greater altitudes. Dense air is susceptible to heating through conduction from warm ground surfaces and from solar radiation. Also, the increased presence at lower elevations of materials such as water droplets and CO_2, both ready absorbers of radiation, helps produce higher temperatures nearer sea level.

The lapse rate should not be confused with a second type of temperature change within the atmosphere. As a given volume of air rises away from the earth's surface, its temperature decreases even when it loses no energy to the space beyond its own limits. This is because as the air expands, the molecules contained within it have more and more room in which to move, and strike each other with less and less frequency. This steady decrease of air pressure, and its parallel decrease in sensible heat, is called the *adiabatic rate*. More specifically, if the temperature of the air, cooling as it rises, has not fallen below the dew point, no precipitation will occur. Air temperature change while in this condition is known as the *dry adiabatic rate* and is equal to approximately 10°C for every 1,000 meters or 5.5°F for every 1,000 feet change in elevation. If the dew point is reached, precipitation follows and heat is released into the atmosphere as water vapor changes to liquid (the latent heat of condensation). This slows the adiabatic rate to about 6°C per 1,000 meters or 3.2°F per 1,000 feet, a condition known as the *wet adiabatic rate*. As precipitation continues, a point may be reached where the air is no longer saturated and precipitation will then cease. Now let us examine the three major

ways in which moist air masses are lifted to elevations where cooling and precipitation can occur.

Convectional rainfall

Imagine a warm day somewhere in the tropics or on the American Great Plains. At 9 A.M. the sky is clear but the air may already seem heavy and humid. As the sun rises hour by hour toward noon, the temperature climbs to 80° and then to nearer 90°F. By twelve o'clock small, puffy cloudlets fill the sky overhead and along the horizon. The day may be quite still, but little cat's-paws of breeze begin to stir the grass and trees. Actually, much of the movement of the air is vertically upward from the baking earth. This convectional flow of air, by itself, would seldom reach more than a few thousand feet from the surface, but if the air is nearly saturated, it may require only a short vertical rise to bring it to elevations where the temperature has decreased to the dew point. Condensation will follow, forming small amounts of rain which may never reach the earth. The latent heat released by the initial condensation will add sufficient energy to the system to actually accelerate the vertical movement of the moist air to greater altitudes. By 3 or 4 P.M. cumulus clouds will begin to boil slowly upward. Somewhere near 10,000 feet (3,200 meters) the dry adiabatic rate will have reduced the temperature of the main air mass sufficiently for much heavier precipitation to occur. Even though the wet adiabatic rate at still higher elevations will be somewhat slower, the cumulus clouds will begin to develop great white domes which push higher and higher. Soon mountains of white cumulonimbus clouds rear 3 to 4 miles into the sky, their bases filled with supersaturated air that may actually be below the freezing point (Figure 15–5A). Humidities of more than 100 percent under these conditions can exist if there are no suitable nuclei around which condensation can occur. The vertical winds which drive the moist air upward quickly push it to elevations where low temperatures permit ice crystals to form. Thus, the tops of thunderheads may be white with ice rather than water droplets. These crystals, falling earthward, enter the lower cloud and provide the solid bits necessary for condensation of the supersaturated air. Violent rains of brief duration follow, adding additional latent heat to the seething cloud mass.

Some particles of ice and water may make several trips up and down through the cloud before their torrential plunge to earth. Layer on layer of water may freeze around the original bits until hail accompanies the thun-

derstorm. Then, as the sun begins to set, energy is removed from the system and its movements begin to ease. The anvil-shaped masses of the mature cumulonimbus start to break up, the accompanying lightning and thunder grow less frequent, and sometime in the night's dark hours the clouds disappear until another day of sun refuels the system. This convectional process is the most dramatic of the three types of rainfall. Nevertheless, it is very likely less important on a world scale than either *orographic* or *frontal* rain-producing systems.

Apollo 9 photo.   This nearly vertical view of thunderclouds over the Amazon Basin, Brazil, was made on the eightieth revolution of the Apollo 9 spaceflight. The energy released by this single storm exceeds that of any weapon devised by man, and yet is so distributed that the selva beneath benefits from its effect. (NASA)

The basic requirement for all types of rainfall is the lifting of moisture-laden air to elevations where prevailing temperatures can cool it below the dew point. Obviously, such air masses also must have sufficient water vapor and condensation nuclei within them to bring about precipitation. In areas where prevailing winds encounter hills and mountains, the horizontally moving air is pushed up and over those barriers. Somewhere up the windward slope rain or snow occurs in large quantities; thus the name for this type of rain derives from the Greek word *oreos*, meaning "mountain" (Figure 15–5*B*).

Heavy annual rainfall resulting from these conditions is typical of the western margins of the continents between 40° and 60° latitude. This is particularly true in the Western Hemisphere, where the Cascade Mountains in North America and the Andes in South America thrust up major barriers into the path of westerly winds. Another smaller but effective barrier, the Olympic Mountains just west of the Cascades in Washington State, receives more than 180 inches of rain annually. When such moisture turns to snow in the winter months, the result can be spectacular. There was a record-breaking accumulation of more than 1,000 inches of snow on Mount Rainier in the Cascades in 1971–1972. Even where mountain elevations are not as great, slight lifting through orographic processes can result in heavy rain. The western British Isles and parts of Norway and northwestern Spain are noted for their wet weather, although their rocky heights are considerably lower than the Cascades or Andes.

Another part of the world where orographic lifting is important is on the subcontinent of India. The monsoon winds, moving in from the Bay of Bengal, encounter the foothills of the Himalayas, particularly the Khasi Hills in Assam Province just north of the Bangladesh border. A weather station located there in the town of Cherapunji consistently records incredible amounts of rain. The most spectacular quantity was 905 inches of

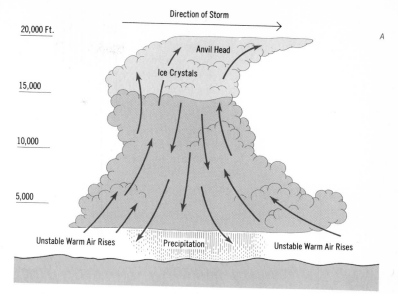

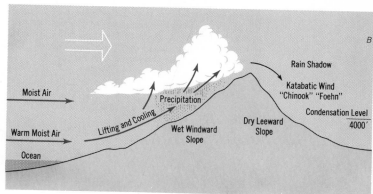

Figure 15-5 Convectional and orographic rainfall. *A.* Anatomy of an altocumulus cloud with convectional rainfall. *B.* Orographic rainfall
Moist air must be cooled below the dew point in order for precipitation to take place. Two occasions on which this happens are when convectional air currents lift air masses to altitudes where lower temperatures prevail, and when winds force moist air up mountain slopes into similar conditions. Altocumulus clouds or thunderheads (*A*) are frequently associated with the first method; orographic rainfall on the windward slopes of mountains accounts for the second (*B*), (*A,* after Joseph E. Van Riper, *Man's Physical World,* Copyright 1962, 1971 McGraw-Hill Book Co., New York, fig. 6–31, p. 232.)

Energy and the Earth: The Hydrologic Cycle

rain measured there in 1861; during that year, in the month of July alone, 366 inches fell.

The lee sides of mountain barriers can be as dry as their windward sides are wet. Once air has been pushed to elevations where it gives up its moisture, the winds may continue over the mountains and down the far side. The descent serves to compress and heat the air at the dry adiabatic rate of 10°C per 1,000 meters (5.5°F per 1,000 feet). As the air warms, its ability to hold moisture increases and the land in its path is dried out. These drying, descending winds are technically called *katabatic winds*, but wherever they are found they have colorful local names. The *chinook* which blows down the eastern slopes of the Rocky Mountains and the *foehn* sweeping out of the Alps are two famous examples.

The overall effect of orographic processes is to create belts of heavy rainfall on the windward sides of mountains and *rain shadows* and deserts on the lee sides. Where mountain ranges are aligned at right angles to the winds, as they are along the west coasts of North and South America, a pattern of wet and dry lands develops paralleling the coastline (Figure 15–6). In other places, mountains may be oriented in the same direction that the winds blow. This is the case in Europe, where much moisture-laden air carried in

Figure 15-6 World pattern of average annual precipitation   The occurrence of precipitation on a worldwide basis provides good examples of the climatic controls discussed in the text. Parallel bands of different rainfall intensities trend north-south along the Pacific coast of both North and South America. This reflects the barrier effect of mountain ranges. Deserts (less than 10 inches or 25 centimeters rain) mark much of the zone of subtropical high pressure. The west coasts of the continents at higher latitudes are well watered by storms brought on by westerly winds. These are only a few of the numerous examples shown by this map.

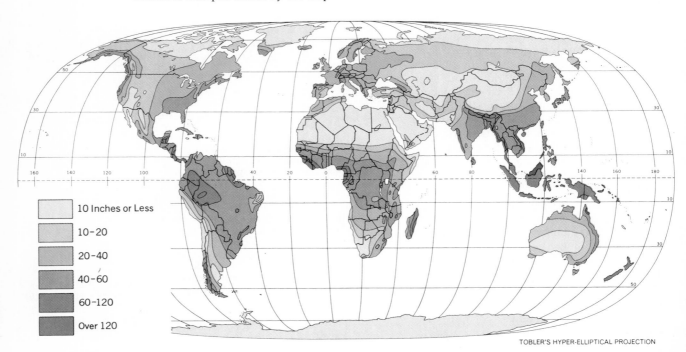

10 Inches or Less

10-20

20-40

40-60

60-120

Over 120

TOBLER'S HYPER-ELLIPTICAL PROJECTION

286

from the sea by the westerlies penetrates beyond the hills of the British Isles and southern Scandinavia. The main mountain barrier in Europe is the Alpine system running from the Pyrenees in the west to the Carpathians and Pontic Mountains in the east. Much of Europe's wet weather is kept north of this impressive barrier. The result is a relatively large area along the Mediterranean Sea which is warmer and drier than might otherwise be expected without the sheltering mountains. Here, too, we find a distinctive spatial pattern of rainfall (Figure 15–6) and a parallel set of human activities marking mankind's utilization of this special distribution of resources.

Cyclonic systems and frontal rainfall

Entire continents, or better yet, whole hemispheres, are the arena where the processes producing frontal rainfall take place. Precipitation of this origin occurs when major masses of warm and cold air encounter each other with subsequent lifting and mixing of warm, moist air with that which is dry and cold. To understand these gigantic meetings, we must consider that the lower atmosphere is divided into two major types of air. The first is the colder air of higher latitudes, viewed by meteorologists as a series of *polar air masses.* The second is the warmer air of lower latitudes made up of *tropical air masses.*[1]

Polar and tropical air masses are further subdivided according to the water vapor they contain, which is, in turn, a function of their continental or marine origins. These various masses of air correspond closely to the low- and high-pressure cells described in the preceding chapter. Thus, we find three polar air masses alternating across the northern part of the Western Hemisphere (Figure 15–7). The North Pacific is the source of cool, moist, maritime polar air. (The notation for this is mP.) Northern Canada produces cold, dry, continen-

tal polar air (cP). The North Atlantic is again the source of mP air masses. Far to the south, similar tropical air masses also form. Warm, moist, maritime air masses (mT) develop over the Pacific southwest of California, over the Gulf of Mexico, and over the Atlantic southeast of the United States. A fourth and smaller continental tropical (cT) air mass noted for its dry air and high temperatures occurs above the American southwest in the summer.

In their totality, these tropical and polar air masses remain remarkably distinct from one another. Their zone of contact is called the *polar front* and stretches around the world in the middle latitudes. High-pressure cells associated with this polar air mass rotate in a clockwise direction, resulting in a flow of cold winds from east to west along the polar front. The tropical counterpart of this flow moves from west to east as the result of a basic counterclockwise movement. As the warm and cold air masses come into contact with each other, a series of eddies occur along the front formed by their opposing flows. The dense polar air tends to push into the warmer, lighter tropical air as a rather steep or blunt-nosed intrusion, a *cold front.* The tropical air takes the form of a thinner wedge which slides up over the colder air against which it moves. This advance is known as a *warm front;* both are shown in Figure 15–8. As the cold limb of the original eddy pushes farther into the warm air mass, and in turn, as the warm air is deflected over the polar air, a prong of warm air can be caught between the two limbs of the polar mass. Since a cold front generally moves more rapidly than does a warm front, the advancing cold air sometimes overtakes and pushes under the warmer air. The result is that warm air is trapped above the colder air as the advancing limb of the cold front catches up with the warm front. When this occurs, the trapped overriding warm air forms what is called an *occluded front.* As major masses of cold and warm air advance across the land, their zone of contact is marked by precipitation and the release of energy through the latent heat of condensation. Two mechanisms, therefore,

[1] It should be noted in passing that these terms are something of an oversimplification since their major source areas are in the *sub*arctic and *sub*tropical areas of the world.

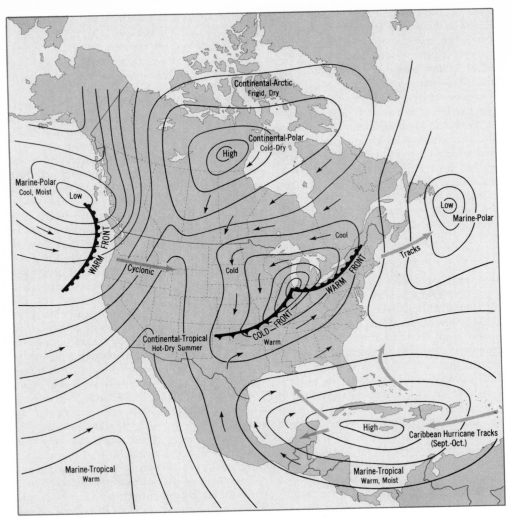

Figure 15-7 Typical North American weather system and air masses
The pattern shown here represents an arrangement of the basic air mass
components described in the text. Two low-pressure cells are crossing North
America, bringing frontal systems and the storms associated with them.
Rain and perhaps violent squall lines will occur where the continental polar
air over northern Canada is being pumped southward into the low-pressure
cell over the Eastern United States. The zone of contact between tropical
and polar air masses would mark the polar front.

are working to lift moisture-bearing air to
higher elevations. The first is a wedging effect
which drives warm air over cold air; the second
is a version of the convection processes described in the preceding paragraphs. The two

in combination produce significant amounts
of precipitation and sometimes, particularly
along the advancing edge of a cold front,
spectacular and violent storms.

Squall-line storms are a frequent occurrence

accompanying the advance of cold fronts across the Great Plains and the Midwest (Figure 15−9). These storms are marked by violent gusts of wind, heavy rain of brief duration, thunder, lightning, and tornadoes. These latter winds with their funnel-shaped clouds and shattering violence travel in association with the most turbulent portions of cumulonimbus buildups. They advance in the general direction of the squall line's movement at speeds from 25 to 40 miles per hour, but within their funnel winds may sometimes exceed 500 miles per hour.

Because the central United States has virtually no natural barriers running in an east-west direction, polar and tropical air masses meet in unrestricted battle more frequently here than anyplace else in the world. The advancing limbs of high-pressure cells, that is, the cold fronts which we have just mentioned, are moving in a counterclockwise, or southwest to northeast, direction by the time they have reached the Midwest. Thus, the most frequent path of squalls and tornadoes is toward the northeast in this part of the world. Moving eastward into densely settled areas, tornadoes have become part of American folklore and fiction. There would be no Dorothy and no Toto and no Judy singing "Somewhere Over the Rainbow" without the famous Kansas "twisters." In reality, and on a far grimmer note, the death and destruction from these storms is tremendous. Figure 15−10A shows the occurrence of tornadoes by one-degree squares in the United States from 1953 to 1969. Contrary to popular belief, although tornadoes are generally more frequent in the Great Plains states, such as Kansas and Texas, their destructive potential to human life is far greater in Illinois, Indiana, Michigan, and some parts of the Eastern United States. This is a function of population density. Figure 15−10B shows the *potential* casualties from tornadoes per square mile. Note the northeastward shift of the high-risk areas when the distribution of population is taken into account.

Less dramatic but just as familiar is the slower advance of a warm front.

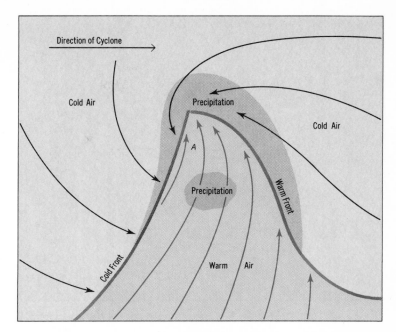

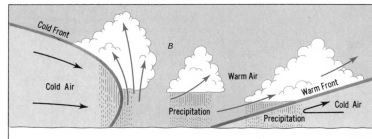

Figure 15-8 Low-pressure cell with associated frontal systems The cyclone shown here would be located in the Northern Hemisphere and is rotating in a counterclockwise direction. Tropical air from the south is coming in contact with cold air from the north. Cold air, being heavier, overrides the warm air and advances more rapidly than does the warm front moving toward the northeast. Precipitation occurs along both frontal systems, although the lifting mechanisms are somewhat different. (After Joseph E. Van Riper, *Man's Physical World,* copyright 1962, 1971, McGraw-Hill Book Company, New York, fig. 6−24, p. 224.)

Mares' tails
And mackerel scales

Bring lofty ships
With lowered sails.

Energy and the Earth: The Hydrologic Cycle

289

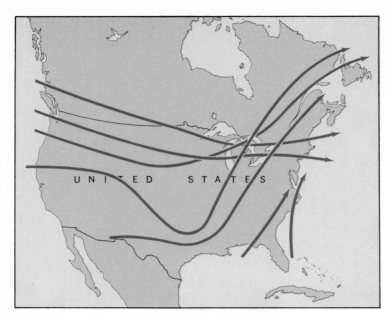

Figure 15-9 Storm tracks across North America
The mid-latitudes experience a steady progression of high- and low-pressure cells which move from west to east. The frontal systems associated with these cells produce the storms whose "tracks" can be traced across the continent. In the summertime, tropical air masses move far to the north and the frontal systems and their storms pass most frequently across Canada. In the winter, polar air masses push far south, bringing storms into the Central and even Southern United States. It should be noted that this figure includes two tracks of hurricanes, which are associated with another set of conditions.

This traditional jingle describes the first messengers announcing a warm front weather change. Because it overrides rather than wedges beneath the cold air mass before it, a warm front first reaches any given location not at ground level but high overhead (Figure 15–11). The first clouds formed along its leading edge are high-altitude *cirrus*, known to most "folk meteorologists" as *mares' tails*. Just behind them, and somewhat lower, will come either a thin veil of *cirrostratus* clouds that put a "ring around the sun," or sometimes the evenly distributed and puffy *cir-*

rocumulus clouds called *mackerel scales*. Still farther behind the leading edge of warm air, and lower still, will come *altostratus* clouds. At last, reaching down to the earth's surface, will come *stratus* and rain-heavy *nimbostratus* layers. This is the second major type of rain production associated with frontal or cyclonic systems. The somewhat more complicated precipitation mechanics of an occluded front will not be treated here. It is enough to say that an occluded front again involves a combination of wedging and convectional turbulence.

Water on the Ground

Once moisture has changed state from vapor to liquid and fallen to the earth, its most direct route back to the sea involves infiltration into the soil and the runoff of any excess. Let us, for the moment, assume that frozen precipitation melts and joins rainwater with no further complications. The accumulated moisture either soaks into permeable surfaces or runs off those which are impermeable. *Permeability* is a measure of how easily or quickly moisture can travel through a substance and depends on the connectivity between existing air spaces within it. *Porosity* describes the amount of empty space within a substance, that is, the enclosed volume not taken up by solid particles. Most rock, unless it is broken or shattered or unless it has solution cavities within it, may be considered impermeable. Rain falling upon it will simply flow elsewhere as surface *runoff*. In most cases rock is neither permeable nor porous. Soil, on the other hand, incorporates varying degrees of these two qualities depending upon its own characteristics.[2] Loose sand is highly permeable, as every child who ever tried to fill a lake in his sandbox knows. Sand is also porous, with its porosity depending upon the size and shape of the grains. On the other

[2]Soil is a complex substance needing special consideration. We ask the reader's indulgence in our use of the term at this point before we define and discuss it in a later chapter.

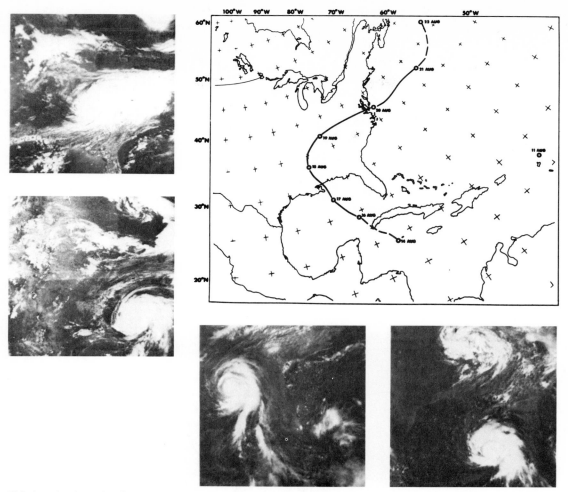

This is a daytime, day-by-day photographic history of hurricane Camille, one of the deadliest hurricanes in recent history. These pictures were taken by the National Aeronautics and Space Administration's Nimbus III meteorological satellite as the storm developed into a tropical storm, slammed into the coast of the United States on the Gulf of Mexico, and traveled northeast out into the Atlantic. These pictures show that the storm continued to pack a wallop even as it was moving across Virginia toward the ocean. (NASA)

end of the continuum of soil textures are colloidal and coarser clays. These are composed of microscopic platelets of a number of different minerals. When the platelets are all oriented in the same direction, clay is nearly impermeable, but surprisingly, its porosity still is very great. If you pour a cup of water on a lump of freshly dug clay, it will run off. But the same lump of clay, which may appear almost dry at first, often will become soaking wet after continued kneading. The manipulation of the clay between your hands will dis-

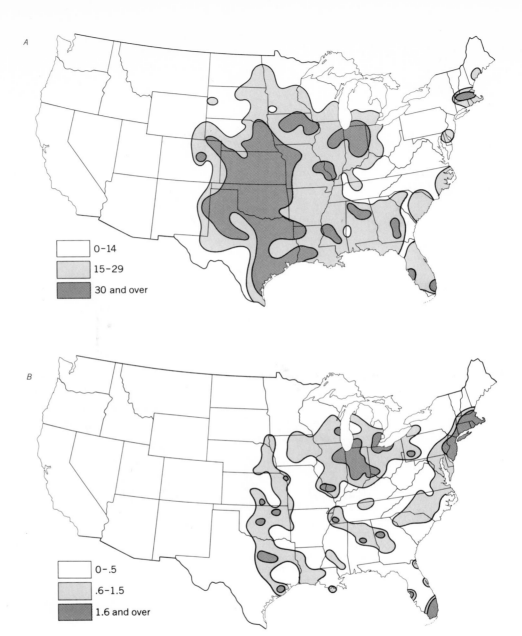

Figure 15-10 *A*. Occurrence of tornadoes by one-degree squares, 1953-1969. Distribution of tornadoes reported during the seventeen-year period cited. Note the dominance of the southern Great Plains and Texas Gulf Coast. ***B*. Potential casualties from tornadoes per square mile.** This map has been weighted in two ways: the area of each one-degree square actually swept by tornadoes during the seventeen-year period was carefully estimated; the 1970 population of each square was considered to be evenly distributed

Legend A:
- 0–14
- 15–29
- 30 and over

Legend B:
- 0–.5
- .6–1.5
- 1.6 and over

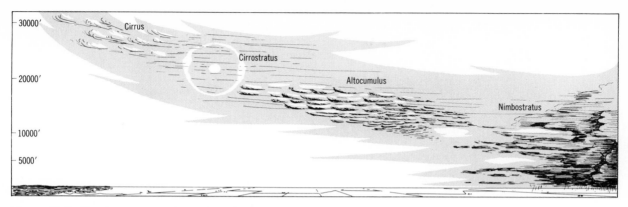

Figure 15-11 Cloud sequence of an advancing warm front   As the warm, moist air overrides the cold air before it, clouds form along the zone of contact. An observer looking directly overhead at the passing clouds would first see cirrus clouds composed of ice crystals at very great heights. The sequence of clouds that follows the cirrus approaches nearer and nearer the ground, becoming more and more dense, until nimbostratus clouds bring drizzling rain.

turb the orientation of the platelets of which it is composed, thus freeing the water trapped between them.

Soil may be compared to a sponge in its ability to absorb a certain amount of water but no more. Hold a dry sponge under a faucet. At first its hard surface will shed water, but as its fibers soften, more and more is absorbed. Finally, when every cavity and pore space is filled, water will once more flow directly from the surface of the sponge. The baked soils of summer and those of all arid regions are usually slow to absorb the rain that falls upon them. (Loose sands, which are not true soils, are an exception to this.) If the downpour is of brief duration, very little water can soak in locally. Instead, a film of water may run off downslope, gaining vol-

ume and depth as it goes. This *sheet flooding* eventually accumulates in river valleys and often creates *flash floods* of brief duration. Desert thunderstorms are a common source of flash flooding, and many an unwary traveler camped in some cool arroyo or wadi far downstream from a rainy area has drowned in an unexpected flood.

Where the soil is more moist and porous and where precipitation is slow and steady rather than torrential, water soaks readily into the surface. If enough water is available, it will seep downward until solid rock or other impermeable material is encountered. The water begins to build up from that level and soon fills the pore space of the overlying materials. The stored water thus accumulated in this *saturated zone* is called *groundwater*,

across the square, allocated on a per-square-mile basis, and multiplied by the number of square miles touched by tornadoes in each cell. This gives a *potential* rather than an actual value for tornado casualties. It should be noted that in reality, more tornado deaths occur in Arkansas, Louisianna, Mississippi, and Alabama than in Northern states with much higher potentials. This is considered by Sims and Baumann to reflect a difference in the perception of tornado hazard between Northern and Southern populations. (Maps based on data reported in A. Sadowski, "Potential Casualties from Tornadoes," National Weather Service, Washington, D. C., 1965 and 1972. See also John H. Sims and Duane D. Baumann, "The Tornado Threat: Coping Styles of the North and South," *Science*, vol. 176, 1972, pp. 1386–1392)

Energy and the Earth: The Hydrologic Cycle

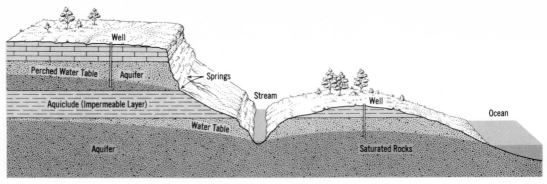

Figure 15-12 Groundwater The unconsolidated mantle of soil serves as a reservoir for underground water. The top of the completely saturated zone is called the *water table*. Wells may penetrate to it, and the water table may also intersect the sides of valleys, creating springs. In general, the water table roughly parallels the contour of the surface above it.

and its upper surface, that is, the top of the saturated zone, is referred to as the *water table*. Above the water table the soil is partially filled and may serve as a container for more moisture or may become a zone of upward water migration if the surface is dry and the energy in the air above it is great enough.

Groundwater moves slowly through the soil and upper layers of the earth wherever permeability permits. The water table tends to follow the contour of the land surface above it. Nevertheless, this water is under the influence of gravity as much as any surface water. Therefore, as a general rule, the water table is farthest from the surface on the tops of hills. Farther downslope the water table may actually intersect the sides of valleys, where it appears as a series of springs (Figure 15–12). In this and other ways water may reach the surface and return to the saturated zone several times on its trip to the sea. Once there, some water actually travels underground beyond the margins of the land and wells up as freshwater springs on the ocean floor of the continental shelf.

Water may also penetrate beneath the unconsolidated upper covering of earth materials into the rock layers or strata beneath. Certain strata, such as the famous St. Petersburg sandstone that underlies much of the Great Plains, carry large quantities of water. These water-rich layers, or *aquifers*, are important sources for irrigation and city water systems in many parts of the world. Other strata may be impermeable and dense and are known as *aquicludes*. Aquicludes prevent the passage of water and form effective traps or barriers. Sometimes a locally occurring aquiclude may hold a lens of groundwater above the normal water table. *Perched water tables* such as these offer short-term benefits to small populations who use them, but are often easily exhausted with intensive use.

In any case, when the storage capacity of the soil is filled and additional precipitation occurs, the excess must run off on the surface as streams and rivers. Lakes may also form as the result of damming or in natural and man-made basins. In terms of the hydrologic cycle, one of the most important aspects of rivers and lakes is the evaporation of water from their surfaces. The development pattern for a river in humid regions is to grow progressively larger as it nears the sea. Each side-stream tributary adds its bit to the total volume of water flowing from the land, and if energy demands of the atmosphere are not too great, precipitation can keep pace with or exceed evaporation. In arid climates, particularly at low latitudes, where the dry air of the subtropical high-pressure belt dries out the land beneath, rivers may actually grow smaller as they near the sea. Typical of such streams are the Nile in North Africa and the Orange River which rises in Lesotho and flows westward across the Republic of South Africa. In both cases the sources of these rivers are at high elevations in better-watered regions. Their downstream portions at lower elevations cross deserts where no tributaries enter. *Exotic streams* such as these give up enormous quantities of moisture to the air and in the case of the Orange River may actually have a dry streambed downstream while water still flows near the source.

Water in Vegetation

The above description has treated all water as simply a flowing mineral substance without reference to its place in life processes of plants and animals. We must now come closer to the earth and choose a still larger scale at which to view the hydrologic cycle. It is in its use within life forms that the true miracle of water occurs.

"Willow weep for me," once sang a popular entertainer. Anyone who stands beneath a willow tree on a hot day will be bathed in a fine mist dropping from its leaves. Desert streams lined with vegetation flow on the surface at night during periods of low energy demand. In the daytime the plants along the bank can draw so much water from the streambed that if the streams are small, they may actually go temporarily dry. Water is essential for plant growth and for plant health. It constitutes a major portion of active plant tissue; it is a reagent in the photosynthetic process, and a solvent which serves as a carrier transporting salts, sugars, and other dissolved materials throughout the plant. Just as important is water's role in maintaining the energy balance of every living thing, including vegetation. When air temperatures are high and radiation is intense, the body heat of a plant may increase to the point where chemical and other processes within it can be seriously and perhaps permanently impaired. Vegetation overcomes this problem by releasing water in vapor form from small openings, or *stomata*, on leaf surfaces. This process is known as *transpiration* and in many ways is the equivalent of perspiration in animals. The change in state of the water from liquid to vapor removes excess heat from the plant tissue. If, for example, a leaf 10 square centimeters in area (1.55 square inches) gives up only 0.005 gram of water each minute, this can produce an energy loss of 3 calories and a lowering of tissue temperature by as much as 15°C (59°F). The need for water is real and immediate. For example, a single corn plant can transpire as much as 204 liters (54 gallons) of water during its growing season. An acre of corn containing 6,000 plants would need 1,225,000 liters (324,000 gallons). A similar study has found that, in addition, an amount equal to somewhat more than 40 percent of the water used in transpiration *evaporates* from a corn plant. In other words, an additional 83 liters (22 gallons) of water would pass from the surface of the plant to the atmosphere.

The combined demands placed upon available water supplies by both evaporation and transpiration have been given the term *evapotranspiration*. In high-sun periods the *potential evapotranspiration* possible if water were available in unlimited quantities can actually exceed the *actual evapotranspiration* that takes place. When the difference between these two quantities is negative, a *water deficit* occurs. If the deficit is great enough, plants will be forced to give up part of the water normally stored in their tissues. Depending upon the type of plant, permanent wilting will occur after from 25 to 75 percent of their water content is lost. Obviously, the water needs of plants will vary from season to season and from region to region. We will discuss these matters in greater detail in Chapter 17. For the moment, it is only necessary to add that man often intercedes and attempts to provide needed moisture for his thirsty crops through irrigation.

Evapotranspiration: A national balance sheet

The complexity of the hydrologic cycle with its hierarchy of shorter cycles nested within ones of longer and longer duration prevents

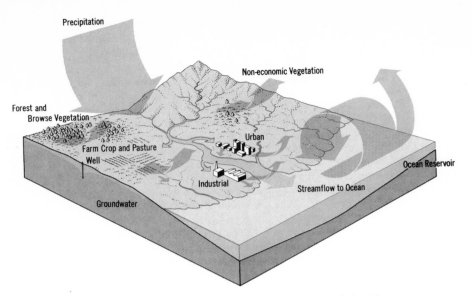

Precipitation

Non-economic Vegetation

Forest and
Browse Vegetation

Farm Crop and Pasture

Well

Urban

Industrial

Ocean Reservoir

Streamflow to Ocean

Groundwater

Figure 15-13 United States water balance (hydrologic cycle) It is estimated that nearly 5,000 million acre-feet of water are precipitated on the
United States each year. If this constitutes 100 percent of the total (actually,
an additional 6 million acre-feet of water are mined from aquifers), then an
equal amount must eventually find its way back into the oceans and the
atmosphere in order to maintain the system in reasonable equilibrium. Much
of the total is evaporated from farmland and noneconomic vegetation back
into the atmosphere. A small amount is used by municipalities and industry. The water which runs off into the sea eventually evaporates and
returns to the land as precipitation. See Table 15–1 for the amounts indicated by each arrow. (Based on data in "Water Resources," Report to the
Committee on Natural Resources of the National Academy of Sciences,
National Research Council Publication 1000-B, Washington, D. C., 1962)

our making exact statements about it. It is
useful, however, to attempt to balance the
ledger of precipitation and evapotranspiration
for a large area like the United States. Figure
15–13 presents such an effort in graphic form.
The source of all but a small portion of the
moisture is assumed to be the atmospheric
reservoir. In this case, only the estimated
amount of precipitation has been taken into
consideration. Though precipitation appears
in the diagram to fall and evaporate only once,
the same molecule of water might, in reality,
make several cycles.

Nearly 5 billion acre-feet of water are involved. By *acre-foot* we mean the amount of
water necessary to cover 1 acre to the depth
of 1 foot, a total of 43,560 cubic feet, or 326,700
gallons. The first debit in our national ledger

is somewhat more than 3.3 billion acre-feet
which are evaporated and transpired from all
the nonirrigated land in the United States.
Note that this constitutes 70 percent of the
total, nearly half of which (38 percent) is used
by plants which are in some way utilized by
man and his animals. The remaining 30 percent runs off the land or falls upon lakes and
streams to become the total stream flow within
the nation. At this point water stored in
aquifers in previous years, perhaps as long
ago as the last ice age, is pumped out for a
variety of human uses including irrigation.
This water is mined just as we might mine
petroleum or solid minerals. Once such water
is removed, there is little or no chance of its
being replaced within our lifetime.

Of the 1.376 billion acre-feet found in American streams, about 340 million are withdrawn for human use for varying lengths of time. Most of this is utilized in irrigating farm crops; a surprisingly small amount is permanently removed for industrial or municipal purposes. Some water flows directly to the sea; the remainder, minus only about 100 million acre-feet, is returned to the river system. Finally, the ocean reservoir returns the balance to the atmosphere. For all practical purposes, all the precipitation that falls finds its way back, or perhaps even somewhat more returns than fell if we wish to include mined water.

In view of the above figures, we can once again raise the question, *if water is essentially available in quantities many times greater than current human needs, and if practically all of it is recycled, why do we face a growing water crisis?*

The answer is as complicated as the hydrologic cycle itself. In a later section of this book we will analyze cases demonstrating why water is scarce and growing scarcer. A quick reply to our own question at this point needs to emphasize the *quality of the water supply* and its *distribution in time and space.* A common perception of stream use by city residents is that upstream water flowing to the city should be pure and drinkable. On the other side of the city, rivers are seen as convenient sewers for the citizens and industry. The difficulties, of course, are that usually more than one city utilizes a given river; that population is not always located where water supplies are most abundant; and that a serious lack of fit often occurs between the spatial organization of human systems and the inherent spatial structuring of natural ones. We will return to these and related matters in the pages ahead.

Table 15-1   U.S. Water Balance (estimated)

	Millions of Acre-feet	% of Total Precipitation
Annual Precipitation over Entire U.S.	4,750	100%
Nonirrigated land	3,380	70
Stream flow	1,370	30
Returned to Atmosphere by Evapotranspiration and Evaporation	3,471	74
Nonirrigated land		
Farm crop and pasture	1,100	23
Forest and browse vegetation	750	16
Noneconomic vegetation	1,530	32
Irrigation	9	2.0
Industry	3	0.1
Municipal	3	0.1
Returned to Sea by Stream Flow	1,247	26
Streams (stream flow not withdrawn)	1,035	22
Irrigation (water returned to a stream)	64	1.4
Industry (water returned to stream)	156	3.3
Municipal (water returned to stream)	25	0.5
Total Water Diverted for Use:	345	7.-
In:		
Irrigated cropland	159	3.4
Industry	159	3.4
Municipalities	27	0.6

Note: Approximately 6 maf are added to water from aquifers. Water may be held for varying lengths of time in the various parts of the cycle.
Source: Based on data from Abel Wolman, "Water Resources, a Report to the Committee on Natural Resources of the National Academy of Science," *National Research Council, Publication 1000-B,* Washington, D.C., 1962.

Energy and the Earth: The Hydrologic Cycle

16 | ENERGY AND THE EARTH'S CRUST: THE LITHOLOGIC CYCLE

Moving water is the plane which smooths the earth. Streams and rivers are the major transporting agents for weathered materials. Thus, the *lithologic cycle*, which incorporates the wearing down and rebuilding of the continents, is in a very real way tied to the hydrologic cycle. The geologic processes involved in continental growth and destruction operate at longer time scales than do hydrologic ones, but we must still consider them in order to round out our picture of the dynamic planet on which we live. To do this, we will start with a small portion of exposed rock at the earth's surface, and follow a few grains of its material as they are weathered free, transported, incorporated in new rocks, depressed beneath the earth's surface, altered, and finally raised again and reexposed through erosion to another round of the *lithologic*, or *rock*, *cycle*. The path (or paths) followed by such material is shown in Figure 16-1. While we are fairly certain about the surface processes the diagram depicts, our ideas concerning subsurface processes within the earth are being radically revised in this decade. Therefore, we will do our best to tell you something about both the old and the new theories of the earth's crust and its formation.

Elevation, relief, and the conversion of energy

The unequal distribution of energy across the surface of the earth results in its flow from one place to another. Winds and currents are the principal components of such systems; the hydrologic cycle is another such principle component. Whenever an energy flow, in any form, encounters some obstruction, turbulence occurs and work is done. One form of work is the movement from place to place of part of the materials which make up the earth's crust. High peaks, craggy shorelines, and steep slopes of all kinds make excellent barriers to energy flow. As a result, turbulence, work, and erosion are often concentrated at such places. This is a function of both *elevation* and *relief*. By *elevation* we mean distance above sea level. For example, the Tibetan Plateau has an average elevation of more than 10,000 feet although its surface is relatively smooth and horizontal. The Tibetan Plateau, therefore, has high elevation and relatively low relief. A sea cliff which reaches only a few hundred feet above the surf has low elevation, but its relief is great. These relationships are shown in Figure 16-2. Water

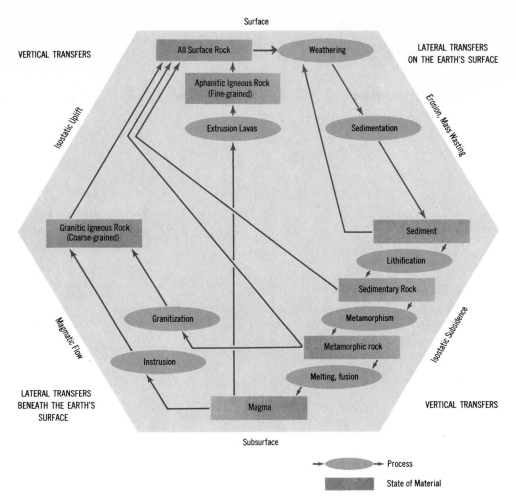

Figure 16-1 The lithologic cycle Materials of the earth's crust are in continual movement from subterranean depths to the tops of mountains and back again. This diagram shows several of the paths that a particle of rock might follow during this process. Movement is clockwise in the diagram. The longest cycle would go from surface rock to sediment, to sedimentary rock, to metamorphic rock, to magma, to coarse-grained igneous rock, and back to surface rock. The processes would involve weathering, sedimentation, lithification, metamorphism, melting, intrusion, and uplift. Other, shorter cycles can also be traced.

raised to high elevations has significant amounts of potential energy capable of performing large amounts of work. Steep slopes, that is, high relief allow the ready conversion of potential energy into kinetic forms. For this reason weathering and erosion are intense near the summits of steep mountains, and that is where we will go to choose the rocky material we will trace throughout the lithologic cycle.

Energy and the Earth's Crust: The Lithologic Cycle

Figure 16-2 Elevation and relief By *elevation*, we mean the altitude or distance above sea level; *relief* means whether or not steep slopes exist. Thus, plateaus can have high elevation and yet be flat and with little relief. The various combinations of these two elements are shown in the diagram. *A.* Mountains—high elevation, high relief. *B.* Plateaus—high elevation, low relief. *C.* Sea cliffs—low elevation, high relief. *D.* Delta—low elevation, low relief.

Types of weathering

The play of atmospheric energy upon the rock surface beneath results in two basic types of rock alteration and disintegration. Stony materials can be literally broken up into smaller and smaller grains under the influence of *mechanical weathering*. Frost is the predominant agent in this process. Moisture in small amounts penetrates cracks and crevices within the rock and upon freezing expands with great force, thereby wedging off particles from the parent mass. Abrasion of surfaces by particles borne by wind and water may also be considered mechanical in character, but it is difficult to draw the line between the breaking up of rock (weathering) and its being transported elsewhere (erosion). Another form of weathering occurs when gases and water from the atmosphere combine with rock-forming minerals to cause chemical decomposition of the stone. *Chemical weathering* of this sort includes *solution, hydration,* and *oxidation*. Mechanical weathering is most common at high elevations and high latitudes where freezing and thawing regularly take place. Chemical weathering predominates in warm, moist climates, particularly in the lower-latitude tropics.

If we begin our rocky odyssey with a granite

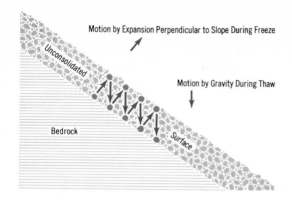

Motion by Expansion Perpendicular to Slope During Freeze

Unconsolidated

Motion by Gravity During Thaw

Bedrock

Surface

Figure 16-3 Downslope progress of a pebble in freeze and thaw cycle The process of freezing lifts the pebble at right angles to the surface, but when thawing occurs, the force of gravity moves the pebble vertically downward. This results in a gradual progression downslope of the surface mantle. Other processes serving to move materials downslope would be slump, slippage, and transport by running water.

outcrop high on a mid-latitude peak, it is likely that a combination of mechanical and chemical weathering will help free the particles we seek. The rock there can be penetrated by microscopic portions of water, which working inward from the surface by means of a series of ionic exchanges can cause changes in the chemistry of the surface layer and bring about its subsequent expansion. Free water might also freeze and thaw in tiny cracks caused by the swelling of the altered rock-forming minerals. All this results in a spalling off of layer after thin layer of rock, much as the dry outer skin of an onion wears away. This process is called *exfoliation* and results in rounded boulders such as those Robinson Jeffers describes as "blunt bear's teeth."

In other climes, at other places, rock might be dissolved by a weak *solution* of carbonic acid often formed by a mixture of water and decaying organic matter. Limestone is particularly susceptible to this kind of destruction. Sometimes the dissolving action of water is more direct if the rocks contain soluble salts. Where chemical bonding takes place (as with our exfoliating granite), the process is termed *hydration*. If oxygen from the air and/or water combines with other elements, *oxidation* may result. Oxides are often soft and easily worn away, though sometimes concentrations of less soluble oxides can result when silica (SiO_2) is removed by alkaline solutions.

Figure 16-4 Stream patterns formed by surface runoff Runoff on unconsolidated or unstructured materials often results in stream patterns which are treelike (dendritic), as shown in *A*. If a central high point exists, such as a volcano, the runoff may form a radial pattern (radial), as in *B*. Where parallel layers of rock crop out on the surface, thereby giving considerable structure or grain to the land—as in the Appalachian Mountains—the stream patterns draining the area may resemble a trellis (*C*), with short stretches crossing the ridges of more resistant rock at right angles to longer stretches in valleys formed on softer materials.

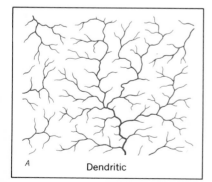

A   Dendritic

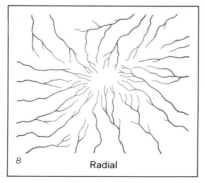

B   Radial

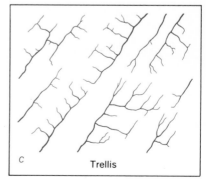

C   Trellis

An approaching dust storm. Colorado, 1938. Wind erosion aided by man's loosening of the topsoil and his destruction of its natural grass cover. (U.S. Dept. of Agriculture photo)

Gully erosion resulting from water running across improperly prepared and contoured fields. The farm has been abandoned. (U.S. Dept. of Agriculture photo)

Erosion by wind and water

The grains and pieces of granite removed by weathering fall from the parent surface and come to rest nearby or a distance away, depending upon the steepness of the mountain slope. Thereafter, their journey might continue in one of at least four ways until the grains are caught up by some stream. *Wind* might transport smaller particles for a distance. If rain were to fall at such a height, the runoff moving across the surface as a thin sheet might carry materials along by *sheet flooding*. If conditions were right, the material might fall upon either a snow and ice field or a glacier surface and begin a slow downhill movement by *glacial transport*. Finally, under somewhat different conditions, *mass wastage* might serve as the transporting agent. Mass wastage requires little or no water, and then only as a lubricating medium for the downhill movement of materials. Sometimes this form of movement will be abrupt, as when a landslide releases millions of tons of materials in some spectacular plunge. At other times the process will be imperceptibly slow. For example, a sand grain, pebble, or even a boulder resting on a slight slope may be lifted at right angles to the slope by the expansion of water freezing in the surface layer of soil. When the frozen ground melts, gravity will bring the particle vertically back to the slope in its thawed configuration. Figure 16–3 shows the millimeter-by-millimeter progress of a pebble down a shallow slope by this method of freezing and thawing.

At some point, however, it is likely that the material we are following will fall into or be washed by water running in a stream. Depending upon the geologic history of the area and the structure of the underlying rock strata, streams represent various patterns of line–area relationships. Where the underlying material is of relatively uniform hardness and texture, the runoff from the surface can take a general treelike configuration, or *dendritic* pattern (Figure 16–4). If the water flows from the slopes of an isolated peak, the stream pattern can be *radial*, but if the underlying

Table 16–1 Rates of Regional Erosion in the United States

Drainage Region	Drainage* Area Km² (thousands)	Runoff m³/sec	Load tons Km²/yr			Erosion cm/1000 yr	% Area Sampled	Average Years of Record
			Dissolved	Solid	Total			
Colorado	629	0.6	23	417	440	17	56	32
Pacific slopes, California	303	2.3	36	209	245	9	44	4
Western Gulf	829	1.6	41	101	142	5	9	9
Mississippi	3238	17.5	39	94	133	5	99	12
South Atlantic and Eastern Gulf	736	9.2	61	48	109	4	19	7
North Atlantic	383	5.9	57	69	126	5	10	5
Columbia	679	9.8	57	44	101	4	39	<2
Totals	6797	46.9	43	119	162	6		

*Great Basin, St. Lawrence; Hudson Bay drainage not considered.
Source: Sheldon Judson, "Erosion of the Land, or What's Happening to Our Continents," *American Scientist*, vol. 56, no. 4, 1968, table 1, p. 363.

rock consists of alternating layers of hard and soft material, the result can be either *trellis* or *annular* drainage patterns. In every case, the immediate effect of the streams will be to carry away weathered materials. This removal can be either of solid materials or of dissolved materials in solution.

Where rainfall is relatively scarce, as in the basin of the Colorado River, the amount of solid material removed from a unit of land by a stream will be much greater than the material carried off in solution. Conversely, in humid regions less solid stuff will be removed from the land by running water, but the stream load of dissolved materials will go up proportionately. Table 16–1 gives some regional erosion rates in the United States.

Material carried to the oceans by streams and rivers moves by one or more of four ways: *sliding, rolling, saltation (skips and jumps)*, and *suspension*. Generally speaking, these methods of locomotion along a stream channel are listed in order of decreasing particle size and increasing speed of water. The smaller a particle, the less energy will be required to lift it from the bed of the stream and to carry it freely in suspension. Extremely fine mate-

rials like clays and silts will cling to the bottom longer than sand grains which have more surface exposed to the force of the water, but once in suspension fine particles will travel farther than large, heavy ones.

Just as water molecules make many trips between heaven and earth during the hydrologic cycle, so do eroded materials pause frequently in their trip to the sea. Our original particles would come to rest after each period of sheet flooding had passed, or when freezing and thawing were inactive. Once in a stream, they subsequently might be deposited temporarily as *sediment* along the banks of some winding, or *meandering*, river. They might also come to rest temporarily in a lake or reservoir where the energy of the flowing water is dissipated into the larger body of water. Shifting of the river meanders could eat away the deposited sediments and bring them back into motion. Or again, through continued downcutting, the lake might eventually disappear or the silted reservoir be scoured clean. All this deposition and removal depends upon the dynamic equilibrium of the stream. Near its headwaters, every river system has a zone of active channel

Energy and the Earth's Crust: The Lithologic Cycle

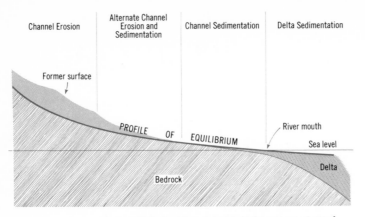

Channel Erosion | Alternate Channel Erosion and Sedimentation | Channel Sedimentation | Delta Sedimentation

Former surface

PROFILE OF EQUILIBRIUM

River mouth

Sea level

Delta

Bedrock

Figure 16-5 Profile of a graded stream at equilibrium A stream is probably seldom in a state of perfect equilibrium. However, in a perfectly stable stream system the volume of the materials eroded away from the headwaters of the stream would be deposited in its lower reaches so as to form a smooth, equilibrium profile.

erosion where constant downward cutting takes place. Farther downstream a transitional zone is found where sedimentation alternates with further erosion. Still nearer the mouth of the river is another zone of active deposition where waterborne sediments, or *alluvium*, at last come to rest (Figure 16–5). The steady extension of sedimentary deposits into the relatively still water of the sea results in the formation of deltas such as that of the Nile River shown in Figure 13–5. The velocity of stream water entering a larger body of water diminishes directly with distance from the river mouth. As a result, heaviest materials are deposited nearest the shore, smaller grains are dropped beyond them, and fine particles extend outward still farther. Dissolved substances travel farthest of all and are precipitated under special conditions in the centers of basins.

All of this relates to the concept of the *base level*, or lowest point, toward which the streams are flowing. At the lowest point, which ultimately is mean sea level, the potential energy of the water is completely exhausted. The ability of the water to perform work is ended, and all transport ceases. Lakes along the course of a stream, or interior basins with no outlets to the sea, may create *local base levels* which may seem quite permanent to us, but in a geologic sense exist for only one wink of eternity's eye. If the streambed is viewed in its entirety from headwaters to mouth and delta foot, we can talk about the *stream profile*. When the energy of the flowing water is evenly distributed along the length of the profile, we say the stream is in equilibrium. The profile of a stream in *equilibrium* would look something like that in Figure 16–5.

Erosion and the role of man

The above discussion may seem very far from our earlier discussion of city models and

This photo and the next two show a river system at different places along its length. In this picture, water in a small stream high in the mountains begins its trip to the sea near Ketchum, Idaho, during the spring thaw. (U.S. Dept. of Agriculture photo)

the works of man. In reality, erosion and deposition of earth materials concern us all and are affected significantly by human actions. We have already commented on how man's activity has increased world erosion rates about 2.5 times. Such an increase is geographically unequally distributed in terms of types of land utilization. A recent study of the Washington, D.C., area by M. G. Wolman has estimated the rates at which the surface of the land has been lowered by erosive forces. In precolonial times the forest floor lowered at about 0.2 centimeters every 1,000 years. As the colonists cut the trees and plowed the ground, the rate increased to nearly 10 centimeters for the same unit of time. Then, with the expansion of the city and the abandon-

The Snake River near Route 26 in the Salmon National Forest. The river is larger now and is a major erosive agent. (U.S. Dept. of Agriculture photo)

The Columbia River downstream from its confluence with the Snake River. A giant river providing quantities of hydroelectric power as well as being a major transporter of sedimentary materials. The Dalles Dam, Oregon. (Photo by J. Nystuen)

Energy and the Earth's Crust: The Lithologic Cycle

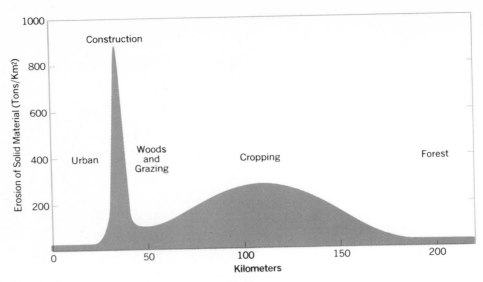

Figure 16-6 The city as a focal point of erosion   Little or no erosion can take place within the paved limits of the city. On the suburban periphery, where construction is in progress and the protective layer of vegetation has been removed, erosion rates are greatest. Abandoned farmland just beyond has a slow rate of erosion which rises slightly in still more remote areas of active cropping. Untouched forest experiences rates of erosion almost as low as paved areas, but what a difference! It is interesting to note that the original figure suggested by Wolman used time rather than distance as the measure along the abscissa. Thus, he considered a single location once in a forest but now at the urban core, and what happened to it over the century or more during which its use shifted from one activity to another. In this case, time and space have an interesting substitutability. (Suggested by Wolman, *American Scientist*, vol. 56, 1968, figure 9, p. 363)

ment of farmland on its edges, second-growth woodlots and temporary pasture reduced erosion to about 5 centimeters per 1,000 years. When modern construction began, rates as high as 10 meters per 1,000 years were reached for short periods of time at active sites. Only when the completely paved city took over did erosion drop to a negligible amount. While Wolman discusses erosion in a historical perspective, it is possible for us to view the city as a kind of time machine with the urban center representing the most recent types of human occupance and the spatial sequence of land use leading away from the center paralleling the city's historic sequence of growth. Figure 16–6 illustrates

the city as the focal point for various rates of erosion based on different land uses.

It would be a bit too fanciful to change scales and talk about the urban areas of the world being surrounded by concentric zones of erosion rates (as we spoke in Chapter 12 of the world's being organized around an urban core), but it is quite reasonable to predict that as more and more humans harness and use more and more energy for construction purposes and for increased agricultural production, significant changes in global geology may well occur. The only thing that makes this prediction conjectural is the short time man has been an effective agent on earth. Urbanization of any note has taken place only in the last 2,000 years; city growth covering significant areas is less than 100 years old. Man, in one form or another, has occupied the earth for something in the neighborhood of 2 million years, a mere tick of the geologic clock. It looks as if our chances of lasting as long as the giant dinosaurs did, some 100 million years, are none too certain. But if we do survive, the earth will be a different place geologically as well as geographically because of us. If we survive. . . .

Subsurface Processes

Our particles have by now found their way into the ocean waters surrounding the continent of which they were a part. From here on, their subsequent travels and transformations can be learned only by indirect observation. As a result, we must present at least two theories of continental formation. The first, and until recently accepted, one is based on the concept of stable continental masses being renewed by essentially vertical convection currents in the earth's interior. This can be called the theory of *isostatic equilibrium*. The second theory, which is currently being explored and tested, is based on a more dynamic model of the earth where large lateral movements occur over vast periods of time. This is referred to as the *plate tectonic theory*. Both of these theories consider operations at continental and global scales. Before discussing their details let us look quickly at the changes in quality and composition that rock-forming materials can undergo when caught up in such giant processes.

Rocks and rock formation

As an offshore area receives more and more waterborne sediments, layer on layer of unconsolidated materials pile up. Near the shore they will consist of sands. Farther out silts and clays will be deposited. Finally, in some areas calcareous, or limey, deposits will be formed from either the shells of sea animals or the precipitation of materials carried in

solution. As the weight of the overlying sediments increases, materials in the lower layers will become compacted and eventually cemented together. Sands will form sandstones; silts and clays will become shales; and calcareous materials will change to limestone. All such rocks which are formed from sediments are called *sedimentary rocks* and are characterized by their occurrence in layers, or strata, and by their relative softness.

With increasing depth beneath the pile of sediments, pressure and temperature increase. Sedimentary rocks can be subjected to great lateral pressure near the surface as well as intruded by molten materials from below. Such rocks can also be depressed to great depths beneath the crustal zone. In any of these events, the pressed, baked, and distorted rocks assume new characteristics. These processes of change are called *metamorphism*, and the rocks which result are known as *metamorphic rocks*. Sandstones become quartzites; shales transform to slate; and limestone turns to marble in the earlier stages of metamorphism. Further melting and fusing or perhaps chemically induced changes at lower temperatures create *gneiss* and other metamorphic rocks.

When rocks have been so transformed and melted that they become molten, or behave at great depth as viscous substances, we refer to them as *magma*. Magmas can move vertically or horizontally and often intrude into the solid rock surrounding them. After their intrusion they cool, and if the rate of cooling is slow, new rock will form, composed of crystals large enough to be seen by the unaided eye. These include the light-colored *granites* and their darker cousins the *gabbros*. If magma breaks through to the surface and extrudes as *lava*, the subsequent cooling will be quick and the rocks will be fine-grained. *Basalts* are typical of these. In either case, rocks with magmatic origins are given the general term *igneous*.

Though we have described this transition from one rock type to another as an unbroken sequence, the lithologic cycle has many loops

Energy and the Earth's Crust: The Lithologic Cycle

of different dimensions within it. Thus, sediments, sedimentary rock, metamorphic rock, and igneous rock may all be exposed to the atmosphere and subsequently weathered and eroded. The multiple paths in Figure 16-1 are indicative of this.

Isostasy and geosynclinorial theory

With few exceptions the view held by earth scientists of the internal structure of the earth and of its crust was until recently a static one. It was, in brief, something as follows. The earth is layered like an onion, with a dense core and thin outer skin. The *innermost core*, with a specific gravity of from 14.5 to 18 times that of an equal volume of water, has a radius of approximately 780 miles. It exhibits the properties of a solid body, but this is conjectural because of the difficulties of observation. The next 1,380 miles of radius behave as a viscous *liquid outer core*. Beyond that for another 1,800 miles is the *mantle* of the earth. The mantle, while dense and rigid, flows under the immense pressure of overlying rock. One might think of it as something like tar or silicone putty (though much more dense) which will break if struck a sharp blow but which will slowly spread if given enough time. Floating on the mantle and constituting the *crust*, or outermost zone, of the earth "onion" is a layer of crystalline rocks. This crust is from 10 to 25 miles thick and is separated from the mantle by a clear-cut discontinuity of rock type. Called the *Mohorovičić discontinuity*, or simply the *Moho*, after its discoverer, a Yugoslavian seismologist, this discontinuity is revealed by the sharp change in velocity that earthquake waves make when passing across it.

The crust, being outermost and being the home of man, attracts the most attention. It is composed of a lower, continuous layer of dark, heavy, basaltic rock with a specific gravity of about 3.2. Composed of *si*lica and ferro*ma*gnesium minerals, it is called the *sima*. Floating on the sima just as a coin can float on a pool of mercury are discontinuous "islands" of lighter, granitic rock with a specific gravity of 2.6. These islands which form the continents consist of *a*luminum-, potassium-, sodium-, and calcium-rich minerals which also have *si*lica as a major constituent. They are called the *sial*. A kind of equilibrium exists between the sialic blocks, their thickness, and the manner in which they ride—like an iceberg in the ocean—in the sima. Near the center of the continents where the sial is thick, a corresponding root of granitic material rides like a deep keel beneath the mountains on the surface. On the margins of the continents where the blocks taper out, the continental edges, which are submerged by overlapping sea water, are underlain by relatively little sial. Beyond the edges of the continents are the open ocean basins floored with basaltic sima. The submerged margins of the continental blocks, the *continental shelf*, extend with surprising regularity to a depth of about 100 fathoms (600 feet). At that depth they are abruptly terminated in many places by a steep slope which plunges to the extreme depths of the open sea. These relationships are shown in Figure 16-7.

In accordance with the above ideas, it was thought that as erosion lowers the interiors of the continents, the sediments deposited on the continental shelf or in the near-shore depths stack up layer on layer of strata until immense prisms of sedimentary rock are formed. The weight of the overlying materials presses those beneath deeper and deeper into the lower layers of the crust until their relative buoyancy prevails and brings them back to the surface. The process of downwarping and accumulation occurring in *geosynclines* is followed by another in which the geosynclinal prism is raised during periods of *isostatic uplift*. These latter periods can be thought of as times of *orogeny*, or mountain building. If the pressure is great enough, the lower portions of the geosyncline may fuse or be invaded by magma from beneath. This accounts for some lateral transfer of materials deep within the earth. Given enough time, such massive movements of the earth, or *tectonic* activity, will return the particles we are tracing to the tops of new mountains where they will again be in position to begin another trip through the lithologic cycle.

Continental drift and plate tectonic theory

Finding a suitable explanation for the subterranean lateral transfer of materials presented some difficulty in the theory of isostatic adjustment. Also, if geosynclinical accumulations of immense size occurred in the past, they should have contemporary counterparts, but no neat corollaries can be found today. This lack of contemporary examples runs counter to the concept of *uniformitarianism*, basic to all geologic thought. First suggested by James Hutton, the theory of uniformitarianism states that the geologic processes going on at present are the same as those processes which in the past created the earth features we now observe. This and other contradictions made scientists look for a more comprehensive theory to account for continental construction and crustal tectonics.

Four major and many minor clues led to the currently developing notions about the crust of the earth. (1) In 1912 A. Wegener pointed out that by removing the Atlantic Ocean a remarkably close fit existed between the continents of the Eastern and Western hemispheres (Figure 16-8). He suggested that these continental blocks had split apart and drifted away from each other across the underlying sima. However, many people found it difficult to imagine "ships made of thick continental crust plowing through a passive sea of oceanic crust." (2) In the years that followed, other scientists observed that evidence of ancient glaciation as well as the spatial distribution of many fossil life-forms occurring on the continents of the Southern Hemisphere could best be explained if those land masses had at one time been continuous. (3) Little was done to

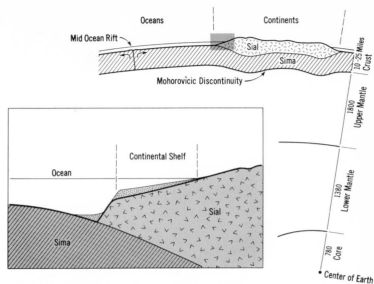

Figure 16-7 Structural and lithologic relations of the earth's crust From a geographic point of view, the thin crustal layer of the earth is most important. It consists of two types of materials, sima and sial. Sima is a dark rock which underlies the continents and covers the floors of the ocean basins and is heavier than sial, which constitutes the continents. The two materials are separated from the upper mantle of the earth by a discontinuity which shows up in the different rates at which earthquake waves travel above and below it. Sial floats upon the sima much as a coin might float on a puddle of mercury.

actively investigate Wegener's *hypothesis of continental drift* until after World War II, when oceanographic explorations in the mid-Atlantic discovered a major north-south trending ridge, or mountain chain, midway between Europe and America. Subsequent investigations of this ridge and the ocean floor on either side of it revealed facts of major importance. The ridge itself had along its center a gigantic, steep-sided valley much like the rift valleys of East Africa. At the same time, dredging and coring of the ocean floor showed that the sediments near the ridge were thin and young, while those progressively farther from it were thicker

Energy and the Earth's Crust: The Lithologic Cycle

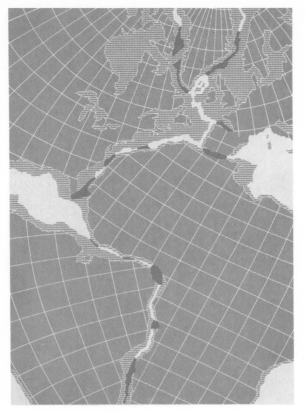

Figure 16-8 The matching of continental forms according to Wegener's hypothesis As early as 1912, W. Wegener had observed that if the oceans of the world were removed, it would be possible to fit the continents together into one or two super-continental blocks. His theory suggested that the continents had "floated" apart over millions of years. Subsequent developments in plate tectonic theory indicate that Wegener was largely correct in his hypothesis. The continental forms shown in the diagram are outlined not at sea level but rather at the edge of the continental slope. Areas of overlap and open, unfilled areas are surprisingly scarce.

and contained older sediments. The implication was that the sea floor of the mid-Atlantic was spreading outward away from the ridge with new material welling up from great depths. In other words, *new area was being created in mid-ocean* and by its appearance was forcing the continents farther apart. (4) The fourth major clue came when the epicenters, or exact location of greatest intensity, of all earthquakes that occurred during the period 1961–1967 were plotted on a world map. The plotted points (Figure 16–9) revealed major zones of tectonic activity and earth movement on a hitherto unappreciated global scale. The plotted earthquake locations also outlined huge platelike areas of the earth's crust. These plates included not only whole continents but also portions of the major ocean basins. In other words, according to the *theory of sea-floor spreading*, the continents were not drifting away from each other across the underlying sima so much as that the crustal plates described above were growing on one side. But what was happening on their opposite edges?

It had long been recognized that the Pacific Ocean, in particular, is surrounded by a series of arc-shaped island archipelagoes, famous for their active volcanoes, such as the islands of Japan. Similarly, the American shores of the Pacific have inland chains of active or recently active volcanoes paralleling them. Furthermore, just seaward of the Asian island arcs are deep sea trenches of enormous depth. It was along these trenches and islands that the plotted earthquakes indicated significant tectonic activity. The epicenters of the earthquakes showed that they occurred near the surface of the earth's crust in the ocean trenches and at progressively greater depths within the crust back under the island arcs and toward the mainland of the continents. The outcome of all these observations was the discovery that the crustal plates which were forming along the Atlantic Ridge were in all likelihood disappearing or being subducted again into the earth along the island arcs. Movements along the descending plate accounted for the earthquakes at increasing depths away from the oceanic trenches which marked the line of underthrusting (Figure 16–10). *Area was literally being created in one place and consumed in another.*

Mountain building, too, can now be given a

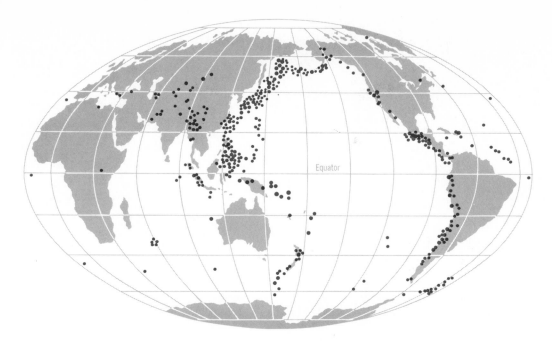

Figure 16-9 Earthquake epicenters The epicenters of major earthquakes are plotted on this map. The pattern reveals the midocean ridges important in plate tectonic theory. It also shows the subduction zones along the island arcs of the Pacific. Volcanic activity is also closely associated with the pattern of epicenters. Thus the "Rim of Fire" title given the volcanoes bordering the Pacific Ocean gains new significance.

new interpretation. The accumulation of sediments beneath sea level on the continental margins eventually is brought into contact with other continental portions of the moving crustal plates (Figure 16–11). The subsequent pressures crumple the geosynclinal masses much as a specially designed car bumper forms accordion pleats in order to take up the shock of a collision. In most cases a continental block with its shield of sedimentary deposits will strike against an outlying island arc. However, in at least one case, where the subcontinent of India appears to be being subducted under the Tibetan or greater Asian continental mass, two continental blocks have come into contact. Figure 16–12 gives some indication of the crumpled topography where they meet. The result is the highest mountains in the world, the Himalayas. Though our knowledge of plate tectonics is as yet incomplete, our view of the world as a dynamic place is enormously enhanced by these new ideas. In the same way, the particles of sediment which we have followed from mountaintop to ocean basin can now be raised upward again through the crumpling of the continental margins. Then, too, the enormous forces involved in these processes allow us to imagine rocks at great depths being metamorphosed, magmatized, and injected to become crystalline granites or extruded as fine-grained basalts. Thus, for the time being, we can consider as complete the round trip of the rock particles we have been following.

Energy and the Earth's Crust: The Lithologic Cycle

An Earth Resources Technology Satellite I photo taken from 914 km (568 miles) of the Allegheny Mountains, which run diagonally from lower left to upper right. The Susquehanna River cuts across them as a strong black line. The ridges and valleys, which form a zigzag pattern, are typical of the pressure ridges along the contact zones of tectonic plates (see Figure 16-11). (NASA photo)

Human implications of crustal formation

It may seem overbold to consider man and his activities in terms of the immensities of time and space involved in crustal dynamics. And yet the deck of spaceship earth upon which we tread can toss like that of a ship on a stormy sea. People living in earthquake zones, those tectonically active areas of the earth's crust, must take special precautions or pay the price. The price can be a high one, too. On January 24, 1556, approximately 830,000 people died as

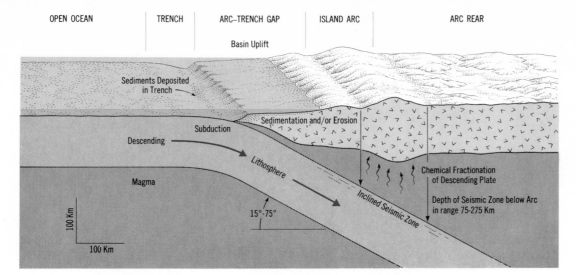

Figure 16-10 Generalized section of an arc-trench system According to plate tectonic theory, surface is continually produced along midocean rifts and continually consumed along the edges of the island arcs. This diagram shows the zone of subduction where materials return to the depths of the crustal zone. The oceanic trenches found in front of the island arcs mark the zone of subduction.

the result of an earthquake in Shensi Province, China. December 16, 1920, another 180,000 died in the neighboring Kansu Province. The famous Tokyo quake of September 1, 1923, killed 143,000, while on August 19, 1966, another 2,529 people perished at the village of Varto in eastern Turkey. In fact, a very conservative estimate of the number of people killed by earthquakes since 1500 exceeds 2,250,000.

We cannot go into a lengthy discussion of

Figure 16-11 Mountain-building sequence According to plate tectonic theory, orogeny, or mountain building, takes place when materials are carried up against the continental blocks by moving plates of the lithosphere. The resulting collision, although taking place over immense stretches of geologic time, nevertheless crumples the materials at the point of contact. The subsequent pressure folds and upthrusting of materials produce mountain systems parallel to the zone of plate contact.

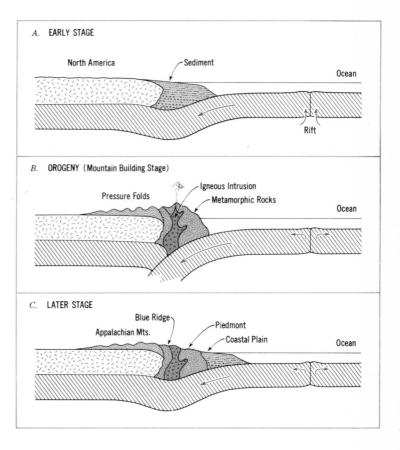

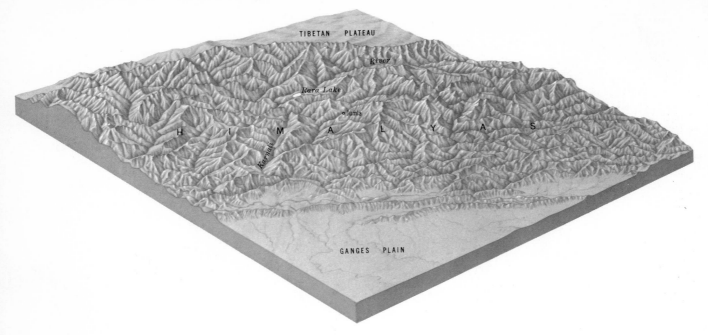

Figure 16-12 Mugu Karnali region of Nepal This diagram shows the incredibly rugged terrain along the Himalayan front. It is theorized that this marks the line of contact between two colliding blocks of continental materials. The Gangetic Plain in the foreground and the Tibetan Plateau beyond the mountains represent those blocks. The Himalayas represent the crumpling resulting from the ongoing orogenic process.

the exact causes of earthquakes beyond those we have already implied. However, there are a variety of reasons why so many people die when earthquakes strike. In China, Shensi and Kansu Provinces are essentially treeless, and many of their inhabitants dwell in unsupported caves dug into thick layers of wind-deposited soil called *loess*. The slightest earth tremor can collapse these caves upon their helpless inhabitants. The Tokyo quake took its toll because the city at that time lacked earthquake-proof buildings on firm foundations. In many parts of the world, including the Mediterranean region and Turkey, buildings either are poorly built or consist of stacked stone walls held together by simple mortising. These too collapse quickly and with little warning when earthquakes strike. While we do not want to sound like doomsayers, San Francisco

and other coastal California towns are located literally on top of the San Andreas *fault zone* along which crustal plates move horizontally in opposite directions relative to one another. Such *transform faults,* as they are known in the parlance of plate tectonic theory, can produce earthquakes as dangerous to man as those occurring along subduction zones, like the one that wrecked Tokyo. Proper construction techniques, building codes permitting only low structures with proper reinforcement, and avoidance of steep hillsides and actual fault areas can all reduce the loss of life from earthquakes. As yet we have no real way of predicting when an earthquake will take place. Research may help us in the near future to foretell such events, but an ounce of prevention is still worth many pounds of cure. The San Francisco earthquake of April 18, 1906, took 700 lives,

Side-looking radar image of the terrain near San Francisco, California. In this image the Golden Gate and Oakland Bay Bridges can be seen clearly. (NASA photo)

This picture is taken from a slightly different angle from the one above. San Francisco airport is marked by the X of crossed runways in the top center. The San Andreas Fault is clearly marked by the strong linear topographic elements across the center of the picture. The diagonal white slash above the fault in the right half of the picture is the mile-long track of Stanford University's experimental linear accelerator. This seems a strange site for such a delicate instrument. Plate tectonic movements take place along the fault line, causing linear displacement of the areas on either side of it. (NASA photos)

and that was at a time when the relatively few people who lived in the area occupied, for the most part, flexible wood frame buildings. The possibility of another major quake in California is very real; the results could be calamitous. There is talk of reducing the threat of big earthquakes by triggering a series of smaller ones along major fault zones by the injection of lubricating liquids into deep wells or even by exploding small atom bombs beneath the surface. But who will be able to take the responsibility of such an experiment, or who would

dare? It seems that earthquakes will remain a major problem for a long time to come.

On the positive side, some imaginative scientists view subduction zones as a possible means of disposing of our dangerous waste materials. The reasoning behind this idea is that holes could be drilled into those portions of the crustal plates which are in the process of descending beneath the overiding crust (Figure 16–13). However, before this can be put into practice we must be certain that the sedimentary layer containing radioactive and toxic

Energy and the Earth's Crust: The Lithologic Cycle

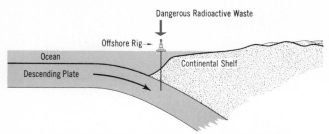

Figure 16-13 Proposal for long-term disposal of radioactive wastes The proposal to dispose of dangerous radioactive wastes takes advantage of the subduction zone in the plate tectonics process. Wastes could be implanted in deep wells penetrating the zones. Thereafter, plate movement would carry the materials deep into the earth's crust. They would remain there for millions of years before being cycled back to the surface.

wastes would not simply be scraped off and returned in a relatively short time to the surface. Much more research is needed before this disposal plan could become a reality, although it has fascinating possibilities as the solution to this very urgent problem.

The orders of relief

A complete discussion of man's occupance of the earth's crust could fill a volume by itself. Instead of continuing, let us end this chapter from a slightly different point of view. We have already referred to the difference between relief and elevation. Relief can be though of as the steepness of the slope separating the highest and lowest portions of the earth's surface

Figure 16-14 Reduced arc segment of the earth.

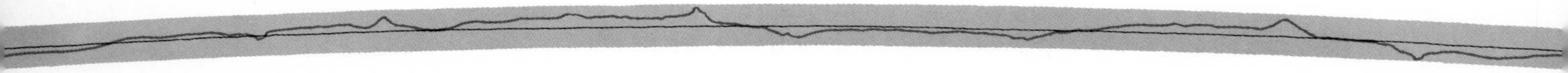

at any given scale. For convenience, we distinguish three major orders of relief. The first is at a global scale and considers only the relative elevations of the ocean basins and the continental blocks. The second order of relief views the surface of the continental blocks in particular—although we could also include the floors of ocean basins as individual entities for this purpose. When a single continent is our frame of reference, the second-order variations in the relief of its surface that would be most prominent are mountains, plateaus, and plains. At an even larger scale, a mountain, or a plateau, or a plain will have a multitude of smaller features upon its surface. These valleys, hills, swales, closed depressions, and numerous other minor topographic elements make up the third order of relief.

The highest point on earth is Mount Everest, 29,028 feet above sea level. The lowest point is the bottom of the Mariana Trench just east of Guam in the Pacific Ocean, 36,198 feet beneath the surface. The distance between these highest and lowest points is just about 65,000 feet, or 12 miles. Figure 16–14, below, shows a small arc segment of a circle 10.7 feet in diameter. If the earth were reduced in size to a sphere just that large, the 12 miles of first-order relief described above would be contained in the 2/10-inch-thick band we show. Embedded in this band is a thin line only 1/60 of an inch in width. This thin thread represents the 5,280 feet which would contain that portion of the earth, between sea level and one mile high, where most of the world's population is found. Such are the dimensions of our abode.

17 | EARTH AS THE ECOLOGIC NICHE FOR LIFE: CLIMATE AND EVAPOTRANSPIRATION

Life exists in a thin film on the surface of the earth, spread like an oil slick on water. And like an oil slick reflecting sunlight, it is colorful, complex, and always changing. We are part of that film and depend upon it for our existence. Life-forms constantly influence one another by changing each other's environments, sometimes benefiting, sometimes destroying, a particular species. In recent centuries man has become the dominant ecologic element in the total life environment. Many of the changes we are causing have ominous consequences for our own survival. We are well advised to appreciate and protect other life-forms such as vegetation and the organisms which live in the soil. To do this we must first understand the processes of which they are parts.

The possibilities for life vary greatly over the surface of the earth. Life-forms are configurations of giant molecules that use energy to maintain internal organization and local environmental conditions, to pass material through their systems, and most remarkably, to create organic structures which are capable of reproduction. This process requires a physical and chemical environment which cannot vary beyond certain limited ranges. The planet earth seems to be a rather special place where such environmental ranges can occur.

If we seek beyond our own world for other life-forms, we may find it lonely in our corner of the galaxy. Conditions suitable for sustaining life as we know it are seldom found on the planets. It is most unlikely that we have living neighbors in the solar system. Mercury shows one burning face always to the sun; the other is forever frigid and dark. Venus is too dry and too hot and is choked in carbon dioxide. Mars may have simple forms of life, but its atmosphere is unsuitable for humans and its temperatures are too low for comfort. The outer planets—Jupiter, Saturn, Uranus, and Neptune—are relative giants with dense, freezing atmospheres of hydrogen and helium. Pluto is so far from the sun that it remains frozen and dim. It is most unlikely that there are any planets suitable for humans circling nearby stars. Since we are far removed from inventing and perfecting an interstellar spaceship drive, we had better learn to live with and within the thin skin of habitable earth environments we have inherited.

Earth Climates as Earth Environments

Energy—predominantly solar energy—acts upon the atmosphere, hydrosphere, and lithosphere of the earth. Materials at and near the surface are constantly reworked and rearranged into forms and distributions which, in various combinations, provide homes for many types of life. We have already discussed the distribution in space and time of insolation upon the surface of the earth. We have also given some indication of the movement of air, water, and crustal materials from place to place, and of the consequent redistribution of available energy and moisture.

A broad view is necessary in order to understand the environments created on the earth's surface by the above processes. In the words of Barry Commoner, ''Everything depends on everything else.'' This attitude forms the basis for the geographic concept of *environmental unity*, and provides a suitable mode for summing up much of the subject matter presented in the preceding chapters. Such a summary can for convenience be phrased in the familiar terms of climatic distributions. Climate is an in-place characterization of the combined effects of energy and moisture availability. Weather can be considered a moving phenomenon. A squall line marches across the landscape; great pinwheels of high- and low-pressure cells spin majestically from coast to coast. Conversely, we always think of climate's being associated with a particular spot. Thus, the combined effect of many different kinds of weather makes up the climate of a given area.

Plants as indicators of climatic characteristics

Climate is an abstraction. Conditions of moisture, temperature, wind, and many other variables change from moment to moment at any given point. If we attempt to summarize the elements of climate at some geographic location, we will be faced with two problems. We must choose a time span of suitable duration and we must specify the limits of the area. In essence, the dividing of the world into climatic zones is an exercise in region building. To make such regions, we must generalize the data available to us. While this can be done in a

Figure 17-1 World climates

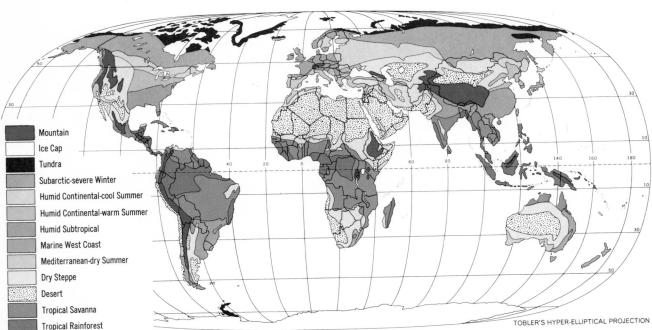

Mountain
Ice Cap
Tundra
Subarctic-severe Winter
Humid Continental-cool Summer
Humid Continental-warm Summer
Humid Subtropical
Marine West Coast
Mediterranean-dry Summer
Dry Steppe
Desert
Tropical Savanna
Tropical Rainforest

TOBLER'S HYPER-ELLIPTICAL PROJECTION

318

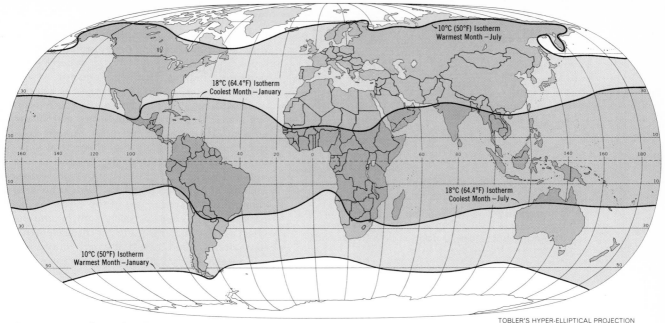

Figure 17-2 10° C (50° F) isotherms of warmest month—18° C (64.4° F) isotherms of coolest month An isotherm is a line of equal temperature. The 10°C isotherms for the warmest month (July in the Northern Hemisphere) mark the most poleward extension of trees—the arctic tree line. The 18°C isotherms for the coolest month define a band around the equator where true palm trees are able to survive.

variety of ways, one of the quickest is to let nature help out. Vegetation of all kinds is a sensitive indicator of the natural conditions generalized as climate. Every plant has a particular set of physical needs for energy and moisture, and such needs must be met throughout the entire year in a fixed sequence of events. Thus, the timing of climatic events is as important to a plant as are absolute annual accumulations of water and solar energy. If vegetation is allowed to develop relatively undisturbed by human activities and for a long enough period of time, the geographic distribution of plants will reflect in large part the geographic distribution of climatic types. There are many exceptions to this rule, particularly where man is concerned, and it must be used with caution. Nevertheless, most climatic distribution maps such as that shown

in Figure 17–1 are in the final analysis based on the distribution of vegetative types.

Two examples should illustrate this point. The location of an isoline marking the distribution of points having an average July temperature of 50°F, or 10°C, (Figure 17–2) roughly corresponds to the poleward limit of normal tree growth. Thus, the July 50°F isotherm in the Northern Hemisphere is sometimes called the *arctic tree line* and marks the transition between the summerless climates of the high latitudes and the mid-latitude climates where summer alternates with winter. Conversely, true palms survive only equatorward of the isoline marking approximately 18°C (64.4°F) during the coolest month of the year (Figure 17–2). In each of these cases, special microenvironments may encourage the growth of these plants beyond their stated geographic limits,

Earth as the Ecologic Niche for Life: Climate and Evapotranspiration

319

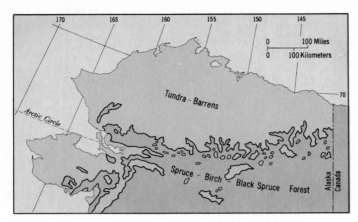

Figure 17-3 Arctic tree line The arctic tree line viewed at a neighborhood scale reveals interfingering and isolated patches of both tundra and trees.

If the world were a completely homogeneous sphere without land and water or variations in topography, there would be an orderly temperature gradient from the equator to the poles. Climates would be arranged as a series of latitudinal bands girdling the earth with symmetrical occurrences on either side of the equator. However, many other climatic controls serve to scramble this theoretical symmetry. The list of controls that follows should not be considered complete, although it does include the major elements which help to shape the climate regions of the earth. We, in passing, will mention each control and its effect on climate. Since some of these elements have already been treated at length, only a few will receive special attention at this time.

Latitude-temperature

Pressure belts and winds

Land-water relationships

Ocean currents

Cyclonic systems (pressure cells)

Mountain barriers and highlands

Latitude-temperature We have already mentioned the temperature gradient from the equator to the poles. It is interesting to note that just as ancient Greek geographers spoke of the "torrid, temperate, and frigid" zones, it is convenient to broadly specify three climatic types: (1) the equatorial-tropical group, which has no true winters; (2) the middle-latitude group, where winter alternates with summer; and (3) the arctic-polar group, which has no true summers. We can use this observation to summarize many of the others we already have made on temperature distributions. The three temperature zones are shown in Figure 17-2.

Pressure belts and winds So much has already been said on these twin subjects that we summarize them in the briefest possible manner. While recognizing that the latitudinal

but such occurrences are relatively rare. In the case of climatic maps, as in the case of city maps, our perception of the edge of a particular region depends upon the scale and detail with which the maps are drawn. It also is important to remember that the neat lines on maps showing the break between climatic regions are in reality zones of transition between sets of conditions which themselves may contain considerable variance. For example, the arctic tree line viewed at a larger scale (Figure 17-3) actually interfingers with the tundra to its north. Finally, the oceans have climates just as much as does the land, although many climatic maps neatly terminate the conditions they depict at the water's edge.

Nevertheless, the relationship between vegetation and climate is such that we need to discuss it at some length. The response time of plants to climatic conditions provides us with a convenient time scale for looking at environmental events since humans also operate in nature within approximately the same temporal dimensions. However, before going on to the vegetative and soil systems which support mankind, let us attempt a quick synthesis of the variables which account for the world distribution of climatic types.

distribution of high and low pressure rarely takes the form of neat "belts," it is still possible to identify bandlike pressure regions alternating from the equator to the poles. The equatorial low-pressure area is associated with convectional rainfall; subtropical high-pressure areas are typified by general aridity; the subpolar low-pressure belts are less well defined but correspond with relatively greater precipitation; finally, the poles are noted for their piled-up masses of frigid, dry air and scant precipitation. Only the lack of solar energy, and consequent low polar and subpolar temperatures, allows the accumulation of surface water in large quantities at high latitudes.

Land-water relationships Climates can also be divided into two classes based on their association with bodies of either land or water. *Marine climates* are relatively mild with warm but not hot summers and cool but not cold winters. This is the result of the insulating effect of water as compared with land. These climates are also noted for winter precipitation maxima associated with storms originating at sea. *Continental climates,* on the other hand, tend to be much more extreme, with hot summers and cold winters. Again, the poor insulating quality of the land accounts for this. For the same reason, isotherms bend equatorward over the centers of continents in the wintertime and poleward in the summer. The annual range between highest and lowest temperatures is far greater for continental climates than for marine ones. Precipitation is usually greatest in the summertime and derives from convectional showers over the heated land. Also, in the interiors of the continents, far from the oceanic sources of atmospheric moisture, aridity can be a problem. At the same time, high summer temperatures over the land can produce low-pressure areas which, in turn, allow the onshore movement of marine tropical air masses. The mechanism for such transfers is incompletely understood, but the famous Indian monsoon winds with their accompanying rains and the autumn hurricane season along the southeastern coast of the United States are undoubtedly associated with this. The result is that the southeastern shores of the continents in the Northern Hemisphere are often better watered than might be expected.

Ocean currents We have already described the movement of warm and cold currents along the continental shores. Such currents tend to bend isotherms poleward along the west coasts of the continents, while shores at comparable latitudes on the eastern coasts are comparably much colder. This effect is shown in Figure 14–8. Since cold currents cool the air above them just as warm currents somewhat heat the atmosphere, there is a distinct correlation between cold currents and dry coasts and warm currents and moister shores. Warm, moist air moving inland is lifted and cooled, thus often giving up precipitation. Cold, dry air moving onto the shore is warmed and takes up additional moisture. The former condition contributes to the humid character of eastern coasts, while coastal deserts such as the Namib in South-West Africa and the Atacama in Peru owe their existence to the presence of the cold Benguela and Humboldt Currents, respectively.

Cyclonic systems (pressure cells) Alternating masses of dense, cold air and lighter, warmer air move eastward around the globe in a stately procession at mid-latitudes. Originating over the major bodies of land and water, these pressure systems are most evident in the Northern Hemisphere in the winter months when their tracks swing southward. The contact between warm and cold air results in the frontal precipitation relied on by so many of the world's people.

Mountains barriers and highlands Topographic barriers are important elements in the production of orographic rainfall like that of the northwest Pacific Coast and the Khasi Hills of India. Mountains also serve as major barriers limiting certain kinds of weather and climate. We have already mentioned the north-south orientation of climatic regions in the western United States as op-

Fog over San Francisco Bay The low mountains and hills on the ocean side of San Francisco Bay are sufficient to hold back the ocean fog, which dissipates as it descends on their landward flanks. The fog is able to enter San Francisco Bay through the gap of the Golden Gate, and it is along this route that the fog for which the city is famous travels into the city. The landward suburbs are usually clear. Courtesy of A. Miller, Meteorology, California State University, San Jose.

posed to the east-west trend of similar climates in Europe. Both owe their alignment to major mountain chains. There are other cases where a mountain barrier has profound effects. The Tsing Ling Mountains of central China effectively halt the northwestward movement of the monsoonlike winds that blow onto the China coast from the South China Sea. The southern Andes deflect the eastward movement of cyclonic storms and create the Patagonia Desert in Argentina. Even small barriers like the hills of San Francisco, California, can hold back masses of air (above photo). Sausalito, on the eastern side of the Marin County Peninsula, will oftentimes be sunny and in the clear while the oceanside is shrouded in fog. The same thing is true to the south, where Palo Alto frequently has open skies while fog fingers poke unsuccessfully through the Santa Cruz Mountains to the west.

Where plateaus and major uplands stretch for miles, the effect is the creation of new climatic regions. The wet-and-dry, semiarid uplands of East Africa are a case in point. The highlands of Kenya counteract that nation's equatorial location insofar as a wet-and-dry, semiarid climate prevails there instead of the year-round convectional rainfall normally expected at the equator. The Tibetan Plateau and the Altiplano of Bolivia also represent large upland areas with colder, drier climates than their latitudinal locations alone would dictate.

World Climate Regions

A number of scientists have attempted to devise logical regional classifications of world climates. The most famous is that of the Austrian Wladimir Köppen, whose work illustrates the idea that the distribution of vegetation is a clue to the distribution of climate types. A somewhat more recent classification by C. W. Thornthwaite, an American, also concerns itself with the relationship of vegetation to moisture and solar energy but takes these three elements into consideration in a more systematic manner.

Köppen's method of classification is operational at three scales: global, continental, and subcontinental. At each scale letters of the alphabet are assigned to indicate different climatic elements. At the global scale he distinguished five major climatic types which can be areally designated. These are the (A) tropical rainy, (B) arid, (C) mid-latitude humid cool winter, (D) mid-latitude humid cold winter, and (E) polar climates. The polar climates are separated from the mid-latitude climates thermally at the 10°C (50°F) isotherm which we have already noted approximately parallels the arctic tree line. Tropical climates fall between the 18°C (64.4°F) isotherms north and south of the equator. The two mid-latitude climates are further subdivided thermally and spatially by the −3°C (26.6°F) isotherm, while a somewhat more complicated formula plotting the excess of evaporation over precipitation defines the boundary between wet and dry regions.

At a slightly larger scale Köppen distinguished three types of tropical climates: rainy, wet-and-dry, and monsoon. Arid climates were subdivided into steppe and desert. Mid-latitude climates fall into five categories (shown in Table 17–1), and polar climates become tundra and ice cap. The effect of this further subdivision is the creation of twelve types of climate regions in place of the original five. He continued his exercise in regionalization by adding eight possible sub-subdivisions to the tropical climates; six sub-subdivisions to the arid climates; thirteen to the mid-latitude humid climates; but no finer subdivisions to the polar category. The end result is a system of spatial classification with at least twenty-seven possible subdivisions. This proved so complicated that the geographer Glenn T. Trewartha simplified the scheme and used only seventeen categories. The system of climatic classification proposed in 1931 by Thornthwaite calculated the ratio

Table 17–1   Köppen's System of Climate Classification

A	Tropical rainy climates
	Af rainy
	Aw wet and dry
	Am monsoon
	+8 sub-subdivisions
B	Arid climates
	BS steppe
	BW desert
	+6 sub-subdivisions
C	Mid-latitude humid cool winter climates
	Cf Temperate, moist year round
	Cs Temperate, dry summer
	Cw Temperate, dry winter
D	Mid-latitude humid cold winter climates
	Df Cold, moist year round
	Dw Cold, dry winter
	+13 sub-subdivisions for C and D combined
E	Polar climates
	ET Tundra
	EF ice cap
	no sub-subdivisions

Note: The upper- and lower-case letters preceeding the climatic descriptions were used by Köppen, Geiger, and others as a shorthand or code for convenience. As such, they do not concern us here. Any standard work on climatology discusses the code in detail.

of precipitation to evaporation and another index showing the relationship of temperature and evaporation. The combination of these elements resulted in at least thirty-two types of climate regions.

We have already mentioned some of the major weaknesses of schemes such as these. Boundaries are shown as clean lines of demarcation rather than as more realistic transition zones. Moreover, vegetation distributions and climatic conditions do not clearly parallel each other everywhere on earth. It is also important to note that when seventeen or twenty-seven or thirty-two regional types are applied across the heterogeneous earth with

*Earth
as the Ecologic
Niche for Life:
Climate and
Evapotranspiration*

subsequent repetition of the same type in several spots, the maps that result can be difficult to interpret. In this sense, the above methods of describing and locating climate regions of the world become ends in themselves. That is, the resulting maps become the reasons for the effort it takes to produce them.

If our intentions are more practical and are oriented toward the definition and subsequent solution of geographic problems, we must ask ourselves the reasons why we want to define and locate types of climates. Our questions are threefold: What kind of environments have resulted from interactions between the energy and moisture systems we have already described? What kind of human interactions take place with different types of environments? And what are the spatial relationships between different subsets of the total human-environment system? Therefore, our knowledge of climate should give us some method of understanding the dynamic elements underlying a given distribution of climate types, as well as a simple way of classifying energy-moisture environmental relationships. Having these in hand when we turn to the real world, either Köppen's or Thornthwaite's maps of climate distributions will serve our purposes, while the number of climate subtypes we use should reflect our own judgment of the number we need.

Climatic controls—a simple synthesis

The list of climatic controls briefly reviewed in the last few pages offers us a quick and relatively simple method of understanding climatic distributions. If we create a hypothetical continent like the shield-shaped one shown in Figure 17-4, we can endow that continent with a few basic characteristics drawn from our list. The shield shape roughly approximates the shape of at least three world land masses. At the same time, we can move our continent of Hypothetica to any latitudinal position we wish.

We have chosen in Figure 17-4 to place Hypothetica at the same latitude as North America. We thus expose it to various condi-

tions of aridity and moisture based on the world pressure belts shown in Figure 17-4A. Next we add a slightly drier interior portion of the country as well as a better-watered southeast coast (17-4B), in recognition of warm offshore currents and the monsoon effect. The result is a continent having the basic moisture regions shown in Figure 17-4C. We next impose temperature zones on this configuration. Such zones are the simple three-way division discussed earlier. The only embellishment to this triple scheme is a slight north-south skewing of the bands as the result of ocean currents (Figure 17-4D). The result shown in Figure 17-4E comes close to the actual pattern of climates in North America. It would be even more similar if we were to add a major topographic barrier along the west coast. However, we leave this to your imagination.

Beginning in the extreme south near the equator, let us quickly comment on the eight climate regions we have specified. A small bit of the rainy tropics comes first. This would correspond to portions of Central America. Directly to the north is an area where a wet season alternates with a dry one. This area is still within range of the vertical rays of the sun during the June solstice and receives convectional rainfall for part of the year. When the sun's vertical ray is in the Southern Hemisphere, this same area experiences a winter dry season. As we move farther north up the west coast, we encounter increasing aridity reflecting the subtropical high-pressure belt as well as more localized aridity resulting from cold offshore currents. Gradually semiarid conditions give way to a true desert regime. This region of little water is extended inland and to the north by the effects of the dry continental interior far from sources of moisture. North of the west coast deserts the Mediterranean and marine west coast climates show seasonal variations paralleling in time the movement of the vertical ray of the sun farther to the south. The Mediterranean climate region receives winter rainfall as the westerly storm tracks shift southward in the winter. But the summer is long and dry as the wet winds and cyclonic systems shift northward. The marine west coast type of climate is much the same but being farther north receives more rain in winter from westerly storms as well as some precipitation. Energy demands on moisture in the marine west coast climate region are considerably less because of the lower angle of the sun's rays.

Along the east coast the monsoon effect in large part offsets the aridity of the subtropical high, although not completely. At the same time, the warm, moist offshore air masses make this southeastern coast mild and moist. These are the humid continental climates of the eastern parts of the continents. Finally, all across the north, increasing aridity related to the polar high-pressure area is matched by increasing cold. What moisture is available seldom escapes from its frozen state on the surface. These arctic-polar climates are rela-

Figure 17-4 Hypothetical continent The effects of the energy and moisture conditions create climatic regions postulated for a hypothetical continent. *A.* Pressure—precipitation. *B.* Moisture conditions: continentality and east coast monsoon. *C.* Moisture regions. *D.* Temperature zones. *E.* Climatic regions.

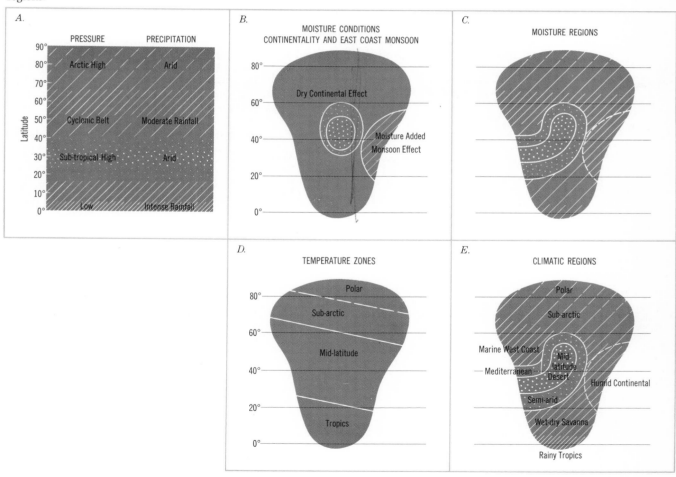

tively undifferentiated across the roof of the world. In all cases, we have created a reasonably accurate pattern with references to only a few variables. Our continent of Hypothetica cannot match the complexities of a real continent, but with a little thought you should be able to derive most of the major climatic regions of the world by moving Hypothetica into new positions and considering the same variables that we have. A final word of advice might be to pay somewhat greater attention to the effect of mountain barriers and highland areas when looking at South America, Europe, and Asia.

Energy-moisture environments—a simple classification

We do not need an elaborate classification of energy-moisture relationships in order to dis-

cuss man-environment systems at a general level. A very simple 3 × 3 matrix with very few modifications provides us with a simple classification which matches equator-to-pole energy-moisture environments with reasonable accuracy. Figure 17–5 has three rows or divisions along the ordinate corresponding to equatorial-tropical, mid-latitude, and arctic-polar climates. The three columns represent arid, semiarid, and humid moisture conditions. The nine cells formed by the intersecting rows and columns need only slight changes to match the climates described for the continent of Hypothetica. In this preliminary diagram the box representing arctic-polar humid conditions has been crossed out because nowhere in high latitudes does the polar high-pressure cell permit heavy precipitation. Other changes relate to the availability of energy and moisture as expressed by the vegetation which flourishes under various conditions. In order to modify the matrix, let us consider how vegetation relates to energy and moisture.

Evapotranspiration and the Water Balance

As the energy available in the atmosphere increases, plants maintain proper body temperatures by increased transpiration from their stomata. Evaporation from leaf surfaces also helps to cool plant tissue. *Evapotranspiration* indicates the combined water needs of vegetation. *Potential evapotranspiration* is the water that would be used if unlimited amounts were available, while *actual evapotranspiration* is the amount of water actually passed through the earth-plant-atmosphere system. The negative difference between these two amounts is a measure of the resulting water shortage or deficit. C. W. Thornthwaite has devised a technique for computing the balance between water need and water availability. Examples of this method are presented in the diagrams in Figure 17–7.

The Mediterranean climate offers a good example of the march of the seasons in terms of water and energy availability. Figure 17–6 shows the water balance for Antalya, Turkey, a small town on the south coast. Typical of

Figure 17-5 Matrix of climates A classification of climates by combinations of energy and moisture conditions creates a matrix which may be used to describe world climates.

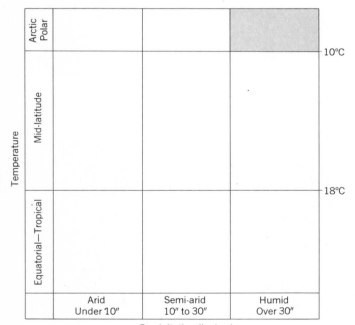

Mediterranean regimes, rainfall occurs almost entirely in the winter or low-sun months. This is indicated by line *p—p,* while line *o—o* shows the increasing energy, that is, the potential for evapotranspiration, within the environment as the summer advances. In the winter months, available water exceeds the water needed to meet the combined demands of plant transpiration and evaporation. By April, rainfall has dropped off to practically nothing, while the sun at noon rides higher and higher each day in the southern sky. Potential evapotranspiration increases steadily, and at first, the negative difference between potential and actual evapotranspiration, the water deficit, is replaced by groundwater drawn from the soil reservoir by the roots of the plants. However, as the summer progresses, the ground gives up at a slower and slower rate what little water it still holds. The water shortage increases, and by summer's end and the coming of the first fall rains a significant deficit exists. If this deficit cannot be satisfied, growing plants will experience severe drought. By September increasing rainfall has filled the lesser demands placed upon the system by the sun as it retreats into the Southern Hemisphere. November and December rains actually exceed potential evapotranspiration, and in those months excess water refills the dry soil reservoir. The soil becomes full as the new year approaches, and additional rains in January, February, and March form runoff on the land surface. Thereafter, as spring turns into summer, potential evapotranspiration once more increases; the rains diminish; and the cycle repeats itself.

The amount of water available to plants depends not only upon precipitation, but also upon the water storage capacity of the soil involved and the depth to which plant roots can reach. The water deficit is shown in Figure 17–6 by the solid red pattern between the lines indicating potential and actual evapotranspiration. As we have mentioned earlier, loamy soils combine storage capacity with permeability, which makes an ideal combination not only for storing water but also for retrieving it with minimum difficulty. Thus,

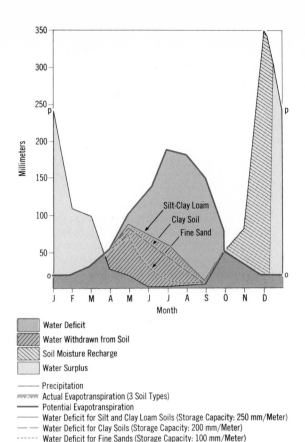

Legend:
- Water Deficit
- Water Withdrawn from Soil
- Soil Moisture Recharge
- Water Surplus
- —— Precipitation
- ≡≡≡ Actual Evapotranspiration (3 Soil Types)
- —— Potential Evapotranspiration
- —— Water Deficit for Silt and Clay Loam Soils (Storage Capacity: 250 mm/Meter)
- – – Water Deficit for Clay Soils (Storage Capacity: 200 mm/Meter)
- ----- Water Deficit for Fine Sands (Storage Capacity: 100 mm/Meter)

Figure 17-6 Water balance diagram of Antalya, Turkey The diagram is a monthly summary of the energy and moisture conditions affecting vegetation growth. The potential evapotranspiration is the amount of water, measured in inches, which would be drawn into the atmosphere if an unlimited supply of ground moisture were present. The actual evapotranspiration is the transfer of available water to the atmosphere. If potential exceeds actual, a water deficit condition exists. This depends, in turn, upon the amount of incoming precipitation and the water storage capacity of the soil.

loamy soils give up water to plants during a drought better than would either clays or sands. Clays might contain a large amount of moisture but would lack permeability, while sands are too permeable and lose their contents either to evaporation or to underground

Earth as the Ecologic Niche for Life: Climate and Evapotranspiration

runoff. The increasing water deficit resulting from different types of soils is shown in the diagram by each added increment of sipling. It should also be noted that this diagram shows conditions relating to deep-rooted crops such as alfalfa, pasture grasses, and grapevines. Crops with more shallow root systems (beets, carrots, peas, etc.) or moderately deep roots (corn and cotton) would have less groundwater available to them and would wilt sooner. Orchards and mature forest with longer roots could survive the onslaught of drought somewhat longer.

Other climate regimes are shown in Figure 17–7A through J. In 17–7E an east coast situation with year-round humid climate has a relatively insignificant water deficit during the peak period of potential evapotranspiration. This situation at Seabrook, New Jersey, is interesting, for even with these humid conditions, carefully controlled irrigation applied with the use of water balance analysis yields surprising increases in crop yields. Soil type also makes a difference. Just a few miles south of Seabrook in the Pine Barrens of New Jersey, loosely packed, sandy soils a low rapid escape of precipitation. The result is a region of dry soils and large water deficits suitable only for drought-resistant pines.

The next water balance (Figure 17–7D) is from Manhattan, in the Flint Hills of eastern Kansas. There, native grasses can reach a height of 6 feet but few trees grow. In that area the winter and spring surplus of water is just about equal to the summer deficit. The annual net water balance, therefore, equals zero. Thornthwaite has observed that grasses such as these often make up the native vegetation in regions where the net water balance shows neither a large surplus nor a deficit. In this particular case, the potential evapotranspiration peaks almost at the same time as does precipitation, although a significant water deficit does occur in late summer.

The ranchers of the Flint Hills recognize a relationship between the growth cycle of the native grasses and their own activities as cattlemen. Native grasses provide the most nutritious forage during the months of April, May, and June. July marks the beginning of the summer drought, and the grasses no longer use quantities of plant nutrients for stem and leaf formation. Instead, nutrients are translocated into the root systems of the plants and stored in order to provide energy for the next year's growing season. Another portion of the nutrients is utilized for seed formation. The result of this natural adjustment to the onslaught of drought is that after the first week of July the grass has roughly "the same nutritional value as baling wire."

The stockmen recognize this and also know that their cattle gain at least 80 percent of their summer weight before the July water deficit begins. Supplemental feeding is expensive; and a good hay crop cannot be cut from the pastures, because the split-second timing necessary to catch the grass at its maximum growth but before it loses its nutrients is next to impossible. As a result, few local ranchers attempt year-round operations, and instead, most buy feeder cattle in the spring, fatten them on the early grass, and sell them as late summer comes on. All of this illustrates an important aspect of energy-moisture relationships. Timing is extremely important. The annual rainfall in the Flint Hills of eastern Kansas is between 31 and 38 inches, which places the region well within the humid set of climates. The late summer drought, however, influences the natural vegetation, the cattle that eat it, and the humans who utilize the cattle. Thus, time and space, energy and moisture, man and nature are all important in defining the environments upon which we depend.

Climate as Evapotranspiration Types

The example of the Flint Hills can be expanded to other environments, other climates. Our view is that climate, vegetation, and soils are completely interconnected. More important, we consider their definition and their potential use as resources to be defined by human perception and human activities. We have already described three different water balances; we now offer seven more. The ten diagrams

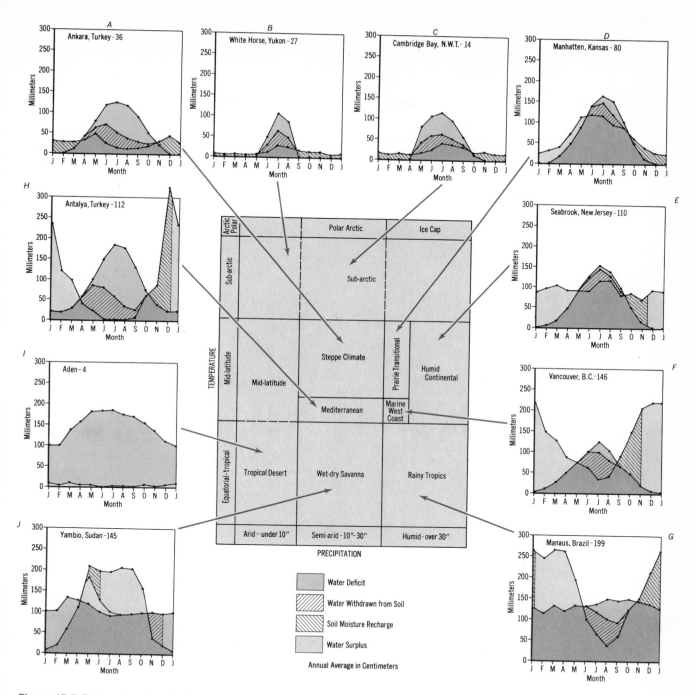

Figure 17-7 Revised matrix of climates with sample water balance diagrams

shown in Figure 17–7 form a simple and useful introduction to world climates with the exception of the polar ice caps. Using these, we will discuss some climatic sequences in terms of the vegetation, soil, and human systems that help define them.

The table in Figure 17–7 is a revision of the simple 3×3 matrix of energy and moisture in Figure 17–5 and reflects the ten water balances shown. Remember, this is not a map, although some of the suggested climatic juxtapositions can and do occur in nature. Mid-latitude and tropical deserts are treated together. There are differences between the two, but the overriding consideration is the continuous water deficit. This is shown by the extreme case of Aden on the southwest corner of the Arabian peninsula. Next, a distinction must be made between two types of tropical and mid-latitude semiarid climates, those which have a distinct dry season followed by a distinct rainy season and those which have some but not much precipitation throughout the year. The former, savanna-type climates, are most often associated with periods of high and low sun; the latter are often on the margins of true deserts or behind mountain barriers which block rain-bearing winds and are associated with steppe regions. The Mediterranean climate is also a wet-and-dry climate and is distinguished in the diagram from the semi-arid steppe climates of the middle latitudes. The humid continental climates can be divided into cool and cold winter types, but we con-

sider this unnecessary for our purposes. However, it is useful to distinguish the climate of both the long-grass prairies and the marine west coast type. The former receives more than 30 inches of rain but shows distinct semiarid characteristics, while the latter has seasonal periodicity resembling wet-and-dry climates but nevertheless has an annual total precipitation far in excess of 30 inches. We next recognize a poleward portion of the mid-latitudes which because of lower temperatures can retain precipitation, however scant, long enough for tree growth to occur. This is the subarctic climate that overrides all three moisture types. Finally, the arctic-polar climates form another group, again cutting across the three categories of moisture. Within this latter set it is possible to distinguish *arctic climates* where some vegetation can grow and *ice cap climates* which are sterile and locked in ice and cold. Each water balance chart gives a reasonable description of the moisture-energy relationships prevailing under the condition it represents. Plant life has made adjustments to each of these environments. In fact, we often name the climate type after the vegetation that grows in association with it, for example, the savanna climates. Having set the scene, in the next chapter we will consider how vegetation and soils relate, on the one hand, to the climatic environments they occupy, and on the other, to the human resource–utilizing systems which in large part define them.

18 | EARTH AS THE ECOLOGIC NICHE FOR LIFE: VEGTATATION AND SOILS

Life is an edge dweller. It takes sustenance from air, water, and land. However, the bulk of material found in organisms is composed of elements which in their pure form at earth temperatures are gases. We consist, for example, largely of hydrogen, carbon, oxygen, and nitrogen. Of these, even carbon assumes a gaseous form as carbon dioxide (CO_2). More than 99.5 percent of the biomass of the earth—that is, the entire mass of all living earth organisms, ourselves included—is by weight composed of these materials.

Although life-forms are made up of materials which occur in the atmosphere in large quantities, water is the medium through which they enter the stream of life as chemical compounds dissolved in water. Land—that is, the solid material of the earth's crust—also provides many metals and other elements critical to life.

In this chapter we will examine the manner in which air, water, and land interact to provide a suitable environment for all kinds of life. Of all life forms, consider vegetation first, for plants are the basic converters of air, water, and land into compounds upon which animal life depends. In this chapter we begin by discussing molecular processes at scales smaller than the individual. The reasons for this choice of scale should become apparent from the discussion that follows.

Nutrients, Plant Life, and Earth Systems

The fact that plants can use elements only in the form of water-soluble compounds is sometimes a problem. In regions of heavy rainfall, plant nutrients—that is, the chemical compounds just mentioned—may be leached out of the soil and washed away. In other words, they are dissolved by water percolating down through the soil and carried off by groundwater. In addition chemical barriers in water sometimes prevent plants from receiving nutrients. By this we mean that the soil moisture available to plants may have an excess of hydrogen ions (H^+) and be too acidic, or a shortage of hydrogen and an excess of hydroxyl ions ($-OH$) and be too basic. The amount of hydrogen ions in solution is expressed by a numerical index. This number, termed the pH, is the reciprocal of the logarithm of the degree of dilution of the hydrogen ions and ranges from 0 to 14. The water content of a soil may give a reading from pH 3 (very acid) to pH 10 (very basic or alkaline). Most plant growth requires a soil pH that does not vary from the neutral value pH 7 by more than 2 points either way. Marine organisms live only in a more restricted pH range from about pH 7.5 to pH 9. The problem is that the water solubility of chemical compounds changes with the pH. Plant nutrients can either precipitate out of solution or be blocked from access to the plant's system if the pH of the soil shifts outside the tolerable range. Also, certain parts of the plant organism may actually dissolve if the safe pH range is exceeded.

In every case, certain key processes associated with vegetative growth make inert elements available to all forms of life. *Photosynthesis* is one of the most important of these. The photosynthetic process is one in which green plants possessing chlorophyll convert solar energy into chemical energy which is stored in the form of glucose. Carbon dioxide, water, and energy are thus converted into sugar, with oxygen molecules as a by-product. Glucose is a basic building block from which most of the other compounds needed by living organisms are made. Plant sugars are also the "fuel" by means of which animals, most of which cannot manufacture the basic organic compounds upon which they depend, maintain their cellular activities.

Another key process is *nitrogen fixation*, in which nitrogen gas (N_2) is combined with hydrogen to form amino ions ($+NH_2$), which are the raw materials for amino acids. Amino acids are used in the synthesis of proteins and enzymes which make up the incredibly complex structures and control mechanisms of life-forms. Despite its importance, free nitrogen gas, which makes up 79 percent of the atmosphere, is unavailable for the great majority of life-forms, which cannot use it directly. It must first be "fixed" by a few organisms capable of combining it in compounds which can be incorporated into other life-forms. Most nitrogen is fixed by microorganisms which inhabit the soil in association with certain plants such as legumes. Among other nitrogen fixers are the blue-green algae, of particular interest because they are also photosynthesizers.

Man has learned to produce fixed nitrogen industrially. Fritz Haber and Karl Bosch developed a process in Germany in 1914 primarily to meet the demand for nitrates for explosives in World War I. These processes are in sharp contrast to those in nature. The nitrogen fixed by man requires temperatures of 500°C and several hundred atmospheric pressures. Bacteria accomplish the same thing with the help of special enzymes. Their process requires normal temperatures and one atmosphere of pressure. The human process uses nickel as a catalyst to bring about the necessary reactions, while bacteria need trace amounts of cobalt and molybdenum.

The need for heavy metals is an example of the third medium vital to plant growth. For example, legumes such as beans until recently could not be grown in many parts of Australia. After much research it was discovered that as little as 2 ounces of molybdenum per acre counteracted poor soil conditions and stimulated plant growth.

The many elements and minerals required from the land are made available by weathering of rocks from the surface of the continents. The root systems of plants take up elements in ionic form as they come into solution in the soil. Ocean life depends upon the presence of such ions in the discharge from rivers. Since the original occurrence of trace elements in the lithosphere is limited to a very few spatial locations, the redistribution and diffusion of crustal materials by the hydrologic-lithologic cycle are vital geographic aspects of worldwide plant nutrition.

One ominous fact is that while many elements are needed for life processes, certain heavy metals and other substances found in the earth are poisonous to life. Human activity in recent centuries has resulted in an increase in the amount of these substances available to various organisms. Mercury mined from the earth, concentrated, and subsequently dumped as waste in lakes and streams is one example. At the same time, we are adding new and poisonous compounds to those already in nature, particularly in and near cities. Chlorinated hydrocarbons including the DDT family of pesticides are among the most important of these. In this case the diffusion of toxic materials by wind and water works against, rather than for, man's benefit. The dispersion of local concentrations of industrial and urban waste does not mean getting rid of the dangerous substances. They often are reconcentrated in other locations and continue to be hazardous to all kinds

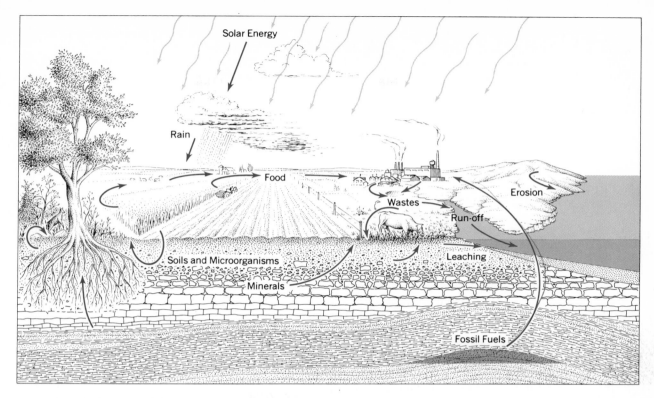

Figure 18-1 Biologic cycles and energy cycles The major inanimate inputs to biotic cycles are solar energy, water, and minerals from the lithosphere. The human food system is part of the biotic system and results in spatial transfers of nutrients, which must be taken into account in order to sustain viable agricultural production.

of life. We will return to these problems in the chapters ahead. At this time we wish only to point out that the systems and processes which produce and sustain life can be contaminated as well as enhanced by human works.

In summary, the interdependence of organisms is a major characteristic of biological systems. Biotic processes are cyclic and tied inextricably to earth processes. Material is captured and processed by plants using energy from the sun. Animals live on plants, and both plants and animals die and return to the soil. Microorganisms in the soil complete the cycle by breaking down dead materials through decay into forms which serve as plant nutrients. The major inanimate inputs are solar en-

ergy, water, and minerals from the lithosphere. Losses from this system (Figure 18–1) occur when materials are transferred out of it either by wind and water or leaching and erosion or when man harvests and exports plants and animals to distant areas. Other losses or negative inputs can occur when materials are changed into unusable or dangerous compounds. In every case equilibrium must be maintained within the system. A lack of critical components or excessive losses at any geographic site will cause the decline of the ecosystem at that location. Conversely, adding missing elements can restore the system and allow increases in the biomass produced at a given site. These ideas give us a key to understand-

Earth
as the Ecologic
Niche for Life:
Vegetation
and Soils

ing why we find certain types of vegetation and soil in certain places, and also suggest strategies which can be employed to improve life environments.

Soil Systems and Classifications

The cloak of soil that rests so lightly on earth's shoulders is a strange garment. We take soil for granted, scarcely recognizing that it is a complex mixture of gases, liquids, weathered rock, humus or dead vegetation, and microorganisms. Soil is formed by the action *in time* of climate and living organisms—both plants and animals—on the rocky surface of the earth. Moreover, soil reflects variations in the relief of the surface upon which it is formed. Vegetation and soils are so interrelated that it is impossible to describe either one as the "egg" and the other as the "chicken" in answer to the question of which develops first. We offer only as a matter of convenience this brief discussion of soils and their classification before talking of soils and vegetation in combination.

The processes which form soils are in large part represented by the vertical movement of liquids and gases through weathered materials. In humid regions, which we somewhat arbitrarily designate as those with more than 30 inches of rainfall annually, a layer of plant debris will cover undisturbed soil. This surface mat of organic material consists of recent leaves and grasses at its top and of *humus*, i.e. decomposed organic matter, lower down which gradually shades into weathered rock and the parent lithosphere as one digs deeper and deeper. Water filters down through these layers. The organic materials form weak solutions of carbonic and other acids which leach out the uppermost layer of weathered, rocky stuff. Still deeper in earth's unconsolidated mantle the dissolved minerals may precipitate out again, and microscopic, colloidal bits of altered clay from the leached stratum also may be deposited. Fully developed soils under these conditions often exhibit distinct strata or horizons from top to bottom, composed of an organic layer, a leached layer (called the *A horizon*), a layer of deposition (called the *B*

horizon), and a layer of relatively unleached and uncontaminated but weathered materials (the *C horizon*).

These acidic and leached soils often have iron (fe) and aluminum (al) removed from the A horizon and reconcentrated in the B horizon and are called *pedalfers* to indicate this. They usually represent open systems in that energy, water, and some earth and organic materials move through them from top to bottom where either colloidal materials or materials in solution can be carried away by groundwater.

In regions with less than 30 inches of rainfall—or more accurately in those places where only the upper layers of the ground become wet and surface water does not seep down until it reaches the water table—a different process takes place. If the land is too dry for much plant growth, the surface organic layer may be sparse. Considerably less leaching takes place in the A horizon. Instead, the vertical movement of water in the soil is often upward and a layer of carbonates may be deposited when soil moisture evaporates near the surface. These precipitates can actually form a hard, sometimes impenetrable, crust anywhere from a few inches to a few feet beneath the surface. This *hardpan* or *caliche* is the extreme result found under these conditions, particularly where mineralized groundwater may continually move to the surface by capillary action in response to high temperatures. Soils of this type are called *pedocals* in reference to the process of calcification which has taken place. Here the system is a closed one, at least for the mineral substances held temporarily in ionic form in the intermittently moist surface layers. Water and energy may move through such systems, but little else escapes.

If we consider the variety of climates on a world scale, as well as variations in vegetation and rock type, it is not surprising that a multitude of soils and soil regions can be distinguished. Defining and classifying soils, therefore, represent the same problems as do defining and classifying climates. We may distinguish very few soils and the areas they occupy, or we may divide and subdivide them into an almost infinite number of types. Typical of soil conditions which could allow impossibly small microregions is the *soil catena*. This term is used to describe the variation in soil types which occurs from the top to the bottom of a hill. The parent rock may be everywhere the same, but differences in soil moisture and the depth of the water table create a variety of moisture conditions which in turn affect soil chemistry and the intensity of microbiotic activity.

This raises the question of choosing a useful soil classification. Two systems are currently used to designate soil categories. The first, and oldest, was first suggested by V. V. Dokuchaiev, a Russian soil scientist, and was subsequently modified for use by the United States Department of Agriculture. This classification recognizes three basic orders of soils: the *zonal*, the *azonal,* and the *intrazonal*. Zonal soils have well-developed profiles and reflect the climatic and vegetative conditions under which they have developed. Soils with poorly developed profiles or with none at all are called *azonal*. Such soils are essentially recently deposited and were borne by wind and water to their resting places. Some specialists do not recognize these as true soils because of their undeveloped layering. Intrazonal soils reflect special local conditions such as excess water (*hydromorphic soils*), excess salt or alkali (*halomorphic soils*), and excess lime (*calcimorphic soils*). A three-level classification based on the three orders is shown in Table 18–1.

The new soil classification subsequently used by the Department of Agriculture is known as the *Seventh Approximation* in reference to the manner in which it was devised. It creates ten soil orders based on the morphology and formative processes of each. In view of our intent to deal with man's use of the environment we will refrain from the lengthy description necessary to make the Seventh Approximation's terminology intelligible to non-soil scientists. There is much to recommend this new classification, but Dokuchaiev's has the advantage of being relatively simple as well as being still widely used. Therefore, we will return to our discussion of zonal soils.

Table 18–1 Zonal, Intrazonal, and Azonal Soils

Order	Suborder	Great Soil Group
Zonal soils	1. Soils of the cold zone 2. Soils of arid regions	Tundra soils Sierozem Brown soils Reddish-brown soils Desert soils Red desert soils
	3. Soils of semiarid, sub-humid, and humid grasslands	Chestnut soils Reddish chestnut soils Chernozem soils Prairie or brunizem soils Reddish prairie soils
	4. Soils of the forest-grassland transition	Degraded chernozem Noncalcic brown
	5. Podzolized soils of the timbered regions	Podzol soils Gray wooded, or gray Podzolic soils Brown podzol soils Gray-brown podzolic soils Sol brun acide Red-yellow podzolic soils
	6. Lateritic soils of forested warm-temperate and tropical regions	Reddish-brown lateritic Soils Yellowish-brown lateritic Soils Laterite soils
Intrazonal soils	1. Halomorphic (saline and alkali) soils of imperfectly drained arid regions and littoral deposits	Solonchak or saline soils Solonetz soils (partly leached solonchak) Soloth soils
	2. Hydromorphic soils of marshes, swamps, seep areas, and flats	Humic gley soils Alpine meadow soils Bog and half-bog soils Low-humic gley soils Planosols Groundwater podzol soils Groundwater laterite soils
	3. Calcimorphic soils	Brown forest soils Rendzina soils
Azonal soils		Lithosols Regosols Alluvial soils

Source: Charles B. Hunt, *Geology of Soils*, W. H. Freeman, San Francisco, copyright © 1972, table 8–1, p. 175.

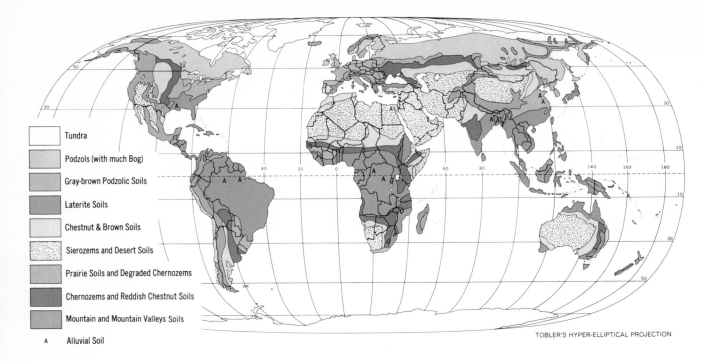

Legend:
- Tundra
- Podzols (with much Bog)
- Gray-brown Podzolic Soils
- Laterite Soils
- Chestnut & Brown Soils
- Sierozems and Desert Soils
- Prairie Soils and Degraded Chernozems
- Chernozems and Reddish Chestnut Soils
- Mountain and Mountain Valleys Soils

A Alluvial Soil

TOBLER'S HYPER-ELLIPTICAL PROJECTION

Figure 18-2 Major soil regions Zonal soils reflect the climates under which they developed. Notice the similarity in patterns on this map and those in Figure 17-1, *"World Climates."* The classification shown here is very broad. Great differences in soils exist within the classes shown, depending upon parent material, time in place, vegetation cover, slope, and other conditions.

Zonal soils are most widespread and dominate any world map of soil distributions such as that in Figure 18-2. At this scale, azonal and intrazonal soils either occur in areas which are too small to be distinguished, or merge with nearby zonal soils, or are included among those soils designated as mountain and mountain valley types. Only nine categories are used, and a few of the semiarid to semihumid soils have been lumped together for convenience. Another way of organizing our perceptions of soil variations is to use a variation of the 3 × 3 matrix introduced earlier in Chapter 17. Figure 18-3 shows the distribution of nine soils in terms of their energy-moisture corollaries. In the next section we will describe the major humid soil sequence from the equa-

tor to the tropics and another one in the midlatitudes from humid to dry conditions. In this diagram, notice how low energy conditions at high latitudes override moisture conditions and create world-circling bands of tundra and podzol soils. Notice too that moisture-energy conditions in the marine west coast and Mediterranean areas resemble east coast humid and prairie conditions sufficiently to produce similar soils.

Major soil-vegetation sequences:
The Arctic to the humid tropics

To begin our examination of the combinations of soils and vegetation shown in Figure 18-3 and 18-4 we will look at the series of humid environments ranging from ice cap to tropical

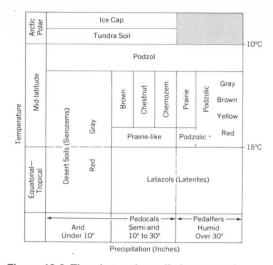

Figure 18-3 The nine major soils in terms of energy/moisture content Soil types reflect the moisture and energy conditions (shown as temperature) in which they develop. This diagram is not a map, but because moisture and energy conditions vary systematically over a continent, so too do the soil types. Each continent has a soil covering which resembles at least part of this sequence, depending upon its location on the globe.

tundra region border the Arctic Ocean and extend inland for varying distances. There, despite scanty precipitation, what little water exists is locked up within the soil for most of the year by low summer temperatures and long, cold winters. When the weak summer sun finally brings 24 hours of daylight to the area north of the Arctic Circle, melting occurs and the surface is turned into a swampy maze. In many places it is difficult to tell whether it is land with a lacework of water or water with a lacework of land. Permanently frozen ground called *permafrost* underlies much of the area, sometimes to a depth of a hundred feet or more. Only the uppermost portion thaws each year during the brief summer. Then, as winter settles in, the surface freezes. This makes a sandwichlike structure with frozen materials both above and below a soggy filling. Sometimes hydrostatic pressure builds up and mud

Figure 18-4 Major vegetation sequences The vegetation sequences found on the continents are associated with the corresponding sequences of soil types shown in Figure 18-3.

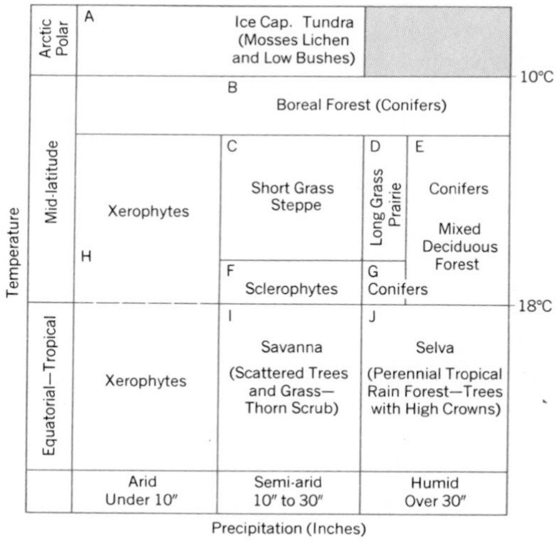

conditions. While the nature of the ice caps of the world is of considerable interest and significance—remember, three-fourths of all fresh water is locked up in glaciers and ice caps—they do not concern us here. Where rocky islands or *nunnataks* thrust out of ice fields, no soil exists, only sometimes a bit of pulverized rock. Let us pass on, for at the same time no vegetation beyond the rare occurrence of a few lichens and mosses graces such inhospitable surfaces.

Tundra soils and vegetation In arctic areas where ice does not prevail, a kind of soil forms which is almost like a pudding. Soils of this

Earth as the Ecologic Niche for Life: Vegetation and Soils

volcanoes and great blisters, or *pingos*, erupt on the surface.

The soil itself that forms under these conditions is extremely shallow, perhaps only a foot or two deep. A third of its depth will be an acidic, humus-rich mixture of clay and sand particles with considerable undecomposed organic matter within it. This is particularly common because of the small amount of bacterial action possible under extreme cold. The remaining soil which rests upon the permafrost is gray and waterlogged, and if the rocky lithosphere is near the surface, it may contain chunks of rock shattered and freed by winter freezing. No normal trees can grow under these conditions, although sometimes dwarf willows less than a foot high exist. The usual plant life is composed of low arctic shrubs, reindeer moss, lichen on the bare rock, grasslike sedges, and a few flowering plants.

This combination of shallow soil and plants with poorly developed root systems presents particular problems for human use. No domesticated vegetation does well on tundra soils, and even better soils which are sometimes underlain by permafrost heave and buckle from differential heating if they are plowed and planted. More tragic is what happens when dangerous atmospheric pollution such as the dust from the Russian hydrogen bomb tests on the arctic island of Novaya Zemyla is blown onto these areas by the polar easterlies. Much of the resulting fallout rests upon bare rock; the remainder is caught in the shallow surface layer that thaws and freezes, for the underlying permafrost effectively prevents such materials from being carried to deeper levels or from being transported out of the region by underground waters. Mosses and lichens, which have no true roots, and all the other plants mentioned above, which have very shallow roots, thus quickly absorb the radioactive materials. Reindeer eat the moss and other vegetation and in turn become radioactive. Hunters and herdsmen of the Arctic depend upon these animals for survival and in their turn absorb large amounts of radioactivity. Though official sources seldom discuss such matters, there is evidence that natives of the Arctic are perhaps the most radioactively contaminated people in the world, and dangerously so.

Podzol soils and the boreal forests   At the margin of the tundra region, dwarf vegetation gives way to true trees. Because plant growth ceases when temperatures go below freezing, these trees are dormant for great portions of the year. Despite the fact that they are frozen solid for part of their lives, they still survive. In some places these northern, or *boreal, forests* will colonize tundra territory underlain with permafrost. Small tundra vegetation has growth cycles adjusted to the long daylight hours of the short summers. The invading trees, however, are perennials which slowly grow larger until their roots extend down to the permanently frozen ground which they cannot penetrate. This places a limit on the size of the trees, and in some particularly cold years the soil does not thaw deeply. This means that the working root systems of the trees are too small to provide for the bulk of the aboveground portion. The trees cannot transpire sufficient water and die of thirst while water stands on the surface all around. As the result of this, sometimes large tracts of small, perfectly formed hemlocks or spruces, all the same size and all dead, can be observed on the boreal forest–tundra boundary. Tundra vegetation eventually reclaims the region, and the boundary is therefore a changing and irregular line. Forests of these extreme northern regions are of no commercial value.

Well south of the arctic tree line but still within the subarctic region, the boreal forests consist of nearly solid stands of spruce and hemlock and cover vast territories in Canada and Siberia. Another name for these forests is the *taiga*, by which they are known in Russia. Several inches of needles and twigs usually carpet the ground under the trees. The soil beneath this cover is called *podzol* soil, a Russian word meaning "ash," for it is the color and consistency of ashes. Podzols are highly acidic and infertile. This is because both chemical and organic actions are slowed by the cold of these regions and the organic cover

Tundra vegetation alternating with open puddles. This is summer in the Arctic, and the surface layer of the permafrost has melted. (Photo by S. Outcalt)

on the forest floor does not decompose very rapidly. Unlike the leaves of deciduous trees at lower latitudes, the pine needles of the taiga, or boreal forests, contain few nutrients and are mostly cellulose. Moreover, by their very nature they form acidic solutions when they do decay. Organic acids leach out not only calcium, potassium, and other nutrients, but also iron and aluminum oxides which normally color the soil with red to brownish hues. The silicon oxides that are left behind explain the gray ash appearance which gives the podzols their name.

Trees along the southern margins of the boreal forests can be used for the production of paper and wood pulp. Regrowth is slow, however, and the land is used for this purpose largely because it has practically no other agricultural value. The needle-leaf conifer forests of the subarctic need only small

A boreal forest, or taiga. Aspen and balsam fir form a two-story cover of relatively small trees. (U.S. Dept. of Agriculture photo)

amounts of plant nutrients such as potassium and phosphate, for their bulk is primarily cellulose. This means, however, that their leaves are of no value as fodder and their organic debris is of no use as green mulch. This accounts in large part for the lack of northward expansion of the agricultural and dairy belts from Megalopolis in the eastern United States. Here is one instance where Thünen's land use rings are distorted by natural causes.

In areas such as the Maritime Provinces of Canada where the weather is more moderate, these soils can be successfully farmed with proper treatment and choice of crops. Cranberries, which require acid soils, potatoes and other root crops, and some fruit trees are grown. The soil must be limed (calcium carbonate is added to neutralize the acid in the soil), and fertilizer with the primary macronutrients, nitrogen, potassium, and phosphate, must be added. This condition does not substantiate the popular image of an agricultural frontier waiting for settlers in the subarctic.

Podzolic soils and mid-latitude deciduous forests Underlying the mixed deciduous hardwood and coniferous softwood forests of the eastern United States are soils typical of the forests found south of the taiga wherever sufficient moisture is available. The hardwoods include the familiar maple, beech, oak, walnut, and hickory. Deciduous trees, which lose their leaves every winter, and especially nut producers bring nutrients up from the B horizons of the soil and the parent material. Such trees produce abundant organic material which each season is released as the leaves change color and fall to the ground along with the nuts and seeds. This organic debris is mineral-rich, especially the nuts and seeds, which have more nutrient value than leaves and stems. The soils under these forests are called the *gray-brown podzolics*. When the forests are cleared, the soils may be very productive, while in their natural state under undisturbed forest they support a sizable animal population. However, they are normally too acid for domestic crops and require

liming. They are darker in color than a true podzol because of higher humus content. At the same time, warm summers and generally milder climates allow greater bacterial action.

Mixed livestock—feed grain farming practiced in the Midwest is suited to these podzolic soils. This farm system involves rotating small grains and corn with legumes, hay, and soybeans in order to help restore nitrogen to the soil. Livestock, in previous decades much more than at present, were kept on each farm and fed on feed grains as well as hay, and their manure was returned to the grain fields. These farmers also learned to put phosphate and potash (potassium oxide) on their fields. With such treatment podzolic soils continue to produce a wide range of products, but with poor farming techniques they rapidly deteriorate.

The soils of the humid southeastern United States and of a similar area in China are noticeably red and yellow in color. They are also quite infertile, a condition typical of the *red and yellow podzolics*. The color results from high iron and aluminum content in the clay particles of which they are principally composed. Abundant rainfall, high temperatures, leaching, and bacterial action contribute to this condition. Also, in the southeastern United States, the soils developed on deeply weathered ancient surface material undisturbed by the continental glaciers which never reached so far south. To the north all across the continent, fresh mineral-bearing materials were exposed by the action of the glaciers, either by scraping, by direct deposition, or through action of water and wind associated with the ice front.

The pioneers who came to the southern Piedmont on the seaward flanks of the Appalachian Mountains found a natural vegetation of mixed broadleaf and pine forests. Clearing the forests and raising crops invariably resulted in a very rapid decline in yields. The land was often abandoned after only two or three years. They then moved on to the west to repeat the process. This destructive land use practice is sometimes referred to as "grasshopper farming." Heavy rains caused severe erosion in those bare, abandoned fields. In

(A) Mid-latitude white pine forest in northern Minnesota. These trees are 200 to 300 years old and are remnants of the once extensive forests of the upper Midwest. (U.S. Dept of Agriculture photo)

(B) Mid-latitude hardwood deciduous forest in Wisconsin. Survivors of another age, the trees are, from left to right: maple, elm, black ash, and elm. (U.S. Dept. of Agriculture photo)

(C) Mid-latitude West Coast coniferous forest in northern California. The trees are redwoods. (U.S. Dept. of Agriculture photo)

places, pine forests eventually grew back in place of broadleaf forests. Old field shapes sometimes can still be distinguished in these second-growth pine barrens. This was because pine trees can manage better than broadleaf trees under poor soil conditions. But these podzolics are worthless for agriculture unless very heavily and carefully fertilized.

The chemical nature of the soils in this re-

Tropical rain forest, or selva, showing high-crowned deciduous trees and typical dense growth. Costa Rica. (Photo by B. Begley)

gion can explain why this destructive and poverty-producing sequence occurred. We noticed before that nutrients must be in water solution to be available for plant use. In most soils less than 1 percent of the minerals present are in dissolved form, the bulk being in the solid clay or sand particles. The minerals in solution are contained in water films clinging to the soil particles. As plant roots or leaching action draw the dissolved ions from the water, more ions move into solution from the solid material. The direction and amount of such transfers depend upon the chemical balance available. Plant roots essentially offer hydrogen ions in exchange for other positive ions such as those of calcium ($Ca++$) and magnesium ($Mg++$). Such action is inhibited in acid soils, which by definition have an excess of hydrogen ions ($H+$) already in solution. A soil containing clay particles rich in calcium and other nutrients will slowly release ions into solution as the plants use them up. Such soils are chemically stable and are referred to as being "buffered." The red and yellow podzolics are not buffered at all. The soluble positive ions have moved out of the soil particles due to the long weathering to which they have been exposed, leaving the aluminum and iron oxides behind. The useful nutrients have been leached away.

Humus in the organic layer is normally a good source of recycled plant nutrients. Unfortunately there are also two problems associated with humus in red and yellow podzolics. The first is that there is not much organic material present, a fact that can be deduced from the color. Humus is dark, and soils rich in humus are dark brown or black. These are much lighter and yellower.

The second problem has to do with the quality of the nutrients available to animals, including humans, using the plants grown on these soils as food. Soil microbes, necessary for the decay portion of the plant-soil cycle, under these conditions compete with the plants for proteinaceous food. This is because they are made of proteins themselves. The plant litter under the trees, particularly pine trees in warm, moist regions, is quite carbonaceous.

342

Tropical savanna in which deciduous trees alternate with grass. This area in East Africa has a brief rainy season followed by a long drought. (Photo by A. Larimore)

The trees are little more than cellulose and other carbohydrates which provide an excess of energy food for organisms but little or no growth material.

Therefore the infertility of podzolic soils has a differential quality about it. Fiber and leaf crops such as cotton, sugar cane, and tobacco will do relatively better than protein-rich fodder crops and small grains. Seeds and nuts, being the reproductive parts of plants, require protein nutrients to be viable. Animals fed on protein-deficient fodder grow slowly, do not reproduce well, and are susceptible to diseases. Again, the distribution of crop types in the United States and elsewhere is the result of a combination of both cultural and natural factors. Protein deficiencies, like those described above, also cause malnutrition in human populations. Conditions of this sort also become critical in association with the lateritic soils of both semitropical and tropical regions.

Latasols of the selva We frequently think of tropical rain forests as deep and luxurious. In places that have been relatively undisturbed by man, they are, but as with many other biotic communities, these lush forests rapidly decline under man's impact. Both subsistence and commercial farming contribute to the disappearance of the *selva*, another name for tropical rain forests. The huge biomass built up per unit area within undisturbed tropical rain forest despite its mass constitutes an extremely fragile plant community growing on meager soils. Perhaps only primitive agriculturalists have found a system by which the selva can achieve sustained food crop produc-

Earth as the Ecologic Niche for Life: Vegetation and Soils

tion. Certainly, attempts to convert the apparent plenty of the selva into commercial food crops are often disappointing. There is also evidence that past civilizations have fared poorly in rain forest regions.

Most of the nutrients in a tropical rain forest biosystem are held in the vegetation itself. The plants in this community are dominated by tall trees with high crowns. Little underbrush can grow on the dim forest floor. Our image of impenetrably thick equatorial forests is based in large part on photographs taken from rivers and trails which are lined with dense vegetation taking advantage of the additional sunshine penetrating the forest cover at those places.

Some vegetative cycles exist without benefit of soil in these forests—for example, epiphytes, which grow on other plants but which are not nourished by them, and parasitic plants which live high above the forest floor in the tree canopy. The trees are often evergreen in character and lose their leaves one at a time throughout the year. Thus the high green canopy remains unbroken from season to season. At the same time, very little litter covers the ground beneath, for high temperatures, abundant moisture, and intense bacterial action quickly dispose of any fallen plant materials. Excess water saturates the land, leaching out much of the parent material and weathering the rock to a great depth. The loss of clay silicates in this way creates a crumbly, porous soil rather than a sticky one when wet. In areas where wet and dry seasons prevail, saturation followed by drying out of the soil facilitates oxidation of iron and aluminum compounds. This results in the characteristic red tones associated with the *latasols*.

Under such conditions, nutrients released in the soil are quickly taken up by the roots of existing plants or else are leached away. In places where plant roots cannot reach fresh mineral soil, the plants tend to be protein-poor and to reproduce vegetatively. That is, they send out shoots rather than reproducing by flower and seed. Clearing such forests and replacing them with crops breaks the smooth flow of plant food from roots to canopy to litter and quickly back to the roots. Soils formed under these conditions provide only protein-deficient foods for people and animals. Even the soil microbes, usually thought of as necessary and symbiotic partners in the soil-plant biosystem, begin to compete with plants for growth nutrients. This situation comes about in the following way.

The proportion of carbon to nitrogen in tropical forest litter is out of balance, and nitrogen is in short supply. Plants and animals, including the decay-producing organisms in the soil which break down litter into products usable by vegetation, all compete for the limited supply of proteinaceous minerals. Organic life can be very active in humid, warm environments. Decaying carbohydrate plant parts provide ample energy food but little, if any, protein for growth. Plants requiring seed production on a large scale in their life processed do not do well under these conditions. For example, small grains do not flourish, and starchy crops are grown in their stead.

People who depend upon these tropical crops suffer from malnutrition and conditions such as kwashiorkor, a nutritional disease associated with a starchy diet. Young children in Africa and other tropical areas where carbohydrate-rich subsistence crops such as bananas, cassava (manioc), and maize predominate all suffer from these illnesses. It is significant that most of the original populations of the tropics were concentrated along the shores of lakes, streams, and oceans where fish provided necessary protein supplements. This is still true of places like the Amazon basin, where territories remote from the rivers are nearly empty of people. Since protein-rich crops do not do well under these conditions, it is likely that attempts to improve the health and nutrition of native populations by persuading them to grow imported proteinaceous crops will not succeed. Such crops will not do well without massive inputs to the soil. Such inputs are likely to rapidly wash away, and it may well be cheaper to import food rather than fertilizers directly to such places.

On the other hand, the plants of the tropics

have considerable commercial value. Those best suited for this type of production reproduce vegetatively and yield large quantities of carbohydrates. Tropical lumber is one such crop, although the mixed stands of timber mean high costs on a per tree basis. This limits the present production of tropical woods to those that fetch high prices, such as mahagony and teak. The best commercial crops include sisal, jute, and hemp, which provide a variety of fibers; tea; coffee; sugar cane; and bananas. Spices, for which the tropics are famous, come from seeds (cloves, nutmeg, pepper, and vanilla) as well as from bark and roots (cinnamon and ginger). Spices and medicinal products (quinine bark, for example) very often come from wild trees which must be quite large and old to be productive. Even then their yield is quite small per tree.

Tropical plantations try to overcome some of these problems by raising homogeneous stands of a particular species. However, the continual exporting of nutrients in the form of crops rapidly depletes the soil. Many operators, despite knowledge and use of fertilizers, find it necessary to use land for a few years and then to let it lie fallow for decades or to abandon it altogether. The "hollow frontier" in Brazil is a prime example of this. Coffee plantations are extended into previously unfarmed areas. After a few years the frontier moves forward again, and the land behind it is abandoned, thus making a thin line of active production between the forest and the depleted land.

Humidity and high temperatures encourage all manner of plant and human diseases. The onslaught of Panama disease, or wilt disease, among the banana plantations on the Caribbean shores of Central America in the period from 1890 to 1941 was responsible for the wholesale movement of production to the lowlands on the Pacific side of the isthmus. Similar diseases attacking coco trees in West Africa have also taken a high toll. But even if disease can be controlled, these commercial crops are not products which contribute to the balanced diets of local men and animals. Despite their vast stands of vegetation, the tropics of the world do not offer an easy answer to the search for new lands to farm.

So-called "primitive" systems of agriculture developed by local populations may actually be more sensible in both the short and long run. Such peoples employ variations on a common pattern of *shifting agriculture*, sometimes called *fire-field* agriculture. In this system, small plots are cleared in the forest. Trees are girdled and killed; smaller ones are chopped down and along with brush and grass are burned when they have dried out. The ashes from these fires are mixed in the soil, and crops are planted around the stumps and trunks of the larger trees. Small quantities of maize, cassava, and other plants are removed by harvest for up to three years, and then the fields are abandoned. Nearby plots are opened in the same manner, and the cycle of clearing and abandonment continues. Needless to say, even the nutrients consumed by humans find their way back to the soil as feces and the bodies of each dying generation. When fields are taken out of production, they are quickly reclaimed by grasses and eventually by brush until after 20 years or more the fragile nutrient cycle is restored. As long as populations do not become too large, it is then possible for the farmers to return to their fields or the ones of their fathers.

In the long run, though, even this low intensity of land use cannot endure. More and more of the virgin selva is depleted, and there is evidence that this technique of farming may have contributed to the creation of savanna grasslands in the wet-and-dry tropics.

Savanna and Mediterranean vegetation
The savannas of the world are large tracts of open grassland that merge with the drier margins of the tropical rain forests. Scrub and thorn forest intermingle with patches of open ground, until grassland predominates. These grasslands, however, are unlike those of the middle latitudes in that they are subject to processes of soil formation and laterization similar to those in the selva. The tall grasses which predominate are full of cellulose and particularly when dry are unnutritious and un-

suitable for fodder. Even the wild grazing animals of the area must migrate from pasture to pasture on an annual cycle in order to survive. Thus, a combination of climate, man, and special environmental conditions including those of soil-forming processes helps to create this particular type of environment with its unique problems.

Before discussing the problem of soil laterization in the tropics, let us consider the particular types of plant communities living where year-round high temperatures and wet-and-dry—rather than cold-and-hot—seasons prevail. The savanna areas of the tropics and the Mediterranean environment of the subtropical latitudes fulfill these conditions. Characteristically, the vegetation communities in either type of area would have widely spaced trees alternating with grasslands. Elsewhere, thornbush and scrub create patches of drought-resistant vegetation. While some typologists might object to our discussing the vegetation of these two environments in the same section, a strong similarity exists between Mediterranean and savanna plants. Both vegetative communities must adjust to annual periods of drought followed by rainy seasons of short to long duration. Both kinds of vegetation may become dormant during periods of high temperatures and aridity. This condition is called *estivation*, as opposed to *hibernation*, dormancy during cold, low-sun periods.

In Mediterranean environments, plants sprout new leaves in the autumn with the coming of the first rains. The main growth period when fruit and seeds form is during the milder, winter months. Then as the hot summer approaches, deciduous plants shed their leaves in order to reduce evapotranspiration and water loss. Evergreen oaks such as the cork oak are typical, along with the Aleppo pine. Crops include the olive—the distribution of which defines the geographic extent of the Mediterranean climate in Europe. Where overcutting, overgrazing, and fires have degraded the stands of Mediterranean trees, a thick growth of thorny second-growth scrub often occurs. This is called *maquis*, and during

World War II the famous French Underground Army which resisted the invading Nazis was given the name *maquis* after the thickets where they hid. When maquis vegetation is degraded still further until bare ground with patches of low herbs predominates, the degraded plant community is referred to as *garigue*.

Nearer the equator in the true wet-and-dry tropics, savanna woodland, thornbush and tropical scrub, and true savanna predominate. The woodland has an open, parklike appearance, although dense stands of flat-topped, medium-height trees frequently occur. This vegetation has small leaves and thick, fire-resistant bark, and is adjusted to a long dry season followed by a fairly long rainy one. Elsewhere, thornbush and scrub are even more xerophytic and drought-resistant in character. Such stands are found where rains come in fairly large quantities but for very brief periods, with most of the year hot and dry. True savanna, with its large tracts of open grasslands and scattered, drought-resistant trees, borders on the steppe lands and desert margins of the subtropics and continental interiors.

Laterization

Many tropical soils are characterized by concentrations of aluminum and iron. At the same time, they are low in silica and poor in plant nutrients. A typical soil profile shows practically no organic surface layer of litter. Instead the top inch or so may be a granular, dark-red clay. This gives tropical latasols their typical reddish hues. The rest of the A horizon is somewhat lighter. It is more coarsely granular and penetrated by roots and insect burrows. The B horizon is composed of blocky red clay that may be up to 6 feet deep.

These deeply weathered soils when exposed to the sun and air through removal of plant cover may turn into a bricklike substance called *laterite* (derived from the Latin word for brick). This material is so hard and durable that roads and buildings may actually be built from it. For example, the famous temple of Angkor Wat belonging to the former Khmer civilization in what is now Cambodia was constructed of laterite. This structure has endured unattended in its tropical environment since the sixteenth century and remains in reasonably good shape to the present day.

The Khmer civilization may have perished because of the laterization of the soils upon which its citizens depended for food. As their population increased, they may have pressed upon the fragile biosystem too hard by not allowing sufficient fallow periods between crop cycles. They may also have exposed large tracts to too much sun by removing the natural vegetative cover. In any event, their once populous area is now nearly empty. A similar example can also be found in Central America, where the Mayan civilization may have suffered the same fate. The Mayas occupied an area of lateritic soils, and some of their temples are also constructed of laterite. This may well be more than coincidence. These conjectures linking the decline of civilizations with the destruction of soil resources are not proven, but present-day people attempting to develop tropical agriculture should be concerned with the hazards of laterization.

Relation of soil fertility to population distribution in the tropics

Not all tropical soils are poor. Notable exceptions occur on the flanks of recent or still active volcanoes. Ash and lava are mineral-rich and form the basis for a rich soil. The island of Java in Indonesia and the flanks of Mt. Kilimanjaro in East Africa are examples. Significantly, each of these places supports a very heavy population density. Commercial plantations also tend to cluster in places where rich parent material is available for soil formation.

In the middle latitudes, mountainous terrain is usually the most sparsely settled, with the low plains having more productive soils and carrying the heaviest rural population density. The opposite is often the case in the tropics. The population there is concentrated in the highlands and on steep slopes. One reason for this tendency in the wet-and-dry tropics is that the climate is milder and the

A Maryland farm prospering on well-managed podzolic soils. (U.S. Dept. of Agriculture photo)

"Tall corn" country in the American Midwest. The prairie soils here are among the best in the world. (U.S. Dept. of Agriculture photo)

rainfall more predictable at higher elevations than closer to sea level. Also in the wet-and-dry tropics, the presence of mountains may result in year-round orographic rainfall. Another reason is that the steep slopes and

*Earth
as the Ecologic
Niche for Life:
Vegetation
and Soils*

347

heavy rainfall cause erosion of surface layers at a rate which exceeds the rate of laterization. New mineral soils are therefore continually made available, and populations can depend on the renewal of vital soil resources.

Major soil-vegetation sequences:
Mid-latitude humid to arid environments

The preceding discussion of soils and vegetation from the Arctic to the humid tropics provides us with an introduction to soil-forming processes. We can now take a somewhat briefer look at another basic series of soils and vegetation found in mid-latitude locations. These environments represent the transition from the humid to the arid mid-latitudes. In North America such a sequence occurs along the 40th parallel of latitude from central Ohio through Illinois, Missouri, Kansas-Nebraska, and on into Colorado. In the East, podzolic soils originally developed under hardwood deciduous forests. Even though the forests have been cleared away, with proper care such soils can remain fertile almost indefinitely and produce large yields from a wide variety of crops. Acidic and humus-rich, with proper liming and the application of phosphate, potash, and farm manure, they are among the best in the world.

Prairie and chernozem soils of the semi-humid-semiarid grasslands West of the podzolics of Ohio and Indiana are soils formed under fairly moist conditions but without tree cover. Representative of these are the prairie soils found throughout the Corn Belt. On our transect they occur in parts of Illinois and Missouri and in eastern Kansas-Nebraska. These are formed on deposits left by continental glaciers which once covered the Midwest as far south as the Ohio and Missouri Rivers. The long grasses on these prairies send roots deep into the soil and have concentrated minerals and other nutrients in the A horizon. The flow of nutrients through the grasses, plus the contribution of the grass itself to the humus content of the prairie soils, is a critical factor in the fertility of these soils. Prairie soils are usually quite thick, with a characteristic dark-brown and loamy surface layer which shades gradually into a yellowish-brown B horizon overlying the original glacial clays and sands.

This region receives adequate precipitation throughout the year, and severe droughts are infrequent. While the soil loses some of its fertility once the grasses have been removed and replaced with farm crops, small inputs of phosphate and nitrogen, plus a system of crop rotation involving corn, grains, and nitrogen-fixing plants such as beans or alfalfa, can keep it fertile and farming profitable. The choice of possible crops is nearly as great as those which can be grown on the podzolics, and the title "Breadbasket of the Nation" can apply here as well as to the chernozem soils immediately to the west.

The name *chernozem* means "black earth" in Russian. These are the soils of the Ukraine which have fed generations of East European people, people who in turn have died defending the land and the riches it represents. In America the same type of soil lies just to the east of the 100th meridian, which in turn marks the approximate location of the 20-inch annual rainfall isohyet on the Great Plains. Only slightly leached, they are among the calcium-rich pedocals and need no liming and only small amounts of fertilizer. Adequate but relatively sparse rainfall and cold winters have kept bacterial action at a reasonable level, and the characteristic black color of the A horizon is the result of its rich humus content. A combination of moisture regime and soil type limits the number of crops that can be grown profitably in these parts, but wheat and other small grains do exceptionally well, and here is the source of much of the world's bread. It is also chernozem soils, interesting to note, that underlie the bountiful wheat fields of Argentina. While rainfall diminishes in a westerly direction across the Plains, the chernozems are still watered by nature with reasonable predictability. However, once beyond the 20-inch rainfall line, precipitation comes with less and less regularity. Thus, farming becomes more and more of a gamble as one leaves the black earth and enters into that of the chestnut and brown soils.

Chestnut and brown soils of the short-grass steppes

The area of chestnut and brown soils denotes a true semiarid environment. Rainfall averages between 10 and 20 inches per year. As a consequence very little leaching has taken place. If there is groundwater present, it may move upward through capillary action, leaving behind an accumulation of carbonates in the lower layers. The grasses under which these soils form are shorter than those of the chernozems and long-grass prairies. This reflects the increased aridity with which vegetation must contend. Despite their lower organic content—a function of less moisture and less vegetative cover—these soils can still provide good crops in moist years. However, the general rule is that as the annual amount of rainfall decreases, the unpredictability of its occurrence will increase. This is an important point to which we will return very shortly. Few crops do well under the combination of these conditions, and grains, particularly winter wheat, are the best choice.

Desert soils and xerophytic vegetation

In western Colorado, deep within the continental interior and barred by mountains from rain-bearing winds, we come to the end of this sequence. Here less than 10 inches of rain falls each year. The spatial occurrence of rain is haphazard at best, and its timing is unpredictable. Vegetation under these circumstances enjoys a "boom or bust" type of existence and is adjusted to it. Two types of plants exist: drought evaders and drought resisters. We will have more to say about these in the next chapter when we discuss the strategies men and other life use in their struggle with nature. For now, we will simply point out that desert plants space themselves farther apart than plants in other climates; that they often have thick, waxy skins and small leaves, characteristics which cut down water loss

Sully County, South Dakota. Chestnut brown soils underly the short grasses of this steppeland. (U.S. Dept. of Agriculture photo)

through transpiration; and that they may estivate, that is, go dormant during periods of high temperature rather than during the winter. These plants are highly specialized, so much so that they receive the special name *xerophytes*.

An absence of leaching makes desert soils relatively rich in nutrients. On the other hand, scattered vegetation means much less humus in the surface layer. Altogether, no agriculture is possible under these conditions unless irrigation is practiced. Even then there is need for careful management of the land. Failures can come as frequently as successes, for the heavy concentration of carbonates and salts near the surface of desert soils can be easily dissolved and reconcentrated in quantities deadly to most plants. Many fields in the dry western part of the United States have been abandoned as the white signature of alkali writes "finis" to their productivity.

The Oklahoma dust bowl

Soils are defined by the use to which humans put them. They are defined as well by their

A desert landscape in Arizona—saguaro, barrel, and cholla cacti, as well as palo verde, depend upon irregular occurrences of rain in small quantities. This xerophytic vegetation is well adapted to sierozem or desert soils. (U.S. Dept. of Agriculture photo)

location relative to the rest of the world productive system. The special properties of the natural environments under which they form are also important. We can make this point by talking briefly about the countryside in Oklahoma and northern Texas once known as the "Dust Bowl." That is a semiarid country with short-grass steppeland best suited for grazing moderate numbers of cattle. Chestnut and brown soils predominate; to the east are the belts of chernozems and prairie soils. Farthest away are the Eastern podzolics. Now *by coincidence* (and we emphasize this point), the major markets of the nation are also in the Northeast and are also far from the chestnut-brown soils of the dry, high plains. All this is shown in Figure 18-5.

In the first quarter of the twentieth century events halfway around the world were helping to create the infamous dust bowl of the Depression era. World War I had ended with victory for the Allies but a total disaster within Russia. The war had devastated much of western European Russia and had decimated the generation of young men who made up the rural work force. Revolution followed close on the heels of war, and the famous granaries of the Ukrainian chernozem soils lay idle for long periods. Not only did Russia cease to be an exporter of grain during those years, but famine stalked the land. Even America was involved in trying to restore the Russian economy, and Herbert Hoover, later the thirty-first President of the United States, directed famine relief there for five years. Meanwhile, better times returned to much of the rest of the world. The Roaring Twenties with their boom economy and runaway stock market put new money in people's pockets. In fact, the new prosperity reached much of what we now call the developing nations of the world. There were increased demands for food, and there was money to pay for it. Wheat became a more valuable commodity than it had ever been before. Part of its value was its relatively short supply, which came in part from the loss of production in the emerging Soviet Union.

In the preboom economy of the United States, the low rent-earning ability of wheat had made it uncompetitive with other crops. In accordance with the theories of Thünen its low rent per acre and good transportability meant that it was produced on the outer margins of the rings of agriculture surrounding the northeastern American market (Figure 18-6). This zone of production at that time coincided with the chernozems and other soils of the better-watered plains of Kansas

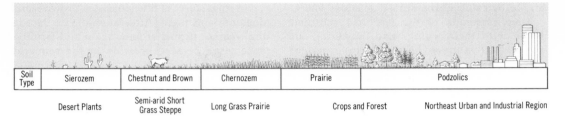

Soil Type	Sierozem	Chestnut and Brown	Chernozem	Prairie	Podzolics
	Desert Plants	Semi-arid Short Grass Steppe	Long Grass Prairie	Crops and Forest	Northeast Urban and Industrial Region

Figure 18-5 Soil types and vegetation and use sequence from humid East to arid West in the United States.

and Nebraska. But when wheat prices soared in response to increased demands on the world market, the competitive position of wheat altered. However, it was still unable to replace corn, cotton, or other crops of the inner rings, for their market prices were also rising. The end result was that the Thünen-like zones of production extended farther into the American heartland, and that the unleached, nutrient-rich but hitherto unfarmed chestnut

Figure 18-6 Thünen-type model of the expansion of agriculture into chestnut and brown soil regions of the Great Plains, 1920–1930 By coincidence, the chestnut brown soils of the Great Plains were distant from the large Eastern markets in the United States, and before the 1920s the area was beyond the agricultural margin. The rise in world and national food demand and food prices during the 1920 boom created a market for crops from this region. In terms of the Thünen agricultural model, the wheat ring expanded out to this formerly marginal land. However, climatic and market fluctuations led to a disastrous decline in the farming system and, in the following decade, to the creation of the Dust Bowl condition during the Depression years.

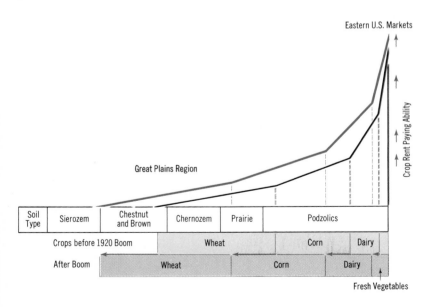

Earth as the Ecologic Niche for Life: Vegetation and Soils

and brown soils now assumed an added allure.

Many veterans of the war had returned home with their savings and mustering-out pay and with a strong desire to be independent farmers. The opportunities offered by the semiarid lands of the Great Plains were quickly noted, and many a farmer went west to buy a small farm with his savings. This condition was also enhanced by the fact that the 1920s were favored with a sequence of relatively wet years in the area of the chestnut-brown soils. And so it happened that the natural grass cover of these areas was plowed under and wheat was planted everywhere. It is an established rule that the drier an area, the less reliable will be its rainfall. Thus, when rain fell for two or three years running in the semiarid west, it was no guarantee that those favorable conditions would last. But the small farmers didn't know that and were caught by surprise when the first years of the thirties ushered in one of the worst droughts on record.

Not only did the weather turn unfavorable in the decade after the chestnut-brown soils came into wheat production, but the great bubble of prosperity burst in October 1929 with a disastrous decline in the stock market. The Great Depression began, and the price of wheat fell very soon thereafter. Once more the Thünen rings adjusted to a new set of conditions. Production shrank back toward the market, and it was no longer profitable to raise wheat so far away. But that scarcely mattered, since the developing Dust Bowl conditions of the 1930s made farming next to impossible in Oklahoma. And so the small farmers lost their land as their mortgages came due. The terrible and tragic trek of the Oklahoma migrants began, and the scenes of social and economic disintegration made vivid in Steinbeck's novel *The Grapes of Wrath* took place.

But the story of the chestnut-brown soils does not end there. After more than a decade the weather turned around again and farming once more became possible in the semiarid west. This time, however, the successful farmer was an entrepreneur with considerable capital and cost accounting skills at his command. Small farms had been consolidated into giant wheat ranches, and the businessman-farmers who controlled them anticipated losses perhaps two years out of three and took this into account in their budgeting. Wheat price subsidies and the soil bank which paid farmers not to plant certain crops became a kind of insurance, while modern farming methods also increased prosperity in the area. At the same time, new deep wells have been drilled throughout this region, and some of the former wheat land is now under irrigation and yielding rich harvests of sugar beets and alfalfa. Prosperity is once more the key word.

We will end this account and this chapter with a thought for the future. The water brought up from the deep wells of the semiarid Great Plains is a nonrenewable resource. Although it exists in large quantities, the aquifers in which it is stored were filled thousands of years ago at the end of the Pleistocene when the continental glaciers melted. Subsequently, less moisture is available and no significant recharging of those deep reservoirs is currently taking place. When the water is exhausted in the foreseeable future, what will happen next to this region? Will water be brought there from thousands of miles away? Will the land revert to modern wheat farming with one good crop for two or three bad ones? Or will some unsuspected use be found for the land? The concluding chapters of this book will consider many questions similar to these as well as others concerning the impact of urbanization on society and nature.

19 | HUMAN ORGANIZATION OF THE ENVIRONMENT: ADJUSTMENTS TO ENVIRONMENTAL UNCERTAINTY

There was a good gardener named Gunn,
Who was growing a cactus for fun,
But whenever his daughter
Tried to give it some water,
He said, "What it needs is more sun."

More potted plants die from overwatering than from thirst. The care you give your windowbox qualifies you as one of the multitude that attempt to manipulate and relate to nature through various strategies. Where in the house is the best spot to grow a pot of chives? Will it rain next Sunday for the wedding reception or should we wait another week? How much grain should the government of India stockpile against possible famine? Thousands of questions like these illustrate why humans constantly play games of chance and strategy with their environments.

For example, a New York apartment dweller owned a cactus. She knew that it shouldn't be watered too frequently, but when? Her solution was to subscribe to an Arizona newspaper and read about the local weather. Whenever it rained there, she watered her plant. It seemed like a great idea, but the cactus still died from overwatering. What our apartment gardener failed to take into consideration was the spatial as well as the temporal character of rainfall in the desert. The newspaper reported rain whenever it fell anywhere within a large area in or near the city. But our friend didn't consider that convectional showers in the desert are of brief duration and highly localized. By noting the occurrence of rainfall within too large an area she overlooked the true nature of an arid environment; the apartment cactus received far too much water; and our gardener lost her game with nature.

During the thousands of years of his existence man has devised numerous strategies to help him survive natural conditions which are often difficult or dangerous. The purpose of this chapter is to outline some of the ways in which we organize our lives and environments to accomplish this. Let us first consider an example drawn from the vast panorama of prehistory and history. The story concerns the buildup of increasingly complex ways of social interaction and resource use and is an example of a deviation-amplifying process.

Resource Use and the Organization of Space: The Tehuacan Valley

Twelve thousand years ago or more a band of Paleo-Indians stood on the hills overlooking the Tehuacan Valley in what today is the state of Puebla, south of Mexico City. The small group probably consisted of two or three couples and their children joined into some type of extended family. They had few material possessions, and their technology at best was able to produce chipped flint tools and weapons: scrapers, gravers, leaf-shaped knives, and some projectile points. Though sometimes described as "big game hunters," they depended mainly on wild plants as well as on small game. Birds, rabbits, and turtles were among the animals cooked at their fires. They seldom were successful in killing anything larger, and as one archaeologist has put it: "They probably found one mammoth in a lifetime and never got over talking about it."

Those people were part of the several migrations of ancient hunters who generations after crossing the Siberian-Alaskan bridge to North America eventually found their way to Central and South America. The Tehuacan Valley before their coming was unpopulated. The climate there in the Mexican highlands at the end of the Pleistocene was a dry one much like that of western Texas today. The valley, while not lush, offered some possibilities for hunting and collecting wild foods; and that group of hunters, or another much like it, descended into the valley and stayed on to become its first inhabitants. The tangible remains of their occupance are like faint shadows on the sand and rock. Eleven of their early hearths or campsites, some in caves, some in the open, have been found by modern scientists.

Nearly 12,000 years later, on another morning, with the clank of light body armor and the neighing of horses, a Spanish patrol also stopped on the hills overlooking the Tehuacan Valley. Their presence marked the end of a distinct and independent Indian culture in that area, as in the rest of Mexico and all of what was to become Spanish America. But that patrol of invading conquistadores did not find a few small and simple groups of hunters and collectors. Instead, the valley presented to them a collection of little kingdoms, each with its towns surrounded by villages and hamlets. Farmers produced a wide variety of domesticated crops, among them maize,

squash, tomatoes, peanuts, and avocados. There were few domesticated animals—only dogs and turkeys—but valley industries produced cotton and salt for export to other regions. An elaborate hierarchy of priests and administrators controlled a population of perhaps a hundred thousand or more people within the valley. The Indian civilization encountered there and elsewhere by the Spanish was nearly as elaborate as their own. Unfortunately for the Indians, the crafts in which the Spanish excelled were iron metallurgy and weaponry, including gunpowder. The destruction of the Indian culture, and its replacement by one based in large part on European norms, is a matter of history.

An amazing sequence of events in that 12,000-year period transformed a small handful of wandering hunters and gatherers into a complex sedentary, agricultural society with thousands of people living in villages and towns. The Indians found by the Spanish possessed a high degree of material civilization, although many of their customs were perhaps still as savage as those of the conquistadores who so thoroughly disrupted them. The whole story of their odyssey through time cannot be told here. What concerns us as geographers is the changing pattern of the way in which those people spatially organized the Tehuacan Valley and its resources.

Why bother to map and analyze an Indian civilization, remote in time and space? The answer is simple. Man organizes the space in which he lives and the resources which he uses in order to deal with the negative aspects and uncertainty of the environments he occupies. Such organization contains within itself a cross-cultural continuity. This means that if we can understand the relationships between man and his environment in cultures using fewer resources and less energy, we can better understand our own behavior. With such understanding we may be able to plot more rational courses into the future. In this chapter we further explore the idea of *spatial hierarchies* as a way of organizing human populations, the resources which sustain them, and the areas they occupy. We then consider other ways in which man solves ongoing environmental problems.

Spatial and social organization for resource use

Before continuing our history of the Tehuacan Valley, let us consider some spatial concepts relating to that or any other area which has been spatially organized for the utilization of its resources. It is often said that man is a gregarious animal following his herd instinct and clustering together whenever and wherever possible. A more intersting explanation, which does not depend upon evoking special hereditary characteristics in order to explain human behavior, is the notion of *convenience and focus*. When John Donne wrote "No man is an island," he referred to the network of reciprocal emotional needs and social actions which bind humanity together. In the same way, not one of us is truly self-sufficient when it comes to providing food, clothing, shelter, and the myriad of other necessities and services upon which we all depend.

Speaking as geographers, we pinpoint the notion of *convenience of location* as one of the key elements in the processes of human resource use, exchange, and interaction. A place near the center of things which offers the greatest opportunity for interaction will be most convenient for the greatest number of people.

A major problem faced by all groups of people is how to organize their lives spatially to achieve satisfactory resource use. People must live far enough apart to ensure the areas necessary for their well-being. Such areas include room for farms, for recreation, and for adequate amounts of fresh air and sunlight. On the other hand, people crowd together in settlements in order to maximize the interaction and the spatial convenience upon which they also depend. A kind of tension thus exists between these two ways of organizing space.

Various cultures at different times in his-

tory have found solutions to the problem of locating people and their activities so as to maximize interaction and still retain sufficient space in which to live and work. Let us return now to the Paleo-Indians who entered the Tehuacan Valley and follow the development of their and subsequent societies in terms of the spatial organizations which evolved.

Spatial organization without domesticates

The earliest people to reach the Tehuacan Valley were well along the road of human technological development. They knew the use of fire and could make chipped stone tools and weapons. They also had considerable knowledge about edible wild plants as well as hunting and trapping skills. This assemblage of skills and knowledge helped them organize their activities in time and space in order to ensure group as well as individual survival. With each seasonal change a new set of resources became available, although not necessarily in the same locality. Overhunting or overcollecting also might exhaust the plants and animals within walking distance of a campsite. To meet these and other circumstances, ancient man from time to time had to relocate himself in the space in which he lived. Carl Sauer in his discussion in *Agricultural Origins and Dispersals* neatly summarizes one interpretation of the basic geographic rationale of early man:

We need not think of ancestral man as living in vagrant bands, endlessly and unhappily drifting about. Rather, they were as sedentary as they could be and set up housekeeping at one spot for as long as they might. In terms of the economist, our kind has always aimed at minimizing assembly costs. The first principle of settlement geography is that the group chose its living site where water and shelter were at hand, and about which food, fuel, and other primary needs could be collected within a convenient radius. Relocation came when it was apparent that some other spot required less effort, as with seasonal changes in supplies. Consumer goods were brought to the

Human
Organization
of the
Environment:
Adjustments to
Environmental
Uncertainty

hearth and processed there. Women were the keepers of the fire, and there prepared the food and cared for the children. They were the ones most loath to move, the home makers and accumulators of goods. The early hearths recovered by archeology are not casual camps, but fire places used so long and sites so significantly altered as to have withstood the obliterating effects of time. The normal primitive geographic pattern is that of a community, a biologic and social group, clustering about hearths at the points of least transport, holding a collecting territory for its exclusive use, and relocating itself as infrequently as necessary.[1]

The natural resources of the Tehuacan Valley than as now imposed certain constraints on the activities of its inhabitants. The valley receives from 500 to 600 millimeters (19.7 to 23.6 inches) of rainfall during its wet season, which begins sometime in April or May and extends through the summer months. The rest of the year is dry. As a result most of the valley is either arid or semiarid in character. In some places streams bring water from the mountains, but many of these flow only intermittently or during the rainy season. Vegetation has adjusted to these conditions and includes a number of edible species including prickly pear, organ cactus, maguey,[2] and the mesquite tree, a legume which during the rainy season produces edible pods. A large variety of small mammals such as cottontail rabbits, gophers, opossums, and ground squirrels live in the area. Larger game in very early times included antelope and a species of

prehistoric horse which later became extinct. Ten thousand years ago the white-tailed deer and peccary were the largest animals in abundance.

Nature's larder used by early people did not include any domesticated plants or animals. It is hard for us to imagine living under such conditions. But early man all over the world survived for at least 1½ million years before gaining the skills and knowledge which led to domestications. The history of the development of the Tehuacan people is closely tied to their gradual mastery of the plants and animals in their environment. The first signs of plant domestication appeared there about 5000 B.C. In the interval from then until about 200 B.C. a permanent system of irrigated agriculture using numerous species of domesticated and hybrid plants was established. Before 5000 B.C. the people depended entirely upon wild foods. To recapitulate, the plants and animals constituting their diet were adjusted to a subtropical wet-and-dry seasonal cycle: a rainy season from May to September alternating with a cooler and very dry period from October to March. Let us now see how these seasons were paralleled by a changing cycle in the types and quantities of wild foods available to them and how they organized their lives spatially and chronologically to meet such fluctuations. As we continue our description, new elements will be introduced, and the emphasis will gradually shift from wild to domesticated sources of food. Another thing that interests us at this point is the gradual development of connectivity and spatial hierarchies within the resource-utilizing systems described.

[1]Carl Sauer, *Agricultural Origins and Dispersals,* American Geographical Society, New York, 1952. p. 12.
[2]The maguey plant resembles the century plant with which we are more familiar. Its heart, or inner portion, can be chewed as a source of nourishment, but only after it has been treated by roasting to remove its incredibly bitter taste. The early Indians gathered these plants and roasted their edible parts in deep pits lined with stones and heated by some slow-burning wood such as oak. The hearts of the maguey were sealed in the pit, and when removed one to five days later, were ready to be eaten. The fibrous remnants of these roasted maguey hearts were spit out and are one of the most common pieces of "garbage" found by archaeologists today. While the maguey was available throughout the year, it was probably considered less desirable than many other types of food.

From wandering microbands to semipermanent villages

In the period before 6800 B.C. the total population of the valley was small. Perhaps three tiny groups, or microbands, wandered through the area collecting and hunting such available food as their technology permitted. In the rainy season their diet consisted in part of mesquite pods and wild avocado supplemented by small mammals such as the jack-rabbit. Life from June to September was relatively easy, and it is likely that members of the microbands moved about at this time less than any other season of the year. Water was available from numerous sources, and plants and small animals were plentiful. As the year advanced into the dry season, plant foods became less abundant, and seasonal streams and springs went dry. Food supplies near the wet-season camps were depleted, and as the dry fall continued, it became necessary to move the group's hearth to a campsite in an area with a different set of resources. Autumn was the season when larger animals were hunted, but large game was always difficult to catch, and plant foods remained a major part of the diet. As wild horses and eventually white-tailed deer became fewer in number and more wary from seasonal harassment, the people were forced to rely more and more upon the maguey plant to sustain them through a period of near starvation at the end of the dry season. This necessitated moving their hearth for at least a third time during the year to an area where maguey plants could be more easily gathered.

Finally, as the dry season neared an end, various cactus fruits such as prickly pear became ripe and available for food. The first rains of a new seasonal cycle wet the parched earth; green shoots heralded a time of abundance. The microband once again moved back to the area where mesquite, avocados, and other plants and small mammals meant full stomachs and relief from hunger. Thus the band moved through space and through time matching its activities to those places within the total valley environment where plants and animals became seasonally available. One of the strategies adopted by these small groups was to choose locations along steep mountain slopes in order to take advantage of different sets of resources available at different altitudes. The three basic moves necessitated by this relatively simple pattern of existence are shown in Figure 19–1A as a spatial pattern superposed upon a circular calendar of the year. Points represent campsites or hearths,

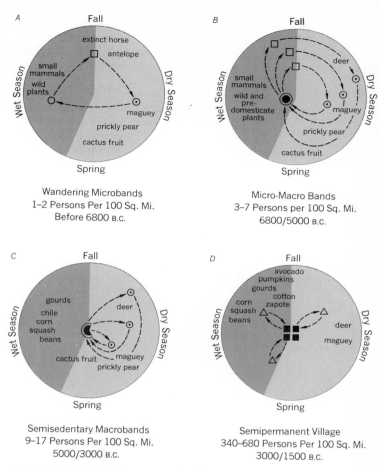

Figure 19-1 **Seasonal movement in the Tehuacan Valley, Mexico.** Archaeological evidence found at ancient campsites has been used to piece together probable movement patterns of these early people. See Figure 19–2 for key to symbols.

and the lines connecting them represent the connectivity of the system. At this stage there was no hierarchical ordering of the space used by the people of Tehuacan. Perhaps the several bands met occasionally by prearrangement or by chance in their wanderings. Perhaps those contacts meant simple trade and friendly exchange; perhaps they were times of hostility. No record of such meetings remains for archaeologists and others to read. And yet the pattern of life within the valley

Human Organization of the Environment: Adjustments to Environmental Uncertainty

357

was slowly changing into new and more complex forms.

In the 1,800 years that followed, slight but significant differences appeared in the resource-using pattern of the Tehuacan people. Plant collecting became more important; certain species like squash, chilies, and ancestral corn may have been gathered and consumed. Analysis of the animal bones dug up from this period indicates that the cottontail rabbit took the place of the jackrabbit as the most important small mammal hunted in the wet season. The people also specialized in hunting the white-tailed deer when the year turned dry. Population had increased about fourfold in the valley. At the same time, the spatial organization of the groups altered somewhat. When food was plentiful in the early part of the wet season, several microbands apparently gathered together in larger, temporary camps. Our knowledge of these early times is scanty and incomplete; but there are strong indications that leadership roles were becoming more specific, at least during the weeks when the microbands came together. There is also some evidence that religion was developing and that part-time shamans engaged in healing ceremonies and other rituals. The space-time chart of this period is shown in Figure 19–1B. Macrobands gathered together in larger campsites during the early rainy season with its abundant food supplies. As the dry season got underway in the fall, the group split into microbands in order to hunt deer and to forage for "starvation foods" like maguey and cactus fruit. The resource system was still dependent upon three or more camps in different localities at different times of the year, but in this case certain hearths had precedence over others as sites for macroband camps. Single-family units probably utilized dry season hearths while extended families or related lineages congregated at spring camps. At that time social organization and interchange increased along with opportunities for group ritual. We can now think of two levels of campsites, with dry-season hearths being subordinate to those of the wet season. It is also likely that some idea of

territoriality, that is, a social group's right to occupy a particular area in order to exploit its resources, came into play at this time.

The years between 5000 and 3000 B.C. saw even more changes. By the end of this period the population of the valley numbered ten times the original. Chilies, squash, corn, beans, and gourds were being cultivated during the rainy season, and domesticated foods constituted about 30 percent of the people's diet. With increased food supplies the smaller microbands could coalesce in the rainy season into semisedentary macrobands, which in the final centuries of this stage lived in village-like clusters of pit houses. However, it was still necessary for the large groups to separate into microbands during the dry season, when they subsisted on deer, maguey plants, and cactus fruit in order to survive until the rains came again the following May. *Incipient agriculture* still acted as only a supplement to the larder of wild foods. During the periods of sedentary life about the larger hearths, new forms of social organization must certainly have developed and leadership and ritual roles must have become more important as larger populations were focused upon such fixed locations. Along with more complex social organization it is likely that the idea of collecting territories and special garden plots developed. Figure 19–1C indicates the annual time span of these semipermanent camps with the complementary scattering of microbands during the dry season. From a spatial viewpoint the wet-season hearths were becoming more and more dominant compared with the dry-season camps, which had scarcely changed from previous times.

The next 1,500 years until 1500 B.C. saw the establishment of full-time agriculture, growing among other domesticated plants hybrid corn, beans, squash, chilies, avocados, pumpkins, and cotton. The population of the valley had increased by then to some forty times the original. We should not think, however, that life was easy by our standards or that domesticated foods had become a major resource. Subsidiary camps were occupied during the dry season for hunting and at other times for planting supplementary crops. The focus of life was a small number of semipermanent or perhaps year-round villages located on terraces near the larger streams. Again we may imagine that the life focused on those more or less permanent settlements included new social forms.

In speculating about the meaning of archaeological evidence, we must always keep in mind how incomplete the record probably is. Nevertheless, the smaller number of settlement sites identifiable for this period can be taken as an indication of a significant change in the settlement pattern. (The frequency of sites in association with other variables is shown in Figure 19–2). As the Indians' ability to support themselves increased, it allowed them to reorganize their lives for greater convenience and intensified social interaction. The spatial expression of such reorganization was a contracting of the scattered population about better locations. This phase, which ended about 1500 B.C., is the last one represented by the time-space diagram in Figure 19–1D. Thereafter, populations were more or less permanently fixed at one location throughout the year.

Permanent settlement hierarchies

In the Tehuacan Valley following 1500 B.C., the number of settlement sites again increased. Such an increase represents the prospering of a larger and more sedentary population. Full-time agriculture which utilized more productive hybrid plants and increasing amounts of irrigation stabilized the population at fixed locations through the annual cycle of climatic events. Improved agricultural technology, which was responsible for this stabilization, can be viewed as ways of rearranging resources in time and space. For example, the availability of water, which normally was found only in a few streams after the rains stopped, was extended in time by storing runoff behind dams and was relocated in space by leading it in canals to distant fields. Soil nutrients and solar energy made available to humans by plants became more accessible

through the efficient production and storage of surplus crops. Even the development of markets and marketing affected the use of resources. As systems of exchange and barter developed in the valley—just as they have done elsewhere in the world at earlier and later times—resources were not only redistributed in space but also redistributed among different groups within the total society. Thus, the period of permanent settlement that the Tehuacan people entered into was very different from the thousands of years of wandering and near-starvation from which they emerged. Additional resources in greater quantities became available to them. In the same way, new spatial and temporal arrangements of those resources and the communities which consumed them appeared with an increasing tempo.

By 3,000 years ago a rich religious life had begun to develop. Priests and chiefs attained more and more power. Artisans learned to make new styles of pottery, and trade or some kind of cultural exchange with areas beyond the valley occurred with greater frequency. The growth of these interregional contacts is inferred from similarities of design and decoration found in many parts of Meso-America including the Tehuacan Valley.

In the years between 900 and 200 B.C. the people became full-time farmers living in small villages which were in turn the satellites of larger settlements containing central religious structures. At first these ceremonial centers were little more than large villages, but change continued after 200 B.C. By A.D. 700 these same settlements had become elaborate hilltop sites with a variety of streets, plazas, courts, and pyramids. New crops were added to the growing list of domesticates: among them peanuts, lima beans, and tomatoes. Irrigation systems were becoming larger and more complex and undoubtedly required managers and engineers. Just who these specialists and administrators were is not certain, but priest-kings may have filled the highest positions. More and more similarities appeared between the valley and other sites in Mexico, indicating increased contacts with the outside.

Human Organization of the Environment: Adjustments to Environmental Uncertainty

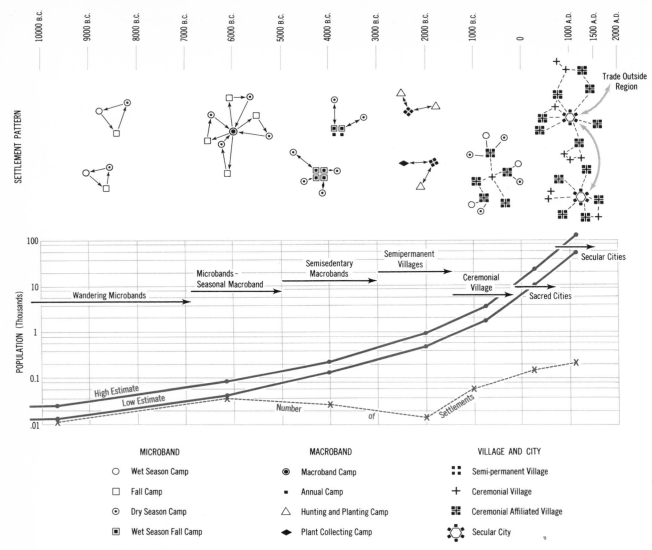

SETTLEMENT PATTERN

10000 B.C. 9000 B.C. 8000 B.C. 7000 B.C. 6000 B.C. 5000 B.C. 4000 B.C. 3000 B.C. 2000 B.C. 1000 B.C. 0 1000 A.D. 1500 A.D. 2000 A.D.

Trade Outside Region

POPULATION (Thousands)

100

10

1

0.1

.01

Wandering Microbands

Microbands – Seasonal Macroband

Semisedentary Macrobands

Semipermanent Villages

Ceremonial Village

Sacred Cities

Secular Cities

High Estimate

Low Estimate

Number of Settlements

MICROBAND		MACROBAND		VILLAGE AND CITY	
○	Wet Season Camp	◉	Macroband Camp	∷	Semi-permanent Village
□	Fall Camp	▪	Annual Camp	+	Ceremonial Village
⊙	Dry Season Camp	△	Hunting and Planting Camp	⊞	Ceremonial Affiliated Village
▣	Wet Season Fall Camp	◆	Plant Collecting Camp	⬡	Secular City

Figure 19-2 Rise of civilization in the Tehuacan Valley, Mexico The migratory habits, population density settlement pattern, and social interaction were all functions of the improved reliability of food supplies that accompanied domestication of plants and animals.

Finally, in the seven centuries before the arrival of the Spaniards, an elaborate system of secular cities, ceremonial centers, villages, and camps or hamlets grew up. Urban centers and the lesser settlements which focused

upon them apparently constituted the realms of minor kings. Only about 15 percent of the people's diet came from wild sources, and industries producing cotton textiles and salt for trade outside the region added to the general prosperity. Much remains to be learned from the records of the Spanish regarding what they found within the valley, and much more remains to be learned through archaeological methods. Nevertheless, the society lacked a detailed written record of its own, and after A.D. 1500 more of the Indian culture was destroyed than preserved by the conquering Europeans.

If we cast back over the 12,000 years encompassing this story of development and seek the geographic features contained therein, we will plot patterns of increasing complexity. Of primary importance to geographers is how the organization of space offered a variety of solutions to environmental problems of resource use. A major element of this organization was the development of a hierarchically ordered group of settlements with a few large cities, more middle-sized towns, and numerous villages and hamlets.

Strategies for Adjustment to Environmental Uncertainty

The above reconstruction of the life and times of the Tehuacan Indians emphasizes the increasingly complex use of space by their society. Embedded within their major solution of environmental problems through spatial organization are a number of other strategies needing further explanation. Rather than repeat their story in great detail, let us present a more systematic review of some of those devices. We will also mention examples from other systems and other cultures and times.

To do this we will refer to the idea of *operators*, that is, routines, techniques, or devices which act to maintain or change conditions within a given system. Let us examine some scale operators, time operators, and site operators.

Scale operators

As with any scale-oriented problem, we must choose the size of the area within which we plan to work. In this case, it is not convenient to divide up the continuum of reality into a great many levels or scales. Instead we can talk of local and global environmental hazards and of the *local* and *global operators* by means of which farmers and others can survive them.

Local operators   Local hazards are those which occur either at points or along lines throughout the environment. The path of a tornado is linear at a regional scale. Actually its swath of destruction can be hundreds of feet wide, but this strip of area reduces to a line in terms of an entire region. This nonareal aspect also would be true of a well which goes dry or of house fires, explosions, and acts of violence, to name a few point-type hazards. In modern cities individual robberies and car crashes can be considered local events.

There are two strategies by which local hazards can be overcome. The first is the *sharing of risk* by a group, the larger the better. Thus, most tribal groups maintain elaborate rituals for dividing up and sharing throughout the community the food found or killed by every single person. In this way, a hunter with a run of bad luck and still count on the food provided by others until his luck changes and he, in turn, must share his kill. It is likely that the early bands of Paleo-Indians in the New World had such arrangements to ensure group survival. In modern society, insurance, family ties, and community obligations help to offset local disasters. Insurance is a good case in point. Many people buy fire and theft insurance with the expectation that only a relative few of the purchasers will need to use it. By paying a small amount we are thus insured in the event of a much larger loss. It is also possible to buy tornado insurance, since when a tornado strikes, only relatively few people are killed or ruined along its path, while the population over a much wider area who feel threatened by the possibility of experiencing a tornado help through their insurance payments to offset the damage. On the other hand, hurricane insurance is not available. This is because hurricanes cover broad areas and affect almost everyone in a community. In that case everyone needs help, not just a few, as with tornadoes.

A hurricane viewed from space. Hurricanes may contain destructive high winds 50 to 100 miles distant from their centers and, when they move on-shore, may damage an area extending over several states. Strategies useful for counteracting local hazards are not effective in such circumstances. In the United States one response is to declare a national disaster area. In this way restorative energies of the entire nation may be brought to bear on the problem. The social/political institution is enlarged to match the scale of the natural phenomena. International relief agencies may offer similar aid to smaller nations in which the storm may be as big as the whole country. (Photograph by NASA from Apollo 7)

The second strategy used against local hazards is *spreading the risk*. In this case, a subsistence-level farmer may own several fields scattered across a wide area. Local occurrences of wind, hail, or insect damage may wipe out part of his harvest, but with luck most of his crops will go unscathed. Again, we do not know enough about Tehuacan society to speak with confidence about their pattern of field distribution, but if other, modern village systems are any indication, there, as elsewhere, fields were scattered for greater security. In another example, the Amish people of North America do not buy tornado or fire insurance on sale to the general public. This is part of their belief in removing themselves from the world at large. However, Amish communities all over the United States will come to the aid of each other in the event of disasters. This private tithing and the donation of food, supplies, money, and labor by widely scattered people ensures the well-being of the group as a whole.

Global operators Hazards that cover entire regions present a different kind of problem for the people involved. It is generally impossible to avoid a drought by having two fields a short distance apart, particularly if rainfall fails across an area as large as southern India or the American Midwest. Another way to imagine global hazards is that they extend beyond the range or effective limits of the social institutions of the system involved. The strategy here is to *discriminate* among minor variations in the macroenvironment. For example, there are areas of higher winter temperatures and milder summers on the lee side of lakes. This results from the greater insulating quality of water and the downwind drift of the air from above the water body. Freezing temperatures are less likely to occur under these conditions, and it is common to find localized areas specializing in apples, berries, flowers, and other frost-sensitive crops in these situations. The eastern shore of Lake Michigan is a good case in point. Another famous example is the vineyards of France. French grape growers rec-

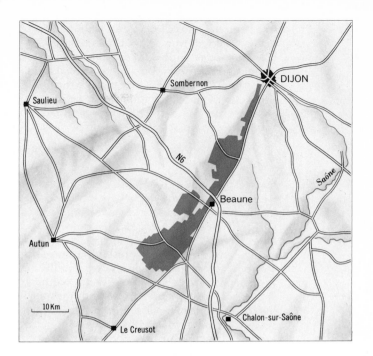

Figure 19-3 Vineyards of Burgundy The best wines of France are produced from grapes grown on small fields possessing a combination of soil, climate, slope, and other conditions which have proved optimum for the purpose. Such areas are known as *climat*. In Burgundy, for example, they occur in narrow bands along hill flanks called *côtes*.

ognize tiny areas with exactly the right conditions suitable for the best grapes which will produce wines near perfection. Such areas are known as *climat* and occur as a precious string of fields along the hill flanks of Burgundy, the Rhone Valley, and in parts of the Bordeaux region (Figure 19–3). The hazard there takes many forms: unsuitable soils, improper soil moisture, too much or too little sun, and dozens of other things. The strategy is to find the best spot and to lavish care and protection upon it. Thus, to return to the Tehuacan example, by the time sedentary agriculture was well established, trial and error had shown the farmers which fields within the generally dry valley retained soil moisture longest. They had also learned to concentrate their efforts upon a relatively

Human Organization of the Environment: Adjustments to Environmental Uncertainty

small group of reliable and durable food plants selected from a much larger number of wild species. In this latter, nondimensional sense domestication became a special kind of discrimination and selection which ensured the food supply of those people. In other words, the system involved deviation-amplifying processes.

Time operators

Just as space can be organized to ensure group welfare, so can time-dependent processes be manipulated for the commonweal. *Storage* of all kinds clearly illustrates this concept. We have already spoken of *food processing* and storage and their role in preserving nutrients and energy for periods of low availability in the annual cycle. In a similar vein, we have spoken of preserving, storing, and transporting foods as one of the linchpins holding urban society together in city locations. But other kinds of storage are equally important. The damming of streams and ponding of water is really nothing more than holding back the flow for use later in time. Certainly, this technique ensured the farmers of Tehuacan larger harvests and more predictable results.

Another technique useful in temporal events is the seasonal or cyclic adjustment of activities. For example, the farmers of the Flint Hills in Kansas sell their herds before the late summer drought comes on. Wheat farmers in the drier parts of the West will "roll with the punch" in dry years and simply write off their crop as a loss early in the season rather than pour good money after bad by attempting to harvest a submarginal crop. The early hunters and gatherers of Mexico also matched the intensity of their activities to the resources available in their environment when their macrobands broke up into smaller units during the dry season. Still another time adjustment that can be made is to compress the time during which certain activities take place. This requires the concentrated effort of everyone involved, but it often pays off in better results. It is a common sight to see harvest work continuing day and night in order to avoid the

onslaught of autumn rains. This can be the case whether the farm is a modern one and the work is done under floodlights or a traditional one where only the flickering light of lanterns helps the laborers. During other seasons other kinds of insurance also exist. If the coming of the rainy season is uncertain, the farmers cannot tell if the first or second rain may also be the last. To counter this, a few seeds may be planted with each rainfall, although some may not survive because of premature germination before adequate soil moisture builds up to see the crop through. On the other hand, the first rains may be the most important, and if they are, some crop is assured.

An example of a way in which the same field and the same time period can serve several purposes takes place during the transition from a subsistence- to market-oriented farm system. Typical of this are the modernizing farmers of southern Turkey who at the present time are changing from an age-old pattern of goat herds and grain fields meant for local consumption to citrus orchards supplying major Turkish and European cities. It takes an orange tree four to six years to grow large enough to produce a profitable crop. If the ordinary farmer had to wait that long for an income, he would starve. But citrus seedlings are interplanted between rows of maize or wheat, and for the first few years both species grow side by side until just as the young trees are large enough to begin shading out the grain crop, the first oranges can be picked and shipped to market.

Site operators

Some survival strategies involve not so much scale differences or the timing of events as they do taking advantage of the special *in-place* characteristics of a given site or creating special conditions at certain spots. For example, in some farm systems *intercropping* is practiced, where different species of crops are grown together. A famous example of this originated in Mexico. There, maize and beans were grown in the same plots. The beans helped fix nitrogen in the soil for the corn, while the corn provided poles, as it were, for the beans to climb upon. But the mutual effectiveness of the two plants did not end with that. *Zein*, the principle protein in corn, in order to form a complete protein suitable for human needs, requires the amino acid *lysine*, which is supplied by beans. Thus, the combination serves not only plants but man as well. It is unlikely that this combination is the result of coincidence. Thousands of years passed during the domestication of these plants, and that time span provided ample opportunity for many plants to be tried and rejected before an adequate dietary combination was found. In any event, this is typical of strategies for human survival where the key is manipulating the elements at the site of operations.

Another reason for mixing the number of species in a garden is the disease control offered by isolating individual plants from others of the same kind by scattering them among unrelated species. The spread of disease through homogeneous stands of vegetation is well known to those American communities which have lost all their shade trees because of Dutch elm disease. The American chestnut was another victim of disease which wiped out the homogeneous groves formed by that species.

Perhaps the most effective site strategy employed by traditional farmers is to seek out multiple environments on steep gradients. On a local scale this can simply mean taking advantage of differences in soil moisture and soil types from the top to the bottom of a hill. But more important are those farmers and herders who utilize entire mountain slopes in their activities. In southern Turkey nomads traditionally wintered in the Mediterranean lowlands near the sea. Then, as summer came on with high temperatures and endemic malaria, they packed their tents and moved in easy stages to high summer pastures with plentiful grass, pure water, and cool temperatures which discouraged mosquitoes. In the same area, seminomadic dirt farmers still occupy villages on the coastal lowland as well as others high in the mountains (Figure 19–4). Winter is spent down below in relative

warmth where early spring crops can be planted or where winter wheat grows throughout the rainy season. Again, as summer conditions make the lower elevations inhospitably hot, entire villages pack up and retreat to fields at heights where lower temperatures prevail. Sometimes even more than one supplemental village is occupied for short periods en route. The overall system has many advantages: summer diseases are avoided; two or three planting and harvest periods can be spaced out instead of one, thus making more labor available; and if crops fail at one elevation, others lower or higher on the mountain can stave off hunger. The similar use of multiple sites in the Tehuacan Valley is an obvious feature of that place.

Counter to the above examples are the homogeneous sites sought by modern farmers using large machines which cannot easily compensate for local variations in vegetation, topography, soil type, and other environmental features. In this case fields with only one kind of crop must be planted. To protect these homogeneous plant communities from epidemics of disease and insects, poisons and medicines must be applied in profusion. High yields are the result, but once a disease does break loose, often the only solution is to abandon one site and to move the entire operation to another location. The spread of Panama disease and the abandonment of the banana plantations of the Caribbean have already been mentioned.

Other Strategies: Magic and *The Farmer's Almanac*

In an earlier discussion concerning the location of the point of minimum aggregate travel, we pointed out that large areas can exist on a transporation cost surface which are either flat or nearly so and that it becomes difficult or impossible to distinguish an absolute optimum point. Hunting and gathering, farming and herding, the day-to-day business of all our lives, present similar situations. In other words, the best strategies people can devise may still leave them with unresolved

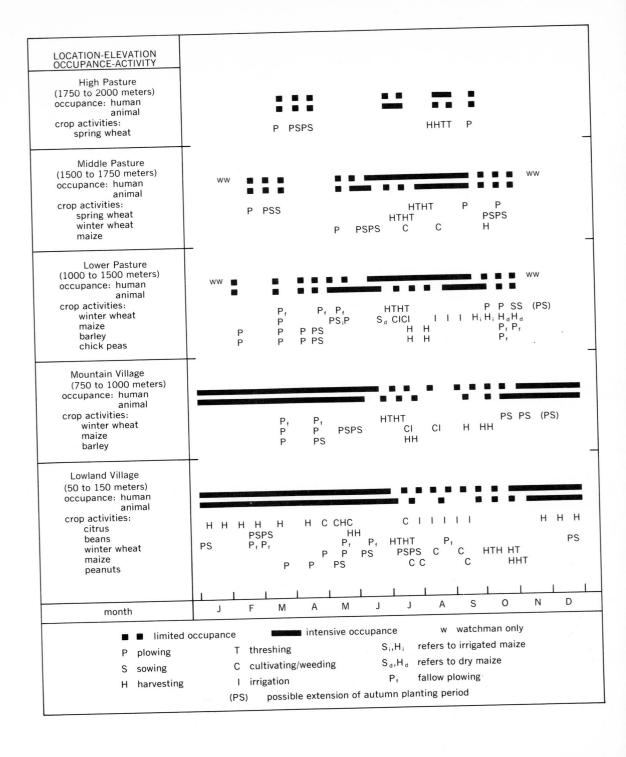

LOCATION-ELEVATION OCCUPANCE-ACTIVITY	month
	J F M A M J J A S O N D

High Pasture
(1750 to 2000 meters)
occupance: human
            animal
crop activities:
  spring wheat
              P PSPS   HHTT P

Middle Pasture
(1500 to 1750 meters)
occupance: human
            animal
crop activities:
  spring wheat
  winter wheat
  maize
  ww   ww
          P PSS   HTHT   P   P
                        HTHT   PSPS
         P PSPS C   C   H

Lower Pasture
(1000 to 1500 meters)
occupance: human
            animal
crop activities:
  winter wheat
  maize
  barley
  chick peas
  ww   ww
           P$_f$ P$_f$ P$_f$ HTHT   P P SS (PS)
           P   PS$_i$P S$_d$ CICI I I I H$_i$ H$_i$ H$_d$H$_d$
    P   P   P PS   H H   P$_f$ P$_f$
    P   P   P PS   H H   P$_f$

Mountain Village
(750 to 1000 meters)
occupance: human
            animal
crop activities:
  winter wheat
  maize
  barley
          P$_f$ P$_f$ HTHT   PS PS (PS)
          P   P   PSPS   CI   CI   H HH
          P   PS   HH

Lowland Village
(50 to 150 meters)
occupance: human
            animal
crop activities:
  citrus
  beans
  winter wheat
  maize
  peanuts
  H H H H   H   H C CHC   C I I I I I   H H H
          PSPS   HH   PS
  PS   P$_f$ P$_f$ P$_f$ P$_f$ HTHT   P$_f$
                    P   P   PS PSPS C   C   HTH HT
            P   P   PS   C C   C   HHT

■ ■ limited occupance	▬▬▬ intensive occupance	w watchman only
P plowing	T threshing	S_i, H_i refers to irrigated maize
S sowing	C cultivating/weeding	S_d, H_d refers to dry maize
H harvesting	I irrigation	P$_f$ fallow plowing
	(PS) possible extension of autumn planting period	

conflicts and decisions. It is at this point that magic, astrology, *The Farmer's Almanac*, and other such devices become useful extensions of rational thought. The seasons do not wait for any man, and indecision may be disastrous. Action, any action, is usually better than none at all. Let us illustrate this with two widely separated examples.

The Naskapi Indians of northern Labrador occupy one of the most difficult environments of North America. They are hunters and gatherers who live in camps which are moved from time to time as the availability of game dictates. Like all other hunters, they possess a large store of knowledge about the animals they seek and about the local habitat and act upon such information in a rational manner. But when game becomes scarce and the vast and bitter landscape offers no clues to the whereabouts of animals, they must nevertheless continue their endless search for food. Now if the hunters always searched in areas where they had most recently been successful, they would soon "overhunt" the game and sensitize it to the point where the animals would hide or run away. It is, therefore, useful for the Naskapi to introduce an element of randomness into their search patterns.

Psychological experiments indicate that it is nearly impossible for humans to act in a purposefully random manner without the aid of some randomizing device. The Naskapi are able to introduce randomness into their hunting patterns by the use of magic. They take the shoulder bone of a caribou and hold it in a forked stick over a low fire. Cracks, checks, and charred spots appear on the bone in a random fashion. The bone is then oriented to the landscape according to another ritual, and the pattern on it is read for the where-abouts of game much as we would read a map. Since the Indians change camps frequently, the randomness of the orientation is further assured. The end result is that the search trips of the Naskapi hunters are varied enough to cover the entire territory and at the same time lack repetition which might drive away needed game.

Divination of all kinds is so similar to modern *games of chance* that sometimes the instrument used can be the same: flipping a coin is a good example. Somewhat different are *games of strategy*, which either are nonrandom in character or which introduce random elements for clearly understood reasons. Before discussing *games against nature* in the next and last section of this chapter, let us consider a modern example of the successful use of nonrational or magical strategies in agriculture.

Tomato farmers in the modern southern United States face an interesting problem each year. They can take advantage of warmer annual temperatures and easily beat Northern farmers to the market with their produce. The earlier their tomatoes are harvested and shipped, the higher the price they will command in Northern cities. Meanwhile, farmers outside the South are also trying to get their plants into the ground and their produce to market as early as possible. Transportation costs on these perishable vegetables are such that when summer blankets the entire country, locally grown Northern tomatoes force Southern tomatoes out of the Northern markets. Thus, tomato farmers must decide upon the earliest possible date that they can plant their tomato seedlings and still avoid possible killing frosts. This is true for Southern as well as Northern farmers, although the chances

Figure 19-4 The seasonal cycle of agricultural activities and occupance patterns as practiced in two seminomadic villages Traditional societies use complex strategies in dealing with the environment. On the Mediterranean coast of Turkey, seminomadic peasant farmers use seasonal variations in conditions on the mountain slopes to optimize their return on labor. (J. F. Kolars, *Tradition, Season, and Change in a Turkish Village*, Research Paper No. 82, Dept. of Geography, University of Chicago, Chicago, Ill., 1963, fig. 14)

of late frosts are considerably less in the South. Tomato growers use three means of predicting the best time to plant. They rely upon their own knowledge of their local environments accumulated from years of experience. This serves them well but leaves them uncertain about global events such as major cold waves originating outside their immediate ken. To anticipate these potential disasters they turn to National Weather Service reports and long-range weather forecasting. But the science of forecasting the weather is still in its infancy, besides which the scale upon which those predictions are made is so gross that the Weather Service's prognostications often do not serve the needs of a particular farmer using a field with a specific microclimate.

At this point the farmer may hit a plateau-like area of knowledge. He can tell that spring is well on its way; he "feels" that the time to plant has come; but no additional amount of rational effort can tell him if the odds are right for him to gamble. Just exactly when is the best day, late enough in the season to be reasonably safe, early enough to beat everyone else to market? What a quandary! It is at this point that many a farmer, frustrated by indecision, turns to that age-old friend *The Farmer's Almanac.* Many different editions of these books exist, and while they contain useful information based on fact, they also give advice on the exact days to plant and other things, all of which, quite frankly, are the creation of the editors' lively imaginations. The advice is not wildly foolish but no better and no worse than any knowledgeable farmer's. However, the air of authority surrounding the *Almanac* is such that the advice is followed when other, more rational, sources of information are inadequate. Action is taken; the crop is planted; most often with a little luck the farmer gains some degree of success and the *Almanac* is vindicated. While the *Almanac* may seem a trick to trap the gullible, actually its function is a good one in a magical sense. It has helped the farmer move off dead center and given him that little additional bit of confidence that everyone needs when

the going gets rough. In this fashion, some of the old folkways of doing things can be effective even in modern times. Now let us consider a more rational attempt to understand nature and its uncertainties and to act accordingly.

Games against Nature

The environment seldom offers a single strategy to the people who depend upon it for survival. Even within the limits of one level of technology there are usually alternative paths of action open to individuals or groups. In their efforts to make rational decisions—and as we have already pointed out, even magic can have its rationale—people engage in activities which have strong counterparts in the *theory of games.* On one side may be an agricultural village, a tribe of hunters, or a large commercial farm; on the other are ranged the forces of an insensate but effective natural environment. (A game of this type, in which only one bona fide player participates, is called a *game against nature.*) Although we must emphasize the lack of consciousness or will in nature, the two may be thought of as players making move and countermove, with the environment presenting a complex and often bewildering array of events to which the human participants respond. Because human knowledge of the environment is always incomplete, and because our predictive ability is often limited where nature is concerned, every farmer anticipates his share of defeat. On the other hand, every producer tries very hard to select the combination of activities which will maximize his returns and minimize his losses as he defines them in terms of his cultural preferences. *Minimaxing* of this sort is a key function of games played against nature.

In applying the theory of games to man-environment systems we make one assumption that varies from reality, and that is that we consider the player called the *environment* to have the same values and motivations as its human opponent. Another way of putting this is that game theory assumes that nature will always do its worst, a point we will return to at the end of this section. In the application of game theory that follows we should also remember that the human participants did not use the analytical methods we employ. They decided upon their strategy through trial and error as well as logical thought applied over many years. Our analysis simply tests the efficiency of their decisions in terms of minimaxing behavior.

The south shore of Jamaica supports a number of fishing villages. One such settlement provides us with an opportunity to apply a game theory interpretation to a human ecosystem. Fishing grounds along that coast extend outward to the 100-fathom line, about 22 miles from shore. The fishing village to which we refer is a small one. About 200 men, women, and children depend upon 94 fishermen to provide a living from approximately 168 square miles of ocean. The fishermen are divided among 26 boats, each captained by its owner. From these boats, fishing pots are set out according to each captain's judgment of the weather, the tides, the configuration of the fishing grounds, the market demand for fish, and the actions of the other fishermen.

The configuration of the fishing grounds is an extremely important factor, for the grounds offer two choices of location. There are *inside fishing grounds* which extend from the shore outward anywhere from 5 to 15 miles. *Outside fishing grounds* make up everything beyond the outer limits of the inner zone out to the 100-fathom line. The outside grounds offer bigger catches of larger fish which command higher market prices. The danger of the oustide areas is that strong, unpredictable currents sweep across them apparently at random. Fishing pots are frequently lost to the currents, the presence of which also requires better, more expensive, and seaworthy canoes for the trip out and back. The inner fishing grounds, on the other hand, are safer, are nearer the village, and have no dangerous currents, all of which means that far fewer pots are lost and that expenses are less. The disadvantage of the inside is that fish are scarcer, smaller, and of poorer quality than those caught on the outside.

The two kinds of fishing environments offer the fishermen three possible strategies for setting their fishing pots. They can always use only the outside grounds, gambling that the currents will run so infrequently that their losses will be offset by larger and better catches. They can always remain on the inside grounds, safe from damaging currents but collecting smaller catches of less valuable fish. They can also form some sort of in-out strategy, placing some pots inside for security and the remainder outside in anticipation of calm seas and exceptional catches.

No one in the village actually uses the first, full-time outside strategy. But it is possible to estimate what the average income from such a plan would be for the days when the currents are running as well as those days when they are not. Field observations also provide us with fairly accurate income figures for the same current–no-current days in terms of fishermen choosing the inside and in-out strategies. We can arrange these data in matrix form, as shown in Table 19–1.

In the terminology of game theory, Table 19–1 represents a two-person–three-strategy, zero sum game offering three different strategies to the fishing village and two to the environment. By *zero sum game* we mean one in which what one player loses the other player gains, with no net increase in the value of the system. Although we know from empirical observation that no one exclusively

Table 19-1 Jamaican Fishing Payoff Matrix

Village Strategy	Environmental Strategy	
	Current	No current
Inside	£17.3	£11.5
In-out	5.2	17.0
Outside	−4.4	20.6

[3]W. Davenport, "Jamaican Fishing: A Game Theory Analysis," *Yale University Publications in Anthropology*, vol. 59, 1961, pp. 3–11.

Human Organization of the Environment: Adjustments to Environmental Uncertainty

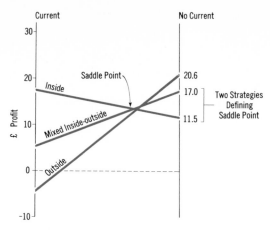

Figure 19-5 Three strategies against two states of nature—Jamaican fishing example (Based on data from W. Davenport, "Jamaican Fishing: A Game Theory Analysis," *Yale University Publications in Anthropology*, vol. 59, 1960, pp. 3–11).

most set of lines (Figure 19–5) represents the minimax (that is, the minimum value of the maximum range of values), and the two lines which define this by their crossing represent the two best strategies. In this case, inside–in-out strategies are better than the other two possible pairs. The example shows only three lines representing three strategies, but any number could be used and reduced to just two as long as the other player's strategies were limited to two to begin with.

The next question is, of the 26 fishing boats, how many ply only inside waters and how many work both in and out? This is solved (Table 19–2) according to game theory techniques by subtracting one element in each row from the other in the same row, disregarding the absolute value (plus or minus), assigning the result to the other row in the 2×2 matrix, and figuring the percentage of the whole that is represented. In this case we find that 67 percent of the boats will fish inside and 33 percent will seek an in-out strategy. In other words, 17 and 9 captains should pilot their canoes to those respective locations. When we compare this predicted figure with what was really done during the period of field observation, we find that 18 canoes, or 69 percent, fished inside.

We have not exhausted the possible manipulations which game theory allows, but the game against nature which the Jamaican fishermen play with the sea serves to illustrate some further points. First, knowing that we can find optimal solutions raises as many questions as it answers. For example, should

uses the outside, game theory allows us to predict the same thing. Thus, we can eliminate one of the village's strategies, thereby reducing the contest to a 2×2 matrix: two players, each with two strategies.

This elimination can be accomplished either by taking every two pairs of strategies and solving them for the maximum payoff to the fishermen or, as Peter Gould suggests, by using a simple graphic method. We can draw two columns representing the two alternatives of nature: current–no-current. Both columns can be calibrated in terms of the values of the alternative strategies of the fishermen. The saddle point or lowest point on the upper-

Table 19–2   Solution of a Two × Two Payoff Matrix

	Current	*No Current*		
Inside	17.3	11.5	$17.3 - 11.5 = 5.8$	$\dfrac{11.8}{5.8 + 11.8} = 67\%$
Inside/outside	5.2	17.0	$17.0 - 5.2 = 11.8$	$\dfrac{5.8}{5.8 + 11.8} = 33\%$

a single fisherman, rather than the group, go outside one-third of the time and inside two-thirds, or should he put one-third of his pots outside at all times? Since these fishermen from a "developing" economy apparently act in a rational fashion in order to maximize income and minimize risk, does this mean that the rational use of space will lead different cultures to similar spatial strategies?

Furthermore, if we turn to game theory for help, we must recognize that such techniques embody assumptions which are pessimistic; that is, they assume that nature will do its worst. We mentioned this point previously and return to it again because of some very fundamental questions it raises about man's role in the natural world. For example, should we consider nature as cruel, indifferent, kind, or impersonal? And how do the attitudes we hold toward nature influence our use of the earth? We have shown in this chapter that man can choose many different strategies for survival. The next chapter considers human perceptions, attitudes, values, and philosophies and how they affect our actions and policies toward the use of resources.

20 | RESOURCES AS CULTURAL APPRAISALS: MAN'S CHANGING WORLD VIEW

The games against nature with which we closed the last chapter assumed that nature would do its worst. But even the phrase "do its worst" implies a kind of consciousness, a humanizing of the environment into something with which we can deal as an individual. How do such attitudes affect our view of resources? We have already commented on the role played by perception in human affairs. For example, the transformation of the "Great American Desert" of the mid-nineteenth century into the "Great American Breadbasket" of the twentieth was a matter of how emigrant farmers interpreted the treeless steppelands of the Great Plains.

Even more complex and subtle than those farmers' views of the environment are the philosophies which provide a basis for all our interpretations of nature. This chapter deals with some of the attempts to explain individual and group behavior with respect to the natural environment. We also look at the role played by perception and attitude in the management of resources. In other words, we view natural resources as cultural appraisals.

Approaches to the Study of Man and Nature

In considering the various interactions between man and his natural environment, we are really referring to two types of studies. The first treats *homo sapiens* as a creature living in a physical environment which satisfies his biological needs and imposes physical limitations on his health and well-being. This type of study tells us such things as how many quarts of water are needed per person per day at certain temperatures, or the manner in which high elevations affect the human body and mind. All such investigations can be grouped under the heading *human ecology*, that is, the biological considerations of man-environment systems. These studies consider human reactions in the same manner as they treat the reactions of all other animals found in ecosystems. However, in considering human use of the earth it becomes difficult to distinguish the purely physical environment from the social one. Therefore, more complex, but to most geographers more interesting, is the study of man-environment systems from the viewpoint of *cultural ecology*. This considers human ecosystems in which man is no longer a simple animal, but rather a carrier of culture with its accumulation of tools, techniques, beliefs, and prejudices.

Our view of the man-environment relationship is similar to that of Harold and Margaret Sprout:

So far as we can determine, environmental fac-

tors (both non-human and social) can effect human activities in only two ways. Such factors can be perceived, reacted to, and taken into account by the human individual or individuals under consideration. In this way, and in this way only, environmental factors can be said to "influence," or to "condition," or otherwise to "affect" human values and preferences, moods and attitudes, choices and decisions. On the other hand, the relation of environmental factors to performance and accomplishment (that is, to the operational outcomes or results of decisions and undertakings) may present an additional dimension. In the latter context, environmental factors may be conceived as a sort of matrix, or encompassing channel, metaphorically speaking, which limits the execution of undertakings. Such limitations on performance, accomplishment, outcome, or operational result may not—often do not—derive from or depend upon the environed individual's perception or other psychological behavior. In many instances, environmental limitations on outcome or performance may be effective even though the limiting factors were not perceived and reacted to in the process of reaching a decision and initiating a course of action.[1]

In other words, the way we feel, whether we are optimistic or pessimistic, energetic and industrious or lazy and slothful, deceitful or honest, *does not derive* from the type of natural environment in which we live. On the other hand, our crops may fail, our bodies may deteriorate, we may starve or grow fat according to our ability to cope with conditions in the natural environment which surrounds us. Furthermore, we need not always know the forces and events coming our way in order subsequently to be affected by them.

Nonenvironmental deterministic theories of human behavior

In all attempts to explain human behavior one or more modes of thought are always ap-

[1]Harold Sprout and Margaret Sprout, *The Ecological Perspective on Human Affairs with Special Reference to International Politics*, Princeton, Princeton, N.J., 1965, p. 11.

parent. The first can be described as *deterministic*. This means "simply that all empirical phenomena of the system under consideration (be it mechanical, biological, or social system) can be predicted by reference to some set of causal laws." Let us first consider some common patterns of nonenvironmental deterministic thought which attempt to explain human behavior. Among these, racial determinism is most prevalent. Thus the idea states that heredity determines all major modes of behavior and that some groups of people sharing a common genetic inheritance will be either superior or inferior to other groups with different genetic legacies. Contrary to uninformed belief there is no evidence that the genetic inheritance of a group of people determines the average intelligence of the group.

We further agree with the recent statement of the American Association of Anthropologists adopted at their 1971 annual meeting that "there is no scientific warrant for ascribing to genetic factors the oppressed conditions of classes and ethnic groups."

Another nonenvironmental type of determinism centers upon the concept of *economic man* and *economic determinism*. This concept views all human activities in terms of profit maximization. No longer taken seriously in its purest form, economic determinism assumes that each person has perfect knowledge and perfect reasoning ability and that everyone acts to earn the highest possible return on his investment of the money, energy, time, and materials available to him. The overly simple notion of economic man has generally been rejected, for while profit maximization seems logical, no one can claim to know everything essential in order to make a completely rational economic decision. Moreover, many people, if not the great majority, will pass up profit in order to attain other kinds of satisfaction. One brief example of this is mountain rescue teams, which are composed almost always of unpaid volunteers. Very few people would tolerate the danger and discomfort of mountain rescue missions if an hourly wage, no matter how much, were attached to such work. Behavior of this kind allows us to substitute the concept of *satisficing man* for economic man. In doing so, however, we introduce so many psychological variables into the picture that simple cause-and-effect relationships become obscured. It is reasonable to say that humans always perceive a limited range of economic possibilities and will often make their selections or choices of activity so as to satisfy their total needs rather than simply to maximize their incomes.

Environmental determinism

Environmental determinism has always been, and remains, a popular explanation of human behavior. We have already given a general definition of deterministic thought. In the present case, the basic idea is that human behavior and human attitudes can be predicted by referring to the characteristics of the natural environment in which the participants are living. Examples of environmental determinism are available from all periods of history.

About 420 B.C. Hippocrates wrote, "The inhabitants of the colder countries are brave but deficient in thought and technical skill and as a consequence of this they remain free longer than others but are wanting in political organization and unable to rule their neighbors. The peoples of Asia on the contrary are thoughtful and skillful but without spirit, whence their permanent condition is one of subjection and slavery." We scarcely need to point out that our Greek philosopher has bracketed his own land and people, the implication being that Greeks are skillful and thoughtful but also freedom loving and quite capable of ruling their neighbors.

Nearly 24 centuries later the French philosopher Soulavie commented, "The inhabitants of basaltic regions are difficult to govern, prone to insurrection, and irreligious." At about the same time, the pithy statement "Basalt is conducive to piety" was published in Germany. These two statements suggest that a person's religious attitudes are in part the result of the rock underlying the place where he lives. The trouble is that the two authors,

typical of those who held this idea, cannot agree on which rock generates which mood and end up contradicting each other.

Geography has had two eloquent spokesmen for environmental determinism. Ellen Churchill Semple, writing at the turn of the century, echoed Hippocrates: "The northern peoples of Europe are energetic, provident, serious, thoughtful rather than emotional, cautious rather than impulsive. The southerners of the sub-tropical Mediterranean basin are easy-going, improvident except under pressing necessity, gay, emotional and imaginative." A moment's thought provides easy contradictions to the above rule. Swedish movie starlets and Old Testament prophets seem to have reversed their assigned roles. The most cautious and persuasive of the American determinist geographers was Ellsworth Huntington. His major interest was climatic change and the effect of climate on man. He proposed that "a certain type of climate prevails wherever civilization is high. In the past the same type seems to have prevailed wherever a great civilization arose." We feel it only fair to point out that when England with its marine west coast climate was inhabited by savage Picts, Rome with its Mediterranean climate was the center of world knowledge. Now Northwest Europe surpasses Italy in research and technology. The jungles of Southeast Asia harbor great ruins which represent civilized societies that grew up under rainy tropical conditions. On the other hand, high-order indigenous civilizations never developed in the jungles of the Amazon or in the marine west coast climate of the Pacific Northwest. With such poor correlations between climate and achievement we must look elsewhere for explanations of human behavior.

What all this stems from is a kind of nonscientific selection of examples to prove the author's point. You look at a man or a nation and decide what you think. Then you engage in what might be called *retrospective inevitabilism*, in which you set out to prove that the end result was predetermined by—what could be simpler?—the climate. We do not for a moment deny that high temperatures and humidities can encourage endemic disease in tropical areas, or that poor soils can lead to malnutrition and slowed human responses. Those conditions are typical of the real effects of the environment of humankind. But what is uncomfortably cold or dry for one human may be too warm or wet for another. In other words the environment offers an incomplete explanation of the causes of human achievement.

Possibilism

The antideterministic arguments given above were worked out in great detail by the generation of geographers following Semple and Huntington. The French geographer Vidal de la Blache, along with Americans like Isaiah Bowman, argued that within a given environmental setting there are a number of choices that humans can make about their activities. The history of any spot in the United States will demonstrate this point. Nowhere has permanent climate change altered the environment in the last four centuries. And yet within that span, or much less in the western part of the country, Indians and settlers and urbanites; hunting, then farming, then industry; camps, villages, towns, and sprawling metropolitan areas have all occurred in rapid sequence. If only one location in space or time were considered, a strong deterministic argument could be made for the particular activity found there. But a step backward from the scene will show many other possible uses or interpretations of any given site. Thus, the message of possibilism is that the environment offers not one, but many, paths for human activities and development. The major caution that must accompany possibilistic thought, however, is the one given by the Sprouts: "Possibilism is not a frame of reference for explaining or predicting decisions. . . ."

Probabilism

Two events are seldom exactly alike no matter how similar the conditions preceding them.

The world is too various for exact copies of things or processes to be other than rarities in themselves. Instead, most of us expect the world to usually live up to our expectations but are not too surprised if the unusual occurs. In other words, we have notions of the *normal* behavior of people and the environments they occupy. These are based on our past experiences and our accumulated knowledge. If the unexpected happens—or for that matter, the less expected—it does so with much less frequency. From this idea we can construct theories of normative behavior. The events which fill our lives and the way in which people will react to different environments can be described in terms of the probability of their occurrence. If we have enough examples, and if the environment has not changed significantly since our preceding observations, we should be able to predict the frequency or expectations of something's happening again.

Much of our activity is based on normative models of human behavior. For example, most people will step off the curb into the path of an oncoming car as long as the traffic light is with them and against the automobile. In most cases the car will stop; in a few instances it will run the light; in a few others it might suddenly turn into a driveway or make a U-turn. The pedestrian assumes that the driver will behave in a normal manner, and he assigns a high probability to that possibility. The application of this idea to geography was apparently first introduced two decades ago by the British geographer O. H. K. Spate when he suggested that a probabilistic view of the world might resolve the argument between determinists and those who advocated free will in human affairs. In any event, predictions based on probabilities can be no more accurate than our knowledge of past events.

Cognitive behavioralism

Our frequent references to the *views* people have of things imply a more dominant role for human thought than deterministic theory allows. We are in great part the product of our education and experience. Twin children, separated at birth and raised in radically different cultures, may share many physical attributes, but their views of the world will depend primarily upon their experiences while growing up and what their foster parents and peers believed. Humans almost always act in terms of what their own cultures value most, and see only those things to which they have been sensitized. For example, coal was only a black rock in ancient times before man learned to burn it as fuel. Similarly, some of the richest deposits of radioactive minerals have been found in recent years by consulting old geological survey reports which simply listed their occurrence as curiosities in the days before atomic technology.

The concept of cognitive behavioralism goes far to explain human actions as long as we are familiar with the minds of those whom we are considering. However there seems to be a randomness that intrudes into real world events and skews our expectations. Disruption by population growth, migration to new environments, the depletion of finite natural resources, the discovery of new ones like atomic energy, and events like war all twist our lives in unexpected ways which exceed our ability to behave according to our expectations and conditioning. Thus human behavior and attitudes cannot be explained in simplistic terms.

Who Owns the Earth?

If we accept the idea that much of our behavior depends upon what we have been conditioned or taught to recognize and value, we come face to face with the current debate on religion and ecology. This issue was brought into the spotlight by Lynn White, Jr., in his discussion of "the historical roots of our ecologic crisis." White's argument is that much of the attitude of Western man (we recognize our use of the nominal term) toward resource use and exploitation stems from Christian theology. He reasons that the ecologic crisis that looms before us results from combining the traditionally speculative and aristrocratic

sciences with more pragmatic and action-oriented technology. The result is a peculiarly "Western" approach to the use of the earth. Moreover, this revolution has swept the world and has so speeded up the pace at which fuels and other resources are being used that it actually threatens the well-being of the next, if not this, generation. White argues further that the roots of such attitudes extend back into history well beyond the Industrial and Scientific Revolutions of the seventeenth and eighteenth centuries. He says:

What people do about their ecology depends on what they think about themselves in relation to things around them. Human ecology [we would say cultural ecology] is deeply conditioned by beliefs about our nature and destiny—that is, by religion. . . .

The victory of Christianity over paganism was the greatest psychic revolution in the history of our culture. It has become fashionable today to say that, for better or worse, we live in "the post-Christian age." Certainly the forms of our thinking and language have largely ceased to be Christian, but to my eye the substance often remains amazingly akin to that of the past. Our daily habits of action, for example, are dominated by an implicit faith in perpetual progress which was unknown either to Greco-Roman antiquity or to the Orient. It is rooted in, and is indefensible apart from, Judeo-Christian teleology. . . .[2]

According to White, in pre-Christian times every item in nature, be it tree, lake, or the landscape itself, was inhabited by spirits which had to be placated and appeased if those things were to be used by man. When Christianity overcame the old gods, man gained the right to use all of nature without thought of the consequences of his actions. In this way he assumed mastery over nature. Thus, our views of natural resources, based as they are on Christian beliefs, are indifferent to any appeal but that of immediate and maximum use.

[2]Lynn White, Jr., "The Historical Roots of Our Ecologic Crisis," *Science*, vol. 155, no. 3767, Mar. 10, 1967, p. 1205.

This argument is countered by that of the geographer Yi-fu Tuan. He reminds us that although early and medieval Christians may have felt that the earth was theirs to use in whatever manner they chose, lack of technology prevented them from seriously disturbing the ecologic balance of man and nature. At the same time Tuan points out that serious destruction of environmental resources had already occurred in China. He quotes songs, instructions to officials, and general written warnings by Chinese living well before the Christian era that the landscape must be saved by careful husbandry or the people would suffer. Deforestation, the manipulation of bodies of water, the creation of entire landscapes for aesthetic purposes were all indications of the Orient's ability to change and destroy the natural order of the world. It is almost a truism among geographers—particularly in grade school courses—to talk about the destruction of the Chinese landscape through deforestation and erosion.

The point of these arguments, it seems to us, is that it is relatively unimportant what beliefs a people or society may have if, whatever those beliefs, and end result is the same. In this case, the issue of Christian versus Oriental philosophies and their subsequent effect on the landscape is a moot one. Instead, the practical problems are those of population pressure, technological developments, and a modern life-style that continues to use up all kinds of resources at an increasing rate.

Resources as cultural appraisals

Resources of all kinds are defined by a complex set of conditions and not by a few lines written in a dictionary. All but one of the elements in this complex definition depend upon the learned behavior of humankind. As we have already said, coal is simply a black rock, a chunk of neutral stuff, until man has learned to burn it and put its energy to his use. Herein lies the key to the definition of resources given by Erich W. Zimmermann. "The word 'resource' *does not refer to a thing or a substance but to a function which a thing or a substance may perform or to an operation in which it may take part,* namely, the function or operation of attaining a given end such as satisfying a want. In other words, the word 'resource' is an abstraction reflecting human appraisal and relating to a function or operation."[3]

When we refer to resource *use*, at least four subsets of conditions have to be met. These relate to (1) physical presence and human awareness, (2) technological availability, (3) economic feasibility and managerial skills, and (4) individual and social acceptability. First and obviously, the material must be physically available and brought to the attention of those people who would use it. This may be more complicated than it appears, for nations like Japan with few natural endowments of their own are able to reach out, nevertheless, and bring raw materials from around the world to their factories. In the same manner, the utility of a substance must be known. That radioactive deposits were only curiosities in the nineteenth century geological literature is a good example of this. Second, the means for acquiring and using the materials must be developed. Fossil water beneath the Great Plains and the Sahara Desert was useful to no one until the technique of drilling deep tube wells was perfected. Similarly, aluminum—one of the most common elements in the earth's crust—was too expensive for common use before the electrolytic refining method was discovered.

Third, and following closely on the heels of our second subset, people must have the financial means to set up the extractive, refining, and manufacturing processes necessary to make something available. More subtle, but just as important, is the need for managerial skills by means of which the factors of production can be brought efficiently together. Many a firm or factory with all the tangible attributes leading to success has failed for want of good management. Fourth, and finally, both individuals and the society to which they

[3]Erich W. Zimmerman, *Erich W. Zimmerman's Introduction to World Resources,* Henry L. Hunker, ed., Harper and Row, Publishers, Incorporated, New York, 1964, p. 8.

belong must find the use of a given resource acceptable. Muslins cannot eat pork although pigs could provide meat to protein-poor areas of the Near East and South Asia. Most Europeans (including ourselves) refuse to eat insects although locusts and grubs are a tasty and welcome supplement to the diets of many people. Alan Moorehead, in his book *Cooper's Creek,* describes how expedition after expedition to the interior of Australia starved because their members would not eat the local and nutritious foods relished by the Aborigines. Land tenure and attitudes toward land ownership also fall within this class of restrictions placed on resource use. Land may be held by individuals, as in the United States and Western Europe; it may belong to the state, as in Communist bloc nations; or it may be the legacy of the tribe or kinship group, as in much of Africa. In each case, the use of the soil and its products is limited or biased by the system involved. At another level, a community may object to the presence of an atomic pile or nuclear reactor in their neighborhood. Objections of this sort rarely depend upon the real issues of safety and cleanliness. Instead, vague fears may be enough to keep power plants of this kind away from urbanized areas. Another example of the sometimes violent reactions to resource use in a modern community is when it is suggested that the drinking water be fluoridated to cut down dental cavities. People will drink substandard water filled with industrial waste or treated sewage, but let someone attempt specifically to add chemicals to the water supply and the trouble starts.

We have emphasized material resources in the above discussion, but less tangible things can also be thought of in the same manner. The climate of a region may allow a variety of uses, but human beings must interpret energy availability, temperature regime, humidity, precipitation, and numberless other things before they can speak of a "vacationland" or an "attractive location for industry." Finally, we emphasize again that from the geographic point of view expressed in this book, *any material or process must enjoy a certain minimum*

locational advantage in order to become a resource in the complete sense of the word.

Perception of Environmental Hazards

We have repeatedly used the term *perception* in our discussion of man-environment systems. Much confusion surrounds the use of this word by geographers, psychologists, and others, but for our purposes we rely on the definition provided by Robert Ward: "Perception is the cognizance of the real world environment as it has been assessed by an individual. This includes the physical, social, and economic complexities of past, present, and future events, and their meanings as they relate to the decision making processes."

The apparent difference between psychologists and geographers in the use of the word *perception* is that psychologists feel that the perceiver "must come into *direct* contact with the stimulus in order to perceive the stimulus." Sometimes the subject reacts to his memory of the stimulus. This memory of his experience and his reactions to that memory are what geographers usually investigate. A geographer would want to find out what memories the inhabitants of a shoreline—across which hurricanes move—have about past disasters and how their evaluations of past events affect their use of the land and their preparations for the next possible storm. "Perception" in this geographic sense is something more than stimulus response and corresponds to what psychologists call *cognition*. This act of cognition according to psychologists relates the physiological awareness of the stimulus to a chain of *memories* which are in turn flavored by the *goals, decisions, actions,* and *consequences* of past events. In accordance with current geographic literature we will use the term *perception* as synonymous with the above definition of *cognition*.

Perception studies in geography cover a wide range of topics. Kevin Lynch, Julian Wolpert, and others have attempted to discover how people view the cities in which they live. Their studies show the different values placed upon elements within the urban en-

Table 20-1   Common Responses to Uncertainty Concerning Natural Hazards

Eliminate the Hazard		Eliminate the Uncertainty	
Deny or Denigrate Its Existence	Deny or Denigrate Its Recurrence	Make it Determinate and Knowable	Transfer Uncertainty to a Higher Power
"We have no floods, here, only high water" "It can't happen here"	"Lightning never strikes twice in the same place" "It's a freak of nature"	"Seven years of great plenty. . . . After them seven years of famine" "Floods come every five years"	"It's in the hands of God" "The government is taking care of it"

Source: Ian Burton and Robert W. Kates, "The Perception of Natural Hazards in Resource Management," reprinted with permission from *Natural Resources Journal* 412 (1964), University of New Mexico School of Law, Albuquerque, New Mexico, table 5.

vironment by their inhabitants. Most important, urban perception studies indicate that modern cities seem fragmentary and uncoordinated to those who inhabit them. The conclusion is that more research is needed in urban design before we can build cities that are perceived and used as "remarkable and well-knit places" in which to live.

Far removed from the city are studies by T. F. Saarinen of the perception of drought hazard in the Great Plains and by Gilbert White, Ian Burton, Robert Kates, and others of storms and flooding. The results of these studies indicate that the adage "familiarity breeds contempt" does not always hold true. In general, people who have had the longest exposure to environmental hazards of this sort score best when asked to estimate the frequency of past floods, storms, and droughts. In the same way, people living in high-hazard areas tend to be more sensitized to the problems facing them than those who encounter such things less frequently. On the other hand, it is human nature to downgrade or discredit the danger of events over which they have little control. People have lived for thousands of years on the slopes of active volcanoes or in low-lying coastal areas subject to typhoons and tidal waves. Their staying in such places may be enforced in part by circumstance and

lack of alternatives, but not always. Table 20-1 lists some of the common responses to natural hazards.

The pragmatic importance of hazard perception studies rests in the realm of public policy making. Should millions be spent to protect summer cottages along open shores? Or would it be better to leave such places unbuilt upon? Once flooding is controlled in a river basin, how best can farmers be persuaded not to make long-term investments in bottomlands despite their perceptions of reduced hazard? Average hazards may be reduced, but exceptionally high flood waters can still occur, topping the levees and causing immense damage and loss. Flood protection is almost always designed to counteract average peak conditions. The cost of protecting against "once in 50 year floods" is prohibitively high.

In the next chapter we will discuss many of the ways in which environments deteriorate, sometimes because of man, sometimes because of agents beyond his control. But before discussing the geographic implications of ecologic deterioration we need to review another significant aspect of human perception.

The world view which each of us nurtures can influence our different theories of human behavior. If we see the world as a series of isolated places and events, we are forced to

Resources as Cultural Appraisals: Man's Changing World View

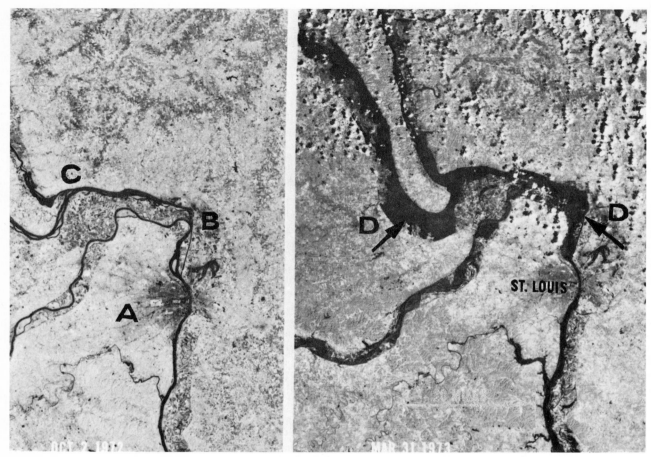

NASA satellite photo shows flooding at St. Louis, Missouri. The St. Louis area
as seen by NASA's Earth Resource Technology Satellite shows the extreme
flooding along the Illinois, Missouri, and Mississippi Rivers. In the photograph on the left, taken Oct. 2, 1972, St. Louis can be located by the letter *A*.
North of St. Louis, the Missouri River joins the Mississippi River at point *B*,
and farther upstream, the confluence of the Illinois and Mississippi Rivers is
noted by the letter *C*. The photograph on the right, taken of the same region on
Mar. 31, 1973, shows areas under water (letter *D*) as a result of the flooding.
In this near-infrared wavelength view, the darkest tones indicate areas of
deepest water. At the time this picture was obtained from space, the
Mississippi River at St. Louis was at a stage of thirty-eight feet, the highest
since 1903. In this frame, about 300,000 acres were already covered by water,
and the river stage was still rising. This flood wave is slowly making its way
downstream, threatening cities and agricultural lands along the entire length
of the Mississippi River. (NASA photo)

seek explanations in terms of site conditions such as environmental characteristics. But if we see the world as a complex network of spatial interrelationships, situational explanations become important.

Maps and the Changing World View

One basic activity of all animals is that of orienting themselves spatially within their environments. That is, they make mental maps and place themselves in them. Even with humans this kind of map making is often intuitive. The child psychologist Piaget points out that babies and small children spend much of their time orienting themselves within their environments. Anyone who has watched an infant crawling or toddling is immediately impressed with the small one's role as an explorer. As adults each one of us carries within himself many maps of the world in which we live. Most of these maps are mental ones, and relatively few are actually drawn on paper. But mapping as such is not limited to modern society. Fragments of ancient maps exist, as do maps drawn by tribal and preliterate people.

People map what interests them. Micronesian charts show the direction of wave fronts (represented by curved palm fronds) and islands (intersection of the fronds) (Figure 20–1). Eskimo maps are among the best made by preliterate peoples. They emphasize the true shapes of land masses and bodies of water, although distances seem to be of little importance. For example, the Netsilik Eskimos drew maps for the arctic explorer Rasmussen. Altogether 532 place names were listed, and of those 498 designated islands, bays, streams, lakes, and fjords. Only 18 showed scattered rocks and ravines, while 16 indicated mountains and hills. For people who earn their living essentially from the sea this is not too surprising. American Indian maps emphasized time rather than spatial relationships. A day's journey was given the same unit length whether the spatial distance was great or small. Travel effort was considered most important, just as modern geographers make maps of travel times in the form of geographic circles. American Indian maps also frequently showed places where important events occurred.

In the final analysis, maps reflect the world view of the people who make them. They can either show limited horizons or actually attempt to chart the universe. Maps also reflect the perceptions and value systems held by their makers. In the United States many maps show where struggles between Europeans and Indians took place; if the white men won, such locations are labeled "battles;" if the red men won, they are called "massacres." We have already mentioned how Canadians map much smaller settlements as towns than do people from the United States. This clearly reflects the Canadian's assessment of their smaller and scattered population.

Figure 20-1 Micronesian navigational stick charts The charts were used for navigating in open boats between islands in the South Pacific. (From a drawing by E. H. Bryan, Jr.; charts are in the collection of Bernice P. Bishop Museum, Honolulu)

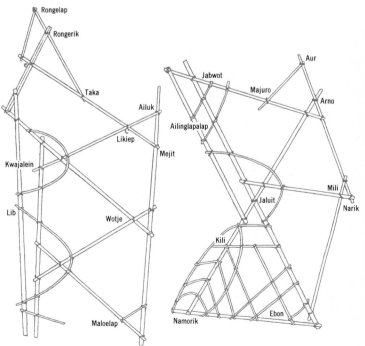

Mental maps

The *mental maps* analyzed by Peter Gould and others illustrate this point. If you, the reader, will stop for a moment and consider the images of the world which you carry in your head and by means of which you navigate from place to place, you will realize that those images incorporate areas of great detail based on intimate knowledge and other places where you could draw nothing meaningful if asked to put it down on paper. The research into mental maps consists of efforts to detect and understand the images of the world that people carry about with them.

One interesting analysis made by Gould was to ask college students at Berkeley (California), Minnesota, Pennsylvania, and Alabama to

Figure 20-2 Student mental maps of desirable places to live Students at four different universities were asked to rank the states in the United States according to their desirability as places in which to live. Places with high value are appealing; places with low value are unappealing. Notice how each group ranked its own location high in desirability. The maps also show some consensus of opinion about certain desirable and undesirable locations; Colorado, for example, is generally highly regarded by all groups. (P. R. Gould, "On Mental Maps," *Michigan Inter-University Community of Mathematical Geographers*, Discussion Paper No. 9, 1966. Reprinted in P. English and R. Mayfield (eds.), *Man, Space and Environment*, Oxford University Press, New York, 1972)

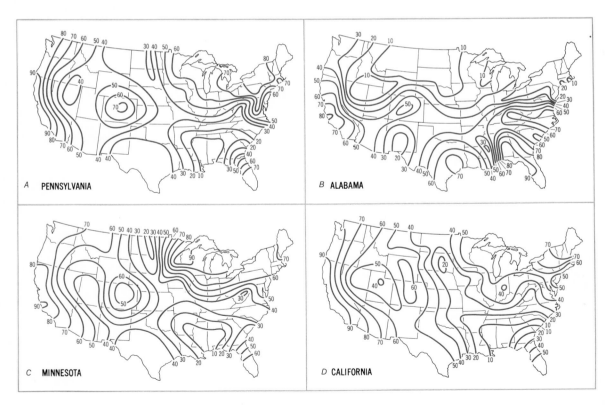

A PENNSYLVANIA

B ALABAMA

C MINNESOTA

D CALIFORNIA

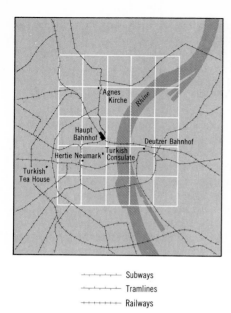

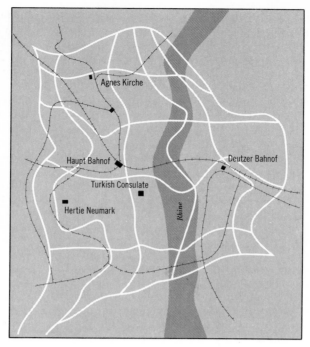

------|--|------ Subways

------|--|------ Tramlines

------|-|-|-|--- Railways

Figure 20-3 Turkish workers' mental map of Cologne, Germany A
sample of Turkish workers in this German city were each asked to draw a
map of the city, showing where they lived, worked, and otherwise traveled.
The maps were combined by averaging the locations of prominent landmarks
identified by the group and comparing this location with the true position
of the landmark as indicated by a large-scale map of the city. A map projection was then calculated that mapped the true position onto the imagined
position. The subsequent stretching of an original square grid in the mental
map shows the nature of the space in the collected image of the city. (The
data collection and analysis were carried out by John Clark, University of
Michigan 1972–1973)

rank the forty-eight coterminus states in order
of their desirability as places in which to live.
The resulting values were summed for the four
different sets of students and plotted on maps
of the United States (Figure 20–2 A to D). High
values show desirable places; low values show
undesirable habitats. We will not take the
space for a detailed examination of the results,
but the reader can take a leisurely look at the
maps and hypothesize for himself why the
peaks and pits of desirability occur as they do.
California is uniformly high (we will return to
the implications of this "Golden State image"

in Chapter 22). The Great Plains are a low and
unappealing plain. Of particular interest is
the way in which all Northern and Western
students rank the Deep South as a homo-
geneously undesirable locality, while Alabama
students are much more discriminating and
see the South as both a varied place and one
which is good to live in.

  This type of map relies upon a standard surveyed base upon which to plot psychological
values gathered by some means of interview or
questionnaire. There is another kind of mental
map which may possibly show the actual per-

*Resources
as Cultural
Appraisals:
Man's Changing
World View*

ception of reality held by individuals or groups. In this case, people are asked to draw maps of the territory in which they live. No one can draw a completely accurate map, but the theory is that people will draw those places they know the best with the greatest accuracy and that they will show the things they deem important in preference to those they don't like or even notice. Comparisons can then be made between the relative positions of features on surveyed maps and those same features on the freehand charts. Figure 20-3 shows such a comparison based on maps drawn by migratory Turkish workers temporarily employed in West Germany. The first diagram simply depicts a rectangular grid which, in this case, was placed across the city of Cologne (Köln) in Germany. The second diagram summarizes how the migratory workers perceived and drew the relative locations of a number of prominent features in the Cologne cityscape. The nearly rectangular grid pattern preserved at the center indicates the greater familiarity of the workers with the center of the city. The distortions at the edges show how

their knowledge of that area diminishes rapidly with distance from the CBD.

Both of these maps offer new clues into the way in which we view our world. If you were to draw a map of the city in which your campus is located, it would predictably differ in many ways from a map of the same area drawn by a businessman, a homemaker, or an inner-city child. Much more research needs to be done on these topics, but the signposts are there. We use and seek out the places and the things we have learned to value. We are more and more urban rather than rural creatures, and more and more our attention focuses upon cities and the resources which support our way of life. If we are to understand the geography of our environments and the problems which beset us in our interactions with the natural as well as the social world, we must use every technique possible to gain useful insights. A knowledge of the way in which we see and map the world around us will help us to understand and, it is hoped, solve man-environment problems, some of which are described in the next chapter.

21 | ENVIRONMENTAL IMBALANCE: MAN'S ROLE IN CHANGING THE FACE OF THE EARTH

For the sword outwears its sheath,
And the soul wears out the breast. . .

(George Gordon, Lord Byron)

Autumn, and the trees shed their leaves; spring and summer with the molting of skin and feather and fur. The carcass in the jungle and the whale awash on the beach. Life is defined by death and cleans itself with a constant sloughing off of old tissue. Even the continents waste into the seas.

In discussing a topic as vast and sensitive as man's role in environmental imbalance we must begin with the idea that the world when healthy is in a constant state of birth, death, decay, and renewal. It is only when the tempo of these processes is changed and when their location is skewed from reasonable to unreasonable distributions that trouble looms. This makes it necessary for us to understand how resources occur in space and time and how policies regarding resource use are tied to human perceptions of their spatial and temporal environments.

Resources in a Time-space Framework

Once we have agreed to designate a set of tangible materials as resources, we must consider the rates at which we utilize the available supply. We must also consider whether the supply is limited or constantly renewable. A basic division of resource types is between renewable and nonrenewable ones. These are also sometimes referred to as *flow* and *fund stocks*. Flow, or renewable, resources are largely biotic. They are usually elements in self-maintaining systems and with proper husbanding can be used over and over. Forest preserves or well-managed fisheries would come under this category. Fund, or nonrenewable resources, exist in a static framework. In other words, the systems that create nonrenewable resources such as mineral deposits operate so slowly that once they are used up, it is unlikely that similar concentrations can be reestablished during a reasonable span of time.

A basic way of looking at renewable and nonrenewable resources is to consider the length of time that must pass before materials can be replaced through the operation of natural processes. Table 21–1 lists some residence times of natural cycles. For example, the average length of time that a molecule of water will remain in the atmosphere before returning to the surface is about 10 days. Terrestrial groundwater requires 150 years to complete its underground circulation. Oxygen incorporated into living tissue will take an average of 2,000 years to pass through the atmosphere, the hydrosphere, and back into the biosphere; while a sodium ion will remain in sea water for 260

Table 21-1 Residence Times of Some Natural Cycles

Earth Materials	Some Typical Residence Times
Atmosphere circulation	
Water vapor	10 days (lower atmosphere)
Carbon dioxide	5 to 10 days (with sea)
Aerosol particles	
Stratosphere (upper atmosphere)	Several months to several years
Troposphere (lower atmosphere)	One to several weeks
Hydrosphere circulation	
Atlantic surface water	10 years
Atlantic deep water	600 years
Pacific surface water	25 years
Pacific deep water	1,300 years
Terrestrial groundwater	150 years (above 2,500 feet (760 meters) depth)
Biosphere circulation*	
Water	2,000,000 years
Oxygen	2,000 years
Carbon dioxide	300 years
Sea water constituents*	
Water	44,000 years
All salts	22,000,000 years
Calcium ion	1,200,000 years
Sulfate ion	11,000,000 years
Sodium ion	260,000,000 years
Chloride ion	Infinite

*Average time it takes for these materials to recycle with the atmosphere and hydrosphere.
Source: *The Earth and Human Affairs,* compiled by National Research Council, National Academy of Sciences, copyright © 1972 by the National Academy of Sciences. By permission of Harper & Row, Publishers (Canfield Press Division), table 2-1, p. 41.

million years. What this means is that given enough time almost all nonliving resources are renewable, but that mankind's sojourn on earth has been so brief and our life-spans are so short that for all practical purposes many of such processes are one-way or irreversible.

Our residence on earth is terrifyingly brief when compared with the total length of earth history. If we were to represent the passage of time by stacking up one sheet of paper for each year as it passes, then the two centuries since the founding of the American Republic would be the equivalent of a book about 1 inch thick. A 5-foot bookshelf would represent all the time since the beginning of the Neolithic Revolution and the domestication of plants and animals. A stack of books 73 feet long would stand for all human history since the beginning of the Paleolithic, and a shelf of books 380 miles in length would mark the elapsed time since the earth itself was formed. It is the lack of fit between cultural processes which consume resources and natural processes which provide them that in many cases creates disharmonies in the man-environment system.

How men of goodwill disagree

A general pattern emerges when we analyze historical sequences of the human development and use of specific resources. At first there is a period of uncontrolled exploitation in which the "cream of the crop" is stripped off. Surface mineral deposits, large stands of accessible timber, herds of wild game all fall prey at this stage. This exploitation leads to the threatended depletion of the resource. Sometimes people don't care—as in the case of the American bison—and replace one resource with another. But oftentimes, as the "bottom of the barrel" gets closer and closer, policy statements are made and regulatory laws are passed. The first thing that happens in this latter stage is a call for and an inventory of the threatened resource. Inventories usually reveal that rates of resource use are exceeding rates of discovery. This causes a flurry of rhetoric, followed by legislation aimed at restoring the original state of plenty. What we witness here is the positive role of negative feedback.

Determining the rate of use

Particularly at this point men of goodwill can violently disagree about what should be done. Resource policies can be quite rational and yet completely opposed to each other, depending upon the perceptions and philosophies of the people involved. The prescriptions that are suggested may include *budgeting the rate of use*. This would be particularly applicable for assigning the rates at which fossil waters or petroleum reserves shall be pumped from the ground. It would also relate to the density of wells drilled per unit area. In this way local capacities may be maintained by regulating the number of users. Too rapid pumping can dry out the space around well shafts and leave valuable liquids stranded or trapped below ground. Slower pumping allows full capillary action and smoother flows, thus assuring

maximum extraction over longer periods of time. In some cases the suggested rates of resource use are unrealistically high. The number of whales that can be slaughtered each year according to international agreement among whaling nations is far in excess of the number actually caught. In fact, the quotas are meaningless, for if they were filled for more than one or two years, whales would become extinct. On the other hand, rates of use can sometimes be too slow. In the absence of natural predators, herds of deer may increase too rapidly, with subsequent overcrowding and starvation if hunting quotas are set too low. A further result can be the destruction of vegetation in such areas through excessive browsing.

Opposed to notions of slow, long-term use are those of *maximizing the flow of profit over a short run*. As we pointed out in Chapter 8, rapid resource exploitation need not be considered completely negative. Sometimes, the quick profits from one area become investment capital in another. Whether or not it is worthwhile to sacrifice one thing for another is something that must be decided—once the facts are gathered—by political and social rather than scientific means.

When a threatened resource is able to renew itself, the rate of use and the rate of renewal become extremely important and subject to debate and legislation. The continuing argument over the national forests is an example of this. How fast should our trees be cut? Are reforestation programs realistic in the estimates of how rapidly new trees can take the place of harvested ones? Is clear cutting (that is, removing every tree from a large tract and then replanting) better than selective logging? Certainly clear cutting is technically easier and cheaper; but will the homogeneous stands of seedlings survive as readily as young trees growing in the shade of older ones? The ideal that all rational users of renewable resources aspire to is that of *sustained yield*.

Alternative uses of a resource

The idea of multiple use is also important. A river should provide drinking water, recrea-

Environmental Imbalance: Man's Role in Changing the Face of the Earth

tion, fishing, and aesthetically pleasing views. But can it at the same time serve as a source of hydropower, a waste disposal system, and a source of irrigation water? High dams and large reservoirs have multiple purposes. For example, hydropower production is maximized by maintaining the ponded water at the highest possible level at all times. Conversely, flood control use would require that the level of the reservoir be lowered to make room for anticipated flood crests. These two uses are largely incompatible with one another, and the policy relating to them must be negotiated. The need for negotiation and compromise is also true for forests. If they are to provide timber, how can they also be places for campers, hunters, and naturalists?

Fitting the policy to the resource

Our perceptions of the spatial and temporal qualities of a resource influence the policies, both public and private, which regulate its use. For example, if a resource is perceived to be in short supply, one response is to *increase the search for new sources*. Sometimes the search goes on inside laboratories. New methods of extracting oil from oil shale, new ways of concentrating low-grade ores, new varieties of faster-growing crops are all examples of this. But spatial search is also important. Oil companies receive a 22 percent tax rebate for use in exploration and drilling new wells. However, policies encouraging search will be effective only where undiscovered stocks still exist. If the total amount of a resource is known, then a policy of protection and allocation is appropriate. We know where the few remaining sequoia trees are growing, and no amount of search will turn up more. The policy decision for protecting them depends upon the value the public places upon them. The national parks which protect unique scenic spots are the result of such considerations. Relative location can be important in these matters. The nearer a natural wonder is to a highly urbanized area, the more difficult it is to preserve it in a pristine state. It may even be difficult to save it from total destruction if the rent-paying ability of other land uses becomes too competitive.

Controls *regulating local capacities* are also important. We mean by this ways in which undesirable concentrations of wastes can be prevented. These may include setting limits or rates on the amount of sewage dumped into a body of water, or the amount of dust and noxious gases that escape from chimneys. It can also mean *zoning laws* which regulate living densities in urban and rural areas.

In all these methods of controlling our use of the environment the twin elements of time and space are important. And in all these cases, sources of conflict constantly occur. Many of the sources of such conflict are specifically geographic in character, and can be described in terms of boundary definition, territoriality, regionalization, and scale differences. The following examples represent only a partial list: *unowned resources*, or those for which ownership is not clearly established; *moving resources* such as spawning fish, migrating wildlife, or running water which cross from one state or nation into another; and *resources* viewed and used simultaneously *at more than one scale*. An example of the last case would be a forest of rare trees. Local townspeople might wish to log off the area, for that would mean jobs and income and prosperity; conservationists scattered across the entire nation and operating with a world view would see the need to preserve the same trees for the good of everyone.

Five Processes Affecting Environmental Equilibrium

Whenever resource policies are made and enforced, parts of society will benefit while others suffer. Much depends upon how various groups of users define the costs which they are willing to pay and the profits with which they will be satisfied. The rapid depletion of resources for short-range profit seems rather foolish, but our interpretation of these matters may be overly pessimistic. We base our views on an analysis of the situation emphasizing five processes through which environmental equilibrium can be disturbed. These are (1)

Table 21-2 Enrichment Factor for Some Common Metals

Metal	Percent in Crust	Percent in Ore	Enrichment Factor*
Mercury	0.000008	0.2	25,000
Gold	0.0000002	0.0008	4,000
Lead	0.0013	5.0	3,840
Silver	0.00007	0.01	1,450
Nickel	0.008	1.0	125
Copper	0.006	0.6	100
Iron	5.2	30.0	6
Aluminum	8.2	38.0	4

*The enrichment factor indicates how many times above its average concentration a metal must be in order to be mined.

Source: *The Earth and Human Affairs*, compiled by National Research Council, National Academy of Sciences, copyright © 1972 by the National Academy of Sciences. By permission of Harper & Row, Publishers (Canfield Press Division), table 4-2, p. 80.

diffusion, (2) concentration, (3) destruction, (4) overproduction, and (5) change of state. The first two processes are distinctly spatial in character. The last three refer to site-connected activities although they too have strong situational overtones. In many cases once such processes are understood and once society has agreed upon a set of goals, it is possible to modify or reverse their negative aspects. One of the most important ways in which resources become depleted is when the rates at which they are accumulated in usable concentrations are exceeded by the rates at which they are diffused across the earth's surface in increments too small to be reused.

Nonreversible diffusion: Mineral depletion

Man's use of minerals is representative of the lack of fit between natural and cultural processes. Although enormous tonnages of the most useful elements exist in the earth's crust, they can be used only when brought together into recoverable concentrations. Table 21-2 lists eight of the most common metals. The total percentage estimated to be in the crust is contrasted with the percent that must occur in an ore for it to be considered minable. The *enrichment factor* represents the number of times above its average concentration a metal must

be in order to be mined. In the entire United States in 1966, more than 90 percent of the production of 16 major minerals and elements was accounted for by the output of only 186 mines. This means that usable concentrations of minerals are quite rare. At the same time, the demand for all kinds of minerals and elements is rapidly increasing. Table 21-3 shows the domestic primary production of nine major minerals as well as additional supplies provided from recycled scrap. The total amount used exceeds those two sources in all cases except uranium, and the difference must be made up by foreign imports. The last column shows the estimated primary demand in the year 2000. The question is, where will those materials come from?

The search for minerals has led deeper and deeper into the earth, and farther and farther from the world's central markets and industrial regions. At the same time, more and more dilute bodies of ore have been tapped in our ceaseless quest. Figure 21-1 shows how this search has progressed in a three-dimensional space defined by distance, depth, and dilution. The distances involved grow greater with every passing year. In the case of iron, the ores of Minnesota are now supplemented and replaced in American mills and foundries by those from Labrador, Venezuela, and

Environmental Imbalance: Man's Role in Changing the Face of the Earth

Table 21-3 Total Annual U.S. Mineral Supplies and Uses

	Domestic Primary Production	Old Scrap*	Total Amount Used†	Projected Primary Demand for 2000 A.D.
Aluminum	450,000	160,000	4,947,000	23,800,000
Copper	1,380,000	422,000	2,122,000	4,860,000
Iron	49,000,000	35,400,000	110,200,000	138,000,000
Lead	517,000	450,000	1,207,000	1,390,000
Mercury	597	378	1,995	2,730
Bituminous coal and lignite	504,000,000	0	504,050,000	900,000,000
Natural gas (dry)	446,000,000	0	465,080,000	1,030,000,000
Petroleum (including natural gas liquids)	508,190,000	0	668,190,000	1,490,000,000
Uranium	9,515	0	9,515	55,800

*Preliminary data for 1971, given in metric tons. Source: First Annual Report of the Secretary of the Interior under Mining and Minerals Policy Act of 1970 (P.L. 91–631), March 1972.
†Including government stockpiling, industry stocks, and exports. The difference between domestic supply and demand is met by foreign imports.
Source: *The Earth and Human Affairs,* compiled by National Research Council, National Academy of Sciences, copyright © 1972 by the National Academy of Sciences. By permission of Harper & Row, Publishers (Canfield Press Division), table 4–1, p. 79.

West Africa. The Kalamazoo copper ores of Arizona are half a mile deep beneath unmineralized rock. If the substance sought is valuable enough, shafts are sunk to even greater depths. Gold mines in South Africa penetrate to depths of more than 12,000 feet. Copper also provides a good example of the use of more and more dilute mineral concentrations. The first copper used by preliterate peoples were nuggets of pure metal pounded into blades, arrowheads, and symbolic tokens. By 1910 copper was mined and extracted from 2 percent ores. By 1970 the average ore used in the United States contained only 0.6 percent copper, and the Berkeley pit in Butte, Montana, operates successfully on 0.2 percent ore.

In some cases, *revolving stocks* of minerals can be established. Gold and copper, for example, are used over and over again. But in many other situations, metals, once used, are lost forever. Silver, an essential ingredient in the emulsion on photographic film, cannot be recovered. One dramatic result of the demand for silver and the nonrecoverable nature of much of its use is the copper and silver *sandwich coins* which have replaced traditional silver currency in the United States. And as one public official has observed: "The island of Jamaica, a huge exporter of bauxite, is gradually drifting—in the form of a unicellular layer of aluminum beer cans—onto the United States and covering us."

Concentration and dispersion of iron ores
Although iron constitutes slightly more than 5 percent of the earth's crust, relatively few deposits are sufficiently concentrated to justify mining them. One of the world's great deposits of pre-Cambrian iron ore was found in the nineteenth century in the northern portions of Minnesota, Wisconsin, and Michigan. A series of individual deposits or ranges including the Marquette, Menominee, Ver-

million, Gogebic, and Mesabi have supplied most of the ore produced domestically in the United States for more than 50 years. Among these, the Mesabi range has been by far the most important. In the years between 1848 and 1930 1.5 billion tons of ore were taken from this district. In 1970 more than 70.2 million tons of iron ore were produced; but by 1980 the shipment of high-grade ores will have dropped to about 5 million long tons. Low-grade ores, called *taconite*, are now being *beneficiated*, that is, brought to economically feasible concentrations, but taconite pellets will amount to no more than 50 million long tons shipped annually from the area. The heyday of those great mines is obviously over. As Table 21–3 shows, the demand for iron will continue to increase and will have to be supplied from other sources. By A.D. 2000 the shipment of conventional ores from that area will be less than 4 percent of the total projected demand for primary ores in the United States.

The lesson should be apparent: 200 years of human activity have used up the materials accumulated by 2 billion years of natural processes. The key to appreciating all this is in the definition of "used up." The world is not less rich today in iron than it was when the first European stood upon the shores of Lake Superior. Only the useful concentrations of iron ore and not the iron itself have been changed. The law of the conservation of matter indicates that, with the exception of atomic reactions, elements are not ultimately altered or destroyed. However, the removal of the iron as ore and its subsequent diffusion across the surface of the earth into a useless film of junk cars, old nails, empty cans, and rust decrease its utility to the point where serious shortages may occur in our lifetime. The use of scrap iron will delay this fate, but an inevitable increment of metal is lost with each production-utilization-abandonment cycle of the system. Even if all the metal lost were eventually to find its way to the sea where it might again be concentrated through geologic or biotic processes, the time required would be of such a magnitude that no one for the next

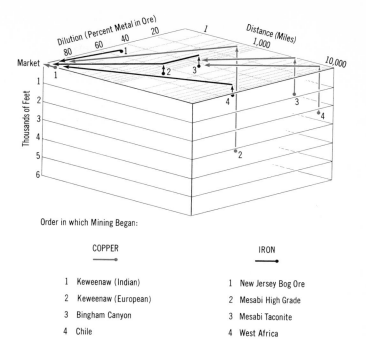

Order in which Mining Began:

COPPER

1 Keweenaw (Indian)
2 Keweenaw (European)
3 Bingham Canyon
4 Chile

IRON

1 New Jersey Bog Ore
2 Mesabi High Grade
3 Mesabi Taconite
4 West Africa

Figure 21-1 Alternatives for exploiting a hypothetical mineral resource   The possibilities for exploiting any mineral in the earth depend upon the distribution of the element in the environment. The cost of recovery is a function of the depth below the earth's surface, the distance from the market, and the degree of dilution of the material. Technological improvements in search methods, transportation, mining, or processing extend the range of exploitation within limits of natural distribution of the material. Not shown on the diagram are recycled wastes from the market, which become more important as only lower and lower-grade ores remain. Copper and iron ore examples shown have different histories.

thousand generations could profit from it. Cultural processes of dispersion operating through a hierarchy of industrial production units and retail distribution centers thus represent our first example of environmental degradation.

As we have said, once the natural and cultural processes inherent in such depletion are understood, it may be possible to slow or reverse the direction of change. It is neces-

Environmental Imbalance: Man's Role in Changing the Face of the Earth

sary, though, for society to agree upon the price it is willing to pay for reliable resources. Metal is a case in point. While consumers pay for the tin cans and automobiles they use and eventually throw away, they are unwilling to pay the costs of salvaging waste materials. Cans are almost always thrown into undifferentiated solid waste and lost in land fills. Abandoned automobiles are such a nuisance that cities like New York cannot find enough places to dump them. Moreover, junk dealers are unwilling to pay the costs of hauling scrap cars off the streets to their crushing machines. One way in which much larger quantitites of scrap could be recycled, thus slowing the rate at which metals are lost in unusable diffusions, would be to pay a recycling tax or deposit on all manufactured objects. Such a tax could work in two ways. The consumer might get back his money by returning the object to a collecting station, or in the case of automobiles and other large objects, the junk dealer could receive a fee from the state for each piece retrieved. This is a small price to pay for resource security; the alternative is that our children and grandchildren will have to do without many materials unless we act now.

Concentration

Our previous discussions lead us to the problem of large numbers of people and their use of resources. Where very large populations are concerned, the ultimate resource may be space itself. Numbers alone are not bad; consumption alone is not bad; there is nothing wrong with the production of waste. The problem is the lack of fit between the numbers of users and the thing used. Whether the resource we are considering is a deposit of iron ore, a school of fish, or adequate land on which to live, we need to balance the carrying capacity of the resource against subtractions from it or additions to it. We have looked at various examples of the destruction or depletion of resources. Now we must look at crowding and pollution, both of which degrade the environment.

Crowding An extreme act of crowding took place on June 20, 1756, during the French and British struggle for India, when the Nawab of Bengal allegedly ordered a captured British garrison consisting of 146 prisoners to be placed in a guardroom chamber measuring only 18 by 14 by 14 feet 10 inches. Two small windows offered the only source of air or outlet for heat. When dawn came and the room was opened, all but 23 prisoners had died of heat prostration and foul air.

This example may seem insignificant, but doom-sayers claim that the world itself is becoming almost as overcrowded. Allowing approximately one square yard of land per person and taking one of the more pessimistic and therefore larger projections of world population growth, estimates show that the last available land will be used up on Friday, November 13, 2104. Obviously, this is an absurd arguement; something will happen before such a situation develops.

What is a reasonable limit on the human use of earth-space and what are its implications concerning crowding? What concentrations of wastes can the human ecosystem tolerate and still remain viable? Put still another way, what is the difference between unpleasant and dangerous crowding and what is the difference between distasteful and lethal accumulations of waste? Unfortunately there are no real answers to any of the above questions. A number of experiments with populations of rats, chickens, and other animals show that several kinds of population controls result from excessive crowding. On the one hand, the reduction of per capita food supplies with increasing populations can bring about starvation and/or decreased sexuality. In other animal communities faced with increasing numbers and finite resources there appears to be some sort of population control through endocrine disturbances brought about by crowding. Social disorders have been observed to develop among Norway rats living under excessively crowded laboratory conditions. Dominant males will control feeding and drinking stations at prime times, but even when they absent themselves from guarding the available resources, the less aggressive rats will refuse to partake and quickly perish. Communities like this are referred to as *behavioral sinks*. But the fact clearly remains that human beings with their large brains and tenacious ability to survive, and also their inherited social systems and other pieces of learned behavior we call culture, are not rats in a maze. It is misleading and dangerous to project and predict human behavior under crowded conditions from instances like those described above.

If we look at the densities at which people have lived for long periods of time, we realize that humans are able to withstand considerable inconvenience. In fact, two kinds of clustering take place. On the one hand is the ghettoization of unwilling minority groups, and on the other we have the self-segregation of the upper-middle and upper classes. Of course, the latter seldom live at high densities, and yet millions of people choose to live on the island of Manhattan, where densities in certain very small areas may reach over 300,000 per square mile. (Seldom do more than a few blocks exist with such populations; this figure is a statistical extrapolation). Table 22–4 gives some peak densities for small areas within cities.

Pollution There are both advantages and disadvantages associated with clustering at such densities. In addition to the personal stress of communications overload, we must also consider the problems associated with the sloughing off of all manner of excess energy and materials. Noise, heat, waste, and trash all create problems when brought together at nearly unbearable concentrations in cities. One example of this is the production of solid waste in American cities. Garbage, rubbish, and junk produced in America amount to 5 pounds per person per day. The grand total is thus more than 500,000 tons per day, or 185 million tons per year, of municipal waste. Moreover, this is increasing at about 4 percent per year. This is in part because of increasing

Table 21–4 Peak Living Densities in Small Areas

Area	Density Per Square Mile
Calcutta, 1951	218,000
London, 1931	152,500
London, 1851	200,000
N.Y.C., 1900	350,000
N.Y.C., 1965	318,000
Paris, 1962	86,300
N.Y.C.,* 1960	7,462†
Manhattan, 1960	75,150†

*Standard metropolitan statistical area.
†Average figure for the total area.

populations. But at least half of the increase in our production of rubbish results from increasing per capita consumption.

The disposal of municipal solid waste is the third highest cost that cities face. We spend about 3.5 billion dollars on cleaning our nests at the present time, but the cost will have tripled by 1980. In some places 10 cents of every tax dollar is spent on waste disposal, and of that money 70 to 80 percent is spent on transportation. This problem remains largely unstudied, and the future is not easy to predict. It is closely linked to the rising amount of synthetic materials which are nonbiodegradable through normal processes of rot or decay. In 1960 wet garbage constituted 5 percent of all wastes, but by 1970 wet garbage had fallen to about half that amount. Paper and single-use paper products have increased their contribution to the national garbage can the most by an impressive 50 to 75 percent. This is due in large part to excessive, poor, and deceitful packaging. More than 3.5 million tons of discarded packaging must be disposed of each year in the United States. Of this 60 percent is paper, 20 percent glass, 16 percent metal, and 4 percent plastic. In the average city, 1,000 tons of paper and 172 tons of metals are discarded each year by every 10,000 people.

All of this represents a kind of negative moving resource which finds its way onto the

Environmental Imbalance: Man's Role in Changing the Face of the Earth

393

common ground. The city and its people are supplied by hierarchies of all kinds which focus all manner of materials and move them into relatively small areas. This represents the basic problem of overconcentration. But the overall problem is greater than might be supposed if we limit our considerations solely to the garbage trucks which munch their way down our streets and alleys every week. Cities are people, millions of people, and people are mouths and stomachs. To feed all those hungry mouths the nations needs livestock of all kinds. In fact in 1970 there were 50 million pigs, 38 million cattle, and 350 million chickens produced in the United States. Feedlots with sometimes more than 50,000 cattle are fairly common in the country today. In fact, there are 256,000 lots of all sizes where cattle are fattened. Since a single animal produces about 80 pounds of urine and excrement each day, the problem of disposing of their wastes equals Hercules' labor of cleaning the Augean stables.

Polluted water draining away from a cattle feed lot. (Dept. of Agriculture photo)

Feeder lots are growing progressively larger and larger, thus forcing out smaller and more evenly distributed ones. The spatial implications of this again can be expressed in terms of concentration. For example, six counties in Colorado fed approximately 5 percent of all the cattle fattened in the United States in 1963. Ten years later, in the states composing the basin of the Missouri River there was a per capita equivalent feeder cattle population greater than the human population in terms of the wastes produced. The results of all this range from half a million fish killed in Kansas by runoff from cattle feedlots to major nitrogen pollution of municipal water supplies.

If we return to our earlier notions of a hierarchically organized world with supplies from all over the world flowing into central urban locations, the picture becomes even more grim. Frances Moore Lappé reports that 700,000 tons of fishmeal were imported into the United States from Chile and Peru in 1968. Although this material can be used as a human food supplement, it was fed to American animals. However, because of the relative inefficiency of animal metabolisms relatively little found its way into the flesh that was subsequently consumed by humans. Instead, most passed through the animals and on into the streams and lakes of the nation. Just as the trend is to concentrate feedlots and cattle, we may also picture a parallel system of concentration bringing nutrients from the vast waters of the southeast Pacific to a relatively small area half a world away in the central United States. Such concentrations overwhelm the capacities of local systems to carry off wastes and render them harmless through dilution and biodegrading.

It would be possible to continue with example after example of systems which bring together concentrations of materials which cannot be dispersed by natural processes. Typical of these would be the problem of urban sewage disposal around and within the Great Lakes. It seems a small matter when one toilet is flushed somewhere within the watershed of the St. Lawrence River. But when we picture feeder sewer lines linked to trunk

Air and water pollution along Lake Erie. Plumes of smoke and dirty water
can be seen streaming to the Northeast.

lines by the millions, and trunk lines pouring into regional conduits, which in turn empty into rivers feeding the Great Lakes, it comes as no surprise that trouble lies ahead. This combination of human and natural waterways brings nutrients in deadly concentrations to larger bodies of water. Lake Erie is particularly susceptible to this kind of pollution by concentration because of its shallow depth and slow currents. The result is eutrophication in the form of the runaway production of algae. This, in turn, reduces the gaseous content of the waters, suffocates the fish, and generally adds to the unpleasant conditions which threaten to destroy the lake. When we consider that the lake has also become the dumping ground for all manner of industrial wastes, it does not seem unreasonable to talk about its imminent death.

Our purpose here is not to discuss lake ecology so much as to point out that the complete tree shape of most hierarchical systems must not be overlooked. In other words, for every system of concentration there should be a system of dispersion of equal magnitude and efficiency. In all the preceding examples the solution lies with considerations of the scale at which things happen. At this point we need to return to our ideas of regional versus local organizations. Most towns and cities operate at local scales when compared with natural systems like rivers and watersheds which exist at regional scales. Little wonder that many small problems result in one enormous one. There is no reason why sewage and other wastes need to destroy the environment through dangerous concentrations. The solution to this problem lies in the creation of regional and national-sized organizations for the disposal of wastes. Certainly, federal regulatory and coordinating agencies need to be created to meet such problems. However, a further word of caution must be included at this point. Assuming that the needed federal agencies existed, their solution to the problem of waste disposal might be to dump everything into the Atlantic and Pacific Oceans. This would be simply failing to face the ultimate facts. The seas cannot cleanse themselves quickly enough of the filth of nations. Only when consumers are willing to pay the costs of adequate sewage treatment and to organize themselves at the same scales as the natural systems upon which they ultimately rely will the environment be truly safe.

Destruction and overproduction

Destruction and overproduction are so closely linked that it is useful to talk about these two causes of environmental imbalance in the same section. Sometimes an animal or a plant can simply be overharvested to the point where it can no longer maintain itself. The destruction of the dodo bird and the great auk, which were used to reprovision sailing ships in the eighteenth and nineteenth centuries, are examples of this. Whales and redwood trees face similar fates unless effective protective action is taken soon. In other cases flora and fauna are simply considered as pests and are wiped out as quickly as possible. Everything from bison to rain forests have met this fate. The defoliation of large tracts of jungle in southeast Asia which were considered a nuisance during the Indochina War will have consequences reaching centuries into the future. Shameful as it is to admit, humans have also actually viewed other humans as pests to be killed and driven from the land. We do not refer to the barbarisms of open warfare but rather to scattered attempts by European settlers in North America, Australia, and Africa to eliminate local hunting and gathering groups by poisoning them or hunting them down.

Extinction sometimes goes unnoticed; but at other times the removal of a species from the ecosystem allows some other plant or animal which was originally held in check by it to experience a population explosion, that is, overproduction. This removal of natural enemies can create monsters out of the mildest creatures through their sheer increase in numbers. At other times, a plant or animal may be introduced into a new land far from its original home. The new arrival may find an open ecologic niche with conditions ideal for its growth and no natural enemies. Again, unchecked population growth can occur with overwhelming results. Perhaps the most famous example of this is the introduction of rabbits into Australia. First brought there from England by early settlers for sport and food, the rabbits quickly began to multiply, with disastrous results. Entire regions were stripped of grass, and valuable water sources were consumed and contaminated. The sheep and cattle industries soon felt the impact of these invaders, and measures were taken to wipe them out. Wholesale hunting proved ineffective. Next rabbit-proof fences were built across the countryside for thousands of miles, but they too proved useless. Biological warfare was also tried with the introduction of myxoma virus. Three years after myxomatosis first decimated the rabbit population the survivors had developed an immunity to the disease and their populations once more increased. Similar stories can be told about the introduction of the mongoose into Jamaica, the European starling into the United States in 1891, and the American gray squirrel into the British Isles in 1876. Figures 21–2 and 21–3 show the diffusion and spread of the latter two of these creatures from their starting points to the far corners of their new homes.

Figure 21-2 Spread of the range of the European starling (*Sturnus vulgaris*) in the United States and Canada from 1891 to 1926 (From T. R. Detwyler (ed.), *Man's Impact on the Environment*, McGraw-Hill, New York, 1971; after M. T. Cooke, *The Spread of the European Starling in North America*, Circular, U.S. Dept. of Agriculture, 40:1–9, 1928)

Insecticides in Sabah The complexities of extinction and overproduction and the role man plays in those processes are illustrated by the consequences of the use of insecticides in Sabah, one of the Borneo states of Malaysia. Commercial coco production was introduced to this equatorial area in 1956. The approach used was typical of man's heavy-handed approach to nature. Large tracts of jungle were cleared, and commercial timber was removed. The remainder of the forest was either burned, or cut and left to rot, or allowed to stand as shade for the coco seedlings. At the present time, coco plantations exist as islands surrounded by secondary growth with the original forest just beyond.

The disrupted territory at the edge of the forest served as an ideal environment for fugitive and volunteer plant species. At the same time, the insects associated with that vegetation have a similar ability to move into new situations and to survive and multiply. As a result, the coco plantations soon fell prey to a series of insect pests which rapidly destroyed more than 20 percent of the coco trees. A ring bark borer, *Endoclita hosei*, which appeared first, was followed by leaf-eating caterpillars, aphids, and mealybugs. By 1961, bagworms, *Psychidae*, which are tent caterpillars and the larvae of moths, threatened the coco fields with a particularly serious outbreak.

During the period of increasing insect infestation, vigorous attempts were made to control all the insects. First, inspection and hand spraying was tried. But this proved too costly and had to be abandoned. After that,

Environmental Imbalance: Man's Role in Changing the Face of the Earth

397

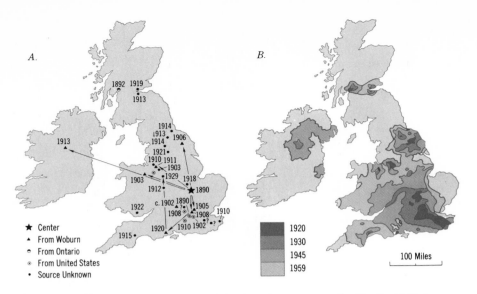

Figure 21-3 Introduction and spread of the American gray squirrel in the British Isles (Monica Shorten, "Introduced Menace," *Natural History Magazine*, December, 1964. Copyright © The American Museum of Natural History, 1964, p. 44.

Legend for map A:
★ Center
▲ From Woburn
◖ From Ontario
◉ From United States
• Source Unknown

Legend for map B:
1920
1930
1945
1959

100 Miles

massive spraying with DDT, BHC, lead arsenate, and dieldrin was carried out. At this point, the peculiar spatial characteristics of the insects involved became very important. Bagworms encase themselves in a tough silk sack covered with twigs and pieces of leaf. When threatened, they retreat completely inside this cover, and while feeding, only a small portion of their bodies extrude. Other pests which also feed on the coco plant bore into its bark and branches and remain covered. In every case, the insects which prey on plants are relatively sedentary, moving about as little as possible and feeding in local concentrations. The natural enemies of these pests are predatory and parasitic and must explore over large territories in order to find their prey. Thus, the coco pests are protected by bags and tunnels and are unlikely to wander into concentrations of insecticides unless those poisons are brought directly to the place where they are feeding. On the other hand, the insects which control them live exposed lives and cover large territories, thereby optimizing the possibility of their contact with insecticides. The results might have been predicted.

The natural enemies of the coco pests were wiped out; the pests themselves were little affected by the poisons, and a runaway overpopulation of insects resulted from man's destruction of first the forest and then the controlling predators.

Gordon R. Conway in his account of the battle to save the Sabah coco plantations points out that the real solution was the cheapest and easiest one. Almost all spraying was stopped, and some of the trees from the secondary growth encircling the fields which had served as hosts for certain of the coco pests were cut down. The predators were able to reestablish their numbers and to move into the plantations and to reduce the coco pests to a level which can be dealt with by human laborers on a selective basis. In this case, man through destruction of a native environment triggered unexpected insect population growth which could be controlled only through reestablishing some kind of natural equilibrium.

The Southern corn leaf blight epidemic
Lest we think that Sabah is too remote or

that examples like this are too rare, let us point out another example of man's tinkering, this time in the United States.

In 1970 the United States corn crop was reduced by more than 700 million bushels. This was the result of a wide-ranging epidemic of the Southern corn leaf blight, a disease caused by *Helminthosporium maydis*. This loss used up most of the reserve stocks of corn and forced prices up. Sorghum, barley, oat, and wheat reserves were used to offset the deficit. The export of grains from the United States was affected, and thus, reverberations of this incident were felt around the world.

Both the causes of the epidemic and the rapid response of agriculturalists which restored corn production to normal by 1972 are very much connected to aspects of both location and environment. The American corn crop depends almost entirely upon hybrid varieties which have the advantages of increased yields and the disadvantage of susceptibility to unexpected disease. In the decade preceding its virulent outbreak, corn leaf blights of all kinds destroyed no more than 2 or 3 percent of the annual crop. Even hybrids were considered to be resistant to such blights. A few reports of susceptibility to blight were reported in 1961, but only in 1968 did the loss of 200,000 pounds of seed corn indicate any serious problem. By 1969 seed fields and hybrid test fields showed indications of an association between hybrid corn with T cytoplasm and the corn leaf blight. By then, however, the development of a virulent strain was well underway and fields of early seed corn in Florida were attacked. By spring of 1970 cornfields in Florida, Georgia, Alabama, and Mississippi were being devastated. The blight had reached all across the Gulf states and up the Mississippi Valley into the Midwest by July. August found it in Wisconsin, Minnesota, and Canada. The dramatic losses which resulted have already been mentioned.

The destruction that resulted from the corn leaf blight is clearly attributable to man. We have bred new varieties and planted homogeneous stands of crops across entire nations. We have thereby created new environments for the overproduction of disease. Again, destruction and overproduction go hand in hand.

On the positive side of things, the problems of genetic homogeneity and hybrid susceptibility are being more and more widely recognized. Plant breeders and seed growers throughout the world attempt to produce a succession of varieties on a regular basis so that there will always be a ready supply of new genotypes as older ones become vulnerable to diseases. The spatial organization of the system helps ensure its success. At present there is an extensive network linking agriculturalists throughout the world. Nations exchange plant information on a regular basis and report the pathogenic responses of plants as soon as they are identified. Once a pathogen is found, growers send their own varieties of the susceptible crops to the infected area in order to identify resistant types. In this way, they prepare well in advance for the invasion of their own fields by virulent strains of disease. Obviously, it is far better to bring a few seeds to the disease than to introduce the disease to new areas for testing purposes. While this technique represents only a small part of an overall program of research and control, the importance of its spatial attributes are undeniable.

Meanwhile, new seed corn lacking T cytoplasm was quickly brought into production from experimental stocks. Some farmers shifted out of corn production for the summer of 1971, while the manual detasseling of some fields of corn also checked the virulence of the blight. Altogether, the organized response of agricultural organizations throughout this country and around the world checked what could have been an even more serious disaster. Nevertheless, the problem of man-made homogeneous environments still remains and someday may be responsible for disasters exceeding our capacity to control.

Change of state

When talking about the dangers of concentration, we have emphasized natural wastes like

*Environment
Environmental
Imbalance:
Man's Role in
Changing the
Face of the
Earth*

399

animal manure. In reasonable quantities manure and other by-products of organic processes can benefit the environment. This is because such compounds are *biodegradable*. This means that they are easily changed from one physical and chemical form to another and that they are quickly rendered harmless by naturally occurring processes. Their basic ingredients are recycled and become available for another round of use.

All biological processes change the state of environmental materials. Life creates complex organic compounds from simple elements. These compounds consist of large molecules, some of which store and transform energy, while others carry genetic codes enabling them to reproduce. All of this results in larger life-forms which, in turn, further order the environments they occupy. But it should be noted that the complete cycle of such systems includes the efficient return of each compound's basic materials into reusable forms. Human activities threaten earth environments by creating artificial compounds which do not easily break down into their basic elements. This is what we mean when we speak of *change of state*.

Man's manufacturing of artificial compounds may be the most dangerous and challenging of all the processes which bring about environmental imbalance. This is particularly true if such materials are allowed to escape into the general environment. Radioactive wastes from atomic power plants are an example of this. The coming decades will see a large increase in the size and number of atomic plants brought into service. The problem of disposing of their wastes will grow proportionately (Table 21–3). Part of the trouble with such materials is that they are produced in solid, liquid, and gaseous states. This means a variety of measures must be devised in order to control them. At the same time, the radioactive half-life (the time necessary for the intensity of radioactive emissions to drop by one-half) of these materials ranges from a few minutes to many years (Table 21–5). We have not yet developed containers for such wastes that will resist corrosion and natural forces

Table 21–5 The Half-Lives of Some Radioactive Materials

Element	Half-Life
Nitrogen-16	8 seconds
Bromine-85	3 minutes
Lead-214	27 minutes
Sodium-24	14.8 hours
Iodine-131	8 days
Polonium-210	138 days
Strontium-90	28 years
Cesium-137	33 years
Radium-226	1,622 years
Carbon-14	5,600 years
Uranium-238	4.5 billion years
Thorium-232	10 billion years

long enough for the contained materials to neutralize themselves. Consequently, dangerous substances may escape into the environment and later be reconcentrated by some of the spatial processes we have already described.

Any nation which wishes to use atomic reactors must face the technological and administrative challenges waste disposal of this kind presents. Fortunately, the problem is well recognized by official and private organizations, and research funds have been made available with which to develop regulatory procedures and control techniques. Such concepts as 100 percent reliable engineering standards and safeguards against sabotage and the theft of fissionable materials, as well as licensing, monitoring, and inspecting atomic facilities, are all being developed. Nevertheless, mistakes have happened and can still happen. For example, we have mentioned the effect of radioactive fallout on the vegetation and animals of the tundra. Similar events in the future are all too possible.

Other important man-made materials which present environmental problems include the biologically inert plastics or polyesters from which containers, drinking straws, film packs, and thousands of other items are made. Produced in prodigious volume and diffused across the countryside, these materials cannot be attacked by decay organisms and do not rot away. This produces a new burden of solid waste that is aesthetically displeasing and may have unforeseen consequences on the environments where such things accumulate. A significant concentration of buoyant plastic materials such as cigarette filter tips and Styrofoam cups has already been reported at the center of the great oceanic gyres. No one is certain what effect such concentrations will have on marine biosystems, but inevitably our children or grandchildren will pay the consequences if there are any.

Even more of a problem and on a par with radioactive wastes are synthetic materials which are active in life processes. More often than not, such materials are dangerous to plants and/or animals. Indeed, these active materials include insecticides, herbicides, and other poisons specifically created to kill unwanted life-forms. Unfortunately, such agents often kill many types of life against which their use was never intended. If the biologically active agents are themselves nonbiodegradable, they can be particularly menacing. DDT and other polychloride chemicals are in this class, as are the residues of 2,4,5-T and 2,4-D, which were the major defoliants used in the Indochina war. 2,4-D is also sold as a commercial herbicide throughout the United States, where 57 million pounds were used in 1968. In 1969 more than a million pounds were used on turf alone, and in the decade from 1960 to 1970 more than half a billion pounds were spread on vegetation in the United States. Residues of these materials can be found in the tissues of most large herbivorous animals found in the vicinity of their use. It is uncertain just what effect their presence will have in the long run, but researchers have already induced malformed births in laboratory animals by exposing them to these substances. The deadly role of DDT is even better known. Its presence in the bodies of birds results in their laying thin and soft-shelled eggs which cannot hatch. A number of species are threatened by this, including the American bald eagle.

DDT and similar agents are called "hard" pesticides because they are not easily broken down into harmless forms by biological action. As a consequence, they become widely dispersed in the environment and then slowly reconcentrate by moving up food chains until they reach lethal dosages in animals such as eagles and other predators high on the chain (Table 21–6). Of course, man is at the top of the food chain and can suffer contamination from eating the flesh of large fish and animals.

These dangers have been recognized, and some action has been taken to prohibit the uncontrolled use of such chemicals. Yet the ultimate control of "hard" compounds can be only partially achieved through a technical program. Society must also decide what it values most and act accordingly. Part of the increase in agricultural production in recent years is the result of the lavish use of pesticides and herbicides. The reduction of their use would help make the environment safer, but crop yields might well decline. This is not always the case, as the example of Sabah shows, but it is more than likely that less food would still be produced. Society, therefore, needs to decide what it wants most, more food or a chemically safe environment.

The Tragedy of the Commons

Extinction and destruction are also the fate of commonly owned resources. This statement sounds harsh and extreme, but there is hardly an exception to the rule thus stated. Garrett Hardin has called this dilemma the *tragedy of the commons*. The tragedy can be illustrated with the following example.

What is it worth to a stockman to add one more steer to a pasture which he shares with other herders, particularly if they are strangers? He must match the benefits against the costs. The benefit is that he has the products of one additional animal. The cost is that the pressure of one more animal unit is directed against the grass resource. The benefit is entirely his; the cost is shared out among all the strangers. Any rational stockman concludes that the only sensible thing to do is to add another animal

Environmental Imbalance: Man's Role in Changing the Face of the Earth

401

Table 21-6 DDT Residues, Selected Sample (in Parts per Million Net Weight of Whole Organism)

Organism	Tissue	DDT Residues PPM
plankton (Long Island, New York)		0.040
shrimp		0.16
crickets		0.23
flying insects, mostly Diptera		0.30
sheepshead minnow		0.94
trout (New Zealand)	whole body	0.7
black duck		1.07
plankton (California)		5.3
bass (California)		4 to 138
grebe (California)	fat	up to 1600
green heron		3.57
penquin (Antarctica)	fat	0.015
herring gull (New York)		7.53
osprey (New York)	abandoned egg	13.8
osprey (Connecticut)	egg	6.5
bald eagle (Missouri)	egg	1.1 – 5.6
dolphin (Florida)	blubber	220.
Man		
(England)		2.2
(France)		5.2
(U.S. average)		11.0
(Israel)		19.2

From G. M. Woodwell, "Toxic Substances and Ecological Cycles," *Scientific American,* vol. 216, no. 3, March 1967, pp. 24–31; and Charles F. Wurster, Jr., "Chlorinated Hydrocarbon Insecticides and the World Ecosystem," *Biological Conservation,* vol. 1, no. 2, 1969, pp. 123–129.

to the commons. In a society composed of rational men, each man is locked into a system that compels him to increase his herd without limit although the world within which he operates is limited. This is the destiny toward which all men rush. Each pursues his own interests in a society that believes in the freedom of the commons. "Freedom in a commons brings ruin to all."[1]

Different societies have devised different

methods of trying to deal with the tragedy of the commons, but success has been evasive. Usually ruin is avoided by removing a resource from common ownership. If this action or something comparable is not undertaken, the resource is destroyed. This was the case with the passenger pigeon, which became extinct because each person killed as many as he wanted. It was nearly so with the American bison. Such a fate now threatens most commercial saltwater fish and sea mammals which are currently being driven to extinction.

The spatial attributes of this problem are

[1] G. Hardin, "The Tragedy of the Commons," *Science,* vol. 162, Dec. 13, 1968, p. 1245.

interesting. The notion of private property plus explicit rules of inheritance removes resources from common ownership. One of the best ways to establish possession of a resource is to tell where it is spatially located and to claim it. This is the time-honored method of *staking a claim*. The identification of spatial jurisdiction both reduces conflict over ownership and allows for reasonable rates of use. Private ownership is an accepted institution in many if not most modern societies. But private ownership works well only if the resource is stationary. The dilemma persists if the resource can move. By crossing property lines a moving resource becomes a common good again. This was the argument between Robin Hood and the Sheriff of Nottingham over the deer in Sherwood forest. Robin Hood was poaching whenever he shot a deer in the King's forest. Now if he had been a freeman with a small parcel of his own land at the edge of the forest, and if a deer from the forest had wandered onto his property, where he then killed it, the act would have been legal by the *rule of capture*. This rule holds that if you can catch a wild thing on your property, it becomes your possession.

As we noted earlier in Chapter 7, the law is a set of rules of conduct. It maintains order by following a set of precedents. When a new situation arises and a decision must be made, the blind following of precedent may not yield reasonable results.

The necessary decisions will require wisdom as well as knowledge, and political action based on social and legal directives. This also means that the perception and value systems of the people must accomodate themselves to new problems. Since these things are all culturally determined inputs to the human ecosystem, we can predict that results will vary from place to place around the world. In any event, this also means that in order to make the right decisions, resource systems must be viewed in their totality. In the next and last chapter we attempt to look at several kinds of geographic systems, including urban ones, and to suggest ways in which the processes of environmental decline can be reversed.

Steel mills pouring out smoke. This represents the "tragedy of the commons," where large organizations take advantage of a common good—in this case the atmosphere. (Environmental Protection Agency photo)

A much too common scene along American roadways. Here, individuals abuse the common good by dumping trash. This "tragedy of the commons" involves individuals as well as corporations. (U.S. Dept. of Agriculture photo)

Our intention in writing this book has been to present the interaction of human and natural systems from a geographic point of view. In doing so, we have discussed many events that contribute to environmental decline and destruction. It is not our intention, however, to become doomsayers, croaking out "Nevermore," like Poe's raven. Undeniably, earth's environments are in serious trouble, but it is our belief that the spatial and natural processes inherent in geographic systems are neutral in character. That is, they are inherently neither good nor bad, but are only what people make of them. We also believe that most processes of environmental decline are reversible. This means that the fate of the earth environments, and, therefore, of ourselves, is up to each and all of us. Our well-being lies in the realm of perception, behavior, and education. There is still time, if we act now, to leave a good earth to our grandchildren. Geographic knowledge of how the world functions should help us appreciate this and suggest to us critical points where individual efforts may be most effective.

Human Environments as Geographic Systems

The following pages present four problem environments in terms of the ideas found throughout this book. These examples are drawn from the past and present and from different cultures. We hope that the geographic insights their analysis provides will suggest guidelines for positive action in other situations. The first case describes how two different cultures obtain and use water from alluvial fans in very different ways. Adjustments to the environmental system in which the actions of each group take place clearly derive from their particular cultures.

Alternative systems of arid-land water procurement

Water for farming in arid lands is scarce, but reliable supplies can be accumulated in several ways by natural systems. One such source of water is located within alluvial fans found at the entrances to valleys or canyons along the flanks of mountains. Even though streams in these locations may flow only intermittently, lenses of fresh water are often present under the loose materials of the alluvial fans (Figure 22–1). Water enters systems such as these when warm winds are forced to rise over the mountains. The rising air mass subsequently cools and yields orographic rainfall. The rain runs off and accumulates in the valleys, whence it flows downstream. If there is sufficient runoff, some will be disgorged into

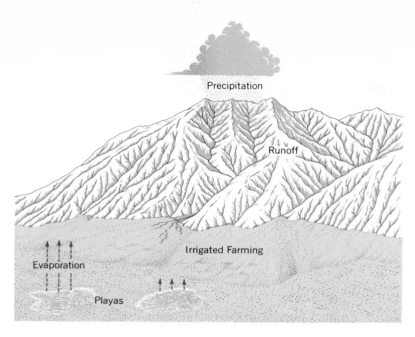

Figure 22-1 Arid lands agriculture In arid lands, a lens of fresh water sometimes exists under alluvial fans along the flanks of mountains. These circumstances present an opportunity for men to put the water to their own use. The natural system is one of concentrating mountain water runoff followed by rapid dissipation through evaporation from the salty playas.

intermontane basins to form shallow, ephemeral lakes which quickly evaporate, leaving behind flat plains of saline silt called *playas.* Water that ponds on these playas is of no use for agriculture or drinking because it is so saline. Another portion of the rainfall infiltrates the surfaces of the streambeds and moves underground into the alluvial fans. There the overlying alluvium protects it from quickly evaporating in the hot sun. Water thus accumulated can remain for long periods before slowly disappearing from the silts, sands, and gravels where it is stored. Evaporation is retarded under such conditions and the water remains fresh while slowly flowing through the fans to the lower playas. A salt-water table is usually found below the fresh water, but because fresh water weighs less, the lens of fresh water rides upon the heavier saline solution. People in arid lands all over

the world have recognized the nature of this resource system and take various actions to utilize the stored water.

The one place man can enter this system is on the alluvial fans. In the western United States one can still find old windmills located on alluvial fans, usually a little to one side of the valley exit to avoid damage from flash floods (Figure 22-2A). Nowadays windmills may be replaced by electric or gasoline-driven pumps. Under these circumstances at least two philosophies of resource use can be practiced: quick pumping for short-term benefits and budgeted water removal for long-term returns. We have already mentioned the problems of too rapidly removing the nonrenewable fossil waters of the Great Plains. In the case of alluvial fan water deposits, there is a steady renewal of the resource but at a slow rate.

Geography: Location, Culture, and Environment

405

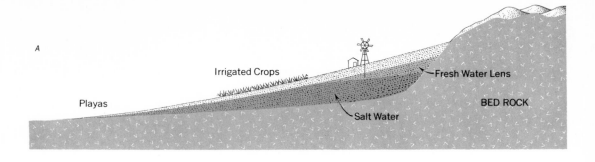

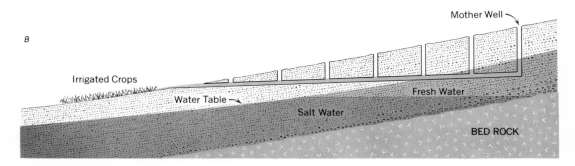

Figure 22-2 **A. Western U.S. alluvial fan** In the Western U.S. arid regions, the fresh water under alluvial fans is exploited by employing wind power or, more commonly now, electric or diesel pumps. **B. Qanats.** In Persia and many other places in the Middle East and North Africa, qanats, or "horizontal wells," are used to tap the alluvial fan water. Gravity is the source of power. The practice is very ancient and requires considerable engineering skill.

Quick pumping might be practiced to provide water for stock or crops over a critical drought period which the farmer anticipates will be a short one. Once the lens of water is gone, it may take many months to completely restore it. For long-term returns, it is likely that the water will be used for stock rather than for crop irrigation. In that case the number of cattle which can be raised on the surrounding steppe or desert range may be controlled by the volume of water which the alluvial fan can produce. That, in turn, depends upon the size of the catchment basin, the height of the mountains, the relative continental location of the entire system, the permeability and po-

rosity of the ground materials, and the capacity and rate of the pumps involved. At the same time, the cattle can move only a few miles from the watering place before they must return for a drink. Thus, the range utilization which accompanies this water use is constrained by special environmental circumstances. If the rancher were to try to increase his herd size by increased pumping, he could only temporarily add to the number of animals dependent upon the system. The temptation presented by pumps utilized fossil fuels for energy is that it is easy to temporarily increase the flow of water and more difficult to foresee the longer-range consequences.

In Iran and other parts of the Middle East and North Africa, similar environmental conditions are found, but the resource is utilized in a significantly different way. In those areas "horizontal wells" called *qanats* are dug in order to tap the freshwater lens (Figure 22–2*B*). A *qanat* is a series of vertical well shafts connected by a slightly sloping tunnel, or *drift*, which leads downhill and out into the valley or basin in front of the fan. The bottoms of the shafts are connected by a tunnel with a very slight gradient. The water reaches the surface by means of gravity flow where the tunnel intersects the slope of the topographic surface. The trick is to keep the gradient of the tunnel shallow enough to prevent erosion and steep enough to encourage a regular flow. The size of the village supplied by such a system (Figure 22–3) is regulated by the amount of water thus made available. The alluvial fan serves as a reservoir which evens out the intermittent and irregular flow resulting from unpredictable desert rains.

The qanat system of irrigation was apparently an ancient Persian invention, and has been utilized there since at least 714 B.C. At present, there are between 20,000 and 40,000 qanats in Iran with an aggregate length of approximately 100,000 miles. Some 20 to 25 percent of all the crops grown each year in that country depend upon qanat water. The advantages are obvious and include low expenditures of fossil fuels and capital equipment to maintain the system. The disadvantage is that these tunnels easily collapse and are difficult to restore. Labor inputs are high although this is in a nation where underemployment is a problem. More important, the work is extremely dangerous for the craftsmen who specialize in digging the tunnels by hand.

The two systems which we have just described have come in direct contact during the earthquakes of the last decade in Iran. At that time, miles of tunnels collapsed, leaving many settlements without water. Those populations might well have died or had to migrate had not relief teams arrived with equipment for drilling deep tube wells. The new wells

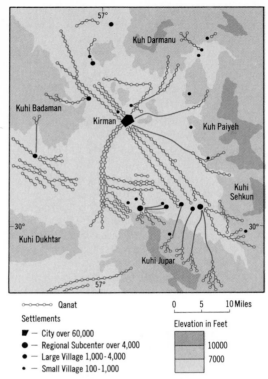

Figure 22-3 Qanats of Kirman Basin Qanats often extend for miles. Notice that the source, or "mother well," is usually at the mouth of a draw or canyon. (Paul Ward English, *City and Village in Iran*, University of Wisconsin Press, © 1967 by the Regents of the University of Wisconsin, p. 32.

were equipped with gasoline pumps and the flow of water actually increased. However, the prosperity which followed may well be ephemeral for the reasons cited in the American example. The rate of water removal is apparently far in excess of the natural system's ability to restore water to the alluvial reservoir. Increased cropland has facilitated parallel increases in local populations, and we are left wondering what the years ahead will bring.

The lesson in this case is clear. Man must assess and respect the rate at which natural systems operate if he attempts to merge his activities with them. If he can speed up the overall system without creating shortages somewhere along its length, well and good.

Geography: Location, Culture, and Environment

But the rates of concentration and dispersal within man-environment systems must be kept in equilibrium throughout all the subsystems, particularly the culturally induced ones, if long-term benefits are to follow.

The Irish famine

The Irish famine and typhoid epidemic of 1845–1847 and an occurrence of blue babies in Decatur, Illinois, in the 1960s make an interesting comparison. Unlike as the two events might at first seem, they have much in common. Both were closely tied to environmental conditions; both depended upon the interpretation of scientific investigations; both hinged upon human value systems and attitudes. The first was an outright disaster and tragedy. The latter case may show mankind's ability to find rational solutions to difficult problems. Our strategy will be to describe the famine and then to describe the situation in Decatur with frequent references to the Irish case.

The "Irish" potato was first domesticated in South America. The particular variety which became so important on European tables apparently came from islands off the coast of Peru. After returning explorers introduced the potato to Europe, its utility was eventually recognized and its use soon spread. Within the next 200 years it became a staple food for many societies. The potato was particularly welcome in places like Ireland where cool, moist conditions, high humidity, and acidic soils made many other crops impractical. Also, its high yields per acre meant that a poor man's large family could be sustained on a small piece of ground. The potato was not what could be described as a reliable crop, however, and failures of varying intensity had plagued the Irish fields from as early as 1728. Total disaster struck finally in 1845, when the entire Irish potato crop was destroyed by a blight caused by the fungus *Phytophthora infestans*. The crop of 1846 fared no better, and by the winter of 1847 the crowded poor were so weakened and brought low that they fell easy victim to a typhoid epi-

demic that killed many who might have survived near starvation.

The spread of the blight from America to Europe, with outbreaks in north Germany, the Isle of Wight, parts of the English mainland, and later in Ireland, is a good example of spatially dependent *contagious diffusion*. The fungus attacked both stored potatoes and those still in the ground, turning them into a black, soggy, and totally inedible mass. The Reverend M. J. Berkeley, typical of the "gentleman" scientists of eighteenth and nineteenth century England, recognized the fungus as the source of the blight and reported on it in the *Journal of the Horticultural Society* of London in 1846. His ideas contradicted the generally accepted notion that the fungus was the effect and not the cause of the blight and were rejected by the scientific community with no effort to prove them right or wrong. If the truth had been accepted, the crops might have been saved by spraying them with Bordeaux mixture and other copper compounds.

At the same time, the Irish peasantry were ill prepared to withstand the pressures placed upon them by crop failures and a hostile or at best indifferent occupation by the English, who had dominated Ireland since Elizabethan times. The Irish population was reduced in almost all cases to an ignorant and agricultural servitude, particularly after Oliver Cromwell had crushed their uprising against him. The penal laws, 1695 to 1829, had prevented Irish Catholics from purchasing land and from participating in the military, in commerce, or in formal systems of education. At the same time, large estates were carved from Irish lands and given to absentee English landlords as rewards for service to the crown. Taxes levied against the tenants were high and had to be paid with produce such as grains, since money was scarce. A farmer who failed to pay his taxes was almost certain to be evicted and had little choice except to flee to the cities if he and his family were to have any chance of survival. One of the few kinds of aid available to the huddled urban poor was *outdoor relief*, working on public projects in the worst kind of winter weather. To top it all off, the English Parliament thoroughly believed in *laissez faire* economics and thought that an uncontrolled economy would force prices low enough for the poor to enter the market economy, something which did not occur. One incredible consequence of all this was that during the famine, Ireland continued to export grain in payment of rent.

All of this paved the way for the typhoid that followed. The sequence has been described by George Carey and Julie Schwartzberg:

1. The potato failure led to famine.
2. Famine led to indigence and the selling of property for food.
3. The sociopolitical structure drove people to urban centers.
4. Outdoor winter work relief in the towns led to further weakness and illness.
5. The ragged, weakened people in the urban centers huddled together for warmth.
6. As they huddled together, lice spread through their rags, carrying typhus.[1]

The result of all this was wholesale migration to North America and England of those most able to survive. The population of Ireland was significantly reduced, and it assumed an age structure with the elderly predominating and late marriages the rule.

In this case special factors in the natural and human environments encouraged reliance on monocropping for subsistence purposes. At the same time, the social and political organization of the local Irish and occupying English prevented quick, rational responses to the situation. The overall effect can be pictured as a wave of blight moving eastward out of North America which in turn triggered a diffusion of Irish culture to the United States and other places. The attitudes and values associated with the various participating groups are of particular importance in understanding the situation.

[1]George W. Carey and Julie Schwartzberg, *Teaching Population Geography,* Teachers College, New York, 1969, pp. 27–28.

In the Irish case, the ruling class identified with the outlook and perspectives of the English squire. Since they were, by choice, urban dwellers, frequently living abroad, the west country Irish peasant was outside of their realm of perception. From this stemmed illusions such as the naive assumption that most Irish families were within the cash economy, and that fiscal policies might alleviate the disaster.

The inflexible adherence to preconceived ideology was not limited to the governing classes, however. Scientists committed to a specific theory of fungus propagation rejected a hypothesis which would have proven correct regarding the cause of the blight, eschewing the possibility of empirical testing in favor of a test by dogma.

On the other hand, the world view of the Irish peasant had been rigidly constricted and circumscribed by generations of policy directed towards limited his access to media of communication and circumscribing his arena of choice, so that although he was caught in the maelstrom of the disaster, he lacked the facilities for fully communicating his plight to the government whose views were formed behind the filtered lenses of their faulty perceptions.[2]

Nitrate pollution in an Illinois community

Barry Commoner in his book *The Closing Circle* discusses an ecologic problem facing the people of Decatur, Illinois, and its agricultural hinterland. It is useful to compare his example with that of the Irish famine because of similarities underlying the two systems. On the other hand, the two events stand in vivid contrast to one another because of the very different human responses which their situations evoked.

The community of Decatur provides goods and services to the farms which surround it. In many ways the prosperity of those farms underlies the prosperity of the town. Modern farming techniques necessitate the use of large amounts of nitrogen fertilizer which dramatically increase corn yields. At the same

[2]Ibid.

time, unused nitrogen washes from the fields into the streams, lakes, and wells upon which the farm and urban populations depend for drinking water. There is strong evidence that when the nitrate level in water rises above the recommended limit of 45 parts per million, infants, particularly girl babies, may suffer and even die from oxygen starvation; that is, they may become "blue babies." This happens when dissolved nitrates are converted by intestinal bacterial action into nitrite. Nitrite is taken up by the hemoglobin in the blood, and the methemoglobin which results prevents oxygen from being carried through the infant's system in sufficient quantities. The citizens of Decatur are, therefore, faced with a real dilemma: must they give up their agriculturally based prosperity in order to have healthy children? The following account outlines their situation in greater detail and reveals the importance of maintaining good communication channels in human ecosystems.

The podzolic soils of the Midwest are well suited for the mixed grain–livestock farming that typifies the area. In previous decades green manure from harvested crops, as well as the manure of animals, was returned each year to the fields. This restored vital amounts of organic nitrogen to the soil and kept crop yields reasonably high. In recent years, however, the situation has changed. It has become too expensive and inefficient for the farmers to return waste products to the land. As a result, natural fertility has declined and the soil must be restored by large inputs of man-made fertilizers. As more and more nitrogen is ap-

plied, crop yields increase dramatically (Table 22-1). It should be noted though that the first 100,000 tons applied to Illinois fields produced a 40 percent increase in yield, while the next 300,000 tons produced an additional increase of only 36 percent. In other words, a point is reached where each added increment of fertilizer produces less of an increase than the one before. Nevertheless, the farmers must use heavy applications of nitrogen fertilizers to make a profit. As you will recall from the discussion of Thünen's theory of land use, this is a high-rent area for agriculture. In fact, corn must return about 80 bushels per acre for the farmer to break even. His profits are made by the additional bushels of corn he can force from the land by adding more and more fertilizer. If he can produce 95 bushels per acre, he makes 15 bushels profit. But the extra fertilizer he adds to get those additional bushels of profit is used less and less efficiently. The nitrogen which is not taken up by the plants simply washes off the land.

Now let us pause for a moment and compare this and the previous example. In both nineteenth century Ireland and twentieth century Illinois relative location and site conditions played important parts in the development of the respective patterns of land use. In both cases, climate and soil required either special crops or special technology for optimum yields. From the point of view of a possibilist, many choices were open to the people occupying the land, but in more pragmatic terms potatoes and corn were good answers to the question of which crops to plant. Not the least of their choice depended upon the need for high yields. In the first case, potatoes supported large populations of rural poor on small tracts of land. In the latter, high production costs necessitate large yields for reasonable profits.

Once more considering Decatur and its problems, the effects of excess nitrate are not immediately apparent, and for a long time there was doubt in some people's minds that the high level of nitrate in Illinois rivers was directly the result of the increased use of fertilizer. Barry Commoner had scarcely presented a paper on this topic at the annual

Table 22-1 The Relationship of Crop Yields to the Application of Fertilizer Nitrogen

Time Period	Amount Applied to Illinois Fields	Yields per Acre, Bushels
1945–1948	Minimal amounts	50
1958	100,000 tons	70
1965	400,000 tons	95

Source: Barry Commoner, *The Closing Circle*, Bantam Books, New York, 1972, p. 81.

meeting of the American Association for the Advancement of Science when his conclusions were challenged by representatives of the fertilizer industry as well as some agricultural scientists who had helped perfect the use of nitrogen fertilizers on Midwestern farms. This is an example of what we have called "when men of goodwill disagree." The issue at question was not the agricultural benefits resulting from fertilizer use but rather the importance of the long-range consequences possibly associated with that use. Despite the fact that some of those involved maintained a "My mind is made up. Don't disturb me with the facts" attitude, there was sufficient freedom and objectivity of thought to launch a thorough investigation of the matter, and various groups within the scientific community established the clear-cut relationship between intensive fertilization and the increased nitrogen content of Illinois streams. This is a far cry from the closed minds and indifference with which Reverend Berkeley's conclusions were greeted by English savants a century and a half earlier.

Commoner's next step was to communicate directly to the people concerned. In 1970 he and others reported their findings to health department officials, farmers, and agronomists at a special seminar held in a local high school. This "grass roots" method of action was an effective one. Though not everyone could immediately accept the implications of those reports, the basic goodwill and cooperation of the entire community in the face of environmental threat soon became apparent. As a result of that meeting, efforts were intensified to find alternative ways to maintain crop yields at high levels without the overuse of nitrogen. At the same time, once the farmers were made aware of the possible side effects of their fertilizers, they indicated their willingness to substitute those alternative farm methods wherever possible.

The issue is still far from resolved, but the situation around Decatur stands in sharp contrast to the narrow-minded and predetermined attitudes of the nineteenth century politicians responsible for the ineffectual response to the great potato famine. Here,

then, is another insight into effective environmental management: every effort must be made to maintain and increase the level and efficiency of communication flow and information handling. In other words, the need for education and research concerning critical issues never ends. Well-informed minds will not do away with differences in opinion about what is best, but they vastly improve the chances of working out compromises acceptable to all.

Los Angeles as a human ecosystem

In order to understand the Los Angeles region in terms of the ideas introduced throughout this book, let us first diagram the general system which it represents. The interlocking flow of natural and cultural processes and elements which constitute the system known as Los Angeles is shown in Figure 22–4. On the far left are listed major characteristics of the atmosphere, hydrosphere, and lithosphere in Southern California. There are an infinite number of things that might be shown, but we have chosen a few which we think are critical. First is the land itself, a coastal plain backed by the San Bernardino Mountains of the Coast Range. Behind the mountains to the east the Mojave Desert merges with the higher deserts of Nevada and Arizona.

Geologically speaking, this is an unstable area with numerous fault zones either penetrating it or located on its boundaries. These include the San Gabriel fault complex, the Newport-Inglewood system, and the Santa Ynez, which crosses both Ventura and Santa Barbara Counties. Tremors are a frequent occurrence and major earthquakes have occurred in almost every decade. At the same time, despite the presence of fault zones, the sedimentary rocks of the Los Angeles lowlands contained valuable petroleum deposits.

The general location of Southern California at 34° north latitude places it within the influence of the subtropical high-pressure system. A Mediterranean climate prevails, with mild and often rainy winters and long, dry summers. At the same time, the hydrology of the area reflects its global position as well as

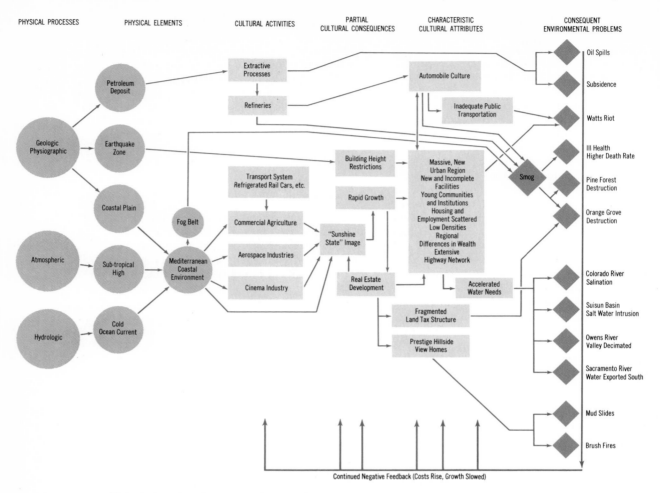

Figure 22–4 Los Angeles basin physical/cultural system. A systems diagram of the Los Angeles Basin, including both natural and social elements. The many inputs combine in complex ways, some of which create unexpected and unwanted consequences. These act as negative feedbacks to further influence the system. The diagram is not meant to be complete and does not imply that any equilibrium state is in sight.

Nature and Man in a Spatial Context

more local influences. The California Current that flows offshore from north to south is relatively cool. When the land warms, local offshore breezes move inland, bringing fog which is suitable for certain kinds of agriculture. But the warming air increases its ability to hold moisture and the land beneath is dried out as the cool sea breezes warm and rise over the land.

The result of all this and more is a Mediterranean coastal environment well suited for specialized agriculture. Here then are some of the major physical elements and processes which have been discussed elsewhere in this book. Let us begin with them and thereafter by adding human activities follow through some of the sequences of events that affect Southern California.

The felicitous environment of Southern California was particularly good for agriculture, but little except local production took place until the railroads with refrigerator car technology pushed through to the city. The combination of improved transportation and suitable year-round growing conditions allowed the development of commercial agriculture which at first emphasized citrus fruits. The orange seems like a small sun itself, and it was only a matter of a few years until someone first called California the *Sunshine State*. The movie industry, which had its early beginnings in New Jersey and elsewhere in the East, was attracted by the warm and cloudless weather which allowed outdoor filming every month of the year. People who watched the silver screen knew where the "movies" and then the "talkies" were made, and those sunny skies got good publicity. The aircraft industry also chose Southern California because of the weather, although its arrival was considerably later. Clear skies allowed testing throughout the year, and warm temperatures made it unnecessary to build well-insulated or heated hangers. Aircraft are complex machines requiring skilled workers and engineers, and one of the selling points employment agencies gave for moving out to California became the good climate, which compensated in large part for the state's remote location on the far side of the continent. Real estate developers and the chamber of commerce went to great lengths to promote the "Sunshine State" image. This perception of California as a desirable place to live and work prevails to the present time. This is shown by the high ranking given it on Peter Gould's mental maps described in Chapter 20.

Early rapid population growth began in the 1880s when the Santa Fe Railroad reached Southern California. The original little Spanish settlement, which in 1800 had only 300 residents, had swelled to 50,000 by 1890. (The first oil field began production in 1892 and added to the image of limitless riches.) The second rapid increase in population came soon after the Union Pacific was completed to the city in 1905. At that time, small local industries provided for the population's needs, but the range of those goods was insufficient for them to compete in Eastern markets. Meanwhile, the increased agriculture and the increased population required more water than the plan could provide. The Los Angeles Aqueduct was built to the east side of the Sierra Nevada Mountains in 1913, and the extra water which this brought provided the means for Los Angeles to grow by annexing thirsty communities on its borders. Here was one of the first resource conflicts between the city and the land.

The first search for additional water led the city to the Owens River, 223 miles north at the foot of Mt. Whitney. But the water taken from there was not enough. Los Angeles by the 1920s had purchased water rights in the northern Owens Valley. Crawley Lake Reservoir and the Mono Extension Canal followed by 1935. The result was the near depopulating of the Owens Valley and the death of Owens Lake as its waters were diverted to the city. Two-thirds of the water used in the modern metropolitan region still comes from that area, but the demand continues to grow and more water is now brought from central California. The resources of one area are being moved to another and millions of people are benefiting from such a transfer, but the end is not in sight. Water is also being brought from the Colorado River via the Colorado River Aqueduct. The removal of those fresh waters from the river plus the addition of mineralized drainage water from irrigation projects has resulted in an increased salt content in the river flow crossing the border into Mexico. In the international agreement regulating use of the river the amount of water that the United States must pass on to Mexico was agreed upon but nothing was said about its salinity. Once again, the finite nature of a resource has led to ill feeling between two

Geography: Location, Culture, and Environment

413

groups of well-meaning, but self-serving, people. Even the Sacramento River northeast of San Francisco has been used to meet these increasing water demands. Now, thirsty Southern Californians are eyeing the water resources of the extreme northern part of their state. The manipulation of California's waters has centered, in large part, upon the California Water Plan, which was authorized by the state legislature in 1947. The plan utilizes the Sacramento River, with much of its water being diverted to the south. The Oroville Dam, a major part of the Feather River Project on a tributary of the Sacramento, also provides water for urban populations to the south. But the real prize for which Californians yearn is the abundant waters of the Pacific Northwest. However, the prospective use of their waters outside of their own region is viewed with no enthusiasm by the people of Washington, Oregon, and British Columbia, and the federal government has banned the majority of feasibility studies of such projects. It would seem that the answers to water shortages in the Los Angeles area must come from within its own region, or if not, at least from within the American Southwest.

In this way, we can trace a path through the general system from hydrosphere to climate, on through the influence of man and his perceptions of the area as a desirable place to live and of water as a freely expendable resource. We come at last to the negative results brought to water source areas beyond the city. But as water demand continues to grow, word of water shortages diffuses outward to the rest of the nation. This has in a small way formed a deviation dampening mechanism or negative feedback which may discourage further migration to the state. Whether or not it and others will come in time to take the pressure of excess population off the Los Angeles area is debatable, but before translating the question of crowding and the subsequent runaway use of resources into a more general case, let us look at some related problems of pollution and environmental degradation in Southern California.

This time let us begin with the geology and quickly move on to the petroleum deposits and their exploitation. We have already mentioned the discovery of oil in 1892. In the dozen years between 1917 and 1929, fifteen new oil fields were discovered in the Los Angeles basin. The coastal stretch became important with the Huntington Beach field in 1920 and the Signal Hill field in 1921. Refineries and tank farms were quick to follow, and the state became an exporter of petroleum products to Eastern markets via the Panama Canal. In 1936 an important new field was opened at Wilmington near the harbors of Los Angeles and Long Beach. Although the field's production varied in the next three decades, a total of 913 million barrels of oil, 484 million barrels of water, and 832 million MCF of gas (MCF = 1,000,000 cubic feet) have been removed from about 10 square miles of territory. The removal of all that material had the same effect as a leak in a water bed. Subsidence of the surface of the land above the deposits was detectable by 1941. The rate of subsidence has been carefully measured and reached its peak in 1951 with 2.37 feet per year, the same year in which maximum pumping of 140,000 barrels of oil per day from the field was attained. The nearby Signal Hill field also contributed to the sinking of the earth. Altogether the land sank 27 feet at the center of this depression (Figure 22–5).

The solution to this problem was twofold. At first, levees, bulkheads, and retaining walls were constructed. But dire predictions of further subsidence forced the city and the producers to take a more rational look at the problem. The final solution was to repressurize the field by pumping specially treated water back into the ground. As a result of this action there has been up to 15 percent rebound of the initial subsidence, which has in general been checked. It is interesting to note from a geographic point of view that the runaway exploitation—particularly of Signal Hill—created the most serious obstacle to repressurizing. The deposit was owned and tapped by 117 producers, all of whom had to agree to such drastic measures. Coordinating them and forming them into a single oper-

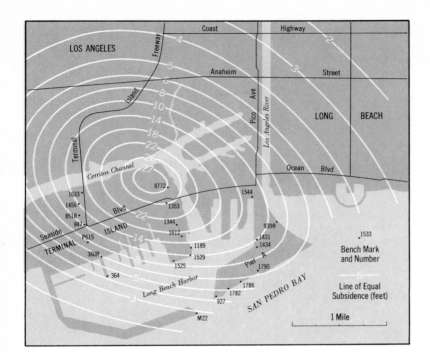

Figure 22-5 Long Beach harbor area, California, subsidence from 1928 to 1962 (J. F. Poland, and G. H. Davis, "Land Subsidence Due to Withdrawal of Fluids," *Reviews in Engineering Geology*, The Geological Society of America, vol. 2, 1969)

ating unit was much more difficult than the engineering problems involved.

Here we have followed one path through our system showing Los Angeles. Let us retreat partway along it and look at another problem. The search for oil has taken drilling rigs out to sea. Southern California has its share of offshore wells, particularly in the Santa Barbara Channel opposite the city of the same name. One such well "blew" on January 28, 1969, when workmen pulled the drilling bit from the hole. While wells can usually be quickly capped under these circumstances, the well casing in this instance scarcely penetrated beneath the ocean floor. The escaping oil burst out through shattered rock of an adjacent fault and flooded to the surface. For eleven days, while crews worked around the clock trying to stanch the flow,

an estimated 21,000 barrels per day escaped. The slick that spread out on the surface eventually covered 800 square miles. Despite frantic efforts of thousands of conservationists, beach bums, businessmen, dowagers, and the general public, the loss of marine birdlife was extreme. Sea mammals and fish also perished from being coated with the sticky mess. The well was eventually closed off; the oil was finally cleaned up; the dead wildlife was buried or drifted out to sea; but the questions raised by this and other disasters such as the wreck of the tanker the *Torrey Canyon* off the coast of Cornwall, England, cannot be overlooked. Safety measures adequate to meet the problems of dangerous geology or wreck-proof ships are too expensive for board chairmen to justify to their stockholders. The result is that too often the costs are pushed

Geography: Location, Culture, and Environment

off on the general public, who must clean up the mess or go without beaches and birdlife. In terms of what we have said before, the ocean belongs to no one. It is the *commons* all over again, and there is nobody to protect it.

Again we move back along our systems path, this time to the refineries which produce gasoline for the thousands and thousands of automobiles in the city. These same refineries also emit fumes into the polluted skies over Los Angeles. Refinery fumes, hydrocarbon exhaust gases from automobiles, and the famous California fog combine to make an eye-smarting, acrid, debilitating smog. Though few people die from its effects, orange groves have suffered a decline in production and quality of fruit, while vast tracts of pine forest in the mountains beyond the city are dying from the same cause. Most of the blame can now be traced to automobile exhausts, which contribute about 90 percent by weight of the total air pollutants. Pollution control devices on automobiles help to some extent, but the number of cars is increasing so rapidly that major efforts at control result in only small gains. Table 22–2 shows some of the tonnages of pollutants entering the air in Los Angeles County each day.

Table 22–2 Emission of Air Pollutants in Los Angeles County

Year	Source	Amount, Tons per Day
1950	Transportation	6,888
	Other	3,240
	Total	10,128
1965	Transportation	13,054
	Other	1,792
	Total	14,846
1970 (projected)	Transportation	10,083
	Other	1,770
	Total	11,853

Source: "Summary of Total Air Pollution Data for Los Angeles County: A Report of the Engineering Division," Air Pollution Control District, County of Los Angeles, January 1965, pp. i–ii and 1–41.

Again the commons and its tragedy come to the fore. Which among us is willing or able to give up his car for the good of the public? If this is difficult for the average American, it would be well nigh impossible for the citizens of spread-out, freeway-laced Southern California where no adequate public transport exists.

Effecting Change in Geographic Systems

What can be done about pollution of the air, the waters, and the land? Even uncluttered space has become a dwindling resource as urban sprawl increases. More generally, how can rational change for the better be implemented in geographic systems? Although the nature and sources of trouble vary from one location to another, the basic issues remain the same. The problem may be air pollution in one place and solid waste in another, but in every case, underlying similarities catch our attention. Air pollution is a suitable topic with which to begin our discussion, but let us leave California and consider such matters in a broader context. After all, Los Angeles is everywhere.

An analysis of the spatial and temporal aspects of air pollution suggests some remedial strategies. First, we must recognize that serious localized air pollution episodes occur when the normal diffusion action of the atmosphere fails to dissipate pollutants because of certain meteorological conditions. Such dangerous concentrations are localized in time and space. They take place sporadically and with varying frequency, but not entirely in an unpredictable manner. Given sufficient knowledge of the weather, these events can be forecast (Figure 22–6). As our meteorological knowledge improves and as our capacity to monitor the atmosphere increases, we can expect pollution forecasts to become more accurate. Data gathering and surveillance of the total environment thus become important parts of any remedial program. But facts alone do not produce solutions; those must be based on policy agreements among the parties involved.

Our concern here is with the interplay between physical processes and cultural ones. If the physical system temporarily assumes a particular configuration like an inversion layer over a city, it may be possible for the cultural system to respond by changing its configuration during the period of crisis. If over a long period of time the natural system simply cannot meet the demands placed upon it, it may be possible to modify the long-range behavior of the society involved. On the other hand, technological improvements such as emission control devices on automobiles may become economically feasible and remove unmanageable burdens from the natural system.

In the case of air pollution, if early warning devices give sufficient advance notice, measures can be taken such as shutting down incinerators, factories, and power plants which emit large quantities of pollutants into the atmosphere. Traffic can also be curbed, and the populace told not to burn trash or leaves. Control systems similar to this already exist in Los Angeles, the New York–New Jersey region, and elsewhere, although as yet they are not totally successful.

Strategies of this kind represent the least-cost approach to adequately controlling short-duration events. Costs include the disruption of normal affairs and the price of the early warning system. Legal and institutional arrangements must be agreed upon and implemented in such a way that when action is necessary, affected segments of society will accept the disruptions and inconveniences and act responsibly. This includes specific agreements with factories and businesses that they will shut down or cut back their operations. The Los Angeles petroleum refineries have already accepted such measures. But the public must also be involved in the remedy. They must be educated to the dangers of the situation and kept informed. For example, the "murk" index of pollutants contained within the atmosphere is a good daily measure often reported on radio and television. The question is, once the public is informed, how can individuals

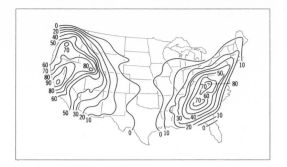

Figure 22-6 Frequency of high air pollution potential The number of days that widespread high air pollution potential was forecast throughout the United States are shown in this map from the Environmental Sciences Services Administration. The program began in the East on Aug. 1, 1960, and in the West on Oct. 1, 1963. Between these respective dates and Apr. 3, 1970, there were thirty-nine episodes in the West and seventy-five in the East. The numbers indicate the days a particular area was affected by a high air pollution potential forecast, for example, the area between the line marked "0" and the line marked "10 days." This map does not show the many additional days of bad air pollution weather of less than 75,000 square miles extent, or of less than thirty-six hours duration, or both. (© 1971 Committee for Environmental Information. Reproduced from "Episode 104" in *Air Pollution* by Virginia Brodine by permission of Harcourt Brace Jovanovich, Inc.)

be persuaded to do their bit, to accept their share of inconvenience? Effecting change in mass attitudes and behavior is perhaps the most difficult thing to do. As Pogo says, "We have met the enemy and he is us."

One tragedy of the commons is the difficulty of charging individuals for their use of a moving resource. The air we breathe has traditionally been considered a "common good." It costs nothing, is found everywhere, and moves unimpeded across jurisdictional boundaries. However, as Roger Revelle points out:

With an inversion at 1,000 feet over a crowded city, the weight of the column of air available at any given time near the ground is about 100 tons per person. If the air is to remain breathable (carbon dioxide concentration less than 1 per cent), the amount required each day for com-

In this oblique air photograph of Los Angeles, in 1967, the San Gabiel Mountains are clearly seen in the distance. However, at lower elevations a temperature inversion exists which has trapped a flat-topped smog layer visible over the city center in the middle distance of the picture. This is a typical condition in the basin, which is open to the ocean to the west but surrounded by mountains in the other directions. Automobiles are the primary source of air pollutants from the vast urban development on the basin floor. (Photo by J. Nystuen)

*Nature
and Man
in a Spatial
Context*

418

bustion of gasoline, fuel oil, diesel oil, coal, and natural gas at rates of use prevailing in 1965 is close to 6 tons per person. Thus, if the inversion process persists, the city air needs to be completely changed at least once every 17 days. Periods of near stagnation lasting four or five days occur several times a year over large parts of the United States. It is clear that, even with present population densities and rates of use of fossil fuels, our cities are coming uncomfortably close to using up all their available air.

Under these circumstances, we can no longer think of urban air as a "free Good." Instead, it must be thought of as a natural resource—that is, as part of the natural environment for which the demand is liable to outrun the supply, and to which a cost can be attached.[4]

Technological, Legal, and Behavioral Solutions to Environmental Problems

The rights of private ownership as well as typical economic attitudes do not apply when the common good is threatened. For example, as the air becomes polluted, public policy based on informed debate is needed to establish the acceptable quality that the air must have. Further debate and arbitration must determine how that quality shall be reached and maintained. This brings us face to face with three different types of policy suggestions. These can be called *technological, legal, and behavioral solutions to environmental problems.*

For example, Revelle considers and rejects a technological solution which has already become the mode of operation in many cities. "The number of automobiles operating in the city at any one time might be lowered by greatly enlarging the area covered by freeways and parking lots, which would speed up traffic and reduce the time spent in cruising the streets, looking for a place to park. . . ."

Typical of legal solutions is the Federal Environmental Protection Agency's sugges-

[4]Roger Revelle, "Pollution and Cities," *The Metropolitan Enigma*, James Q. Wilson (ed.), Chamber of Commerce of the United States, Washington, D.C., 1967, pp. 86–87.

tion that gasoline rationing and extra gasoline taxes may be needed to reduce the severity of air pollution in Los Angeles.

A third type of behavioral solution was initiated in 1969 to deal with traffic congestion in the nation's capital. The Northern Virginia Transportation Committee and the Metropolitan Washington, D.C., Council of Governments with help from the United States Department of Transportation set aside two traffic lanes on the Shirley Highway leading from Virginia into Washington, D.C., for exclusive use by express buses. This was an attempt to modify the spatial behavior of commuters by rewarding them with quick, comfortable trips if they left their cars at home. By 1972 more people were riding the buses during rush hours than were using private automobiles. Quantitatively, bus passengers increased from less than 2,000 per day in 1969 to more than 18,400 per day in 1972. Such experiments follow B. F. Skinner's ideas of behavior modification through rewards (i.e., faster commuting service) rather than threats (i.e., dire predictions of environmental disaster) or punishment (i.e., rationing and taxes). Another example of behavior modification through rewards further illustrates this point. The San Francisco Toll Bridge Crossing Authority now charges different toll rates for automobiles depending upon the number of people each car carries. The more passengers, the less the toll. As many as 1,400 fewer automobiles per day are now entering the city as the result of this project. A decrease in air pollution inevitably will follow. The additional benefits of lowered congestion and less noise are also obvious.

Let us see how these strategies might apply equally well to the problem of urban water shortages. We have already said that there is sufficient water in the world for everyone, but the introduction of cultural subsystems into the hydrologic cycle can upset its equilibrium. As a result, many cities face increasing water shortages. Again, three types of remedies can be applied. Technologically, bigger and longer aqueducts can be built.

But we have already pointed out that interregional water transfers are becoming increasingly difficult to arrange because the people in source areas are unwilling to part with scarce resources. From a geographic point of view transportation costs also tend to make such plans less feasible with every mile of distance added. In like manner, spatial systems of concentration, even of water, may tend to overload the carrying capacities of local environments.

Legally and economically, water would become more abundant if its true costs were charged. According to Theodore Schad, executive director of the National Water Commission created in 1968 by President Johnson, "Water is so important that the country can't afford in the future to give it away or make it available at less than cost."[5] We agree with Schad's statement when we consider the activities of the Army Corps of Engineers and similar government agencies over the last 50 years. Numerous dams, canals, levees, drainage projects, and other waterworks have been provided at little or no direct cost to their users but rather have been charged against the pocketbook of the general taxpayers. This has led to contradictory situations. For example, in 1972 the government paid farmers to keep upward of 50 million acres of land out of production; at the same time it paid as much as 90 percent of the cost involved in reclaiming 9 million acres of land per year. At city scales, water users are very often charged a flat rate or one based on some arbitrary measure. For example, New York City assesses water charges by the front foot of property rather than by the actual amount used. But to charge the true costs of water by legal fiat would go in the face of the voting public.

A third solution is suggested by a program of the Washington, D.C., Suburban Sanitary Commission (WSSC). A predicted

[5] Quoted by Constance Holden, "Water Commission: No More Free Rides for Water Users," *Science*, vol. 180, no. 4082, Apr. 13, 1973, p. 165.

and serious water shortage faces suburban Washington, especially every summer. To counteract it the WSSC in April 1972 began an experiment including improved technology and consumer education. A test area consisting of 2,400 households in Cabin John, Maryland, was chosen and its inhabitants exposed to a thorough campaign of community education. Radio, television, and newspaper spots were used to sensitize the public to the problem. Neighborhood meetings were held to answer questions, slide shows were given, and informative publications were distributed to consumers. Water users were made aware of the relationships that existed between their individual uses of water, the impending shortages, and the resulting over-load on sewage treatment facilities.

At the same time, flow reduction devices were installed on faucets, showerheads, and water closets in the 2,400 houses. Preliminary results of a 17-month trial period show that per capita water consumption in the test area has been reduced by 30 to 50 percent. At the same time, carefully developed relationships with the consumers have ensured that few complaints occurred. The result is an encouraging pilot model for similar plans being initiated elsewhere around the nation. It is this combination of several strategies which brings the best results.

Poco a Poco

The message of woe in our discussion of Southern California was that little by little, *poco a poco*, things can go wrong. Geographically speaking, the tiny contributions of low-order elements in hierarchically ordered space can swell into a flood of trouble. This is undeniably true. Although the organization of space by human cultures is of itself neither good nor bad, the runaway movement of materials through geographic systems can cause imbalances of grave import. But systems depend upon the flow of ideas as well as materials, and ideas can change the character of any system in which man is involved. It is often said that we already have the technology necessary to solve the earth's environmental ills but that we cannot agree on how to use it. The truth is that technology without continuing education and subsequent changes in behavior cannot save the world. The examples in the above pages, however, indicate that much can be done to improve things through a combination of technology, legal and political action, and behavior modification. *Poco a poco* an informed public and a responsible government can reverse environmental decline if the right approach is chosen. We have tried in this book to make suggestions about such an approach from a geographic point of view. The rest of the job is up to you.

REFERENCES TO PART TWO

CHAPTER 13
Cited References

Bunge, William, *Field Notes,* Discussion Paper No. 1, The Detroit Geographical Expedition, Detroit, Mich., July 1969.

Chorley, Richard J., and Barbara Kennedy, *Physical Geography: A Systems Approach,* Prentice-Hall, Englewood Cliffs, N.J., 1972.

Johnson, Ross B., "The Great Sand Dunes of Southern Colorado," *Geological Survey Research, 1967,* United States Geological Survey Professional Paper 575-C, pp. C177–C183.

Maruyama, Magoroh, "The Second Cybernetics: Deviation-Amplifying Mutual Causal Processes," *American Scientist,* vol. 51, 1963, pp. 164–179.

Selected Readings

Buckley, Walter (ed.), *Modern Systems Research for the Behavioral Scientist,* Aldine Publishing Co., Chicago, 1968. A collection of some of the best, most understandable articles on general systems theory. A good place to begin studying this subject.

Curry, Leslie, "Chance and Landscape," *Northern Geographical Essays in Honor of G. H. J. Daysh,* ed. by J. W. House, Oriel Press, Newcastle-upon-Tyne, 1966, pp. 40–55. This essay relates ideas of landscape format on, systems theory, and probability theory in a highly readable manner.

McArthur, Norman, "The Demography of Primitive Populations," *Science,* vol. 167, no. 3921, pp. 1097–1101. A note of warning is sounded in this article concerning attempts to estimate populations without adequate data.

Zelinsky, Wilbur, *A Prologue to Population Geography,* Prentice-Hall, Inc, Englewood Cliffs, N.J., 1966. A precise and relatively brief discussion of the historical, cultural, economic, and political factors that account for different types of populations and their distributions.

CHAPTER 14
Cited References

Oort, Abraham, H., "The Energy Cycle of the Earth," *The Biosphere,* A Scientific American Book, W.H. Freeman and Co., San Francisco, 1970, pp. 14–23.

Riehl, Herbert, *Introduction to the Atmosphere,* McGraw-Hill Book Co., New York, 1965.

Trewartha, Glenn T., Arthur H. Robinson, and E. H. Hammond, *Physical Elements of Geography,* 5th ed., McGraw-Hill Book Co., New York, 1967.

Van Riper, Joseph, *Man's Physical World,* 2d ed., McGraw-Hill Book Co., New York, 1971.

Selected Readings

Hare, F. K., *The Restless Atmosphere,* Harper & Row Publishers, Inc., New York, 1963.

Kuenen, P. H., *Realms of Water,* John Wiley & Sons, Inc., New York, 1955. A smooth blend of technical and literary styles, worth reading despite its age.

Odum, Howard T., *Environment, Power, and Society,* Wiley-Interscience, New York, 1971. A stimulating book relating man's use of power to all phases of life and society. Packed with ideas but not light reading.

Scientific American, *The Ocean,* A Scientific American Book, W.H. Freeman and Co., San Francisco, 1969. Ten essays covering a wide range of subjects on the physical and biological processes of the world's oceans.

————, "Energy and Power," special issue, vol. 224, no. 3, September 1971. Eleven essays on energy, ranging from sources throughout the universe to those utilized by a hunting society.

Strahler, A. N., *Introduction to Physical Geography,* John Wiley & Sons, Inc., New York, 1965. A well-illustrated standard physical geography text.

————, *The Earth Sciences,* 2d ed., Harper & Row Publishers, New York, 1971. A fuller treatment of the same physical geography material.

The Doors, "Horse Latitudes," *Strange Days,* Elektra Records No. EKS 74104, New York, 1967.

CHAPTER 15
Cited References

Chorley, R. J. (ed.), *Water, Earth and Man,* Methuen & Co., Ltd., London, 1969.

Foster, E. E., *Rainfall and Runoff,* The Macmillan Co., New York, 1949.

Mason, B. J., *Clouds, Rain and Rainmaking,* Cambridge University Press, Cambridge, 1962.

Thornthwaite, C. E., and J. R. Mather, *The Water Balance, Publications in Climatology,* vol. 8, no. 1, Drexel Institute of Technology, Laboratory of Climatology, 1955.

Tuan, Yi-Fu, *The Hydrologic Cycle and the Wisdom of God—A Theme in Geoteleology,* University of Toronto, Department of Geography Research Publication No. 1, 1968.

Wolman, Abel, "Water Resources, A Report to the Committee on Natural Resources of the National Academy of Science: National Research Council," *Publication 1000-B,* National Academy of Science, National Research Council, Washington, D.C., 1962.

Selected Readings

Blumenstock, David I., *The Ocean of Air,* Rutgers University Press, New Brunswick, N.J., 1959. A very readable book relating the atmosphere and the working of its climates and weathers to the concerns of man.

Penman, H. C., "The Water Cycle," *The Biosphere,* A Scientific American Book, W.H. Freeman and Co., San Francisco, 1970, pp. 38–45. A clear, precise, well-illustrated discussion of this complex system.

Vonnegut, Kurt, *Cat's Cradle,* Delacorte Press, New York, 1971. Vonnegut at his best, with the geography of the imagination much in evidence.

References

CHAPTER 16
Cited References

Callender, E., and R. Rossmann, "Sea Levels during the Past 35,000 Years," *Science,* vol. 162, Dec. 6, 1968, pp. 1121–1123.

Dickenson, William R., "Global Tectonics," *Science,* vol. 168, June 5, 1970, pp. 1250–1259.

————, "Plate Tectonics in Geologic History," *Science*, vol. 174, Oct. 8, 1971, pp. 107–113.

Heezen, Bruce C., "200,000,000 Years Under the Sea: The Voyage of the U.S.N.S. 'Kane,'" *Saturday Review*, Sept. 7, 1968, pp. 63–88.

Hunt, Charles B., *Physiography of the United States,* W.H. Freeman and Co., San Francisco, 1967.

Knopoff, L., "The Upper Mantle of the Earth," *Science,* vol. 163, Mar. 21, 1969, pp. 1277–1287.

Miller, D. H., *The Energy and Mass Budget at the Surface of the Earth,* Association of American Geographers, Washington, D.C., 1968.

Scientific American, *Continents Adrift,* A Scientific American Book, W.H. Freeman and Co., San Francisco, 1972.

Wolman, M. G., "A Cycle of Sedimentation and Erosion in Urban River Channels," *Geografiska Annaler,* vol. 49A, 1967, pp. 385–395.

Selected Readings

Engel, A. E. J., "Time and the Earth," *American Scientist,* Winter 1969, pp. 458–483. A thorough review of the earth's history in terms of the varying estimates of time required for certain events to have taken place.

Golomb, Berl, and Herbert M. Eder, "Landforms Made by Man," *Landscape,* vol. 14, no. 1 (Autumn 1964), pp. 4–7. A speculative review of man's impact on erosion and other landform processes, as well as a call for further study of the subject.

Ittelson, W. H., *Environment and Cognition,* Seminar Press, New York, 1973. "This volume is perhaps the first to bridge the gap between contemporary psychology and environmental perception and cognition." Contributions from many fields, including geography.

Lessing, Doris, "Report on the Threatened City," *The Temptation of Jack Orkney and Other Stories,* Alfred A. Knopf, Inc., New York, 1972. Frightening science fiction account of an unsuccessful attempt to warn San Franciscans that an earthquake is about to destroy the city.

McAlester, A. Lee, *The History of Life,* Prentice-Hall, Inc., Englewood Cliffs, N.J., Foundations of Earth Science Series, 1968. A concise, readable account of life on earth from its beginnings. Evocative comments on the role of blue-green algae and the ozone shield in shaping life environments.

CHAPTER 17
Cited References

Ahlmann, H. Wilson, *Glacier Variations and Climatic Fluctuations,* The American Geographical Society, New York, 1953.

Carter, Douglas B., Theodore H. Schmuddle, and David M. Sharpe, "The Interface as a Working Environment: A Purpose for Physical Geography," *Commission on College Geography Technical Paper No. 7,* Association of American Geographers, Washington, D.C., 1972.

Chang, Jen-hu, *Climate and Agriculture,* Aldine Publishing Co., Chicago, Ill., 1968.

Dole, Stephen H., *Habitable Planets for Man,* Blaisdell Publishing Co., a Division of Ginn and Co., Waltham, Mass., 1964.

Gates, David M., *Man and His Environment: Climate,* Harper & Row, Publishers, Inc., New York, 1972.

Landsberg, Helmut, *Physical Climatology,* Gray Printing Co., Inc., DuBois, Pa., 1958.

Sellers, William D., *Physical Climatology,* The University of Chicago Press, Chicago, Ill., 1965.

Thornthwaite, C. W., and J. R. Mather, "Instructions and Tables for Computing Potential Evapotranspiration and the Water Balance," *Publications in Climatology,* vol. 10, no. 3, Drexel Institute of Technology, Laboratory of Climatology, Centerton, N.J., 1957.

————, "An Approach toward a Rational Classification of Climate," *Geographical Review,* vol. 38, no. 1, 1948, pp. 55–94.

Selected Readings

Murchie, Guy, *Song of the Sky,* The Riverside Press, Cambridge, Mass., 1954. A lovely and personal description of everything that goes on in the atmosphere.

Shapley, Harlow (ed.), *Climatic Change: Evidence, Causes, and Effects,* Harvard University Press, Cambridge, Mass., 1953. Twenty-two essays on a wide variety of subjects relating life processes to those of climate and climatic change.

Sloane, Eric, *Look at the Sky, and Tell the Weather,* World Publishing Co., New York, 1970. Sloane at his anecdotal best, giving a combination of technical and folksy information about the weather.

Stewart, George R., *Storm,* Random House, New York, 1941. A novel, the central figure of which is a great storm moving slowly across the continent.

CHAPTER 18
Cited References

Anderson, Edgar, "Hybridization of the Habitat," *Evolution,* vol. 2, no. 1, 1948, pp. 1–9. Also Bobbs-Merrill Reprint Series G-5.

Buckman, Harry O., and Nyle C. Brady, *The Nature and Properties of Soils,* 7th ed., The Macmillan Co., New York, 1969.

Budowski, Gerardo, "Tropical Savanna, A Sequence of Forest Felling and Repeated Burnings," *Tursialba,* vol. 6, 1956, pp. 23–33. Also Bobbs-Merrill Reprint Series G-29.

Chang, Jen-hu, *Climate and Agriculture, An Ecological Survey,* Aldine Publishing Co., Chicago, Ill., 1968.

Edwards, Clive A., "Soil Pollutants and Soil Animals," *Scientific American,* vol. 220, no. 4, April 1969, pp. 88–99.

References

424

McNaughton, S. J., and L. L. Wolf, "Dominance and the Niche in Ecological Systems," *Science,* vol. 167, Jan. 9, 1970, pp. 131–137.

Strahler, Arthur N., "Climate, Soils, and Vegetation," Part III of *Physical Geography,* 3d ed., John Wiley & Sons, Inc., New York, 1969.

Watts, David, *Principles of Biogeography,* McGraw-Hill Book Co., New York, 1971.

Selected Readings

Anderson, Edgar, *Plants, Man and Life,* University of California Press, Berkeley, 1967. Discusses man's symbiotic relationship with weeds and crop plants.

Brown, Lester R., *Seeds of Change,* Frederick A., Praeger, Inc., New York, 1970. A discussion of the "green revolution" brought about by new types of crops, with some cautionary advice.

Darling, F. Fraser, and J. P. Milton (eds.), *Future Environments of North America,* The Natural History Press, Garden City, New York, 1966. Projections into the future of the impact of man on North American environments.

Hunt, Charles, B., *Geology of Soils,* W.H. Freeman and Co., San Francisco, 1972. A comprehensive account of soils and soil-forming processes.

Kellog, Charles E., "Soil," *Scientific American,* vol. 185, July 1950, pp. 30–39. Outlines the relationship between soils and vegetation.

Odum, Eugene P., *Ecology,* Holt, Rinehart and Winston, Inc., New York, 1963. A brief, well-written technical account of biosystems, from microscopic to regional scales.

CHAPTER 19
Cited References

Burton, I., and R. W. Kates, "The Floodplain and the Seashore: A Comparative Analysis of Hazard-zone Occupance," *Geographical Review,* vol. 54, 1964, pp. 366–385.

Curry, Leslie, "Climate and Economic Life: A New Approach," *Geographical Review,* vol. 42, 1952, pp. 367–383.

Flannery, Kent V., "Archeological Systems Theory and Early Mesoamerica," *Anthropological Archeology in the Americas,* Washington, D.C., 1968.

Gould, Peter R., "Man Against His Environment: A Game Theoretic Framework," *Annals of the Association of American Geographers,* vol. 53, no. 3, September 1963.

Grigg, David, *The Harsh Lands,* Macmillan and Co., Ltd., London, 1970.

Isaac, Erich, *Geography of Domestication,* Prentice-Hall, Inc., Englewood Cliffs, N.J., 1970.

Kolars, John, "Locational Aspects of Cultural Ecology: The Case of the Goat in Non-western Agriculture," *Geographical Review,* vol. 56, 1966, pp. 577–584. Also Bobbs-Merrill Reprint Series G-241.

Leeds, Anthony, and Andrew P. Vayda, *Man, Culture, and Animals—The Role of Animals in Human Ecological Adjustments,* American Association for the Advancement of Science, Pub. 78, Washington, D.C., 1965.

MacNeish, Richard S., "Ancient Mesoamerican Civilization," *Science,* vol. 143, no. 3606, Feb. 7, 1964, pp. 531–537.

—, Paul C. Mangelsdorf, and Walton Galinat, "Domestication of Corn," *Science,* vol. 143, 1964, pp. 538–545.

Struever, Stuart (ed.), *Prehistoric Agriculture,* American Museum Sourcebooks in Anthropology, Natural History Press, Garden City, New York, 1971.

White, G. F., *Choice of Adjustment to Floods,* University of Chicago Department of Geography Research Paper No. 93, Chicago, Ill., 1964.

Selected Readings

Adams, Robert McC., *The Evolution of Urban Society,* Aldine Publishing Co., Chicago, Ill., 1966. Early Mesopotamia and prehispanic Mexico: a comparative study of one of the great transformations in the history of man.

Albrecht, William A., "Soil Fertility and Biotic Geography," *Geographical Review,* vol. 47, 1957, pp. 86–105. Also Bobbs-Merrill Reprint Series G-4. A discussion at a regional scale of the relationship of soil fertility to crop nutrition for animals and men.

Barth, Frederick, "Ecologic Relationships of Ethnic Groups in Swat, North Pakistan," *American Anthropologist,* vol. 58, 1956, pp. 1079–1089. Also Bobbs-Merrill Reprint Series A-9. An analysis of the adjustment of ethnic groups to ecological niches located on steep slopes. Emphasizes the importance of interaction between the ethnic groups with different resource bases.

Braidwood, Robert, and Gordon R. Willey, *Courses toward Urban Life,* Aldine Publishing Co., Chicago, Ill., 1962. Archaeological considerations of some cultural alternatives.

Brown, Lester R., and Gail W. Finsterbusch, *Man and His Environment: Food,* Harper Row, & Publishers, Inc., New York, 1972. Concerned with the development, current state, and immediate future of world food production.

Burton, I., and R. W. Kates (eds.), *Readings in Resources Management and Conservation,* University of Chicago Press, Chicago, Ill., 1965. Selected readings on the origins and development of public conservation policy.

Carol, Hans, "Stages of Technology and Their Impact upon the Physical Environment: A Basic Problem in Cultural Geography," *Canadian Geographer* vol. 8, no. 1, 1964, pp. 1–8. A theory of the interaction between technology and environment.

Porter, Philip, "Environmental Potentials and Economic Opportunities—A Background for Cultural Adaptation," *American Anthropologist,* vol. 67, 1965, pp. 409–420. Also Bobbs-Merrill Reprint Series G-186. Applies water balance concepts to the evaluation of agricultural uses in traditional African societies and analyzes the survival strategies employed by these societies. An excellent study.

CHAPTER 20
Cited References

Barrows, Harlan H., "Geography as Human Ecology," *Annals of the Association of American Geographers,* vol. 13, 1923, pp. 1–14.

Clarkson, James D., "Ecology and Spatial Analysis," *Annals of the Association of American Geographers,* vol. 60, 1970, pp. 700–716.

Glacken, Clarence J., *Traces on the Rhodian Shore,* University of California Press, Berkeley, 1967.

Huntington, Ellsworth, *Mainsprings of Civilization,* John Wiley & Sons, Inc., New York, 1945. A chapter of this book, "Regions and Seasons of Mental Activity," pp. 343–367, is reprinted in Fred E. Dohrs et al. (eds.), *Outside Readings in Geography,* Thomas Y. Crowell Co., New York, 1955, pp. 146–156.

Moorehead, Alan, *Cooper's Creek,* Harper & Row Publishers, Inc., New York, 1964.

Murphey, Rhoads, "Man and Nature in China," *Modern Asian Studies,* vol. 1, no. 4, 1967, pp. 313–333.

Platt, Robert S., "Environmentalism Versus Geography," *The American Journal of Sociology,* vol. 53, no. 5, March 1948, pp. 351–358.

Robinson, Arthur H., *Elements of Cartography,* John Wiley & Sons, Inc., New York, 1953.

Saarinen, Thomas Frederick, *Perception of the Drought Hazard on the Great Plains,* University of Chicago Department of Geography Research Paper No. 106, Chicago, Ill., 1966.

———, "Attitudes Toward Weather Modification: A Study of Great Plains Farmers," *Human Dimensions of Weather Modification,* Research Paper No. 105, ed. by W. R. Derrick Sewell, Department of Geography, University of Chicago, Chicago, Ill., 1966.

———, *Perception of Environment,* Association of American Geographers, Washington, D.C., 1969.

Schaefer, Fred K., "Exceptionalism in Geography: A Methodological Examination," *Annals of the Association of American Geographers,* vol. 43, 1953, pp. 226–249.

Semple, Ellen C., *Influences of Geographic Environment,* Henry Holt and Co., Inc., New York, 1911.

Spate, O. H. K., "Toynbee and Huntington: A Study in Determinism," *The Geographical Journal,* vol. 118, part 4, December 1952, pp. 406–428.

———, "How Determined Is Possibilism?" *Geographical Studies,* vol. 4, 1957, pp. 3–7.

Spoehr, Alexander, "Cultural Differences in the Interpretation of Natural Resources," *Man's Role in Changing the Face of the Earth,* ed. by William L. Thomas, Jr., University of Chicago Press, Chicago, Ill., 1956.

Tuan, Yi-Fu, "Attitudes Toward Environment: Themes and Approaches," *Environmental Perception and Behavior,* Research Paper No. 109, ed. by David Lowenthal, Department of Geography, University of Chicago, Chicago, Ill., 1967.

———, "Discrepancies between Environmental Attitude and Behavior: Examples from Europe and China," *Canadian Geographer,* vol. 12, no. 3, 1968, pp. 176–191.

Vidal de la Blache, Paul, *Principes de géographie humaine,* Paris, 1922. Trans. as *Principles of Human Geography,* Henry Holt and Co., Inc., New York, 1926.

Ward, Robert M., *Cold and Wind Hazard Perception by Orange and Tomato Growers,* Michigan Geographical Publication No. 9, Department of Geography, University of Michigan, Ann Arbor, Mich., 1973.

Selected Readings

Marsh, G. P., *Man and Nature,* Scribner and Sons, New York, 1864; ed. by David Lowenthal and reprinted by Belknap Press, Cambridge, Mass., 1964. This is the pioneering work on man's modification of the earth and the concept of conservation.

Platt, John R., *Perception and Change: Projections for Survival,* The University of Michigan Press, Ann Arbor, Mich., 1970. Deals with the need to control the effects of modern technology in order to create peace and a livable environment.

Thrower, Norman J. W., *Maps and Man,* Prentice-Hall, Inc., Englewood Cliffs, N.J., 1972. "An examination of cartography in relation to culture and civilization."

Tuan, Yi-Fu, "Man and Nature," *Commission on College Geography Resource Paper No. 10,* Association of American Geographers, Washington, D.C., 1971. A good introduction to perception of nature studies.

Vayda, Andrew P., (ed.), *Environment and Cultural Behavior,* Natural History Press, Garden City, N.Y., 1969. "Ecological studies in cultural anthropology."

CHAPTER 21
Cited References

Conway, Gordon, R., "A Consequence of Insecticides," *Natural History* supplement, February 1969, pp. 46–51.

Glaser, Peter E., "Power from the Sun: Its Future," *Science,* vol. 162, 1968, pp. 857–861.

Jackson, J. F., *Landscapes,* ed. by E. H. Zube, University of Massachusetts Press, Amherst, Mass., 1970.

Jones, Lawrence W., "Liquid Hydrogen as a Fuel for the Future," *Science,* vol. 174, October 1971, pp. 367–378.

Singer, S. Fred, "Global Effects of Environmental Pollution," *Science,* vol. 162, December 1968, p. 1308.

Smith, J. E., *"Torrey Canyon" Pollution and Marine Life,* University Press, Cambridge, England, 1968.

Woodwell, George M., Paul P. Craig, and Horton A. Johnson, "DDT in the Biosphere: Where Does It Go?" *Science,* vol. 174, December 1971, pp. 1101–1107.

Selected Readings

Commoner, Barry, *The Closing Circle,* Alfred A. Knopf, Inc., New York, 1971. Well-written analysis of ecological problems with prescriptions for technological, political, and social counteractions.

Deshler, Walter, "Livestock Trypanosomiasis and Human Settlement in Northeastern Uganda," *Geographical Review,* vol. 50, 1969, pp. 541–554. An example of the interrelatedness of man's actions and biotic processes in an African setting.

Detwyler, Thomas R., *Man's Impact on Environment,* McGraw-Hill Book Co., New York, 1971. A survey and critical commentary on environmental impact studies. Many detailed and informative examples are given.

Ehrlich, Paul R., and Anne H. Ehrlich, *Population, Resources, Environment—Issues in Human Ecology,* W. H. Freeman and Co., San Francisco, 1970. Relationship of overpopulation and population dynamics to demands on food, resources, and the environment. A world view of the social, political, and technological action needed for a brighter prospect for mankind.

Hardin, Garrett, "The Tragedy of the Commons," *Science,* vol. 162, December 1968, pp. 1243–1248. An exposition of the difficult institutional and ethical problem associated with the exploitation of "common" resources.

Montague, Katherine, and Peter Montague, *Mercury,* Sierra Club, San Francisco, 1971. An account of the deadly accumulation of mercury in the marine food chain.

Thomas, W. L. (ed.), *Man's Role in Changing the Face of the Earth,* University of Chicago Press, Chicago, Ill., 1956. This large collection of papers on all aspects of man's impact on the environment is the result of a symposium on the topic. The quality of the papers varies greatly, but many are very good.

Wagner, Richard H., *Environment and Man,* W. W. Norton and Co., Inc., New York, 1971. A well-written, informative book on man's increasing impact on his environment. The author is a botanist.

Whiteside, Thomas, *The Withering Rain: America's Herbicidal Folly,* E. P. Dutton & Co., Inc., New York, 1971. A description of defoliation in Vietnam and use of herbicides in American agriculture.

Wood, Nancy, *Clearcut,* Sierra Club, San Francisco, 1971. A criticism of the most common method of lumbering in the United States.

CHAPTER 22

Cited References

Jacoby, Louis R., *Perception of Air, Noise and Water Pollution in Detroit,* Michigan Geographical Publication No. 7, Department of Geography, University of Michigan, Ann Arbor, Mich., 1972.

Landsberg, Hans H., *Natural Resources for U.S. Growth,* The Johns Hopkins Press, Baltimore, Md., 1964.

Nicholson, Max, *The Environmental Revolution,* McGraw-Hill Book Co., New York, 1970.

Steinhart, Carol E., and John S. Steinhart, *Blowout,* Duxbury (Wadsworth) Press, Belmont, Calif., 1972.

Selected Readings

Albaum, Melvin, *Geography and Contemporary Issues: Studies of Relevant Problems,* John Wiley & Sons, Inc., New York, 1973. A collection of geographic studies of poverty, racism, pollution, and crowding.

Bernarde, Melvin A., *Our Precarious Habitat,* W. W. Norton and Co., Inc., New York, 1970. A review of a wide range of problems created by man's use of his environment.

Detwyler, Thomas R., and Melvin G. Marcus, *Urbanization and Environment,* Duxbury Press, Belmont, Calif., 1972. A collection of essays on the interaction between urbanization and the physical environment.

Fabricant, Neil, and Robert M. Hallman, *Toward a Rational Power Policy: Energy, Politics, and Pollution,* George Braziller, New York, 1971. A factual approach written in terms of the practical problems facing metropolitan planners.

Farber, Seymour, "Quality of Living—Stress and Creativity," in F. Fraser

Darling and John P. Milton, *Future Environments of North America,* Natural History Press, New York, 1966.

Holdren, John P., and Paul R. Ehrlich (eds.), *Global Ecology,* Harcourt Brace Jovanovich, Inc., New York, 1971. A set of readings on a multiplicity of ecological crises, with emphasis on global problems.

Hoyle, Fred, "Welcome to Slippage City," *Element 79,* A Signet Book, The New American Library, New York, 1967, pp. 50–65. Fantasy fiction, but the account of Los Angeles couldn't be more true.

Ward, Barbara, *Spaceship Earth,* Columbia University Press, New York, 1966. A popular work calling for a balanced world ecology and a revision of the notion of material progress.

Wilson, James Q. (ed.), *The Metropolitan Enigma: Inquiries into the Nature and Dimensions of America's "Urban Crisis,"* Chamber of Commerce of the United States, Washington, D.C., 1967. An informative and comprehensive series of essays. "Pollution and Cities," by Roger Revelle, pp. 78–121, is of particular interest.

INDEX

INDEX

Page numbers in *italic* indicate illustrations.

Index

439

New York City:
 hinterland boundary, 161, *162*
 information for urban dweller, 122
 location of corporation head-
  quarters, *116*
 milk market, *55*
 water rates, 419
Newspaper distribution in Frank-
 furt, Germany, *57*
Newsprint, consumption of, by
 country, *119*
Night soil, 184
Nile valley, 246–247
Nimbostratus clouds, 290, *293*
Nineteenth-century cities:
 U.S. industrial development,
  133–139
 urban characteristics, 33
Nitrate pollution, 409–411
Nitrogen fertilizer, 409–411, *410*
Nitrogen fixation, 332, 340, 364
Nitrogen production, 332
Nodal regions, 159–161
Nominal classification, 8–9
Nominal locations, 8–9
Nonrenewable resources, 385
 aquifers, 352
Nonreversible diffusion, 389–390
Nordbeck, Stig, 46–47
Normal lapse rate, 263
Normative models of human be-
 havior, 375
North Africa, qanats, 406
North America:
 migration to, 409
 storm tracks, *290*
North American weather systems,
 288
North Beach, San Francisco, 177–*179*
North Equatorial Current, 273
North Pole, 257–259
North Star (Polaris), 257
Northeast trade winds, 268
Northern Hemisphere:
 climates, 324–330
 isotherms, *319*
 pressure system, 271
 water movement, *271*
Nuclear energy, 255
Nunnataks, 337
Nutrient concentrations, 394
Nutrients in soil-vegetation, 331,
 336–352
Nutrition, world, 4, *8*

Occluded front, 287, 288
Ocean currents, *272–275, 273*
 effect on climate, 321

Oceanic circulation, 277
Oceans:
 in hydrologic cycle, 278–281
 as source of water, 278
Oil:
 cost of moving, *153*
 Los Angeles, 414–416
 offshore wells, 415
 (*See also* Petroleum)
Oil companies, 388
Oil pollution, 415–416
Oil reserves use, 287, *289*
Oil shale, 388
Oklahoma dust bowl, 349–350
Old Order Amish, 97
Old Order Mennonite, 96–99
Omaha, Nebraska, 90
Ontario, shopping habits in, 96–*98,
 99*
Open system, 248
Operators, 361–365
Optical air path, 257
Orbit, earth, 257–*259, 258*
Ore:
 concentrations of metal, 388, *389–
  393*
 cost of transport, *154*
Organization of space, Tehuacan
 Valley, 353–360
Oriental philosophy of resource use,
 377
Orogeny, 308, *313*
Orographic rainfall, 284–286, *285*
Orwell, George, 245
Overload in information system,
 104–105
Overproduction, 396–400
 effect in environmental equilib-
  rium, 388
Over-the-road cost in transportation,
 153
Owens Valley, 413
Oxidation in chemical weathering,
 300–301
Oxygen time in biotic cycle, 385, *386*
Oyashio Current, 274
Oysters, boundary dwellers, 176, *178*

Pacific Northwest, water resource,
 414
Packaging waste, 393
Paleo-Indians, 353–360
Panama disease, 345
Paper waste, 393
Pattern:
 of daily water use, *249*
 global: demographic, *173*
  technological, *172*

Pattern:
 of movement and resource use of
  early man, 357–360
 of resource use, 387, 403–404
 of world precipitation, *286*
 of world pressure belts, *268*
 of world winds, 267–269, *268*
Pedalfers, 334
Pedocals, 334, 348
Per capita income:
 Europe, 3, *6*
 level of living, 242
 world, *6*
Perception, cultural: of desirable
  places to live, 413
 of environment, mental maps,
  381–384
 of environmental hazard, 378–
  381
 of food, 188–189
 of resources, 388, 403–404
 of settlement, 124
Perched water table, 294
Periodic markets in China, 86–89
Perishability of food, 186
Permafrost, 337–338
Permeability, 290
 water storage, 327
Persia, qanats in, 406, *407*
Personal communication field, 126,
 126
Personal space, 25
Pesticides, 397–402
Petroleum:
 Los Angeles, 411, 414–416
 (*See also* Oil)
Petroleum reserves, 387
Peutinger Map, *15*
pH tolerance of plants, 331–332
Phonographs, increase in numbers
  of, 119
Phosphate, 340, 348
Photosynthesis, 332
Piaget, 381
Picadilly Circus, population, 48
Pingos, 338
Pipelines to move fuel, *153*
Plane of the ecliptic, 257, *258, 259*
Plant distribution, soil-vegetation
  sequences, 336–352
Plant nutrition, 331, 336–352
Plants:
 domestication, 185, 354–358, 361
 indicators of climate, 318
 as self-maintaining systems, 252
 water availability, 327–328
 water in, 295
Plastics, 401
Plate tectonic theory, 307, 309–312

World distribution:
  of technical skills, 242, 243
  of telephones, 115, 120
  of urbanization, 47–48, 52, 53
  of water, 278
World growth rate, 7
World nutrition, 4, 8
World ocean currents, 273
World population curve, 48–50
World precipitation pattern, 286
World pressure pattern, 268
World rubber production, 192

World winds, 267–269, 268

Xerophytic plants, 346, 349

Yields (agricultural), 199–202, 336–352
  caloric, 224
  on cleared forest land, 340
  of corn, 409, 410
  modern and traditional farming, 365

Yields:
  of potatoes, 223, 408
  of wheat, 223

Zein, 365
Zero sum game, 369–370
Zimmerman, Erich W., 377
Zonal soils, 335
Zone of transition around CBD, 36
Zoning laws in resource use policy, 388
Zuider Zee, 207, 209